Labour Standards in International Economic Law

Henner Gött
Editor

Labour Standards in International Economic Law

Springer

Editor
Henner Gött
Georg-August-University Göttingen
Institute of International and European Law
Göttingen, Germany

ISBN 978-3-030-09889-6 ISBN 978-3-319-69447-4 (eBook)
https://doi.org/10.1007/978-3-319-69447-4

Softcover re-print of the Hardcover 1st edition 2018

Printed on acid-free paper

This Springer imprint is published by Springer Nature
The registered company is Springer International Publishing AG
The registered company address is: Gewerbestrasse 11, 6330 Cham, Switzerland

Preface

Ensuring a decent level of worker protection in the globalized economy remains one of the central challenges of economic globalization. This profoundly intricate issue will likely remain unresolved until all its aspects are properly understood. The present volume assembles timely analyses, written by expert scholars and experienced practitioners, of the most pressing legal questions arising in the field. It bridges existing gaps between the different sub-fields of law and surpasses the boundaries of professional and epistemic communities, to foster a more comprehensive understanding of labour standards in international economic law.

Most contributions to this volume were inspired by presentations given at the Göttingen Conference on Labour Standards in International Economic Law, convened on 1–2 October 2015 by the Institute of International and European Law's Department of International Economic and Environmental Law in Göttingen. Additional chapters on further important issues were included to round off the compilation.

It is a keen pleasure to acknowledge all those who have made this volume possible. First and foremost, I wish to express my sincere gratitude to *Peter-Tobias Stoll*, whose expertise and unfailing and dedicated support have made both the conference and this volume possible. Special thanks are due to all the authors for their invaluable contributions to this book and to the conference. Furthermore, I wish to thank *Mary Footer*, *Pablo Lazo Grandi*, *Inmaculada Martínez-Zarzoso*, *Frank Schorkopf*, *Friedl Weiss* and *Ruben Zandvliet* for enriching the conference as speakers and chairs. Last but not least, I am grateful to *Anna Kozyakova*, *Mauricio Pacheco*, *Doris Ruhr*, *Laura Wanner*, *Oskar de Wyl* and *Jia Xu*, who served as members of the conference organization team, and to *Jasmin Evers*, *Laura Wanner* and *Oskar de Wyl* for assisting me with the edition of the manuscript.

Göttingen, Germany
August 2017

Henner Gött

Contents

Contributors

Patrick Abel Georg-August-University Göttingen, Institute of International and European Law, Göttingen, Germany

Nazli Aghazadeh Georg-August-University Göttingen, Institute of International and European Law, Göttingen, Germany

Thomas Cottier University of Berne, World Trade Institute, Berne, Switzerland

Franz Christian Ebert Max Planck Institute for Comparative Public Law and International Law, Heidelberg, Germany

Katja Gehne BASF, Ludwigshafen, Germany

Henner Gött Georg-August-University Göttingen, Institute of International and European Law, Göttingen, Germany

Till Patrik Holterhus Georg-August-University Göttingen, Institute of International and European Law, Göttingen, Germany

Claire La Hovary University of Glasgow, School of Law, Glasgow, Scotland

Franziska Humbert University of Berne, Berne, Switzerland

Oxfam Germany, Berlin, Germany

Rüdiger Krause Georg-August-University Göttingen, Institute of Labour Law, Göttingen, Germany

Deborah Martens Ghent University, Ghent, Belgium

Tonia Novitz University of Bristol Law School, Bristol, UK

Jan Orbie Ghent University, Ghent, Belgium

Lore Van den Putte Ghent University, Ghent, Belgium

Anja Seibert-Fohr Ruprecht-Karls-University, Heidelberg, Germany

Peter-Tobias Stoll Georg-August-University Göttingen, Institute of International and European Law, Göttingen, Germany

Anne Trebilcock Georg-August-University Göttingen, Institute of Labour Law, Göttingen, Germany

Former Legal Adviser and Director of Legal Services, International Labour Organization, Geneva, Switzerland

Reingard Zimmer Berlin School of Economics and Law, Berlin, Germany

Labour Standards in International Economic Law: An Introduction

Henner Gött

Content

The ever-progressing globalization of the economy and the growing economic interdependence of states has a profound and lasting impact on the world of labour. As the International Labour Organization (ILO) has pointed out in its 2008 Declaration on Social Justice for a Fair Globalization, this impact is ambivalent:

> [O]n the one hand, the process of economic cooperation and integration has helped a number of countries to benefit from high rates of economic growth and employment creation, to absorb many of the rural poor into the modern urban economy, to advance their developmental goals, and to foster innovation in product development and the circulation of ideas[.]
>
> [O]n the other hand, global economic integration has caused many countries and sectors to face major challenges of income inequality, continuing high levels of unemployment and poverty, vulnerability of economies to external shocks, and the growth of both unprotected work and the informal economy, which impact on the employment relationship and the protections it can offer.[1]

Against this backdrop, securing and improving adequate levels of worker protection while preserving the benefits of globalization has become an issue of utmost importance.[2] What is at stake is not only to ensure effective compliance and implementation as a factual matter. Rather, there is also the normative question which level of protection is adequate, or, in other words, how labour standards *should* be protected and promoted in the light of the challenges posed by a

[1] ILO Declaration on Social Justice for a Fair Globalization, adopted on 10 June 2008.

[2] The ILO has conceptualized this question in its Decent Work Agenda, as laid down in its 2008 Declaration on Social Justice for a Fair Globalization. See International Labour Office (1999) and Vosko (2002).

H. Gött (✉)
Georg-August-University Göttingen, Institute of International and European Law, Göttingen, Germany
e-mail: hgoett@gwdg.de

H. Gött (ed.), *Labour Standards in International Economic Law*,
https://doi.org/10.1007/978-3-319-69447-4_1

globalized economy.[3] Given the complexity of both the factual and the normative dimension, it can hardly be surprising that no coherent, sustainable and satisfying solution has been identified so far.

The status quo is that the protection and promotion of labour standards within the context of economic globalization is dealt with in numerous contexts, which have spawned a variety of different and disparate approaches both within and beyond the confines of international law.[4]

Within the realm of international law, the two areas of prime relevance are international labour law on the one hand and international economic law on the other.

International labour law is concerned with the formulation and implementation of internationally recognized labour standards, rights and policies. With its origins dating back to the so-called 'first globalization' at the end of the nineteenth century, it has demonstrated remarkable long-term viability.[5] The ILO, the central international organization in the field, has developed a comprehensive body of treaties, recommendations, declarations and other instruments and a rich organizational practice on the creation and implementation of labour standards. As to the current economic globalization, the ILO has engaged in various initiatives to secure adherence and to further promote labour standards.[6] For one part, it has engaged in both revisions and a prioritization of its numerous instruments. This resulted, most prominently, in the identification of fundamental labour standards in the 1998 Declaration on Fundamental Principles and Righta at Work, which has become a point of reference both for a realignment of resources and activities inside the ILO and for numerous instruments and initiatives developed elsewhere. Moreover, the ILO has defined and committed to pursue strategic objectives (job creation, fundamental principles and rights at work, social protection and social dialogue, as well as gender equality as a crosscutting objective) in its Decent Work Agenda, manifested in its 2008 Declaration on Social Justice for a Fair Globalization. At the same time, the ILO has continued to experience major challenges to its work, both internally and externally, some of which have the potential to substantially compromise its impact and, ultimately, even its relevance.

The second central body of law, international economic law, including international trade law as well as international investment law and the law of international financial institutions, frames and accompanies economic globalization through a

[3]This normative dimension is relevant both for those concerned with positive international law and those concerned with developing and changing this law as a matter of politics.

[4]To promote coherence between these contexts has time and again amounted to a challenge in itself. A prominent example is the—eventually unsuccessful—attempt to introduce labour standards into the law and practice of the WTO, on this see e.g. Leary (1997) and Weiss (2005). Another example is the lengthy struggle to achieve at least some coherence between the so-called EWI indicators used in the World Bank's Doing Business Reports and the implementation and further promotion of ILO conventions, Bakvis (2009).

[5]On the origins and development see Servais (2014), p. 19 et seqq.

[6]Maupain (2013), p. 51 et seqq.

rapidly developing body of norms. These norms are mostly laid down in multilateral, regional and bilateral treaties and are significantly developed further by the practice of powerful international organizations, such as the World Trade Organization (WTO), the Organization for Economic Co-Operation and Development (OECD) or the Bretton Woods Institutions. These treaties and organizational practices have had a profound impact on the current state of economic globalization. In this context, they have also contributed to (re-)configuring the parameters within which contemporary industrial relations take place. That being said, labour standards have never been a central concern in international economic law—indeed, they have at times been facing outright opposition.[7] Yet, their role appears to be slowly increasing at least in certain areas, for example in the context of regional trade agreements.[8]

While international economic law and international labour law are two central fields of concern, it would be negligent not to look beyond these two bodies of law. With the international legal order being more developed and multifaceted than ever before in history, it is only natural that the issue of protecting and promoting labour standards in the globalized economy also touches on other areas of international law, such as international institutional law or international human rights law.[9] Certain human rights guarantees in regional and universal human rights instruments have become central points of reference, like Art. 11 ECHR and the corresponding jurisprudence of the European Court of Human Rights, to name one prominent example. In a similar vein, there are important links to the level of domestic law.[10]

What is more, labour standards play an increasing role in transnational economic and social self-regulation by non-state actors. Non-state actors, such as enterprises, trade unions and NGOs, have always played an important part in the formulation and implementation of labour standards, both on the domestic and the international level.[11] As economic globalization coincides with diminishing regulatory capacities of states, self-regulation by non-state actors becomes more relevant also for other parts of the international economic order.[12] Many non-state actors have developed own approaches to the protection and promotion of labour standards,

---

[7]See e.g. the WTO's refusal to include labour standards in its work, as prominently spelled out in Singapore Ministerial Declaration, 18 Dec 1996, WT/MIN(96)/DEC, para. 4.

[8]Including in recent major trade agreements, see e.g. Chapter 23 CETA. According to a 2016 ILO study, 'nearly half of trade agreements with labour provisions came into existence since 2008 and over 80 per cent of agreements entering into force since 2013 included them', ILO (2016), p. 22.

[9]See e.g. Kolben (2010) and Swepston (2013).

[10]As a general matter, international labour law heavily relies and depends on its implementation through national legislators and authorities, see e.g. the obligations in Art. 19 (5) ILO Constitution. Moreover, the issue of protecting labour standards in a globalized economy can become relevant in civil litigation before domestic courts, see e.g. the pending case of Regional Court (*Landgericht*) Dortmund, *Mohammad Jabir et al. v. KiK Textilien und Non-Food GmbH*, Case-No.7 O 95/15.

[11]The most prominent example is the ILO's tripartite structure, Art. 3 (1) and Art. 7 (1) ILO Constitution. On further examples see Hepple (2005), p. 69 et seqq.

[12]For a more general account see Peters et al. (2009).

some of which are transcending (or even clearly lying beyond) the realm of international law in the traditional sense. Intricate examples for unilateral or contractual cross-border self-regulation by enterprises, trade unions and NGOs can be found in corporate codes of conduct, international framework agreements or social labelling schemes.[13] While evidently introducing normative propositions on labour standards in globalization, the legal quality and relevance of these private initiatives remain—at least from an international lawyer's point of view—highly uncertain.

The approaches to the protection and promotion of labour standards that can be found in each of the aforementioned areas differ significantly as to their respective rationale, scope, means and efficacy. Each of them has its own objectives, characteristics, potentials and pitfalls. These divergencies in substance go along with a considerable separation, and at times isolation, of professional and epistemic communities of those who are concerned with international economic law and those concerned with the protection and promotion of labour standards, both in academia and in practice. This multidimensional fragmentation has repeatedly resulted in remarkable misunderstandings, such as an unbalanced perception of labour standards as mere obstacles to doing business, or unfortunate limitations of political debates, e.g. when the question of how to improve labour chapters in trade agreements is reduced to the issue whether these chapters should be enforceable by temporary suspensions of trade benefits (so-called 'trade sanctions') or not. Perhaps more than ever before, there is a need for increased coherence between approaches, as there is a need for enhanced mutual understanding between communities.

This volume addresses some of the most pressing issues arising at the tangent of international economic law and international labour standards. It deliberately adopts a comprehensive perspective, covering the manifold approaches and the different professional backgrounds mentioned above. Its aim is to provide analysis and assessment of the law and practice, to broaden the perspective beyond sub-fields and communities and to combine the threads in a single volume in order to provide guidance to academics and practitioners who are facing the challenge of securing adequate levels of worker protection in the globalized economy.

The first part of the volume prepares the ground for the discussions in the subsequent parts by elucidating the historical, organizational and conceptual background which informs labour standards and their role in international economic law today.

The protection and promotion of labour standards in the international economic order is by no means a new issue. As *Peter-Tobias Stoll* points out in his contribution, it has been a recurring issue ever since the end of the nineteenth century. In order to shed light on the multiple connections and divisions between the economic and social dimensions of international law and relations, he embarks on a historical and analytical *tour d'horizon*. *Claire La Hovary* picks up in the present, assessing

[13] See e.g. Davarnejad (2011), Burkett (2011) and Seidman (2009).

the ILO's mandate and capacity to create, proliferate and supervise labour standards in the globalized economy. Tripartism, the ILO's most important foundational feature, and its operationalization have come under severe pressure in the course of the ILO's post-2012 constitutional crisis. Yet, despite current difficulties, *La Hovary* argues that 'the current crisis affecting the ILO also suggests that the organization does matter, as does its supervisory system'. While the ILO will remain an institution of paramount importance in the field, it must not be overlooked that contemporary labour law has transcended the traditional structures of domestic and international law. It operates, in the words of *Anne Trebilcock*, 'within, between and beyond States to form a type of (imperfect and incomplete) multi-layered global governance'. In her contribution, *Trebilcock* points out why this shift from international to transnational labour law matters for labour standards. She concludes that transnational labour law's 'broader vision of reuniting the social and the economic [...] seems at least theoretically better placed to test different solutions until the most promising can emerge within a particular context'.

After the scene is set, the contributions in the volume's second part explore the role of labour standards in the most prominent fields of international economic law, which are trade, investment and finance.

Given that initiatives to include provisions on labour into the multilateral trade regime failed both in the case of the General Agreement on Tariffs and Trade (GATT) and again when establishing the WTO, *Thomas Cottier* explores whether the recent WTO *EC - Seals* case will be of help in this regard. He concludes that the WTO's case law is worth studying and that such studies will likely reveal some policy space 'to support and pursue labour standards and human rights abroad, using the means and instruments of trade policy in a well-calibrated manner'. *Franziska Humbert,* in focusing on child labour, advocates in favour of an ILO-WTO implementation mechanism. This institutional solution, she argues, can be seen in line with a 'constitutionalist approach'.

Many of the preferential trade agreements that have recently been concluded or are currently being negotiated to try to rectify the WTO's refusal to address labour standards. As *Tonia Novitz* explains, in EU trade agreements, there is 'an apparent shift away from a human rights [...] perspective to one more focused on sustainable development', which in her view warrants caution. The same holds true in view of the involvement of the civil society in this context, as *Jan Orbie, Lore Van den Putte* and *Deborah Martens* conclude after a look to the actual practice of such civil society mechanisms in the light of their objectives. Their analysis reveals that civil society involvement in free trade agreements lacks a clear definition of purpose. As they put it: 'It appears unclear what exactly civil society should be doing in this regard.'

The relevance of labour provisions in trade agreements largely depends on their implementation and enforcement mechanisms. The North American Free Trade Area (NAFTA) side agreement on labour employed a specific arbitration model, which the US has used, with certain modifications, in its subsequent trade agreements. As *Patrick Abel* points out in his comparative analysis, however, these mechanisms suffer from 'an unsuitable procedural and institutional design', which may explain that the mechanisms have only poorly been used and have not lived up to expectations. Drawing from these findings, *Henner Gött* explores the potential of 'an Individual Labour Complaint Procedure for Workers, Trade Unions, Employers and NGOs in Future Free Trade Agreements'. This proposal is aiming at endowing those actors which have a genuine interest in the implementation of labour chapters in trade agreements with the procedural means to do so, thus enhancing the chapter's overall performance. The debate on labour chapters in trade agreements has an immediate and continuing practical relevance. The EU-Canada Comprehensive Economic and Trade Agreement (CETA), which was signed in October 2016 and is being provisionally applied at the time of this writing, has received widespread public attention and criticism in Europe. The same is true for the envisaged EU-US Transatlantic Trade and Investment Partnership (TTIP), which, despite its fate being uncertain after the last presidential election in the USA, is likely to remain a point of reference in future trade negotiations. *Reingard Zimmer* analyses these agreements with a special focus on social standards. She is particularly concerned about the far-reaching mechanisms for regulatory cooperation and investment protection.

Next to trade provisions, investment liberalization and protection is an integral part of recent trade agreements. *Henner Gött* and *Till Patrik Holterhus* discuss whether the combination of investment and labour chapters in recent free trade agreements may enhance the role of labour standards in international investment law. They conclude that there are indeed 'opportunities to promote an adequate balance of investor and labour concerns', but the provisions in contemporary agreements and drafts 'do not in themselves sufficiently steer towards this goal'.

Besides trade and investment, the law of international financial institutions is the third important pillar of international economic law. In historical perspective, the World Bank Group member organizations' approaches to labour standards have repeatedly led to conflicts and critique. *Franz Christian Ebert* explains that, in 2016, the World Bank has 'for the first time [set out] detailed labour standards requirements for both the Bank's staff and its borrowers', which, however, have their shortcomings.

The volume's third part addresses the numerous and diverse non-state actor approaches to enhance the protection and promotion of labour standards in the globalized economy.

The inclusion of labour standards in self-imposed corporate codes of conduct has received wide resonance in academia and practice, including both appraisal and critique. *Katja Gehne* approaches this phenomenon from a practitioner's point of view. Finding that 'soft standards at the international level have emerged as a standard of responsible business management', she argues that they 'could be part of a (para-)legal answer to deficiencies of national states' human rights protection systems'. To step in governance gaps is also the purpose of joint endeavors of trade union federations and multinational groups to strengthen labour standards in corporate governance by way of international framework agreements. In his contribution, *Rüdiger Krause* highlights that the success of such agreements largely depends on them being implemented in strong and resilient industrial relations, which in turn they are able to reinforce. Therefore, he calls for the conclusion of more robust international framework agreements in the future. Exploring unilateral enforcement of international labour standards through adjudicatory means, *Anja Seibert-Fohr* discusses the domestic enforcement of international labour standards under the US Alien Tort Claims Act. While recent decisions have put up considerable substantive and procedural hurdles, she concludes that 'the door is not closed and federal courts are still in the process of delimiting the exact scope of ATS litigation'. She argues that jurisdiction could and should be assumed in cases of violations of sufficiently established international labour standards with a territorial link to the USA. Turning to more indirect and promotional approaches, *Nazli Aghazadeh* examines the effectiveness of social labelling to implement labour standards along global supply chains. Using the example of three social labelling schemes, she finds that all three of these schemes by and large fail to minimize the 'information asymmetry' between consumers and producers, mainly because of NGOs' lack of capacity to monitor producers' adherence to the schemes. She proposes that this issue be addressed by regulation and cooperation with the ILO.

Instead of a summing up, the volume's fourth part offers a conclusion of a different kind. *Peter-Tobias Stoll*, *Henner Gött* and *Patrick Abel* present a textual proposal for a labour chapter to be included in future EU trade agreements. This model labour chapter has been published and publicly debated in the context of pending EU trade negotiations and revisions of major trade agreements. It has been informed by—and is in many ways the result of—the extensive research, analyses and discussions conducted on the protection and promotion of labour standards in international economic law in politics, society and academia. The model labour chapter aims at making a practical and constructive contribution to the ongoing debate on the protection and promotion of labour standards in the globalized economy.

References

Bakvis P (2009) The World Bank's doing business report: a last fling for the Washington consensus? Transfer: Eur Rev Labour Res 15(3–4):419–438

Burkett BW (2011) International framework agreements: an emerging international regulatory approach or a passing European phenomenon. Can Labour Employ Law J 16(1):81–114

Davarnejad L (2011) In the shadow of soft law: the handling of corporate social responsibility disputes under the OECD guidelines for multinational enterprises. J Dispute Resolut 2011 (2):351–385

Hepple B (2005) Labour laws and global trade. Hart Publishing, Oxford

ILO (1999) Decent work: Report of the Director-General to the International Labour Conference, 87th Session 1999. ILO, Geneva

ILO (2016) Assessment of labour provisions in trade and investment agreements. Studies on growth with equity. ILO, Geneva

Kolben K (2010) Labor rights as human rights? Virginia Journal of International Law 50:449–484

Leary VA (1997) The WTO and the social clause: post-Singapore. Eur J Int Law (1):118–122

Maupain F (2013) The future of the International Labour Organization in the global economy. Hart, Oxford

Peters A, Koechlin L, Förster T, Zinkernagel F (eds) (2009) Non-state actors as standard setters. Cambridge University Press, Cambridge

Seidman G (2009) Social labeling in export supply chains: can voluntary certification programs end child labor? India in transition. University of Pennsylvania, Philadelphia

Servais J-M (2014) International labour law, 4th edn. Kluwer Law International, Alphen an den Rhijn

Swepston L (2013) The International Labour Organization and international human rights system. In: Sheeran S, Sir Rodley N (eds) Routledge handbook of international human rights law. Routledge, London, pp 339–352

Vosko LF (2002) 'Decent work': the shifting role of the ILO and the struggle for global social justice. Glob Soc Policy 2(1):19–46

Weiss F (2005) Trade and labor I. In: Macrory PFJ, Appleton AE, Plummer MG (eds) The World Trade Organization: legal, economic and political analysis, vol II. Springer, New York, pp 571–596

Part I
Setting the Scene

International Economic and Social Dimensions: Divided or Connected?

Peter-Tobias Stoll

Contents

P.-T. Stoll (✉)
Georg-August-University Göttingen, Institute of International and European Law, Göttingen, Germany
e-mail: pstoll@gwdg.de

H. Gött (ed.), *Labour Standards in International Economic Law*,
https://doi.org/10.1007/978-3-319-69447-4_2

1 Introduction

The recent discussions on trade and labour standards as reflected in this book mirror the widespread concern that today's international legal framework for globalization does not sufficiently address labour conditions and, more generally, social justice.[1] As is often observed, it appears that globalization moves on with the help of creating and further developing international 'economic' institutions and rules, while the 'social' aspects are left behind and marginalized. Often, this goes along with statements indicating that economic and social concerns have been more closely linked in the past and that they should come this close again. A historical and analytical *tour d'horizon* might help to give context to the recent discussion by offering a short overview over a bit more than a century of international relations and some reflections on what has been understood to be 'economic' and 'social' and how the two are or should be interrelated.

2 The Interwar Period: The International Labour Organization and Stubborn Nationalism in Economic Affairs

A look to the past may start with the establishment of the International Labour Organization in the aftermath of World War I in 1919. Indeed, the establishment of this organization as a part of the Versailles peace treaty has made labour conditions and social justice a permanent international concern, closely linked to peace.[2] In its preamble, the ILO constitution explicitly states that a 'universal and lasting peace can be established only if it is based upon social justice'[3] and furthermore acknowledges that 'conditions of labour exist involving such injustice, hardship and privation to large numbers of people as to produce unrest so great that the peace and

[1]See for instance, the labour chapters in prominent free trade agreements: Chapter 23 Trade and Labour of the Comprehensive Economic and Trade Agreement (CETA) and Chapter 19 Labor of the Trans-Pacific Partnership (TPP), consolidated text available at https://ustr.gov/trade-agreements/free-trade-agreements/trans-pacific-partnership/tpp-full-text. Accessed 22 Dec 2016.

[2]Treaty of Peace between the Allied and Associated Powers and Germany, signed at Versailles, 28 June 1919, 225 CTS 188, Part XIII Labour; see also Schorkopf (2010).

[3]Preamble (1) ILO Constitution, signed 28 June 1919, 15 UNTS 30, 15 UNTS 40.

harmony of the world are imperilled'.[4] Drawing from earlier international developments, including international conferences convened and some international agreements concluded to improve the situation of workers before World War I,[5] the ILO was tasked with the creation of international labour standards. ILO activities in this regard were quite successful.[6] However, these improvements of labour conditions hardly came to bearing, as the working class, just as the societies at large, greatly suffered from the world economic crisis.[7]

This economic crisis has been importantly aggravated by the lack of willingness of States to cooperate. Instead, a beggar-thy-neighbour policy[8] prevailed, with governments resorting to national approaches at the expense of other states. The League of Nations was poorly equipped to address the issue as it was neither mandated to do so nor had institutional structures at hand. Both the 1922 Genoa[9] and the 1933 London[10] conference failed to achieve a consensus of States to jointly address the challenges of the world economic crisis.[11]

When looking at this period, it appears fair to conclude that it has seen impressive international progress in labour rights, while turning the working classes into mass unemployment and misery as a result of the inability of governments to cooperate to cope with the great depression and the world economic crisis and a general destabilization of Europe in the wake of World War II.[12]

3 Uniting Economic and Social Dimensions? Early Institution Building After World War II

This important failure has been quite influential in the process of institution building after World War II. As early as 1941, the leaders of the United Kingdom and the United States, Churchill and Roosevelt, laid down their visions for the future world order in the Atlantic Charter.[13] The document can be understood as an embryonic master plan for the establishment of the later United Nations and the post-war world order, prominently featuring its economic and social dimensions. The Atlantic Charter addresses economic issues like liberalization and non-discrimination in

[4]Preamble (2) ILO Constitution, signed 28 June 1919, 15 UNTS 30, 15 UNTS 40.

[5]Such as the Convention respecting the Prohibition of Night Work for Women in Industrial Employment, signed 26 September 1906, 203 CTS 4; see Sauer (2014).

[6]Troclet (1952), p. 421 and Haas (1964), pp. 148 et seqq.

[7]Adamthwaite (2016), pp. 216 et seqq. and Overy (2016), pp. 99 et seqq.

[8]Bowles (2009), p. 127 et seqq. and Overy (2010), pp. 53 et seqq.

[9]Conference of Genoa, 10 April–19 May, 1922; Overy (2010), pp. 53 et seqq.

[10]The London Economic Conference, 12–27 July 1933; see Clarke (1973), pp. 19 et seqq.

[11]See Clarke (1973), p. 2.

[12]Haas (1964), pp. 154–155; Troclet (1952), pp. 422 and 710 and Rodgers et al. (2009), pp. 97 et seq.

[13]United States, Office of War Information, Division of Public Inquiries (1941) The Atlantic Charter. http://digital.library.unt.edu/ark:/67531/metadc581/. Accessed 22 Dec 2016.

trade, access to raw materials and economic prosperity,[14] economic advancement and a cooperation of States in economic matters, and at the same time alludes to the social dimension in mentioning labour standards and social security.[15] 'Economic advancement' in this context can be considered to address both social and economic issues.[16] To the more, in alluding to a freedom from fear and want,[17] a wording that Roosevelt had introduced some months earlier in his State of the Union Address, the Charter introduces a key term for the later development of human rights.[18] In Roosevelt's words: 'freedom from want (. . .), translated into world terms, means economic understandings which will secure to every nation a healthy peacetime life for its inhabitants—everywhere in the world.'[19]

3.1 The ILO and the 1944 Philadelphia Declaration as an Early Starter

In the early institutional building after World War II, there was a short moment when the International Labour Organization was considered to play a major role also in cooperation for economic policy-making. The so-called Philadelphia Declaration, adopted in 1944 at the 26th International Labour Conference in Philadelphia, envisaged that the ILO should play a central role in economic policy-making by endowing it with a competence to scrutinize the work of other international economic organizations as to social aspects.[20] The declaration reiterates the relevance of social justice for a lasting peace and goes on in stating that

> all human beings, irrespective of race, creed or sex, have the right to pursue both their material well-being and their spiritual development in conditions of freedom and dignity, of economic security and equal opportunity (II a).

---

[14]The fourth paragraph of the Charter reads: 'Fourth, [the United Kingdom and the United States] will endeavor . . . to further the enjoyment by all States, great or small, victor or vanquished, of access, on equal terms, to the *trade and to the raw materials of the world* which are needed for their *economic prosperity*;' (emphasis added).

[15]The fifth paragraph of the Charter reads: 'Fifth, they desire to bring about the *fullest collaboration between all nations in the economic field with the object of securing, for all, improved labor standards, economic advancement and social security*;' (emphasis added).

[16]Ibid.

[17]The sixth paragraph of the Charter reads: 'Sixth, after the final destruction of the Nazi tyranny, they hope to see established a peace which will afford to all nations the means of dwelling in safety within their own boundaries, *and which will afford assurance that all the men in all lands may live out their lives in freedom from fear and want;* '(emphasis added).

[18]The term resurfaces e.g. in the preamble of the 1948 Universal Declaration of Human Rights, UN GA Res. 217(III) A.

[19]Roosevelt (1941).

[20]ILO Declaration Concerning the Aims and Purposes of the International Labour Organisation (Declaration of Philadelphia), adopted on 10 May 1944.

The declaration went on in stating that

> (b) the attainment of the conditions in which this shall be possible must constitute a central aim of national and international policy;
>
> (c) all national and international policies and measures, in particular those of an economic and financial character, should be judged in this light and accepted only insofar as they may be held to promote and not to hinder the achievement of this fundamental objective;
>
> (d) it is a responsibility of the International Labour Organization to examine and consider all international economic and financial policies and measures in the light of this fundamental objective;
>
> (e) in discharging the tasks entrusted to it the International Labour Organization, having considered all relevant economic and financial factors, may include in its decisions and recommendations any provisions which it considers appropriate. (II lit. a, b, c, d and e).

The Philadelphia Declaration, which eventually was annexed to the revised ILO Constitution in 1946, can be seen as a milestone in view of the ILO and its work. It has importantly broadened the objectives of the organization in applying a more general and human-rights-type language and in referring to economic security as a broader term, encompassing both macroeconomic elements as well as a human rights-type approach.[21] However, the aspirations concerning the role of the ILO as voiced in the declaration were obviously too ambitious and at the same time not specific enough to materialize. At the time of the adoption of the Philadelphia Declaration, plans were underway firstly to create much more specific and functional international structures and secondly to establish a much broader and general international organization, namely the United Nations.[22] Obviously, the protagonists of the United Nations were eager to equip that organization with the maximum amount of competencies and were reluctant to give established pre-war institutions much of a say.[23]

3.2 The World Bank Group and Keynesian Thought

The formation of today's international system after World War II has particularly focused on this aspect of economic cooperation, which had been combined from the very beginning with a social dimension. Alongside to the establishment of the United Nations, the World Bank Group was founded.[24] The International Bank

[21] Maul (2012), pp. 83 et seqq. and Monteiro (2014), pp. 213 et seqq.

[22] Swepston (2013), pp. 339 et seqq.

[23] UN, Report of the Preparatory Commission, 23 Dec 1945, PC/20, pp. 40 et seqq.; Haas (1964), p. 163 and Meng (2012), Art. 57, paras. 31 et seqq.

[24] The World Bank Group is comprised by five institutions: The International Bank for Reconstruction and Development (IBRD), The International Development Association (IDA), The International Finance Cooperation (IFC), The Multilateral Investment Guarantee Agency (MIGA) and The International Centre for Settlement of Investment Dispute (ICSID). See on the nomenclature Ragazzi (2014), mn. 1 et seq.

for Reconstruction and Development, now known as the World Bank, was established already in July 1944 as an institution to finance the reconstruction of those countries and regions devastated by World War II.[25] To the more, the World Bank had a more general mandate to finance development, which today is its main purpose. The International Monetary Fund (IMF) as established in December 1945 was designed as a mechanism for a joint response to monetary problems.[26]

The founding documents of both these instruments are noteworthy as they clearly involve a social element. According to Art. I (III) of its Articles of Agreement,[27] the purpose of the World Bank is

> [t]o promote the long-range balanced growth of international trade and the maintenance of equilibrium in balances of payments by encouraging international investment for the development of the productive resources of members.

However, the provision goes on in adding

> thereby assisting in raising productivity, the standard of living and conditions of labor in their territories.

Accordingly, Art. I of the IMF's Articles of Agreement[28] set out that the purpose of the Fund is

> (ii) [t]o facilitate the expansion and balanced growth of inter-national trade, and to contribute thereby to the promotion and maintenance of high levels of employment and real income and to the development of the productive resources of all members as primary objectives of economic policy.

Both these institutions were deeply influenced by Keynesian thought and moreover by John Maynard Keynes in person, who acted as a British delegate in those negotiations.[29] As is well known, the inclusion of employment and the raising of incomes into the agenda of economic policymaking has been one of his most significant findings.[30]

3.3 *The United Nations: World Economic and Social Governance*

The formation of the United Nations as the universal and general organization follows this pattern. The most visible institutional manifestation of the close link between economic and social issues certainly has been the establishment of the

[25] Articles of Agreement of the International Bank for Reconstruction and Development, 27 Dec 1945, 2 UNTS 134.

[26] Articles of Agreement of the International Monetary Fund, 22 July 1944, 2 UNTS 39.

[27] See Fn. 26.

[28] See Fn. 27.

[29] For an overview see e.g. Kitanovic and Kozuharov (2012), pp. 83 et seqq.

[30] See for instance: Keynes (1935).

Economic and Social Council (ECOSOC) as one of the principal organs of the organization.[31] In substantial terms, the link is most importantly reflected by Art. 55 UN Charter, which can be seen as the 'work programme' of ECOSOC. It reiterates the link between peace and economic and social progress as originally introduced by the ILO Constitution. Moreover, it is much more explicit about economic aspects, including their social dimension. In this vein, Art. 55 lit. a refers to

> higher standards of living, full employment, and conditions of economic and social progress and development;

and in this way alludes to the Keynesian ideas as reflected in the Articles of Agreements of the World Bank and the IMF. Art. 55 (b), jointly with Art. 56, calls for a co-operation in matters of *inter alia* 'economic, social, health, and related problems' and (c) addresses the issue of human rights.[32]

3.4 The Universal Declaration of Human Rights: Social Rights and Human Rights

In 1948, the General Assembly adopted the Universal Declaration of Human Rights (UDHR),[33] which set out the UN human rights agenda for the years to come and can be seen as a forerunner for the two 1966 United Nations Human Rights Covenants.[34] Most importantly and in contrast to the constitutions of many member States, the UDHR embraces both political and civil as well as economic and social rights. In the latter regard, it features a number of rights which have a close connection to labour standards and rights, as is true for instance for the right to form unions (Art. 23 (4)), the right to equal pay (Art. 23 (2)), the right to rest and leisure, a reasonable limitation of working hours and periodic holidays with pay (Art. 24). Furthermore, a number of rights reflect the idea of social security, just as the right to protection against unemployment (Art. 23 (1)) and the right to a just and favourable remuneration and means of social protection (Art. 23 (3)). Furthermore and without a link to labour and employment, the UDHR in the sense of more general social rights stipulates in Art. 25 (1) a right to an adequate

> standard of living (...) including food, clothing, housing and medical care and necessary social services, and the right to security in the event of unemployment, sickness, disability, widowhood, old age or other lack of livelihood in circumstances beyond his control.

Altogether, the Declaration is a cornerstone of the international human rights system and its further development. It is even more relevant in the context discussed

[31] Art. 61 UN Charter.

[32] Stoll (2012), Art 55 (a) and (b), paras. 12–13 and Riedel and Arend (2012), Art 55 (c), para. 8.

[33] Universal Declaration of Human Rights, UN GA Res. 217(III) A.

[34] International Covenant on Economic, Social and Cultural Rights, 16 Dec 1966, 993 UNTS 3; International Covenant on Civil and Political Rights, 16 Dec 1966, 999 UNTS 171.

here, as it explicitly stipulates 'social' rights, and thereby translates ideas of social justice into individual entitlements.

3.5 *The 1948 Havana Charter: A World Economic and Social Order Under the Auspices of the UN*

Within the United Nations and more particularly under the aegis of ECOSOC, initiatives have been taken to establish an institutional framework and rules for the world economy in conformity with the more general objectives and principles voiced by Art. 55 UN Charter.

Driven by quite some optimism as to what world governance may achieve in international economic relations, an agreement was negotiated in this regard, which included a number of issues, such as trade, economic development, raw materials and competition. To implement and administer these rules, an international organization, named the International Trade Organization was envisaged, which was supposed to work as a specialized agency under the supervision of ECOSOC.[35] This impressive international instrument, named the Havana Charter,[36] did address several pertinent economic policy issues. This is true for Chapter III on economic development and reconstruction as well as for Chapter VI on commodities and commodity agreements.

Even more impressive is its chapter II on 'employment and economic activity', which links economic and social dimensions in several ways. Arts. 2 to 6 reflect contemporary—or more clearly: Keynesian—economic thought by calling for employment and economic growth and by addressing some particular aspects of economic policy. The often-cited Art. 7 relates to 'fair labour standards' and this way links to the work of the ILO. The article acknowledges

> that measures relating to employment must take fully into account the rights of workers under inter-governmental declarations, conventions and agreements.

Furthermore, the provision speaks about the 'common interest of members in the achievement in maintenance of fair labour standards related to productivity and thus in the improvement of wages and working conditions as productivity may permit.' Also, Art. 7 (1) Havana Charter addresses the linkage to trade in pointing out that unfair labour conditions may create difficulties in international trade. At this point, Art.7 Havana Charter called on members to take whatever action may be appropriate and feasible to eliminate such conditions within its territory. It furthermore envisages consultations and a co-operation with the ILO.[37]

---

[35]Stoll (2012), Art 55 (a) and (b), para. 44.

[36]Havana Charter for an International Trade Organization, 24 March 1948, UN Doc E/CONF.2/78.

[37]Art 7 (3) of the Havana Charter reads: 'In all matters relating to labour standards [. . .] it shall consult and cooperate with the International Labour Organisation.'

After having been concluded in 1948, the Havana Charter eventually failed after the US Senate had indicated that it would not ratify the instrument.[38]

3.6 An Early Divide: The GATT Agreement

During the negotiations of the Havana Charter, tariff reductions had been agreed among parties based on reciprocity in the context of the trade chapter of the Charter. To implement those achievements as early as possible, these tariff reductions, together with provisions of the trade chapter, were applied provisionally. After it became clear that the charter would not come into force, those few trade rules, together with the tariff concessions, were separately framed as the General Agreement on Tariffs and Trade (GATT),[39] which did not embody the aforesaid labour-related provisions of the Havana Charter. The GATT was applied provisionally based on a Protocol on Provisional Application.[40] This development can be seen as a divide, as the GATT and its provisions on the promotion of international trade were applied, whereas the manifold other provisions of the Havana Charter, which did address 'social' aspects, were dropped.

3.7 In Sum: Important Achievements and Pragmatic Promotion of Economic Cooperation

Altogether, the desire to combine economic and social dimensions and to promote international cooperation in these areas has largely guided the architecture of the post-war international order. The institutional setup of the United Nations as well as the World Bank group reflect this desire, based on contemporary economic thought. Even more, some of the main ideas of social justice and labour standards were translated into individual entitlements with the UDHR, which guided the further development of the international human rights system. However, the impressive project to create a more concrete institutional and normative frame for the world economy along those lines—the Havana Charter—failed. In a very pragmatic way, a small fragment of the Charter dealing with trade was separately applied, while the rest of the ambitious project was dropped. What is more, the World Bank quickly adopted a remarkably narrow interpretation of its own mandate, striving to isolate financial considerations from seemingly 'political' issues, including labour and human rights issues.[41]

[38] See Sacerdoti (2014), para. 10.

[39] General Agreement on Tariffs and Trade 1994, Marrakesh Agreement Establishing the World Trade Organization, 15 Apr 1994, Annex 1A, 1867 UNTS 187, 33 I.L.M. 1153 (Hereinafter cited as 'GATT').

[40] Protocol of Provisional Application of the General Agreement on Tariffs and Trade, 30 Oct 1947, 55 UNTS 308.

[41] Maupain (2013), pp. 73 et seqq.; Janse (2014) and Cissé (2012), pp. 78 et seqq.

4 Development as a 'Social' Concern and the New International Economic Order

Decolonization quickly became a main issue in the work of the United Nations.[42] After having attained their political independence, the new States were heading for economic independence and development. The formation of a group of developing countries in the UN General Assembly, the Group of 77, created a strong political momentum to put the issue of development on the agenda of the UN and to create new bodies such as UNCTAD and UNDP and many others.[43]

The four UN development decades and a number of GA declarations set the scene for a long-lasting process by which developing countries aimed to adapt the world economy and its rules to accommodate to what they saw as priorities for development.[44] The main concept behind this development agenda can be seen as a 'social' one, as it was based on an idea of a responsibility of the state community or more specifically of the developed countries to assist developing countries by financial and other means and to cooperate with a view to change the rules for international economic activities to the benefit of developing countries.[45]

Development in those days was primarily defined with a view to the national economy and macroeconomic parameters such as the gross national product, economic growth and the per capita income of the population. The closing of the 'gap' between developed and developing countries was taken as a major benchmark in the various decisions and texts at the time. Also, development was seen in the context of independence, and thus had a strong link to sovereignty. In terms of theory, the gap-theory, the *dependencia*-theory and several postmarxist approaches were quite influential.[46] Particularly the *dependencia*-theory is worth mentioning, as it saw developing countries as being dependent on an unjust world economic order. In this way, the existing international economic system was considered to

---

[42]See i.e. Declaration on the Granting of Independence to Colonial Countries and Peoples, 14 Dec 1960, UN GA A/RES/15/1514.

[43]Fabbricotti (2009); Fortin (2013) and Schoiswohl (2013).

[44]It nevertheless had the effect of mobilizing them to obtain reforms and concessions, often in the form of UN General Assembly resolutions: Resolution 1710 (XVI), 19 Dec 1961; Resolution 2626 (XXV), 24 Oct 1970; Resolution 35/56, 5 Dec 1980 and Resolution 45/199, 21 Dec 1990 concerning the Development Decades; Resolutions 3201 (S-VI) and 3202 (S-VI), 1 May 1974 on the New International Economic Order; Charter of Economic Rights and Duties of States, Resolution 3281 (XXIX), 12 Dec 1974; Resolution 3362 (S-VII), 16 Sep 1975 on development and international economic co-operation and Resolution 34/150, 17 Dec 1979 on the principles of the new international economic order. But in 1986, the developing countries did not succeed in winning general acceptance or recognition of the right to development, GA Res 41/128, 4 Dec 1986.

[45]See for instance Charter of Economic Rights and Duties of States, GA Res. 3281 (XXIX), 12 Dec 1974.

[46]James (1997), pp. 205 et seqq.

represent a double standard of morality, a term which clearly alludes to the question of social justice.

In substance, the concept of development in those days focused on industrialization,[47] while other issues such as agriculture or the basic needs of individuals were only added later. The issue of labour conditions was hardly ever mentioned. In view of the international economy, the discussions focused on whether developing countries should become an integrated part of the world economy, what benefits they could achieve this way and how their situation could be improved.[48] Besides industrialization in general, one relevant point in this regard was the export of commodities; in respect of which several details were discussed, including the stabilization of commodity prices, trade policy, the shipment of such commodities, competition issues, investment for extractive activities, and the role and conduct of multinational enterprises.[49] The declaration on the permanent sovereignty over natural resources[50] was a major cornerstone in this regard, which was later complemented by the Declaration and Programme of Action of a New International Economic Order[51] and by the Charter of Economic Rights and Duties of States.[52]

This period of the development of international economic law with its focus on development saw some achievements. One such achievement was the granting of preferential market access for developing countries in the context of GATT,[53] by GATT decisions addressing economic development and the special and differential treatment of developing countries,[54] including the insertion of a Chapter IV to GATT and the adoption of the enabling clause.[55] Another was the establishment of UNCTAD's commodity programme.[56] Furthermore, codes on restrictive business

[47]Yusuf (2009), pp. 5 et seqq.

[48]See e.g. World Bank, World Development Report 1978.

[49]Ibid. pp. 19 et seq.

[50]GA Res. 3281 (XVII), 12 Dec 1974.

[51]GA Res. 3281 (XXIX), 12 Dec 1974 and GA Res. 3202 (S-VI), 1 May 1974.

[52]Charter of Economic Rights and Duties of States, GA Res. 3281 (XXIX), 29 Sess., 12 Dec 1974, UN Doc. A/RES/29/3281.

[53]Especially concerning the Generalised System of Preferences (GSP) and the concept of Special and Differential Treatment. See also: WTO Committee on Trade and Development (2013) Special and Differential Treatment Provisions in WTO Agreements and Decisions, WT/COMTD/W/196.

[54]See e.g. Report of the Review Working Party (1955) Quantitative Restrictions, BISD III, Supp 170 and Report of the Review Working Party (1955) Schedules and Customs Administration, BISD III, Supp 205. Furthermore, see Committee on Trade and Development (1980) Note by the Secretariat, COMTD/W/311. See as an example WTO, *India – Quantitive Restrictions on Imports of Agricultural, Textile and Industrial Products*, Report of the Panel, 6 April 1999, WT/DS90/R. Tortora (2003), p. 5.

[55]World Trade Organization (1979) Differential and More Favourable Treatment: Reciprocity and Fuller Participation of Developing Countries, WTO Doc No L/4903; see also: http://www.wto.org/english/docs-e/legal-e/enabling-e.pdf. Accessed 1 Sept 2016.

[56]UNCTAD, Integrated Programme for Commodities, 30 May 1976, TD/RES/93 (IV).

practices[57] and technology transfer[58] were concluded in UN bodies, albeit there was a lack of consensus to undertake the further step to translate them into binding agreements.

4.1 International Investments in Focus: CSR and International Investment Law

A particularly contested issue in these discussions in the UN and outside has been the role of foreign economic activities and primarily foreign direct investment and the activities of multinational enterprises. The issue played a role in the aforementioned negotiations on restrictive business practices and technology transfer.

4.1.1 From the United Nations Code of Conduct on Transnational Corporations to Corporate Social Responsibility

However, the key project in this regard has been the elaboration of a United Nations Code of Conduct on Transnational Corporations (UNCTAD MNE Code) within UNCTAD with the help of a United Nations Centre on Transnational Corporations (UNCTC) that was established in 1974.[59]

The relevance of the issue in terms of international economic and social policy is evidenced by the very fact that it—and UNCTAD's ambitions in this regard—provoked two other international bodies to engage and to come up with their own projects in the matter. Ironically, these two activities succeeded early and quickly, whereas the UNCTAD project eventually failed after some difficult negotiations in 1992.[60]

One of these projects was the OECD Declaration on International Investment and Multinational Enterprises which was adopted in June 1976.[61] The OECD addressed the issue early on by a Committee on International Investment and Multinational Enterprises.[62] The declaration contained various elements. Its most

[57]The Set of Multilaterally Agreed Equitable Principles and Rules for the Control of Restrictive Business Practices, Dec 1980, A/RES/35/63. See also UN (1981) Doc TD/RBP/ CONF/10/Rev.1.

[58]UNCTAD Secretariat Report (1975) An International Code of Conduct on the Transfer of Technology, UN Doc TD/B/C.6/AC.1/2/Supp 1/Rev. 1. See Patel et al. (2000).

[59]Sauvant (2015).

[60]Ibid., p. 34.

[61]See OECD Declaration on International Investment and Multinational Enterprises, 21 June 1976, C(76)99 (Final). For the most recent version see http://www.oecd.org/daf/inv/investment-policy/oecddeclaration anddecisions.htm. Accessed 15 Sep 2014. As of late 2014, all 34 OECD member countries and 12 non-OECD members had adhered to the Declaration.

[62]OECD Resolution of the Council establishing a Committee on International Investment and Multinational Enterprises, 21 Jan 1975, C(74)247(Final).

prominent part surely was the 'Guidelines for Multinational Enterprises' as attached to the Declaration. These guidelines, which explicitly were characterized as legally non-binding, included provisions on economic issues such as competition, taxation and technology, but also a chapter on 'Employment and Industrial Relations'. Apart from these guidelines, the declaration contains elements concerning the treatment of foreign investors. These are 'National Treatment' and 'International Investment Incentives and Disincentives'. In regard to the former, a 'Decision of the Council on National Treatment' is annexed that calls for national treatment of enterprises from other OECD member States. As is sometimes observed, the declaration and its elements aim at promoting rights and obligations of multinational enterprises in a balanced way.

The other project, which paralleled the elaboration of the UNCTAD MNE Code was the 1977 ILO 'Tripartite Declaration of Principles Concerning Multinational Enterprises and Social Policy'.[63] It focused on the role of such enterprises and spelt out respective obligations of States and enterprises in view of employment, training, 'conditions of work and life', 'industrial relations', the 'examination of grievances' and the settlement of 'industrial disputes'.

Both these projects later on became the starting point of a number of developments, which aimed at establishing principles and standards of corporate social responsibility.

4.1.2 The Emergence of International Investment Law

The critical views on the role of foreign economic activities in developing countries voiced in the United Nations and the discussions and negotiations on various new agreements to control such activities caused quite some concern among developed countries.[64] The clear tendency among developing countries to subject expropriations and the treatment of foreign direct investments to their national laws and courts was felt to importantly put into question the legal stability and credibility necessary for promoting foreign direct investments. Furthermore, it was feared that these activities could undermine the existing customary international law standards for the protection of property of foreigners.[65]

The OECD Declaration had attempted to address the legitimate interests of enterprises together with their responsibilities. However, a number of developed countries were seeking protection of their enterprises and investors on a bilateral track outside the heated debates in the United Nations and without linking such protection to certain responsibilities.[66] With the 1959 Germany Pakistan Bilateral

[63]ILO Tripartite Declaration of Principles Concerning Multinational Enterprises and Social Policy, adopted on 16 Nov 1977.

[64]Schill et al. (2015), pp. 21 et seqq.

[65]See for instance Francis and Nicholson (1965).

[66]Dolzer and Schreuer (2008), pp. 3 et seqq.

Investment Treaty a new development started[67] which resulted in over 3200 bilateral investment treaties (BITs) today.[68] As an alternative to submitting disputes concerning foreign direct investment to host state rules and courts, industrialized countries promoted the concept of settling investment disputes at international level under the auspices of international law.[69] In order to furnish their project with the credibility of an international institution, they initiated the establishment of a mechanism for investor-state dispute settlement within the World Bank Group, the International Centre for the Settlement of Investment Disputes (ICSID).[70] Early BITs were mainly focused on the protection of the investor in view of its investments. However, the scope of application of BITs expanded considerably over time. In later agreements, even rights in view of the pre-investment stage were added.[71]

4.2 The Development of the Global Human Rights System

Also in the 1960s, and roughly 20 years after the Universal Declaration of Human Rights, the United Nations succeeded in adopting important human rights instruments. The International Covenant on Civil and Political Rights[72] and the International Covenant on Economic, Social and Cultural Rights[73] were adapted in 1966 and reflected related parts of the UDHR. The ILO, having administered the only universal supervisory system until then, assisted in the drafting of the UN Covenants and influenced the provisions related to labour rights.[74] Particularly the ICESCR contained a number of rights, which can be considered to parallel labour standards.

---

[67]Treaty between the Federal Republic of Germany and Pakistan for the Promotion and Protection of Investments, signed on 25 Nov 1959, 457 UNTS 23.

[68]See http://investmentpolicyhub.unctad.org/IIA. Accessed 1 Sept 2016.

[69]Reinisch and Malintoppi (2008).

[70]Convention on the Settlement of Investment Dispute between States and Nationals of Other States (ICSID Convention), 18 Mar 1965, 575 UNTS 159.

[71]For instance, pre-investment rights protection could be found in 'US model' bilateral investment treaties and the investment chapters of free trade agreements such as NAFTA; see also Houde and Yannaca-Small (2004).

[72]International Covenant on Civil and Political Rights, 16 Dec 1966, 999 UNTS 171.

[73]International Covenant on Economic, Social and Cultural Rights, 16 Dec 1966, 993 UNTS 3.

[74]Alston (1979) and Rodgers et al. (2009), p. 39. See also the express references to the ILO Freedom of Association and Protection of the Right to Organise Convention 1948 (No. 87) in the final text of Art. 22 (3) ICCPR and Art. 8 (3) ICESCR.

4.3 In Sum: Ideologic Battles and Some Progress

It appears that in this era of international relations, the issue of labour conditions and social justice was fully absorbed by the many heated debates about development and the justice of the world economic system. Development was seen strictly as a sovereignty issue, which made it difficult to address the situation of certain groups or individuals in particular countries. However, beyond the many debates and negotiations, which did hardly succeed, some achievements have to be noted, such as the codification of social human rights and tariff preferences for developing countries, which later on served as vehicles for imposing labour conditionalities on developing states. Just as the GATT can be seen as a pragmatic turn to simple trade facilitation after the failure of a much more comprehensive project, the emergence of investment protection can be seen as the very simple and pragmatic outcome, which neglected the highly contested issue of a responsibility of foreign enterprises and investors.

5 The 'Era of Globalization'

The fall of the Berlin wall is often seen as a major turning point in international relations. The dissolution of the USSR and the Warsaw Pact as well as the transition of many formerly socialist states to market economy sparked new developments in the international economic and social order.[75]

5.1 Sustainable Development: The 1992 Rio Conference

The first United Nations event which took place after these groundbreaking historical events was the 1992 Rio de Janeiro United Nations Conference on Environment and Development.[76] The Rio Conference was a follow-up to earlier United Nations conferences on the environment[77] and its main achievements has been the conclusion and signature of two prominent international environmental agreements, namely the Convention on Biological Diversity and the United Nations Framework Convention on Climate Change.[78] However, as its title already indicates, the

[75]Kolodko (1999) and Stoll (2009), pp. 273 et seq.

[76]United Nations (1992) Report of the United Nations conference on environmental and development, 3–14 June 1992, A/CONF.151/26.

[77]United Nations (1972) Report of the United Nations Conference on the Human Environment, 5–16 June 1972, A/CONF.48/14Rev.1.

[78]Convention on Biological Diversity, concluded 5 June 1992, 1760 UNTS 79 and United Nations Framework Convention on Climate Change, signed on 9 May 1992, 1771 UNTS 107. See also Dupuy (2013), pp. 11 et seqq.

conference was based on a new approach which combines environmental protection with economic and social development. This conceptual frame, which was coined as sustainable development, was based on the understanding that economic development and the preservation of the environment have to go hand in hand.[79]

In view of the social dimension of the sustainable development concept, the conference and its most important outcome documents, the Rio Declaration on Sustainable Development and the Agenda 21, feature a comprehensive understanding of development, which considerably deviates from earlier concepts. Poverty eradication figures prominently in this concept. Furthermore, particular groups of society, such as women, children and particularly indigenous groups and communities are mentioned.[80] Thus, the concept of development became less focused on particular states and their sovereignty and independence but rather began to address individuals, groups and societies. Moreover in view of the 'economic' dimension of development inherent in the sustainable development concept, the texts reflect a much friendlier attitude towards free and open markets both inside countries as well as at the international level. In this perspective, the two documents broadly address issues of international trade and in particular the on-going Uruguay round of multilateral trade negotiations and foreign investments.[81]

5.2 The Establishment of the World Trade Organization

Only 3 years later, states concluded the Uruguay round of multilateral trade negotiations and established the WTO as of January 1, 1995.[82] The WTO administers a comprehensive set of trade rules which is based on the old GATT but contains a large number of additional and more precise agreements, including the ones on intellectual property rights and trade in services.[83] Furthermore, the dispute settlement system of the GATT was developed into a compulsory procedure featuring an appellate review.[84]

---

[79]Stoll (2012), Art. 55 (a) and (b), paras. 63 et seqq. and Stoll (2009), pp. 291.

[80]Ulrich (2009), pp. 716 et seqq.

[81]Principle 12 UN Rio Declaration on Environment and Development, 12 Aug 1992 and Chapter 2 (A) UN Agenda 21, adopted by United Nations Conference on Environment and Development, 3–14 June 1992.

[82]Marrakesh Agreement Establishing the World Trade Organization, 15 Apr 1994, 1867 UNTS 154, 33 I.L.M. 1144.

[83]Agreement on Trade-Related Aspects of Intellectual Property Rights, Marrakesh Agreement Establishing the World Trade Organization, 15 Apr 1994, Annex 1C, 33 I.L.M. 1197 and General Agreement on Trade in Services, Marrakesh Agreement Establishing the World Trade Organization, 15 April 1994, Annex 1 B, 33 ILM 1168. See Stoll (2009), pp. 279 et seqq.

[84]Art. 17 DSU, Dispute Settlement Rules: Understanding on Rules and Procedures Governing the Settlement of Disputes, Marrakesh Agreement Establishing the World Trade Organization, Annexs 2, 33 I.L.M. 1226.

During the negotiations for the WTO agreements and in the ministerial conferences of the organization, various attempts have been made to specifically address labour and other public interest issues. To a large extent, these initiatives centred on introducing a 'social clause' into WTO law, which was aspired to strengthen the role of labour standards in the new global trade system.[85] Unfortunately, however, all those initiatives failed.[86] In the famous 1996 Singapore Ministerial Declaration, the WTO Ministerial Conference essentially expelled labour standards from the WTO's ambit.[87]

5.3 *Social Development and Decent Work: UN and ILO Activities*

At the time of the establishment of the WTO, a World Summit took place in Copenhagen to elaborate on the issue of social development as one pillar of the concept of sustainable development.[88] In line with the Rio Conference, the Copenhagen Declaration calls for 'plac[ing] people at the centre of development'[89] and highlights that employment policies have to be elaborated and implemented with 'full respect for workers' rights'.[90]

It was then that ILO Director-General Hansenne first outlined what would be the first of several stages for renewal: The prioritization of certain labour standards as fundamental.[91] From 1995 onwards, reinvigorated inter alia by the confirmation of its mandate to pursue social justice by the WTO's 1996 Singapore Declaration, the ILO started activities in this regard. In 1998, the ILO International Labour Conference adopted the ILO Declaration on Fundamental Principles and Rights at Work, which highlighted that in maintaining 'the link between social progress and economic growth, the guarantee of fundamental principles and rights at work is of particular significance'.[92] The declaration went on in stating that the ILO is the

[85]See Weiss (2005), pp. 574 et seqq.

[86]See i.e. Leary (1997).

[87]The fourth paragraph of the Declaration reads: 'We renew our commitment to the observance of internationally recognized core labour standards. The International Labour Organization (ILO) is the competent body to set and deal with these standards, and we affirm our support for its work in promoting them. We believe that economic growth and development fostered by increased trade and further trade liberalization contribute to the promotion of these standards. We reject the use of labour standards for protectionist purposes, and agree that the comparative advantage of countries, particularly low-wage developing countries, must in no way be put into question. In this regard, we note that the WTO and ILO Secretariats will continue their existing collaboration.'

[88]See Copenhagen Declaration on Social Development, Annex I, A/Conf. 166/9, para. 5.

[89]Ibid., para. 26 (a).

[90]Ibid., para. 28, Commitment 3.

[91]Hansenne (1994). Regarding the four stages see Maupain (2013), p. 51.

[92]ILO Declaration on Fundamental Principles and Rights at Work and its Follow-up, International Labour Conference, adopted on 18 June 1998 and Annex revised 15 June 2010, para. 5.

'constitutionally mandated international organization and the competent body to set and deal with international labour standards, and enjoys universal support and acknowledgement in promoting fundamental rights at work as the expression of its constitutional principles'.[93] Importantly, the 1998 Declaration stipulated that all ILO members were bound to adhere to the four fundamental principles and rights at work solely by virtue of their membership in the organization and established a special follow-up.[94] The prioritization of certain labour standards has resulted in much of the ILO's resources being focused on these fundamental standards.[95]

One year later, the ILO Director-General issued a report to the 87th session of the International Labour Conference, which aimed at directing the future work of the organization. The report carried the title 'Decent Work' and defined an agenda of work for the organization. Decent work was further defined in the report as comprising four strategic objectives which were fundamental principles and rights at work, employment and income opportunities for women and men, social protection and social dialogue and tripartism. This definition of objectives was considerably broader than the traditional scope of activities of the organization and took into consideration many other international developments, including the concept of sustainable development.[96] The issues of development, social dimensions and labour conditions and their interaction with the liberalization of trade and the globalization of the economy was taken up again by the 2000 United Nations Millennium Declaration, which used the notion of decent work in one instance.[97] In 2008, the ILO addressed the issue of globalization in its 'Declaration on Social Justice for a Fair Globalization'.[98] In doing so, the International Labour Conference particularly highlighted its decent work agenda, which thenceforth has informed virtually all the ILO's activities. In 2015, the issue of decent work was addressed at the United Nations summit for the adoption of the post-2015 development agenda. The resulting 2030 Agenda for Sustainable Development defined a number of sustainable development goals. Goal 8 envisages to '[p]romote sustained, inclusive and sustainable economic growth, full and productive employment and decent work for all'.[99]

[93] ILO Declaration on Fundamental Principles and Rights at Work and its Follow-up, International Labour Conference, adopted on 18 June 1998 and Annex revised 15 June 2010, para. 6.

[94] Maupain (2013), pp. 51–52.

[95] Alston (2004), pp. 509 et seqq. and Kellerson (1998), pp. 223 et seqq.

[96] Rodgers et al. (2009), pp. 222 et seqq.

[97] United Nations Millennium Declaration, GA Res. 55/2, 8 Sep 2000, para. 20.

[98] ILO Declaration on Social Justice for a Fair Globalization, adopted on 10 June 2008.

[99] Transforming our World: the 2030 Agenda for Sustainable Development, GA Res. 70/1, 25 Sep 2015.

5.4 *Labour Clauses in GSPs*

In parallel to the developments at global level, a number of initiatives were taken to include labour provisions in a number of trade agreements. The EU's Generalized System of Preferences must be mentioned here, which roots back to 1971 and has its origins in the more general international discussions on the preferential treatment of developing countries in the world economy. In the 1990s, the system was furnished with a 'GSP+' element, which offered developing countries additional trade benefits conditioned upon the ratification, implementation and observance of a number of international agreements in the area of sustainable development and good governance, including various global human rights standards, but also the eight ILO fundamental labour conventions.[100] A monitoring is provided in this regard and procedures are in place for cases of a 'serious and systematic violations of principles laid down in the conventions' which ultimately can result in the suspension of trade benefits.[101] A similar mechanism had been established even earlier by the USA, which, from 1984 onwards, included a catalogue of 'internationally recognized workers' rights' into their GSP.[102]

5.5 *Labour Clauses in Free Trade Agreements and Bilateral Investment Agreements*

At the same time, labour provisions became an element of trade agreements. In 1994, the North American Free Trade Agreement (NAFTA) was concluded between Canada, Mexico and the USA. NAFTA was accompanied by a 'side agreement', the North American Agreement on Labor Cooperation (NAALC), in which the parties committed to effectively enforce their domestic labour laws. The NAALC also introduced an inter-state dispute settlement mechanism which, as a final resort, spelled out the possibility to suspend trade benefits granted in the

---

[100] Convention concerning Minimum Age for Admission to Employment (No. 138); Convention concerning the Prohibition and Immediate Action for the Elimination of the Worst Form of Child Labour (No. 182); Convention concerning the Abolition of Forced Labour (No. 105); Convention concerning Forced or Compulsory Labour (No. 29); Convention concerning Equal Remuneration for Men and Women Workers for Work of Equal Value (No. 100); Convention concerning Discrimination in Respect of Employment and Occupation (No. 111); Convention concerning Freedom of Association and Protection of the Right to Organize (No. 87) and Convention concerning the Application of the Principles of the Right to Organize and to Bargain Collectively (No. 98). See e.g. Art. 9 and EU Parliament and Council Regulation 978/2012 *applying a scheme of generalised tariff preferences and repealing Council Regulation (EC) No 732/2008*, O.J. L 303/1 (2012), annex VIII, part A.

[101] See e.g. European Parliament and Council Regulation 978/2012 *applying a scheme of generalised tariff preferences and repealing Council Regulation (EC)*, O.J. L 303/1 (2012), Art. 19 (1) (a).

[102] Alston (2004), pp. 497 et seqq. and Compa and Vogt (2001).

NAFTA in order to coerce the respondent to adhere to its obligations under the NAALC. The NAALC has served as the blueprint for all subsequent US and Canadian FTAs containing chapters on labour.[103] From the mid-1990s, the EU followed suit in linking trade and labour issues in its trade agreements, as well as in its more comprehensive Economic Partnership Agreements and its Association Agreements. However, the EU's approach, especially to enforcement, was slightly different in relying less on adjudicatory dispute settlement and more on dialogue and consensual solutions.[104] Furthermore, labour chapters have also been included in FTAs concluded by other countries, e.g. Chile or New Zealand.[105] Labour chapters have sparked hopes that the trade-labour linkage, which had been rejected at WTO level, could be effectuated at least at regional or bilateral level. To date, practice has not lived up to these aspirations.

Unlike trade agreements, bilateral investment agreements hardly ever contain references to labour standards.[106]

5.6 *Corporate Social Responsibility*

The potential responsibility of international enterprises was taken up again in international debates from 2010 onwards. As seen above, the issue had already been addressed in the 1970s by the UNCTAD, the OECD and the ILO. Thereafter, it has been treated with low priority only. In 1999, UN Secretary-General Kofi Annan initiated a global compact as a principle-based framework for businesses, based on 10 principles regarding human rights, labour, the environment and anti-corruption. More than 10,000 businesses around the world joined the framework and endorsed the principles. In addition, the issue of business and human rights was explored by the United Nations Human Rights Council and the United Nations Special Representative for Business and Human Rights, John Ruggie. In 2011, the United Nations Human Rights Council adopted his Guiding Principles on Business and Human Rights.[107] Principle No. 12 sets out that '[t]he responsibility of business enterprises to respect human rights refers to internationally recognised human rights - understood, at a minimum, at those expressed in the International Bill of Human Rights and the principles concerning fundamental rights set out in the International Labour Organization's Declaration on Fundamental Principles and Rights at Work'. These developments, which altogether were referred to as corporate social responsibility,

---

[103]On the incremental development of US and Canadian FTA labour chapters see Bolle (2016), pp. 2 et seqq. and Lazo Grandi (2009), p. viii.

[104]Bartels (2012) and also Novitz (2017).

[105]Lazo Grandi (2009).

[106]Gordon et al. (2014), pp. 10 et seqq.

[107]UNHR, Office of the High Commissioner (2011) Guideline Principles on Business and Human Rights, HR/PUB/11/04.

were taken up by the European Union and other States which established regional or national frameworks and legislation to implement this international principles on the responsibility of businesses.[108]

5.7 Summary: Diversity of Approaches and Bilateralism

In overview, the many developments after the fall of the Berlin Wall evidence an important progress in conceptualizing the relationship between economic development, social justice and labour standards. In addition, the approaches diversified and new actors, such as corporate businesses, came into play. Initiatives for social justice and labour rights were importantly promoted by UN conferences, the Secretary General and human rights institutions, whereas the ILO played a rather reactive role. On the other hand, trade policy played quite a role. While the WTO, the multilateral flagship institution for economic globalization, kept its focus on trade liberalization, a number of bilateral—or better: non-multilateral—initiatives were taken to link trade preferences to the implementation of labour standards.

6 Analysis

The short historical overview has covered a small selection of a bundle of developments of ideas, concepts, institutions, rules and their relationship at international level. Nevertheless, it did hardly more than scratching the tip of an iceberg. Many more events, projects and activities have taken place at international, regional and national levels to promote economic growth and social development. How these two aspects are or should be connected and whether there is a divide will be assessed differently by academics, governments, trade unions, civil society and businesses.

However, the short account of international developments is indeed telling in regard to one particular dimension, which concerns progress in international regulation and its coverage. Separately applying the trade chapter of the Havana Charter while dropping the rest of the agreement with its various rules on a variety of 'social' aspects certainly can be considered a key case for 'economic' issues to progress, while 'social' aspects were left behind. The same holds true for the conclusion of investment protection by bilateral agreements and by the establishment of the ICSID in parallel to, but outside a much more encompassing discussion

[108]See e.g. European Commission (2011) A renewed EU strategy 2011–2014 for Corporate Social Responsibility, COM(2011) 681 and European Parliament and Council Directive 2014/95/EU *amending Directive 2013/34/EU as regards disclosure of non-financial and diversity information by certain large undertakings and groups*, O.J. L 330/1 (2014).

in the UN in regard to foreign business activities in developing countries, including negotiations on instruments for the conduct of multinational enterprises. Certainly also, the establishment of the WTO as a pure trade organization must be mentioned in this regard, in the context of which initiatives to include labour rights and environmental protection were dismissed at the time of the final negotiations as well as in the later Ministerial Conferences.[109]

However, this account of some missed opportunities scratches the surface only. Without some further reflection, it is hardly convincing to criticise particular steps to advance trade and foreign investments to be taken without involving a 'social element' or even to claim that one should not be agreed upon without the other.

Analytically, 'economic' and 'social' are quite ambitious concepts if it comes to international relations and law and this is even more so the case in view of their potential interrelatedness. There is obviously some relation between the two. Economic growth and welfare have a 'social' dimension. Conversely, labour conditions have an 'economic' aspect, as a well-situated and skilled workforce is necessary for economic development and a continuous consumption and demand. Art. 55 Charter of the United Nations reflects that economic and social well-being and development go hand in hand. We can conclude at this point that the economic and social aspects of well-being and development cannot be divided and that—normatively—Art. 55 UN Charter reflects this close interrelationship.

The ways to achieve economic and social well-being and development around the world have been discussed for a long time. These debates concerned the proper allocation of authority and action at national and international levels and appropriate international mechanisms, including institutions and rules. The experiences of the interwar period have shown that the development of international labour standards is futile if States fail to agree on cooperative responses to economic crisis.

On the other hand, economic cooperation in the postwar area and particularly the development of the international trade system arguably has been an achievement both in economic and social terms. There is hardly any doubt that the improvement of living conditions and particularly the release of a great number of people from conditions of extreme poverty is due to a significant part to the liberalization of international trade and the promotion of foreign investments.

However, employment and labour conditions in different regions of the world and more specifically in certain branches and among different groups can hardly be said to have improved accordingly. What is more, the promotion of these conditions through international labour standards did not advance much. While a huge number of standards have been produced by the ILO, their implementation and enforcement considerably lags behind.

Indeed, there is still a divide—a divide between the overall economic welfare vis-à-vis poor employment and living conditions in many places and a divide between the progress made in international economic cooperation as compared to

[109]See Fn. 87.

the rather poor advances in securing acceptable living conditions and labour standards around the world.

However, these real-world findings do not readily support the conclusion that the promotion of trade and of social justice and labour standards should mandatorily be linked if it comes to international rules and arrangements. Technically speaking, international trade rules and international rules on social justice and labour standards are quite apart in view of subject matter and institutional machinery. There is good reason to believe that in an ideal world, separate regimes should be in place for these different objectives.

However, under real world conditions, interest and power come into play and the benefits of a trade agreement may well give a momentum which could be used to persuade States to ratify and implement labour standards. For obvious reasons, this type of a linkage has been rejected more than once in the multilateral trade system. Again, for obvious reasons, such linkage has been successfully established in preferential trade agreements. Using the bilateral track, however, comes with a political cost. It may well impair the relevance of multilateral institutions such as the WTO and the ILO. This way, bilateral linkages of trade and labour may end up in another divide. They may end up in drawing dividing lines between bilateral arrangements and multilateral governance.

References

Adamthwaite A (2016) 'A low dishonest decade'?: war and peace in the 1930s. In: Doumanis N (ed) The Oxford Handbook of European history 1914–1945. Oxford University Press, Oxford, pp 207–222

Alston P (1979) The United Nations' specialized agencies and implementation of the international covenant on economic, social and cultural rights. Columbia J Transl Law 18:79–118

Alston P (2004) 'Core labour standards' and the transformation of the international labour rights regime. Eur J Int Law 15(3):457–521

Bartels L (2012) Human rights and sustainable development obligations in EU free trade agreements, University of Cambridge Faculty of Law Research Paper No. 24/2012

Bolle MJ (2016) Overview of Labor Enforcement Issues in Free Trade Agreements. US Congressional Research Service

Bowles P (2009) 'Beggar-Thy-Neighbour' and 'Mercantilism' In: Kenneth A, Reinert A, Rajan RS (eds) The Princeton encyclopedia of the world economy, vol I. A-H. Princeton University Press, Princeton

Cissé H (2012) Should the political prohibition in charters of international financial institutions be revisited? In: Cissé H, Bradlow DD, Kingsbury B (eds) The World Bank legal review, vol 3. The World Bank, Washington, pp 59–92

Clarke SVO (1973) The reconstruction of the international monetary system: the attempts of 1922 and 1933. Princeton Studies in International Finance No. 33

Compa LA, Vogt JS (2001) Labor rights in the generalized system of preferences: a 20 year review. Comp Labor Law Policy J 22:199–238

Dolzer R, Schreuer C (2008) Principles of international investment law. Oxford University Press, Oxford

Dupuy PM (2013) International environmental law: looking at the past to shape the future. In: Dupuy PM, Viñuales JE (eds) Harnessing foreign investment to promote environmental protection. Cambridge University Press, Cambridge, pp 9–24
Fabbricotti A (2009) International Trade Centre UNCTAD/WTO (ITC). In: Wolfrum R (ed) Max Planck Encylopedia Of Public International Law. Oxford University Press, Oxford. Available via DIALOG. http://opil.ouplaw.com/home/epil. Accessed 9 Aug 2017
Fortin C (2013) United Nations Conference on Trade and Development (UNCTAD). In: Wolfrum R (ed) Max Planck Encyclopedia of Public International Law. Oxford University Press, Oxford. Available via DIALOG. http://opil.ouplaw.com/home/epil. Accessed 9 Aug 2017
Francis J, Nicholson SJ (1965) The protection of foreign property under customary international law. Boston Coll Law Rev 6:391. http://lawdigitalcommons.bc.edu/bclr/vol6/iss3/1. Accessed 1 Sept 2016
Gordon K, Pohl J, Bouchard M (2014) Investment treaty law, sustainable development and responsible business conduct: a fact finding survey. In: OECD Working papers on international investment. OECD Publishing, Paris. Available via DIALOG. https://doi.org/10.1787/5jz0xvgx1zlt-en. Accessed 22 Jan 2017
Haas EB (1964) Beyond the nation state. Stanford University Press, Stanford
Hansenne M (1994) Defending values, promoting change: social justice in a global economy, an ILO agenda
Houde M, Yannaca-Small K (2004) Relationships between international investment agreements. OECD Working Papers on International Investment, 2004/01. OECD Publishing, Paris
James P (1997) Post-dependency: the third world in an era of globalism and late capitalism. Altern Glob Local Polit 22(2):205–226
Janse R (2014) (Why) was the World Bank supposed to be a nonpolitical organization? An interpretation of the original meaning and rationale of article 4 (10) of the articles of agreement of the International Bank for Reconstruction and Development, 1941–1948. J Hist Int Law 16: 113–155
Kellerson H (1998) The ILO declaration of 1998 on fundamental principles and rights: a challenge for the future. Int Labour Rev 137(2):223–227
Keynes JM (1935) The general theory of employment, interest, and money. Cambridge University Press, Cambridge
Kitanovic VS, Kozuharov S (2012) The international monetary fond as a creator of the global financial system. UTMS J Econ 3:83–90
Kolodko GW (1999) Transition to a market economy and sustained growth. Implications for the post-Washington consensus. Communis Post-Commun 32:233–261
Lazo Grandi P (2009) Trade agreements and their relation to labour standards: the current situation. International Centre for Trade and Sustainable Development, Geneva
Leary VA (1997) The WTO and the social clause: post-Singapore. Eur J Int Law (1):118–122
Maul D (2012) Human rights, development and decolonization. In: The International Labour Organization (ed) International Labour Organization century series. Palgrave Macmillan, London
Maupain F (2013) The future of the International Labour Organization in the global economy. Hart, London
Meng W (2012) Art 57 UN charter. In: Simma B, Khan DE, Nolte G, Paulus A (eds) The charter of the United Nations, 3rd edn. Oxford University Press, Oxford, pp 1611–1649
Monteiro A (2014) Ethics of human rights. Springer, Berlin
Novitz T (2017) Labour standards and trade: need we choose between 'human rights' and 'sustainable development'? In: Gött H (ed) Labour standards in international economic law. Springer International Publishing, Cham. this volume
Overy RJ (2010) The interwar-crisis, 2nd edn. Routledge, London
Overy RJ (2016) The origins of the second world war. Routledge, London
Patel SJ, Roffe P, Yusuf A (2000) International technology transfer: the origins and aftermath of the United Nations negotiations on a draft code of conduct. Kluwer Law International, Alphen aan den Rijn

Ragazzi M (2014) World Bank Group. In: Wolfrum R (ed) Max Planck Encyclopedia of Public International Law. Oxford Universtiy Press, Oxford. Available via DIALOG. http://opil.ouplaw.com/home/epil. Accessed 9 Aug 2017

Reinisch A, Malintoppi L (2008) Methods of dispute resolution. In: Muchlinski P, Ortino F, Schreuer C (eds) The Oxford handbook of international investment law. Oxford University Press, Oxford, pp 692–720

Riedel EH, Arend J-M (2012) Art 55 (c) UN charter. In: Simma B, Khan DE, Nolte G, Paulus A (eds) The charter of the United Nations, 3rd edn. Oxford Universtiy Press, Oxford, pp 1565–1602

Rodgers G, Lee E, Swepston L, Van Daelen J (2009) The International Labour Organization and the quest for social justice, 1919–2009. ILO, Geneva

Roosevelt FD (1941) State of the Union Address 'The four Freedoms', 6 Jan 1941

Sacerdoti G (2014) Havana Charter (1948). In: Wolrum R (ed) Max Planck Encyclopedia of Public International Law. Oxford University Press, Oxford. Available via DIALOG. http://opil.ouplaw.com/home/epil. Accessed 9 Aug 2017

Sauer H (2014) International Labour Organization (ILO). In: Wolfrum R (ed) Max Planck Encyclopedia of Public International Law. Oxford University Press, Oxford. Available via DIALOG. http://opil.ouplaw.com/home/epil. Accessed 9 Aug 2017

Sauvant KP (2015) The negotiations of the United Nations code of conduct on transnational corporations. Experience and lessons learned. J World Invest Trade 16:11–87

Schill SW, Tams CJ, Hofmann R (2015) International investment law and development: friends or foes? In: Schill SW, Tams CJ, Hofmann R (eds) International investment law and development: bridging the gap. Edward Elgar, Cheltenham, pp 3–42

Schoiswohl M (2013) United Nations development programme. In: Wolfrum R (ed) Max Planck Encyclopedia of Public International Law. Oxford University Press, Oxford. Available via DIALOG. http://opil.ouplaw.com/home/epil. Accessed 9 Aug 2017

Schorkopf F (2010) Versailles peace treaty (1919). In: Wolfrum R (ed) Max Planck Encyclopedia of Public International Law. Oxford University Press, Oxford. Available via DIALOG. http://opil.ouplaw.com/home/epil. Accessed 9 Aug 2017

Stoll P-T (2009) Le droit international economique face aux défis de la mondialisation. Revue Générale de droit Int Public 113:273–303

Stoll P-T (2012) Art 55 (a) and (b) UN charter. In: Simma B, Khan DE, Nolte G, Paulus A (eds) The charter of the United Nations, 3rd edn. Oxford University Press, Oxford, pp 1535–1564

Swepston L (2013) The International Labour Organization and international human rights system. In: Sheeran S, Sir Rodley N (eds) Routledge handbook of international human rights law. Routledge, London, pp 339–352

Tortora M (2003) Special and differential treatment and development issues in the multilateral trade negotiations: the skeleton in the closet. UNCTAD, Geneva

Troclet L-E (1952) Législation sociale international. Librairie Encyclopédique, SPRL

Ulrich B (2009) Sustainable development. In: Wolfrum R (ed) Max Planck Encyclopedia of Public International Law. Oxford University Press, Oxford. Available via DIALOG. http://opil.ouplaw.com/home/epil. Accessed 9 Aug 2017

Weiss F (2005) Trade and labor I. In: Macrory PFJ, Appleton AE, Plummer MG (eds) The World Trade Organization: legal, economic and political analysis, vol II. Springer, New York, pp 571–596

Yusuf S (2009) Development economics through the decades. The World Bank, Washington

The ILO's Mandate and Capacity: Creating, Proliferating and Supervising Labour Standards for a Globalized Economy

Claire La Hovary

Contents

Abstract This chapter explores the International Labour Organization's (ILO) mandate and capacity to create, proliferate and supervise labour standards through the lens of the operationalization of tripartism. Tripartism, a foundational feature of the ILO which implies the active participation of representatives of Governments, Employers and Workers in all aspects of the Organization, is essential to both the Organization's mission of pursing social justice and the generation of international labour law more generally. Changes in the balance of power between the three groups inevitably have an impact on international labour law and on its supervision; such changes, in particular between Workers and Employers, have been taking place since 1989 and have taken a dramatic turn in 2012. The crisis that occurred that year and that has been unfolding since could have an impact beyond the ILO, by not only challenging the independence and the role of ILO supervisor bodies—and therefore reducing their influence—but also by having highly negative consequences for existing International Labour Standards which could be weakened.

This chapter draws on La Hovary (2015c), pp. 204–236.

C. La Hovary (✉)
University of Glasgow, School of Law, Glasgow, Scotland
e-mail: Claire.LaHovary@glasgow.ac.uk

H. Gött (ed.), *Labour Standards in International Economic Law*,
https://doi.org/10.1007/978-3-319-69447-4_3

1 Introduction

Deficient working conditions worldwide are creating immense human suffering, threatening stability, and nourishing inequality. In view of these circumstances, the International Labour Organization's (ILO) mandate to pursue social justice through the improvement of the conditions of work worldwide is clearly as relevant now as it was in 1919 when the Organization was founded. Amongst the initiatives taken to assist it in its mandate, the ILO has produced an impressive number of conventions, protocols and recommendations (these constitute international labour standards or 'ILS') as well as some important declarations. The ILO has also developed a complex supervisory mechanism to monitor the application in law and in practice of ILS, as well as to respond to complaints. The Organization has, more generally, demonstrated significant capacity for innovation over the almost 100 years of its existence, as well as achieved important milestones. These successes have occurred in the face of major difficulties.

At the same time, however, while the ILO has never had an easy task, it is arguably currently operating in a particularly difficult global environment and faces huge difficulties in achieving its mandate. This is all the more so as the Organization's means and scope for action have been affected by a range of external and internal factors.[1] In particular, in terms of its internal governance, it is more specifically confronting some very serious challenges with regard to the dynamics and operationalisation of its unique tripartite structure which, because of the central importance of tripartism to all of the Organization's actions, poses a considerable hurdle to its smooth functioning. As this chapter will examine, tripartism, which refers to a form of governance involving not only governmental representatives of the ILO's now 187 member states, but also representatives of Employer and Workers' organizations from each of these states, has a central place in the shaping of ILS, not only in relation to the choice of the topic of standards, their elaboration and their adoption, but also with regards to their supervision. Its operationalisation therefore has an impact on the ILO in general, but more specifically on ILS and the ILO's supervision system.

Of course, difficulties in the operationalization of tripartism are not new and their impact on ILS and the supervisory system are not new either. As Maupain has stated for example, tensions between tripartism *within* the ILO and realities *outside* the ILO have often reached 'rupture point',[2] while the tension between the growing mandate of the ILO and the narrower representativity of the ILO's constituents has

---

[1]See Maupain (2013). As Langille notes, more generally, 'the ILO is centred upon the most sensitive political nerve of all modern societies - the relationship of markets and politics and the questions of both the virtues and limits of markets. In the ILO this general question is focused upon the most central and most difficult of all markets - the labour market - a market in people, not commodities', Langille (1999), p. 234. Considering that the orthodoxy within dominant economic thought tends towards a desirability for de-regulating labour issues, this makes law-making in the field particularly difficult.

[2]Maupain (1999a), p. 336.

always been problematic. However, as Trebilcock has highlighted in 2010, the ILO is facing particularly testing times characterized by an unprecedented absence of consensus between the Organization's constituents.[3] This crystallized in a spectacular institutional crisis relating to the right to strike in June 2012 and the resulting change in the balance of power between the tripartite groups could have a significant impact not only on the ILO and ILS but also on other fields of international law, in particular international economic law.[4] Indeed, beyond their important influence in the domestic sphere, ILS are referred to or included in diverse ways in numerous international initiatives such as free trade agreements, investment treaties, or in the International Financial Corporation's standards of performance, for example, and they are also used, along with the ILO supervisory bodies' comments, by international or regional tribunal or bodies. Any change affecting the dynamic of the ILO from within and thus the shape and supervision of its ILS is therefore important to understand when one studies the role that ILS have or may have in other platforms.

To grasp the extent of the possible repercussions of the difficulties the ILO is facing in terms of its tripartite structure, this chapter revisits the central place that tripartism holds in the constitutional landscape of the ILO, focussing on its role in the shaping of ILS and their supervision, before turning to the events that have escalated the crisis within the supervisory bodies and the impact that this has had so far. Unless the ILO can overcome the current crisis of tripartism, it will struggle to have an impact and effectively implement its mandate to improve workers' conditions worldwide. In particular, this will affect both the content of international labour law as developed by the ILO, as well as the way that it is engaged with outside of the ILO.[5]

2 Tripartism in the ILO: What Impact on ILS?

It is useful to recall certain aspects about the origins of tripartism in order to situate its currently difficult operationalization. On the one hand, the objective of tripartism was, at the time of the creation of the ILO, 'to enable the workers and the employers to exercise their own influence upon, and make their own contributions to, the

[3]Trebilcock (2010), pp. 566–567. See also Novitz (2009–2010).

[4]The connection between the two fields was established in 1919 and recalled in the Declaration of Philadelphia in 1944, annexed to the ILO's Constitution in 1946. For an overview, see for example Diller (2013), pp. 128–147.

[5]This chapter draws on primary and secondary written material, but also on oral interviews conducted between February and August 2014 with individuals from the ITUC, national confederations, the ILO (ACTRAV, ACTEMP, as well as current and retired civil servants), and Workers' organizations. Individual interviewees are not identified but indications are given where specific insights from these interviews have been taken. This research was supported by the University of Glasgow and the Carnegie Trust for the Universities of Scotland.

discussions of industrial matters'.[6] On the other hand however, the instable context in which tripartism was established also had an influence on its birth: it was very clear at the time that in order to create an organization which might credibly provide an answer to Bolshevism and be an alternative to revolution—or, an 'insurance against revolution'[7]—it needed to include workers and provide them with a voice.[8]

2.1 *The Institution of Tripartism*

Tripartism is established in the ILO's Constitution which, with other texts, details how Members of the ILO will be represented and will participate in the Organization. As is well known, the ILO is made up of three entities: the Governing Body, the International Labour Conference (ILC) and the International Labour Office (Office). The first two entities are tripartite. The Governing Body is composed of 28 government members, 14 employer members, and 14 worker members,[9] and the ILC is composed of delegations from each member state consisting of two Government delegates, one Employer delegate and one 'workpeople' delegate.[10] Both institutions have important functions,[11] and decisions on all matters are reached by consensus or votes.[12] Each delegate to the ILC and each member of the Governing Body has the right to vote individually (2/1/1) unless they are in Committees, where each group has an equal vote (1/1/1). This latter deviation gives more weight to Employers and Workers as, for example, the decisions of ILC committees are adopted normally without modification by the ILC—this is particularly important with regards to ILS as they are adopted within a Committee.

---

[6]ILO (1956), para 9.

[7]Maul (2012), p. 2. Also Cabanes (2014), p. 79 and Cox (1973), p. 102.

[8]Helfer (2006), p. 679, referring to Cox (1973), p. 102. Also Béguin (1959), p. 6. As is well known, it is, with the help of visionaries, the combination of the industrial revolution in the nineteenth century—which had led to the proliferation of abysmal working conditions—the ravages of the First World War and the rise of Bolshevism that led to the ILO's creation.

[9]See Art. 7 of the Constitution. There are also 66 deputy members (28 Government members, 19 Employers members and 19 Workers members)—Section 1.1.1, Standing Orders of the Governing Body.

[10]See Art. 3 of the Constitution.

[11]These include, for the Governing Body, appointing the Director-General who carries out his functions according to its instructions (Art. 8 (1)), directing the Office's activities (Art. 10), deciding the agenda of the ILC (Art. 14 (1)) as well as several important matters concerning the supervision of ILS (and ILO (2011), paras 5–6). The ILC discusses and adopt ILO instruments, discusses policies, adopts the Organisation's programme and budget, and elects the Governing Body, for example.

[12]The International Trade Union Confederation (ITUC) and the International Organisation for Employers (IOE) provide secretarial support to, respectively, the Workers and Employers' groups, and have a key role in formulating the groups' responses at the Governing Body and the ILC.

The process of nominating non-Government delegates to the ILC, which is fundamental to the functioning of tripartism, is governed by Article 3 (5) of the Constitution establishing the obligation for Members of the ILO to 'undertake to nominate non-Government delegates and advisers chosen in agreement with the industrial organizations, if such organizations exist, which are most representative of employers or workpeople, as the case may be, in their respective countries'.[13] Delegates to the ILC elect members of the Governing Body: Government members in the Governing Body, representing their own national Governments, are elected by the Government delegates to the ILC, while employers and workers' members, representing *their groups*, are elected by their respective groups at the ILC (Article 7 (2) and (4) of the Constitution). This latter provision contributes to the autonomy of the non-governmental members.[14]

The third component of the ILO, the International Labour Office, is a secretariat of civil servants, responsible for, *inter alia*, collecting and distributing information, studying issues for the adoption of ILS by the ILC and carrying out technical assistance, in particular with regards to national labour law reforms.[15] Albert Thomas, the first Director General of the ILO, and the public international lawyer Georges Scelle were however convinced that the Office had a crucial—even vital—role as an arbitrator, a researcher, an idea provider,[16] even as an advocate for the workers,[17] and its role—and that of the Director-General—has clearly expanded since the ILO's inception,[18] to the extent that both have even been credited for the ILO's survival so far.[19] Certainly, Maupain argued in 1999 that the Office went beyond the most basic common denominator when it makes suggestions to the ILC or the Governing Body, and that its role is to help overcome oppositions between

[13]This article has been interpreted by the Permanent Court of International Justice (PCIJ) in an advisory opinion of 1922 that still guides the ILO, see PCIJ, *Designation of the Workers' Delegate for the Netherlands at the Third Session of the International Labour Conference*, Advisory Opinion, PCIJ Series B No. 1, pp. 23, 25. In particular, the PCIJ established that Workers' delegates should represent *all* workers (not only unionised workers)—the same goes for Employers' delegates, who should represent all employers.

[14]See Art. 10 of the Constitution. See generally Jenks (1970), p. 70.

[15]There is however a bureau of Workers' Activities (ACTRAV) and of Employers' Activities (ACT/EMP) within the Office.

[16]See the works of Albert Thomas and Georges Scelle, cited in Maupain (1999a), p. 364. See also Jenks (1970), pp. 517–518.

[17]Maupain (1999a), p. 366. Thomas justified his role by arguing that the Organisation had been created 'for the workers and to improve their conditions', Phelan (1936), p. 246.

[18]See Cox's account (1973) and Jenks (1970), pp. 517–518—Jenks explains that it is precisely because he was elected by the combined votes of Employers and Workers that Albert Thomas was able to act the way he did.

[19]Helfer (2006), pp. 681 et seqq.

different interest groups within these organs.[20] The role of the Office has changed in this regard, however, and it has become very cautious, or more passive,[21] in recent years. This is said to have been further combined with a deprofessionalization of civil servants within the office.[22] This has important consequences for the ILO, as we will see in the last part of this chapter. The Office does have an important role—supportive and substantive—with regards to ILS and their supervision. Amongst the ILO's unique specificities however, is the fact that ILS are both adopted and supervised within its tripartite institutional structure.

2.2 ILS and Their Supervision

The ILO strives to achieve its mandate by, *inter alia*, promoting ILS of which an impressive number has been adopted: 189 conventions and 205 recommendations, of which 77 and 84 respectively, as well as six protocols, are considered up-to-date today.[23] Tripartism has a key influence on these ILS. First and foremost, tripartism intervenes during the elaboration and adoption of ILS. After a topic for standard setting is suggested to the Governing body, including by employers or workers' organizations,[24] it is discussed and a decision is taken whether to place it on the agenda of the ILC.[25] Once this has been decided, a two-year process normally takes place before the final draft of a convention or recommendation is discussed in the ILC and put to a vote for its adoption. This process involves Governments, Employers and Workers.

In order to avoid that an instrument be adopted by one group only, a draft needs two-thirds of the votes cast by the delegates present at the ILC to be adopted (Article 19 (2) of the Constitution)—this is to ensure that Workers and Employers cannot, on their own, adopt an instrument without the support of Governments—

[20]Maupain (1999a), pp. 365–366. The Office usually makes suggestions to add items on the agenda, Haas (1964), p. 213. The role that Phelan had in drafting the Declaration of Philadelphia, and the role that Maupain had regarding the 1998 and 2008 Declarations are well known, for example.

[21]As Maupain states, the 'tripartite compromise' or the 'excess of tripartite zeal' of the Office raises the 'risk [...] that in anticipation of negative reaction from one group or another, certain topics might be given up completely, or that controversial conclusions might be emasculated', Maupain (2013), p. 122.

[22]See Standing (2008), pp. 372–373 and Rodgers et al. (2009), p. 234.

[23]In September 2015. An amendment to the Constitution, adopted in 1997, which facilitates the abrogation of obsolete conventions has entered into force in October 2015.

[24]Art. 14 (1) of the Constitution states that the agenda of the Conference is 'settled by the Governing Body, which shall consider any suggestion as to the agenda that may be made by the government of any of the Members or by any representative [employers' or workers'] organization [...] or by any public international organization'.

[25]Article 14 (1) of the Constitution and Art. 34 and Art. 35. *Standing Orders of the Conference*, for complete details.

and a quorum needs to be reached (Article 17 (3)). The quorum was almost not reached when the Declaration on Fundamental Principles and Rights was adopted in 1998, testifying to the difficult discussions which preceded its adoption. Generally, it is quite unusual for a draft not to be adopted, considering that ILS reflect extended discussions, concessions, and compromises made by the three groups. They are moreover generally quite broad. This does not mean that the adoption of ILS always gains the support of all three groups. In particular, many conventions did not get the support of all Employers.

Furthermore, many aspects of the ILS supervisory mechanisms are tripartite in nature or have involved tripartite decision making to be set up.[26] This is particularly the case of the Committee of Expert on the Application of Conventions and Recommendations (CEACR), whose independent legal experts are appointed by the tripartite ILO Governing Body based on proposals put forward by the Office, the tripartite Committee on the Application of Standards (CAS) of the ILC, and the tripartite Committee on Freedom of Association (CFA), which is made up of representatives nominated by each group and is chaired by a neutral academic, with all members approved by the Governing Body. These have all been affected by the current crisis of tripartism, examined in the last part of this chapter.

More specifically, the supervisory system deals not only with ratified conventions, but also with non-ratified conventions and recommendations. It has two main components: the 'regular supervision' and the 'special procedures. The regular supervision is based on the provision of periodic reports by Member States, as required by the ILO Constitution, on the application in law and in practice of ILS.[27] These reports are first examined, along with comments from Workers and Employers' organizations (Art. 23 of the Constitution), in an independent legal manner by the 20 experts of the CEACR. The CEACR makes, with regard to ratified conventions, *observations* on fundamental issues as well as more technical *direct requests*; these determine whether the requirements of conventions are met, in law and in practice.[28] The CEACR also writes a General Survey each year, which examines a specific topic. This General Survey is based on all the reports due according to the Constitution—on ratified and non-ratified conventions and on recommendations—and on the information received from Employers and Workers' organizations. It also recapitulates the observations that the Experts have made over the years and it identifies difficulties or gaps in the application of ILS. The annual report of the CEACR[29]—and a General Survey—is adopted at the end of the yearly two-week meeting of the Experts. This annual report is submitted to the ILC where

[26]The ILO supervisory system has been described extensively—see e.g. Maupain (1999b), pp. 273–293; Servais (2011) and Valticos (1994).

[27]See Art. 19 and Art. 22 of the Constitution.

[28]The work of the CEACR is enormous—ILS had received 8003 ratifications in September 2015 and they are constantly the object of new ratifications—22 ratifications were registered between May and August 2015, for example (see ILO website). ILS also keep on being adopted with important instruments adopted in the last ten years.

[29]Direct requests are not published in this report but are available on the ILO website.

it is discussed, with a political outlook, by the tripartite representatives in the CAS, a standing committee of the ILC. Because of lack of time, only the worst cases of violations are examined by the CAS.

Further supervisory procedures provide an opportunity for any employers' and workers' organizations to bring a complaint before the CFA for the violation of freedom of association by a member State (regardless of whether the State concerned has ratified the relevant conventions or not). The CFA was established by the ILO's Governing Body in 1951 and has examined over 3200 cases, from which 1125 principles and decisions have been extracted so far.[30] These principles provide key guidance to understand the meaning of freedom of association and collective bargaining in practice, and have played a crucial role in the development of the right to strike in the ILO. A 'special procedure' also provides the possibility for Employers and Workers' organizations to make *representations*, and States, delegates to the ILC or the Governing Body to make *complaints*, regarding the failure to give effect to conventions (Article 24 and Art. 26 of the Constitution). Both of these procedures have not been used as much as it was initially hoped when the ILO was founded, and the 'regular' supervision by the CEACR and the CAS has become *de facto* the central part of the ILO supervisory system and the one which is most visible outside the ILO.[31] This is particularly the case of the CEACR which, in verifying application of conventions, clarifies their meaning[32]—a function that has partly triggered the 2012 crisis.

3 Current Difficulties in the Operationalization of Tripartism and the 2012 Crisis

Most Employers and many Governments in the ILO generally hold the opinion that overly regulating working conditions has adverse effects on economic growth, and this has translated in a reticence to adopt new standards granting more protection to workers.[33] One of the main reasons that motivated the Employers and most Governments to support the adoption of ILS—the fear of Communism—disappeared with the fall of the Berlin wall. After the end of the Cold War, the tripartite groups put a stop to the role-playing that they had adopted which allowed the West to offer a united front vis-à-vis the East. In many ways, Employers returned to their initial 1919 position, which Béguin describes as being 'indifferent

[30]ILO (2006).

[31]See Maupain (2013).

[32]See La Hovary (2015b).

[33]Rodgers et al. (2009), p. 24. Also Sengenberger (2013), p. 65.

if not openly hostile to the principle of international labour legislation'.[34] This geopolitical development, which also took place in a context of ever-increasing global neo-liberalization, has naturally led to tensions within the ILO and, as we have seen in the first part of this chapter, the scope for these tensions to have an impact on ILS and their supervision is extremely broad.

3.1 The Crisis of 2012 and Its Consequences

After the end of communism, Employers in the tripartite CAS started to voice discontent with the fact that the independent CEACR was, when interpreting ILS, 'expanding' them.[35] This disapproval crystallized around the issue of the right to strike and initially remained very much within the CAS without, however, visibly affecting its proceedings or those of other supervisory bodies.[36] This long-standing disagreement escalated during the June 2012 ILC when the Employers insisted that a disclaimer be added to the CEACR's annual report indicating that its work was not 'an agreed or determinative text of the ILO tripartite constituents'.[37] They moreover also refused to include any case that dealt with the right to strike in the list of ILS violation cases discussed each year within the CAS if such a disclaimer were not added. As the Workers refused to negotiate this list under such conditions, the CAS did not proceed to study any cases of violations in 2012, despite such an exercise being an intrinsic element of the ILO supervisory system since 1927.[38] The developments during the 2012 ILC resulted in a 'unique situation' according to the Reporter of the CAS and for most involved, the Employers' actions were clearly a surprise.

In fuelling this outcome, Employers escalated their negotiations tactics by not only rejecting the role that the CEACR has had in providing clarifications to ILS and the inherent nature of the right to strike to freedom of association but also paralyzing the work of the CAS and breaking the precarious trust between Employers and Workers.[39] The crisis is not yet resolved. Despite intervention by

[34]Béguin (1959), p. 7. The position of the IOE is that although there is a role for ILS, 'the ILO is harming its credibility by continuing to adopt standards that are increasingly less ratified', France (2001), p. 63.

[35]As Cox notes, the Director-General and some others in the Office 'played a broker's role' in the resolution of this crisis, Cox (1973), p. 107.

[36]It should be recalled here that the right to strike is not explicitly mentioned in Convention No. 87 on Freedom of Association but has been interpreted by the CEACR as an inherent element of freedom of association since the 1950s, following the conclusions of the CFA in this regard.

[37]ILO (2012a), para. 150.

[38]Ibid., para. 22. The CEACR and the CAS were both set up in 1926.

[39]Ibid., para. 213 and information obtained from interviews.

the Governing Body in support of the supervisory mechanism,[40] discussions surrounding the possible use of legal solutions provided by the Constitution,[41] and the clarification by the CEACR of its mandate,[42] the crisis intensified during 2014, and persisted in 2015.[43] These developments, which have been studied elsewhere,[44] obviously go well beyond the existence or not of a right to strike however and signal some changes in the practice of tripartism within the ILO as well as, unavoidably, broader changes in the Organization. These changes relate *inter alia* to the functioning and impact of ILO supervisory bodies, as well as the actions of the Office, and signal a break-down of trust between the parties and another stage in the way of doing business within the ILO with the Employers setting the terms. The post-Cold War indifference or resistance of Employers towards ILS has therefore developed into an additional opposition against the ILO supervisory bodies which, until now, they had not attacked in such a frontal manner.

Several explanations can be put forward for the changing power play between Workers and Employers in the ILO. On the one hand, Employers have clearly increasingly felt in the post-Cold War period that they have a free hand to push for a deregulation of international labour law and for a reform of the ILO's supervisory system. This however is something which they feel is extremely pressing as the potential for ILO supervisory bodies to have influence outside the ILO is changing.[45] In particular, Employers suggested in 2012 that 'the critical issue was that [the CEACR's] observations were being viewed by the outside world as a form of soft law labour standards jurisprudence'.[46] It is certainly true that there are a growing number of initiatives taken outside the ILO as well as judicial decisions that make reference to ILS and/or the supervisory bodies' pronouncements. Furthermore, with the consolidation of the concept of fundamental principles and rights at work, increasing reference has been made outside the ILO to the eight fundamental conventions that underpin these, and Employers are concerned that the interpretation that the CEACR is giving to these conventions will not remain limited to dealings within the ILO.[47] On the other hand, however, Employers'

[40]Reaffirming *inter alia* that 'in order to exercise fully its constitutional responsibilities, it is essential for the ILO to have an effective, efficient and authoritative standards supervisory system commanding the support of all constituents', ILO (2014a), para. 40–43.

[41]Art. 37 provides a legal answer to such deadlocks: Art. 37 (1) concerns referral to the ICJ for 'any question of dispute' relating to the interpretation of the Constitution or of Conventions and Art. 37 (2) concerns the setting-up of a Tribunal for matters related to the interpretation of Conventions. Resort to Art. 37 needs to be decided by the Governing Body, through a vote or consensus.

[42]ILO (2013a), para. 33 and ILO (2015), para. 46.

[43]La Hovary (2015a).

[44]This crisis has been examined from different angles by a range of scholars, including Bellace (2014); La Hovary (2013) and Maupain (2013), pp. 117–165.

[45]See e.g. Maupain (2013) and La Hovary (2015b).

[46]ILO (2012a), paras. 49 and 82.

[47]ILO (2012b), p. 3.

organizations are (again) facing increasing disapproval from their members at the national level with regards to which ILS or which policies have been approved in the ILO. Certainly, the Employers' group has not always managed to block the initiatives they have opposed due to the ILO's tripartite decision-making structure, and this has had a cost on their credibility.[48] This disapproval from national members may lead to decreases in membership at a time when organizations need more members to be credible and financially viable.

Employers, while reiterating 'their full commitment' to both the ILO supervisory system and tripartism,[49] have stated that the ILO's supervisory system as a whole is in 'crisis',[50] to the extent that the IOE explicitly called for a 'change [to its] functioning'.[51] Yet, efforts to improve ILS and the supervisory bodies have been on-going in the Governing Body, and a number of steps have already been taken in this regard.[52] However, employers are pushing for their own changes. The choice to appoint a practising lawyer, clearly not that interested in compromising, as Employers' spokesperson in the CAS in 2012 was perceived by the Workers as a 'game changer' which 'is undermining tripartism'.[53] Indeed, previous spokespersons of Employers in the CAS, such as Ed Potter (2005–2011), while defending an employers' perspective, clearly believed in the necessity of promoting ILS and had always pursued a constructive dialogue. This new trend is spreading throughout the ILO supervisory bodies as the Employers' spokesperson in the CAS referred to above was elected as Employer Vice-Chairperson of the CFA by the Governing Body. The work of the CFA—which is behind many of the clarifications of the right to freedom of association and collective bargaining including the confirmation of the right to strike in 1952—will most certainly be severely affected by this development, both in terms of how issues are dealt with in the cases preliminary prepared by the Office and in terms of the discussions between the members of the CFA and the adoption of conclusions. Certainly, clear indications have already been given to that effect by the International Organization of Employers (IOE).

Furthermore, as the Workers remarked, the CEACR has changed its practice after the Employers' 2012 'coup'. Indeed, the CEACR made more 'direct requests' in its 2014 report, which are less visible and less accessible than 'observations' and are not the object of discussions in the CAS, and it has at the same time reduced the length of its observations.[54] The length of the CEACR Report has been the object of many criticisms in the past, but the Workers rightly expressed concern that the

---

[48]Information obtained from interviews.

[49]ILO (2014c), paras. 11 and 228.

[50]ILO (2013c), paras. 19–20.

[51]See IOE (2013).

[52]See the ILS Policy and the documents adopted by the Governing Body's Committee on Legal Issues and International Labour Standards.

[53]One in five Employer representative in the CAS is said to come from a company—the others all belong to law firms.

[54]ILO (2014c), para. 67.

substance of the comments might be affected, and that this may contradict the supervisory and advisory functions of the CEACR. They expressed further concern that some cases were being deferred and they warned about the effect of this 'self-censorships' on Governments' feeling of impunity.[55] The Employers on the other hand, noted these changes with satisfaction, claiming that they had asked the independent CEACR to make these changes in order to enable more 'room for inputs from constituents', arguing that this would 'strengthen the credibility and acceptance of the supervision of ILO standards'.[56]

It is however difficult to understand how such changes would impact positively on a body which has the role of verifying in an independent manner the application of ILS in practice. Indeed, such changes will clearly profoundly affect the supervisory system—both in terms of its potential usefulness and, possibly, its reputation.[57] Until now, and despite many difficulties and criticism which will not be dealt with here,[58] the CEACR offered an independent (or non-tripartite) view on the application of ILS at national level. While it is not inconceivable that the objectives of the ILO might be better pursued with the CEACR taking on different roles and practices,[59] reform of the supervisory system has until now always been undertaken within the Governing Body, in a way that respects the views of all. By taking unilateral action, the Employers clearly risk reducing the legitimacy, impact, visibility and coherence of the supervisory system (which is likely to be their objective).

Further effects might be felt within the Office. Indeed, the Office, or part of it, has become extremely aware of the need to keep the constituents content and its attitude has certainly changed over the years in this regard. The Office traditionally held a 'leadership role in promoting the objectives of the ILO' and officials considered themselves as 'collaborators in the pursuit of social justice',[60] with the Director-General in particular having substantial powers. These role, powers and scope of action have all been receding over the years for various reasons. The accusations of Employers that the Office was not neutral when it contributed to the CEACR reports—the important role of the Office in this regard has never been a

[55] Ibid., para. 67.

[56] Ibid., para. 55. At the Employers' request, the CEACR met with the Workers' and the Employers' Chairpersons before its meeting, in an unprecedented move, ILO (2013a), para. 10. As a result, the Experts declared that 'some adjustments been made' as to the length and the presentation of information to the 2014 CEACR report, see ILO (2014b), para. 26.

[57] The events of 2012 have been brought to the attention of national and international courts to dispute the CEACR's work (see e.g. ECHR, *RMT* v. *United Kingdom*, Appl. No. 31045/10, 8 Apr 2014, para. 69—while the ECHR stated that it was not reconsidering the CEACR's role as 'a point of reference and guidance for the interpretation of certain provisions of the Convention'—at para. 97, it did not, however, apply the CEACR's jurisprudence on sympathy strikes, which are crucial in a globalized world).

[58] La Hovary (2013), pp. 345–346 for a summary.

[59] Maupain has suggested a re-balancing of the available means of supervision, Maupain (2013).

[60] Leary (1992), p. 613.

secret[61]—will only make the Office even more cautious. Certainly, the times when Director-Generals either 'controlled' or 'ignored' ILO constituents are gone,[62] but it is clear that a strong Office, acting as a 'broker' as it did during the Cold War, would help resolve this crisis. Since 2012, it has been extremely difficult to bring Employers to compromise.

3.2 Underlying Challenges for Tripartism

Despite the fact that it has been widely hailed as *the* feature setting the ILO apart and providing it with a 'unique advantage',[63] especially in terms of the legitimacy it brings to its actions, tripartism has attracted a lot of criticism: some commentators have argued that the Organization is 'trapped' within its particular governance structure,[64] while others contend, for example, that tripartism is the reason why ILO conventions have such a low ratification rate.[65] Or, on a broader level, tripartism is simply not considered to promote any dynamism or legitimacy anymore, with some commentators going so far as to describe the Organization as 'stuck in a time-wrap'.[66]

Tripartism in the ILO has never had a smooth existence, however. Freedom of association is central to the ILO and to tripartism. Yet, as it is still not a reality in many countries, significant tensions emerged between tripartism within the ILO (whereby each delegate has an independent vote), and the national reality of tripartism, or rather its absence when there are no independent organizations. Very serious tensions arose specifically because organizations, and therefore their delegates, were not independent. Despite this, demanding the existence of independent organizations was deemed to de facto exclude the nomination of delegates from a significant number of countries, creating a situation which would have been contrary to the principle of universality of the ILO.[67] Problems of the representativity of constituents groups, which relates to the difficulty of representing the

[61] See ILO (2012a) para. 153; Cox (1973), p. 112 and Creighton (2004), p. 261.

[62] Information obtained from interviews.

[63] ILO Declaration on Social Justice for a Fair Globalization, adopted on 10 June 2008.

[64] Standing (2008), pp. 379–80. These debates are by no means new, however. For example, in 1959, Béguin was already writing that '[w]hether or not tripartism still has a contribution to make in enabling the organization to 'work more effectively' on its future tasks, and whether new interpretations can be given to this form of collaboration are the questions that face [the] ILO as it enters its fifth decade', Béguin (1959), p. 33.

[65] Peters (2009), p. 321.

[66] Klabbers (2014), p. 185.

[67] For thorough survey of these issues, see Tikriti (1982), pp. 339–346 and Maupain (1999a), pp. 333–344. Furthermore, since 1919, the demand for tripartism within the ILO has been seen as a means of promoting tripartism and freedom of association within countries, e.g. Bonvin (1998), pp. 68–69. The role of the ILO is still very much seen in this way today.

conflicting and fragmented interests of workers and employers, have now become more acute, and it is said that current developments in the world of work are seen as 'threaten[ing] to explode the tripartite categories'.[68]

Critiques concerning representativity are not new.[69] However, issues of representativity are today linked to broader economic processes—e.g. 'neo-liberalism', 'globalization', 'financialization', 'deregulation'—as well as more general issues of governance and development. The extent to which these processes make the operationalisation of tripartism and the ILO irrelevant is debatable, however, especially in the absence of an alternative institution at the international level with any legitimacy. Representing fully the diverse and fragmented nature of both capital and labour has moreover always been unrealistic, and at least *some* aspects of the conflict between capital and labour are captured through the ILO's constituents. Workers and Employers do represent real and conflicting general interests, and this has led to a range of initiatives, with a much broader reach than these organizations' particular interests, being adopted within the ILO (the ILO is not only concerned with narrowly defined 'employees' but with all human beings who work, and 'work' is understood in its broadest sense). It is clear however that in view of the challenges faced, continuous efforts need to be put in place to improve formal representativity.

The need for clearer, greater and stronger participation by civil society has often been raised,[70] notably by successive Director Generals of the ILO, not least by Albert Thomas in the 1920s.[71] More recently, Michel Hansenne and Juan Somavia both suggested to engage with civil society,[72] and the current Director-General, Guy Ryder, also attempted to re-open the door in its 2013 report to the ILC.[73] All these attempts have been met with resistance from Employers and Workers, however. This resistance is understandable,[74] but there are also vested interests in maintaining the status quo. The IOE exists only because of the ILO,[75] and it might not want to see its existence threatened. Trade unions on the other hand, might not

[68]Maupain (2013), p. 10. Generally, see Hepple (2005), pp. 53–54 and Cooney (1999), pp. 370–373.

[69]See ILO (2013b), para. 90.

[70]Civil society is not completely absent from the ILO however—civil society representatives' consultation and participation in debates is provided for in the Constitution and Standing Orders and some ILS make specific reference to their involvement. Moreover, so-called 'Tripartite plus meetings are quite frequent within the ILO in practice.

[71]Albert Thomas attempted to give a formal role to cooperatives, Louis (2013), p. 25.

[72]ILO (1994), p. 35 and ILO (1999), p. 40.

[73]ILO (2013b), para. 98. The 2008 Declaration on Social Justice stated explicitly the need to cooperate with new actors (II.A)v.

[74]Inter alia, NGOs are not necessarily representative or independent either, their presence might create geographical imbalance, their lifespan is not necessarily very long, they are numerous, and their selection would not be straightforward. Maupain (1999a), p. 384 and ILO (1999), p. 40. See also Charnovitz (1997), pp. 75–77; Nolte and Lagodinsky (2004), p. 325 and Baccaro (2001).

[75]Bonvin (1998), p. 69. Similar comments have been voiced about the ITUC on the workers' side—Standing argues that the ILO 'is one of the very few means by which to retain international legitimacy (and financial assistance for its members)', Standing (2008).

want to experience a further loss of influence.[76] The boundaries and operationalization of tripartism will in any case not change without the agreement of the constituents. Things might be changing, however. Although a lot of resistance is still voiced by individuals on both sides,[77] Workers may feel that in the present context, they need as much support as they can get from the labour movement beyond trade unions. Hoffer has voiced the opinion that there is a need to broaden 'alliances of organizations and initiatives fighting for social justice and the rights and dignity of people in the world of work'. Although this strategy would 'raise challenging and complex political questions', he argues that 'as business as usual is no longer an option thinking the unthinkable might be a good start'.[78] This change—or a change—might be brought about by the 2012 crisis, which may act as a catalyst for change.

Ultimately, the crisis and the processes described above have been the product of broad shifts in global geopolitics, not just in ideological terms, but also in terms of the rise of new regional and national configurations of power. On the one hand, as Sengenberger remarks, the rise of some regions over others has translated in much more vocal and proactive representatives of developing countries in the ILO.[79] On the other hand, this shift has also allowed Employers to be more vocal in their demands, as the rising BRICS (Brazil-Russia-India-China-South Africa) powers may be generally less inclined to social regulation,[80] and States are not taking the side of Workers as they used to.[81] Furthermore, the events shaking the ILO are happening in a broader context where States have been losing control over the issues dealt within the ILO, some more willingly than others, making their intervention to restore a fair balance within the ILO more difficult.[82]

---

[76]Standing goes much further, arguing with regard to representativity in the Governing Body, that both Employers and Workers want 'to retain their exclusive, monopolistic position and control the agenda with which they are most comfortable [and] each would support the other if any effort was made to broaden representativity', Standing (2008), pp. 379–380. Others have pointed out that some Employers and Workers members stay on 'well past their 'use by' date' and make little positive contributions, Creighton (2004), p. 266. See also Maupain (1999a), p. 249. The Workers' Group has been addressing these issues however.

[77]Information obtained from interviews.

[78]Hoffer (2014), p. 246. Frank Hoffer works in ACTRAV.

[79]Sengenberger (2013), p. 63. This was manifest in the 2011 discussions of the Convention No. 189 on Domestic Workers. Generally, Sengenberger points out to the fact that 'the ILO framework of international governance may be said to be more democratic and more up-to-date with the distribution of the present economic and political weight in the world than the system of governance of the international financial institutions', Sengenberger (2013), p. 63.

[80]Maupain (1999a), p. 59 referencing them as the BRIC States, as they then were.

[81]Haas, for example, argued that while historically some Governments were likely to take the side of the Workers, the State is now supporting capital, Haas (1964), p. 213 and also Landelius (1965), p. 522. It can certainly be contended that it has abandoned its mediating role between capital and labour, Chhachhi (2014), p. 902. Information also obtained from interviews.

[82]Information obtained from interviews.

4 Conclusion

Several conclusions can be drawn from this overview of the ILO, ILS, and tripartism. The first is of course that the ILO is not static and this is something to keep in mind when examining ILS and analysing their reception in other fields of law or the influence they might have. The second conclusion is that the current crisis has been, in part, provoked by this very interest in ILS and international labour law. The ILO's mandate has therefore not changed, but its capacity to create and supervise ILS in a manner that is coherent with its mandate seems to have been affected by the current crisis.

Recent events have illustrated how despite States formally having more power than Workers and Employers within the ILO,[83] the latter two groups actually have the necessary leverage to influence and even change the course of the ILO. This is, however, especially the case when one constituent is in a position of strength vis-à-vis the other, as is currently true of Employers vis-à-vis Workers. The end of the Cold War, and the rise of neo-liberalism as a dominant global ideology, revealed the extent to which tripartite consensus was linked to the ILO's origins as a rampart against communism. After 1989, maintaining common objectives among the ILO constituent groups that went beyond their own particular interests has clearly proven to be difficult, and the necessity for the Organization's ILS to be backed-up by its current supervisory system has been challenged (the mere fact that this crisis is on-going is already negatively affecting both the ILO and its supervisory system). This latter issue is fundamental and will inevitably entail a repositioning of the constituents within the ILO. This repositioning however needs to be done in a way that respects the Constitution's premises and principles, including first and foremost the core mission to pursue 'social justice' and the famous motto that 'labour is not a commodity'. This latter principle, which seems at times forgotten and relegated to a lofty ideal, should be of central concern in our contemporary times of economic crisis and inequality; indeed, it is not out of the question that the initial role of the ILO as a 'revolution insurance' comes to the fore again.

This being said, the current crisis affecting the ILO also suggests that the Organization does matter, as does its supervisory system, otherwise Employers would not have bothered to attack it. Although the operationalization of tripartism at the international level has posed, and continues to pose, important difficulties, it is—as a former ILO Director-General has stated—'a precious institution',[84] which

[83]Indeed, Governments have half the votes compared to a quarter each for Employers and Workers in plenary meetings and they are the only constituents empowered to vote on the ILO's budget, which they finance. They are moreover the only constituents directly consulted by the Office during the preparation of ILS—ILS are addressed to them, although the procedural rules provide they do need to consult Employers and Workers—and they nominate the Workers and Employers representatives to the ILC, Haas (1964), p. 213.

[84]ILO (1994), p. 35.

is a unique feature of the ILO. There is no doubt that tripartism 'is only as valuable as it is effective',[85] but the onus should very much be on reforming and improving a system that has proven its worth for almost 100 years now rather than letting it become irrelevant. This is all the more the case considering that any multilateral organization concerned with labour issues and social justice must clearly be able to represent more than a single interest, and in this respect, no better solution than tripartism has come to the fore.

References

Baccaro L (2001) Civil society, NGOs, and decent work policies: sorting out the issues. Discussion Paper DP/127/2001. International Institute for Labour Studies, ILO, Geneva

Béguin B (1959) ILO and the tripartite system. Carnegie Endowment for International Peace, New York

Bellace J (2014) The ILO and the right to strike. Int Labour Rev 153(1):29–70

Bonvin J-M (1998) L'Organisation internationale du Travail: Étude sur une agence productrice de normes. Presses universitaires de France, Paris

Cabanes B (2014) The great war and the origins of humanitarianism – 1918–1924. Cambridge University Press, Cambridge

Charnovitz S (1997) Two centuries of participation: NGOs and international governance. Michigan J Int Law 18(2):183–286

Chhachhi A (2014) Introduction: the 'Labour Question' in contemporary capitalism. Dev Change 45(5):895–919

Cooney S (1999) Testing times for the ILO: institutional reform for the new international political economy. Comp Labour Law Policy J 20(3):365–399

Cox RW (1973) ILO: a limited monarchy. In: Cox RW, Jacobson HK (eds) Anatomy of influence; decision making in international organization. Yale University Press, Yale/London, pp 102–138

Creighton B (2004) The future of labour law: is there a role for international labour standards? In: Barnard C et al (eds) The future of labour law. Hart, Oxford, pp 253–274

Diller J (2013) International labour law and the challenge of pluralism in the international order. Manch J Int Econ Law 10(2):128–147

France D (2001) Employers and the international labour organisation. In: Blanpain R, Engels C (eds) The ILO and the social challenge of the 21st century. Kluwer Law International, The Hague

Haas E (2008, first published 1964) Beyond the nation-state – functionalism and international organization. ECPR Press, Colchester

Helfer L (2006) Understanding change in international organizations: globalization and innovation in the ILO. Vanderbilt Law Rev 59(3):650–726

Hepple B (2005) Labour laws and global trade. Hart, Oxford

Hoffer F (2014) When very little is already too much: the struggle for international labour standards'. In: Sandbrook R, Güven AB (eds) Civilizing globalization. State University of New York Press, pp 233–249

ILO (1956) Committee on freedom of employers' and workers' organisations. GB.131/7/8. ILO, Geneva

[85] Ibid., p. 35.

ILO (1994) Report of the Director-General, defending values, promoting changes. ILC, 81st session
ILO (1999) Director General Report, decent work. ILC, 97th session
ILO (2006) Digest of decisions and principles of the Freedom of Association Committee ILO. ILO, Geneva
ILO (2011) Compendium of rules applicable to the Governing Body of the International Labour Office. ILO, Geneva
ILO (2012a) Report of the Committee on the Application of Standards: General Report. Record of Proceedings, No. 19(Rev)/Part 1. ILC, 101st Session
ILO (2012b) Report of the Committee on the Application of Standards: Submission, Discussion, and Approval. Record of Proceedings, No. 27. ILC, 101st Session
ILO (2013a) Report III (Part 1A) Report of the Committee of Experts on the Application of Conventions and Recommendations. ILC, 102nd Session
ILO (2013b) Director General Report, Towards the ILO centenary: realities, renewal and tripartite commitment. ILC, 102nd Session
ILO (2013c) Matters arising out of the work of the International Labour Conference, Governing Body, 317th Session. GB.317/INS/4/1. ILO, Geneva
ILO (2014a) The standards initiative: follow-up to the 2012 ILC Committee on the Application of Standards. GB.320/LILS/4. ILO, Geneva
ILO (2014b) Report III (Part 1A) Report of the Committee of Experts on the Application of Conventions and Recommendations. ILC, 103rd Session
ILO (2014c) Record of Proceedings No. 13 Part I. ILC, 103rd Session
ILO (2015) Report of the Committee on the Application of Standards, Provisional Record No. 14 Part one. ILC, 104th Session
IOE (2013) News release, employers call for a change to the functioning of the ILO regular supervisory system. IOE, Geneva
Jenks CW (1970) The international protection of trade union freedom. Stevens & Sons, London
Klabbers J (2014) Marginalised international organizations: three hypotheses concerning the ILO. In: Blanpain R, Liukkunen U, Yifeng C (eds) China and ILO fundamental principles and rights at work. Kluwer, The Hague, pp 181–196
La Hovary C (2013) Showdown at the ILO? A historical perspective on the Employers group's 2012 challenge to the right to strike. Ind Law J 42:338–368
La Hovary C (2015a) The ILO's supervisory bodies' soft law jurisprudence. In: Blackett A, Trebilcock A (eds) Research handbook on transnational labour law. Edgar Elgar, Cheltenham, pp 316–328
La Hovary C (2015b) The 2015 ILC and the right to strike: business as usual? Int Union Rights J 22 (2):16–17
La Hovary C (2015c) A challenging ménage à trois? Tripartism in the International Labour Organization. Int Organ Law Rev 12(1):204–236
Landelius T (1965) Workers, employers and governments: a comparative study of delegations and groups at the International Labour Conference, 1919–1964. Norstedt & Söner, Stockholm
Langille B (1999) The ILO and the new economy: new developments. Int J Comp Labour Law Ind Relat 15(3):229–258
Leary V (1992) Lessons from the experience of the international labour organisation. In: Alston P (ed) The United Nations and Human Rights: a critical appraisal. Clarendon Press, Oxford, pp 580–619
Louis M (2013) Syndicats contre coopératives? L'OIT et la représentation des acteurs de la société civile. Relations internationals 154(2):21–32
Maul D (2012) Human rights, development and decolonization: the International Labour Organization, 1940–70. Palgrave/ILO, Geneva
Maupain F (1999a) L'OIT, la justice sociale et la mondialisation. Collected Courses of The Hague Academy of International Law 278

Maupain F (1999b) The settlement of disputes within the International Labour Office. J Int Econ Law 2(2):273–293

Maupain F (2013) The ILO regular supervisory system: a model in crisis? Int Organ Law Rev 10 (1):117–175

Nolte G, Lagodinsky S (2004) The role of non-governmental organizations in the International Labor Organization. In: Benvenisti E, Nolte G (eds) The welfare state, globalization, and international law. Springer, Berlin/Heidelberg, pp 321–341

Novitz T (2009–2010) Connecting freedom of association and the right to strike: European dialogue with the ILO and its potential impact. Can Labour Employ Law J 15(3):465–494

Peters A (2009) Dual democracy. In: Klabbers J, Peters A, Ulfstein G (eds) The constitutionalization of international law. Oxford University Press, Oxford, pp 263–352

Phelan E (1936) Yes and Albert Thomas. Columbia University Press, New York

Rodgers G et al (2009) The ILO and the quest for social justice. ILO, Geneva

Sengenberger W (2013) The international labour organization: goals, functions and political impact. Friedrich Ebert Stiftung, Berlin

Servais J-M (2011) International labour law. Kluwer Law International, Alphen aan den Rijn

Standing G (2008) The ILO: an agency for globalization? Dev Change 39(3):355–384

Tikriti AK (1982) Tripartism and the international labour organisation: a study of the legal concept — its origins, function and evolution in the law of nations. Almqvist and Wiksell, Stockholm

Trebilcock A (2010) Putting the record straight about international labor standard setting. Comp Labor Law Policy J 31(3):553–570

Valticos N (1994) Once more about the ILO system of supervision: in what way is it still a compliance model? In: Blokker NM, Muller S (eds) Towards more effective supervision by international organizations: essays in honour of Henry G. Schermers, vol I. Martinus Nijhoff, Dordrecht, pp 99–113

Why the Shift from International to Transnational Law Is Important for Labour Standards

Anne Trebilcock

Contents

Although the term 'transnational law' was introduced by Philip Jessup as early as 1956, it has come into frequent use only over the past decade or so. For Jessup, it referred to 'all law which regulates actions or events that transcend national frontiers,'[1] and could involve a wide group of actors. Transnational law was initially most closely associated with 'thin' conceptions of law, sidelining economic and social rights. This began to change with the acceleration of modern-day globalization as from the 1990s, leading David Trubek in 2006 to point to the 'emergence of transnational labour law'.[2]

Today transnational labour law is seen as operating within, between and beyond States to form a type of (imperfect and incomplete) multi-layered global governance.[3] As Peer Zumbansen has observed, transnational law remains contested terrain,[4] and this is particularly so when labour rights meet other fields such as trade and investment law. Asymmetries of power characterize not only the Global South and the Global North, but also the actors within each of them. These

[1]Jessup (1956).

[2]Trubek (2006), pp. 725–733.

[3]Blackett and Trebilcock (2015), p. 3–31. For an in-depth review of governance aspects, see Halliday and Shaffer (2015).

[4]Zumbansen (2012), pp. 898–925.

A. Trebilcock (✉)
Georg-August-University Göttingen, Institute of Labour Law, Göttingen, Germany
e-mail: annetrebilcock@gmail.com

H. Gött (ed.), *Labour Standards in International Economic Law*,
https://doi.org/10.1007/978-3-319-69447-4_4

imbalances are mirrored in international legal constructs, such as increasingly free movement of goods, services and capital alongside tightened restrictions on the movement of people. Drawing on forces that gave birth to labour law in a prior era, transnational labour law is always in search of new methods to ensure respect for labour rights. The move from international to transnational labour law lies precisely in transnational labour law's capacity to be counter-hegemonic.

1 Transnational Labour Law Brings in Actors Other than States

Expanding the sources and nature of law-making is one aspect of such counter-hegemony. The enhanced importance of non-State actors is one of the main features of transnational law. Representatives of employers and workers have been embedded alongside governments in the ILO's governing structure since its inception. In other international law circles, recognition of the role of non-State actors in the development of global rule-making has been a more recent and more tentative phenomenon. Within the ILO, the incumbent non-State actors resist dilution of their own role in favour of non-governmental organizations or other groups, questioning the latters' legitimacy to engage in rule-making.

The increased role of a wide range of actors is in fact a two-edged sword in relation to labour standards. On the positive side, the involvement of actors who understand diverse realities on the ground expands the possibility of having global norms that reflect real awareness of what is important and what could function well in various contexts. Bringing more potential actors into the mix augments the number of possible pressure points towards an outcome. New opportunities emerge for the forging of strategic alliances. More resources and networks may be marshalled to campaign for respect for rights at work.

On the negative side, the involvement of more actors—many of which have no accountability to those who are the 'subjects and objects' of labour rights and labour protection—can create of a dispersion of norms. A confused landscape of 'public,' 'private' and 'privatized' norms leads to a loss of legal coherence. The phenomenon of non-State actors forming law-generating communities breaks traditional rule hierarchy. By decentering political law-making, a new frame emerges which 'can only be heterarchical.'[5]

Thus while the existence of diverse regulatory arrangements offers potential for innovation and adaptation, high levels of fragmentation bring limited potential for structural change.[6] There is also a risk of watering down or twisting a public norm, such as through a less stringent definition of a term.[7] Similarly, danger lies in the

[5]Peters et al. (2009), p. 550 et seq.

[6]Pekdemir et al. (2015), p. 226.

[7]See e.g. Bellace (2014), pp. 175–198.

selective use of indicators to measure some but not all important aspects of respect for fundamental principles and rights at work.[8] At the same time, however, as key elements of transnational labour law become more embedded in private action, this may contribute to enhancing respect for public norms.[9] In this connection, developments relating to follow-up to the UN Guiding Principles on Business and Human Rights merit attention, especially regarding use of the due diligence paradigm.[10] In short, the shift from international to transnational law offers both opportunities and threats in relation to labour rights.

2 Transnational Labour Law Grapples with Accountability in Global Value Chains

For much of the ILO's history, the predominant model in its Member States featured national industrial policy, production of most non-agricultural goods or services within the same territorial space, and national trade unions whose members were mostly male breadwinners. The focus was on encouraging Member States, seen as the sources of power, commit to and comply with international labour standards. Today, except for the national character of most trade union organizations, these features are no longer typical. Some multinational firms have resources that far outstrip those of a number of countries. Finished goods and services emerge from what is often a long 'value chain' that crosses many borders. The way firms operate has changed in fundamental ways. Production is outsourced and subcontracted without ownership, and the buying firm is not the legal employer, even though it has significant impact on conditions of work.[11]

So too has the picture of the workforce changed. It is increasingly diverse, although bias persists on grounds of gender, race and other categories.[12] Worldwide, traditional employment relationships and social security protection are not enjoyed by the growing ranks of the 'precariat'.[13] Many workers already or will soon face a digitalized gig economy where artificial intelligence is reinventing work in many fields.[14] Patterns of union membership may vary by country, but all are struggling to seek means of pinning responsibility on ever more footloose

[8]For an example, see the indicators developed for use in the World Justice Index, which is oriented mainly towards civil and political rights. A broader examination of issues around indicators is provided by Barenberg (2015), pp. 76–92.

[9]Van der Heijden and Zandvliet (2015), pp. 170–189.

[10]Trebilcock (2015), pp. 93–107.

[11]ILO (2016a), p. 8. See also ILO (2016a), No. 14 Part two and ILO (2016b).

[12]Lansky et al. (2016).

[13]ILO (2016c) and ILO (2016f), pp. 22–25.

[14]ILO (2015).

corporations.[15] How to guarantee sufficient incomes and adequate levels of social protection in this new scenario is not yet clear. This is a particular challenge along global supply chains.[16]

3 Transnational Labour Law Features Hybrid Arrangements in Search of Remedies

The centrality of collective action—and the freedom of association that underpins it—is a key element of transnational labour law. This in turn sparks interest in transnational labour law methods such as international framework agreements,[17] which span jurisdictions and involve non-State actors beyond national borders. An even greater magnet for attention has been the range of responses to the 2013 Rana Plaza factory collapse in Bangladesh.[18] The horrific event itself revealed fundamental flaws in the subcontracting paradigm that permits consumers in the Global North to buy cheap, trendy goods produced within very tight time-frames, under poor conditions and at very low wages, mostly in the Global South.

The Bangladesh Accord on Fire and Building Safety and the Arrangement on Payments to Victims and their Families offered the most intriguing approaches to corporate responsibility, the relationship between public and private roles, and the means of remedying and preventing harm from unsafe workplaces. Illustrating several features of transnational labour law, they combine traditional international labour law with a new role for the ILO,[19] elements of private and public international law,[20] networking among a wide range of actors, time-bound goal-setting and use of indicators in monitoring. The post-Rana Plaza response has also combined litigation-type efforts with social campaigning, although this strategy has many earlier precedents.

For many years the possible remedies for infringement of trade agreements, especially trade sanctions, have been held up as a gold standard in comparison to the relative mildness of what is foreseen under international labour Conventions. Although ratifying States are required to given them effect,[21] and some

[15]Sukthankar (2015), pp. 37–50. The business models that make effective strategies difficult to devise are summarized by Martin (2015), pp. 51–64.

[16]ILO (2016f), pp. 22–25.

[17]Drouin (2015), pp. 217–229.

[18]These are set out briefly in Compa (2015), pp. 127–131.

[19]See Diller (2015), pp. 336–342 and Reinecke and Donaghey (2015), pp. 257–277.

[20]The Arrangement uses the ILO Employment Injury Benefits Convention (No. 121), a public international law instrument unratified by Bangladesh, as the basis for income replacement. Disputes between the parties to the Accord are to be referred under rules set by the New York Convention on the Recognition and Enforcement of Foreign Arbitral Awards, drawing on private international law.

[21]Art. 22 ILO Constitution.

Conventions specify that legislative measures and penalties are to be enacted, many leave it up to the State itself to decide how to ensure their application. The ILO monitoring system, while robust in human rights circles, pales in comparison to what the WTO Appellate Tribunal can do in the face of violations of the underlying legal instrument.

At the same time, however, trade measures may be ill-suited to actually grappling with a problem in relation to respect for labour law. Not only trade measures but also trade sanctions can cause job losses. There has been great reluctance to invoke potentially available procedures, much less envisioned compliance measures, as illustrated by the experience under the labour side agreement to the North American Free Trade Agreement.[22] One problem is that the notion of 'country of origin' has become anachronistic. In addition, trade adjustment schemes will leave remediless those who could not prove a close enough connection between the trade violation and the harm caused. While the ILO has of course welcomed the increased references to labour provisions appearing in recent trade agreements, it also recognizes that problems of sustainability of impact, coherence and cooperation remain.[23]

Similar scepticism has accompanied the motivation of consumers to support better respect for workers' rights. While there can be some impact when an upper-tier product with consumer visibility is involved, serious questions of sustainability persist.[24] The UN Guiding Principles' emphasis on due diligence as a means of embedding better practices in firms has gained considerable traction, despite its many shortcomings. The tripartite resolution adopted following discussion of decent work in global supply chains at the International Labour Conference in 2016, for instance, was infused with references to due diligence procedures.[25] Fortunately, the resolution also refers to actions ensuring that workers have access to legal remedies.[26] This should dovetail with the calls to continue development under the UN Guiding Principles for effective remedies in case of violations of labour rights. A Working Group of the Human Rights Council is considering the development of a binding instrument on the human rights responsibility of enterprises, but opinions differ as to the wisdom of such a proposal. On a more philosophical plane, Yossi Dahan and others have argued for seeing global labour rights as duties of justice.[27]

And there are many other ways in which a corporate entity might be held responsible for legal violations committed by an intermediary. Admittedly, however, such attempts provoke push-back by enterprises. There are also numerous

[22] Compa and Brooks (2015).

[23] ILO (2016d).

[24] Kolben (2015), pp. 361–373. See also Barry and Macdonald (2016), pp. 92–118 and ILO (2016f), pp. 22–25.

[25] ILO (2016e), see for instance paras. 16 (d), (e) and (f), Art. 18 and Art. 23 (f).

[26] Ibid. para. 23 (b) concerning the ILO's own programme of action on the topic.

[27] Dahan et al. (2016), pp. 53–91.

hurdles to jump, from the interpretation of *forum non conveniens* to limits placed on court-awarded damages. Depending on the national and sectoral context, some useful avenues for recourse may lie in seemingly unlikely areas of law, outside the traditional areas of either trade or labour. Examples include creative use of fiduciary duties, consumer protection measures, tort law, aspects of corporate law, export credits, tax law and even criminal responsibility.[28] The distinct logics of other legal regimes are not, however, without complications.[29] Instead, Alan Hyde has proposed an ILO standard on remote responsibility to correct violations of core labour standards.[30] If politically feasible, it would be a welcome addition to the arsenal of transnational labour law. To have a meaningful impact, such an instrument would need wide acceptance and additional buttressing by a wide range of actors.

4 Transnational Law Reinforces the Need for Interdisciplinary Analysis and Monitoring

In contrast to what often become temporary alliances around the most recent outcry over labour exploitation, alignment of interests can be key to sustaining improvement in global supply chains, as shown by Daniel Berliner et al.[31] These researchers' findings reinforce and refine Richard Locke's conclusion that private efforts to improve working conditions will be sustainable only alongside stronger public action.[32] Some ideas for such action will lie in other areas of law. Moreover, an understanding of what will be needed to effect long-lasting change in various contexts will come not simply from labour law—international or national—but will rely as well on findings of anthropologists, economists, sociologists, statisticians, labour relations professionals and political scientists. Transnational law is up front about its reliance on inter-disciplinarity,[33] which enriches discourse and widens horizons.

Even in the past, most ILO Conventions were developed taking into account statistics and economic and other analysis in addition to legal considerations. With employers' and workers' organizations free to provide comments on Government reports and to participate fully in Conference proceedings at which instruments are

[28]See for instance Deva and Bilchiltz (2013), Murray (2015), pp. 337–366; Carse and Njoya (2015), pp. 311–335; Sukthankar (2015), pp. 37–50 and Trebilcock (2015), pp. 104–106 respectively.

[29]See examples provided by Sukthankar (2015), pp. 37–50.

[30]Hyde (2016), pp. 209–236.

[31]Berliner et al. (2015).

[32]Locke (2013).

[33]See for instance, the website of the Transnational Law Institute, Dickson Poon School of Law, King's College London: https://www.kcl.ac.uk/law/tli/index.aspx. Accessed 08 Aug 2017.

adopted, it is an iterative process for those involved. The social partners' familiarity with actual practice in the world of work informs the contextual crafting of legal instruments.[34]

A different story has emerged so far when it comes to monitoring of implementation. Various formulations are used in ILO Conventions regarding the means for giving them effect; reference is often made to laws and regulations, collective agreements, arbitral awards or court decisions. Some call on Member States to provide statistical data and other information in reporting on their application of ILO instruments.[35] In addition, the report form approved by the ILO Governing Body for governments to use in showing how they apply an instrument will often specify what information is required. In practice, however, the vast majority of information provided in response relates only to legal provisions and the occasional court decision.

With its much greater reliance on indicators, transnational labour law promises to raise the bar when it comes to more meaningful reporting on implementation. Despite all the caveats that justifiably accompany such efforts, considerable progress has occurred both within and outside the ILO in better measurement of respect for rights at work.[36] Using better metrics would generate a more extensive information base. A range of actors could draw in it in pushing for greater respect for labour rights. In a network, such actors could also become effective diffusers of information about compliance.

5 Final Comments

As the International Labour Conference concluded in 2016, 'There is concern that current international labour standards may not be fit for purpose to achieve decent work in global supply chains'.[37] Aside from some encouraging exceptions like the Decent Work for Domestic Workers Convention, 2011 (No. 198), the generation of international labour law has in recent times been slow-moving and sometimes politically paralysed. A similar comment would describe recent efforts towards successful negotiation of significant trade pacts. Where traditional tripartite dialogue is unable or unwilling to move outside a narrow comfort zone, transnational labour law—with its broader vision of reuniting the social and the economic—seems at least theoretically better placed to test different solutions until the most promising can emerge within a particular context.

The shift from international to transnational labour law is well underway, but remains very much in evolution. It holds risks as well as promise. Actors dedicated

[34]For a description of how the process operates, see Trebilcock (2010), pp. 553–570.

[35]See ILO (2006), paras. 96–99.

[36]In addition to Barenberg (2015), see e.g. Sari and Kuchera (2011) and Kucera (2007).

[37]ILO (2016b), para. 25.

to the improvement of working conditions around the world will continue to push its limits in favour of greater respect for rights at work.

References

Barenberg M (2015) International labour indicators: conceptual and normative snares. In: Blackett A, Trebilcock A (eds) Research handbook on transnational labour law. Edward Elgar, Cheltenham, pp 76–92

Barry C, Macdonald K (2016) How should we conceive of individual consumer responsibility to address labour injustives? In: Dahan Y, Lerner H, Milman-Sivan F (eds) Global justice and international labour rights. Cambridge University Press, Cambridge, pp 92–118

Bellace JR (2014) Human rights at work: the need for definitional coherence in the global governance system. Int J Comp Law Ind Relat 30(2):175–198

Berliner D, Greenleaf AR, Lake M, Levi M, Noveck J (2015) Labor standards in international supply chains: aligning rights and incentives. Edward Elgar, Cheltenham

Blackett A, Trebilcock A (2015) Conceptualizing transnational labour law. In: Blackett A, Trebilcock A (eds) Research handbook on transnational labour law. Edward Elgar, Cheltenham, pp 3–31

Carse A, Njoya W (2015) Labour law as the law of the business enterprise. In: Bogg A, Costello C, Davies ACL, Prassi J (eds) The autonomy of labour law. Hart, Oxford, pp 311–335

Compa L (2015) Commentary: the ILO committee on the application of standards on Bangladesh and the Rana plaza collapse. Int Labor Rights Case Law 1:127–131

Compa L, Brooks T (2015) NAFTA and NAALC: twenty years of trade-labour linkage. Wolters Kluwer Law & Business, New York

Dahan Y, Lerner D, Milman-Sivan F (2016) Global labour rights as duties of justice. In: Dahan Y, Lerner H, Milman-Sivan F (eds) Global justice and international labour rights. Cambridge University Press, Cambridge, pp 53–91

Deva S, Bilchiltz D (eds) (2013) Human rights obligations of business: beyond the corporate responsibility to protect. Cambridge University Press, Cambridge

Diller J (2015) Pluralism and privatization in transnational labour regulations: experience of the International Labour Organization. In: Blackett A, Trebilcock A (eds) Research handbook on transnational labour law. Edward Elgar, Cheltenham, pp 329–342

Drouin R-C (2015) Freedom of association in international framework agreements. In: Blackett A, Trebilcock A (eds) Research handbook on transnational labour law. Edward Elgar, Cheltenham, pp 217–229

Halliday T, Shaffer G (eds) (2015) Transnational legal orders. Cambridge University Press, Cambridge

Hyde A (2016) To what duties do global labour rights correlate? Responsibilty for labour standards down the productive chain. In: Dahan Y, Lerner H, Milman-Sivan F (eds) Global justice and international labour rights. Cambridge University Press, Cambridge, pp 209–236

ILO (2006) Manual for drafting ILO instruments. ILO, Geneva

ILO (2015) World employment social outlook: the changing nature of jobs. ILO, Geneva

ILO (2016a) Report IV, decent work in global supply chains. ILC, 105th Session. ILO, Geneva

ILO (2016b) Report of the committee on decent work in global supply chains. Provisional Record No. 14 Part two. ILC, 105th Session. ILO, Geneva

ILO (2016c) Resolution and conclusions concerning decent work in supply chains. ILC, 105th Session. ILO, Geneva

ILO (2016d) Non-standard employment around the world: understanding challenges, shaping progress. ILO, Geneva

ILO (2016e) Assessment of labour provisions in trade and investment agreements. ILO, Geneva

ILO (2016f) Resolution concerning decent work in global supply chains, ILC, 105th session. ILO, Geneva
Jessup PC (1956) Transnational law. Yale University Press, New Haven
Kolben K (2015) Transnational private labour regulation, consumer-citizenship and the consumer imaginary. In: Blackett A, Trebilcock A (eds) Research handbook on transnational labour law. Edward Elgar, Cheltenham, pp 361–373
Kucera D (2007) Qualitative indicators of labour standards: comparative methods and applications. Springer, Dordrecht
Lansky M, Ghosh J, Méda D, Rani U (eds) (2016) Women, gender and work: social choices and inequalities, vol 2E. ILO, Geneva
Locke R (2013) The promise and limits of private power: promoting labor standards in a global economy. Cambridge University Press, Cambridge
Martin I (2015) Corporate governance structures and practices: from ordeal to opportunities and challenges for transnational labor law. In: Blackett A, Trebilcock A (eds) Research handbook on transnational labour law. Edward Elgar, Cheltenham, pp 51–64
Murray J (2015) Conceptualizing the employer as fiduciary: mission impossible? In: Bogg A, Costello C, Davies ACL, Prassi J (eds) The autonomy of labour law. Hart, Oxford, pp 337–366
Pekdemir C, Gasbergen P, Cörvers R (2015) On the transformative capacity of private fair labour arrangements. In: Marx A, Wouters J, Ryp G, Beke L (eds) Global governance of labour rights: assessing the effectiveness of transnational public and private policy initiatives. Edward Elgar, Cheltenham, pp 209–229
Peters A, Koechlin L, Fenner Zinkernagel G (2009) Non-state actors as standard setters: framing the issue in an interdisciplinary fashion. In: Peters A, Koechlin L, Förster T, Fenner Zinkernagel G (eds) Non-state actors as standard setters. Cambridge University Press, Cambridge, pp 550–551
Reinecke J, Donaghey J (2015) The accord for fire and building safety in Bangladesh' in response to the Rana plaza disaster. In: Marx A, Wouters J, Ryp G, Beke L (eds) Global governance of labour rights: assessing the effectiveness of transnational public and private policy initiatives. Edward Elgar, Cheltenham, pp 257–277
Sari D, Kuchera D (2011) Measuring progress towards the application of freedom of association and collective bargaining rights: a tabular presentation of the findings of the ILO supervisory system. ILO Policy Integration Department Working Paper No. 99. ILO, Geneva
Sukthankar A (2015) Global organizing and domestic constraints. In: Blackett A, Trebilcock A (eds) Research handbook on transnational labour law. Edward Elgar, Cheltenham, pp 37–50
Trebilcock A (2010) Putting the record straight about international standard setting. Comp Labor Law Policy J 31(3):553–570
Trebilcock A (2015) Due diligence on labour issues – opportunities and limits of the guiding principles on business and human rights. In: Blackett A, Trebilcock A (eds) Research handbook on transnational labour law. Edward Elgar, Cheltenham, pp 93–107
Trubek D (2006) Review essay: the emergence of transnational labor law. Am J Int Law 100:725–733
Van der Heijden P, Zandvliet R (2015) The rapprochement of ILO standards and CSR mechanisms: towards a positive understanding of the 'privatization' of international labour standards. In: Marx A, Wouters J, Ryp G, Beke L (eds) Global governance of labour rights: assessing the effectiveness of transnational public and private policy initiatives. Edward Elgar, Cheltenham, pp 170–189
Zumbansen P (2012) Transnational law, evolving. In: Smits JM (ed) Elgar Encyclopedia of comparative law. Edward Elgar, Cheltenham, pp 898–925

Part II
Labour Regulation of Trade, Investment and Finance

The Implications of *EC – Seal Products* for the Protection of Core Labour Standards in WTO Law

Thomas Cottier

Contents

Abstract This paper offers a brief history of labour standards in international trade regulation, recalling that negotiations have not yet materialised achieving a stronger nexus. Yet, efforts to bring about linkages with non-trade concerns have been developing in WTO dispute settlement. The paper discusses the implications of *EC - Seals* and expounds and the relevant passages of the reports of the Panel and the Appellate Body. In applying deference to the notion of public morality and in applying standards of necessity and a balance of interests involved, the

T. Cottier (✉)
University of Berne, World Trade Institute, Berne, Switzerland
e-mail: Thomas.cottier@wti.org

H. Gött (ed.), *Labour Standards in International Economic Law*,
https://doi.org/10.1007/978-3-319-69447-4_5

paper argues that the case is of paramount importance in assessing the policy space of Members of the WTO in establishing closer linkages between trade and labour standards.

1 International Trade Regulation and Labour Standards

1.1 Introduction

Since the first wave of globalization in the nineteenth century, the relationship of trade and labour standards has been at the heart of interfacing open markets, competition and social policy. Labour, amounting to one of the key factors of production next to capital and natural resources, is a key determinant in defining comparative advantages. Trade and employment economics explore the interdependence of the two fields and discuss the impact of trade liberalization on employment and vice-versa in controversial terms.[1] From the very beginning, harmonization and approximation of levels of labour standards has been a core motivation to bring about level playing fields and equal conditions of competition in international trade. The creation of the Bureau International de Travail (BIT) and the International Labour Organization (ILO) not only was a response to the Bolshevik revolution at the end of World War I; it was equally driven by the need to create equal level playing fields in international trade.[2] The same motivations, forty years later, were driving social standards in the European Economic Community in terms of gender equality.[3] Today, the issue is mainly discussed in regard to the triangle of labour migration, trade and investment.[4]

Yet, while trade and labour are inextricably linked, the areas have largely stayed separated in institutional terms. The same is true for investment. Despite the fact that the WTO is hosted in the former premises of the ILO—work depicted in realist sculptures and art deco murals—the WTO treaties, without the exception of prison labour, do not establish explicit legal linkages between the two fields. Much like trade and human rights, they developed in isolation for many years and decades, once the project of linking them in the Havana Charter was rejected and had failed. Except for addressing prison labour, the WTO does not seem suitable to address the issue. Social dumping is not captured by the Anti-dumping Agreement. Countervailing duties based upon subsidization are not to the point in addressing

[1] For a comprehensive survey see Jansen and Lee (2007).

[2] See generally Kaufmann (2007) and Belser (2007).

[3] Art 119 EEC Treaty (1957); see in particular CJEU, *Defrenne/SABENA*, Case C-43/75, EU:C:1976:56.

[4] See Panizzon et al. (2015).

low labour standards in exporting countries. The two fields, however, are legally closer than many would think. They may meet in WTO dispute settlement.

The paper briefly recalls the history of failed negotiations and turns to the implication of WTO dispute settlement. So far, no case explicitly focused on the linkages to labour standards. Yet, legal developments mainly triggered by environmental and moral concerns will not remain without implications for fostering the linkage between trade and labour standards in the case law of the WTO. Of particular importance is the 2014 ruling in *European Communities – Measures Prohibiting the Importation and Marketing of Seal Products*.[5] The paper explores the implications for unilateral protection of labour standards and human rights and to what extent such measures may affect producers in other markets.

1.2 Negotiations

Several attempts were made to link labour standards and GATT and WTO law. Upon the failure of the Havana Charter and its farsighted treaty text,[6] industrialized countries, in particular the US, repeatedly attempted in trade rounds to establish minimal labour standards in the multilateral system.[7] All these efforts failed, mainly due to resistance of developing and emerging economies stressing the need of growth and fearing to lose comparative advantages of cheap labour, inducing higher production costs, strengthening of trade unions and enhanced international monitoring and control of powerful employers. The tripartite system of the ILO and its

[5]WTO, *EC – Measures Prohibiting the Importation and Marketing of Seal Products*, Report of the Appellate Body, 22 May 2014, WT/DS400/AB/R, WT/DS401/AB/R; WTO, *EC – Measures Prohibiting the Importation and Marketing of Seal Products*, Report of the Panel, 25 Nov 2013, WT/DS400/R, WT/DS401/R, para.1.

[6]Havana Charter for an International Trade Organization, 24 March 1948, UN Doc E/CONF.2/78. Art. 7 on Fair Labour Standards reads:

> 1. The Members recognize that measures relating to employment must take fully into account the rights of workers under inter-governmental declarations, conventions and agreements. They recognize that all countries have a common interest in the achievement and maintenance of fair labour standards related to productivity, and thus in the improvement of wages and working conditions as productivity may permit. The Members recognize that unfair labour conditions, particularly in production for export, create difficulties in international trade, and, accordingly, each Member shall take whatever action may be appropriate and feasible to eliminate such conditions within its territory.
> 2. Members which are also members of the International Labour Organisation shall cooperate with that organization in giving effect to this undertaking.
> 3. In all matters relating to labour standards that may be referred to the Organization in accordance with the provisions of Art. 94 or 95, it shall consult and co-operate with the International Labour Organisation.

[7]See Charnovitz (1987); see also on the debate at the time Cottier and Caplazi (1998), Edgen (1979), Eglin (1997), Weiss (1996) and de Wet (1995).

reporting system, at best allowing for naming and shaming, was preferred and left international labour standards largely in the realm of non-enforceable international obligations. Renewed efforts were made during the Uruguay Round of multilateral negotiations and resulted in a work programme addressing trade and labour. Yet, the 1996 Singapore ministerial conference agreed to leave responsibilities essentially with the ILO. Trade should contribute to labour standards by means of stimulating enhancing economic growth.[8] The statement was affirmed in the 2001 Doha Declaration.[9] It has not been given further effects ever since. Instead, a compromise reached in 1998 resulted in the elaboration of core labour standards by the ILO *Declaration on Fundamental Principles and Rights at Work and its Follow-up (1998)*, binding upon all Members of the ILO[10]:

> 2. Declares that all Members, even if they have not ratified the Conventions in question, have an obligation arising from the very fact of membership in the Organization to respect, to promote and to realize, in good faith and in accordance with the Constitution, the principles concerning the fundamental rights which are the subject of those Conventions, namely:
> (a) freedom of association and the effective recognition of the right to collective bargaining;
> (b) the elimination of all forms of forced or compulsory labour;
> (c) the effective abolition of child labour; and
> (d) the elimination of discrimination in respect of employment and occupation.

The Declaration provided the foundation for sanctions against Myanmar,[11] but has not otherwise served as a basis for reprisals against violations of core labour standards expounded in the instrument. The relationship of the standards to WTO law, however, was left open and remains to be defined.[12]

Negotiated linkages are more advanced in preferential trade agreements.[13] NAFTA includes a side-agreement on labour standards.[14] The approach is mainly educational and based upon dialogue between the tripartite partners. The promotion

---

[8]WTO, Singapore Ministerial Declaration, 18 Dec 1996, WT/MIN(96)/DEC: 'We renew our commitment to the observance of internationally recognized core labour standards. The International Labour Organization (ILO) is the competent body to set and deal with these standards, and we affirm our support for its work in promoting them. We believe that economic growth and development fostered by increased trade and further trade liberalization contribute to the promotion of these standards. We reject the use of labour standards for protectionist purposes, and agree that the comparative advantage of countries, particularly low-wage developing countries, must in no way be put into question. In this regard, we note that the WTO and ILO Secretariats will continue their existing collaboration.'

[9]WTO, Doha Ministerial Declaration, 20 Nov 2001, WT/MIN(01)/DEC/1.

[10]ILO Declaration on Fundamental Principles and Rights at Work and its Follow-up, International Labour Conference, adopted on 18 June 1998 and Annex revised 15 June 2010.

[11]See International Labour Conference, Resolution concerning the measures recommended by the Governing Body under Art. 33 of the ILO Constitution on the subject of Myanmar, 14 June 2000.

[12]Cf. https://www.wto.org/english/thewto_e/minist_e/min99_e/english/about_e/18lab_e.htm. Accessed 5 Mar 2016. The status quo is discussed by Choudhary et al. (2011).

[13]See Addo (2015).

[14]North American Agreement on Labor Cooperation (NAALC), concluded 13 Sep 1993; Addo (2015), pp. 216–221.

of labour standards forms part of Economic Partnership Agreements of the European Union with developing countries[15] or its more recent FTAs.[16] The recently concluded Transpacific Partnership Agreement (TPP) fosters labour standards following the NAFTA approach in addition to fostering Corporate Social Responsibility (CSR) and to strengthening dispute settlement on labour standards beyond complicated NAFTA procedures never used so far. International obligations essentially address domestic enforcement and implementation and explicitly exclude extraterritorial outreach of enforcement measures in Labour Chapter Art. 19.5 (3) TPP, using somewhat ambiguous language originally drafted, and partly based upon NAFTA, in the 2004 US-Central America-Dominican Republic Free Trade Agreement (CAFTA-DR)[17]:

> Article 19.5: Enforcement of Labour Laws
>
> 1. No Party shall fail to effectively enforce its labour laws through a sustained or recurring course of action or inaction in a manner affecting trade or investment between the Parties after the date of entry into force of this Agreement.
>
> 2. If a Party fails to comply with an obligation under this Chapter, a decision made by that Party on the provision of enforcement resources shall not excuse that failure. Each Party retains the right to exercise reasonable enforcement discretion and to make bona fide decisions with regard to the allocation of enforcement resources between labour enforcement activities among the fundamental labour rights and acceptable conditions of work enumerated in Article 19.3.1 (Labour Rights) and Article 19.3.2 (Labour Rights), provided that the exercise of that discretion, and those decisions, are not inconsistent with its obligations under this Chapter.
>
> 3. Nothing in this Chapter shall be construed to empower a Party's authorities to undertake labour law enforcement activities in the territory of another Party.

1.3 Unilateral Linkages

Failure to agree on trade related labour measures in the WTO and elsewhere has not excluded the adoption of unilateral measures. The United States unilaterally banned products made by child labour.[18] The United States and the European Union both linked their General System of Preferences (GSP) to compliance with international labour standards.[19] Developing countries failing to adhere and implement minimal standards run the risk to see their zero or preferential import tariff rates suspended. Moreover, government procurement may be linked to the respect of social

[15]E.g. Arts. 71 (b) and (c), Art. 73 and Arts. 191–1993, 224 note 1 Economic Partnership Agreement, between the Cariforum States and the European Community and its Member States, O.J. L 289/1/3 (2008).

[16]For example, Art. 13 EU-Singapore Free Trade Agreement concerning trade and sustainable development.

[17]For a survey of US labour provisions in bilateral Trade Agreements see OECD (2012).

[18]See Humbert (2009), pp. 318–322.

[19]See Addo (2015), pp. 147–172 and Thomas (2009).

standards in different jurisdictions of WTO Members. In the EU, public authorities need to respect local labour laws in procuring goods and services supplied by foreign operators essentially working under different and separate contractual arrangements in their home countries.[20]

1.4 WTO Dispute Settlement

None of these, nor other unilateral measures, have been tested in WTO dispute settlement so far. India challenged the linkage to labour standards in *European Communities – Conditions for the Granting of Tariff Preferences to Developing Countries*,[21] but eventually withdrew the particular complaint. As of today, no Member of the WTO has ever brought a case based upon violation of labour standards or alleging excessive outreach of imposing domestic labour standards affecting conditions of production abroad. Nor has the WTO seen complaints, based upon violations of obligations to protect from unfair competition, seeking the enforcement of labour standards to which adherence was pledged by companies in their statements of Corporate Social Responsibility. So far, the traditional divide and segmentation has persisted. *European Communities – Measures Prohibiting the Importation and Marketing of Seal Products*[22] may have changed this equation for coming years.

2 EC – Seal Products

2.1 Facts and Results

The European Union banned the placing on the EU market of seal products from commercial production and channels in Regulation 1007/2009 adopted by the European Parliament and the Council[23] and implemented by the Commission with additional Regulation 737/2010.[24] The ban resulted from successful efforts

---

[20]See EU Parliament and Council Directive 96/71/EC *concerning the posting of workers in the framework of the provision of services*, O.J. L 18/1(1997). The directive is currently under review seeking to increase standards from minimal wage requirements to local tariff levels.

[21]WTO, *EC – Conditions for the ranting of Tariff Preferences to Developing Countries*, Report of the Appellate Body, 7 Apr 2004, WT/DS246/AB/R; see Thomas (2009), p. 266.

[22]WTO, *EC – Measures Prohibiting the Importation and Marketing of Seal Products,* Report of the Appellate Body, 22 May 2014, WT/DS400/AB/R, WT/DS401/AB/R. For the subsequent discussion of the case, see also Humbert (2018).

[23]EU Parliament and Council Regulation 1007/2009/EC *on trade in seal products*, O.J. L 286/36 (2009).

[24]European Commission Regulation 737/2010 *laying down detailed rules for the implementation of Regulation 1007/2009/EC of the European Parliament and the Council on trade in seal products*, O.J.L 216/1 (2010).

of the animal rights and protection movement and took issue with the traditional manner and methods of stunning (clubbing and shooting) and bleeding seals in order to protect the integrity of the fur. The regulation entailed a general ban with three particular exceptions: The report of the Appellate Body characterised the schemes as follows:

> 1.4. The EU Seal Regime prohibits the placing of seal products on the EU market unless they qualify under certain exceptions, consisting of the following: (i) seal products obtained from seals hunted by Inuit or other indigenous communities (IC exception); (ii) seal products obtained from seals hunted for purposes of marine resource management (MRM exception); and (iii) seal products brought by travellers into the European Union in limited circumstances (Travellers exception). The EU Seal Regime lays down specific requirements in respect of each of these exceptions.[25]

Unlike the title of the case indicates, the measures were drafted as an internal market measure. However, since most of the products originate outside the Union, the measure mainly affected imports from commercial hunting predominant in Canada and Norway while the exception for Inuit and other indigenous communities (IC) de facto mainly benefited exports from Greenland. While subject to sovereignty of Denmark, Greenland is not a member of the Union and, legally speaking, imports are from without the common market and pertain to external relations of the European Union.

The regulations were challenged by Canada claiming a violation of the TBT Agreement, and Norway essentially claiming violations of Art. I:1 and III:4 GATT.[26] The Panel qualified the measure as a technical regulation under Annex A of the TBT Agreement and dealt with the matter accordingly under this Agreement. It concluded that the regulation could be justified under Art. 2.2 TBT, invoking public morals in defence of prevailing perceptions in Europe. In assessing the measure and its regulatory distinctions, the Panel referred to jurisprudence under Art. XX GATT and incorporated considerations relating to public morals and the chapeau in reading the respective provisions of the TBT Agreement. The Panel held that the measure offered reasonable regulatory distinctions but failed to respond to obligations of conformity assessment under Art. 5.1.2 TBT. The Panel proceeded to examine the matter under Art. I and III and XX of GATT by importing its analysis made under the TBT Agreement.

Upon appeal, the Appellate Body rejected the integrated analysis of the TBT and GATT Agreements by the Panel and exclusively dealt with the matter under the

---

[25]WTO, *EC – Conditions for the ranting of Tariff Preferences to Developing Countries*, Report of the Appellate Body, 7 Apr 2004, WT/DS246/AB/R. All subsequent quotes are indicated at the outset by the respective number of paragraph of the Appellate Body and Panel Report, respectively; all footnotes omitted.

[26]While the parties initially claimed that the ban violates Art. XI:1 GATT, subsequent arguments limited the scope of this claim to the modalities of the exceptions and was eventually refuted by the Panel and not appealed; see WTO, *EC – Measures Prohibiting the Importation and Marketing of Seal Products*, Report of the Panel, 25 Nov 2013, WT/DS400/R, WT/DS401/R, paras. 7.652–7.663.

provisions of the General Agreement. The measure was found to be an import restriction devoid of the requirements of a technical regulation under Annex A of the TBT Agreement. Violations of Art. I:1 and III:4 GATT were affirmed. The Appellate Body, however, developed a new argumentation under the chapeau of Art. XX GATT and found discriminatory treatment due to lack of precision of the regulations and de facto advantages granted to export from Greenland.

The Appellate reiterated the function of Art. I and III GATT on non-discrimination of providing equal conditions of competition:

> 5.82. Finally, we observe that, notwithstanding the textual differences between Articles I:1 and III:4, each provision is concerned, fundamentally, with prohibiting discriminatory measures by requiring, in the context of Article I:1, equality of competitive opportunities for like imported products from all Members, and, in the context of Article III:4, equality of competitive opportunities for imported products and like domestic products. It is for this reason that neither Article I:1 nor Article III:4 require a demonstration of the actual trade effects of a specific measure.

The main issue of the case thus relates to the question whether the regulations could be justified under Art. XX GATT which follows a two-tier test.

> 5.169. As established in WTO jurisprudence, the assessment of a claim of justification under Article XX involves a two-tiered analysis in which a measure must first be provisionally justified under one of the subparagraphs of Article XX, before it is subsequently appraised under the chapeau of Article XX. As the Appellate Body has stated, provisional justification under one of the subparagraphs requires that a challenged measure 'address the particular interest specified in that paragraph' and that 'there be a sufficient nexus between the measure and the interest protected'.

Assessing the impact of public morals invoked and necessity amount the most important considerations of the case in assessing its impact for the protection of labour standards. It is of interest to recapitulate the reasoning within Art. XX GATT in some detail.

2.2 *Public Morals*

The European Union defended the regulations by invoking public morals under Art. XX (a) GATT as its main defence of the measure. The measures were argued to be necessary to protect widely perceived standards in Europe on animal welfare, witnessed and evidenced by majorities in the legislative process. Canada argued instead that the invocation of public morals must be supported by an existing risk which the defendant failed to demonstrate. The argument drew from an analogy to Art. XX (b) SPS Agreement where restrictive measures in support of public health need to be based upon the existence of a scientifically proven risk and in accordance with an appropriate level of risk as defined by the regulator. The Appellate Body, however, held that the perception of public morality as a moral and not scientific category is not suitable to such a requirement:

> 5.198. However, the notion of risk in the context of Article XX (b) is difficult to reconcile with the subject matter of protection under Article XX (a), namely, public morals. While the focus on the dangers or risks to human, animal, or plant life or health in the context of Article XX (b) may lend itself to scientific or other methods of inquiry, such risk-assessment methods do not appear to be of much assistance or relevance in identifying and assessing public morals. We therefore do not consider that the term 'to protect', when used in relation to 'public morals' under Article XX (a), required the Panel, as Canada contends, to identify the existence of a risk to EU public moral concerns regarding seal welfare.

Secondly, it was argued that recourse to public morality failed to be sufficiently precise. The argument of a double standard, however, was not upheld by the Appellate Body. Instead, and referring to previous cases, the perception and definition of public morals, while an international law standard, enjoys significant deference and is largely left to the state invoking the notion in defence of the measure at hand:

> 5.199. For this reason, we also have difficulty accepting Canada's argument that, for the purposes of an analysis under Article XX (a), a Panel is required to identify the exact content of the public morals standard at issue. The Panel accepted the definition of 'public morals' developed by the Panel in *US – Gambling*, according to which 'the term 'public morals' denotes 'standards of right and wrong conduct maintained by or on behalf of a community or nation''. The Panel also referred to the reasoning developed by the Panel in *US – Gambling* that the content of public morals can be characterized by a degree of variation, and that, for this reason, Members should be given some scope to define and apply for themselves the concept of public morals according to their own systems and scales of values.

Canada further argued that the standard of morality must be consistent and applied to animal welfare and husbandry in general. European practices in treating cattle and other animals were held inconsistent with the strict moral standards applied to the killing of seals. Again, this argument draws from the requirement of consistency of Art. 5.7 SPS Agreement. The Appellate Body rejected the analogy in relation to perceptions of morality:

> 5.200. Finally, by suggesting that the European Union must recognize the same level of animal welfare risk in seal hunts as it does in its slaughterhouses and terrestrial wildlife hunts, Canada appears to argue that a responding Member must regulate similar public moral concerns in similar ways for the purposes of satisfying the requirement 'to protect' public morals under Article XX (a). In this regard, we note that the Panel in *US – Gambling* underscored that Members have the right to determine the level of protection that they consider appropriate, which suggests that Members may set different levels of protection even when responding to similar interests of moral concern.

2.3 Necessity and Alternative Measures

Upon approving recourse to public morality, similar to the Panel, the Appellate Body thus turned to the analysis of necessity of the measure. It engaged in a process of weighing and balancing the importance of the objective in relation to the instruments deployed and assessed whether less restrictive measures—such as labelling—could adequately substitute while achieving the purpose of the measure:

> 5.169 [. . .] As the Appellate Body has explained, a necessity analysis involves a process of 'weighing and balancing' a series of factors, including the importance of the objective, the contribution of the measure to that objective, and the trade-restrictiveness of the measure. The Appellate Body has further explained that, in most cases, a comparison between the challenged measure and possible alternatives should then be undertaken. The burden of proving that a measure is 'necessary to protect public morals' within the meaning of Article XX (a) resides with the responding party, although a complaining party must identify any alternative measures that, in its view, the responding party should have taken.

The Appellate further elaborated this requirement as follows:

> 5.214. [. . .] As the Appellate Body has stated, '[i]t is on the basis of this 'weighing and balancing' and comparison of measures, taking into account the interests or values at stake, that a Panel determines whether a measure is 'necessary' or, alternatively, whether another WTO-consistent measure is 'reasonably available" Such an analysis, the Appellate Body has observed, involves a 'holistic' weighing and balancing exercise 'that involves putting all the variables of the equation together and evaluating them in relation to each other after having examined them individually, in order to reach an overall judgment'.

In assessing necessity, the Panel and the Appellate Body examined alternative measures proposed by the complainants. Instead of the ban of marketing commercial seal products, they argued that less intrusive measures are equally able to achieve the defined policy goals. They suggested recourse to: (1) the prescription of animal welfare criteria, (2) the application, monitoring, and enforcement of animal welfare criteria and (3) certification and labelling of compliance with animal welfare criteria. The Panel report offers a succinct summary of arguments made before it:

> 7.4 Factually, the parties debated extensively whether humane killing methods can be applied, monitored, and enforced in seal hunts. The European Union's justification of its measure is based on the premise that the application and enforcement of humane killing methods in seal hunting are not always feasible because of inter alia the unique environmental conditions in which the hunting takes place. The European Union asserts that due to the 'inherent' inhumane nature of the hunts, particularly hunts conducted for commercial purposes, the European public is ethically and morally repelled by the presence on the EU market of seal products. Hence, a general ban as designed under the current measure is the only effective way to protect the public moral concerns. The complainants argue that humane killing methods can be properly enforced in seal hunts. Further, they underline that as the current measure does not condition market access on the humaneness with which seals are killed, seal products derived from seals killed inhumanely may be allowed on the EU market. This, in their view, proves that the current measure is not capable of protecting the welfare of seals. Both sides have submitted a voluminous amount of evidence, mostly based on scientific studies and expert statements, pertaining to whether the application and monitoring of humane killing methods can be enforced in seal hunting practices.

> 7.486. Canada and Norway state that the alternative proposed measure is reasonably available to the European Union for the following four reasons. First, it is feasible to prescribe animal welfare criteria applicable to the hunting of seals based on existing scientific evidence that would ensure the minimization of suffering. Second, once established, animal welfare criteria can be effectively monitored and enforced in the context of seal hunting. Third, a system of certification of conformity with animal welfare

requirements is feasible and reasonably available. Fourth, animal welfare labelling of seal products is reasonably available contrary to the preamble recital of the EU Seal Regime that a labelling scheme would not be cost effective.

7.487. Further, both Canada and Norway reference the European Union's policy in related product areas as evidence of the feasibility of prescribing animal welfare requirements and monitoring killing for animal welfare compliance. With respect to the certification of animal welfare compliance, Canada and Norway specifically contend that certification would not need to be on a seal-by-seal basis to achieve a level of contribution to seal welfare that is equal to or greater than that of the EU Seal Regime. In this respect, the complainants suggest options drawing upon other certification schemes that include regional/geographic certification and hunter licensing.

The European Union replied before the Panel that these measures were not in a position to appropriately achieve the policy goals set forth:

7.488. The European Union responds that the complainants' proposed alternative is similar to the same measure which had been proposed by the European Commission during the legislative process. However, this measure was deliberately rejected by EU legislators because 'although it could be possible, in theory, to prescribe a humane method for killing seals, in practice the unique conditions in which seal hunting takes place would render it impossible to apply and enforce such method in an effective and consistent manner.' In particular, the European Union disputes various distinct components of the proposed alternative.

In discussing these arguments upon appeal, the Appellate Body first reiterated the case law standards applied to alternative measures as follows:

5.261 [...] An alternative measure may be found not to be reasonably available where it is merely theoretical in nature, for instance, where the responding Member is not capable of taking it, or where the 'measure imposes an undue burden on that Member, such as prohibitive costs or substantial technical difficulties.' Furthermore, in order to qualify as a 'genuine alternative', the proposed measure must be not only less trade restrictive than the original measure at issue, but should also 'preserve for the responding Member its right to achieve its desired level of protection with respect to the objective pursued.' The complaining Member bears the burden of identifying possible alternatives to the measure at issue that the responding Member could have taken.

The Appellate Body examined the arguments which were set forth by the Panel as follows:

7.502 As described above, the alternative measure as proposed by the complainants appears to span a range of possible regimes of varying stringency and leniency with respect to animal welfare requirements and accuracy of certification. On the one hand, more stringent and accurate regimes would appear to pose precisely the 'prohibitive costs or substantial technical difficulties' that can prevent an alternative measure from being considered to be reasonably available. On the other hand, more lenient regimes would call into question the degree to which the alternative measure can contribute to the welfare of seals. Moreover, an alternative measure within this range may give rise to an increase in the number of seals hunted with the accompanying risks to seal welfare through restored market opportunities within the European Union. This may undermine the objective of the EU Seal Regime of reducing the overall number of seals killed inhumanely. We recall in this regard the Appellate Body's guidance that a responding Member cannot be reasonably expected to employ an alternative measure that involves a continuation of the very risk that the challenged measure seeks to halt.

The Appellate Body confirmed the reasoning of the Panel and found:

> 5.269. As we see it, in addressing whether the alternative measure was reasonably available, the Panel was exploring the hypothetical implications for the European Union's ability to achieve its objective of addressing seal welfare concerns. There were several recurring elements in its analysis. We note, for instance, the Panel's explanation that it was undertaking an analytical exercise in which the contours of the animal welfare standards required as part of the alternative measure were not clearly defined, and that this had a bearing on the range of hypothetical versions of the alternative measure that the Panel was being asked to examine. As the Panel stated: 'Based on the differing views on what would constitute adequate welfare standards, and absent a clearly articulated standard from the complainants, the requirements under the alternative measure could possibly span a range of different levels of stringency or leniency.'
>
> 5.272. We do not consider the Panel's reference to more stringent hypothesized regimes as somehow suggesting that it was comparing the alternative measure against a benchmark of complete fulfilment of the objective. Rather, we understand the Panel to have suggested that even the more stringent certification systems presented significant difficulties in terms of both their reasonable availability and their contribution to the objective. As the Panel stated, more stringent certification systems would likely present difficulties in terms of ensuring adequate animal welfare standards and accurately distinguishing between humanely and inhumanely killed seals, and lead to increased market access accompanied by more seal killings, and, consequently, more inhumanely killed seals. Indeed, the Panel did not suggest that the stringent alternative measure achieved complete fulfilment, but rather that it would be difficult to implement and enforce, and would lead to increased numbers of inhumanely killed seals. Alternatively, the Panel noted, a more lenient regime might very well attenuate some of these limitations, but then would have the consequence – by more weakly enforcing animal welfare standards and any distinctions drawn between humanely and inhumanely killed seals – of achieving a weak contribution in respect of EU public moral concerns regarding seal welfare. The fact that the Panel entertained, and compared, the possibility of stringent versus lenient versions of a certification system, in order to consider how a loosely defined alternative measure might contribute to the identified objective, confirms in our view that the Panel was undertaking considerable efforts to understand how such variations of the alternative measure might operate. We understand the Panel to have concluded that, irrespective of the level of stringency, a certification system would be beset by difficulties in addressing EU public moral concerns regarding seal welfare.

2.4 Discriminatory Treatment Under the Chapeau of Art XX GATT

Upon completing the analysis, the Appellate Body turned to assessing the measure under the criteria of the chapeau which essentially serves the purpose of avoiding abuse of rights and to preserve the balance of rights and obligations within the multilateral trading system:

> 5.297. The function of the chapeau of Article XX of the GATT 1994 is to prevent the abuse or misuse of a Member's right to invoke the exceptions contained in the subparagraphs of that Article. In that way, the chapeau operates to preserve the balance between a Member's right to invoke the exceptions of Article XX, and the rights of other Members to be

> protected from conduct proscribed under the GATT 1994. Achieving this equilibrium is called for 'so that neither of the competing rights will cancel out the other and thereby distort and nullify or impair the balance of rights and obligations constructed by the Members themselves'. As the Appellate Body stated in *US – Gasoline*, the burden of demonstrating that a measure provisionally justified under one of the exceptions of Article XX does not constitute an abuse of such an exception under the chapeau rests with the party invoking the exception. The Appellate Body explained that this is a heavier task than that involved in showing that an exception [...] encompasses the measure at issue.

Since the chapeau of Art. XX cannot simply repeat discrimination found in violation of other GATT provisions, such as MFN and national treatment, discriminatory treatment is further qualified and essentially relates to the issue whether it can be justified in relation to the policy objective of the measure:

> 5.306. One of the most important factors in the assessment of arbitrary or unjustifiable discrimination is the question of whether the discrimination can be reconciled with, or is rationally related to, the policy objective with respect to which the measure has been provisionally justified under one of the subparagraphs of Article XX.

Taking these elements into account, the Appellate Body assessed the measures at hand. It found the carve-out for IC hunts short of any criteria relating to human killing of seals inconsistent with the stated goals of protecting public morals:

> 5.320. The first relevant question before us is thus whether the European Union has sufficiently explained how the manner in which the EU Seal Regime treats IC hunts as compared to 'commercial' hunts can be reconciled with, or is related to, the policy objective of addressing EU public moral concerns regarding seal welfare. We note that the different regulatory treatment of IC hunts, as compared to 'commercial' hunts, takes the form of a significant carve-out of the former from the measure's ban on seal products. The European Union has sought to explain why it decided not to impose the ban on the importation and placing on the market of seal products derived from IC hunts. Yet, the European Union has failed to demonstrate, in our view, how the discrimination resulting from the manner in which the EU Seal Regime treats IC hunts as compared to 'commercial' hunts can be reconciled with, or is related to, the policy objective of addressing EU public moral concerns regarding seal welfare. In this connection, we note that the European Union has not established, for example, why the need to protect the economic and social interests of the Inuit and other indigenous peoples necessarily implies that the European Union cannot do anything further to ensure that the welfare of seals is addressed in the context of IC hunts, given that 'IC hunts can cause the very pain and suffering for seals that the EU public is concerned about'.

The Appellate Body noted the irrelevance of killing methods in IC hunting and the degree of commercialization of such hunts and the broad discretion in determining such hunts:

> 5.326. Given these significant ambiguities and the broad discretion in the application of the IC requirements, we are troubled by the European Union's position that, once a seal hunt has been classified as an IC hunt, the degree of commercialization is 'irrelevant'. In particular with regard to borderline cases, the 'subsistence' and 'partial use' criteria would appear to call for, if not continuous, at least regular reassessments, at a sufficiently disaggregated level, of whether the requirements of the IC exception are fulfilled. We note in this regard that the evaluation of whether a given seal product complies with the requirements of the IC exception is left entirely to the 'recognized bodies' designated pursuant to Article 6 of the Implementing Regulation. Given the ambiguities that can arise

> with respect to at least two elements of the IC requirements, the recognized bodies would appear to enjoy broad discretion in applying the IC requirements, which could allow for instances of abuse of the IC exception, even where the recognized body is acting in good faith. Depending on how strictly the IC requirements are applied, seal products derived from what should in fact be properly characterized as 'commercial' hunts could thus enter the EU market under the IC exception in some instances. As we see it, the European Union has not sufficiently explained how such instances can be prevented in the application of the IC exception.

In conclusion, the Appellate Body held that the disconnection to public morals, broad levels of discretion, the lack of criteria of IC hunts and lacking efforts to include Canadian Inuits created 'arbitrary or unjustifiable discrimination between countries where the same conditions prevail'. The measures failed to pass the test of the Chapeau of Art. XX GATT:

> 5.338. In sum, we have identified several features of the EU Seal Regime that indicate that the regime is applied in a manner that constitutes a means of arbitrary or unjustifiable discrimination between countries where the same conditions prevail, in particular with respect to the IC exception. First, we found that the European Union did not show that the manner in which the EU Seal Regime treats seal products derived from IC hunts as compared to seal products derived from 'commercial' hunts can be reconciled with the objective of addressing EU public moral concerns regarding seal welfare. Second, we found considerable ambiguity in the 'subsistence' and 'partial use' criteria of the IC exception. Given the ambiguity of these criteria and the broad discretion that the recognized bodies consequently enjoy in applying them, seal products derived from what should in fact be properly characterized as 'commercial' hunts could potentially enter the EU market under the IC exception. We did not consider that the European Union has sufficiently explained how such instances can be prevented in the application of the IC exception. Finally, we were not persuaded that the European Union has made 'comparable efforts' to facilitate the access of the Canadian Inuit to the IC exception as it did with respect to the Greenlandic Inuit. We also noted that setting up a 'recognized body' that fulfils all the requirements of Art. 6 of the Implementing Regulation may entail significant burdens in some instances.

3 Assessment

WTO cases are fact-intensive. The report of the Panel in *EC – Seal Products* amounts to 186 pages, not taking into account exhibits of the case. The Appellate Body Report amounts to 192 pages. The legal assessment of what is a fairly straightforward ban on marketing seal products subject to three exemptions amounts to a complex legal operation, the results of which cannot readily be generalized and abstracted from the specific context. Yet, the decision is a landmark case which may have implications for various regulatory fields, including the protection of labour standards. To what extent can general lessons be learned and conclusions drawn? In a cautious manner, the following observations may be submitted.

3.1 Deferential Standards of Public Morals and Evidence

The Panel and the Appellate Body confirm the possibility of WTO Members to justify trade restrictions by invoking their own standards of public morality. Despite the notion, entailed in Art. XX (a) GATT, as a norm of WTO and public international law, a standard of deference is applied in line with the standards adopted earlier in *United States – Measures affecting the Cross-Border Supply of Gambling and Betting Services*.[27] WTO law, however, requires sufficient evidence of broad acceptance of values expressed; it cannot be invoked to simply justify *ex post* a measure which was adopted on other grounds. The case affirms that moral standards may lawfully vary from country to country. Morality, moreover, is not subject to evidence of risk, unlike the protection of public health, and it is devoid of scientific support. Morality does not need to be consistent across the board. The Appellate Body accepts that animal welfare standards do not need to be reasonably uniform, and thus may target a particular population.

3.2 The Issue of Extraterritorial Effects

The European Union strongly emphasised the impact of the measure on its own territory. It was designed to protect public morality perceptions within the Union. Canada and Norway opted to concur and to refrain from developing an argument based upon extraterritorial effects of the measure. While protecting morals at home, the measures deploys significant impact as to how products destined for exports to Europe are processed and produced within the territory of Canada, Greenland and Norway. Communities and commercial producers and the administration of marine management in these countries clearly are affected. The Panel did not address the issue, and the Appellate Body was unable to deal with it simply due to lack of substantial arguments made. The Appellate Body cautioned as follows:

> 5.173 Finally, we note that, in *US – Shrimp*, the Appellate Body stated that it would not 'pass upon the question of whether there is an implied jurisdictional limitation in Article XX (g), and if so, the nature or extent of that limitation'. The Appellate Body explained that, in the specific circumstances of that case, there was 'a sufficient nexus between the migratory and endangered marine populations involved and the United States for purposes of Article XX (g)'. As set out in the preamble of the Basic Regulation, the EU Seal Regime is designed to address seal hunting activities occurring 'within and outside the Community' and the seal welfare concerns of 'citizens and consumers' in EU member States. The participants did not address this issue in their submissions on appeal. Accordingly, while recognizing the systemic importance of the question of whether there is an implied

[27] WTO, *US – Measures affecting the Cross-Border Supply of Gambling and Betting Services*, Report of the Appellate Body, 7 Apr 2005, WT/DS285/AB/R. For a discussion see Wu (2008), pp. 215–251 and Leroux (2008). For an early assessment of Art. XX (a) GATT see Charnovitz (1998), p. 689.

jurisdictional limitation in Article XX (a), and, if so, the nature or extent of that limitation, we have decided in this case not to examine this question further.

The doctrine of nexus was developed in the context of Art. XX (g) GATT. Does it also apply to the protection of morals of consumers within the territory when practical effects on producers are mainly deployed abroad? A nexus clearly exists if the conduct regulated translates into the quality of the product and the difference can be felt in products imported into the territory of the country invoking public morals. *EC – Seal Products* clearly found that products can be banned even though conduct aimed at on grounds of morality does not leave physical traces in the product potentially imported. This leads to the issue of PPMs.

3.3 Production and Process Methods (PPMs)?

The objective of the regulations and ban clearly is to avoid inhumane killings of seals. The objective, in other words, does not relate to the product as such, but to the manner how seal products are being obtained. It thus would seem at first sight that the measure at hand is concerning a so-called Production and Process Method (PPM) which are of increasing importance in international trade regulation; for example in the field of energy and climate change mitigation and which lead to differential treatment of like products.[28] In *Canada – Feed-In Tariffs*, the Appellate Body concluded that markets of electricity stemming from renewable (solar, wind, hydro, thermal) and from non-renewable energy (coal, gas, oil) are different; a conclusion the Panel did not draw with all its implications on like product analysis.[29]

Closer analysis, however, reveals that the measure at hand is not based upon performance requirements, but establishes a general ban subject to three exceptions. These exceptions are motivated by socio-economic (IC exception), conservationist (Marine management) and practical reasons (travel exception). They, however, do not rely upon PPMs. Production methods properly speaking (albeit the term was not used) were discussed as alternative measures submitted by the complainants. Canada and Norway argued that less intrusive methods, discussed above, exist. These related to animal welfare standards of human killing, certification and labelling. The Panel and the Appellate Body rejected this approach as not sufficiently conducive, thus affirming the necessity of the measure in order to effectively protect public morals. At the same time, the Appellate Body held that the lack of

[28]For a careful discussion of PPM related legal issues see Holzer (2014), pp. 91–177 and Conrad (2011).

[29]WTO, *Canada – Certain Measures affecting the Renewable Energy Generation Sector*, Report of the Appellate Body, 6 May 2013, WT/DS412/AB/R; WTO, *Canada – Measures relating to the Feed-in Tariff Program*, Report of the Appellate Body, 6 May 2013, WT/DS413/AB/R, paras. 5.167–5.179.

animal welfare standards for IC hunts and the lack of performance requirements frustrate the overall goal of protection of public morality and created arbitrary or unjustifiable discrimination in relation to ban commercial hunting. The Appellate Body thus implies that the EC, in revising the regulations and rendering them WTO compatible, is obliged to introduce performance requirements, and thus production and process methods applied to the three exceptions, in particular IC hunts in order to sustain the ban on commercial hunting.

The ruling thus accepts the ban on commercially hunted seals products on ground of public morality, but requires more detailed PPMs where trade should be allowed in light of the objective of protecting public morals. In other words, short of a complete ban of imports, imports need to be accompanied by PPMs sufficiently responding to the objectives of protecting public morality. These implications, induced by the interpretation and application of the Chapeau of Art. XX GATT, amount to one of the puzzles of the case: Why, if future PPMs are required for IC hunts, could the same standards not apply to all commercial hunting, and thus recourse would be taken to alternative means of protection by way of general welfare standards, certification and labelling? The differentiation may be justified by looking at the quantities killed by commercial operations and the difficulties to monitor the operations abroad short of extensive international cooperation. Perhaps, in other configurations, it could be addressed by means of quantitative restrictions, short of a full ban. Conceptually, the rejection of alternative means of protection while imposing them for IC hunts leaves a question mark behind. It certainly indicates that partial bans of products cannot operate without PPMs.

4 The Prospects of Enforcing Labour Standards

Translating the findings of *EC –Seal Products* to the realm of labour standards, given a completely different context, seems farfetched, at least at first sight. Yet, the ruling is of general importance, and also in the field of prime interest in this volume and paper. What are the implications for unilateral protection of labour standards, in the absence of agreed avenues of enforcement and the lack of harmonization within the WTO and other international trade agreements?

4.1 Recourse to Public Morals

EC – Seal Products and former precedents confirm that trade measures may be taken on the basis of ethical concerns. Recourse to public morals provides a door of entry of such concerns into the trading system. The notion is construed with deference, and members of the WTO may bring to bear their particular concerns, provided that they are broadly supported in society as evidenced in legislative processes and comparable, but not necessarily identical, levels of protection, exist in domestic law. Recourse to public morals thus is more readily available than compliance with Art. XX (d) GATT which allows taking flanking measures necessary to implement domestic measures which are not inconsistent with GATT rules, and which so far have remained largely untested. A WTO member may for example adopt trade restrictions in textiles in order to secure decent salaries for textile workers relative to general levels of income in the country of origin and to combat practices of exploitation and social dumping, but short of forced labour. The fact that no multilaterally agreed standards on minimal wages exist today does not stop the member from invoking public morals, and without facing, according to *EC – Seal Products*, a test of consistency with salaries in other and comparable sectors at home. Not the cause and objective, but the proper means and instruments discussed below will be controversial. *EC – Seal Products*, however, also clarifies that WTO law does not allow invoking public morals as a post argument in defence of trade measures taken mainly for different reasons.

The standard of deference does not limit public morals to domestic perceptions but *a fortiori* includes internationally accepted moral standards. Labour standards contained in international agreements and supported by a large number of countries, but foremost core labour standards belong to this realm. Restrictions of goods and services related to violation of core labour standards discussed at the outset enjoy moral support beyond a particular country and form part of an international consensus. Partly, this has been recognised in treaty law. The EU CARIFORUM Economic Partnership Agreement explicitly recognises that public morals can be invoked to combat child labour.[30] Restrictions may serve to support freedom of association of trade unions, combatting forced labour and exploitation and discriminations at the workplace. In the case of child labour, measures may arguably be justified in addition on the basis of *jus cogens*, and thus violations *erga omnes* which entitle countries to adopt appropriate counter-measures and reprisals irrespective of recourse to public morals and other clauses authorizing such measures in treaty law.

The same holds true for human rights of which many important labour standards are part of. If *EC – Seal Products* allows invoking domestic standards, it *a fortiori* allows for recourse to standards universally accepted in treaties or as a matter of general principles of law. Some of these rights pertain to *jus cogens* and deploy effects *erga omnes*, the violation of which amounts to a common concern of humankind.[31] In my view, this is particular the case for exploitation of children in the workplace short of adequate education.[32] Others will be based upon

[30]Note 1 ad Art. 224 *Economic Partnership Agreement, between the Cariforum States and the European Community and its Member States*, O.J. L 289/1/3 (2008) reads: 'The Parties agree that, in accordance with Chap. 5 of Title IV, measures necessary to combat child labour shall be deemed to be included within the meaning of measures necessary to protect public morals or measures necessary for the protection of health.'

[31]Cottier (2016) and cf. also Cottier et al. (2014), pp. 293–324.

[32]See Humbert (2009), pp. 114–120, 337/378 and Humbert (2018).

customary law or accepted as principles of law, in particular the ILP core labour standards, or by treaty law, in particular human rights standards of the UN Human Rights Covenants. The broader a standard is accepted, the less invocation of public morals as its foundation should be controversial and contestable in the WTO. Again, the main issue relates to appropriate measures rather than the objective protected by the invocation of public morals.

According to *EC – Seal Products*, invocation of public morals, and thus of labour standards and human rights, does not require proof of risks comparable to invocations of public health concerns. It is based upon societal, moral and philosophical values and judgment, and the sole requirement consists of broad societal support as evidenced in the domestic legal order and culture. According to *EC – Seal Products*, these values may focus on a particular walk of life and need to be consistently applied throughout society. Again, the standards show considerable deference and policy space. Future developments of case law may refine this proposition. Coherence may be required in support of showing widespread support of the concern. If it is limited to a particular issue—such as child labour or forced labour—yet without extending to other forms of severe discrimination at home and abroad—the moral claim may not be convincingly demonstrated in terms of evidence required within a particular society. The analysis under the chapeau of Art. XX GATT and Art. XIV GATS, serving the purpose to avoid the abuse of rights, offers room to take inconsistencies into account which, under current cases, are ignored in assessing preliminary justification under public morality. The less coherent moral values or rights are pursued, the more they are open to criticism of disguised restrictions to trade and protectionism under the chapeau of these provisions. Incoherent measures taken by recourse to public morals may indicate that the prime motivation is not justice and fairness, but the pursuit of disguised protectionism motivated by economic interests.

4.2 Extraterritorial Effects

The lawfulness of invoking public morals to support workers abroad and protecting consumers at home inherently deploys extraterritorial effects. Linking public morals and international trade inherently affects producers and workers abroad. The requirement of a nexus, discussed, as mentioned above, by the Appellate Body's obiter dictum, was developed in the context of environmental protection. Whatever its merits (for example as applied to climate change and the protection of the atmosphere), it cannot be relevant in the present context.[33] It is interesting to observe that Canada and Norway did not advance and press the argument in the present case in challenging regulations which, in their view, strongly focused on the problem of marketing seal products within the European common market and

[33] See also Charnovitz (2002).

clearly did not show the nexus found in *United States – Import Prohibition of Certain Shrimp and Shrimp Products*.[34] Limitations to extraterritorial effects cannot be located in public morals, but in the subsequent examination of necessity, abuse of rights and duties to negotiate prior to taking unilateral action.

EC – Seal Products confirms that domestic legislative measures can be adopted which deploy effects abroad. A regulation seeking to secure certain labour or human rights standards within the domestic market may affect foreign producers seeking exports to that market. Such linkages are well accepted when conditions and methods of production impact on the quality of the product consumed within the jurisdiction of the importing country. *EC – Seal Products* confirms that such effects may also be deployed when conduct does not translate into the physical properties of the product. They are usually based upon defined PPMs. The case, however, shows such effects may also be justified in light of the objective of the measure and without defining PPMs, at least to the extent that the measure applies to all configurations alike and no exceptions are being made. As *EC –Seal Products* is based upon an outright ban, it does not discuss consumer preferences to justify differential treatment of physically like products. It could have done so, in particular if PPMs were employed. Labour standards and human rights standards may induce differences in consumer preferences, and thus allow particular privileges accorded to products complying with the PPM standard defined.

4.3 Necessity

The requirement of necessity obliges to balance the importance of the concern and the trade measures taken. *EC – Seal Products* allowed for a categorical ban of marketing and imports of seal products, and thus taking recourse to the most restrictive trade measure available. Recourse to Production and Process Methods (PPMs), discussed below, is not inherently required due to the challenges of enforcing and implementing such requirements in practical terms. The case law, however, also shows that determination of necessity is strongly dependent upon the particularities of the case and its findings cannot be readily generalized. But what in principle is valid for animal welfare standards is, *a fortiori*, valid for fundamental values in human rights and labour standards. It may be argued that the realization of core labour standards, given their importance and broad acceptance, may thus justify the banning of imports without the need to take recourse to PPMs and complex mechanism of monitoring, leaving decisions to consumers. Yet again, the proposition depends upon configuration of the particular case and may not be readily generalized.

[34]WTO, *United States – Import Prohibition of Certain Shrimp and Shrimp Products*, Report of the Appellate Body, 12 Oct 1998, WT/DS58/AB/R, para. 133.

EC – Seal Products deals with a complex constellation of partially banning like products, while allowing marketing and imports under three exceptions, and without considering the methods of killing. It essentially is an argument of consistency and coherence. The Appellate Body considers the lack of concern for methods of killing in the exceptions undermining the objective of protecting public morals. It required the EU to define PPM based standards for the exceptions. This is relevant in labour rights constellations where different standards are applied among different countries taking into account different levels of social and economic development. For example, if child labour and imports derived from it are tolerated from least developed countries but excluded from other, more advanced economies under a philosophy of graduation and progressive regulation[35] and the philosophy of progressive realization of social and economic rights, conditions for accepting child labour, for example the amount of schooling required as a minimum, would need to be defined in terms of PPMs. The case law does not allow operating a ban while allowing unfettered imports under exceptions without consideration given to the main objectives of regulation.

Weighing and balancing different components in assessing a regulation under the necessity text may often lead to recourse to PPMs, in particular performance standards, certification and labelling schemes. Recourse to banning trade can only be justified in the pursuit of fundamental norms of protection, but not otherwise. It is here that the government and the law may trump consumer choice. Less intrusive restrictions creating greater transparency to consumers often will be the appropriate answers while excluding outright prohibitions. Labour standards outside the realm of core human rights and labour standards, such as those relating to salary and remuneration, welfare, and access to education and social services, may not qualify for banning related products unless it can be shown that PPM-based measures are practically excluded and ineffective and do not allow to successfully implement the measure abroad.

The ban in *EC – Seal Products* related to products directly derived from conduct considered unethical and contrary to public morals. In the case of core labour standards, products may be targeted which are produced upon violation of the standard. There needs to be a sufficient link between the insufficient adherence to the standard and the product subjected to trade restrictions. *EC – Seal Products* would not support the proposition that WTO allows for smart sanctions targeting products unrelated to the violation of the standard. Such measures fall under the ambit of international security and either require a threat to national security or clearance by the United Nations Security Council.

---

[35]See Cottier (2006).

4.4 Abuse of Rights and the Duty to Negotiate

Trade restrictions taken for reasons of public morality face detailed scrutiny under the chapeau of the exception clauses. The avoidance of abuse of rights, disguised protectionism and arbitrary discrimination between members where the same conditions prevail, apply to all labour standards- and human rights-based restrictions. The provision does not exclude categorisation, as *EC – Seal Products* shows. But it is important to treat similar configuration in different countries similarly.

The chapeau requires that efforts at finding a negotiated settlement are undertaken. Unilateral measures only can be taken upon failure of such negotiations. *EC – Seal Products* expounds this fundamental principle established in case law in *US – Shrimps*[36] and confirmed and elaborated in a follow-up complaint by Malaysia[37]:

> 5.43 As mentioned above, the Appellate Body, as part of its process of determining whether the original measure had been applied in a manner that constituted a means of 'unjustifiable discrimination', addressed the issue of international negotiations, an issue which is raised by Malaysia before this Panel. After having considered that the lack of flexibility to take into account the different situations in different countries amounted to unjustifiable discrimination, the Appellate Body added that:
>
> '166. Another aspect of the application of Section 609 [US Public Law 101-102 of 1989] that bears heavily in any appraisal of justifiable or unjustifiable discrimination is the failure of the United States to engage the appellees, as well as other Members exporting shrimp to the United States, in serious, across-the-board negotiations with the objective of concluding bilateral or multilateral agreements for the protection and conservation of sea turtles, before enforcing the import prohibition against the shrimp exports of those other Members.'
>
> 5.44 As underlined by the Appellate Body itself, Section 609 (a) directs the US Secretary of State inter alia to initiate negotiations as soon as possible for the development of bilateral or multilateral agreements with other nations for the protection and conservation of sea turtles. This as such is not a ground for a finding of unjustifiable discrimination unless, in implementing Section 609 (a), the United States authorities have discriminated between exporting countries by negotiating seriously with some and less seriously or not at all with others.
>
> 5.45 However, the Appellate Body did not conclude its analysis at that point. It also noted that 'the protection and conservation of highly migratory species [...] demand concerted and cooperative efforts on the part of the many countries whose waters are traversed in the course of recurrent sea turtle migrations.' The Appellate Body went on to recall that the need for and the appropriateness of such efforts had been recognized by the WTO itself as well as in a significant number of other international instruments and declarations. In addition, the Appellate Body recalled that the United States had actually succeeded in negotiating an international agreement for the protection and conservation of sea turtles, namely the Inter-American Convention. In the conclusion to its analysis, the Appellate Body also stated that 'the unilateral character of the application of Section 609 heightens the disruptive and discriminatory influence of the import prohibition and underscores its unjustifiability'.

---

[36]WTO, *United States – Import Prohibitions of Certain Shrimp and Shrimp Products*, Report of the Appellate Body, 12 Oct 1998, WT/DS58/AB/R, paras.166 et seqq.

[37]WTO, *United States – Import Prohibitions of Certain Shrimp and Shrimp Products*, Report of the Appellate Body, 21 Nov 2001, WT/DS58/AB/RW; Recourse to Article 21,5 of the DSU by Malaysia.

> 5.46 The approach of the Appellate Body leads us to conclude that it is not solely the fact that the United States negotiated seriously with some Members and less seriously with others which is at the origin of its finding of unjustifiable discrimination in relation to negotiations, even though it would have been sufficient in itself to justify such a conclusion. We believe that another reason for the Appellate Body finding is that the United States, by unilaterally defining and implementing criteria for applying Section 609, failed to take into account the different situations which may exist in the exporting countries. In other words, the United States failed to pass the 'unjustified discrimination' test by applying the same regime to domestic and foreign shrimp.

Whether a ban is contemplated or PPMs to address the moral concern expressed in labour and human rights standards, cooperation needs to be sought in seeking redress and improvement, often entailing incentives, before recourse to policies of unilateral sticks are being deployed in legislation or trade policy.

5 Conclusions

Trade regulation, labour standards and human rights so far have been assigned to different communities and institutions on the multilateral level. Accordingly, linking the fields in the process of negotiations has largely failed except in the realm of preferential trade agreements. While there is no shortage of labour and human rights standards, appropriate mechanisms to enforce them internationally do not exist under these agreements, properly speaking. Cooperation is based upon moral suasion, naming and shaming, education, but short of deploying trade measures and economic sanctions with very few exceptions in international relations.

The clinical isolation and fragmentation, however, is overcome in assessing unilateral measures taken in support of labour standards and human rights implementation by means of trade restrictions. Labour, human rights and trade finally meet in WTO or special RTA dispute settlement, interfacing areas otherwise dealt with in isolation. It is there that the fundamental contribution of case law and precedent in addressing complex configuration in the legal process of law-making and application is evident. WTO Members enjoy policy space to support and pursue labour standards and human rights abroad, using the means and instruments of trade policy in a well-calibrated manner. Tools include import bans but also PPMs which essentially leave decisions to informed consumers. Companies, in return, are obliged to consider these concerns and take commitments to corporate and social responsibility seriously. Further studies will need to assess to what extent preferential trade agreements expand or limit the scope available under WTO law. Ideas to further institutional cooperation, also at the level dispute settlement, are worthwhile pursuing.[38] At any rate, trade will be able to do more in the pursuit of human rights and labour standards than the soft law inherent to these fields if dealt with institutionally in splendid isolation.

---

[38] See the dispute settlement proposal by Humbert (2018).

References

Addo K (2015) Core labour standards and international trade: lessons from the regional context. Springer, Heidelberg
Belser EM (2007) The White Man's Burden: Arbeit und Menschenrechte in einer globalisierten Welt. Staempfli Verlag, Bern
Charnovitz S (1987) The influence of international labour standards on the world trade regime: a historical overview. Int Labour Rev 126:565–584
Charnovitz S (1998) The moral exception in GATT. Virginia J Int Law 38:689
Charnovitz S (2002) The law of environmental 'PPMs' in the WTO: debunking the myth of illegality. Yale J Int Law 27:59–110
Choudhary B, Gehne K, Heri S, Humbert F, Kaufmann C, Nadakavukaren Schefer K (2011) A call for a WTO ministerial decision on trade and human rights. In: Cottier T, Delimatsis P (eds) The prospects of international trade regulation: from fragmentation to coherence. Cambridge University Press, Cambridge, pp 323–358
Conrad CR (2011) Processes and production methods (PPMs) in WTO law. Cambridge University Press, Cambridge
Cottier T (2006) From progressive liberalization to progressive regulation in WTO law. J Int Econ Law 9:779–821
Cottier T (2016) Improving compliance: Jus Cogens and international economic law. Neth Yearb Int Law 46:329–354
Cottier T, Caplazi A (1998) Labour standards and world trade law: interfacing legitimate concerns. In: Geiser T, Schmid H, Walter-Busch E (eds) Arbeit in der Schweiz des 20. Jahrhunderts. Haupt Verlag, Bern/Stuttgart, pp 469–510
Cottier T, Aerni P, Karapınar B, Matteotti S, de Sépibus J, Shingal A (2014) The principle of common concern and climate change. Archiv des Völkerrechts 52:293–324
de Wet E (1995) Labour standards in the globalized economy: the inclusion of a social clause in the general agreement on tariffs and trade/world trade organization. Hum Rights Q 17:443–642
Edgen G (1979) Fair labour standards and trade liberalisation. Int Labour Rev 118:523–536
Eglin R (1997) Core labour standards and the WTO. Int Trade Law Rev 3:101–104
Holzer K (2014) Carbon-related border adjustment and WTO law. Elgar, Cheltenham
Humbert F (2009) The challenge of child labour in international law. Cambridge University Press, Cambridge
Humbert F (2018) The WTO and child labour: implications for the debate on international constitutionalism. In: Gött H (ed) Labour standards in international economic law. Springer International Publishing, Cham, this volume
Jansen M, Lee E (2007) Trade and employment: challenges for policy research. A joint study of the international labour organization and the secretariat of the world trade organization. ILO/WTO, Geneva
Kaufmann C (2007) Globalisation and labour rights: the conflict between core labour standards and international economic law. Hart Publishing, Oxford/Portland
Leroux EH (2008) From periodicals to gambling: a review of systematic issues addressed by WTO adjudicatory bodies under GATS. In: Panizzon M, Pohl N, Sauvé P (eds) GATS and the regulation of international trade in services. Cambridge University Press, Cambridge, pp 236–275
OECD (2012) Policy priorities for international trade and jobs. OECD, Paris
Panizzon M, Zürcher G, Fornale E (2015) The Palgrave handbook of international labour migration. Palgrave Macmillan, Houndsmill
Thomas C (2009) WTO and labor rights: strategies of linkage. In: Joseph S, Kinley D, Waincymer J (eds) The world trade organization and human rights: interdisciplinary perspectives. Edward Elgar, Cheltenham, pp 257–284
Weiss F (1996) Internationally recognized labour standards and trade. Leg Issues Eur Integr 23:161–178
Wu M (2008) Free trade and the protection of public morals: an analysis of the newly emerging public morals clause doctrine. Yale J Int Law 33:215–251

The WTO and Child Labour: Implications for the Debate on International Constitutionalism

Franziska Humbert

Contents

Abstract Child labour remains a widespread problem around the world. According to global estimates published by the International Child Labour Organisation in 2017, 152 million children can be regarded as child labourers and 73 million children are in hazardous work. Despite many efforts to reduce child labour in global supply chains, children are still involved in either manufactured or agricultural products for export. This article is based on the assumption that in order to solve this problem, global solutions including trade measures are needed. Analysing some key legal issues relevant for the WTO law-compatibility of trade measures on child labour, it submits that under the current status of WTO law, some trade measures on child labour may be found to be WTO law-consistent. However, it holds that an ILO-WTO implementation mechanism *de lege ferenda* would be a more effective solution to combat child labour. In this context, the article briefly discusses new approaches to international law and argues that the constitutional approach to international law will help to provide answers how such a new governance framework for the issue of trade and child labour should be shaped.

F. Humbert (✉)
University of Berne, Berne, Switzerland

Oxfam Germany, Berlin, Germany
e-mail: fhumbert@oxfam.de

H. Gött (ed.), *Labour Standards in International Economic Law*,
https://doi.org/10.1007/978-3-319-69447-4_6

1 Introduction

Child labour still is a major challenge of today's globalization and needs to be addressed by the international community, inter alia by using trade measures as a measure of last resort.[1] This has been one lesson learnt by the ILO's International Programme on the Elimination of Child Labour (IPEC).[2] The IPEC explicitly stated that international action was necessary to prompt governments to initiate policies and programmes to abolish child labour.[3] Also, recent phenomena such as the prevalence of child labour in global value chains as well as the trade and labour linkage in regional trade agreements prove that child labour cannot be perceived as a purely national problem but requires international solutions. Already the Preamble of the ILO Constitution as established by the Treaty of Versailles stated that unfair labour conditions in one country might impact on the welfare of other countries:

> [. . .] Whereas also the failure of any nation to adopt humane conditions of labour is an obstacle in the way of other nations which desire to improve the conditions in their own countries; [. . .].[4]

Similarly, US trade laws such as the Generalized System of Preferences (GSPs),[5] Section 301 of the Trade Act of 1974[6] and the amended Section 307 of the Tariff Act of 1930[7] are based on the assumption that unfair working conditions abroad have a bad impact on US commerce and jobs, and should be tackled by trade measures.[8]

Moreover, given the almost universal ratification of the Convention on the Rights of the Child[9] and the possible classification of child labour as a contemporary form of slavery, it can be argued that the prohibition of child labour forms part

---

[1]On the use of trade measures on child labour, see Humbert (2009), pp. 373–375.

[2]ILO (2006), para. 162 and ILO/IPEC (2002), p. 18.

[3]Ibid.

[4]ILO Treaty of Versailles, Treaty of Peace between the Allied and Associated Powers and Germany, signed at Versailles 28 June 1919, 225 CTS 188, Part XIII Labour, Section I.

[5]Trade Act of 1974, US Code Title 19—Customs Duties, Chapter 12, Subchapter V, Generalized System of Preferences.

[6]Trade Act of 1974, US Code Title 19—Customs Duties, Chapter 12, Subchapter III, § 2411; Pub. L. 93-618, Title III, § 301, as added Pub. L. 96-39, title IX, § 901, 26 July 1979, 93 Stat. 295; amended Pub. L. 98-573, title III, § 304 (a)–(c) and (f), 30 Oct 1984, 98 Stat. 3002, 3005; Pub. L. 100-418, Title I, § 1301 (a), 23 Aug 1988, 102 Stat. 1164; Pub. L. 103-465, Title III, § 314 (a)–(c), Title VI, § 621(a) (9), 8 Dec 1994, 108 Stat. 4939, 4940, 4993; Pub. L. 104-295, § 20 (c) (4), 11 Oct 1996, 110 Stat. 3528.

[7]Tariff Act of 1930, US Code Title 19—Customs Duties, Chapter 4, Subtitle I—Harmonized Tariff Schedule of the United States, Section 1307, 17 June 1930, Chapter 497, title III, § 307, 46 Stat. 689; Pub. L. 106-200, title IV, § 411 (a), 18 May 2000, 114 Stat. 298.

[8]See Humbert (2009), pp. 284 et seqq. with further references.

[9]Convention on the Rights of the Child, GA Res. 44/25, 20 Nov 1989. As of 15 December 2015, 196 states were participants to the treaty, the US is a signatory.

of *ius cogens*[10] and as such part of those obligations that the International Court of Justice (ICJ) considered to be 'obligations of a state towards the international community as a whole', which are 'the concern of all states' and for whose protection all states have a 'legal interest', i.e. they apply *erga omnes*.[11] This prohibition of child labour in international law with *ius cogens* character does not encompass all forms of child work. The relevant UN and ILO Conventions generally differentiate between tolerable child work and exploitative child labour. They prohibit all three categories of child labour distinguished by the ILO, i.e. labour that is performed under the minimum age for this kind of work, and thus likely to impede a child's education and full development, hazardous work and the unconditional worst forms of labour including trafficking, debt bondage and prostitution.[12] As will be discussed later, under the rules on state responsibility for internationally wrongful state acts,[13] violations of *ius cogens* norms may be argued to be remedied by taking recourse to trade measures. The following section will analyse key issues regarding the compatibility of existing trade measures on child labour with WTO law in order to draw lessons for future global strategies to combat child labour.

2 WTO Law and Child Labour: Key Legal Issues

The legal analysis will concentrate on trade in goods since it is this area where to date most controversial issues have arisen. Existing trade measures on child labour are for example the US import ban on goods produced with forced or indentured child labour[14] or the Belgian Social Label Law.[15] The latter provides for the granting of a social label to products produced in accordance with the ILO core labour conventions as set out in the ILO Declaration on Fundamental Rights and

[10]On the *ius cogens* nature of the prohibition of child labour, see Humbert (2009), pp. 114–119.

[11]ICJ, *Barcelona Traction, Light and Power Company, Ltd. (Belgium v. Spain)*, Judgment, ICJ Rep. 1970, p. 32: 'In particular, an essential distinction should be drawn between the obligations of a state towards the community as a whole and those of a state vis-à-vis another state in the field of diplomatic protection. By their very nature, the former is the concern of all states. In view of the importance of the rights involved, all states can be held to have a legal interest in their protection; they are obligations *erga omnes*.'

[12]For a thorough discussion of the scope of the prohibition of child labour in international law, see Humbert (2009), pp. 14–121.

[13]ILC, Draft articles on responsibility of states for international wrongful acts, Yearbook of the International Law Commission, 2001, vol. II, Part Two.

[14]Tariff Act of 1930, US Code Title 19, Section 307.

[15]Loi visant à promouvoir la production socialement responsible de 2002. Belgium never enforced the law.

Principles at Work[16] including the prohibition of child labour. Other measures comprise for example the US and the EU GSPs[17] setting forth labour conditionality schemes, the Kimberley Process Certification Scheme on conflict diamonds,[18] or the 2003 US Burmese Freedom and Democracy Act banning all goods coming from Myanmar.[19] Since these measures raise many additional legal issues, they will be given less consideration in this paper.

Before starting to discuss the legal issues under the relevant provisions, it should be stated that under WTO terminology, child labour can be said to be a non-product-related process and production method (PPM) in contrast to product-related measures such as content requirements or product-related process and production methods such as regulations on the use of pesticides or asbestos.[20] This classification is important for the so-called PPM-debate,[21] which is a central issue when discussing for example the consistency of trade measures on child labour with the non-discrimination obligations contained in the General Agreement on Tariffs and Trade (GATT)[22] and the Agreement on Technical Barriers to Trade (TBT-Agreement).

2.1 The Non-discrimination Obligations of GATT Art. I and III

The two main pillars of the GATT are the non-discrimination obligations contained in GATT Art. I and III. The most-favoured nation (MFN) clause requires WTO members to accord any advantage, favour, privilege, or immunity that they grant to any imports to all like products imported from any WTO member immediately and without conditions. GATT Art. I:1 reads:

---

[16]ILO Declaration on Fundamental Rights and Principles at Work and its Follow-up, International Labour Conference, adopted on 1998 and Annex revised 15 June 2010.

[17]EU Parliament and Council Regulation 978/2012 *applying a scheme of generalised tariff preferences and repealing Council Regulation*, O.J. L 303 (2012).

[18]www.kimberleyprocess.com/documents/10540/11192/KPCS%20Core%20Document?version=1.0&t=1331826363000. Accessed 23 Dec 2015.

[19]US Burmese Freedom and Democracy Act of 2003. For details see Humbert (2009), pp. 188–190. In May 2013, the House of Representatives introduced a resolution to renew the import restrictions contained in the US Burmese Freedom and Democracy Act of 2003, which has so far not been enacted.

[20]See for example OECD (1997).

[21]For a thorough discussion of the product-process doctrine and an overview of the debate see for example Cottier and Caplazi (1998), Howse and Regan (2000) and Conrad (2011).

[22]WTO General Agreement on Tariffs and Trade of 1994. The WTO legal texts are embodied in the Final Act Embodying the Results of the Uruguay Round of Multilateral Trade Negotiations.

General Most-Favoured-Nation-Treatment

1. With respect to customs duties and charges of any kind imposed on or in connection with importation or exportation or imposed on the international transfer of payments for imports or exports, and with respect to the method of levying such duties and charges, and with respect to all rules and formalities in connection with importation and exportation, and with respect to all matters referred to in paragraph 2 and 4 of Article III, any advantage, favour, privilege or immunity granted by any Member to any product originating in or destined for any other country shall be accorded immediately and unconditionally to the like product originating in or destined for the territories of all other Members.

Thus, it prohibits discrimination among like products originating in or destined for other countries. The national treatment clause of GATT Art. III requires the treatment of imported goods no worse than that of like domestic products. The text of the relevant provisions read:

1. The contracting parties recognize that internal taxes and other internal charges, and laws, regulations and requirements, affecting the internal sale, offering for sale, purchase, transportation, distribution or use of products, and internal quantitative regulations requiring the mixture, processing or use of products in specified amounts or proportions, should not be applied to imported or domestic products so as to afford protection to domestic production*.

2. The products of the territory of any contracting party imported into the territory of any other contracting party shall not be subject, directly or indirectly, to internal taxes or other charges of any kind in excess of those applied, directly or indirectly, to like domestic products. Moreover, no contracting party shall otherwise apply internal taxes or other internal charges to imported or domestic products in a manner contrary to the principles set forth in paragraph 1*.

4. The products of the territory of any contracting party imported into the territory of any other contracting party shall be accorded treatment no less favourable than that accorded to like products of national origin in respect of all laws, regulations and requirements affecting their internal sale, offering for sale, purchase, transportation, distribution or use. The provisions of this paragraph shall not prevent the application of differential internal transportation charges which are based exclusively on the economic operation of the means of transport and not on the nationality of the product.

The asterisks refer to the *Ad* Note to GATT Art. III which reads:

Any internal tax or other internal charge, or any law, regulation or requirement of the kind referred to in paragraph 1 which applies to an imported product and to the like domestic product, and is collected or enforced in the case of the imported product at the time or point of importation, is nevertheless to be regarded as an internal tax or other internal charge, or a law, regulation or requirement of the kind referred to in paragraph 1, and is accordingly subjected to the provisions of Article III.

Paragraph 2

A tax conforming to the requirements of the first sentence of paragraph 2 would be considered to be inconsistent with the provisions of the second sentence only in cases where competition was involved between, on the one hand, the taxed product and, on the other hand, a directly competitive or substitutable product which was not similarly taxed.

Hence, questions as to the meaning of 'likeness' and 'less favourable treatment' play a central role when deciding whether a measure is discriminatory or not. With regards to child labour, the question is for example whether coffee made with child labour may be judged to be distinct from coffee not made with child labour. If not, the legality of the measure depends on whether it discriminates between the two products, and whether such discrimination can be justified. If yes, the analysis would end here and the measure would not contravene GATT Art. III or I. In the context of the MFN clause, a related question is whether it is allowed to impose non-product related conditions on the advantage conferred to WTO members. This was denied by the panel in the old GATT case *Belgium–Family Allowances*, where Belgium introduced a tax law granting exemptions to goods from countries with a similar system of family allowances to the Belgian system.[23] However, some authors rightly argue that this case is not a complete rejection of non-product related conditions since these conditions were clearly discriminating on the basis of origin.[24]

The first panel making the case for the so-called product-process doctrine under GATT Art. III was the panel in the first *US-Tuna I* case.[25] Referring to the Working Party Report on Border Tax Adjustments of 1970,[26] it held that PPM-measures, in this case the prohibition of certain harvesting methods, were even excluded from the scope of GATT Art. III because they did not affect tuna 'as a product'.[27] While this argumentation can easily be defeated pointing to the fact that in this case, PPM-measures would generally be treated better than product-related measures that have to be GATT consistent, the second *US–Tuna case II*[28] was more convincing raising the issue of extraterritoriality. When arguing that the US measure was contrary to GATT Art. III, it relied implicitly on the fact that foreign products did not have to comply with domestic policies of the importing country. Indeed, the issue of extraterritoriality, and implicitly the sovereignty of WTO members, is at the heart of the debate and has been taken up by following cases dealing with PPM-measures such as *US-Shrimps*,[29] where the Appellate Body discussed it under the general exceptions clause of GATT Art. XX. While the Appellate Body to date has refused to explicitly decide on the issue of extraterritorial jurisdiction, this paper will argue that the issue can be solved by applying general rules of public international law, and by developing substantive criteria on how potential abuse of process-oriented criteria can be avoided.[30]

---

[23]WTO, *Belgian Family Allowances*, Report of the Panel, 7 Nov 1952, BISD 1S/53 (1953) (hereinafter *Belgium Family Allowances*).

[24]Hudec (1999), pp. 41 et seqq.

[25]WTO, *United States – Restrictions on Imports of Tuna*, Report of the Panel, not adopted, 1993, BISD, 39S/155 (hereinafter *US–Tuna I*), para. 5.15.

[26]GATT, Report of the Working Party on Border Tax Adjustments, 2 Dec 1970, BISD 18S/97, para. 18.

[27]Ibid.

[28]WTO, *United States – Restrictions on Imports of Tuna*, Report of the Panel, not adopted, 1994, ILM 33:839-903 (hereinafter *US–Tuna II*).

[29]WTO, *United States – Import Prohibition of Certain Shrimps and Shrimp Products*, Report of the Appellate Body, 12 October 1998, WT/DS58/AB/R (hereinafter *US–Shrimps*).

[30]For an elaboration of the latter argument see Jackson (2000), p. 304.

In *US-Gasoline*, the Appellate Body explicitly stated that the WTO agreement should not be read 'in clinical isolation from public international law'.[31] And Art. 3 (2) of the Dispute Settlement System (DSU) calls for an analysis of WTO law in accordance with customary rules of international law for treaty interpretation, i.e. the Vienna Convention on the Law of Treaties (VCLT). Art. 31 (3) (c) of the VCLT says that any rule of international law applicable in the relations between the parties can be referred to in the interpretation. Thus, when discussing 'likeness' und GATT Art. III, or deciding whether there is an implied jurisdictional limitation in GATT At. XX (a), it is possible to refer to general rules of public international law such as the law on countermeasures and the responsibility of states. According to Art. 48 (1) (b) of the Draft Articles on the Responsibility of States for Internationally Wrongful Acts, third party countermeasures are possible in case a norm applicable *erga omnes* is violated. As stated above, it is possible to argue that the prohibition of child labour is a norm of *ius cogens* and applicable *erga omnes*. And in contrast to forcible countermeasures that are prohibited by Art. 2 (4) UN Charter, economic measures are in principle not prohibited by public international law.[32] Moreover, as regards the use of forced child labour, the case of Myanmar shows that Art. 33 ILO Constitution can be read as to allow for the adoption of (non-binding) recommendations of economic measures by the International Labour Conference to its constituents.[33] This possibility does however not solve the question of how such trade measures may be enforced, which has to be resolved according to WTO law und the law on countermeasures. Hence, *argumentum a maiore ad minus*, origin-neutral trade measures with extraterritorial effects taken to address the issue of child labour such as a social label or an import ban for goods made with child labour should be possible if otherwise consistent with WTO law. In conclusion, PPM-measures should not be considered as generally contrary to WTO law.[34] However, robust legal tests are needed under the non-discrimination and exception clauses to achieve acceptable results.

The so called 'aim and effects' test developed by cases such as *US–Automobiles*[35] and *US–Beverages*[36] could be such a robust legal test. According to this test, the aim and effect of a measure should be relevant when determining its consistency with GATT Art. III. However, this test should not be used, as suggested by these cases, to determine whether products are 'like', but whether there is less favourable treatment of foreign products under GATT Art. III or whether an advantage is conferred unconditionally under the MFN clause. This has been established by

---

[31]WTO, *United States – Standards for Reformulated and Conventional Gasoline*, Report of the Appellate Body, 20 May 1996, WT/DS2/AB/R, p. 18 (*US-Gasoline*).

[32]Cf. Schröder (2004), p. 588.

[33]For a thorough discussion of the Myanmar case see Humbert (2009), pp. 183–192.

[34]For a discussion of PPMs and the *EC–Seals* decision see Cottier (2017).

[35]WTO, *US – Taxes on Automobiles*, not adopted, ILM 33:839-903 (hereinafter *US–Automobiles*).

[36]WTO, *US – Measures Affecting Alcoholic and Malt Beverages*, Report of the Panel, 19 June 1992, BISD 39S/206 (1993) (hereinafter *US–Beverages*).

convincing case law such as *EC–Asbestos*[37] and *Chile–Alcoholic Beverages.*[38] The Appellate Body in *EC–Asbestos* held that the determination of 'likeness' related to the competitive relationship between products.[39] It rightly maintained that the only place where the regulatory purpose of a measure could come in when determining 'likeness' would be under the Working Party criterion of 'consumer preferences', if, for example, consumers opine that coffee made with child labour is distinct from coffee made without child labour.[40] With regard to discriminatory treatment, the Panel and Appellate Body in *Chile–Alcoholic Beverages* convincingly argued that the aim of a measure as manifested in the design was extremely important when interpreting whether the measure was applied 'so as to afford protection',[41] a term that informs the interpretation of the whole GATT Art. III. The purposive connotation of the words 'as to' suggests that the aim of a measure is relevant. In order to achieve fair and objective results, it is also convincing that the aim has to be discernible in the structure of the law. And since the words 'so as to' also refer to the manner of how potential measures are used, the measure also needs to have potential disparate trade effects on different groups of products to be found to be discriminatory.[42] However, it has to be admitted that the Appellate Body in the case *US–Clove Cigarettes* rejected any consideration of the regulatory purpose of the measure in contrast to Art. 2.1 TBT Agreement, where it considered it appropriate to inquire into the legitimate objective of the measure.[43] It confirmed its position in *EC–Seals* but at least made a cautious suggestion that in case of any imbalance arising out of neglect of the regulatory purpose, it would be for the member states to remedy this problem.[44] While *Howse* argues some language in the decision leaves some room for taking into account the regulatory purpose, the decision on the whole seems to follow the path of *US–Clove Cigarettes.*[45] However, in the view of the author, the language of GATT Art. III is a compelling argument for considering the regulatory purpose of the measure. Most importantly, taking into account the aim of a measure ensures fairer results when deciding a case. For example, the aim can

[37]WTO, *European Communities–Measures Affecting Asbestos and Asbestos – Containing Products*, Report of the Appellate Body, 12 Mar 2001, WT/DS135/AB/R (hereinafter *EC–Asbestos*).

[38]WTO, *Chile – Taxes on Alcoholic Beverages*, Report of the Appellate Body, 13 Dec 1999, WT/DS87/ABR, WT/DS110/AB/R (hereinafter *Chile–Alcoholic Beverages*).

[39]*EC – Asbestos*, para. 37.

[40]Cf. ibid., para. 117.

[41]*Chile – Alcoholic Beverages*, para. 71.

[42]For an elaboration of an 'asymmetric impact test' of potential trade effects see Ehring (2002), pp. 921–978.

[43]WTO, *United States–Measures Affecting the Production and Sale of Clove Cigarettes*, Report of the Appellate Body, 4 Apr 2012, WT/DS406/AB/R (hereinafter *US–Clove Cigarettes*), paras. 161–236.

[44]WTO, *European Communities–Measures Prohibiting the Importation and Marketing of Seal Products*, Report of the Appellate Body, 22 May 2014, WT/DS400/AB/R, WT/DS401/AB/R (hereinafter *EC–Seals*), para. 5.125.

[45]Howse (2014).

come in when trade effects of a measure are unclear, complementing the analysis of the discriminatory impact of a measure. This could help to rescue innocent trade measures on social and environmental issues with disparate trade impacts on goods manufactured in different countries. If, for instance, it is unclear whether the Belgium Social Label Law has a detrimental trade effect on goods imported by the complainant, its *bona fine* aim could help to save the law. It should however be noted that in relation to GATT Art. I, it is more difficult to argue in favour of a consideration of the regulatory purpose, because this norm lacks the words 'so as to afford protection', the legal basis of the interpretation suggested here.

2.2 *The General Exceptions Clause of GATT Art. XX*

One of the central GATT clauses is the general exceptions clause of GATT Art. XX, which allows WTO members to condition market access to achieve certain policy objectives, including the protection of public morals or human, animal or plant life. In order to be justified under GATT Art. XX, a measure has to fall within the scope of one of the possible exceptions for certain policy objectives, it has to be 'necessary' to achieve the desired policy goal or, depending on the different exceptions contained in the sub-paragraphs, has to have some other degree of connection to the objective, and, in any case, must not constitute arbitrary or unjustifiable discrimination. The latter obligation is contained in the so-called chapeau of GATT Art. XX, its introductory paragraph. With regard to child labour, the most relevant exceptions clauses are the ones just mentioned, i.e. the public morals and the health exception. Since the public morals exception is potentially broader including all aspects of child labour, and since there have been new cases such as *EC–Seals*, this paper will focus on the public morals clause.[46]

In *US–Gambling*, the panel held that the term 'public morals' referred to 'standards of right or wrong conduct maintained by or on behalf of a community or nation'.[47] It also stated that the term 'public morals' was an evolutionary concept that varied in time and space and was determined by factors such as social, ethical and religious values.[48] It found that members should be given some scope to define and apply for themselves the concepts of 'public morals' and 'public' order' in their respective territories, according to their systems and values.[49] With regard to child labour, it appears to be obvious to classify the prohibition of child labour as a standard maintained by a community and determined by social values. Indeed,

[46]For a thorough discussion of the scope of public morals exception as construed by the *EC–Seals* decision see Cottier (2017).

[47]WTO, *United States–Measures Affecting the Cross-Border Supply of Gambling and Betting Services*, Report of the Panel, 20 Apr 2005, WT/DS285/R (hereinafter *US–Gambling*), para. 6.462.

[48]Ibid. para. 6.461.

[49]Ibid.

Marceau argues that human rights measures may be allowed under the public morals exception.[50] Most importantly, the *EC–Seals* decision has made clear that the term 'public morals' has a broad scope going beyond issues such as gambling, sex or drugs trade and extends to animal welfare.[51] Thus, trade measures on child labour may possibly fall within the scope of the public morals exception. However, further thoughts are needed as to what other labour standards may come within the meaning of this term.

It should be noted that in case of child labour, it is also possible to apply Art. 31 (3) (c) VCLT and refer to the CRC or the ILO Convention on the Worst Forms of Child Labour[52] when construing the term 'public morals'. As will be recalled, under this norm, it is possible to refer to any rule applicable between the parties. Since the CRC and the Convention on the Worst Forms on Child Labour are ratified by the majority of states, they will in most cases be applicable to 'the parties', no matter whether this term refers to the parties of the dispute or all WTO members.[53] Also, considering that the prohibition of child labour forms part of *ius cogens* that applies *erga omnes*, i.e. to all WTO members, it is a rule that is 'applicable between the parties'.

With regard to the issue of extraterritoriality of trade measures on child labour, it is possible to argue that the prohibition of child labour is part of *ius cogens* and since *ius cogens* norms apply *erga omnes*, the morals of the international community are concerned and no problem of extraterritoriality exists. While the Appellate Body in *EC–Seals* has not decided the issue of extraterritoriality because the parties did not raise the issue, it rightly stated that the EU Seal Regime both addressed seal welfare concerns of EU citizens and seal hunting in and outside the EU.[54] That is, although the public morals of the population of the importing state are concerned, the EU Seal Regime still has extraterritorial effects. However, as discussed with regard to GATT Art. III, in case of child labour, this issue can be resolved by referring to rules of public international law including the concept of *ius cogens*, rules of state responsibility and the law of countermeasures. It can be argued that *argumentum a maiore ad minus*, origin-neutral measures on child labour with extraterritorial effects should be possible in case they otherwise comply with the necessity test and the chapeau of GATT Art. XX.

The necessity test under the health exception has evolved from a less-trade-restrictive means test into a broader proportionality test or a 'weighing and

[50] Marceau (2006), p. 206.

[51] *EC–Seals*, paras. 5.14–5.203.

[52] ILO Convention concerning the Prohibition and Immediate Action for the Elimination of the Worst Forms of Child Labour No. 182, International Labour Conference, 7 June 1999.

[53] For an elaborate discussion of the meaning of the term 'the parties' see Marceau (2002), pp. 780–783.

[54] *EC–Seals*, para. 5.173.

balancing' test.[55] The most important case in recent case law is *Brazil–Retreaded Tyres*, which has held that a panel must

> consider the relevant factors, particularly the importance of the interests at stake, the extent of the contribution to the achievement of the measure's objective, and its trade restrictiveness. If this analysis yields a preliminary conclusion that the measure is necessary, this result must be confirmed by comparing the measure with possible alternatives, which may be less trade restrictive while providing an equivalent contribution to the achievement of the objective. This comparison should be carried out in the light of the importance of the interests or values at stake.[56]

Further, it stated that the

> weighing and balancing is a holistic operation that involves putting all variables of the equation together and evaluating them in relation to each other after having examined them individually, in order to reach an overall judgement.[57]

The Appellate Body in *EC–Seals* also conducted such a thorough weighing and balancing operation with regard to the public morals exception.[58] However, criticizing the weighing and balancing test, some authors have maintained in the past that the Appellate Body cannot balance national policy interests with trade interests underlying the WTO agreements as a result of any proportionality requirement.[59] They held that such a test required strong democratic legitimacy, which would not be the case with the WTO bodies.[60] Yet, in the view of the author, decisions such as *EC–Seals* or *US–Shrimps* demonstrate that the WTO adjudicating bodies are able to properly taking non-economic issues into account.[61] And in the light of the fact that a reasonable balancing and weighing process is at the core of constitutionalism, it has convincingly been submitted that this recent trend of the WTO jurisprudence towards proportionality can be called a 'constitutionalization in a modest sense'.[62]

In relation to trade measures on child labour, it is certainly important to discuss the contribution of such measures for the actual reduction of child labour in poor countries where financial resources are lacking. It is for example questionable whether blanket import bans without some flanking educational and financial measures can be considered to contribute to the reduction of child labour, and

[55]Important cases discussing the necessity test are *Korea – Measures Affecting Imports of Fresh, Chilled and Frozen Beef*, Report of the Appellate Body, 11 Dec 2000, WT/DS161/AB/R (hereinafter *Korea–Beef*) and *EC–Asbestos*.

[56]WTO, *Brazil–Measures Affecting Imports of Retreaded Tyres*, Report of the Appellate Body, 17 Dec 2007, WT/DS332/AB/R (hereinafter *Brazil–Retreaded Tyres*), para. 178.

[57]Ibid., para. 182.

[58]*EC–Seals*, paras. 5.204–5.290.

[59]Desmedt (2001), pp. 469 et seqq.; Blüthner (2004), pp. 128 et seqq. and Neumann and Türk (2003), pp. 214 et seqq.

[60]Neumann and Türk (2003), pp. 214 et seqq.

[61]For example, in *US–Shrimps*, the Report of the Appellate Body took due account of relevant international environmental law. In *EC–Seals*, it duly considered the issue of animal welfare.

[62]Cottier (2000), p. 221.

thus be 'necessary'. Given the comprehensive and elaborate assessments of existing trade measures of WTO members by the WTO adjudicating bodies reflected also in the length of panel and Appellate Body reports in cases such as *EC-Seals* or *US-Tuna* amounting to almost 200 pages, it would be legitimate to require panels to assess whether additional measures are necessary to make an import ban necessary. This is in fact what the Appellate Body did when criticizing the EU in *EC–Seals* for not having done 'anything further to ensure that the welfare of seals is addressed in the context of IC hunts, given that 'IC hunts can cause the very pain and suffering for seals that the EU public is concerned about'.[63] By contrast, more comprehensive measures such as the Belgium Social Label Law would possibly pass the necessity test.[64]

Finally, the measure must comply with the chapeau, i.e. it must not constitute 'arbitrary or unjustifiable discrimination between countries where the same conditions prevail, or a disguised restriction on international trade'. To date, it has been well-established in case law and legal literature that the *chapeau* is an expression of good faith[65] and should prevent abuse of exceptions, embodying the doctrine of *abus de droit*.[66] The analysis focussed on the application of a measure. For example, the Appellate Body in *US–Shrimps* held that the application of a measure through administrative acts or guidelines must not be coercive on foreign policies but leave them enough flexibility.[67] This interpretation of the chapeau has now been challenged by Bartels who contends that it is incorrect to distinguish between the contents and the application of a measure. Instead, the chapeau comprises a set of conditions that on the one hand prohibit measures that arbitrarily or unjustifiably discriminate between countries where the same conditions prevail, and on the other hand measures that are a 'disguised restriction' in international trade, i.e. adopted for explicit protectionist reasons but with an 'ostensible legitimate objective'.[68] In his view, the discriminatory elements of the measure should exclusively be assessed under the chapeau. These elements should be the ones found discriminatory already under the non-discrimination obligations of GATT Art. III and I. They could then be justified if either the conditions are different in different countries, or on another ground that is not related to the objective.[69] The test under the subparagraphs would target the trade-restrictiveness of the measure.

[63] *EC–Seals*, para. 5.320. See also Cottier (2017) rightly holds that the Appellate Body in *EC–Seals* implies that the EU is obliged to introduce performance requirements, i.e. PPMs to make the partial ban consistent with WTO law.

[64] For a presentation of the Belgium Social Label Law, see Humbert (2009), pp. 323–329.

[65] Marceau (2009), p. 552.

[66] See for example cases such as *US–Shrimps*, paras. 158–159, para. 158; *US–Gasoline*, p. 22 or Marceau (2009), p. 553.

[67] *US–Shrimps*, para. 161.

[68] Bartels (2015), p. 97.

[69] Ibid., p. 124.

This interpretation appears to be especially appealing in cases where the differentiation between the content and the application of a measure is difficult, for example in case of labelling schemes such as the Belgian Social Label Law where the specific requirements could be termed ‘content’ or ‘implementation measures’. Furthermore, it is very convincing to take into account the conditions, i.e. the circumstances of the countries, in particular in case of environmental and social regulation that bears on the financial resources of countries. For example, possible discrimination of Indian goods could be justified because the conditions in Belgium and India with regard to child labour are quite different. Also, it seems to be logical not to require that the rationale for the justification is related to the objective of the measure especially in the case of an exception as in *EC–Seals*, because in most cases, the exception by its nature will not relate to the objective of the rule.[70] However, there are many open questions as to for example the possible grounds for justifications of discriminatory measures other than having different conditions. Also, it is questionable whether the scope of application of the subparagraphs of GATT Art. XX would not be unduly restricted if the discriminatory elements of the measures are exclusively assessed under the chapeau. For to violate the non-discrimination obligations of GATT Art. I, Art. III or Art. XI, a measure has to have discriminatory elements, which would be tested under the chapeau and could be found to be justified. This could make the legal tests of the subparagraphs superfluous unless one supports the view that GATT 1994 also prohibits measures that are solely trade restrictive. This is subject to debate. In sum, further thoughts are needed to elaborate on this approach. With regard to the Belgian Social Label Law, results would probably be the same, i.e. the law would probably pass the chapeau under both readings since there is no discriminatory element discernible in its implementation clauses.

2.3 The Agreement on Technical Barriers to Trade

Finally, the question is whether trade measures on child labour come within the scope of the TBT Agreement. This agreement contains specific requirements for ‘technical regulations’ and is potentially broader than the GATT to the extent that it also explicitly refers to trade-restrictive measures that have to be ‘not more trade-restrictive than necessary’ to fulfil a ‘legitimate objective’, Art. 2.2 TBT Agreement. Hence, the crucial question is whether non-product-related PPM measures such as trade measures on child labour are covered by the term ‘technical regulation’. The recent decision of *EC–Seals* could be read as to argue rather against the inclusion of such measures into the scope of the TBT Agreement, having assessed the EU Seal Regime under GATT Art. III and Art. XX.[71] However, the Appellate

[70]Ibid.

[71]*EC–Seals*.

Body explicitly refused to make a finding on whether the exceptions to the import ban of seal products amounted to related PPM measures within the meaning of the definition of technical regulations.[72] In the view of the author, given the rather technical nature of the TBT Agreement, it seems more appropriate to restrict the scope of application to more product-related labelling measures on child labour but to assess for example trade bans on products made with child labour with a looser product nexus rather under the GATT and its Art. XX. Thus, the Belgian Social Label Law would then have to be assessed under the TBT Agreement, i.e. under its Code of Good Practice since it is not a mandatory label. As such, according to Annex 3.D and E TBT Agreement, it would also have to be neither discriminatory nor 'more trade restrictive than necessary'. Since both tests can be read to be similar to the necessity test under GATT Art. XX, the Belgian Social Label Law is likely to be held as consistent with the TBT Agreement.

2.4 Concluding Remarks on the WTO Law Compatibility

Whilst there are still many open questions as to WTO law compatibility of trade measures on child labour, some measures such as the Belgian Social Label Law could certainly be considered to be consistent with the relevant norms of the GATT and the TBT Agreement. However, this is still very much debated in legal literature and certainly not established in WTO jurisprudence. The product-process doctrine is still the common legal doctrine. Also, it is not entirely sure that issues of extraterritoriality would be solved. As regards GATT Art. XX, it is still open to question whether trade measures on child labour would be held to address the public morals, whether they pass the necessity test and to comply with the requirements to the chapeau. In sum, there is no legal predictability for trade measures on child labour.

Furthermore, while some unilateral measures might be held compatible with WTO law, such an approach is not the most appropriate for adequately resolving the issue of child labour and trade. For at the moment, trade and human or labour rights are still separate regimes, there is no cooperation between the WTO and the ILO or the UN. In order to obtain satisfactory solutions, as a minimum, the WTO adjudicating bodies should consult for example with UN and ILO institutions and base their decisions on respective jurisprudence. It would also be desirable to have some labour experts involved in the (judicial) decision making. Also, private complaints on behalf of concerned children are not possible under the WTO Dispute Settlement. Finally, it is questionable whether trade measures without flanking educational measures and financial support are desirable and effective in combating child labour. Thus, it might be more appropriate to devise a joint ILO-WTO regime *de lege ferenda* on child labour that could serve as a model also for other labour

[72] Ibid., para. 5.69.

standards. The next section will briefly discuss whether new approaches to international law would help to devise such a regime by offering a legitimate basis and an adequate legal framework for such a solution.

3 A Constitutional Approach to International Law?

Legal scholars have been discussing for quite some time whether new approaches to international law would help to find feasible options to overcome the shortcomings of the current order. While all of the different theories attempt to respond to the challenge of fragmentation of international law and questions of legitimacy of the current international legal order, they differ as to the underlying law concepts.

One school of thought seeks to solve the challenge of fragmentation of international law through traditional methods of legal reasoning.[73] Legal scholars defending this approach hold that conflict rules provided by international law already offer a coherent theory of conflict of norms, i.e. that international law offers sufficient techniques to deal with challenges of fragmentation and coherence.[74] While this approach indeed offers valid solutions to the problem of child labour and trade, it does not offer a conceptual framework for curing the legitimacy deficit in the international order including private actor participation in the international decision-making and judicial procedures.

While equally taking conflicts between regulatory systems as a starting point, the conflict law approach draws on lessons from private international law to resolve policy coordination problems between different governance systems including the lack of participation of non-governmental bodies in the management of public affairs.[75] The conflicts-law approach to transnational governance is appealing since international private law indeed has an important role in social regulation through for example laying down rules for transnational corporate behaviour and its impacts on society. However, this approach does not answer pressing questions concerning the role of the state and private actors in the international order.

The school of global administrative law seeks to remedy accountability deficits in the growing exercise of transnational regulatory power emerged as a consequence of globalized interdependence in such fields as security, environmental protection and labour standards by creating a 'global administrative space' that is governed by global administrative law.[76] However, the approach does not answer

[73]See for example ILC, Fragmentation of International Law: Difficulties Arising from the Diversification and Expansion of International Law, ILC Report to the GA, A/61/10, 13 April 2006, A/CN.4/L.682 (hereinafter: A/CN.4/L.682); Pauwelyn (2003) and Neumann (2003).

[74]Pauwelyn (2003), p. 490 and A/CN.4/L.682, para. 20.

[75]See instead all Joerges (2011) and Wai (2011).

[76]See for example Kingsbury et al. (2005), pp. 15–61 and Grant and Keohane (2004).

the fundamental question on what basis such principles may be applied to the international order and what the normative basis of a global legal order should be.

There are a variety of approaches to international law that build upon constitutional theory and multilevel governance. *Petersmann* argues for a multilevel constitutionalism in order to overcome collective action problems.[77] In particular, taking EU law as a model, *Petersmann* argues for a human rights approach to trade that calls for a human rights interpretation of WTO obligations; for democratic functions of WTO rules that empower citizens to invoke WTO guarantees of freedom and non-discrimination in domestic courts and for more democratic participation inside intergovernmental organization through consultative parliamentary bodies and consultation or participation of representative non-governmental organizations.[78]

Peters' main thesis is that in an era of increasing interdependence of states and governance at the global level, the on-going de-constitutionalization at the national level should be compensated by a constitutionalization at the international level.[79] Since governmental functions such as guaranteeing human security, freedom and equality are more and more transferred to higher levels and governance is exercised beyond national constitutional confines, only the various governance levels taken together can provide full constitutional protection.[80]

Cottier's basic premise is that with governance expanding into international law, twenty-first century constitutionalism can no longer be limited to nation states.[81] He puts forward the idea of a 'Five Storey House' where all the different governance layers together, as a whole, constitute the constitutional system.[82] Such a new system should be based on principles such as the rule of law, human rights, equal legitimacy of the different layers, an appropriate allocation of power between the different levels, adequate representation and voice at all layers and effective decision making and dispute resolution including participation of private actors.[83]

All the different constitutional approaches seem to offer valid analytical frameworks for an ILO-WTO implementation system. They all suggest building a new approach to international law exactly on the elements such as human rights and participation of private actors that had been identified as missing to solve the problem of trade measures on child labour. However, a variety of critical views exists as to this constitutional approach reaching from schools conceiving international law rather as a sort of faith[84] to realist schools.[85] For example, the realist

---

[77]Petersmann (2011), pp. 5–57.

[78]Ibid., pp. 19–28.

[79]Peters (2006), pp. 579–610 and Klabbers et al. (2009).

[80]Peters (2006), p. 580.

[81]Cottier and Hertig (2003), p. 299.

[82]Ibid., p. 301.

[83]Cottier (2006), pp. 526–532.

[84]Koskenniemi (2011), pp. 331–361.

[85]Goldsmith and Posner (2005).

school holds that states only seek to maximize their interest and reject a more integrated global order. However, as the analysis has shown above, state action is already very much determined by foreign and intergovernmental action. Thinking of the US import ban on goods made with child labour, national regulators already have to regard foreign law when regulating child labour in their country. Also, the WTO is constitutionalizing when trade values are balanced against non-trade values, thus, a globally integrated order already exists to a certain extent.

4 Recommending an ILO-WTO Regime on Child Labour

In conclusion, it seems to be possible to use the constitutional approach to international law to suggest new regimes on issues of global concern such as child labour and trade. The constitutional approach as suggested by the three mentioned authors is a useful tool for devising an ILO-WTO enforcement regime built on desirable principles such as human rights, democratic participation, interaction of different layers, effective dispute resolution including private actors and substantial coherence between both the trade and the human rights regime.

To put it more concrete, an ILO-WTO enforcement regime built on the suggested principles would contain elements such as the following: Complementing national domestic legal regimes, it would contain child labour standards that in certain cases such as export-related child labour could be subject to a dispute settlement resulting in trade measures as measures of last resort. In addition to the intergovernmental dispute settlement system, there should also be a private complaints mechanism where non-governmental organizations on behalf of children could bring certain complaints against companies and governments along the lines of the procedures under the National Contact Points under the OECD Guidelines and the public communication procedure of the North American Agreement on Labour Cooperation,[86] the side-agreement on labour to the North American Free Trade Agreement. Complaints against governments may result in dispute resolution ending with trade measures. Panels would include ILO experts and decisions would be based on UN and ILO jurisprudence. The institutional structure should consist of a ministerial trade and child labour council as well as a parliamentary assembly to enhance democracy and participation at the global level. The council would be the decision-making body where experts from civil society and companies should be given consultative status. The parliamentary assembly should meet annually and also have decision making power. The main activities of the decision-making bodies would consist of monitoring and devising policy reviews with resulting child labour programmes in cooperation with the ILO. Another focus

[86]North American Agreement on Labor Cooperation, between the Government of the United States of America, the Government of Canada and the Government of the United Mexican States, Final Draft, 13 Sept 1993.

should be on devising trade incentives regimes where preferences are given for implementation of national child labour programmes.[87]

To conclude, the constitutionalist approach offers a valid solution how to devise new international regimes in the twenty-first century where private actors have a role and human rights are taken into account also on the international level.

References

Bartels L (2015) The chapeau of the general exceptions in the WTO GATT and GATS agreements: a reconstruction. Am J Int Law 109:95–125

Blüthner A (2004) Welthandel und Menschenrechte in der Arbeit, The compatibility of human rights at work with the WTO-system. Peter Lang/Europäischer Verlag der Wissenschaften, Frankfurt am Main

Conrad CR (2011) Processes and production methods (PPMs) in WTO law : interfacing trade and social goals. Cambridge University Press, Cambridge

Cottier T (2000) Limits to international trade: the constitutional challenge. In: American Society of International Law (ed) International law in ferment: a new vision for theory and practice. Proceedings of the 4th Annual Meeting, Washington, DC, pp 220–222

Cottier T (2006) Towards a five storey howse. In: Joerges C, Petersmann E-U (eds) Constitutionalism, multilevel trade governance and international economic law. Hart, Oxford, pp 495–532

Cottier T (2017) The implications of *EC – Seal Products* for the protection of core labour standards in WTO law. In: Gött H (ed) Labour standards in international economic law. Springer International Publishing, Cham, this volume

Cottier T, Caplazi A (1998) Labour Standards and World Trade Law: Interfacing Legitimate Concerns. In: Geiser T, Schmid H, Walter-Busch (eds) Arbeit in der Schweiz des 20. Jahrhunderts. Paul Haupt, Bern, pp 469–507

Cottier T, Hertig M (2003) The prospects of 21st century constitutionalisation. Max Planck Yearb U N Law 7:261–328

Desmedt A (2001) Proportionality in WTO law. J Int Econ Law 4(3):441–480

Ehring L (2002) De facto discrimination in world trade law – national and most-favoured-nation treatment or equal treatment? J World Trade 36:921–978

Goldsmith JL, Posner EA (2005) The limits of international law. Oxford University Press, Oxford/New York

Grant RW, Keohane RO (2004) Accountability and abuses of power in world politics. International Law and Justice Working Paper 7. Global Administrative Law Series. Institute for International Law and Justice, New York

Howse R, Regan D (2000) The product/process distinction – an illusory basis for disciplining 'unilateralism' in trade policy. Eur J of Int Law 11:249–289

Howse R (2014) Sealing the deal: the WTO's appellate body report in EC–Seal products. Am Soc Int Law Insights 18(12)

Hudec RE (1999) Essays on the nature of international trade law. Cameron & May, London

Humbert F (2009) The challenge of child labour in international law. Cambridge University Press, Cambridge

ILO/IPEC (2002) IPEC Action against child labour: highlights 2002. ILO, Geneva

ILO (2006) The end of child labour: within reach, Global report under the follow-up to the ILO declaration on fundamental principles and rights at work. ILO, Geneva

[87] For more details on how such an enforcement could look like, see Humbert (2009), pp. 376–385.

ILO (2013) Marking progress against child labour – global estimates and trends 2000–2012. ILO, International programme on the elimination of child labour, Geneva
Jackson J (2000) Comments on shrimp/turtle and the product/process distinction. Eur J Int Law 11:303–307
Joerges C (2011) Three-dimensional conflicts law as constitutional form. In: Joerges C, Petersmann EU (eds) Constitutionalism, multilevel trade governance and international economic law. Hart, Oxford
Kingsbury B, Krisch N, Stewart RB (2005) The emergence of global administrative law. Law Contemp Probl 68:15–61
Klabbers J, Peters A, Ulfstein G (2009) The constitutionalization of international law. Oxford University Press, Oxford
Koskenniemi M (2011) The politics of international law. Hart, Oxford/Portland
Marceau G (2002) WTO dispute settlement and human rights. Eur J Int Law 13:753–814
Marceau G (2006) The WTO dispute settlement and human rights. In: Abbott F, Breining-Kaufmann C, Cottier T (eds) International trade and human rights, foundations and conceptional issues. University of Michigan Press, Ann Arbor, pp 181–258
Marceau G (2009) Trade and labour. In: Bethlehem D, McRae D, Neufeld R, Van Damme I (eds) The Oxford handbook of international trade law. Oxford University Press, Oxford, pp 539–569
Neumann J (2003) Die Koordination des WTO-Rechts mit anderen völkerrechtlichen Ordnungen, Konflikte des materiellen Rechts und Konkurrenzen der Streitbeilegung. Duncker & Humblot, Berlin
Neumann J, Türk E (2003) Necessity revisited – proportionality in world trade organization law after Korea–Beef, EC–Asbestos, EC–Sardines. J World Trade 37:199–233
OECD (1997) Process and production methods (PPMs): conceptual framework and considerations on use of PPM-based trade measures, OCDÈ/GD(97)137. OECD Publishing, Paris
Pauwelyn J (2003) Conflicts of law in public international law, how WTO law relates to other rules of international law. Cambridge University Press, Cambridge
Peters A (2006) Compensatory constitutionalism: the function and potential of fundamental international norms and structures. Leiden J Int Law 19:579–610
Petersmann EU (2011) Multilevel trade governance in the WTO requires multilevel constitutionalism. In: Joerges C, Petersmann EU (eds) Constitutionalism, multilevel trade governance and international economic law. Hart, Oxford/Portland
Schröder M (2004) Sanktionen. In: Graf Vitzhum W (ed) Völkerrecht, 3rd edn. De Gruyter, Berlin, pp 582–588
Wai R (2011) Conflicts and comity in transnational governance: private international law as mechanism and metaphor for transnational social regulation through plural legal regimes. In: Joerges C, Petersmann EU (eds) Constitutionalism, multilevel trade governance and international economic law. Hart, Oxford/Portland

Labour Standards and Trade: Need We Choose Between 'Human Rights' and 'Sustainable Development'?

Tonia Novitz

Contents

1 Introduction

This chapter examines the links made between labour standards and trade, in the context of an apparent shift away from a human rights (HR) perspective to one more focused on sustainable development (SD). The approach taken by the European Union (EU) is taken here as an example of this evolution in approach. My concern is whether this shift of language could entail a change in content. Can the justificatory basis for inclusion of labour standards make any difference to the efficacy of trade conditionality? My suggestion is that there may be benefits to supplementing bare HR compliance with a richer and more nuanced SD perspective, but that we have yet to see trade instruments which realize that ambition.

T. Novitz (✉)
University of Bristol Law School, Bristol, UK
e-mail: tonia.novitz@bristol.ac.uk

H. Gött (ed.), *Labour Standards in International Economic Law*,
https://doi.org/10.1007/978-3-319-69447-4_7

2 The Ambitions of Human Rights and Sustainable Development

Before commencing discussion of concrete texts and their implications, some careful discussion of HR and SD is called for; neither is an altogether natural home for 'labour standards' in respect of which there has been a struggle for independent recognition in trade conditionality. I want to make clear at the outset that is not my intention to suggest that the concepts of HR and SD cannot interrelate, such that sustainability is understood to be contingent on HR protection. Indeed, as I argue below, Amartya Sen's work on the notion of 'development as freedom'[1] and Martha Nussbaum's articulation of 'central human capabilities'[2] would suggest otherwise. Rather, I wish to suggest that it is possible to conceptually distinguish the aims and objectives of two recognisably distinct discourses, which can operate in discrete ways and have been known to do so in recent history.

This chapter explores that history of ideas and considers whether a SD discourse could embrace HR concerns while allowing a richer engagement with labour-related issues. The second part of the chapter provides a preliminary investigation into whether this possibility is being realized or is likely to be realized in practice.

2.1 *Human Rights Conditionality*

Labour standards have come to be included in trade conditionality as 'human rights' (HR) over a number of years. The language of HR is arguably one of imperatives, namely the entitlements of persons (by virtue only of being human beings) which their dignity demands must be protected over and above other objectives. Hence Dworkin's characterization of such rights as 'trumps'.[3]

The inclusion of explicit HR protection in binding international law instruments, under the International Covenant on Civil and Political Rights (ICCPR) and the International Covenant on Economic, Social and Cultural Rights (ICESCR) both adopted in 1966, can be seen as the continuation of a post-Second World War concern with the basic protection of all human beings. That concern had already been expressed in instruments such as the International Labour Organisation (ILO) Declaration of Philadelphia 1944, as well as the United Nations (UN) Charter 1945 and the Universal Declaration of Human Rights 1948. The Declaration of Philadelphia indicated that the fundamental objectives of the ILO, which included freedom of association and protection from forced labour and discrimination,

[1] Sen (1999).

[2] Nussbaum (1997, 2000, 2003, 2011).

[3] Dworkin (1977).

were not to be compromised by economic and financial policies.[4] In this sense, HR conditionality can be seen as an ethical constraint on the otherwise utilitarian practices of trade. HR instruments (and international supervisory bodies) tend to defer to ILO instruments in this regard (and to the findings of ILO supervisory bodies).[5]

The question then is to what extent labour standards fit within the rubric of HR (as opposed to broader social policy objectives which could be constrained by such rights). Certainly, some labour standards, such as freedom of association and freedom from forced labour, easily meet the criteria for protection as civil and political rights.[6] That propensity for protection of the worker under a HR discourse was the subject of extensive comment in the wake of identification of 'core labour standards' in the ILO Declaration of Fundamental Principles and Rights at Work 1998 and eight 'fundamental' ILO Conventions. The danger identified was that this shift in policy orientation potentially narrowed the remit of legitimate ILO objectives and its role in the international community.[7] One might see the deliberate expansion of an ILO 'Decent Work Agenda' as a response, in that this agenda encompasses not only protection of human rights at work, but also promotion of job opportunities, social protection and social dialogue.[8] That said, there has been no official expansion of the ILO 'core' to encompass other entitlements, such as to health and safety or adequate remuneration.

Of course, labour rights may be seen not only as those specified in the ICCPR but also the ICESCR. There might seem to be a barrier to effective implementation of labour standards that are termed 'socio-economic' as opposed to 'civil and political', conventionally characterised as progressive (as opposed to immediate), group-oriented (as opposed to individual in character), resource-dependent and ultimately policy oriented rather than justiciable.[9] By way of contrast, it has been argued by various authors that the multi-faceted need for protection of the interests of workers

---

[4]ILO Declaration concerning the aims and purposes of the International Labour Organisation, adopted on 10 May 1944, Art. II(C).

[5]Art. 22 of the ICCPR endorses a 'right to freedom of association', while Art. 8 of the ICESCR requires States Parties to undertake to ensure 'the right to strike', but both provisions conclude with an express reminder that nothing is to prejudice the guarantees provided for in ILO Convention No. 87. See also the Singapore Declaration of the WTO Ministerial Conference 1996 recognizing the competence of the ILO to 'set and deal' with core labour standards, including freedom of association. For discussion of the problem of a hierarchy of norms, see Novitz (2014b), pp. 358–360.

[6]Civil and political rights can be claimed by an individual who may—or may not—choose to do so collectively. The option to claim collectively is, for example, offered by Art. 34 European Convention on Human Rights 1950.

[7]http://www.ilo.org/declaration/lang--en/index.htm. Accessed 13 Nov 2015. See comment by a number of authors: Alston (2004, 2005), McCrudden and Davies (2000) and Murray (2010).

[8]http://www.ilo.org/global/about-the-ilo/decent-work-agenda/lang--en/index.htm. Accessed 12 Nov 2015. See also ILO Declaration on Social Justice for a Fair Globalization, adopted on 10 June 2008, Article IA.

[9]For an example, see Hare (2002).

may traverse traditional boundaries between civil and political and socio-economic rights in a variety of ways.[10] Such entitlements may have both individual and collective dimensions[11]; and can in some contexts be enforceable by a sole litigant whether on an international or national stage, while in others best realized through bargaining at the workplace or species of policy implementation and regulatory innovations.[12] The creation of an individual complaints procedure with respect to the ICESCR may indicate that these prejudices are gradually being overcome in the international community.[13] Similarly, Article 21 of the revised Treaty on European Union (TEU) indicates that the EU is under an obligation to treat all human rights as 'indivisible'.

In initial EU trade agreements, labour standards had to be understood as 'human rights' in the sense of civil and political rights to achieve some semblance of protection through trade.[14] Examples included freedom of association and protection from forced labour or slavery. Early incarnations of protection of labour standards under the EU Generalized System of Preferences are indicative of taking (certain) human rights seriously.[15] Even this form of conditionality was extremely politically sensitive as indicated by the rejection by the World Trade Organisation (WTO) of the 'social clause' proposed by the EU and the United States (US) in Seattle.[16] Instead the architecture of international economic law does not require but permits such conditionality, subject to other WTO instruments and provisions, such as the Enabling Clause[17] or Art. XX of the General Agreement on Tariffs and Trade (the GATT).[18]

'Core' standards as identified by the ILO have come to feature as the subject matter of protection under EU GSP (and subsequently GSP+)[19] alongside a variety

---

[10]See Mantouvalou (2012), for example, who reaches beyond the positivistic approach to labour rights which might take the Covenants as a starting point.

[11]Novitz (2002) and Churchill and Khaliq (2004).

[12]Ewing (1999); Fenwick and Novitz (2010) and Novitz (2012), pp. 161–165.

[13]Optional Protocol to the International Covenant on Economic, Social and Cultural Rights, GA Res. A/RES/63/117, which provides the Committee competence to receive and consider communications; Vandenhole (2003).

[14]Novitz (2008).

[15]Tsogas (2000) discussed in Novitz (2005), p. 231.

[16]Summers (2001).

[17]Enabling Clause: 'Differential and More Favourable Treatment Reciprocity and Fuller Participation of Developing Countries'—WTO, *Differential and More Favourable Treatment Reciprocity and Fuller Participation of Developing Countries*, L/4903, 28 Nov 1979—appended to GATT (which continues to apply as part of GATT 1994 under the WTO). See for discussion Bartels (2003).

[18]Howse (2003).

[19]Hepple (2006), Chapter 6; see European Council Regulation 2501/2001, O.J. L 346/1 (2001); European Council Regulation 732/2008 *applying a scheme of generalised tariff preferences for the period from 1 January 2009 to 31 December 2011 and amending Regulations (EC) No 552/97, (EC) No 1933/2006 and Commission Regulations (EC) No 1100/2006 and (EC) No 964/2007, O.J. L 211/1 (2008) and Council Regulation 978/2012*, O.J. L 303/1 (2012).

of EU trade agreements.[20] That apparent spread of labour standards protection as a species of HR under the 1998 Declaration and ILO 'fundamental' conventions was, it seems, one of the factors that prompted the revolt by the employer group within the ILO. The employer representatives expressed concern that ILO Conventions were 'embedded' in other international institutions and instruments; so that findings of the ILO Committee on the Application of Conventions and Recommendations (CEACR) had increasing relevance.[21] Even the fact that implementation of EU GSP tends to centre on the findings of the Conference Committee on the Applications of Standards (CAS), a tripartite body in which employers have demonstrated that they can exercise a veto on identification of concern,[22] did not appease them. Such norms may be agreed by all governments (and indeed by the social partners at the ILO) to deserve impact, but their content remains a matter over which there will be fierce dispute, not only regarding the principles stated but the processes through which they are articulated.[23]

2.2 *Sustainable Development*

The 'malleability' of 'sustainable development' (SD) as a concept has been the subject of academic comment for some time[24]; and we have seen its evolution to encompass a blend of objectives. The Rio Declaration on Environment and Development 1992 began the process and the established position is best stated in the Johannesburg Declaration on Sustainable Development 2002, paragraph 5 of which states that:

> we assume a collective responsibility to advance and strengthen the interdependent and mutually reinforcing pillars of sustainable development — economic development, social development and environmental protection — at the local, national, regional and global levels.

Labour standards are now understood to come within the 'social' and 'economic' pillars, but there has been recent consensus identification of a fourth 'cultural' pillar

[20] Orbie et al. (2009) and van den Putte and Orbie (2015).

[21] See ILO (2012) Record of Proceedings, 101st ILC, Part I/16, para. 146. For comment, see Bellace (2014), La Hovary (2013) and Swepston (2013). For apparent reconciliation of this dispute, see ILO (2015) Tripartite Meeting Report, TMF APROC/2015/2.

[22] For criticism of the EU approach, see Vogt (2015), p. 293 where he notes that the Commission requires recommendation of a 'special paragraph' by the CAS, a rarity that certainly will not apply every year. In this way Bangladesh and Guatemala have been protected from potential withdrawal of trade preferences; discussed by Vogt (2015), pp. 300–301.

[23] See ILO (2014) and also La Hovary (2017).

[24] See Robinson (2004) and Novitz and Mangan (2011), p. 2.

which also has relevance to work in various ways.[25] This addition may be indicative of how the meaning of SD remains contested and is still shifting.[26]

In 2012, in a compelling analysis of recent international trade initiatives, Lorand Bartels observed that SD chapters were emerging in economic partnership agreements which made reference to protection of labour standards.[27] These chapters (as opposed to the standard HR clauses) were the new method by which to pursue EU ethical foreign policy objectives. Bartels placed this development at 2008, but Lore Van den Putte and Jan Orbie see this as a programmatic change introduced by Peter Mandelson as Commissioner for DG Trade in 2005 instantiated in EU GSP from 2005 and in all free trade agreements from EU-Korea in 2011.[28]

A further issue is the potential for this apparent change to affect the content of the labour norms promoted through such trade agreements. Does it necessarily indicate a dilution of labour standards from the imperative human right to 'malleability' in the face of other objectives which are environmental or economic in nature? Or could such an approach be a way to more effective inclusion of socio-economic as well as civil and political rights facets of labour standards into trade—and from a more pragmatic perspective? Further, might this discourse affect the acceptance by the South of conditionality in that it appears to enable more discursive and gradual forms of development also applicable to the North?

Contemporary academic opinion is critical of this shift. Van den Putte and Orbie see the policy framework of SD as 'reframing' labour provisions in ways that are 'more blurred' and 'ambiguous'.[29] In particular, putting labour standards:

> on the same level as environmental standards, is problematic from a human rights perspective and also has legal consequences. While implicitly they are also part of the essential elements clause, mentioning them also in the chapter on trade and sustainable development harms the indivisibility of human rights. In addition it is not clear how a violation of social norms should be handled: by taking appropriate measures as the violation of essential elements prescribes, or by referring it to the specific dispute settlement mechanism as described in the chapter on sustainable development, they are too different with regard to their objectives and measures to combine them in one oversight mechanism.

Bartels expresses comparable misgivings, namely that if 'core labour standards' are seen as HR they can be subjected to dispute settlement in a way which contemplates suspension of trade concessions, but not if they are considered a matter for SD where softer measures apply. He highlights the obligation within the EU to view civil, political and social rights as indivisible and identifies a lack of 'internal coherence' in EU conduct.[30]

---

[25]http://www.agenda21culture.net/index.php/docman/-1/393-zzculture4pillarsden/file. Accessed 12 Nov 2015.

[26]See also Schrijver (2008).

[27]Bartels (2012), p. 1.

[28]Van den Putte and Orbie (2015), pp. 281–282. For further discussion of this trend, see De Schutter (2015).

[29]Van den Putte and Orbie (2015), p. 281.

[30]Bartels (2012), pp. 18–19.

These are serious concerns and deserve more careful attention than has been the case to date. Certainly, EU policy documents seem to skirt around these issues and trade conditionality is such a sensitive issue for both the ILO and the World Trade Organisation (WTO) that little analysis or advice is forthcoming from either institution. The guidance from the WTO on trade conditionality is that, in terms of compliance with the Enabling Clause, the same preferences need not be given to developing countries, as long as their treatment can be transparently determined and justified with reference to their distinctive developmental needs.[31] However, while relevant to 'development' per se, this does not assist in terms of assessing what might be meant by 'sustainable' development and how labour standards come within this contested frame.

2.2.1 The Idea of 'Sustainability'

The Declaration on the Right to Development 1986 refers to the 'indivisibility' of rights such that 'equal attention and urgent consideration should be given to the implementation, promotion and protection of civil, political, economic, social and cultural rights'.[32] In other words, all facets of HR protection are recognized to be necessary to development. However, there is no mention of the element of 'sustainability' which surfaces only later. The genesis of that term seems to begin with the Brundtland Report, which considers that sustainability arises where a policy 'meets the needs of the present without compromising the ability of future generations to meet their own needs'.[33] This widely cited definition[34] gives us some sense of what relevance labour standards might have then for both the needs of the present (in terms of the economy and social well-being) while ensuring ongoing welfare for the future, such that environmental concerns might (for example) act as a constraint on the subject matter of collective bargaining over new technologies. In an extremely helpful commentary on the treatment of 'sustainable development' under international law, Virginie Barral goes on to understand the term according to the combination of two principles: intergenerational and intragenerational equality.[35] The latter speaks of 'fair economic and social development'[36] with which labour lawyers are usually concerned.

What is evident from the UN Declaration of 1986, the Rio Declaration of 1992 and the Johannesburg Declaration of 2002 is that the right to development

---

[31]WTO, *European Communities – Conditions for the granting of Tariff Preferences to Developing Countries*, WT/DS246/AB/R, 7 Apr 2004.

[32]Declaration on the Right to Development GA Res. 41/128, 4 Dec 1986, Art. 6 (2) and also see Art. 9.

[33]WCED (1987), p. 51.

[34]Villiers (2011), pp. 48–49; Barral (2012), p. 378 and also Bartels (2012), p. 10.

[35]Barral (2012), p. 380.

[36]Ibid.

recognized therein is not just an entitlement to certain outcomes but also to be an active participant in the process by which those outcomes are achieved. So, for example, Article 1 (1) of the UN Declaration not only stressed that development is a human right, but that it is one 'by virtue of which every human person and all peoples are entitled to participate in, contribute to, and enjoy.' Principle 10 of the Rio Declaration likewise observed that 'environmental issues are best handled with participation of all concerned citizens [...]' Fleshing out the concept requires a normative vision of what labour rights might secure enduring present and future well-being. I have argued elsewhere that the experience of labour lawyers (and trade unions) may well be relevant here, in so far as the idea of sustainability is dynamic (or as Barral puts it 'not a static concept').[37] Further, it would seem that the sustainability of development (and our evolving appreciation of what this might entail) requires active forms of voice from workers and their representatives as well as other citizens.[38]

In October 2015, the UN adopted 17 'Sustainable Development Goals' (SDGs) replacing the Millennium Development Goals (MDGs). These encompass a broader conception of 'sustainability' as opposed to MDG relief from the most extreme forms of poverty. The most obviously relevant for the purposes of labour standards and trade conditionality is Goal 8: 'Promote sustained, inclusive and sustainable economic growth, full and productive employment and decent work for all.'[39] This general aspiration is accompanied by a more concrete list of objectives concerning creation of job opportunities, generation of greater social equality, prevention of child labour and forced labour, as well as provision of safe and secure working environments. In this respect, the proposed UN instrument self-consciously reflects various aspects of the ILO's Decent Work Agenda (not just the core labour standards).[40] One difference, which one hopes is not significant, is that social dialogue is not mentioned in Goal 8 but in Goal 16: 'Promote peaceful and inclusive societies for sustainable development, provide access to justice for all and build effective, accountable and inclusive institutions at all levels.' Trade unions are not mentioned specifically under this head, but there is recognition of the need to 'ensure responsive, inclusive, participatory and representative decision-making at all levels'.[41]

---

[37]Ibid., p. 382.

[38]Novitz (2015).

[39]Transforming our world: the 2030 Agenda for Sustainable Development, GA Res 70/1, 25 Sep 2015.

[40]This inclusion was pre-empted by the final resolution to the 2012 Rio +20 summit which also makes reference to 'decent work'. See UN (2012) Doc A/RES/66/288, para 23.

[41]See Transforming our world: the 2030 Agenda for Sustainable Development, GA Res 70/1, 25 Sep 2015, SDG 16.7.

2.2.2 The Link Between Labour Rights and Environmental Concerns: To What Extent Can They Stand Alone?

Barral's conception of SD might seem a narrow one, for she sees development as sustainable 'only when both intergenerational (environmental protection) and intragenerational (fair economic and social development) are guaranteed and this is to be achieved through their integration'.[42] As such, it might seem that labour standards could never stand alone in a SD clause to be worthy of protection separately from the environmental matters.

On the other hand, one could say that the environmental, economic and social dimensions of sustainability need to be jointly *and severally* enforceable as the component parts of development. My suggestion is that social policy, including labour standards and HR, are a vital pillar in the process of SD. While mutually reinforcing the other pillars, they need to be enforceable alone or the entire edifice of sustainability (durable progress) is threatened.

There is arguably some evidence of such an approach in the UN SDGs, which are described as 'integrated' and 'interdependent',[43] but where environmental protection is not explicitly mentioned in each discrete goal (and sub-goal). Specific measures are to be taken in respect of each SDG that do not necessarily entail environmental measures, although it would be peculiar were any measures taken in relation to an SDG that did not also pay attention to environmental as well as economic and social aspects of sustainability.

Certainly, core labour standards, which can also be viewed as HR, are a vital precursor to other forms of economic wellbeing and environmental protection. Without freedom of association we cannot have the voice to integrate environmental concerns into the workplace.[44] Without protection from discrimination we devalue the capacity of all people to contribute to our environmental protection, economic wellbeing and social policies; and without that broader holistic support, the achievement of these goals is unlikely to be possible. Further, protection from child and forced labour ensures that workers cannot be coerced into doing what is bad for them, their community or their planet. It can also be observed that the prohibition of child labour contributes to the greater aim of inter-generational justice and thereby, not only the environmental, but also economic and social well-being of future generations.[45]

We can integrate this discourse with Amartya Sen's idea of 'Development as Freedom'. In particular, Sen's notion of 'capabilities' offers the argument for 'both

[42]Barral (2012), p. 380.

[43]See Transforming our world: the 2030 Agenda for Sustainable Development, GA Res 70/1, 25 Sep 2015, para. 5.

[44]See Galgoczi (2014), p. 63; Lund (2004), pp. 45–48 and Räthzel and Uzzell (2013). See also ETUC (2010), ILO (2010) and TUC (2014) which offers six case studies in which trade unions have assisted in enabling environmental change in the workplace.

[45]I am grateful to one of the editors, Henner Gött, for initially making this observation, which I include here.

processes that allow freedom of actions and decisions, and the actual *opportunities* that people have [. . .]'[46] This is a 'freedom to do' (rather than the classical neo-liberal 'freedom from'). The focus is on the ability to achieve human 'functionings', namely 'the various things a person may value doing or being',[47] the value of which is to be determined by discursive processes.[48] In his account, the significance of workers' capabilities is explicitly acknowledged.[49]

His is not a complete normative theory,[50] but Martha Nussbaum builds on this assessment by identifying what she regards as 'central human capabilities' required for living a life of dignity: life, bodily health, bodily integrity, senses, imagination and thought, emotions, practical reason, affiliation, connection with other species, play and political and material control over one's environment. To the extent that HR as we currently understand them feed into these capabilities, they are to be protected. In this way Nussbaum offers an alternative perspective on debates regarding civil and political and socio-economic rights and their value.[51] Her formulation of capabilities contributes arguably to a deeper understanding of how we value other species and our environment; our functionings being formed by them and our actions having the capacity to nurture them. How humans do this seems potentially to link to our ability to engage in affiliative thought and action or, as it might be termed, freedom of association and collective voice.

In this way, we can understand HR (and workers' freedoms to organize and speak) as constitutive of the ongoing sustainability of development. Indeed, this is acknowledged in SDG 16.10 which requires governments to 'ensure public access to information and protect fundamental freedoms, in accordance with national legislation and international agreements'. Their protection can be achieved alongside economic or environmental objectives; but their freestanding guarantee offers potential for durable social solutions to connected development-related problems.

2.2.3 Does Sustainable Development Lead Us Beyond Labour 'Rights' into a Broader Decent Work Agenda or Just 'Soft(er)' Law?

A concern raised by the term 'sustainable development' is that, while it can encompass (or presume) the protection of rights, it is itself merely a 'political objective', rather than a legal term capable of enforcement.[52] It is this idea that

[46]Sen (1999), p. 17.

[47]Sen (1999), p. 75.

[48]Ibid, p. 119. Deakin and Wilkinson (2005), p. 286.

[49]Sen (1999), pp. 27–30 and 112–116.

[50]For this debate from labour lawyers, see Langille (2005), Fudge (2007, 2011) and also Bogg (2015).

[51]Nussbaum (2003), p. 36 and Nussbaum (2000), chapter 1. For further discussion, see Novitz (2014a).

[52]Barral (2012), p. 379 reviews this literature.

Barral investigates. She demonstrates, subsequently, how SD may play various 'interpretive functions' in legal proceedings. For example, in *Shrimp-Turtle*, the WTO Appellate Body drew specific legal consequences from the principle.[53] Further, using the International Court of Justice judgment in the *Pulp Mills* case,[54] she shows how SD may be seen variously as an objective, a means and as a mode of measurement.[55] The difficulty for our purposes is that legal respect for the principle of SD requires potentially rebalancing of entitlements. For example, the Judgment in *Pulp Mills* refers to 'this interconnectedness between equitable and reasonable utilization of a shared resource and the balance between economic development and environmental protection that is the essence of sustainable development'.[56] There is the potential predicament that placing labour rights, which might seem to be neatly defined HR, under the rubric of SD then opens them up to this act of potential 'balancing', thereby undermining the certainties with which they have previously been associated as strong claims. There are at least two answers which could be offered here.

The first answer is that few human rights have ever been regarded as unqualified and freedom of association, non-discrimination, child labour and forced labour have been subjected to careful interrogation and points of compromise in various international instruments. The ILO Conventions (and accompanying Recommendations) are themselves illustrative of this need for debate and concession, as are some of the provisions set out in the ECHR (not to mention the ICCPR and ICESCR). Therefore, that economic and environmental (or even cultural) concerns might be important constraints on the exercise of, for example, on freedom of association and collective bargaining is not entirely new or unacceptable.[57] It is harder to see how economic or environmental concerns could affect obligations not to allow forced or child labour; but one can imagine cases of indirect discrimination justifiable by virtue of such factors.[58] It is possible that unscrupulous members of the employers' group at the ILO might use the language of 'sustainable development' as a further opportunity to revisit the content of established core labour standards, such as freedom of association (and the right to strike)[59]; but the economic and political climate generated by the financial crisis is such that it is arguable that the International Organisation of Employers (IOE) would be lobbying

[53]WTO, *US - Import Prohibition of certain Shrimp and Shrimp Products*, WT/DS58/AV/R, 12 Oct 1998, paras. 127–31; cited in Barral (2012), p. 386.

[54]ICJ, *Case Concerning Pulp Mills on the River Uruguay (Argentina v. Uruguay)*, ICJ Rep. 2010, 20 Apr 2010.

[55]Barral (2012), pp. 388–397.

[56]See *Pulp Mills* above, para. 177.

[57]The case law on Art. 11 (2) ECHR is illustrative of the application of principles of proportionality and a margin of appreciation for State parties.

[58]See for recent (albeit critical comment) on the readiness of the UK courts to adopt such an approach, O'Cinneide and Liu (2015).

[59]See ILO (2014) and La Hovary (2017).

for diminution of labour rights in any case.[60] What should matter are the arguments that can be put forward to protect labour standards, which remain compelling and far-reaching. Indeed, their very mention in trade agreements is a concession that this is widely accepted.

The second answer is that labour standards and their conditionality in trade should, as various commentators noted in response to the introduction of a focus on 'core labour standards', be concerned with more than that bare minimum. The scope for intersection of the social with the economic and environmental arguably opens possibilities for the pursuit of the broader ILO 'Decent Work Agenda' encompassing not only rights at work (which remain subject to protection as HR), but promotion of jobs, extension of social protection and greater social dialogue.[61] In pursuit of these broader objectives, the Preface to the 2008 ILO Declaration indicates that the instrument.

> contributes to policy coherence for sustainable development in national policies, among international organizations and in development cooperation, bringing together social, economic and environmental objectives. In this regard, it highlights that international and regional organizations with mandates in closely related fields can play an important role in the implementation of the integrated approach required and invites them to promote decent work.[62]

This is evident from the ILO commitments as regards implementation of the 2008 Declaration which explicitly seeks to promote SD.[63]

Arguably, what SD offers is not so much another reason to compromise core labour rights, but to add new labour standards as worthy of protection and to seek durability of a fairer economic settlement for workers. With this, there is scope to build new alliances between workers' organizations and NGOs or other groups seeking moderation in the pursuit of economic interests. Also, arguably, the SD discourse allows engagement not only with the bare compliance with a discretely defined human right but the broader social effects of trade agreements, which are unsustainable in the longer term where the operation of trade provisions (for example, relating to trade in services) can cause illness, poverty or other forms of harm.[64] In this sense, then, the 'redefinition of conventional obligations' that Barral identifies as a facet of an international doctrine of SD could be useful for workers in their resistance to trade rules such as those relating to services which corrode national labour laws.[65]

---

[60]See Supiot (2010).

[61]http://www.ilo.org/global/about-the-ilo/decent-work-agenda/lang--en/index.htm. Accessed 12 Nov 2015. See also ILO Declaration on Social Justice for a Fair Globalization, adopted on 10 June 2008, Article IA.

[62]ILO Declaration on Social Justice for a Fair Globalization, adopted on 10 June 2008, p. 3.

[63]Ibid, Articles IIA(ii) and IID.

[64]For example, for analysis of the potential effects of the Trans-Pacific Partnership, see Kelsey (2013) and Backer (2014).

[65]See Novitz (2014c) and also Kelsey (2008).

For these reasons, there is nothing intrinsically objectionable about either the treatment of labour rights as HR within EU trade agreements or with a broader agenda of SD (encompassing labour rights) opening out scope for further deliberation. The two could even be mutually reinforcing aspects of an overarching conditionality. What obviously matters is the ways in which trade agreements operationalize both HR and SD.

3 The Practice of Human Rights Protection and Sustainable Development

The study of the practice of utilisation of HR approaches and their comparison with those associated with SD is a subject more suited to the international relations specialist than an international lawyer (or even a labour lawyer). To this extent, Van den Putte and Orbie's concerns must be taken seriously, for these stem from their own empirical studies of the application of sustainable development chapters.[66] Nevertheless, there are some preliminary observations that can be made on the basis of documentation already available, regarding current practice, and the potential for its further improvement.

In this section of the chapter, I begin with a brief review of the use of labour standards conditionality in EU GSP before and after the introduction of mention of 'sustainable development', suggesting that the promise identified in the prior section of this chapter has not been realized. Indeed, the change of wording would seem to have made little if any practical difference. My second observation regards the potential for the realization of human capabilities under sustainable development clauses as they have emerged in FTAs to which the EU is a party. Provision for civil society voice seems a positive development, but its implementation has not enabled effective voice. Finally, with reference to the current draft of the EU-Canada Comprehensive Economic Trade Agreement (CETA)[67] and the preliminary text issued in respect of the EU–US Transatlantic Trade and Investment Partnership (TTIP),[68] I argue that the realization of HR and SD may not be best achieved by a single essential elements clause or a (marginalized) SD chapter in an FTA but rather by specific safeguards 'mainstreamed' into trade provisions.

---

[66] Van den Putte and Orbie (2015).

[67] Agreed text (not legally binding) is available at: http://ec.europa.eu/trade/policy/in-focus/ceta/. Accessed 12 Nov 2015.

[68] The most recent documentation was released by the European Commission on 6 November 2015, http://trade.ec.europa.eu/doclib/press/index.cfm?id=1393. Accessed 7 Nov 2015.

3.1 EU GSP Before and After

In 1994, the EU GSP regulatory framework made provision for tariff preferences to be temporarily withdrawn in whole or in part in circumstances including the practice of any form of forced labour as defined in the Geneva Conventions of 25 September 1926 and 7 September 1956 and ILO Conventions Nos 29 and 105.[69] This provided the legal basis for subsequent withdrawal of trade preferences from Burma/Myanmar.[70] In 2001, a particular 'special incentive arrangements for the protection of labour rights' was introduced.[71] That arrangement was kept notionally separate from environment, development and drugs and there remained reference to 'fundamental' ILO Conventions[72] which enabled withdrawal from general preferences where there was a breach of core labour standards (or where prison labour was at issue).[73] Arguably, the 2001 Regulation, by offering specific protection of labour standards *per se*, rather than a general human rights clause or treatment of labour standards as a facet of sustainable development, was a superior approach to that which we generally see in trade agreements, enabling recognition of the specificity of labour-related issues, even if restricted to core labour standards. However, this was not to last long, given the successful challenge by India to the problematic drug arrangements.[74]

The EU's response to the findings of the WTO Appellate Body in that case was to incorporate the 'fundamental ILO Conventions' in an overarching 'special incentive arrangement for sustainable development and good governance chapter' (which has come to be known as 'GSP+')[75]; an approach that has been maintained in the current incarnation of the GSP.[76] However, whereas the 2008 GSP+

[69]See European Council Regulation 3281/94 *applying a four-year scheme of generalized tariff preferences (1995 to 1998) in respect of certain industrial products originating in developing countries,* O.J. L 348/1 (1994), Art. 9 and European Council Regulation 1256/96 *applying Article 6 of Regulations (EC) No 3281/94 and (EC) No 1256/96 on multiannual generalized tariff preferences schemes in respect of certain industrial and agricultural products originating in developing countries,* O.J. L 160/1 (1996), Art. 9.

[70]European Council Regulation 552/97 *temporarily withdrawing preferences from Myanmar,* O.J. L 085 (1997).

[71]European Council Regulation 2501/2001 *applying a scheme of generalised tariff preferences for the period from 1 January 2002 to 31 December 2004,* O.J. L 346/1 (2001), Art. 2 (b).

[72]Ibid., Art. 14 (2) and Art. 26.

[73]Presumably, the reference to prison labour was returned by virtue of its specific mention in Art. XX GATT.

[74]WTO, *European Communities - Conditions for the granting of Tariff Preferences to Developing Countries*, 7 April 2004, WT/DS246/AB/R.

[75]European Council Regulation 732/2008 *applying a scheme of generalised tariff preferences for the period from 1 January 2009 to 31 December 2011 and amending Regulations (EC) No 552/97, (EC) No 1933/2006 and Commission Regulations (EC) No 1100/2006 and (EC) No 964/2007,* O.J. L 211/1 (2008), Chapter 2, Section II.

[76]European Council Regulation 978/2012, *applying a scheme of generalised tariff preferences and repealing Council Regulation (EC) No 732/2008,* O.J. L 303/1 (2012).

Regulation concerned with 'effective implementation' of the core labour standards, the 2012 Regulation merely applies where there is no 'serious failure' to implement. Further, action to withdraw the special preferences is reliant on extreme breach of labour rights as identified by the ILO Committee on the Application of Standards in a 'special paragraph'. The result is that only Myanmar and Belarus have had general GSP benefits withdrawn and failure to effectively implement ILO Conventions has little impact on GSP+ eligibility.[77]

What is evident from this brief overview is that the shift in terminology to that of 'sustainable development' does not necessarily make a difference to the EU's approach or the outcomes of conditionality. Only core labour standards (what might have been termed properly HR) have been considered suitable as the subject of concern apart from prison labour—which could be regarded as a species of forced labour. It is notable that this was the case before the term sustainable development was used and remains the case afterwards (from 2008 onwards). More needs to be done than a change of title to ensure that a broader range of labour standards are protected.

3.2 Dialogue and Capability in SD Chapters

The 'sustainable development' chapters inserted by the EU into FTAs have introduced new mechanisms for monitoring their implementation. These mechanisms, although not identical in all agreements, tend to take two forms. The first is a 'Domestic Advisory Group' (or DAG) representing civil society reflecting broadly environmental, labour and business interests which advises on domestic concerns relating to the impact of the FTA on sustainable development. The second is a transnational 'Civil Society Dialogue' (CSD) which enables EU civil society representatives to meet with their counterparts in the other State parties so as to discuss implementation of the sustainable development chapter.[78] These mechanisms might seem to offer the potential for coalitions between labour and other representatives within a broader frame of sustainable development offering consolidation of voice. Indeed, there is scope here to see a sustainability approach as enhancing 'capability' for social actors on the ground, so that they can realize their own vision of development.[79]

While such an approach could have benefits, there are also risks. One is that the local domestic actors lack the capacity to perform the role that they have been given.

---

[77]See Vogt (2015), p. 287 who notes at p. 298 that Georgia was granted GSP+ status despite ongoing violations of ILO standards.

[78]For a (critical) overview of their operation, see the ETUI Policy Brief by Van den Putte et al. on the social face of EU FTAs http://www.ugent.be/ps/politiekewetenschappen/en/research-groups/centre-for-eu-studies/news-events/news/etuipolicybrief. Accessed 13 Nov 2015.

[79]Cf. Sen (1999) and Nussbaum (2000) discussed above. See also ILO (2013), pp. 105–106.

Such a concern has recently been highlighted by Franz Ebert who notes that the DAG under the EU-Korea FTA, which is the longest in operation, has been plagued by 'concerns regarding the independence of civil society representatives, and reluctance of the Korea Government to engage with civil society'.[80] His suggestion is that the DAG mechanism can only work if the EU, as the US has started to do, devotes development aid to the active building of such capacity. If we are to give a richer and more nuanced understanding to SD, incorporating understandings of 'development as freedom' (as taken from Sen) together with Nussbaum's treatment of affiliation, some correction of this state of affairs is vital.[81]

There is also a lack of linkage between the operations of the DAG or CSD and action regarding compliance. Karin Ulmer has noted that participation in Korean DAG and CSD proves 'time-intensive' for NGOs and trade unions alike, but is thwarted by the fact that any recommendations made are unenforceable.[82] If States (or the EU) are not likely to act under the wider dispute settlement mechanisms, the purpose of civil society engagement is lost and genuine participation and voice is likely to fade.

The request of the EU DAG to the EU Commission to activate dispute settlement under the EU-Korea agreement in 2014 could be seen as a mark of its success, given that it led to re-engagement with ILO standards, and in particular the need to ratify ILO Conventions on forced labour and freedom of association.[83] Nevertheless, the fact of ratification still seems some way off. Given that the EU-Korea FTA has been in force for 4 years, this is hardly rapid progress towards improvement of labour standards.

3.3 Chapters and Mainstreaming: CETA and TTIP

Third and finally, there may be a danger in expecting the mere inclusion of an SD chapter to achieve all the objectives of SD identified above. This may be illustrated by analysis of the sustainable development chapter (Chapter 22) linked to chapters on 'trade and labour' (Chapter 23) and on 'trade and environment' (Chapter 24) in CETA, the full text of which is available as at February 2016,[84] and a comparable set of provisions now proposed by the Commission in respect of TTIP.[85]

[80]Ebert (2016), p. 412.

[81]See again Sen (1999) and Nussbaum (2003).

[82]Ulmer (2015), pp. 320–321.

[83]See the record of the September 2015 CSD meeting. http://www.eesc.europa.eu/resources/docs/eu-korea-csf-conclusions_september-2015_en_final-version.pdf. Accessed 13 Nov 2015.

[84]See http://trade.ec.europa.eu/doclib/docs/2016/february/tradoc_154329.pdf. Accessed 21 Mar 2016.

[85]EU Textual Proposal, 'Trade and Sustainable Development' set out at http://trade.ec.europa.eu/doclib/docs/2015/november/tradoc_153923.pdf. Accessed 13 Nov 2015. See especially Section 2, but note that implementation measures are yet to be proposed. Note that this is an interesting contrast to the now (as of 5 Nov 2015) released draft of the text of the Trans-Pacific Partnership

Notably, human rights clauses have been a rarity between developed countries and, even when agreed in trade agreements, have seldom been invoked by the EU to suspend trade benefits.[86] In the text of CETA (still to be ratified) and the Commission's proposal for TTIP, the decision to opt for supplementary SD chapters which incorporate labour standards is then very interesting indeed.[87]

In some ways, these two texts are, from an SD perspective, much that we might wish for. They include not only the core labour standards mentioned in the 1998 Declaration but also key aspects of the Decent Work Agenda.[88] There is likewise stress placed on the desire of both parties to 'continue to improve those laws and policies' and a 'right to regulate',[89] such that there will not be static minimal levels of protection but dynamic enhancement of work-related protections. Provision for a civil society dialogue and potential engagement with labour law expertise accompanies the CETA chapters,[90] while under the Commission's proposed SD chapter for TTIP civil society is to be engaged in the delivery of transparency and public participation measures (for trade and investment) and in the review of 'sustainability' impacts.[91] However, this apparent promotion of SD may cloak other deficiencies in the drafting of these trade instruments.

The Commission has said that fuller proposals for enforcement of the TTIP SD chapter will be offered in later negotiations.[92] However, one might wonder whether either side of an EU-Canada or EU-US agreement would actually make use of dispute settlement procedure provided with reference to labour standards, or whether the parties are more likely to reach the political settlement that will always be permitted, leaving civil society (or labour law experts) a role in making recommendations but possibly achieving little else. It remains entirely possible that labour-related issues will be 'traded off' against other trade interests and that

(TPP) to which the US is a party which only refers to core labour standards from the 1998 Declaration in a 'Labour' chapter (Chapter 19), mentioning none of the ILO Conventions (to which the Commission's TTIP draft refers).

[86]Bartels (2005), pp. 32–40.

[87]European Commission DG for Trade (2015) EU to pursue the most ambitious sustainable development, labour and environmental provisions in TTIP, Press Release. See also European Commission DG Trade (2015) Trade for all: Towards a more responsible trade and investment policy EU, pp. 22–26.

[88]Part 24 and Art. 3 CETA and TTIP 'Trade and Sustainable Development' Proposal, Art. 4 and Art. 5; although greater attention is paid to the minutiae of all the core labour standards in Art. 5–8.

[89]Part 24 and Art. 2 CETA and TTIP 'Trade and Sustainable Development' Proposal, Section 1, Art. 3.

[90]Chapter 22, Art. 22.5 CETA refers to a joint 'Civil Society Forum' which the Parties shall facilitate to be convened once a year and Chapter 23, Art. 23.10 makes provision for a 'Panel of Experts' with 'specialised knowledge in labour law, other issues addressed in [...the SD chapter...], or the resolution of disputes arising under international agreements'.

[91]TTIP, 'Trade and Sustainable Development' Proposal, Section 1, Art. 18 and 19 respectively.

[92]http://trade.ec.europa.eu/doclib/press/index.cfm?id=1393. Accessed 13 Nov 2015.

problems with enforcement identified in respect of the EU-Korea FTA will reoccur here.[93]

Further, neither the CETA nor the proposed TTIP SD chapter, makes direct reference to the ways in which trade rules may impact on labour standards. Experience in the EU regarding the application of trade rules might make us cautious in this respect. The comparison between the EU and other inter-State trade regimes (such as those arising under the WTO or by virtue of WTO recognised FTAs) is not straightforward in that EU law enables private actors to defend their entitlements, whereas these other agreements are a species of public international law whereby the onus is usually on States to act. However, the impacts of trade law on work have been more fully explored under EU law[94] and bring an interesting point of reference for understanding the effects of WTO and FTA rules and operations. In particular, warning bells ring when we consider cases like *Viking*[95] relating to the desire of employers to prevent strikes which would obstruct opportunities for establishment and investment and *Laval*[96] which suggests that a service provider should always know in advance what the costs of carrying out a business abroad will be. We are now aware of various examples where labour standards have been identified by private corporate investors as the basis of illegitimate 'indirect expropriation' and challenged through arbitral proceedings under bilateral investment treaties (BITs). Examples include *Noble Ventures v Romania* (in 2005—concerning the alleged failure of the Romanian state to adequately prevent or police unlawful strikes)[97] and *Veolia v Egypt* (raised in 2012 and still ongoing at the time of writing—concerning a rise of the monthly minimum wage).[98]

These precedents would seem to indicate that protection of labour standards may need to be embedded in the core trade rules relating to investment and services (as opposed to being placed in a discrete chapter towards the end of a lengthy document). Claims need to be able to be brought by workers and their organisations akin to the voice given to investors; and there needs to be capacity for trade unions to respond to State and investor claims regarding breaches of trade provisions which would have implications for labour standards. Freedom of speech, freedom of association and access to justice demands as much. In this respect, Goal 8 and Goal 16 of the new Sustainable Development Goals adopted by the UN General

---

[93]Discussed in Sect. 3.2 of this chapter above.

[94]See recently, Freedland and Prassl (2014), Countouris and Freedland (2013) and Evju (2013a, b).

[95]CJEU, *Case C-438/05 ITF and FSU v Viking Line*, 11 Dec 2007, EU:C:2007:772.

[96]CJEU, *Case C-341/05 Laval un Partneri v Svenska Byggnadsarbetareförbundet*, 18 Dec 2007, EU:C:2007:809. See for the further application of this principle in respect of the status of collective agreements and their enforceability in the context of public procurement, CJEU, *Case C-346/06 Rüffert v Land Niedersachsen*, 3 Apr 2008, EU:C:2008:189.

[97]Available at http://www.italaw.com/documents/Noble.pdf. Accessed 15 Nov 2015. Note the case was decided in Romania's favour after arbitration.

[98]For the ICSID case reference see http://www.italaw.com/cases/2101. Accessed 12 Nov 2015. Not yet concluded. See discussion available at http://aftinet.org.au/cms/veolia-vs-egypt-workers-2014. Accessed 13 Nov 2015.

Assembly on 25 September 2015 have particular significance. Otherwise, it is arguable that, whether formally referred to in terms of HR or SD, labour standards will be meaningless.

4 Conclusion

The use of SD chapters in trade agreements to incorporate labour standards is not objectionable *per se*. Indeed, it offers opportunities to add to a HR discourse centred on core labour rights enabling to a broader, more inclusive approach to a Decent Work Agenda. Inclusion of labour interests alongside those of the environment, economy and even culture need not preclude prioritisation of the most compelling claims by labour or eclipse the necessity of protection of some labour rights as human rights. There is scope within a SD frame to utilise trade union strength within society to promote a dynamic, forward looking and durable approach to trade. However, the realization of SD is not straightforward.

A brief investigation of the practical application of SD to trade and labour standards has led here to three preliminary observations. First, the use of the language of SD in trade instruments does not offer any guarantees that worker protections will be enhanced; this is evident from EU GSP which does not go beyond the core labour standards and associated ILO Conventions. Second, while SD opens vistas to human freedom and capability, leading to constructive dialogue and genuine voice regarding the labour implications of trade agreements, we need to build capacity on the ground for this to become any kind of reality. The establishment of institutions without this infrastructure cannot achieve SD. Third, to achieve HR protections and SD, labour standards need to be mainstreamed into the terms of trade. They need to operate as an ongoing limit on trade freedoms claimed by States and private actors. In this respect, a discrete chapter at the end of an FTA titled 'SD' is too weak a device. Instead, labour standards have to be foregrounded in a preliminary section, understood to inform all aspects of the agreement and be actionable by workers and their representatives. SD may be a worthy ambition, but its current manifestation in trade instruments seems unlikely to promote greater protection of labour standards.

References

Alston P (2004) 'Core labour standards' and the transformation of the international labour rights regime. Eur J Int Law 15:457–521

Alston P (2005) Facing up to the complexities of the ILO's core labour standards agenda. Eur J Int Law 16:467–480

Backer LC (2014) The Trans-Pacific Partnership: Japan, China, the U.S., and the emerging shape of a new world trade regulatory order. Wash Univ Glob Stud Law Rev 13:049

Barral V (2012) Sustainable development in international law: nature and operation of an evolutive legal norm. Eur J Int Law 23(2):377–400
Bartels L (2003) The WTO enabling clause and positive conditionality in the European Community's GSP program. J Int Econ Law 6(2):507–532
Bartels L (2005) Human rights conditionality in the EU's international agreements. Oxford University Press, Oxford
Bartels L (2012) Human rights and sustainable development obligations in EU free trade agreements. Legal studies research paper series, University of Cambridge Faculty of Law, Paper No. 24/2012
Bellace J (2014) The ILO and the right to strike. Int Labour Rev 153(1):29–70
Bogg A (2015) Labour law and the trade unions: autonomy and betrayal. In: Bogg A, Costello C, Davies ACL, Prassl J (eds) The autonomy of labour law. Hart Publishing, Oxford, pp 73–106
Churchill R, Khaliq U (2004) The collective complaints system of the European Social Charter - an effective mechanism for ensuring compliance with economic and social rights? Eur J Int Law 15(3):417–456
Countouris N, Freedland M (eds) (2013) Resocialising Europe in a time of crisis. Cambridge University Press, Cambridge
De Schutter O (2015) Trade in the service of sustainable development: linking trade to labour rights and environmental standards. Hart/Bloomsbury, Oxford
Deakin S, Wilkinson F (2005) The law of the labour market: industrialisation, employment and legal evolution. Oxford University Press, Oxford
Dworkin R (1977) Taking rights seriously. Duckworth, London
Ebert F (2016) Labour provisions in EU trade agreements: what potential for channelling labour standards-related capacity building? Int Labour Rev 155(3):407–433
European Trade Union Confederation (2010) Resolution on a sustainable new deal for Europe and towards cancun. ETUC, Brussels
Evju S (ed) (2013a) Cross-border services, posting of workers, and multilevel governance. University of Oslo, Oslo
Evju S (ed) (2013b) Regulating transnational labour in Europe: the quandaries of multilevel governance. University of Oslo, Oslo
Ewing KD (1999) Social rights and constitutional law. Public Law:104–123
Fenwick C, Novitz T (2010) Regulating to protect workers' human rights. In: Fenwick C, Novitz T (eds) Human rights at work: perspectives on law and regulation. Hart Publishing, Oxford, pp 585–615
Freedland M, Prassl J (eds) (2014) Viking, laval and beyond. Hart Publising, Oxford
Fudge J (2007) The new discourse of labor rights: from social to fundamental rights? Comp Labor Law Policy J 29:29–66
Fudge J (2011) Labour law as a 'fictive commodity': radically reconceptualizing labour law. In: Davidov G, Langille B (eds) The idea of labour law. Oxford University Press, Oxford, pp 120–136
Galgoczi B (2014) The changing role of trade unions in the sustainable development agenda. Int Rev Sociol 24(1):59–68
Hare I (2002) Social rights as fundamental human rights. In: Hepple B (ed) Social and labour rights in a global context: international and comparative perspectives. Cambridge University Press, Cambridge, pp 153–181
Hepple B (2006) Labour laws and global trade. Hart Publishing, Oxford
Howse R (2003) Back to court after *Shrimp/Turtle?* Almost but not quite yet: India's short lived challenge to labor and environmental exceptions in the European Unions' generalized system of preferences. Am Univ Int Law Rev 18(6):1333–1381
ILO (2010) Cancun agreement: ILO highlights call for a 'Just Transition' with green jobs and decent work. ILO, Geneva
ILO (2012) Record of Proceedings, 101st ILC, Geneva
ILO (2013) Social dimensions of free trade agreements. ILO, Geneva

ILO (2014) Governing body employer proposal concerning the standards initiative. ILO, Geneva
ILO (2015) Tripartite Meeting Report, TMF APROC/2015/2, Geneva
Kelsey J (2008) Serving whose interests? The political economy of trade in services agreements. Routledge, Abingdon
Kelsey J (2013) The Trans-Pacific Partnership Agreement: a gold-plated gift to the global tobacco industry? Am J Law Med 39:237–264
La Hovary C (2013) Employers' group 2012 challenge to the right to strike. Ind Law J 42 (4):338–368
La Hovary C (2017) The ILO's mandate and capacity: creating, proliferating and supervising labour standards for a globalized economy. In: Gött H (ed) Labour standards in international economic law. Springer International Publishing, Cham, this volume
Langille B (2005) Core labour rights – the true story (reply to Alston). Eur J Int Law 16:409–437
Lund HL (2004) Strategies for sustainable business and the handling of workers' interests: integrated management systems and worker participation. Econ Ind Democr 25(1):41–74
Mantouvalou V (2012) Are labour rights human rights? Eur J Int Law 3(2):151–172
McCrudden C, Davies ACL (2000) A perspective on trade and labour rights. J Int Econ Law 3 (1):43–62
Murray J (2010) Taking social rights seriously: is there a case for institutional reform of the ILO? In: Fenwick C, Novitz T (eds) Human rights at work: perspectives on law and regulation. Hart Publishing, Oxford, pp 359–382
Novitz T (2002) Are social rights necessarily collective rights? A critical analysis of the collective complaints protocol to the European Social Charter. Eur Hum Rights Law Rev 1:50–66
Novitz T (2005) The European Union and international labour standards: the dynamics of dialogue between the EU and the ILO. In: Alston P (ed) Labour rights as human rights. Oxford University Press, Oxford, pp 214–241
Novitz T (2008) Legal power and normative sources in the field of social policy: normative power Europe at work? In: Orbie J (ed) Europe's global role: external policies of the European Union. Ashgate, Aldershot, pp 139–156
Novitz T (2012) Labour rights and property rights: implications for (and beyond) redundancy payments and pensions. Ind Law J 41:136–165
Novitz T (2014a) Information and communication technology and voice: constraint or capability? In: Bogg A, Novitz T (eds) Voices at work. Oxford University Press, Oxford, pp 436–454
Novitz T (2014b) The internationally recognized right to strike: a past, present, and future basis upon which to evaluate remedies for unlawful collective action? Int J Comp Labour Law Ind Relat 30(3):357–380
Novitz T (2014c) Evolutionary trajectories for transnational labour law: trade in goods to trade in services? Curr Leg Probl 67:239–271
Novitz T (2015) The paradigm of sustainability in a European social context: collective participation in protection of future interests? Int J Comp Labour Law Ind Relat 31(3):243–262
Novitz T, Mangan D (eds) (2011) The role of labour standards in development: from theory to sustainable practice. British Academy/Oxford University Press, London, Oxford
Nussbaum M (1997) Capabilities and human rights. Fordham Law Rev 66:273–300
Nussbaum M (2000) Women and human development: the capabilities approach. Cambridge University Press, Cambridge
Nussbaum M (2003) Capabilities as fundamental entitlements: Sen and social justice. Fem Econ 9:33–59
Nussbaum M (2011) Creating capabilities: the human development approach. Belknap Press/ Harvard University Press, Cambridge (Mass)
O'Cinneide C, Liu K (2015) Defining the limits of discrimination law in the United Kingdom. Principle and pragmatism in tension. Int J Discrim Law 15(1–2):80–100
Orbie J, Gistelinck M, Kerremans B (2009) The social dimension of EU trade policies. In: Orbie J, Tortell L (eds) The European Union and the social dimension of globalization: how the EU influences the world. Routledge, Abingdon, pp 148–165

Räthzel N, Uzzell D (eds) (2013) Trade unions in the green economy. Routledge, Abingdon
Robinson J (2004) Squaring the circle? Some thoughts on the idea of sustainable development. Ecol Econ 48:369–384
Schrijver N (2008) The evolution of sustainable development in international law: inception, meaning and status. Martinus Nijhoff, Leiden/Boston
Sen A (1999) Development as freedom. Oxford University Press, Oxford
Summers C (2001) The battle in Seattle: free trade, labor rights and societal values. Univ Pa J Int Law 22:61–90
Supiot A (2010) A legal perspective on the economic crisis of 2008. Int Labour Rev 149 (2):151–162
Swepston L (2013) Crisis in the ILO supervisory system: dispute over the right to strike. Int J Comp Labour Law Ind Relat 29(2):199–218
Trades Union Congress (TUC) (2014) The union effect: greening the workplace. TUC, London
Tsogas G (2000) Labour standards in the generalized system of preference of the European Union and the United States. Eur J Ind Relat 6:349–370
Ulmer K (2015) Trade embedded development models. Int J Comp Labour Law Ind Relat 31 (3):305–329
Van den Putte L, Orbie J (2015) EU bilateral trade agreements and the surprising rise of labour provisions. Int J Comp Labour Law Ind Relat 31(3):263–283
Vandenhole W (2003) Completing the UN complaint mechanisms for human rights violations step by step: towards a complaints procedure complementing the international covenant on economic, social and cultural rights. Neth Q Hum Rights 21(3):423–465
Villiers C (2011) Directors' duties and the company's internal structures under the UK Companies Act 2006: obstacles for sustainable development. Int Comp Corp Law J 8:47–75
Vogt J (2015) A little less conversation: the EU and the (non) application of labour conditionality in the generalized system of preferences (GSP). Int J Comp Labour Law Ind Relat 31 (3):285–230
World Commission on Environment and Development (WECD) (1987) Our common future, The Brundtland Report. http://www.un-documents.net/our-common-future.pdf. Accessed 12 Nov 2015

Civil Society Meetings in EU Free Trade Agreements: The Purposes Unravelled

Jan Orbie, Lore Van den Putte, and Deborah Martens

Contents

Abstract In the last decade the EU has embarked on a series of deep and comprehensive Free Trade Agreements (FTAs). Each of these agreements includes a chapter on trade and sustainable development, encompassing labour (and environmental) provisions. Against the background of increased liberalization and rising attention paid to sustainable development, EU FTAs set up civil society mechanisms to advance the implementation of these commitments. While civil society meetings have become increasingly important in practice, the assessment of their success differs widely among actors. While some see it as a 'fig leaf' or 'talking shop', others are more optimistic about its potential to empower marginalised groups within EU trading partners. Evaluations will continue to diverge as long as the exact purposes of the civil society meetings have not been clarified. This chapter is a first attempt to uncover the purposes behind them. By combining a content analysis on the legal texts and political discourse we identify four

The authors would like to thank the participants of the Conference on Labour Standards in International Economic Law (Göttingen, 1–2 October 2015) and in particular Peter-Tobias Stoll and Henner Gött, for their comments, as well as Myriam Oehri and Ferdi de Ville for their substantial feedback.

J. Orbie (✉) • L. Van den Putte • D. Martens
Ghent University, Ghent, Belgium
e-mail: jan.orbie@ugent.be; lore.vandenputte@ugent.be; Deborah.Martens@UGent.be

H. Gött (ed.), *Labour Standards in International Economic Law*,
https://doi.org/10.1007/978-3-319-69447-4_8

analytically distinct purposes: instrumental (gathering support for the FTA), functional (monitoring and information gathering on the implementation), deliberative (promoting democratic governance) and policy influence (advising the governments). We do not aim to prioritise one purpose over another. However, we do argue that the primordial purpose of the mechanisms should depend on the domestic setting of the trade partner country and on the matureness of the mechanism.

1 Introduction

The European Union (EU) has always been one of the global frontrunners in trade policy. Since the 1990s two evolutions have taken place in this policy field. Not only has the labour dimension of EU trade agreements increased, at the same time civil society has become more important in trade policy discussions. Labour rights have been promoted in EU trade arrangements since the mid-1990s. While original references mostly referred to social security rights for migrant workers, in the past decade the EU has widened and deepened both the substance of and the approach to the trade-labour rights nexus through the inclusion of core labour standards as defined by the International Labour Organization (ILO) in its Generalized System of Preferences (GSP) and its bilateral trade agreements.[1] The substance has broadened from 'labour rights' to 'sustainable development', an evolution that is discussed in Novitz' contribution to this volume. Since the battle of Seattle in 1999, the involvement of civil society in EU trade policy debates has increased. In the last decade, with the advent of the so-called 'new generation of FTAs',[2] the involvement of civil society has become more important. In this chapter, we focus on a prominent manifestation of these two trends, the 'civil society meetings' set up to advance the labour (and environmental) objectives in EU trade agreements.

Such civil society meetings have become a standard element of the chapters on trade and sustainable development (SD Chapters) of the new generation of EU trade agreements. These meetings assign a central role to civil society (in particular labour, environmental and business groups) for discussing and monitoring sustainable development aspects of trade relations between the governments. While these civil society meetings seem to have become increasingly important, it remains unclear what their goal should be. Are they supposed to provide (binding?) recommendations for the governments? Or are the meetings intended to foster a dialogue between civil society members, some of whom may not have a voice within the domestic political landscape? Or should they focus primarily on the shortcomings in the governments' compliance with the agreement? Finally, and more cynically,

[1]See Van den Putte and Orbie (2015).

[2]In this chapter, the term 'Free Trade Agreement' covers all variations of preferential trade agreements concluded by the EU such as Association Agreements, Deep and Comprehensive Free Trade Agreements or Economic Partnership Agreements.

would we dare to say that the meetings essentially serve to buy off public support for the trade agreement?

Thus, our central question is what the aim(s) of the civil society meetings are. Academic research on the purpose(s) of these civil society mechanisms is timely for mainly two reasons. First of all, these meetings are a prominent feature of the so-called 'cooperative' EU approach, which emphasises dialogue and cooperation over the so-called 'sanctions-based' approach of the US (and Canada).[3] While US and Canadian trade agreements include some civil society involvement, it is clearly more elaborated in EU agreements.[4] Much criticism has focused on whether this 'soft' approach of the EU can be effective,[5] but empirical or theoretical research into the potential contribution of the civil society meetings is quasi-absent.[6] Second, the International Institute for Labour Studies pointed out that the inclusion of civil society in the implementation of labour provisions could be a way to make the social dimension of bilateral trade agreements more effective.[7] This can not only increase the legitimacy of the labour provisions, but it could also provide the trade partners with additional expertise.

A debate on the relevance of these meetings has started to emerge in policy circles and in academia. While some see it as a 'fig leaf' or 'talking shop', others (not surprisingly also the European Commission) are more optimistic. However, evaluations will continue to diverge as long as the exact purposes of the civil society meetings have not been clarified. Lacking clear benchmarks about how to evaluate success, the debate on whether the civil society meetings have at least the potential for improving labour rights will remain inconclusive and speculative.

This chapter aims to provide a better guide in this debate by dissecting the different purposes that can be (and have been) ascribed to the civil society meetings. We will show that the civil society meetings can serve four analytically distinct purposes: instrumental (gathering support for the free trade agreement), functional (monitoring & information gathering on the implementation), deliberative (promoting democratic governance) and policy purposes (advising the governments). Two notes of caution need to be mentioned. First, we look at formal as well as informal purposes. While some are derived from legal texts, others are based on political discourse. Second, the four purposes are not mutually exclusive. They can co-exist, interrelate and even reinforce each other. However, the analytical

---

[3]See Oehri (2014) and Postnikov and Bastiaens (2014).

[4]The US tradition of involving civil society in the trade-labour nexus, both domestically and in relation to the trade partner country, dates back to the 1990s but differs from the recent EU civil society meetings in many ways. For more information, see Van den Putte (2015). In addition, it is interesting to note that these civil society mechanisms are becoming a global trend, as we recently witnessed in the labour chapter of the Trans-Pacific Partnership.

[5]See Burgoon (2009), Horn et al. (2010), Orbie and Van Roozendaal (2017), Meunier and Nicolaïdis (2006) and Vogt (2014).

[6]One of the exceptions is the research by Postnikov and Bastiaens (2014). However, this deals with civil society involvement in general in the implementation of EU trade agreements.

[7]IILS (2013).

distinction between them will prove to be useful since some actors emphasise certain purposes more than others. Moreover, it is not inconceivable that conflicts between different purposes emerge. For example, the need for an open discussion and wide representation of civil society might be more important from a 'democratic governance' than from a 'monitoring and information' perspective.

The purposes are based on a content analysis of official documents (including legal text of the trade agreements), speeches (including debates in the European Parliament) and interviews with actors involved in the civil society meetings. The next section briefly discusses the establishment of civil society meetings under the SD chapters of EU trade agreements. Subsequently, we elaborate on each of the four purposes. Finally, we end with conclusions and a research agenda.

2 Civil Society and EU Free Trade Agreements

For a long time, trade was a relatively shielded policy domain involving mostly officials of the European Commission, senior experts of the member states and lobbyists from specific business interests. However, organizations independent from the state (here broadly referred to as 'civil society'[8]) have become increasingly involved in discussions on EU trade policy. The institutionalized involvement of civil society in EU trade agreements is a relatively new phenomenon. As mentioned in the introduction, it is also distinctive to the EU's approach to trade policy-making, as opposed to other trading powers such as the US and Canada. The inclusion of civil society in EU trade policy can be traced back to external and internal factors.[9] Externally, there are the protests against trade liberalization since the famous protest during the Ministerial Conference of the World Trade Organization (WTO) in Seattle, when it became clear that trade policy goes beyond tariffs and has a strong impact on aspects of daily life. This 'battle of Seattle' made it clear to trade policy-makers that discussions with civil society are important in order to gain public support for trade agreements. The EU's negotiations of Economic Partnership Agreements with its former colonies, which started in 2002 and are still ongoing for some countries, further fuelled civil society criticism against the

[8]'Civil society' and 'non state actors' are fuzzy concepts. The definition of civil society is often vague and diverse in EU policy documents. It is used as a container concept, encompassing such diverse actors as trade unions, NGOs and the private sector, see Peels (2012). In this paper we adapt the European Commission definition of civil society being comprised of a very wide range of actors see European Commission (2012b). These include: community-based organizations, non-governmental organizations, faith-based organizations, foundations, research institutions, Gender and LGBT organizations, cooperatives, professional and business associations, and the not-for-profit media, trade unions and employers' organizations.

[9]Armstrong (2002), Slob and Smakman (2007) and Smismans (2003).

'undemocratic' and 'neoliberal' tendencies of EU trade policy.[10] Internally, the EU has suffered from a democratic deficit in the face of the perceived alienation of the Commission from the wider public.[11] From the very beginning of European integration, the European Commission has been eager to consult external interests and experts. Besides its constant need for expertise, the Commission's chronic understaffing attracted it to the idea of gaining diverse stakeholders as allies for its legislative proposals. However, the participation of civil society organizations to EU policy was characterised as 'participation by grace and favour' meaning that it hinged largely upon the discretion of individual civil servants.[12] Thus, from a normative perspective, the creation of formal civil society platforms can be seen as an inclusive evolution that improves the democratic character of the EU.

Against this background, DG Trade organised the first Trade Civil Society Dialogue in 1998. The process, promoted mainly by political entrepreneurs such as Trade Commissioner Pascal Lamy and his Director for civil society relations Robert Madelin, was intended to provide a regular and structured approach to discussing EU trade issues with European civil society organizations.[13] The discussions take place in face-to-face meetings including Commission officials from DG Trade and other DGs working in relevant policy areas. Since it was created the Civil Society Dialogue has been reassessed several times. Even though the participants' expectations are partially met, and those who engage in the process see its value, there are underlying frustrations. One of the main frustrations is (and has been) the perceived lack of influence.[14]

Also in its external relations, the EU started to emphasize the involvement of civil society more. Already in the EU-Chile Association Agreement (signed in 2002) civil society mechanisms were mentioned. The EU-CARIFORUM agreement (2008) created a Consultative Committee, which is composed of representatives of civil society of both Parties. The 2010 EU trade strategy 'Trade, Growth and World Affairs' explicitly refers to cooperation of the Commission with civil society in the context of sustainable development.[15] However, it is only since the South-Korea agreement (2010)[16] that these civil society mechanisms have become a standard and quite prominent feature of EU trade agreements and more

---

[10]Del Felice (2014).

[11]Slob and Smakman (2007).

[12]Friedrich (2008).

[13]Kohler-Koch and Quittkat (2013).

[14]Coffey (2014) and Slob and Smakman (2007).

[15]European Commission (2010).

[16]Apart from the agreement with South-Korea, provisions for civil society meetings have been formally mentioned in all the concluded agreements, namely Peru-Colombia (2012), Central America (2012), Ukraine (2014), Georgia (2014), Moldova (2014), Singapore (2014), Canada (2014) and Vietnam (2015). In practice, civil society meetings have only taken place so far in the context of the agreements with CARIFORUM, South-Korea, Peru-Colombia, Central America, and Moldova.

specifically of the SD chapter.[17] Such a chapter is included in all of the EU's new generation 'deep and comprehensive' trade agreements. In this chapter, the parties commit to adhere to several international environmental and labour conventions as well as certain sustainability principles. Specifically, the agreements foresee the set-up of domestic and transnational civil society meetings. More concretely, each Party convenes a domestic advisory group (DAG) that consist of a selected number of civil society organizations representing specific interests. For example the EU-Central America agreement stipulates that

> The Advisory Groups of the Parties shall comprise independent representative organizations, in a balanced representation of economic, social and environmental stakeholders including, among others, employers and workers organizations, business associations, non-governmental organizations and local public authorities (Art. 294.4).

In addition to these DAGs, transnational civil societies are also established in the SD Chapters. Here civil society organizations of both Parties meet. In the case of the EU-Central America agreement

> The Parties agree to organise and facilitate a bi-regional Civil Society Dialogue Forum for open dialogue, with a balanced representation of environmental, economic and social stakeholders (Art. 295.1).

Even though based on the same template, there is variation in SD chapters and in the constellations and organization of the domestic and transnational civil society meetings of the different EU trade agreements.[18] In addition to the variation in formal provisions between the agreements (*de jure* component), the implementation and thus *de facto* realisation of the civil society meetings differ as well, leading to an even more complex ensemble of civil society meetings in EU trade agreements. More fundamentally, it is not always clear for which purpose the civil society meetings have been established. Whereas there is a vague but common understanding that they should give a human face to free trade, correct the negative impact of liberalization, contribute to sustainable development, and be involved in decision-making on this topic, it remains unclear what exactly is (are) the (main) purpose(s) of the meetings. Since different concerned actors attribute different purposes to the civil society meetings, it is essential to distinguish and understand the implications of these purposes.

---

[17]Other forms of civil society involvement, also outside the SD chapter, are possible but will not be discussed in this chapter. The Cotonou Agreement (2000) with the ACP countries was the first EU agreement providing ample attention to the involvement of 'non-state actors', albeit not specifically in the context of trade. The recently concluded Association Agreements (Central America, Ukraine, Moldova and Georgia) establish additional civil society meetings in the General Provisions. In contrast to the civil society meetings discussed in this chapter, their agenda not specifically related to trade. The EU-Canada Comprehensive Economic and Trade Agreement (CETA) and draft Transatlantic Trade and Investment Partnership (TTIP) suggest stakeholder consultation concerning regulatory cooperation.

[18]Delving into these small but significant differences would divert us from the objective of this contribution. Therefore, we will not discuss this further.

3 Purposes of Civil Society Meetings

In this section, we will show that the civil society meetings can serve four analytically distinct purposes. Partly drawing on Friedrich,[19] we make a distinction between instrumental (gathering support for the free trade agreement), functional (monitoring & information gathering on the implementation), deliberative (promoting democratic governance) and policy influence (advising the governments) purposes. Hereafter we set out each purpose, illustrating it with quotes from the agreements and from different actors involved in the meetings.

3.1 Instrumental Purpose: Supporting the Free Trade Agreement

Civil society meetings have arguably been established in order to guarantee political support for EU trade agreements. Since the Global Europe trade communication in 2006 the EU has been negotiating trade agreements at a tremendous pace. Indeed, the EU is a strong proponent of the view that trade liberalization is necessary for economic growth (especially since the crisis).[20] This new generation of FTAs struggles with a tension between the creation of an economic project that focusses on global expansion and competition and a political project that pays attention to concerns such as social justice and sustainability.[21] It is therefore not surprising that FTAs have become increasingly contested by civil society organizations. Overall there is generally a mistrust and opposition of labour, human rights and environmental groups against trade liberalization.[22]

The growing politicisation of trade agreements already became clear with the protests in Seattle (1999) against the launch of a new round of WTO trade negotiations as mentioned above and with the 'Stop EPA Campaign' (2006) against the Economic Partnership Agreements (EPAs) between the EU and the countries from Africa, the Caribbean and the Pacific (ACP). Apart from civil society movements (both in the EU as well as in trade partner countries), members of the European Parliament (EP) have voiced critical concerns. The Lisbon treaty, which entered into force in late 2009, increased the competences of the EP. Due to its enhanced formal role, the EP should be regularly updated on where negotiations are going and is required to give its consent to any trade agreement. The rejection of the ACTA sent a clear message that the EP is able and willing to use its additional power.[23] In this capacity, the EP has repeatedly

[19]Friedrich (2008).

[20]European Commission (2006, 2010, 2015) and Siles-Brügge (2011).

[21]Ford (2013) and Ulmer (2015).

[22]EESC (2012).

[23]Van den Putte et al. (2014).

emphasised her requirements concerning the inclusion of human and labour rights and civil society involvement in trade agreements through resolutions as well as oral and written questions.[24]

In the run up to the EU-Peru-Colombia FTA, the EP, concerned about the human rights situation in those countries, explicitly advocated on several occasions a 'strengthening of the monitoring and dispute settlement mechanisms for breaches of human rights and sustainable development and the involvement of civil society in the implementation process'.[25] In response to this, European Commission officials and trade commissioners often stress the inclusion of such mechanisms in speeches. During the debate in the EP on the same, FTA Commissioner De Gucht had to reply to requirements such as

> Against this background, Parliament is, of course, investigating very carefully, [. . .] whether this trade agreement with Colombia and Peru meets these requirements [. . .]. The issues include the extent to which civil society is included in the process of implementing the trade agreement, the independence of its involvement and the options for instigating complaint procedures.

And along the same line:

> We also want to see both in Peru and Colombia the establishment of permanent institutionalised mechanisms that guarantee the role of civil society.[26]

Since the start of the negotiations on a Transatlantic Trade and Investment Partnership (TTIP) in 2013, public scrutiny of EU trade negotiations has only increased.[27] While some oppose 'neoliberal' free trade per se, others warn against the possible negative social impact of free trade if its development is not managed well. Creating civil society meetings in the context of the SD chapter indicates not only that the trade agreements have a social and environmental face, but also that the parties intend to involve civil society actors in policy-making on these issues. It solidifies the belief that the EU and the third country government are not only interested in free trade, but also in a genuine partnership that promotes sustainable development. This could foster a broader support for the overall trade agreement, including its liberalization schedules and regulatory commitments. At least, it signals the parties' intention to balance these market-enhancing provisions with more interventionist policies. Or to put it in Commissioner De Gucht's words:

---

[24]European Parliament Resolution 2009/2219(INI) *on human rights and social and environmental standards in international trade agreements*, P7 TA(2010)0434 and European Parliament Resolution 2010/2026 (INI) *on the European Union's trade relations with Latin America*, P7_TA (2010)0387.

[25]Council Note 9463/12 *Summary record of the meeting of the European Parliament's Committee on International Trade (INTA)*, 25–26 Apr 2012, p. 5.

[26]European Parliament Debate *on the EU trade agreement with Columbia and Peru*, CRE 22/05/ 2012-14.

[27]De Ville and Siles-Brugge (2015).

> With all of these safeguards, I hope you will agree that the agreement is strong enough to ensure that the parties' commitments on labour, human rights and the environment are consistently upheld.[28]

At most, it suggests that trade and non-trade objectives are compatible and mutually reinforcing. In this view, trade liberalization will be beneficial for sustainable development, and the civil society meetings play a role in this achievement. As is stated in the EU-Peru-Colombia trade agreement:

> The Parties recognise international trade, productive employment and decent work for all as key elements for managing the process of globalisation, and reaffirm their commitments to promote the development of international trade in a way that contributes to productive employment and decent work for all. (Art. 269.1)

The literature on global governance has long recognized that involving public participation in global governance arrangements (such as a trade agreement) can help to improve the democratic legitimacy of such arrangements.[29]

Not surprisingly, however, this purpose can also be interpreted in a less optimistic manner. Some observers have lamented the SD chapter and the civil society meetings as a 'fig leaf'. The criticism reads that these ostensibly progressive elements effectively hide the real objectives of the agreement, which are to create free trade in line with the economic priorities of the parties (and particularly of the EU which is usually the stronger partner). They may indeed forge a broader support for the approval of the agreement, thereby helping the parties to 'sell' the agreement to their constituencies and can thus be reduced to a PR stunt to improve the reputation of the trading partners. Questions can be raised about whether they will effectively be implemented once the ratification has been secured. In this regard one Peruvian NGO representative remarked that the EU civil society mechanisms are not designed for civil society to monitor the implementation of labour norms, but rather as a good news show for governments to show civil society which actions they have undertaken in the past months (2015).

Moreover, a perverse effect from the establishment of civil society meetings may be that potential critics are being co-opted. By involving civil society in the implementation mechanism of an agreement to which they are opposed, opposition can be diluted and neutralized. Civil society is in this case again confronted with the insider versus outsider dilemma.[30] One participant of these civil society meetings expressed it as follows:

> You see, this is a governmental process and then we're asked to come in already to basically defend these free trade agreements. Now many of us [...] have substantial conflicts and issues with the kind of free trade agreements and the economic agenda behind it. And for the Commission, for the government, this is a way to say we're smoothing with the edges and we get civil society in there and they can help us to address the worst issues. But the fundamental drivers and the way we design trade relations remain contentious. At least for us. [...] It's a way to invite the protest on the street into the agreement[31]

---

[28]De Gucht (2012).

[29]Meunier (2003) and Scholte (2004).

[30]Spalding (2008).

[31]European NGO (2014).

Our own participatory observation also showed that organizations in Colombia, when engaging in a dialogue with the EU, discipline each other in coming forward with constructive proposals on the basis of acceptance of the agreement instead of continued questioning of free trade. This was also confirmed in other research where groups who at the start wanted to challenge the neoliberal paradigm, were transformed during the process.[32]

According to this purpose the outcome of the meetings is not that important: what counts is merely the fact that civil society is involved in the implementation. It will be successful if it has managed to neutralize opposition against the trade agreement. However, other purposes come to the fore once an agreement has been ratified, as will be explained in the next section.

3.2 Functional Purpose: Monitoring and Information

Second, the civil society meetings were established to monitor the implementation of the SD chapter, report on the advancements and signal possible defaults. This monitoring and gathering of information is seen as an important purpose both in the texts of the agreements, as they are sometimes included under the heading 'institutional and monitoring mechanism', as well as in EU discourse. For example, former trade commissioner Karel De Gucht stated that the goal is to raise concerns: 'As governments we will depend on their active support in bringing their concerns on labour or environmental matters to our attention'.[33] The EU's current trade commissioner, the Swede Cecilia Malmström, puts it like this: 'We also need to make sure that civil society and business organizations are properly consulted and integrated in our work so we have the right information'.[34] Involved civil society actors also confirm this role as illustrated in the minutes of a EU-Central American civil society meeting: 'Those present reiterated their commitment to fulfilling the role laid down in the Trade and Sustainable Development Title of the Association Agreement, namely to monitor implementation of the Title and to provide advice to the Parties to the Agreement'.[35] (The mentioned purpose 'providing advice' will be handled as a separate purpose in a distinct section below).

According to this logic, civil society organizations are experts on the ground who bring together information and can detect and then signal problems with implementation. This implies that the EU and the partner country delegate the monitoring of the implementation of the sustainable development commitments (partly) to the civil society bodies. This might be more efficient given that these often have more expertise on the ground than the parties do. For example, the

[32]Hopewell (2015).

[33]De Gucht (2012).

[34]Malmström (2015).

[35]EESC (2015).

European Commission and its DG Trade have been criticized for not having sufficient expertise in monitoring the sustainable development and human rights conventions of the GSP(plus) system, whilst relying mostly on a superficial assessment of the reports of international monitoring bodies (such as the ILO).[36]

Their monitoring and information role does not necessarily mean that civil society can advise the governments on policy matters. Although policy advice may be the ultimate goal (see below), this purpose is analytically distinct from monitoring and information gathering. According to the monitoring task civil society should provide information without giving indications as to what should be done with it by the governments. The main goal of the meetings is then not to provide concrete recommendations for cooperation as such (and thus to make sure that the provisions are implemented) but rather to provide information and detect problems (and thus to verify whether the provisions are not violated). To some extent civil society organizations are the ears and eyes of the European Commission and its trading partners on the ground; and it is up to the parties to decide how the information will be followed up. In the EU-Central American Association Agreement this resulted in the following explicit footnote: 'For greater certainty, policy making and other such typical government functions shall not be delegated to the Civil Society Dialogue Forum' (2012).

3.3 *Deliberative Purpose: Dialogue and Deliberation*

Third, the civil society meetings aim to provide a forum for dialogue and deliberation, thereby contributing to the purpose of democratic governance. Instead of emphasizing effective monitoring (outcome-oriented goal), this purpose emphasizes more the intrinsic democratic and empowering potential of the discussions with(in) civil society (process-oriented purpose). In other words, organizing a structured dialogue between members of civil society and/or with the government (s) is seen to contribute to the democratic quality of the agreement and the quality of democracy in general. This is not so much about the substance of the discussions (sustainable development in a trade context) but most of all about the (deliberative) process in which this is addressed. Not only is it important to engage in a dialogue between the governmental parties to the agreement, but members of civil society should also be involved in open and transparent discussions on the trade agreement. The underlying assumption of such a 'governance' approach is that it makes the political decision-making system more democratic.[37] The increased democratic potential relates to the openness of the discussions and the involvement of non-governmental actors, which would ultimately also lead to better decisions.

[36]Orbie and Tortell (2009) and Velluti (2016).

[37]Scholte (2001).

According to suggestions by some actors, the civil society meetings should open up space for an open and critical dialogue beyond the (governmental) parties of the agreement. Their main added value, according to this perspective, lies not so much in the monitoring of compliance with labour standards, but more fundamentally in their potential to foster a better understanding of common concerns. For example, the document on the EU DAG for the Korea agreement states: 'In spite of the differences in terms of culture and approaches, both parties showed a strong willingness to have a dialogue and reach reciprocal understanding.'[38] The rules of procedure of the EU-Korea Civil Society Forum stipulate: 'The Civil Society Forum is a platform in which the organizations of civil society in Korea and in the European Union can exchange views and discuss matters related to the sustainable development aspects of the trade relations between the parties.' Participants of the EU-Korea civil society meetings confirm:

> A key objective should be to devise a system for continuous improvement of standards, with a monitoring mechanism including representative and independent social partners. So far as the monitoring mechanism is concerned, we believe that the Domestic Advisory Groups and Civil Society Forum set up under EU-Korea provides the foundation on which to build, though specific issues have arisen such as the representativeness of members.[39]

The notion of 'dialogue' is also referred to in the EU-Peru-Colombia agreement, where Art. 282 includes 'a session with civil society organizations and the public at large, in order to carry out a dialogue on matters related to the implementation of this Title' as well as in the EU-Central America Agreement Art. 195 (2): '[. . .] the Civil Society Dialogue Forum may express its views and opinions in order to promote dialogue on how to better achieve the objectives of this Title.'

Perhaps even more importantly, these dialogues can empower certain civil society actors. While the process of empowerment is typically a process that should originate from the inside, actors like the EU can facilitate this process by promoting social dialogue or establish venues for participation.[40] They make it possible for previously marginalized actors to transcend the domestic political arena and have their voice heard within a wider, transnational setting. They create a new 'opportunity structure' which creates possibilities for actors to raise their concerns and understand the power structures they are a part of. The head of the Unit on GSP and Sustainable Development puts it like this: 'But we do think that this is a very important element, and it is thanks to our FTA that we have given a voice to those trade unions in the trade context on labour rights.'[41] Commissioner Malmström's spokesperson mentioned the same potential regarding the civil society involvement in a future FTA with Malaysia (negotiations are on hold since 2012):

> As in other FTAs, the Commission will pursue ambitious provisions aiming at fostering governments' accountability and civil society empowerment – and thereby strengthening a

[38]European Commission (2012a).

[39]Jenkins (2014).

[40]Commission for Legal Empowerment of the Poor (2008) and OECD (2012).

[41]Hencsey in Van den Putte (2015).

> supportive environment for human rights. This is the case, for instance, for rules on transparency and on the direct involvement of civil society in the implementation of provisions on trade and sustainable development.[42]

Moreover, the participation of members of civil society allows them to find allies within the other parties of the agreement. In the past trade agreements have led to transnational collaboration between civil society organizations of for example the US and Mexico.[43]

3.4 *Policy Influence: Advising the Governments*

Fourth, by providing relevant information and/or engaging in a deliberative debate (the two previous purposes), civil society meetings can also lead to tailor-made joint recommendations on how the EU and its trade partner should implement the trade agreement in a sustainable way. Whereas this purpose builds on the previous ones, it distinguishes itself by its explicit ambition to formulate policy advice.

According to this view the civil society meetings serve as advisory boards for the governments. They should come forward with concrete suggestions as to how the implementation of labour and environmental provisions should be improved. The difference with the previous purpose of 'monitoring' lies in the *positive* task civil society should take up here: the goal is not (only) to highlight shortcomings in the implementation of the agreement (purpose 2) and/or to engage in a deliberative dialogue on these issues (purpose 3) but also to come up with suggestions for improving this. The ultimate goal would be that such meetings provide the governments with a clear mandate to act with their support. According to this perspective, civil society meetings that do not lead to policy advice would continue to be an empty shell.

The EU-Central America Association Agreement for example sets out in Art. 294.4: 'These groups shall be tasked with expressing views and making recommendations on trade-related aspects of sustainable development and advising the Parties on how to better achieve the objectives of this Title.' Whereas the EU-Korea Agreement stipulates in Art. 13.12 (4): 'Each Party shall establish a Domestic Advisory Group(s) on sustainable development (environment and labour) with the task of advising on the implementation of this Chapter.' According to a union representative from the EU side coming forward with recommendations is the ultimate goal of such meetings: 'Moreover, the monitoring mechanism's mandate provides for specific recommendations and making policy interventions on particular matters.'[44] The rules of procedure of the EU-Korea Civil Society Forum set out: 'Within this area of competence, the Civil Society Forum may express its views in the form of opinions, reports or conclusions or through any other appropriate action.'

---

[42]Tempest (2015).

[43]Compa (2001).

[44]Altintzis (2013).

In addition, in some cases the agreements foresee that the civil society mechanisms can provide advice when a dispute arises between the parties on labour or environmental issues (EU-South Korea, Moldova, Georgia and Canada). In that case, the governments can decide to start government consultations or (if the issue fails to be resolved) a panel of experts where the civil society meetings can be considered as a potential source of advice. For instance, the EU-Moldova Agreements sets out that 'where appropriate, that Sub-Committee may seek the advice of the domestic advisory group(s) of either Party or both Parties or other expert assistance' (Art. 378.5).

Here too, it remains to be seen whether and to what extent (a) the civil society meetings effectively manage to produce policy recommendations, (b) what their quality is in terms of setting out general policy orientations and making specific suggestions for improvement, (c) to what extent they are (and should be) picked up by the governments.

4 Conclusions

In this chapter, we have addressed the question which purposes the civil society meetings, set up in the framework of EU trade agreements with third countries, serve. Civil society seems to have been granted an important role within these agreements' chapters on 'trade and sustainable development'—which also include international labour rights. However, when one examines this more closely, it appears unclear what exactly civil society should be doing in this regard. While it is too early to make a systematic and comparative analysis of these new civil society mechanisms, some of which have only convened a few times at the time of writing, we have made a first attempt to understand the purposes behind them. In particular we have identified four analytically distinct purposes: instrumental, functional, deliberative and policy influence. Thereafter we have shown how these different purposes appear in the legal texts and/or political discourse of relevant actors on the civils society meetings.

We do not aim to prioritize one purpose over another. The main purpose of civil society meetings under a specific trade agreement should depend on the domestic setting of the partner country and on the matureness of the mechanism. For example, if the third country has little experience with social dialogue, the deliberative purpose might be the most important one. In this case, it can be useful to have business and labour groups discussing issues. In addition, these mechanisms need some time to develop. Participants need to get acquainted with each other so that a common purpose can be created. While socialization may not be feasible and even not desirable within these groups, a common sense of the main objectives would be important.

Although the instrumental purpose might seem the most important one at this stage, it is difficult to estimate how these mechanisms will evolve. To make a perhaps simplified comparison: also the International Labour Organization (ILO) was created in order to enhance a broader support for capitalist economy in the face of the Bolshevik threat. Despite its original rather narrow objective, over the past century, the ILO has played a progressive role in global social policy. In any case, as historical institutionalist scholarship has convincingly advanced, over time external bodies may take up a role that was originally not anticipated by the governments that created them.[45] It would anyhow be premature to argue that these civil society meetings are irrelevant. The fundamental question is which purpose(s) is/are being (and should be) pursued. Without having clarified this, any debate on the potential value of the meetings will be trivial. In this regard, we can identify four avenues for further research.

First, the question arises which purposes are emphasized more or less by which actors. While from the EU side there has not been any political objection against the creation of civil society meetings, there seem to be quite different perspectives on their objective. Whereas EU trade officials seem to put more emphasis on the instrumental and functional purposes, members of civil society seem more keen on the normative and policy advising potential of the civil society meetings. Also, it seems that the advisory purpose is emphasized more in the legal texts whereas political discourse puts more emphasis on the monitoring purpose. These are however preliminary observations: the question who wants what, how and why needs to be researched more systematically.

Second, it may not be possible to pursue all the objectives at the same time. We are not so much pointing to practical difficulties, but more fundamentally to inherent tensions that may emerge between the different purposes. Different visions on legitimacy—for example, 'output' versus 'input' legitimacy—of the trading system may not be entirely compatible.[46] If coming to specific output is the principal objective, it might be more convenient to have like-minded people sitting together. If you want to stimulate a democratic debate among actors who are not used to jointly engage in social dialogue, you should make sure that differing interests try to understand each other's viewpoints.

Third, it could be useful to learn from experience with other agreements. For example, the North American Agreement on Labor Cooperation (NAALC) was likewise created in order to gain support for the highly contested North American Free Trade Agreement (NAFTA) in the early 1990s. Nonetheless, studies show that the use of NAALC by civil society resulted in the forging of transnational advocacy networks,[47] formal communication channels for labour representatives and mobilisation between Mexican, Canadian and US civil society members.[48] Thus, even if institutions (like the NAALC) are flawed, they can create spaces for international cooperation and the spread of new norms.

---

[45]Pierson (1996).

[46]For instance De Schutter (2002) and Meunier (2003).

[47]Compa (2001).

[48]Nolan García (2011).

Fourth, the extent to which labour rights are addressed within these civil society meetings requires more in-depth research. Currently these mechanisms bring together labour, business and environmental groups. The attention to labour rights might be diluted by the presence of other, in some cases competing, concerns such as business interests, purely environmental issues, broader human rights and governance issues, animal welfare, etc. In countries where civil society coordination is difficult, it might be worth proposing a separate mechanism on labour issues.

References

Altintzis Y (2013) Civil society engagement and linkages in EU trade policy. In: Takacs T, Ott A, Dimopoulos A (eds) Linking trade and non-commercial interests: the EU as a global role model? vol vol 4. Centre for the Law of EU External Relations, The Hague, pp 27–34

Armstrong K (2002) Rediscovering civil society: the European Union and the white paper on governance. Eur Law J 8(1):102–132

Burgoon B (2009) The distinct politics of the European Union's 'Fair Trade' linkage to labour standards. Eur Foreign Aff Rev 14(5):643–661

Coffey (2014) Evaluation of DG TRADE's Civil Society Dialogue in order to assess its effectiveness, efficiency and relevance. Publication Office of the European Union, Luxembourg

Commission on Legal Empowerment of the Poor (2008) Towards a global social contract: labour rights for legal empowerment of the poor. In: Commission on Legal Empowerment of the Poor & UNDP (eds) Making the law work for everyone: working group reports, vol 2, pp 129–194

Compa L (2001) NAFTA's labour side agreement and international labour solidarity. In: Waterman P, Wills J (eds) Place, space and the new labour internationalisms. Blackwell Publishers, Hoboken, pp 147–163

Council of the EU (2012) Summary record of the meeting of the European Parliament's Committee on International Trade (INTA), Brussels, 25–26 Apr 2012

De Gucht K (2012) EU-Columbia and Peru trade agreement. In: Public Hearing of the Committee on International Trade at the European Parliament, Brussels, 29 Feb 2012

De Schutter O (2002) Europe in search of its civil society. Eur Law J 8(2):198–217

De Ville F, Siles-Brugge G (2015) TTIP: the truth about the transatlantic trade and investment partnership. Wiley, Hoboken

Del Felice C (2014) Power in discursive practices, the case of the stop EPAs campaign. Eur J Int Relat 20(1):145–167

EESC (2012) Civil society in action – monitoring sustainable development and wider FTA implementation: lessons to be drawn from the EU experience, Abstract, Session on 26 Sept 2012

EESC (2015) Summary of the discussion held during the joint meeting of the European and Central American civil society advisory groups. http://www.eesc.europa.eu/resources/docs/en_joint-advisory-groups-document_28-may-2015_final-version.pdf. Accessed 13 Aug 2017

European Commission (2006) Global Europe: competing in the world, COM(2006)567. Brussels

European Commission (2010) Trade, growth and world affairs: trade policy as a core component of the EU's 2020 strategy, COM(2010)612. Brussels

European Commission (2012a) Meeting with the EU Domestic Advisory Group (DAG) under the EU-Korea free trade agreement. http://trade.ec.europa.eu/doclib/docs/2012/october/tradoc_150007.pdf. Accessed 13 Aug 2017

European Commission (2012b) The roots of democracy and sustainable development: Europe's engagement with Civil Society in external relations, COM(2012)492. Brussels

European Commission (2015) Trade for all: towards a more responsible trade and investment policy, COM(2015)497. Brussels
European NGO (2014) Interview on Civil Society Meeting in EU FTA, Interviewer: Van den Putte L. Brussels
European Parliament (2012) Debate on EU trade agreement with Colombia and Peru, 22 May 2012, Strasbourg
Ford L (2013) EU trade governance and policy: a critical perspective. J Contemp Eur Res 9(3):578–596
Friedrich D (2008) Democratic aspiration meets political reality: participation of organized civil society in selected European policy processes. In: Steffek J, Kissling C, Nanz P (eds) Civil society participation in European and global governance: a cure for the democratic deficit? Palgrave Macmillan, Basingstoke, pp 140–165
Hopewell K (2015) Multilateral trade governance as social field: global civil society and the WTO. Rev Int Polit Econ 22(6):1128–1158
Horn H, Mavroidis P, Sapir A (2010) Beyond the WTO? An anatomy of EU and US preferential trade agreements, vol 7. The World Economy
IILS (2013/Revised ed 2015) Social dimensions of free trade agreements. ILO, Geneva
Jenkins T (2014) Discussion points by Tom Jenkins, Chief adviser at the European Trade Union Confederation (ETUC). In: EMPL/INTA hearing on employment and social aspects of TTIP. Brussels
Kohler-Koch B, Quittkat C (2013) De-mystification of participatory democracy: EU-governance and civil society. Oxford University Press, Oxford
Malmström C (2015) The way ahead for the EU-Cariforum Economic Partnership Agreement
Meunier S (2003) Trade policy and political legitimacy in the European Union. Comp Eur Polit 1(1):67–90
Meunier S, Nicolaïdis K (2006) The European Union as a conflicted trade power. J Eur Publ Policy 13(6):906–925
Nolan García K (2011) The evolution of United States-Mexico Labor Cooperation (1994–2009): achievements and challenges. Polit Policy 39(1)
OECD (2012) Decent work and empowerment for pro-poor growth. http://www.oecd.org/dac/povertyreduction/50157792.pdf. Accessed 29 Sept 2016
Oehri M (2014) Comparing US and EU labour governance 'near and far' – hierarchy vs network? J Eur Publ Policy 22(5):731–749
Orbie J, Tortell L (2009) The new GSP+ beneficiaries: ticking the box or truly consistent with ILO findings? Eur Foreign Aff Rev 15(5):663–681
Orbie J, Van Roozendaal G (2017) Labour standards and trade: the need for innovation of instruments and methods. Politics Gov 6(3)
Peels R (2012) Facing the paradigm of non-state actor involvement: the EU-Andean region negotiation process. Katholieke Universiteit Leuven
Peruvian NGO (2015) Interview on Civil Society Meeting in EU FTA, Interviewer: Van den Putte L
Pierson P (1996) The path to European integration a historical institutionalist analysis. Comp Pol Stud 29(2):123–163
Postnikov E, Bastiaens I (2014) Does dialogue work? The effectiveness of labor standards in EU preferential trade agreements. J Eur Publ Policy 21(6):923–940
Scholte JA (2001) Civil society and democracy in global governance. In: Centre for the Study of Globalisation and Regionalisation Working Paper No. 65/01. University of Warwick, Coventry
Scholte JA (2004) Civil society and democratically accountable global governance. Gov Oppos 39 (2):211–233
Siles-Brügge G (2011) Resisting protectionism after the crisis: strategic economic discourse and the EU-Korea free trade agreement. New Polit Econ 16(5):627–653
Slob A, Smakman F (2007) A voice, not a vote. Evaluation of the Civil Society Dialogue at DG Trade. http://trade.ec.europa.eu/doclib/docs/2007/march/tradoc_133527.pdf. Accessed 29 Nov 2016

Smismans S (2003) European civil society: shaped by discourses and institutional interests. Eur Law J 9(4):473–495

Spalding RJ (2008) Civil society engagement in trade negotiations: CAFTA opposition movements in El Salvador. Latin Am Polit Soc 49(4):85–114

Tempest M (2015) Rights abuses revealed in EU free-trade candidate Malaysia. http://www.euractiv.com/sections/global-europe/rights-abuses-revealed-eu-free-trade-candidate-malaysia-318965. Accessed 29 Sept 2016

Ulmer K (2015) Trade embedded development models. Int J Comp Lab Law Ind Relat 31(3):305–329

Van den Putte L (2015) What social face of the new European Union trade agreements? Transcripts, Brussels

Van den Putte L, De Ville F, Orbie J (2014) The European Parliament's new role in trade policy: turning power into impact. In: Van den Putte L, Orbie J (eds) (2015) EU bilateral trade agreements and the surprising rise of labour provisions. Int J Comp Lab Law Ind Relat 31(3):263–284

Van den Putte L, Orbie J (2015) EU bilateral trade agreements and the surprising rise of labour provisions. Int J Comp Lab Law Ind Relat 31(3):263–283

Velluti S (2016) Human rights conditionality in the EU GSP scheme: 'a focus on those in need or a need to refocus?'. In: Ferreira N, Kostakopoulou D (eds) The human face of the European Union: is EU law and policy humane enough? Cambridge University Press, Cambridge, pp 342–366

Vogt JS (2014) Trade and investment arrangements and labor rights. In: Blecher L, Kaymar Stafford N, Bellamy GC (eds) Corporate responsibility for human rights impacts: new expectations and paradigms. ABA Book Publishing, pp 121–176

Comparative Conclusions on Arbitral Dispute Settlement in Trade-Labour Matters Under US FTAs

Patrick Abel

Contents

P. Abel (✉)
Georg-August-University Göttingen, Institute of International and European Law, Göttingen, Germany
e-mail: mail@patrickabel.de

H. Gött (ed.), *Labour Standards in International Economic Law*,
https://doi.org/10.1007/978-3-319-69447-4_9

Abstract Since NAFTA, US free trade agreements cover provisions on labour standards. Noteworthy, these substantive obligations are flanked with compulsory inter-state arbitration procedures, a dispute settlement mechanism known for its effectiveness in international economic law. But in a stark contrast to arbitral practice on trade obligations, states have brought disputes on labour standards only once to arbitration. This submission aims for shedding some light on the reasons for this lack of arbitral practice. For that purpose, it compares US FTAs' arbitration provisions on labour standard disputes to other dispute settlement systems in international law along the functional categories of access to arbitration, jurisdiction *ratione materiae*, legal consequences of an arbitral award and the procedural role of individuals.

The article concludes that the lack of arbitral practice stems at least partly from an unsuitable procedural and institutional design. US FTA dispute settlement provisions on trade-related labour standard obligations in different parts resemble various functional approaches from other branches of international law. However, US FTAs do not succeed in adequately merging these components to a coherent dispute settlement procedure. Instead, their provisions cover elements not suited to the specific constellation of interests in the tripartite labour context in which states, employees and employers are involved. Whereas more recent US FTAs alleviate some deficiencies, important flaws remain even in this newest treaty generation.

Dispute settlement provisions for enforcing labour standards in regional and bilateral free trade agreements ('FTAs') are commonly categorized in two phenotypes: US 'hard' and EU 'soft' approaches. The reason for this characterization is that, even though both US and EU FTAs contain trade-related obligations on labour standards, they fundamentally differ in their enforcement mechanisms. In a remarkable analogy to widespread perceptions of the two entities' general geo-political behaviour, EU FTAs are perceived to focus on diplomatic means of dispute settlement.[1] The contrasting US FTAs' qualification as 'hard' is commonly derived from the inclusion of an enforcement procedure in the form of compulsory arbitration in labour matters ('trade-labour dispute settlement') and the possibility to suspend trade benefits (often also called trade sanctions) as a last resort.[2] The

[1]An elaborate comparison on the US and EU models is conducted by van den Putte et al. (2015), pp. 1 et seqq.

[2]For a critique on the sanctions and complaints based US approach based on international legal theory see Banks (2011), pp. 45 et seqq.

option for a state party to unilaterally initiate arbitral proceedings was firstly introduced in the NAFTA labour side agreement, the North American Agreement on Labor Cooperation (NAALC).[3] Arbitration and enforcement through trade sanctions from then onwards formed an integral part of US FTAs' DNA.[4]

Practice stands in a striking contrast to this perhaps too simplistic juxtaposition of the two approaches. First, US FTAs have a substantial diplomatic practice on labour standard disputes: Roughly more than 40 proceedings have been initiated, mostly under the NAALC.[5] At the same time, so far, US FTAs all together have only generated one arbitral proceeding on labour standard obligations, which is the dispute of *US v. Guatemala* under the Central-American Free Trade Agreement, including the Dominican Republic ('CAFTA-DR'). The Tribunal issued a final report on 14 June 2017, in which it rejected the US claim on the merits.[6]

Why are US FTAs' supposedly 'hard' trade-labour dispute settlement procedures apparently softened in practice? As a complement to literature conducting in-depth analyses of the respective FTA's provisions,[7] this paper aims for discussing the topic from a slightly different angle with the purpose of further clarifying the underlying problems. Arbitration as an adjudicatory method of international dispute settlement is subject of scholarly debate on a more general level, which addresses the functions, commonalities and differences of international dispute settlement tools that are non-exhaustively listed in Art. 33 para. 1 of the UN-Charter.[8] Whereas prominent arbitral dispute settlement regimes such as investor-state arbitration or arbitration under the UN Convention on the Law of the Sea are well researched and understood as parts of the general international dispute settlement world, this seems to be less the case for labour-standard related arbitration in US FTAs. As will be shown, a comparative analysis of US FTAs' trade and labour chapters to other international arbitration systems reveals structural inadequacies in the normative architecture of their dispute settlement provisions.

This submission will proceed in four steps. Firstly, as a background for the analysis, the general reasons shall be recalled for which stakeholders and states strive for arbitration in trade-labour matters (Sect. 1). Then, by way of comparison to other fields of international law and general international law, structural common

[3]NAALC in its final version goes back to political demands by the Democrats in the US Congress, as explained by Bieszczat (2008), pp. 1388–1389; more generally on the role of the US Congress in trade relations see Fergusson (2015), pp. 1 et seqq.

[4]In the FTAs of the US with Australia, Bahrain, Chile, Colombia, Israel, Jordan, Korea, Morocco, Oman, Panama, Peru, Singapore, with states from central America (Costa Rica, El Salvador, Guatemala, Honduras and Nicaragua) and the Dominican Republic in the CAFTA-DR, and in the prospective Trans-Pacific Partnership (TPP); cf. Bieszczat (2008), pp. 1397 et seqq.

[5]Cf. ILO and IILS (2013), pp. 43 et seq.

[6]Arbitral Panel established pursuant to Chapter Twenty of the CAFTA-DR, *In the Matter of Guatemala – Issues Relating to the Obligations Under Article 16.2.1(a) of the CAFTA-DR*, Final Report of the Panel, 14 June 2017, paras. 592–593.

[7]See i.e. Polaski and Vyborny (2006), pp. 100 et seqq.; Lazo Grandi (2009), pp. 7 et seqq.; Vogt (2015), pp. 829 et seqq. and ILO and IILS (2013), pp. 43 et seqq.

[8]For a general perspective on international dispute settlement see i.e. Merrills (2011).

elements of dispute settlement in US FTAs' trade and labour chapters shall be scrutinized on their conceptual adequacy. These elements are the requirements to access arbitration (Sect. 2), the material scope of dispute settlement (Sect. 3), the legal consequences of an arbitral award against a state (Sect. 4) and the procedural role of individuals (Sect. 5).

1 Reasons for Labour Standard Protection in FTAs Through Arbitration

To shed light on why states have not brought any disputes on labour standard obligations under US FTAs to arbitration, it is useful to recall why they created a compulsory arbitral jurisdiction in the first place. Arbitration's appeal as an international dispute settlement method becomes best apparent from a historical perspective. Modern arbitration has its roots in the eighteenth century's arbitration commissions firstly instituted by the famous 1794 Jay Treaty between the US and Great Britain.[9] From thereon, arbitration formed an important practice for the settlement of inter-state disputes, notably with US involvement, and as a result features prominently in the 1899 and 1907 Hague Conventions for the Pacific Settlement of International Disputes.[10] Today, inter-state arbitration before Panels at the WTO as provided in its Dispute Settlement Understanding, flanked with an Appellate Body which effectively operates as an international court,[11] serves as a well-known paradigmatic example for an effective dispute settlement procedure. One of its outstanding properties is that any member can unilaterally initiate arbitration proceedings against another member.[12] Such so called compulsory jurisdiction of international tribunals still remains rather the exception in international law.[13] Many FTAs, including US FTAs, follow the DSU's example in enshrining compulsory jurisdiction of arbitral tribunals for disputes between state parties on the interpretation and application of the FTA. Object and purpose of such

[9]Treaty of Amity, Commerce and Navigation, between His Britannic Majesty and The United States of America, concluded 19 Nov 1794 and entry into force 29 Feb 1796 and cf. Brower (2007), paras. 13 ff.

[10]Hague Convention for the Pacific Settlement of International Disputes, concluded 29 July 1899 and entry into force 4 Sep 1900, 187 CTS 410 and Hague Convention for the Pacific Settlement of International Disputes, concluded 18 Oct 1907 and entry into force 26 Jan 1910, 205 CTS 233.

[11]On the differences between international adjudication and arbitration see i.e. Brower (2007), paras. 4 et seqq.

[12]On the consent-basis of compulsory jurisdiction of international tribunals cf. PCIJ, *Status of the Eastern Carelia*, Advisory Opinion, PCIJ Series B No. 5, p. 27.

[13]On compulsory jurisdiction of tribunals in WTO law see generally Mavroidis (2006), pp. 1–2, 49. Other examples of areas with international tribunals having compulsory jurisdiction are international investment law see i.e. Stoll et al. (2017), p. 34 and regional human rights law see i.e. Abel (2013), pp. 377 et seqq.

an approach is to provide for a rules- rather than power-based enforcement mechanism. In other words, disputes should be solved only on the basis of legal arguments to the exclusion of political or economic aspects in light of the often different political and economic strength of the parties.[14]

As the example of WTO dispute settlement suggests, scholars perceive the ambit of international trade law to have characteristics particularly favourable for such a rule-based enforcement approach. First and foremost, reciprocal obligations between state parties to grant trade concessions comprise a directly identifiable monetary value. Withdrawing these concessions is an economic lever which may result in substantial pressure to comply with legal obligations—if the state party pulling the lever has considerable economic weight in relation to the other.[15] The international trade field with relatively precise and quantifiable economic obligations is an ideal reference point for arbitral remedies and is presumably one of the key reasons why international trade regimes in general work rather effectively.[16] A comparable lever is often not present in other areas of international law. For example in international human rights law, due to the non-reciprocal nature of human rights, a party is barred form suspending human rights obligations owed to the other party in case the other party violates its duties.[17]

In this light, including labour standards into FTAs and their arbitral procedures could arguably connect them with an effective international enforcement mechanism that is rule- rather than power-based.[18] At the same time, if we look into the substantive composition of a FTA, labour standards integrate a social element into the treaty's architecture which focusses largely on reducing barriers to trade,

[14]On the development of the dispute settlement system of the GATT 1947 to the WTO DSU see Stoll (2006), paras. 5–6. Generally on rule-based dispute resolution in international trade law Brewster (2006), pp. 253 et seqq. Of course, the degree to which a dispute settlement system may be described as rules- rather than power-based depends on the procedural design of arbitration in detail.

[15]Disparate economic capacities are a major criticism to the effective functioning of WTO retaliatory remedies, see already Sutherland et al. (2004), para. 243. On the potential leverage see also the high impact of national GSP schemes by economically powerful developed countries, which form tools of high impact for development policies and often are not scrutinized under WTO law because a violation of the MFN obligation under Art. I (1) GATT 1994 is often justified under the Enabling Clause, Art. IX WTO-Agreement or Art. XXIV GATT 1994. See Nottage (2009), pp. 499 et seqq.

[16]However, it must not be forgotten that suspending trade concessions causes trade distortion which runs counter to the principal purpose of international trade law, and that for economically less powerful states, trade remedies may not be a real option, cf. van den Bossche and Zdouc (2013), pp. 200 et seqq. Political and economic reasons for an international organization with enforceable trade obligations lie in the fact that macroeconomic gains from trade may only be reached for the benefit of all states if free-rider effects and financial and political incentives for purely internal benefits through barriers to trade are minimized by a multilateral system, cf. Matsushita et al. (2015), pp. 6 et seqq.

[17]See i.e. on the enforcement of human rights in regional human rights treaties Abel (2013), pp. 388 et seqq.

[18]Elliott and Freeman (2003), p. 73 and ILO and IILS (2013), pp. 6–7.

notably with the important goal to prevent low labour standards from becoming a comparative economic advantage once these barriers have been substantially broken down.[19] To a certain extent, FTA labour chapters also should compensate the lack of hard enforcement mechanisms in the ILO which mainly operates monitoring functions on the basis of naming and shaming.[20]

On the other hand, there was always concern to overload FTAs with social considerations which are often felt to belong to other fields, institutions and treaties of international law such as precisely the ILO or international human rights law.[21] Moreover, developing countries often voiced the concern that labour standards ultimately serve to impose disguised protectionist measures to their competitive disadvantage.[22]

In sum, compulsory arbitration for disputes on labour standard obligations in US FTAs can provide a potentially potent enforcment mechanism as an established rule-based dispute settlement method.[23] As such, it could function as an important complement of diplomatic procedures and practices on labour standard disputes established in US FTAs.[24] But the observed reservations towards role and adequacy of labour standards in US FTAs caused the US and its trade partners to open disputes on labour standards to compulsory adjudication only with limitations and modifications. As will be analyzed in more detail below, they led to rather half-hearted constructions of dispute settlement procedures in US FTAs labour chapters which often constitute obstacles to unfolding the aforementioned desired effect and role of arbitration for the protection of labour standards.

2 Access to Arbitration

Having established that arbitration's appeal for the protection of labour standards in US FTAs stems from positive examples of effective rule-based enforcement in other fields of international law, the differences of arbitration under US FTAs' trade and labour chapters to these other examples of arbitration come into focus. Could

[19]For comparable motives, there is ongoing scholarly debate on bringing in human rights and environmental consideration into international investment law, see for example Berner (2016), pp. 177 et seqq.

[20]On the ILO's supervisory organs and their relation to FTAs see Agustí-Panareda et al. (2014), pp. 22 et seqq.

[21]Accordingly, the inclusion of a social clause into WTO law was heavily debated in the negotiations on a WTO Agreement, see i.e. Leary (1997), pp. 119 et seqq. For a more general critical analysis of the WTO's social dimension see Lang (2011), pp. 23 et seqq.

[22]Cf. Bhagwati (1995), pp. 746 and 753 et seqq.

[23]See Tomuschat (2002), paras. 19 et seqq.; see also the Friendly Relations Declaration, GA Res. 2625 (XXV), 24 Oct 1970 and the Manila Declaration, GA Res. 37/10, 15 Nov 1982.

[24]On the diplomatic dispute settlement methods see Orbie, van den Putte and Martens (this volume); more specifically on CAFTA-DR see Gantz (2007), pp. 391–392.

deviations of the respective procedural and institutional provisions in US FTAs to other fields of international arbitration contribute to an understanding why trade-labour arbitration has not effectively been used so far?

Considering the logical order of a dispute settlement procedure, it is convenient to firstly investigate under which conditions trade-labour arbitration in US FTAs can be initiated. Burdensome requirements for access to arbitration can be a substantial obstacle for its effectiveness. The analysis will first look into the admissibilty requirement of a prior attempt to an amicable solution of the dispute through negotiations and in that regard identify the pecularities of the NAALC (Sect. 2.1). It will then dedicate special attention to the role of national contact points as a gatekeeper to the trade-labour dispute settlement procedure which will prove to be a significant practical hurdle for initiating trade-labour arbitration (Sect. 2.2).

2.1 *The Requirement to Negotiate*

All US FTAs contain a procedure which foresees a diplomatic procedure that states can follow if a dispute on a labour standard obligation arises. These provisions serve a dual function. First and foremost, they provide a framework for inter-state negotiations on such a dispute and support the reaching of an amicable solution. At the same time, they represent an obligatory preliminary phase to be completed before the creation of an arbitral tribunal can be requested. It is this second role as an admissibility requirement of arbitration with which this section is concerned. Such a preliminary obligation to negotiate is well known in many other international dispute settlement procedures as an admissibility requirement for arbitral or judicial proceedings (Sect. 2.1.1). However, under the NAALC, the obligatory preliminary negotiation phase is significantly more complex than the seemingly similar requirement in other international dispute settlement procedures, rendering access to arbitration more difficult (Sect. 2.1.2). More recent US FTAs have a simpler preliminary negotiation phase reflecting a convergence towards the role of an attempt to an amicable solution in other international judicial dispute settlement procedures, and thus prove to be less problematic in this regard (Sect. 2.1.3).

2.1.1 Obligation to Negotiate as a Condition for Adjudication in International Law

The obligation to negotiate as a condition for access to arbitration is not peculiar to US FTAs' trade-labour regime, but a wide-spread admissibility prerequisite in the law of international dispute settlement. Although in general international law, there is no obligation to enter negotiations in case of a dispute between states,[25] most international agreements which enshrine compulsory arbitration or adjudication require that an attempt to negotiate an amicable solution of the dispute must have failed, as for example under the ITLOS[26] and under many BITs.[27] In the WTO, consultations must take place before the establishment of an arbitral tribunal may be requested: Generally, within ten days the member state addressed by the complainant must reply, and within 30 days must enter into consultations. If the states fail to settle the dispute within 60 days or the parties jointly consider that consultations have failed, the complaining party may request the establishment of a Panel.[28] Moreover, compromissory clauses establishing jurisdiction of the ICJ for disputes arising from the interpretation or application of an international agreement are often contingent upon a failed attempt to negotiate. This admissibility requirement was for example decisive in the recent case of *Georgia v. Russia* on the Convention on the Elimination of All Forms of Racial Discrimination before the ICJ.[29] In sum, it does not surprise that not only labour chapters but also general dispute settlement chapters in US FTAs impose a requirement to attempt the reaching of an amicable solution before a party may resort to arbitration.[30]

---

[25]Art. 33 (1) UN-Charter does not prescribe a general obligation to negotiate, but rather in connection with Art. 2 (4) UN-Charter to resort to peaceful means if a state engages in the settlement of a dispute. Further obligations only arise if negotiations are i.e. required under a compromissory clause, for example the procedural obligation to negotiate meaningfully as found by ICJ, *Application of the International Convention on the Elimination of All Forms of Racial Discrimination (Georgia v. Russia)*, Preliminary Objections, ICJ Rep. 2011, pp. 70, 132 et seqq. Moreover, there is no obligation under general international law to exhaust negotiations before resorting to other means of dispute settlement, see ICJ, *Aegan Sea (Greece v. Turkey)*, Jurisdiction, ICJ Rep. 1978, pp. 3, 12 and ICJ, *Military and Paramilitary Activities in and against Nicaragua (Nicaragua v. USA)*, Jurisdiction and Admissibility, ICJ Rep. 1984, pp. 392, 440.

[26]Art. 283 and Art. 286 UNCLOS.

[27]I.e. for inter-state dispute settlement see Art. 9 (1) and (2) Germany Model BIT 2008. In investor-state arbitration investors often must abide by cooling-off periods, see i.e. Art. 24 US Model BIT 2012, which is a different form of linking negotiations with arbitration. Cooling-off periods stipulate that a certain period of time must have lapsed in which the investor and the respective state negotiated on the issue. Only after this time period has lapsed, the investor can initiate arbitration proceedings without a need for negotiations to have deadlocked. This can pose a higher hurdle on access to arbitration than the obligation to attempt to negotiate an amicable solution as there is no way of shortening the defined time period even if negotiations have no prospect. For an overview on cooling-off periods see Waibel (2015), paras. 266 et seqq.

[28]Art. 4 (3)–(7) DSU. Shorter time periods must be met in cases of urgency, Art. 4 (8) and (9) DSU. There is no obligation to apply bona fide efforts, instead it is sufficient that no settlement of the dispute was reached, see *EC – Regime for the Importation, Sale and Distribution of Bananas (Bananas III)*, Report of the Panel, 25 Sep 1997, WT/DS27/R/USA, WT/DS27/R/GTM, WT/DS27/RHND, WT/DS27/R/MEX, WT/DS27/R/ECU, para. 7.19 and *Korea – Taxes on Alcoholic Beverages*, Report of the Panel, 17 Sep 1998, WT/DS75/R, WT/DS84/R, para. 10.19.

[29]ICJ, *Application of the International Convention on the Elimination of All Forms of Racial Discrimination (Georgia v. Russia)*, Preliminary Objections, ICJ Rep. 2011, pp. 70, 121 et seqq.

[30]I.e. Art. 2005 et seqq. NAFTA; Art. 20.4 et seqq. CAFTA-DR and Art. 28.5 et seqq. TPP.

The purpose of this admissibility requirement is to give the potential respondent state at least the chance to react to the allegations and possibly adjust its domestic laws or measures. It also opens the possibility for quick mutually agreed solutions. Lastly, it is a means of delimiting the scope of the dispute more precisely.[31] As is expressly highlighted in the case of the WTO,[32] this often stands in line with a focus on fostering amicable inter-state relations.

2.1.2 NAALC in 1994: Multi-Step Negotiation Procedures

NAALC, forming part of the first modern US FTA,[33] overtook this well established admissibility requirement; however, not without substantial modifications. NAALC prescribes a state party interested in an arbitration on a labour standard obligation to go through a particularly lengthy and complex negotiation procedure, significantly deviating from the aforementioned patterns in other fields of international law. To illustrate its convolutions the procedure shall be briefly outlined in its essential elements:[34] First, national administrative offices (NAOs) created by the state parties as provided in the NAALC receive complaints by stakeholders like trade unions or NGOs. The NAO firstly controls whether the submission meets certain formal minimal requirements. If that is answered to the affirmative, the NAO investigates whether the allegations are substantiated and may conduct public hearings with the claimant for that purpose. Usually, it also requests consultations with the respondent's NAO.[35] After having completed the investigation, it will then issue a public report on whether the allegations are substantiated.[36] Only afterwards, first inter-state ministerial consultations may be conducted.[37] If they do not lead to a mutually agreed solution, a state party may bring the complaint before an Evaluation Committee of Experts (ECE).[38] The ECE analyses in a non-adversarial manner if there is a pattern of violation of certain labour provisions and issues an according Draft Evaluation Report within 120 days that contains an interim assessment of

[31]Cf. ICJ, *Application of the International Convention on the Elimination of All Forms of Racial Discrimination (Georgia v. Russia)*, Preliminary Objections, ICJ Rep. 2011, pp. 70, 124–125.

[32]Art. 3 (7) WTO DSU.

[33]NAFTA covered a series of innovative provisions in comparison to its at least related predecessors, the Treaties of Friendship, Commerce and Navigation. Generally on FCN-Treaties see Paulus (2011).

[34]Generally on the NAALC see i.e. Bieszczat (2008), pp. 1388 et seqq.

[35]Art. 21 (1) NAALC.

[36]For the US NAO procedure see https://www.dol.gov/ilab/trade/agreements/naalcgd.htm. Accessed 7 Dec 2016.

[37]Art. 22 NAALC.

[38]Art. 23 NAALC. Default rules of procedures can be found in Art. 24 NAALC.

the matter with conclusions and practical recommendations.[39] After that, again, both parties may provide submissions to the Committee.[40] Within 60 days, the Committee presents a final report to the Council of Ministers, the organ of NAALC composed of the parties' labour ministers.[41] This report must be followed by another round of consultations and the attempt to reach an amicable solution.[42] If it fails again, any party may request in writing a special session of the Council, in which another attempt to reach an amicable solution has to be made.[43] Only if within 60 days after the special session the dispute is not mutually resolved, the creation of an arbitral panel may be requested.[44] The creation of an arbitral panel is then contingent upon a two-thirds majority in the Council.[45] This means that the third state party not involved in the dispute must take sides with the complainant for an arbitration to be successfully initiated.

Compared with the typical requirements in other fields of international law and their purposes presented above, it is immediately apparent that the obligatory diplomatic phase in the NAALC poses a much greater hurdle to reach arbitration due to the complex multi-stepped structure of the diplomatic proceedings. The different phases of negotiations involve different organs of the NAALC, and thus represent a form of guided or institutionalized negotiation. Therein, the ECE represents a more neutral instance, comprised by labour standard experts, which is supposed to bring an impartial view into the dispute settlement process. But it does not exert any adjudicatory function: Rather, it examines patterns of practice in enforcement of certain labour standards[46] and is thus limited to a factual, non-adversarial analysis without legal conclusions. The other phases of the negotiation procedure involve state representatives on different levels in different institutional contexts of the NAALC and thus aim for providing opportunities for amicable solutions in a successively increasing 'escalation' of the diplomatic negotiation context. And at the end of this long process stands the often politically almost insurmountable obstacle of persuading the third uninvolved NAALC party to affirm the initiation of arbitration. The complainant must likely invest a rather high amount of political capital to compel the third state to vote in its favour. The third state party will typically be reluctant to do so in fear of a dangerous precedent against its own interests in other current or future cases and in consideration of the general diplomatic relations to the respondent state.

[39]Art. 25 (1) NAALC.

[40]Art. 25 (2) NAALC.

[41]Art. 26 NAALC.

[42]Art. 27 (4) NAALC.

[43]Art. 28 NAALC.

[44]Art. 29 (1) NAALC.

[45]Art. 29 (1) NAALC.

[46]See also Art. 24 (1) (c) NAALC which stipulates that ECE members shall be independent and not be affiliated with or take instructions from any party.

In sum, the NAALC's negotiation procedure is a complex multi-stepped framework which has a clear focus on facilitating an amicable solution by complementing negotiations with an institutional setting. This becomes clear if one compares the NAALC's procedure with the much simpler requirement to attempt negotiations before resort to arbitration in other branches of international law. On the one hand, this framework can prove useful for a diplomatic settlement of trade-labour disputes. But on the other hand, it represents a stark obstacle to reaching the arbitral stage up to a point to which a state, considering its options in case of a dispute on NAALC obligations, often cannot consider arbitration as a realistic alternative in the first place. It also politicizes the access to arbitration, in tension to arbitration's raison d'être of offering a rules- rather than power-based setting.[47]

2.1.3 More Recent US FTAs: Simpler Negotiation Procedures

Later US FTAs increasingly simplified the negotiation procedure that must be completed before resort to arbitration is allowed. These FTAs generally foresee a two- or three-steps negotiation procedure. This admissibility requirement either features as an element of a separate dispute settlement procedure for labour standard obligations or forms part of a labour-specific modified application of the FTA's general dispute settlement procedure,[48] or is enshrined in the general dispute settlement regime which is declared applicable to disputes on labour standards without modification.[49]

The preliminary negotiation phase usually starts with consultations arising from complaints filed with national contact points and then mostly envisages to present the complaint before an FTA organ competent for labour issues. This is followed by the possibility to address the highest executive body of the respective FTA, composed by high government representatives of all state parties. The CAFTA-DR may be taken as an example:[50] Firstly, labour consultations must be requested to a national contact point of the other party.[51] Parties can request the Council of Ministers to convene and consider the matter if consultations are not successful.[52] If the parties do not resolve the issue within 60 days and the dispute concerns the obligation to enforce national labour laws, consultations or a meeting of the

[47]Cf. Dombois (2006), p. 248.

[48]I.e. Art. 17.7 and Art. 21.4 et seqq. US-Colombia FTA; Art. 18.6 (4) and Art. 21.5 et seqq. US-Australia FTA and Art. 15.6 (4) and Art. 19.5 et seqq. US-Bahrain FTA.

[49]Cf. Bolle (2016), 2 et seqq. This includes the Trans-Pacific-Partnership (TPP) the fate of which remains unclear because of the US withdrawal. Due to its potential role as a model for future FTAs, even if it eventually does not enter into force, it is nevertheless worth taking into account in the analysis.

[50]Cf. Bieszczat (2008), pp. 1397 et seqq.

[51]Art. 16.6 (1) CAFTA-DR.

[52]Art. 16.6 (4) CAFTA-DR.

Commission on the matter may be requested.[53] That matter may then be brought before an arbitral panel on request of the complaining party.[54]

These more recent US FTAs come much closer in nature and function to according admissibility requirements in other international dispute settlement proceedings. Notably, the time periods set are comparatively short, for instance measured against the WTO's Dispute Settlement Understanding.[55] Although they still complement negotiations with an institutionalized framework, the steps to be taken before an arbitration can be initiated are simpler. In this regard, a clear progress regarding accessibility to arbitration may be observed in the course of the development of US FTAs after the NAALC while preserving the framework favourable to inter-state consultations. At the same time, the lack of arbitral practice in all US FTAs is evidence that an obligatory negotiation phase cannot be the decisive cause for this inaction.

2.2 *The Gateway to Initiate Proceedings: Petitions by Individuals to National Contact Points*

It is submitted that a more important reason for the lack of practice lies in the way individuals are de facto involved in the initiation of inter-state arbitration. To shed light on such access hurdles, it is necessary to dive deeper into the practice of US FTAs' dispute settlement procedures. More precisely it is necessary to reflect on the key role that private actors play in providing the information that forms an indispensable basis for a potential arbitral claim by a state against another state.

2.2.1 Unions and NGOs as De Facto Initiators of Trade-Labour Dispute Settlement

In practice, the incentive for the use of US FTAs' dispute settlement procedures in instances of alleged violations of labour standards came from trade unions and NGOs, sometimes in transnational alliances through petitions to national contact points. In contrast, state parties rarely started inter-state consultations on their own initiative.[56] This shows that trade unions and NGOs provide states with the necessary factual information on violations of trade-labour obligations by filing a petition with a national contact point.[57] As already touched upon briefly, the problem is that

---

[53] Art. 16.6 (6), Art. 20.4 and Art. 20.5 CAFTA-DR.

[54] Art. 20.6 CAFTA-DR.

[55] Cf. on CAFTA-DR see Gantz (2007), p. 399.

[56] Dombois (2006), p. 247.

[57] See US Federal Register, Vol. 71, No. 245 on procedural guidelines for the functioning of contact points for all US FTAs. Cf. Dombois (2006), pp. 247 et seqq.

the role of national contact points in dealing with private actors' petitions is very limited. They represent a certain investigative instance and for that purpose may even conduct public hearings. Still, the depth of analysis is limited, and is not comparable to a judicial or arbitral inquiry.

Importantly, only states have the power to bring the trade-labour dispute settlement procedure to the next phases. They are free to decide whether to take up a complaint by a trade union or NGO and use the factual information provided to initiate ministerial consultations. All the more, they have full discretion whether to initiate arbitration after the respective requirements are met.[58] The decision if and how to initiate and proceed complaints will depend on a variety of general factors and inter-party constellations of interests and relations, such as general political or economic tensions, regulatory culture in labour matters and the volume and relative flows of trade.[59] In practice, states take up only few complaints issued by NGOs and trade unions.[60] Accordingly, Dombois accurately describes this phenomenon as a 'disappointment trap' for these interested non-state actors.[61]

2.2.2 Aligned Interests of Non-State Petitioners and States of Nationality in the WTO and in Diplomatic Protection

The lack of control of labour unions and NGOs on the initiation of arbitration is a clear difference to procedures of mixed dispute settlement in other fields of international law such as human rights or international investment law. There, individuals formally control how the petition proceeds in the different phases of arbitral or adjudicatory proceedings. This includes the decision which argument to raise and which evidence to present as well as to decide when to settle under which conditions. Without surprise, such procedures provide much greater incentives for non-state actors to resort to them. Indeed, the creation of mixed dispute settlement is considered a significant success in these areas of international law for the effective protection and enforcement of international obligations which aim for protecting individual values and rights[62]—a purpose, as we have seen, shared by labour chapters of US FTAs.

---

[58]Already the national contact point has full discretion whether and how to take up a petition. Requirements and criteria may be set in national law, see for the US national contact point US Federal Register, Vol. 71, No. 245. Initiating consultations then is again open to the parties' discretion, as FTAs do not contain any guiding or restricting language on that point, see i.e. Art. 22 NAALC; Art. 16.6 (1) CAFTA-DR and Art. 19.15 (2) TPP.

[59]For a perspective focussing on the choice of conflict or cooperation and on possible normative interests of states in trade-labour matters see Banks (2011), pp. 62 et seqq.

[60]On the roughly 40 cases which were taken up by the national contact points under the NAALC see ILO and IILS (2013), pp. 43 et seqq.

[61]Dombois (2006), p. 247.

[62]See i.e. Tomuschat (1999), pp. 149 et seqq. with comments on the connection to the broader discussion on the individualization of international law.

Still, the lack of non-state actors' control over a dispute settlement procedure that affects their interests is not unique at all to US FTAs' trade-labour arbitration. It is the law of diplomatic protection in which inter-state negotiations or even arbitration between states for the benefit of a state's injured national is well-established. Here, following the *Mavrommatis* fiction, the state brings forward an own right in the person of its national who remains fully mediatized in his or her legal position.[63] A good example is the *LaGrand* case before the ICJ on the basis of the Vienna Convention on Consular Relations.[64] Also in the WTO, inter-state arbitration often is initiated for the benefit of certain disadvantaged industries or companies. In these instances, the state retains full discretion if and how to make use of dispute settlement procedures, and receives the factual background for that purpose from natural or juridical persons. comparable to US FTAs to a certain extent at first glance.[65] As a result, non-state actors such as national industries often try to exert considerable internal political pressure on 'their' state to defend their interests on the international level.[66]

2.2.3 Unaligned Direct Legal Interests of Petitioners and Addressed States in US FTA Trade-Labour Dispute Settlement

However, the constellation of interests between states and non-state actors in US FTAs is in one crucial respect very different than in the aforementioned examples, and indeed more unfavourable to workers, trade unions and NGOs. The reason is that people affected by labour standard violations on one state party's territory must resort to the government of the other state party, as it is only another state that may initiate an inter-state dispute settlement procedure against their home state.[67] For

[63]PCIJ, *Mavrommatis Palestine Concessions (Greece v. Great Britain)*, Jurisdiction, PCIJ Rep. Series A No. 2, paras. 21–22.

[64]ICJ, *LaGrand Case (Germany v. United States of America)*, Judgment, ICJ Rep. 2001, p. 466 (paras. 38, 42).

[65]On diplomatic protection ICJ, *Case Concerning the Barcelona Traction, Light and Power Company, Limited (Belgium v. Spain)*, Judgment, ICJ Rep. 1970, p. 3 (44). On possible restrictions for discretion cf. Dugard (2009), paras. 14 et seqq. On the WTO see van den Bossche and Zdouc (2013), pp. 177–178.

[66]Of course, domestic law may provide procedures for individuals which give the opportunity to the state or even oblige it to make use of diplomatic protection or comparable inter-state dispute settlement procedures; see for example EU Regulation 2015/1843 *laying down Union procedures in the field of the common commercial policy in order to ensure the exercise of the Union's rights under international trade rules, in particular those established under the auspices of the World Trade Organization*, O.J. L 272/1 (2015).

[67]For example, the Monitoring & Enforcement of Trade Agreements Division within the Bureau of International Labor Affairs of the US Department of Labor is the US's national administrative office receiving the complaints filed under US FTAs which include trade-labour dispute settlement procedures. See https://www.dol.gov/agencies/ilab/our-work/trade/fta-submissions. Accessed 7 Dec 2016.

example, if Mexican trade unions want to complain under the NAALC about violations of the obligation to allow for collective bargaining in the Mexican national legal order, they must file a complaint with an US or Canadian national contact point. Other possibilities to make reference to US FTAs' trade-labour dispute settlement procedures are only indirect: They could for example contact US trade unions or individuals and persuade them to file a petition, possibly in a transnational cooperation. The US or Canadian government will then have to decide whether to take up the claim that relates to the Mexican legal order, Mexican workers and trade unions before the NAALC's trade-labour dispute settlement system. The respective US FTA's state party thus does not take up a claim of a violation that *directly* affects its own territory or own nationals.[68]

To be sure, in some occasions, such a petition may coincide with a state's own direct interest, for example when migrant workers of the state party's own nationality are likewise affected by an alleged labour standard violation. However, in tendency, the impact of the claim on the petitioned state party is a rather indirect one: The motivation to prevent low labour standards in the other state party's territory from becoming a comparative advantage. In contrast to diplomatic protection or WTO dispute settlement, the direct legal interests of the petitioner and the state addressed are unaligned.

This constellation of interests is disfavourable, because it requires a higher degree of pressure or persuasion to be exerted on the respective state party in order to convince it to initiate US FTAs' trade-labour dispute settlement procedures. The indirect socio-economic impact on and connection to the state party is more complicated to prove and promote in the political process. It requires greater organizational capacities, preferably cross-border alliances between trade unions that have indeed formed in cases brought before the NAALC.[69] In consequence, campaigns that intend to resort to US FTAs' dispute settlement mechanisms must arguably concentrate on a number of cases against the background of limited organizational and political resources. This correlates with the finding that complaints filed by usually better equipped transnational coalitions were 'three times more likely to be accepted for review by the relevant NAO'.[70]

Still, this constellation of unaligned interests has some potential advantages. Where trade unions and NGOs are given the possibility to address another state party's government, even more through institutionalized avenues such as national contact points, they may find attention of a party more neutral to the concrete dispute. On the other hand, as the petitioned state would have to advocate against

[68]Of course, citizens working in the other state party's labour market may well be affected by a breach of labour obligations in US FTAs. However, these breaches usually concern all workers of a given industry or labour market, which mostly still are nationals of the respective state. The constellation is substantially different from diplomatic protection or the WTO dispute settlement system in which a state's citizen or company operating on the state's territory is typically behind that state's claim against another state.

[69]Cf. Bieszczat (2008), p. 1397.

[70]Bieszczat (2008), p. 1396 and ILO and IILS (2013), pp. 49–50.

certain conditions in another state and might have trade-related interests at stake, the grade of neutrality is naturally questionable. Secondly, the system encourages transnational cooperation of trade unions and NGOs which might bring to bear greater bargaining power and influence on national governments.[71] From a viewpoint focusing on the access to arbitration, however, it is submitted that chances of bringing labour standard violations to a rules- rather than power-based dispute settlement are generally lower than in comparable constellations in other fields of international law.

2.3 Conclusion

The NAALC provides for a complex negotiation procedure which operates as an almost insurmountable hurdle for the access to arbitration. Its focus clearly lies on providing a framework for a diplomatic settlement of labour standard disputes rather than serving as a pre-arbitration phase. Later US FTAs also encompass negotiation procedures as admissibility requirements for arbitration. However, they are more streamlined and resemble more closely comparable admissibility requirements in other judicial dispute settlement procedures of international law. Thus, they do not provide a compelling explanation for the lack of arbitral practice.

A much more important hurdle to arbitration lies in the limited role of trade unions and NGOs in the trade-labour dispute settlement procedures. Through petitions to national contact points, they provide the indispensable factual basis for any inter-state trade-labour dispute settlement. However, states only rarely take up these petitions for the initiation of such procedures. The existence of the NAOs which receive complaints from individuals, and which then freely choose whether to proceed with the matter, seems to resemble constellations in the law of diplomatic protection and the WTO.[72] However, the interests of the different actors involved are differently distributed in US FTAs, because the direct legal interests at stake are often not aligned: States do not take up claims of their nationals, but receive petitions of private actors from the domestic jurisdiction of another state party. They would have to represent the interests of a 'foreign' private actor which is often only of indirect relevance to them in their aim to prevent the misuse of low labour standards as a comparative economic advantage. This provides a disincentive for individuals to file petitions in the first place. There is no procedural or institutional component in US FTAs to alleviate this essential difference.[73]

[71] Dombois (2006), pp. 247 et seqq.

[72] Cf. the observation of potential borrowing from the WTO DSU by CAFTA-DR negotiators Gantz (2007), p. 387.

[73] Options that could have been thought of will be discussed below in relation to the role of individuals in dispute settlement, see Sect. 5.2.

3 The Requirements to Prove Patterns of Violations and an Impact on Trade

A further disincentive for using trade-labour arbitration in US FTAs represent the requirements in US FTAs to prove a pattern of violations of labour obligations as well as an impact on trade (Sect. 3.1). These requirements essentially prevent arbitral tribunals from grounding a violation of a labour standard obligation on a single case. This is an important obstacle for the effectiveness of arbitration (Sect. 3.2). That it is possible to reconcile the addressing of systemic problems and individual violations is shown by the practice of the European and American regional human rights courts. They prove that US FTA's limitation to systemic violations is a conceptual fallacy (Sect. 3.3).

3.1 Proof of Patterns of Violations and Impact on Trade as Requirements Shared by US FTAs' Labour Chapters

US FTAs' arbitration procedures in trade and labour chapters share the requirement that claimants must proof a recurring course of action or inaction in breach of a labour standard and an impact on trade. To understand the reach of these requirements it is necessary to dive deeper into the different substantive labour standard obligations in US FTAs which have evolved in the different generations of treaties over time. These limitations apply without a doubt to two categories of labour standard obligations: First, the obligation not to fail to enforce national labour laws in a manner affecting trade and second, the obligation to enforce a number of listed internationally recognized labour rights or domestic laws related to these.[74] It is clear that, in order to establish a violation of these types of obligations, US FTAs require the claimant firstly to prove that there was a persistent pattern of a series of violations, and secondly, that the lack of enforcement affected trade between the parties.[75] This is expressly stipulated in the FTAs' texts, sometimes framed as a procedural,[76] sometimes as a substantive requirement.[77]

It is less clear whether this qualification also applies to the third category of substantive obligations which was introduced into the latest generation of US FTAs, brought about by the US Bipartisan Trade Deal.[78] That is the obligation to

[74]See Bolle (2016), pp. 2–3.

[75]See Art. 27 (1) and Art. 29 (1) NAALC; Art. 16.2 (1) (a) CAFTA-DR; Art. 18.2 (1) (a) and Art. 18.6 (4) and (5) US-Australia FTA; Art. 15.2 (1) (a) and Art. 15.6 (4) and (5) US-Bahrain FTA and Art. 19.5 (1) TPP.

[76]I.e. Art. 27 (1) and 29 (1) NAALC.

[77]I.e. Art. 17.3 (1) (a) US-Colombia FTA and Art. 19.5 (1) TPP.

[78]On the Bipartisan Trade Deal see critically Cosbey (2007), pp. 2 et seqq.; more generally see Fergusson (2015), p. 7.

adopt and maintain statutes, regulations and practices enshrined in the 1998 ILO Declaration on Fundamental Principles and Rights, including the prohibition to lower labour standards. In a footnote of the respective articles on this new type of substantive obligation, it is mentioned that a party must establish a violation of this obligation by demonstrating that the other party has failed 'to adopt or maintain a statute, regulation, or practice in a manner affecting trade or investment between the Parties'.[79] This provision is laid down separately from the obligation to enforce labour laws, which states: 'A Party shall not fail to effectively enforce its labor laws, including those it adopts or maintains in accordance with Article [. . ., reference to the above mentioned 1998 ILO declaration], through a sustained or recurring course of action or inaction[. . .].'[80] Thus, the requirement to show a systemic pattern of violation is explicitly introduced only in the text referring to the obligation to enforce labour laws, not in the text covering the obligation to adopt and maintain laws in line with the 1998 ILO Declaration. One possible interpretation is to understand the obligation to adopt and maintain on the one hand, and the obligation to enforce on the other hand, as separate. This interpretation is supported by their textual division in two different provisions. It would follow that parties would not need to prove a systemic pattern of non-compliance to show a violation of the obligation to adopt and maintain laws in line with the 1998 ILO Declaration. However, one could also argue that the showing of a systemic pattern is justified by the trade linkage of the US FTAs' labour chapters. In addition, the obligation to enforce labour laws is explicitly connected to laws adopted and maintained in line with the 1998 ILO Declaration, which is another argument to see both provisions in conjunction.

Overall, although the requirement to show a systemic pattern of non-compliance remains to be tested as to its application to the newest category of obligations in the most recent generation of US FTAs, it is not unlikely that it will be extended to these obligations, too.

3.2 Requirements to Prove Patterns and an Impact on Trade as an Obstacle to Arbitral Procedures

The need to present patterns of misconduct and a trade impact is a significant hurdle for the access to trade-labour arbitration.[81] The requirement to prove a sustained or

[79]This limitation is laid down in the respective footnote of Art. 17.2 (1) US-Colombia FTA; Art. 17.2 (1) US-Peru FTA; Art. 16.2 (1) US-Panama FTA; Art. 19.2 (1) US-South Korea and Art. 19.3 (1) and 19.4 TPP.

[80]I.e. Art. 17.3 (1) (a) US-Colombia FTA.

[81]Another restriction present in the NAALC is the scope of obligations which may be subject to dispute settlement. In the course of the negotiation phases until the final stage of arbitration, NAALC successively restricts the list of relevant obligations from phase to phase. Finally, before an arbitral panel, only violations of the obligation to effectively enforce a party's national

recurring course of action or inaction effectively functions as an intensity qualification of substantive obligations on labour standard obligations in US FTAs. Their wording indicates that the claimant cannot limit its claim to single situations of non-compliance, but most show a certain pattern of breaches which have an impact on trade between the parties beyond merely negatively affecting workers or labour unions. For the CAFTA-DR, the arbitral tribunal defined in its final report on the *US v. Guatemala* case these requirements. The notion of a 'sustained or recurring course of action or inaction' in Art. 16.2.1 (a) CAFTA-DR was to be understood as '(i) a repeated behaviour which displays sufficient similarity [referring to the alternative 'recurring'], or (ii) prolonged behaviour in which there is sufficient consistency in sustained acts or omissions as to constitute a line of connected behaviour by a labor law enforcement institution, rather than isolated or disconnected instances of action or inaction [referring to the alternative 'sustained']'.[82] Notably, the Panel stipulated that it is not necessary to show system-wide or pervasive enforcement failures.[83] Such course of action or inaction was found to be 'in a manner affecting trade between the Parties' by the Tribunal 'if its confers some competitive advantage on an employer or employers engaged in trade between the Parties',[84] to be proven by showing that a business is engaged in competitive markets or competes with imports of CAFTA-DR parties and identifying that a failure to enforce labour obligations are sufficient to cause 'some competitive advantage' on the enterprise.[85]

The Panel's findings do not appear as an overly strict interpretation. Notwithstanding, it still follows that information provided by persons or unions on a certain situation in which they allege to be directly affected in a relevant labour standard does not suffice to prove a case. It is important to recall that the state complainants almost always rely on information presented by persons, unions or NGOs in complaints to the respective NAO.[86] For an individual person or a single labour union, it is much harder to gather such information on patterns in breach of labour law policy which meet the requirements mentioned above. The same is true for proof of a sufficient impact on trade. In short, persons or labour unions cannot restrict themselves to present their own case in a complaint to a NAO if they aim for convincing the respective state to take up their complaint with a view to reaching the arbitration stage. In light of limited resources of many trade unions and NGOs,

occupational safety and health, child labour or minimum wage standards may be claimed (Art. 29 (1) NAALC). As this is a rather clear limitation of the effectiveness of arbitration, and was not taken over in later US FTAs, this aspect is left aside in the present analysis. For critical remarks on this procedural property see i.e. Bieszczat (2008), pp. 66–67.

[82]Arbitral Panel established pursuant to Chapter Twenty of the CAFTA-DR, *In the Matter of Guatemala – Issues Relating to the Obligations Under Article 16.2.1(a) of the CAFTA-DR*, Final Report of the Panel, 14 June 2017, para. 152.

[83]Ibid, para. 435.

[84]Ibid, para. 190.

[85]Ibid, para. 196.

[86]See above Sect. 2.2.1.

this procedural property is a significant disincentive for these organizations to promote and try to make use of labour arbitration in US FTAs. Likewise, it falls short from realizing the self-standing purpose of furthering individual labour conditions which is explicitly mentioned in US FTAs.[87] Therefore, both requirements examined here represent an underlying misled design feature of US FTAs' labour chapters.

3.3 Patterns of Violations in Comparison to Regional Human Rights Adjudication

One may object to this critical assessment that in a dispute settlement procedure of a FTA, it is natural to emphasize the systemic nature of labour standard obligations because it is only then that they gain relevance for mutual trade. However, other international judicial dispute settlement procedures prove that justice in individual cases and an investigation into systemic patterns of violations in a domestic jurisdiction can be achieved at the same time. Namely, human rights courts have developed approaches to examine systemic human rights violations while keeping a focus on the protection of individuals in concrete situations.

In the case of the European Court of Human Rights this is realized through the pilot judgment procedure introduced in the case of *Broniowski v. Poland*. In pilot judgment procedures, the Court focusses on a typical pilot case in order to determine 'structural or systemic problem[s] or other dysfunction[s]'[88] and violations of the European Convention on Human Rights. It adjournes similar proceedings in the meantime as appropriate. If it finds for such systemic violations, it can then order the respondent to remedy them at the domestic level.[89] Individuals have still the opportunity to receive just satisfaction. The ECHR may only reserve that question pending the implementation of individual or general measures by the respondent in accordance with the orders of the pilot judgment.[90] The Inter-American Court on Human Rights in a judgment on a specific case can issue fairly detailed and orders in its judgments which can go beyond the concrete individual situation raised and

[87]As examples, see Preamble (10) NAFTA and Preamble (1) and (13) and Art. 19.10 (6) TPP.

[88]Art. 61 (1) and (3) Rules of Court of the ECHR, lastly amended on 14 Nov 2016.

[89]ECHR, *Case of Broniowski v. Poland*, Judgment, Appl. No. 31443/96, 22 June 2004, paras. 188–194; based on Council of Europe, Committee of Ministers, Resolution CM/Res(2004)3 on judgments revealing an underlying systemic problem, 12 May 2004 and Council of Europe, Committee of Ministers, Recommendation Rec(2004)6 to member states on the improvement of domestic remedies, 12 May 2004; today regulated in Art. 61 of the Rules of Court of the ECHR, lastly amended on 14 Nov 2016. See also Abel (2013), pp. 371–372 and 383.

[90]Art. 61 (5) Rules of Court of the ECHR, lastly amended on 14 Nov 2016.

also address systemic deficiencies in a national jurisdiction.[91] This shows that it is possible for an adjudicatory body to deal with systemic shortcomings while at the same time retaining the character of a judicial procedure with the purpose of benefiting the individual through adjudication on concrete cases.

Whereas the two regional human rights courts generally deal with individual claims and, in a second step, may extract systemic patterns and impacts of violations, labour dispute settlement in US FTAs follow a contrary approach. The focus is on patterns of conduct and the impact on trade, and on the occasion, individual cases may eventually be scrutinized in the course of analysis. US FTAs' labour chapter design therein appears more suitable if perceived as an institutionalized setting for general improvements of labour standards; which is one explanation for the practical preponderance of US FTAs' diplomatic labour procedures. At the same time, individuals' and trade unions' incentives to advocate for a use of FTA labour dispute settlement are naturally lower, given that relief for their individual situation is not a primary concern at least considering procedure.

Why does US FTAs' trade-labour arbitration not allow for a greater focus on single cases of labour standard violations? One possible explanation is to see this as a consequence of the trade ambit in which the labour standard provisions are enshrined. Only where a series of violations occur and trade is affected was there a sufficient relevance of labour standard violations for international trade, and FTAs should be limited to trade issues. Related is the fear for disguised protectionism.[92] Although this is in principal a legitimate concern, there is no reason why FTAs' dispute settlement should not address single labour standard violations as a value-based approach to trade relations and their impact on workers; after all, the improvement of individual workers' situation forms an explicit and self-standing purpose of US FTAs.[93] It would be possible to presume that every labour standard violation causes an abstract danger of constituting an unfair competitive economic advantage, and that thus construe a sufficient trade-linkage as inherent in every single violation as such.[94] A certain trade relevance is always indicated by the fact that a state party has found the violation to be relevant enough to initiate inter-state

[91]See i.e. Burgorgue-Larsen (2011), paras. 10.25–10.30 *inter alia* on orders to amend domestic legislation to ensure the non-repetition of violations and on symbolic measures to gradually rebuild a democratic society.

[92]Cf. the concern of developing countries for the inclusion of a social clause into WTO law, reflected in the Singapore Ministerial Declaration, 18 Dec 1996, WT/MIN(96)/DEC which stipulates in its para. 4: '[...] We reject the use of labour standards for protectionist purposes, and agree that the comparative advantage of countries, particularly low-wage developing countries, must in no way be put into question. [...].'

[93]See Fn. 87.

[94]But see Arbitral Panel established pursuant to Chapter Twenty of the CAFTA-DR, *In the Matter of Guatemala – Issues Relating to the Obligations Under Article 16.2.1(a) of the CAFTA-DR*, Final Report of the Panel, 14 June 2017, para. 168 which, in light of the explicit requirement of an impact on trade in CAFTA-DR, rejected to infer such an impact on trade by the mere fact that the labour standard violation occurred in a company engaged in trade, as the requirement then would be superfluous and without effect.

arbitration. Likewise, any disguised protectionism could still be carved out from protection by a teleological interpretation of labour standard obligations.[95] It is submitted that, therefore, not only the requirement of a recurring course of action or inaction is misled, but also the requirement of an impact on trade should be abolished. Instead, US arbitral tribunals on trade-labour could adopt the methodology of one of the two regional human rights courts mentioned above.

3.4 Conclusion

The obligation to enforce national and certain international labour standards in US FTAs requires the claimant to demonstrate a pattern of violations which affects trade between the parties. These requirements prevent that trade-labour arbitration can meaningfully contribute to further individuals' labour conditions and remedy infringements in concrete situations, despite that being an explicit and self-standing purpose of US FTAs. As a consequence, labour unions and NGOs must provide evidence of labour standard violations in a series of instances to prove their case. Because this requires the investment of substantial resources and information, these actors are disincentivized to make use of petitions under the trade-labour dispute settlement procedure in the first place. As a corollary the procedure loses relevance for the envisioned trade-related systemic safeguard against low labour standards becoming a comparative economic advantage. The reason is that states in practice rely on information of the disincentivized stakeholders as a factual precondition for the use of trade-labour arbitration - a vicious circle. It follows that US FTAs thus do not succeed in combining individual justice and systemic improvements. That reconciling the two in international dispute settlement system would be possible shows the example of according international human rights courts' practice in Europe and America.

4 Legal Consequences of an Arbitral Award Against a State: Monetary Assessments

In the chronological order of an arbitral procedure, the legal consequences arising from an award against a state stand at the end. Their properties are just as important for evaluating the potential outcome and effectiveness of a dispute settlement procedure as the aspects already discussed. To recall, the inclusion of the possibility to suspend trade benefits into US FTA's arbitration procedures in trade and labour chapters, at least as a deterring factor, raises the hope of expanding the enforcement

[95]Cf. Polaski (2003), p. 19.

effectiveness of the international trade regime to the protection of labour standards.[96]

In an early generation of US FTAs, this potential is to a large extent lost by their peculiar connection of the suspension of trade benefits with monetary assessments. The connection is as follows: If state parties cannot agree on an action plan based on the arbitral award, or if a state party does not comply with a mutually agreed action plan, the arbitral tribunal may issue a fee against the defendant, a so called 'monetary enforcement assessment'.[97] This fee is not paid to the complainant, but into a fund which shall finance programmes for the general improvement of labour standards, especially in the respondent's territory.[98] Through suspension of trade benefits, complainants can only enforce the duty to pay monetary assessment to a fund.[99] Trade sanctions thus fulfil a substantially different function in comparison to the suspension of trade concessions in the WTO or in the general trade chapters of US FTAs, where the monetary advantages of such suspension remain with the claimant in order to restore the reciprocal balance of trade concessions.[100]

If the respondent profits, at least to a certain degree, from the suspension of benefits issued against it, much of its deterring potential and corresponding incentive to comply with labour standard obligations diminish. The reason is that the funding of labour standard programmes in the non-complying state does not represent an economic lever at all that could prompt the state to comply, especially in comparison with the suspension of trade benefits available under the WTO Dispute Settlement Understanding. The advantage of forcing the financing of a labour programme through arbitration for workers and labour unions often is rather negligible, as the effectiveness of a labour standard improvement programme always depends on the cooperation of the sovereign state on its territory. Even more, the programme is developed and carried out under the auspices of the pertinent FTA's political executive body in which of course the respondent has a say.[101] This leads back to a need for a diplomatic solution of the conflict. To be sure, monetary assessments have merit in attempting to design a remedy with

[96]See above Sect. 1 and Stoll (2011), para. 1.

[97]I.e. Art. 39 (4)–(6) and Annex 39 NAALC; Art. 21.12 US-Australia FTA; Art. 19.12 US-Bahrain FTA; Art. 20.17 CAFTA-DR and Art. 22.16 US-Chile FTA.

[98]I.e. Art. 39 (4) (b), (5) (b) and Annex 39 (3) NAALC; Art. 21.12 (4) US-Australia FTA; Art. 19.12 (4) US-Bahrain FTA; Art. 20.17 (4) CAFTA-DR and Art. 22.16 (4) US-Chile FTA. In addition, see also the problem of low fee caps, existent only in some US FTAs, see i.e. Annex 39 (1) NAALC; Art. 21.12 (2) US-Australia FTA; Art. 19.12 (2) US-Bahrain FTA and Art. 22.16 (2) US-Chile FTA. See also Bolle (2016), p. 5.

[99]I.e. Art. 41 (1) and (2) NAALC; Art. 21.12 (7) US-Australia FTA; Art. 19.12 (6) US-Bahrain FTA; Art. 20.17 (5) CAFTA-DR and Art. 22.16 (5) US-Chile FTA.

[100]Cf. on CAFTA-DR compared to WTO and general CAFTA-DR dispute settlement Gantz (2007), pp. 404–405.

[101]Annex 39 (3) and Art. 9 et seqq. NAALC; Art. 21.12 (4) and Art. 21.1 US-Australia FTA; Art. 19.12 (4) and Art. 18.2 US-Bahrain FTA; Art. 20.17 (4) and Art. 19.1 CAFTA-DR and Art. 22.16 (4) and Art. 21.1 US-Chile FTA.

constructive rather than distortive effects. The point made here is that it may be a meaningful contribution to diplomatic solutions of a dispute, but are not well placed as a part of rule-based labour arbitration in the way provided for in the early generation of US FTAs analysed here.

The picture is different in US FTAs with Peru, Colombia, Panama and South Korea as well as the TPP, all being decisively determined in content by the 2007 US Bipartisan Trade Deal. In these FTAs, the respective labour standard obligations can be enforced by the suspension of trade benefits as a last resort following the WTO model. The inclusion of monetary assessment here is different: After the Claimant declares its intent to suspend benefits, the respondent can avoid the suspension of benefits *unilaterally* if it declares within a certain time frame that it will instead pay a monetary assessment to the claimant. The Parties then must negotiate on the amount of that fee. If they cannot agree, the amount is set at 50% of the level of the benefits the claimant had announced to suspend, or at 50% of the level of benefits determined by the panel to be of equivalent effect in case such procedure had taken place.[102] If the respondent fails to pay, the complaining party may proceed to unilaterally suspend the benefits as announced in the first place.[103] The option to pay monetary assessment thus functions as a unilateral procedural defence of the respondent against the unilateral suspension of benefits by the claimant. The 50% reduction provides an incentive to the respondent to invoke and actually pay the monetary assessment. Furthermore, for the monetary assessment to be paid into a fund instead of directly to the other party, consent of the claimant is necessary.[104] In sum, this approach retains the possibility of a deterring sanction in the form of the suspension of trade benefits as a last resort, while integrating the possibility of the payment of monetary assessment as a less trade distortive, more constructive remedy. This remedial architecture is sophisticated and may provide an important building block for well-functioning trade-labour arbitration in the future. At the same time, it also shows that the drafting of US FTAs made important progress in the past sparked by the influence of the US Congress.

5 Arbitration and Individuals

5.1 Inter-State and Mixed Judicial Dispute Settlement Modes

The analysis so far has established that US FTAs' arbitration procedures in trade and labour chapters show aspects on the different stages from initation to remedies

[102] Art. 21.16 (6) US-Colombia FTA; Art. 20.15 (8) US-Panama FTA; Art. 21.16 (8) US-Peru FTA; Art. 22.13 (5) and (7) US-Korea FTA and Art. 28.20 (12) TPP.

[103] Art. 21.16 (8) US-Colombia FTA; Art. 20.15 (6) US-Panama FTA; Art. 21.16 (6) US-Peru FTA; Art. 22.13 (5) US-Korea FTA and Art. 28.20 (7) TPP.

[104] Art. 21.16 (7) US-Colombia FTA; Art. 20.15 (7) US-Panama FTA; Art. 21.16 (7) US-Peru FTA; Art. 22.13 (6) US-Korea FTA and Art. 28.20 (8) TPP.

that are functionally problematic. An aspect which has already been touched upon as an underlying issue in this inquiry shall now be investigated more explicitly: the *inter-state* nature of US FTAs' labour arbitration and the potential prospects of mixed arbitration in this field. It has already been pointed out that non-state actors such as trade unions and NGOs play a pivotal role in defending and advocating labour standards.[105] It will now be analysed whether the lack of involvement and status of these important non-state actors in US FTAs' trade-labour arbitration - in other words, the lack of *mixed* arbitration - is another more general reason why it is only scarcely used in practice.

In a comparative view, mixed judicial proceedings have proven to be effective in a number of regimes. One of them is investor-state dispute settlement, for example under the ICSID Convention.[106] US FTAs themselves also cover investment protection chapters which include the right to claim violations of investment obligations by investors against the respective state party before an arbitral tribunal.[107] Another example for mixed judicial dispute settlement are the various human rights regimes, in particular regional human rights tribunals in Europe, America and Africa.[108] However, the effectiveness of the WTO inter-state dispute settlement regime makes it clear that it would be a too superficial conclusion to generally place mixed judicial proceedings over inter-state procedures in terms of effectiveness. Instead, one should ask more specifically if and how individuals may contribute to trade-labour dispute settlement in US FTAs.

It was already addressed that US FTAs' objectives do not only relate to furthering trade between states without low labour standards becoming a comparative advantage, but do also aim for furthering the labour conditions of individuals.[109] In most cases, individuals and trade unions (by representing workers or regarding collective labour rights) are directly affected by adverse labour conditions and thus have the greatest insight into possible violations and access to relevant evidence. This is why more and better substantiated claims are likely to arise if individuals are given certain means of procedural participation and control. Such control would prevent the 'disappointment trap'[110] already pointed out above.[111] Furthermore, participation of individuals and trade unions in labour arbitration could be a means

---

[105]On the NAALC Dombois et al. (2004), pp. 170 et seqq.

[106]Even though there are discussions on the qualitative and quantitative empirical effectiveness of international investment arbitration, it is overall fair to name it as one of the most effective examples of international arbitration. See Bungenberg et al. (2015), paras. 1 et seqq.

[107]It is controversial whether investment treaties vest investors with own international substantive or merely procedural rights, cf. Kim (2015).

[108]Abel (2013).

[109]See Fn. 87.

[110]Dombois (2006), p. 249.

[111]See Sect. 2.2.3.

of creating transparency and linkages to civil society, thus, fostering the legitimacy of FTAs and their legal mechanisms.[112]

5.2 *Missed Opportunities in Comparison*

5.2.1 NAEEC as a Dispute Settlement Realm That Connects a Societal Good with Trade

In fact, in other matters, US FTAs themselves already provide for comparatively more extensive procedural rights for individuals. In the second NAFTA side agreement on environmental issues (NAAEC), the environmental dispute settlement procedure is formally initiated by individuals. They file a complaint directly with the Secretariat of the NAAEC Commission for Environmental Cooperation, which is headed by an Executive Director chosen by the parties and who appoints expert staff.[113] In a preliminary stage, the Secretariat reviews the petition. If it considers the petition to be sufficiently substantiated, it requests a response from the respective government.[114] If the Secretariat believes that further investigation is warranted, it can recommend the creation of a factual record to the NAFTA state parties.[115] By a two-third vote, the Council of the NAEEC Commission, which is comprised by cabinet-level or equivalent representatives of the parties, may instruct the Secretariat to work out a factual report. Its final version is submitted to the Council, which in turn decides by a two-third majority whether to make it publicly available.[116]

Thus, under the NAAEC, individuals have a right to issue a review of a petition by an international organ established by the US FTA on the violation of environmental protection standards which goes more into detail than what is procedurally provided for in labour matters for the review of petitions by NAOs. In the NAEEC, it is only after this initiation and preliminary stage that state parties regain control over the dispute settlement procedure. This relatively higher orientation towards mixed dispute settlement at least correlates with a far greater procedural success rate of NAAEC- in comparison to NAALC-dispute settlement.[117] Some commentators argued that a similar independent body should be created within the

[112]For an overview see Matsushita et al. (2015), pp. 99–100. Stressing the function of *amicus curiae* briefs to contribute to an objective assessment of a case rather than participation Steger (2002), pp. 421 et seqq. and Xu (2017); but see Brabandere (2011), pp. 348 et seqq. More generally on transparency in international adjudication see Neumann and Simma (2013).

[113]Art. 11 and Art. 14 (1) NAEEC.

[114]Art. 14 (2) NAEEC.

[115]Art. 9 and Art. 15 NAEEC.

[116]Art. 15 NAEEC.

[117]With figures on year 2005 see Bieszczat (2008), p. 1402 and Knox (2005), pp. 439 et seqq.

NAALC.[118] Importantly, the NAAEC's mechanism allows individuals to complain about shortcomings in the state of their own nationality. Thus, complaints are brought by individuals who are directly affected by allegedly wrongful conduct of the pertinent state. The shortcomings of NAALC's constellation of unalligned interests described above[119] do not arise, and still, individuals are given an objective instance which they may resort to.

5.2.2 European Union and Canada as Systems with a More Prominent Procedural Role for Individuals

A rather far-reaching procedural influence of individuals in a trade dispute settlement system may be observed in the European Union. Even though the EU nowadays is of course much more than a free trade area, namely a project of political integration in many non-economic areas, one of its historically and contemporary most fundamental aims still is the creation of a single European market. The relationship between free trade and the protection of labour standards is not only addressed by the fundamental freedoms under the Treaty on the Functioning of the European Union.[120] It is also subject of specific provisions in the EU Treaties, as well as many European regulations and directives.[121]

When individuals bring claims on trade-labour issues before the Court of Justice of the European Union (CJEU), mostly channelled through the domestic courts,[122] the CJEU not only adjudicates on the individual case, but at the same time may promote and further develop the single European market as envisaged by the European Treaties. The CJEU, activated by individuals through the interplay between domestic courts and the CJEU, thus operates in aligned interests with the EU member states and the EU-Commission in promoting this overall goal. When advocating its own case on the basis of EU law, every individual thus potentially contributes to the described EU's macroeconomic goal. To be sure, the question how social rights and economic considerations eventually are reconciled *materially* is not touched upon in this article. There is intensive debate and criticism on the CJEU's jurisprudence, especially in comparison to the European Court of Human Rights.[123] It is submitted that the procedural activation of individuals does not determine a certain material outcome, which is instead a separate matter of interpretation of the relevant substantive provisions. Nevertheless, the EU provides an

[118]Bieszczat (2008), pp. 1394 et seqq.

[119]See Sect. 2.2.3.

[120]Art. 28 et seqq., Art. 45 et seqq., Art. 49 et seqq. and Art. 56 et seqq. TFEU.

[121]I.e. Art. 114 and Art. 153 TFEU; EU Directive 2003/88/EC *concerning certain aspects of the organization of working time (Working Time Directive)*, O.J. L 299/9 (2003).

[122]Mostly by preliminary rulings, Art. 267 TFEU.

[123]Cf. comparing the EU and NAFTA see Compa (2001), p. 4. With reference to the ECJ cases of *Viking* and *Laval* see Veldman (2013), pp. 105 et seqq.

example how individuals can contribute to a more general trade purpose through adjudication on individual rights.

Another example is Canada which, due to certain autonomy of its provinces and territories as a federal state, concluded the Canadian Free Trade Agreement (CFTA) which entered into force on the 1 July 2017 and replaced the previous Agreement on Internal Trade.[124] It is an inter-governmental agreement between the federal government, the three territories and the ten Canadian provinces. The Agreement encompasses rules against trade barriers, including provisions on environmental protection[125] as well as labour mobility and occupational standards, however to the exclusion of social policy measures including labour standards.[126] Notwithstanding the limited scope on substantive labour standard protection, its dispute settlement provisions are noteworthy. They include both government-to-government and person-to-government arbitration with direct access and control by individuals.[127] 'Persons' are defined as natural persons, enterprises and trade unions as recognized by the applicable legislation of a CFTA party.[128] They are first called to request the pertinent government to initiate government-to-government dispute settlement proceedings on their behalf.[129] If the government addressed refuses to do so, individuals are free to initiate dispute settlement including arbitration subject to a serious of conditions, and have full control over the proceedings.[130] The CFTA thus forms another example of how to connect procedural rights of individuals with the economic goal of reducing trade barriers.

5.3 Conclusion

It is of course true that one cannot expect the same degree of sovereignty renouncement from FTA parties as in the context of the highly integrated EU or a federal state like Canada. However, the example of the NAAEC shows that participation of individuals is not a question of black or white. Rather, one can picture a gradual scale of involvement of trade unions and NGOs in trade-labour procedures, the NAAEC model representing a modest, the EU and the CFTA system a far-reaching approach. States' decision to include labour matters in FTAs should resonate in a greater participation of trade unions and NGOs in trade-labour arbitration than in current US FTAs. To be sure, free trade agreements should not be overloaded with considerations that fit other branches of international law, and inter-institutional

[124] https://www.cfta-alec.ca/canadian-free-trade-agreement/. Accessed 19 July 2017.

[125] Chapter 6 CFTA.

[126] Chapter 7 and more specifically Art. 701 CFTA.

[127] Part A and B of CFTA, respectively.

[128] Art. 1041 CFTA.

[129] Art. 1016 (1) CFTA.

[130] Art. 1018 et seqq. CFTA; already provided for under the preceding Agreement on Internal Trade, cf. Hoekman (2015), p. 621.

interpretative and jurisdictional conflicts and fragmentation should be avoided.[131] However, the procedures would likely be used more often if trade unions and NGOs were involved to a greater extent and could exert direct control over proceedings. The comparative perspective shows that this is also in the interest of the underlying macro-economic goal of promoting trade growth without impairing on labour standards, and at the same time increases the legitimization of FTAs overall.

Moreover, such an approach would alleviate another concern with contemporary US FTAs. The inclusion of investment chapters and investor-state dispute settlement (ISDS) provisions are increasingly subject to criticism. ISDS is sometimes perceived to have an inherent bias in favour of investors.[132] Procedural participation of individuals in trade-labour issues could contribute to balance economic and societal interests in FTAs.[133]

6 Conclusion

The analysis reveals that the reason for the lack of arbitral practice in trade-labour matters in US FTAs lies in a variety of conceptual incongruences of the arbitration procedures. These can be found in different procedural and institutional aspects to varying degrees in the different generations of US FTAs. US FTAs' trade-labour arbitration provisions combine aspects of different other international dispute settlement systems, in which, however, these elements are often differently conceptualized and framed. The mixture of quite different concepts and elements of international arbitration procedures mostly does not yield a coherent result. One of the greatest problems is that US FTAs substantially marginalize the role of individuals, trade unions and NGOs. Only in some parts, the newest generation of US FTAs has alleviated some of these deficiencies. Therefore, US FTAs fall short from providing a rules- rather than power-based setting for the settlement of trade-labour disputes. It follows that US FTAs fail to preserve the inherent qualities and advantages of arbitration as a specific tool of international peaceful dispute settlement.

Trade-labour arbitration's weakness has consequences on the overall balance of US FTAs. Whereas inter-state provisions on liberalization of trade benefit form an accessible and through trade sanctions effectively enforceable arbitral procedure, and whereas investors are provided with likewise effective mixed investor-state arbitration, labour standard obligations mostly do not benefit from similar arbitral enforcement mechanisms. This, in light of the dynamic development of FTAs, can lead to an excessive preponderance of trade liberalization and investor interests and

[131] On the relation of the ILO and FTAs see Agustí-Panareda et al. (2014), p. 26.
[132] See i.e. van Harten (2010).
[133] See in particular the analysis and suggestions by Gött (this volume).

might indeed result in a race to the bottom of labour standards in contrast to the state parties' declared will and the FTAs' explicit purpose.

It is regrettable that US FTAs miss the opportunity to provide for sound enforcement procedures for the protection of individuals' labour conditions. Thereby, the US FTAs fall short from contribution to the improvement of individuals' labour conditions which forms a separate and self-standing purpose in US FTAs in addition to the furthering of trade between the parties. Procedural and institutional role models for improvement may be found in other treaties and regimes on different scales of integration, such as the NAEEC, the EU, and the CFTA that reconcile macro-economic goals and the improving of labour conditions, in particular by providing trade unions and NGOs with own procedural rights.

References

Abel P (2013) Menschenrechtsschutz durch Individualbeschwerdeverfahren: Ein regionaler Vergleich aus historischer, normativer und faktischer Perspektive. Archiv des Völkerrechts 51(3):369–392

Agustí-Panareda J, Ebert F, LeClercq D (2014) Labour provisions in free trade agreements: fostering their consistency with the ILO standards system. ILO, Geneva

Banks K (2011) Trade, labor and international governance: an inquiry into the potential effectiveness of the new international labor law. Berk J Employ Labor Law 32(1):45–142

Berner K (2016) Reconciling investment protection and sustainable development: a plea for an interpretative U-turn. In: Hindelang S, Krajewski M (eds) Shifting paradigms in international investment law: more balanced, less isolated, increasingly diversified. Oxford University Press, Oxford, pp 177–203

Bhagwati J (1995) Trade liberalization and 'Fair Trade' demands: addressing the environmental and labour standards issues. World Econ 18(6):745–759

Bieszczat FH (2008) Labor provisions in trade agreements: from the NAALC to now. Chicago-Kent Law Rev 83(3):1387–1408

Bolle MJ (2016) Overview of labor enforcement issues in free trade agreements. US Congressional Research Service

Brabandere E (2011) Non-state actors in international dispute settlement: pragmatism in international law. In: d'Aspremont J (ed) Participants in the international legal system: multiple perspectives on non-state actors in international law. Routledge, London, pp 342–359

Brewster R (2006) Rule-based dispute resolution in international trade law. Virginia Law Rev 92:251–288

Brower CH II (2007) Arbitration. In: Wolfrum R (ed) Max Planck encyclopedia of public international law. Oxford University Press, Oxford. Available via http://opil.ouplaw.com/home/epil. Accessed 09 Aug 2017

Bungenberg M, Griebel J, Hobe S, Reinisch A (2015) General introduction to international investment law. In: Bungenberg M, Griebel J, Hobe S, Reinisch A (eds) International investment law: a handbook. Nomos, Baden-Baden, pp 1–5

Burgorgue-Larsen L (2011) The right to determine reparations. In: Burgorgue-Larsen L, Úbeda de Torres A (eds) The Inter-American Court of Human Rights: case law and commentary. Oxford University Press, Oxford, pp 217–241

Compa LA (2001) NAFTA's labour side agreement and international labour solidarity. Cornell University ILR School. http://digitalcommons.ilr.cornell.edu/articles/175. Accessed 11 Aug 2017

Cosbey A (2007) Brave new deal? Assessing the May 10th U.S. bipartisan compact on free trade agreements. http://www.iisd.org/sites/default/files/publications/com_brave_new_deal.pdf. Accessed 23 June 2016
Dombois R (2006) Sozialklauseln in US-Freihandelsabkommen: Ein wirksames Mittel internationaler Arbeitsregulierung? Industrielle Beziehungen: Zeitschrift für Arbeit. Organisation und Management 13(3):238–252
Dombois R, Hornberger E, Winter J (2004) Internationale Arbeitsregulierung in der Souveränitätsfalle: Das Lehrstück des North American Agreement on Labor Cooperation zwischen den USA, Mexico und Kanada. Politik, Gemeinschaft und Gesellschaft in einer globalisierten Welt, vol 2. LIT, Münster
Dugard J (2009) Diplomatic protection. In: Wolrum R (ed) Max Planck encyclopedia of public international law. Oxford University Press, Oxford. Available via http://opil.ouplaw.com/home/epil. Accessed 09 Aug 2017
Elliott KA, Freeman RB (2003) Can labor standards improve under globalization? Institute for International Economics, Washington, DC
Fergusson IF (2015) Trade promotion authority (TPA) and the role of congress in trade policy. Congressional Research Service
Gantz DA (2007) Settlement of disputes under the Central America-Dominican Republic-United States free trade agreement. Boston Coll Int Comp Law Rev 30(2):331–410
Hoekman B (2015) Fostering transatlantic regulatory cooperation and gradual multilateralization. J Int Econ Law 18:609–624
ILO, IILS (2013) Social dimensions of free trade agreements. Studies on growth with equity. ILO, Geneva
Kim Y-I (2015) Investment law and the individual. In: Bungenberg M, Griebel J, Hobe S, Reinisch A (eds) International investment law: a handbook. Nomos, Baden-Baden, pp 1585–1601
Knox JH (2005) The 2005 activity of the NAFTA tribunals. Am J Int Law 100:429–444
Lang A (2011) World trade law after neoliberalism: re-imagining the global economic order. Oxford University Press, Oxford
Lazo Grandi P (2009) Trade agreements and their relation to labour standards: the current situation. International Centre for Trade and Sustainable Development, Geneva
Leary VA (1997) The WTO and the social-clause: post-Singapore. Eur J Int Law 8(1):118–122
Matsushita M, Schoenbaum TJ, Mavroidis PC, Hahn MJ (2015) The world trade organization: law, practice, and policy, 3rd edn. Oxford University Press, Oxford
Mavroidis PC (2006) Art. 6 DSU. In: Wolfrum R, Stoll P-T, Kaiser K (eds) WTO - institutions and dispute settlement. Martinus Nijhoff, Boston, pp 337–353
Merrills JG (2011) International dispute settlement, 5th edn. Cambridge University Press, Cambridge
Neumann T, Simma B (2013) Transparency in international adjudication. In: Bianchi A, Peters A (eds) Transparency in international law. Cambridge University Press, Cambridge, pp 436–476
Nottage H (2009) Trade and development. In: Bethlehem D, McRae D, Neufeld R, van Damme I (eds) The Oxford handbook of international trade law. Oxford University Press, Oxford, pp 481–504
Paulus A (2011) Treaties of friendship, commerce and navigation. In: Wolfrum R (ed) Max Planck encyclopedia of public international law. Oxford University Press, Oxford. Available via DIALOG. http://opil.ouplaw.com/home/epil. Accessed 09 Aug 2017
Polaski S (2003) Protecting labor rights through trade agreements: an analytical guide. J Int Law Policy 10:13–25
Polaski S, Vyborny K (2006) Labor clauses in trade agreements: policy and practice. Integration Trade 25:95–124
Steger DP (2002) Amicus Curiae: participant or friend? The WTO and NAFTA experience. In: Bogdandy A, Mavroidis PC, Mény Y (eds) European integration and international co-ordination: studies in transnational economic law in honour of Claus-Dieter Ehlermann. Kluwer Law International, The Hague, pp 419–450

Stoll P-T (2006) Article I DSU. In: Wolfrum R, Stoll P-T, Kaiser K (eds) WTO - institutions and dispute settlement. Martinus Nijhoff, Boston, pp 268–276

Stoll P-T (2011) World trade organization, dispute settlement. In: Wolfrum R (ed) Max Planck encyclopedia of public international law. Oxford University Press, Oxford. Available via DIALOG. http://opil.ouplaw.com/home/epil. Accessed 09 Aug 2017

Stoll P-T, Holterhus TP, Gött H (2017) Investitionsschutz und Verfassung: Völkerrechtliche Investitionsschutzverträge aus der Perspektive des deutschen und europäischen Verfassungsrechts. Mohr Siebeck, Tübingen

Sutherland P, Bhagwati J, Botchwey K, FitzGerald N, Hamada K, Jackson JH, Lafer C, de Montbrial T (2004) Report on the future of the WTO: addressing institutional challenges in the new millennium. World Trade Organization, Geneva

Tomuschat C (1999) International law: ensuring the survival of mankind on the eve of a new century: general course on public international law. Recueil des cours 281:1–438

Tomuschat C (2002) Article 33. In: Simma B, Mosler H, Randelzhofer A, Tomuschat C, Wolfrum R, Paulus A, Chaitidou E (eds) The Charter of the United Nations: a commentary, vol I, 2nd edn. Oxford University Press, Oxford, pp 583–594

van den Bossche P, Zdouc W (2013) The law and policy of the world trade organization: text, cases and materials, 3rd edn. Cambridge University Press, Cambridge

van den Putte L, Orbie J, Bossuyt F, Martens D, de Ville F (2015) What social face of the new EU trade agreements? Beyond the 'soft' approach. ETUI policy brief. Eur Econ Employ Soc Policy 13:1–5

van Harten G (2010) Perceived bias in investment treaty arbitration. In: Waibel M, Kaushal A, Chung LK-H, Balchin C (eds) The Backlash against investment arbitration: perceptions and reality. Kluwer Law International, Alphen aan den Rijn, pp 433–453

Veldman A (2013) The protection of the fundamental right to strike within the context of the European internal market: implications of the forthcoming accession of the EU to the ECHR. Utrecht Law Rev 9(1):104–117

Vogt JS (2015) The evolution of labor rights and trade: a transatlantic comparison and lessons for the transatlantic trade and investment partnership. J Int Econ Law 18(4):827–860

Waibel M (2015) Investment arbitration: jurisdiction and admissibility. In: Bungenberg M, Griebel J, Hobe S, Reinisch A (eds) International investment law: a handbook. Nomos, Baden-Baden, pp 1212–1287

Xu J (2017) The role of civil society in EU preferential trade agreements. European Society of International Law Conference Paper Series. Available via SSRN. https://ssrn.com/abstract=2912010. Accessed 2 Feb 2017

An Individual Labour Complaint Procedure for Workers, Trade Unions, Employers and NGOs in Future Free Trade Agreements

Henner Gött

Contents

H. Gött (✉)
Georg-August-University Göttingen, Institute of International and European Law, Göttingen, Germany
e-mail: hgoett@gwdg.de

H. Gött (ed.), *Labour Standards in International Economic Law*,
https://doi.org/10.1007/978-3-319-69447-4_10

1 Introduction

Labour chapters are, and are likely to remain, a recurring feature of free trade agreements (FTAs).[1] An increasing number of labour chapters, including those in virtually all US, Canadian and EU FTAs, include dispute settlement mechanisms (DSMs) as tools for protecting and promoting labour standards. These DSMs were designed to enhance the protection of labour standards in the context of market liberalization and economic cooperation.[2] Their performance in practice, however, has been rather disappointing: Only a handful of all FTA labour DSMs have ever been activated. So far, most submissions have been filed under the DSM established by the 1994 North American Agreement on Labor Cooperation (NAALC), the first FTA Labour DSM ever installed, and even here, their numbers are decreasing.[3] The recently decided case *In the Matter of Guatemala – Issues Relating to the Obligations Under Article 16.2.1(a) of the CAFTA-DR* between the USA and Guatemala is the only dispute that has ever reached the stage of arbitration.[4]

While some authors highlight certain improvements that have coincided with FTA labour DSMs, such as the increase in transnational cooperation among trade unions and NGOs from different countries,[5] it seems fair to contend that in general, these DSMs have not lived up to expectations.[6]

In the preceding chapter, *Patrick Abel* discusses in more detail the systemic deficiencies of current inter-state labour DSMs in FTAs. In this chapter, I will turn to a possible avenue for reform by proposing elements of an internationalized individual labour complaint procedure to be included in future FTAs. I refer to 'individuals' in a broad sense as non-state actors, including natural persons, but also (and, as a practical matter, primarily) trade unions, employers' associations and non-governmental organizations (NGOs). A textual proposal for a complaint procedure as outlined in this chapter is included in the Model Labour Chapter for Future EU FTAs in the fourth part of this volume.

This chapter has been inspired by various calls for a more active role of individuals in FTA labour chapters, including an enhanced role in dispute settlement.[7] In general, individual complaint procedures are still somewhat exceptional under contemporary FTAs, with investor-state dispute settlement (ISDS) included

[1]This is the case at least as to those states that have hitherto included labour provisions in their FTAs. For an overview, see Lazo Grandi (2009) and ILO (2013).

[2]Upon the NAALC's inception, a range of US officials expected it to bring about changes to Mexican labour law and politics. See Dombois (2006), p. 242 and Human Rights Watch (2001).

[3]ILO (2013), pp. 43 et seqq.

[4]Arbitral Panel established pursuant to Chapter Twenty of the CAFTA-DR, *In the Matter of Guatemala – Issues Relating to the Obligations Under Article 16.2.1(a) of the CAFTA-DR*, Final Report of the Panel, 14 June 2017.

[5]Compa (2001).

[6]Vogt (2015), p. 828.

[7]E.g. Greven (2012), p. 92 and Van Roozendaal and Voogsgeerd (2011), p. 364.

in some agreements[8] and recent drafts[9] being a noteworthy exception. By contrast, outside the FTA context, individual complaint mechanisms have proliferated during the past decades. While many of these mechanisms are not specifically dedicated to labour issues, labour-related cases may still be filed under a good number of them. Examples include the universal and regional human rights regimes, such as the International Covenant on Civil and Political Rights (ICCPR),[10] the International Covenant on Economic, Social and Cultural Rights (ICESCR),[11] the European Convention of Human Rights (ECHR),[12] the European Social Charter (ESC)[13] or the American Convention on Human Rights (ACHR).[14] Under the supervisory mechanism of the International Labour Organization (ILO), workers' and employers' organizations can file complaints with the Committee on Freedom of Association, or make representations pursuant to Arts. 24 and 25 of the ILO Constitution.[15] Compared to these other mechanisms, the limited role of individuals as mere petitioners under contemporary FTAs lags behind. This raises the question how the role of individuals in labour disputes could be enhanced in future FTAs.

While not being indifferent towards political realities, this chapter's focus lies on conceptualization.[16] In Sect. 2, I will first briefly recapitulate three main shortcomings of contemporary inter-state FTA labour DSMs. As a proposal to remedy these shortcomings, I will propose three key elements of an individual complaint procedure in Sect. 3 and present their possible benefits for the implementation of FTA labour provisions in Sect. 4. For the remaining part, I will elaborate on a number of issues that arise when attempting to conceptualize an individual complaint procedure. Thus, Sect. 5 will address the appropriate scope of actionable FTA labour provisions. Section 6 will focus on questions of procedure, with a particular focus on accommodating the political contentiousness of labour disputes within a (more) formalized procedure. The procedure's output and its enforcement are the subject of Sect. 7. Section 8 goes beyond the FTA framework and touches on concerns of increased fragmentation of international labour law. The chapter closes with some final remarks in Sect. 9.

---

[8] E.g. Chapter 11 NAFTA and Chapter 8 CETA.

[9] E.g. Chapter 9 EU-Singapore FTA-Draft.

[10] ICCPR Optional Protocol 1.

[11] ICESCR Optional Protocol 1.

[12] Art. 34 ECHR.

[13] Additional Protocol to the European Social Charter Providing for a System of Collective Complaints, see Churchill and Khaliq (2004).

[14] Art. 44 ACHR.

[15] Senghaas-Knobloch (2004), pp. 144–148.

[16] While individual complaint procedures may well be compatible with a constitutionalist approach to FTAs, and while I do not wish to oppose these approaches here, my argument is more pragmatic, centring on enhancing the efficacy of the implementation of FTA labour commitments and deliberately leaving open possible constitutionalist implications.

2 Three Shortcomings of Contemporary FTA Labour DSMs

The suboptimal performance of existing inter-state FTA labour DSMs can be traced back to three important interrelated aspects: the over-politicization of the procedure (Sect. 2.1), the marginalization of individuals (Sect. 2.2) and a corresponding lack of accountability of governments with regard to FTA labour commitments (Sect. 2.3).

2.1 *Over-Politicization*

A recurring feature of contemporary labour DSMs in FTAs is the high degree of politicization, which is an issue regarding both the institutional and procedural arrangements and the way these arrangements have been used in practice.

As to the institutional and procedural arrangements, from the moment petitions are received by one of the governments until the very last step of implementing the final results, FTA labour dispute settlement heavily depends on the political will and means of the government pursuing a claim and the general state of relations with the responding party.[17] Typically, the first stage in FTA labour DSMs has a political and cooperative character, focusing on political consultations and sometimes expert advice. Both the commencement and the further pursuit of this consultation stage is discretionary.[18] Even where a second stage of dispute settlement with adjudicatory mechanisms exists,[19] key procedural steps, such as their initiation or the enforcement of the decisions, are placed under the control and political discretion of the parties.[20] In addition, depending on the particular agreement, a varying number of mandatory procedural steps has to be taken before the parties can move on to the second stage.[21]

As to use of the arrangements in practice, governments have been overly reluctant to make use of dispute settlement. Although governments have occasionally conducted initial research, they have not made use of their competence to initiate dispute settlement without a preceding petition by trade unions or NGOs.[22] What is more, governments have been even more reluctant in proceeding to further stages of dispute settlement, the *US-Guatemala* case mentioned above being the sole example in which further stages were triggered. No case has ever proceeded to

[17]Ebert and Posthuma (2009), p. 63 (79) and Zimmer (2012), p. 150.

[18]Abel (2017).

[19]Recent major EU FTAs and FTA drafts explicitly exclude labour chapters from inter-state arbitration, see e.g. Art. 13.16 EU-Korea FTA and Art. 23.11 CETA Draft.

[20]Abel (2017).

[21]For an overview over the particularly complex procedure under NAALC see Bieszczat (2008), pp. 1388–1392. More recent agreements tend to reduce the number of steps, Abel (2017).

[22]For US governments see Greven (2012), p. 89.

the stage of enforcement. Rather, virtually all cases accepted for review remained on the consultations stage. Moreover, the average length of this stage has dramatically increased.[23] These shortcomings have partly been traced back to limited resources of the relevant national authorities,[24] but there are also indicators that those authorities are guided, determined and compromised by their own political agenda and external political constraints, whether connected to the particular issue at hand or not.[25] For example, analyses of practice under the NAALC revealed that the three parties to the agreement held opposing views on the general role the labour DSM should play. As a consequence, the parties (a) sought to prevent labour dispute settlement to spark tensions in their mutual (economic) relations and (b) were careful not to create precedents that could turn against them later.[26] This resulted in a 'lowest common denominator-approach' by the governmental and intergovernmental bodies involved.[27] Persisting sentiments on the respondent states' side that the true motivations for initiating labour DSMs were protectionist or in nature and additionally burdened the process.[28]

2.2 *Marginalization of Individuals and the 'Disappointment Trap'*

The second issue is a marginalization of individuals both in the institutional design of labour DSMs and in subsequent treaty practice: Especially trade unions and NGOs have always played a central part in advocating labour provisions during FTA negotiations.[29] Likewise, they have been the key drivers behind attempts to implement these provisions, and particularly for attempts to activate the respective dispute settlement provisions.[30] Apart from taking the initiative, trade unions and NGOs also play an essential role in identifying cases, gathering information and evidence and preparing and following up on submissions. Prior studies highlight that submissions backed by advocacy campaigns and supported by transnational

[23]ILO (2013), p. 45.

[24]Bolle (2016), pp. 5–6 and Finbow (2006), p. 232.

[25]Greven (2012), p. 88; ILO (2013), p. 49 and Nolan Garcia (2009).

[26]Dombois (2006), p. 246.

[27]Dombois et al. (2004), p. 293.

[28]Reportedly, there is little evidence that there has actually been protectionist use of labour provisions, Ebert and Posthuma (2009), p. 25. On specific arrangements in FTA labour DSMs created to avert protectionist abuse, see Polaski (2003), pp. 19–20.

[29]ILO (2013), p. 105.

[30]As mentioned above, to date, virtually all of these attempts originated in petitions by trade unions or NGOs concerning cases of alleged labour law violations, Greven (2012), p. 89.

coalitions of trade unions and NGOs have been significantly more successful than submissions that did not have such support.[31]

Yet, as to institutional and procedural arrangements under present agreements, these groups are typically confined to the role of mere petitioners. The choice of whether to initiate dispute settlement and how to pursue a case is left at the discretion of the governments.[32] The consequence is a disconnection of interest and initiative on the one hand and procedural means on the other.

In past practice, petitions, if they were not dismissed or otherwise discontinued, have been 'taken over' by governmental authorities and 'squeezed' through the over-politicized inter-state mechanism time and again.[33] Even if it cannot be said that the outcomes were entirely fruitless for improving the situation in the respective cases,[34] the claims made in the original petitions were often diverted or diluted. It is reported that this has reduced the credibility of labour dispute settlement among petitioners, some of which perceived it as a 'whitewashing' of their original case.[35] Moreover, even in those instances where improvements actually occurred, it was often hardly possible to determine whether they were actually consequences of the petition or caused otherwise, e.g. through parallel political campaigns.[36] As *Dombois* reports with regard to the NAALC, both developments have led to discouragement among petitioners.[37] From their perspective, he argues, it seemed difficult to justify the investment of time, efforts and resources in an FTA labour petition if this petition has no (or no identifiable) gains.[38]

These developments, coinciding with general scepticism towards trade liberalization and FTAs, appear to have increased disappointment among trade unions and NGOs and decreased confidence in labour petitions—*Dombois*, *Hornberger* and *Winter* refer to these developments as a 'disappointment trap'.[39] FTA labour DSMs thus 'lost' some of those groups whose interest and initiative was vital for their performance.

---

[31]ILO (2013), pp. 43–50 and Nolan Garcia (2009).

[32]See e.g. Art. 11 (3) Canada-Peru ALC. See Abel (2017).

[33]Finbow (2006), p. 232 and Greven (2012), p. 88.

[34]Achievements include 'soft' long-term achievements, such as the creation of transnational networks and an increase in public awareness, ILO (2013), p. 50.

[35]Dombois et al. (2004), p. 268.

[36]Dombois et al. (2004).

[37]Many of whom had already been sceptical about FTA labour provisions before, see Dombois (2006), p. 249.

[38]Dombois (2006), p. 249.

[39]Dombois et al. (2004), p. 267.

2.3 *Lack of Accountability*

A third and correlated issue is the lack of accountability of governments with regard to the implementation of FTA labour commitments.[40] As mentioned earlier, under current FTAs, there are a number of avenues for individuals to bring labour petitions to indicate grievances and request the proper implementation of commitments. However, it is by and large left to the recipient governments what to make of them.[41] The potential of existing DSMs as a tool to enhance accountability is thus significantly diminished.

It is worth noting that the issue has partly been taken up in some recent encounters. For example, pursuant to Art. 19.3 (3) TPP, governments have to provide timely responses, 'including in writing as appropriate', to public submissions in labour matters. If one assumes that this is meant to include giving reasons for action or inaction, this might be one step to increase accountability. Yet, being required to respond does still not limit the governments' discretion whether or not to initiate dispute settlement even where they find a violation of labour provisions. Neither is there any neutral independent and impartial review of the governments' conduct. It will thus have to be seen whether provisions such as Art. 19.9 (3) TPP can help to increase accountability. For the time being, as a general observation, DSMs still fall short of being sufficiently effective tools for holding governments accountable.

3 Conceptualizing an Individual Complaint Procedure

Proposing a way to improve FTA labour DSMs, this section will first coin the shortcomings observed above into general objectives for reform (Sect. 3.1). Subsequently, it will propose three key features of an individual labour complaint procedure in future FTAs (Sect. 3.2).

3.1 *Two Overarching Objectives for Reform*

The experience with existing FTA labour DSMs and their flaws can be translated into two objectives to be achieved when considering reform. Firstly, to prevent the DSM from being obstructed by over-politicization, and, secondly, to increase both

[40]This is not a specific issue of dispute settlement—it is equally relevant with regard to civil society participation in cooperative mechanisms established under FTA labour chapters, see van den Putte et al. (2015), p. 3.

[41]For a recent example under cooperative mechanisms, see van den Putte (2015), p. 229.

efficacy and accountability by better aligning substantive interest in the implementation of FTA labour provisions and the procedural capacity to pursue it.

These two overarching objectives, taken together, serve as a common leitmotif for the following identification of three key elements.

3.2 Key Elements

The three key elements that future FTA labour DSM should comprise are: An increased role of individuals and groups as procedural subjects (Sect. 3.2.1), unobstructed access to review of complaints by an independent and impartial body (Sect. 3.2.2) and a definite case-specific statement on the (non-)violation of FTA labour obligations (Sect. 3.2.3).

Before turning to these elements in more detail, it is important to emphasize that neither the overall aim nor the key elements proposed here necessarily warrant a particular institutional and procedural setting. Rather, they are suggested to be elements that could be embedded in a variety of conceivable arrangements. While the key features bear a semblance of adjudicatory mechanisms, this does not mean that there necessarily has to be something like a fully-fledged 'FTA Labour Court'. Instead, from a negotiator's perspective, it will arguably be easier to build on pre-existing arrangements in FTA labour chapters and develop them with due regard to the particularities of the respective situation of the parties, available resources and political sensitivities. In this respect, substance over form is the order of the day.

Moreover, as will be shown in further detail below, the envisaged individual complaint procedure is not meant as a complete replacement of either inter-state DSMs or cooperative mechanisms foreseen under contemporary FTA labour chapters. With regard to the latter, it will be shown that one benefit of the model proposed here lies precisely in the interplay between the essentially political cooperative mechanisms and a more adjudicatory individual complaints procedure.[42]

3.2.1 Individuals and Associations as Procedural Subjects

At the heart of the present proposal lies the idea of giving a more active role to individuals in future labour DSMs. It is suggested that individuals should be upgraded from mere initiators (and subsequent 'bystanders') of an inter-state DSM to procedural subjects.

Individuals should not only be capable to initiate the procedure by filing petitions to a government, but to further pursue their complaints against the respondent FTA party directly, i.e. without being mediatized by the other FTA party. This

[42]Infra. 4.3.

would particularly include that, in principle, the individual claimant retains the unilateral decision to proceed to further stages of dispute settlement, instead of depending on a political decision of the FTA parties' authorities.

As indicated earlier, the notion of 'individuals' is to be understood in a broad sense, including both individual workers or employers and associations such as trade unions, employers' associations and NGOs. As experience shows, and as a practical matter, the typical complainants would be associations, namely trade unions and NGOs. Still, keeping the procedure open for individual workers and employers accounts for the growing number of non-unionized workers, new forms of associations that might not qualify as trade unions or other non- (or differently) organized claimants, thus responding to the increasing diversification of labour relations in the globalized economy.[43] For greater certainty, this broad understanding of individuals does not mean that the envisaged procedure amounts to an *actio popularis*: As will be discussed further below,[44] it is prudent to restrict the right to action to those complainants who can establish a sufficient interest.

3.2.2 Immediate Review by an Independent and Impartial Body

To counter the over-politicization of labour disputes described above, it is suggested that labour disputes be dealt with by a neutral body, e.g. a Secretariat, a Committee or a Panel.[45] Important, rather than its name, is the composition of that body, which should comprise members with specific expertise in labour law and relations. Current rules on inter-state FTA labour DSMs already contain detailed rules on the required qualification of body members and on the procedure of their nomination, which could easily be imported into the modified framework proposed here.[46] It is important to underline that—as is provided for under some present FTA labour DSMs—individual labour complaints should not be dealt with by trade or investment specialists with no expertise in labour matters.

Depending on what is preferred or suitable, the body could be composed entirely ad hoc, as a special division of a permanent treaty committee (such as the trade and labour committees or subcommittees foreseen in many FTAs[47]) or be in itself a permanent institution. Especially the latter option would also increase the chance that there is a coherent approach to an FTA's labour provisions.

---

[43]On relevant developments see ILO (2006).

[44]Infra. 5.

[45]Similar Greven (2012), p. 93.

[46]See e.g. the special labour rosters created under US FTAs, e.g. Art. 16.7 CAFTA-DR. Under more recent US FTAs, the general DSM provisions apply.

[47]See e.g. Art. 15.4 US-Bahrain-FTA; Art. 19.12 TPP; Art. 13.12 and Art. 15.2.1 EU-Korea-FTA and Art. 22.4 CETA-Draft.

3.2.3 Definite Statement on the (Non-)Violation of Labour Standards

As noted above, one important cause of the 'disappointment trap' was that the groups that had an interest in filing petitions felt this would not change much in the particular cases they brought to the attention of the governments. Indeed, those submissions that actually led to consultations ended on the consultation stage, producing as an output general resolutions instead of case-specific findings.[48] Apart from the fact that the commitments arising from intergovernmental consultations were often rather vague, it appears to be a prudent conclusion that the failure to make definite findings on alleged labour law violations in the respective particular cases has contributed to the 'disappointment trap'.[49] As a consequence, any individual complaint procedure should include in its output a definite legal statement, issued by the neutral body, addressing the specific case at hand, such as a declaration on whether a violation of FTA labour provisions could be determined, as well as the body's reasoning.

4 Envisaged Benefits

For the area of dispute settlement, a DSM with these three key features could yield a number of positive effects: Labour disputes could be less politicized (Sect. 4.1), the implementation of labour provisions could be effectuated (Sect. 4.2), a functional lacuna between inter-state dispute settlement and political cooperation could be closed (Sect. 4.3) and, especially regarding FTAs containing chapters on investment protection, the overall balance among the different enforcement mechanisms could be maintained (or restored) (Sect. 4.4).

4.1 Countering Over-Politicization

The model proposed here would render a labour dispute essentially one between the claimant and the respondent FTA party, as opposed to the inter-state character of disputes under current DSMs. It is suggested that, through this 'bypassing' of the other FTA party, labour disputes are less likely to be adversely influenced by diplomatic ties or other factors extrinsic to the particular case at hand.[50] Furthermore, an individual claim, immediately examined by a neutral and independent

---

[48]Dombois (2006), p. 248. For a close-up analysis of cases see Finbow (2006) and Addo (2015).

[49]Dombois (2006), p. 248.

[50]Notwithstanding the idea of an individual complaint procedure, it is conceivable for the non-respondent FTA party to play an active part in it. Furthermore, it would be possible to retain an inter-state DSM as an additional avenue for dispute settlement.

body, is less likely to be perceived as a disguised measure of protectionism or paternalism than a claim brought by the other FTA party under current inter-state DSMs. The result could be a more rationalized approach to solving labour disputes.[51]

To be sure, the goal here is not to entirely de-politicize the dispute, which would arguably be an unachievable (and potentially undesirable) goal. Rather, the goal is to avoid that the inherently political nature of labour disputes compromises the aspired performance of FTA labour DSMs.

4.2 *Enhancing Efficacy by Aligning Interests and Procedural Capacity*

The 'efficacy argument' draws on the experience that action by individuals and non-governmental entities has been central to initiating and pursuing labour dispute settlement. These actors have the greatest interest and incentive to prepare, file and pursue labour complaints, not least as they are, in most instances, the ultimate beneficiaries of labour provisions in FTAs.

In this context, endowing them with the status and means to pursue a claim on their own behalf serves two interrelated purposes: Firstly, it opens an avenue for individuals to seek redress without having to fear that their original case might be diverted or diluted in the course of intergovernmental consultations. This can, secondly, help to further the implementation of labour provisions as a structural objective of economic and social governance. This 'functional approach' of endowing interest groups with the opportunity to enforce provisions they benefit from has been tested in other areas of law.[52] As to labour standards, there is fair reason to believe that a greater alignment of interest and procedural capacities will similarly induce and effectuate non-state initiatives and thereby enhance the implementation of FTA labour provisions.

4.3 *Complementing Cooperative Mechanisms and Inter-State DSMs in FTAs*

Further benefits surface when putting an individual complaint procedure in context with existing inter-state dispute settlement and political cooperation in labour

---

[51]For comparison, this is a named achievement of ISDS, Schreuer (2009), p. 416 (Art. 27 n. 4) and Bhagnani (2015), pp. 452–453, with further references.

[52]On the national level, examples comprise rights of action for environmental law and consumer protection organizations. A noteworthy example on the international level comprise investor-state dispute settlement or individual complaint procedure under human rights regimes.

matters. The flaws of the former have already been discussed above.[53] As to cooperative mechanisms, the concerns are similar to some extent: Some recent FTAs foresee participatory mechanisms for civil society.[54] While these may well be suitable for broader-ranged projects of cooperation, they rather do not provide sufficient means to address particular instances of FTA labour chapter violations. Firstly, the role of the participating civil society groups is again mostly confined to express views, with the governments retaining discretion whether to take action or not.[55] Secondly, designed as predominantly political fora with a corresponding composition (heterogeneous groups with partly opposing interests) and procedure (usually annual meetings), it is likely that their work will focus on broader issues. Close-up analysis of particular cases might simply 'fly under their radar'.[56] Thirdly, especially EU FTAs frame labour issues in the broader context of sustainable development, which might be favourable in terms of policy coherence, but at same time runs the risk of obstructing specific takes on labour issues.[57]

For clarity, it is not suggested that an individual complaint procedure should (or even could) entirely replace the existing models.[58] Indeed, it appears to be one lesson from both WTO law and investment law that a 'legalization' of dispute settlement, while capable of decreasing politicization in particular cases, cannot completely supersede political debates on economic and social matters. Instead of replacing political debates, the proposed complaint procedure is meant to step in and fill a lacuna left by the existing inter-state DSMs and cooperative mechanisms in order to enhance the implementation and enforcement of FTA labour provisions as a whole. Compared to inter-state DSMs, an individual complaint procedure might increase efficiency and accountability. Compared to cooperative mechanisms including civil society participation, it allows for independent legal scrutiny at the initiative of one particular complainant and with a case-specific and definite outcome. On that note, while the decisions of an individual labour complaint procedure are case-specific, governments and non-governmental actors may bring them back into the political arena. There, they can fulfil important systemic functions, both as clarifications on the law and as 'case studies' highlighting and examining underlying issues and serving as potential starting points for more focused cooperation. Indeed, cooperative activities directly linked to specific cases have reportedly been most effective under existing cooperative

---

[53]See also Abel (2017).

[54]E.g. Art. 13.13 EU-Korea FTA and Art. 22.5 and Art. 23.8 (4) CETA-Draft. Van den Putte (2015) and Xu (2017).

[55]Gött (2016), p. 217; Stoll et al. (2015), p. 29 and van den Putte et al. (2015), p. 2.

[56]Instances like the EU DAG's letter to EU Commissioner de Gucht concerning violations of labour standards in Korea (see van den Putte 2015, p. 229) illustrate potential constraints stemming both from the heterogeneous composition and the limited mandate of civil society mechanisms.

[57]Van den Putte (2015), p. 229 and van den Putte et al. (2015), p. 2. Unlike the civil society bodies, intergovernmental committees envisaged by some recent FTAs can hold 'dedicated sessions' where only labour issues are discussed, e.g. Art. 22.4 (1) CETA-Draft.

[58]Critical as to the sufficiency of adjudicatory mechanisms Banks (2011).

mechanisms,[59] while the absence of systematic approaches has been named one shortcoming of past cooperative activities.[60]

4.4 Maintaining or Restoring 'Enforcement Balance'

Lastly, the individual complaint procedure could remedy disparities between implementation and enforcement mechanisms foreseen in FTAs. Apart from substantive provisions obliging the parties to a different extent, especially recent European FTAs tend to foresee different DSMs for different chapters. Thus, FTA trade provisions can be enforced via inter-state arbitration,[61] complementing the multilateral WTO DSM at bilateral level.[62] If an FTA includes investment chapters, the respective obligations are subject to ISDS. Especially the latter has proven a highly efficient enforcement tool. By contrast, FTA labour DSMs suffer from shortcomings like those sketched above. Even more, under some recent EU FTAs, labour issues are entirely excluded from general FTA DSMs.[63] These agreements merely foresee consultations or an examination by a panel of experts.[64] As a result, particularly between 'strong' ISDS and 'weak' labour DSMs, there is a noteworthy asymmetry. While it is too early to draw definite conclusions from this, there is at least the potential that this 'enforcement imbalance' will be to the detriment of the protection and promotion of labour standards.[65] Enhancing labour enforcement through an individual labour complaint procedure could help to maintain (or restore) a greater systemic 'enforcement balance' throughout the FTA as a whole.[66]

5 Scope of Individual Enforcement

Compared to inter-state DSMs, where the parties themselves enforce their mutually accepted obligations, there is a greater need to define which obligations are enforceable by which individual or group in the context of an individual complaint procedure. As to the scope of enforceable obligations, the heterogeneity of

[59] Polaski and Vyborny (2006), p. 107 and Ebert and Posthuma (2009), p. 26.

[60] Concerning NAALC see ILO (2013), p. 79.

[61] E.g. Chapter 20 NAFTA and Chapter 29 CETA-Draft.

[62] Accordingly, a range of FTAs contain choice of forum clauses, e.g. Art. 2005 NAFTA; Art. 14.19 EU-Korea FTA and Art. 29.3 CETA-Draft.

[63] Art. 13.16 EU-Korea FTA and Art. 23.11 CETA-Draft.

[64] Art. 13.14 and Art. 13.15 EU-Korea FTA and Art. 23.9 and Art. 23.10 CETA-Draft.

[65] Gött (2015).

[66] Gött (2015).

provisions in FTA labour chapters brings up the question whether some of them should a priori be excluded from enforcement (Sect. 5.1). The more promising approach, however, would be to require that complainants establish that they are the envisaged beneficiaries of the allegedly violated FTA labour provision (Sect. 5.2).

5.1 A Priori Exclusion of Certain Obligations from Enforcement?

As a general premise, any DSM should suit the peculiarities of the substantive provisions it seeks to enforce. From a formal perspective, labour provisions in FTAs oblige the parties as subjects of international law, without differentiating between their internal organizational structures. Still, as a practical matter, the respective obligations are heterogeneous, as they may affect some state organs more than others: Some seem to primarily address the legislature by requiring that domestic labour law should embody certain principles or minimum standards.[67] Others, e.g. the obligation to effectively enforce national labour laws,[68] put stronger emphasis on executive activities. A third group focuses on labour policy instead of labour law, e.g. commitments to develop certain policies concerning occupational safety and health.[69] Finally, among all these different obligations, some are perceived to be more politically sensitive than others.

As a consequence of this heterogeneity, one could consider excluding certain FTA provisions from enforcement through an individual complaint procedure, as is the case in a range of (especially older) FTA labour chapters.[70] Indeed, the disparate nature of the obligations might require treating them differently. It seems to be a plausible assumption that—similar to inter-state DSMs—an individual complaint procedure would not be an equally effective and suitable enforcement tool for all obligations alike. Where the substantial legal standards are low or include broad margins of discretion, it might be overly difficult for claimants to establish a violation. Thus, obligations primarily addressing the legislature and national politics might prove more difficult to enforce than obligations addressing the executive, as the work of the former typically comprises the exercise of prerogatives and margins of discretion, whereas the latter typically makes decisions in particular cases. Likewise, provisions that oblige the FTA parties to pursue and reach a certain goal, such as a 'high level of protection'[71] leave broad margins of discretion to

[67]E.g. Art. 23.3 CETA-Draft; Lazo Grandi (2009), p. 34 and Polaski (2003), pp. 15–18.

[68]E.g. Art. 3 NAALC; Art. 15.2(a) US-Bahrain FTA; Art. 13.7(1) EU-Korea FTA and Lazo Grandi (2009), p. 34.

[69]E.g. Art. 23.3 (3) CETA-Draft.

[70]See e.g. the NAALC approach, Addo (2015), pp. 268–274 and Finbow (2006), pp. 66–68. See also the 'Bush era'-template used e.g. in Art. 16.6 CAFTA-DR and Vogt (2015), p. 831.

[71]E.g. Art. 2 NAALC and Art. 192 EU-CARIFORUM.

national politics and legislators, whereas obligations not to infringe on internationally recognized minimum standards are more definite.

On the other hand, other (especially a number of newer) treaties subject all substantial labour provisions to their respective labour DSMs.[72] As a general matter, at least as a starting point, this appears to be the more convincing approach: While the above observations are of great importance both for the efficacy of the procedure and the preservation of policy spaces for the respondent state, they should nevertheless not be taken to support an *a priori* exclusion of certain FTA labour provisions from enforceability. The particular scope of certain obligations is properly understood as a question of the merits of a claim, rather than as a matter of 'justiciability'.[73] A broad obligation is nevertheless a legal obligation principally capable of enforcement, even if cases might be rare.[74] An *a priori* exclusion of certain provisions runs the risk that broad but important obligations remain unenforceable. To properly account for the heterogeneity of substantive obligations, it therefore seems more promising to either integrate political positions in the procedure or to allow for appropriate policy space as a question of the merits of the particular case at hand.[75]

5.2 *Rights of Action*

Since an individual complaint procedure essentially takes away control over the commencement of dispute settlement from the FTA parties, it has to be determined who instead should be competent to initiate the procedure.

In this respect, a number of existing individual complaint mechanisms require the claimant to establish a violation of his own rights, as opposed to rights of third parties, rendering popular actions inadmissible. Recalling that the individual labour complaint procedure is intended to complement cooperative mechanisms, this seems to be one feasible option to focus on particular legal disputes while leaving more general issues to the political arena. Still, two peculiarities have to be considered: Firstly, as mentioned before, FTA labour provisions are often formulated as comparatively broad obligations between the FTA parties. To pay due

---

[72]Bolle (2016), pp. 4–5 and Vogt (2015), p. 831.

[73]Critical with regard to completely excluding political questions from scrutiny ICJ, *Admission of a State to the United Nations (Charter, Art. 4)*, Advisory Opinion, ICJ Rep. 57, 28 May 1948, p. 62 and ICJ, *Legality of the Threat or Use of Nuclear Weapons*, Advisory Opinion, ICJ Rep 226, 8 July 1996, p. 234.

[74]For example, a violation of the parties' obligation to 'make continued and sustained efforts towards ratifying the fundamental ILO Conventions to the extent that they have not yet done so' (Art. 23.3 (4) CETA) might only be found if one party remains entirely inactive on that matter or at least does not make any reasonably sustained effort towards ratification—this situation might be exceptional, but it is not inconceivable.

[75]See infra, 6.

regard to this structural openness, it is suggested that FTA obligations should be deemed actionable by individual complainants whenever the complainant belongs to the intended beneficiaries of that obligation. Secondly, it must be borne in mind that the intended beneficiaries of an FTA labour obligation, particularly individual workers, often lack time, resources and expertise to file a complaint on their own behalf. This could impose a significant obstacle in those cases where there are no simultaneous violations of genuine rights of trade unions or other (more powerful) associations. As possible under some domestic labour laws[76]—and following practice under existing FTA labour DSMs—associations should be enabled not only to file complaints regarding their own rights, but also to complain on behalf of their members or other individuals who agree to be represented by them.

With special regard to the internationalized nature of the dispute, it is then to be determined whether the right to file a complaint should depend on the nationality of the complainants. In other words, should nationals of a FTA party only be admitted to complain against 'their' home state, or should there be a chance to file complaints against either of the FTA parties? On the one hand, labour relations are still considered a primarily domestic matter, and complaints against one FTA party brought by complainants from the other party could face resistance. On the other hand, non-fulfilment of labour obligations in one FTA party can have detrimental indirect effects on workers the other FTA party; for example, if labour standards are lowered to encourage the relocation of businesses from that other party. In some cases, there might thus be good reasons not to *a priori* exclude complaints by foreign individuals or groups. At the same time, leaving this avenue open would not automatically result in overly extensive procedural opportunities of foreign complainants, as it will arguably be much more difficult to establish that (a) an FTA obligation, as a matter of law, is intended to protect foreign complainants and (b) the measure in question, as a matter of fact, actually has an adverse impact on the complainants.

As a further observation in this regard, experience under existing FTA labour DSMs illustrates the important role of transnational alliances between unions, NGOs and other actors, both for strategic cooperation and for enabling groups with few own resources or insufficient expertise to prepare and file a submission.[77] Thus, even if foreign individuals or groups should not be admitted as complainants themselves, there should at least remain opportunities for transnational collaborations among complainants and other groups, particularly between wealthier and poorer countries.

---

[76]E.g. § 11 (2) (4) German Labour Court Law (Arbeitsgerichtsgesetz), BGBl. I 853, p. 1036.

[77]Compa (2001); Dombois et al. (2004), p. 192 and Dombois (2006), p. 247.

6 Accommodating the 'Political Nature' of Labour Disputes

As pointed out earlier, labour disputes tend to have a strong political dimension. At the heart of the 'political nature' of labour dispute settlement lies the exercise of reconciling workers' and employers' rights and interests. For one part, pursuant to the internationally recognized rights to associate freely and bargain collectively, this exercise is left to the social partners themselves. Inasmuch as there remains room for public regulation, the right to regulate labour relations is one aspect of the internationally protected sovereignty of the respondent state. Against this background, dispute settlement under the auspices of an international and neutral body could be considered as more intrusive and illegitimate than the existing inter-state DSMs with their strong consultative components.

Therefore, it is necessary to identify appropriate means to depict underlying political positions and frictions within the context of a more formalized individual complaint procedure. Thus, a major challenge in conceptualizing such a dispute settlement model is to translate the inherently political nature of labour disputes into workable rules of procedure.

6.1 Room for Amicable Settlement

A first option to address these concerns is to maintain an opportunity for achieving amicable settlement. As noted above, under present intergovernmental FTA labour DSMs, this is usually achieved by a mandatory consultations stage. Such a preceding consultations phase could be maintained in the context of an individual complaint procedure (with the consulting parties then being the individual claimant and the respondent state), provided that there is an option for the complainant to unilaterally proceed to the next stage in case negotiations are unsuccessful. Similar 'cooling-off periods' are already well-established in other areas, e.g. international investment arbitration.[78]

6.2 Exhaustion of Local Remedies

For another option, introducing the local remedies rule[79] could yield similar results as far as deference to domestic solutions is concerned. A requirement to exhaust local remedies before commencing an FTA individual labour complaint procedure

[78] OECD (2012), p. 15.

[79] On the local remedies rule in general, see Amerasinghe (2004).

appears particularly worth considering in cases of alleged labour law violations by other individuals, notably employers, as it would require the claimant to primarily seek relief directly from the perpetrator by means of domestic civil (labour) law. An FTA party would thus have an opportunity to reconcile interests domestically in accordance with its FTA labour obligations. However, the local remedies rule only applies if, and inasmuch, local remedies are available and their exhaustion is not unreasonably obstructed.[80] In many countries, insufficiencies of the national labour administration and judiciary pose a major practical obstacle for claimants. In this respect, many present FTAs already lay down minimum procedural safeguards in labour matters,[81] the violation of which could be employed as an indicator for an unreasonable obstruction in the said sense.

6.3 Creating Opportunities to Introduce Perspectives

Thirdly, there are options to formally introduce the views of the social partners into the procedure. While the principal parties would be the individual claimant and the respondent state, there are several conceivable avenues for participation of other individuals or the other FTA party. One of them is to allow submissions by the other FTA party or individuals with a particular interest, e.g. as non-disputing parties or as *amici curiae*.[82] This would be of particular relevance if allegations of labour law violations by employers or other individuals are at stake. Another avenue would be to include other stakeholders in the composition of the body, e.g. as lay assessors.[83] Importantly, however, any tripartite composition must not compromise the neutrality, impartiality and proper functioning of the body.[84]

6.4 Adapting the Standard of Review

A fourth approach is to adapt the standard of review as to the merits of a case. It is a recurring phenomenon in both national and international jurisprudence that dispute settlement bodies depart from the default position of full legal review and adapt their standards in order to give due regard to the case at hand.[85] In labour matters, judicial self-restraint could be exercised in favour of regulatory discretion or

[80] Amerasinghe (2004), pp. 200–215.

[81] E.g. Arts. 4- 6 NAALC; Art. 16.3 CAFTA-DR and Art. 23.5 CETA-Draft.

[82] On these concepts see Sands and Mackenzie (2008).

[83] Lay assessors are a feature of some domestic labour judiciaries, see e.g. § 16 German Labour Court Law (Arbeitsgerichtsgesetz), BGBl. I 853, p. 1036.

[84] On corresponding issues in ILO committees, see La Hovary (2017).

[85] E.g. in ECHR, *Case of Rail, Maritime and Transport Workers Union v. United Kingdom*, Judgment, Appl. No. 31045/10, 8 Apr 2014 and Hilf and Salomon (2014), with further references.

collective bargaining. Care has to be taken, however, not to neglect the abovementioned genuine functions the individual complaint procedure is supposed to fulfil by too readily refusing to decide on 'political questions', as it is the very essence of FTA labour chapters to provide legal standards for an inherently political field of application. Restraint should thus be exercised with caution and on a case-by-case basis. In terms of conceptualizing an individual complaint procedure, it has also to be taken into account that self-restraint is primarily a matter of DSM practice. It might prove challenging to draft treaty language that allows for self-restraint on the one side while ensuring a sufficient level of review.

6.5 Subsequent Policy Space

Finally, there is the option to allow for policy space in the aftermath of a dispute. For example, many contemporary FTAs explicitly provide for legally binding interpretations of treaty provisions to be adopted either by the parties or by FTA committees.[86] Correspondingly, the parties could adopt binding interpretations of labour provisions in order to provide guidance on issues that have surfaced in the course of an individual complaint procedure. Yet, it must be understood that, for reasons of legal certainty, binding interpretations are an instrument to (re-)direct *future* treaty practice, rather than to influence pending cases or even to retroactively 'correct' the outcome of past cases.[87]

7 The Output and Its Effects

It is crucial to ensure that the output of the individual complaint procedure actually has an effect. From a formal perspective, the output could be made legally binding, in the sense that the respondent has an international legal obligation to cease the violation of labour standards specified in the neutral body's findings. The creation of such a concretized obligation might induce states to comply, although it should be noted that, under other international DSMs, there are a range of instances in which formally non-binding decisions have gained substantial normative relevance in subsequent international practice (and, of course, other instances where formally binding decisions have been ignored).

[86] Art. 1135 NAFTA; Art. 10.22 (3) CAFTA-DR and Art. 26.1 (5) (e) CETA-Draft.
[87] Kaufmann-Kohler (2011).

7.1 Monitoring and Follow-Up

What appears to be at least as important is to provide for monitoring and follow-ups in the aftermath of a decision. A number of FTAs leave monitoring primarily to the parties and allocate a complementary role to the (reconvened) adjudicating body.[88] Under individual complaint mechanisms outside the FTA context, monitoring is sometimes vested in international bodies.[89] This might prove a feasible option for an individual labour complaint procedure under future FTAs, too, e.g. by vesting monitoring in the respective intergovernmental treaty committees, civil society fora or dedicated bodies. Critically, however, any such monitoring mechanism should perpetuate the active procedural role of the individual claimants. In this respect, as illustrated by cases under present FTA labour DSMs, there is a need to include enhanced follow-up mechanisms. For example, in US NAO Submission 940003, filed under the NAALC, the initial petitioners filed a follow-up requesting to reopen governmental consultations that had been concluded by a ministerial implementation agreement arguing that the initially claimed violations sustained. The US NAO rejected the request and instead commissioned a follow-up report, which included general conclusions on both improvements and remaining shortcomings,[90] but apparently did not lead to further action. The case illustrates potential for improving follow-up mechanisms. Other international arrangements might provide useful inspiration here.[91]

7.2 Coercive Enforcement?

A good portion of the trade and labour debate has centred on whether compliance with DSM decisions should be enforced by coercion. Among those states that have opted for a coercive enforcement mechanism, the predominant approach is to entitle the other FTA party to suspend trade benefits from the respondent state.[92] Under some treaties, the claimant state is entitled to collect fines from the respondent.[93] Both options, however, have been criticized for their lack of accuracy: Suspending trade benefits targets the respondent state's export industry as a whole, including compliant (and therefore 'innocent') businesses, and risking that

---

[88]E.g. Art. 38 and Art. 39 NAALC and Art. 20.15 and Art. 20.16 CAFTA-DR.

[89]Art. 46 (2) ECHR.

[90]US NAO, Submission No. 940003 (SONY), Follow-up Report, 4 Dec 1996.

[91]For example the monitoring mechanism established by the Council of Europe in the ECHR context. See the Council of Europe, Committee of Ministers, Rules of the Committee of Ministers for the supervision of the execution of judgments and of the terms of friendly settlements, 10 May 2006, Rule 9.

[92]Polaski and Vyborny (2006), p. 101.

[93]Polaski and Vyborny (2006), p. 101.

losses incurred as a consequence from suspension could eventually harm workers, precisely the group intended to be protected.[94] Fines have to be paid by the respondent state, although in many cases, employers are the true perpetrators of labour law violations. Those employers could take this as an incentive to comply even less with labour standards. These difficulties would arguably remain when using suspension of trade benefits or fines as means to enforce the output of an individual complaint procedure. On the other hand, even if not actually put to use, the mere prospect of 'trade sanctions' can induce FTA parties or even employers to voluntarily comply with labour standards.[95] For example, as a reaction to initiation of the US-Guatemala arbitration under CAFTA-DR, Guatemalan enterprises urged the Guatemalan government to address the issues brought forward by the US.[96]

Unlike with negative incentives such as suspension of trade remedies and fines, there have been some promising experiences with positive incentives in the past. Under the US-Cambodia textiles agreement, the US agreed to increase the import quota for Cambodian textiles in case Cambodia effectively implemented certain labour standards defined in the agreement. Adherence to labour standards was subject to annual review.[97] Under this arrangement, incentives to effectively implement the standards were high not only for the government, but also for employers in the textile manufacturing industry. The US Cambodia textiles agreement and the subsequent better factories programme, involving monitoring by the ILO, is often cited as a positive example of promoting labour standards through FTAs.[98] If the parties can agree on a comparable mechanism of positive incentives, this could well be connected with an individual complaints procedure in labour matters. For example, when conducting the annual review, maintaining the increased import quota could be made conditional on the respective state's record of compliance with the decisions of the neutral body. Arrangements such as in the US Cambodia textiles agreement can work in some cases, but might be legally impermissible[99] (or not be the method of choice) in others. Still, as a more general approach, the enforcement of the individual complaint procedure output could be linked to cooperative activities in labour matters under FTAs and could include monitoring or technical assistance by the ILO or other organizations.[100] Caution must be taken, however, not to create an incentive to violate labour standards to obtain benefits, such as development aid.[101]

---

[94] Polaski (2003), p. 21.

[95] Polaski (2003), p. 20. See also Nolan Garcia (2009), p. 44 with further references.

[96] ILO (2013), p. 53.

[97] ILO (2013), pp. 101–103 and Kolben (2004).

[98] ILO (2013), p. 101.

[99] ILO (2013), p. 101. On the compatibility of the US-Cambodia Textiles Agreement with WTO law, see Kolben (2004), p. 11.

[100] See Banks (2011) and Kolben (2004).

[101] Greven (2012), p. 93.

The aforementioned options all refer to enforcement at the initiative of the other FTA party. In theory, both 'trade sanctions' and positive incentives are intergovernmental measures, and thus again vulnerable to political agendas extrinsic to the case at hand, and hence to over-politicization as described above. As individual complaint approach consistently seeking to reduce politicization and to increase performance should hence evaluate genuine options for coercive enforcement. This point shall not be discussed in depth here. For one remark, some other individual-state DSMs provide for compensation, either for economic losses[102] or as just satisfaction,[103] as the case may be, to be granted directly to the applicant.

8 The Issue of Fragmentation

When proposing new or reformed DSMs, it is inevitable to consider not only the role of such a DSM within its 'own' treaty framework, but also to take into account broader implications of what might be considered yet another hire for the rapidly growing orchestra of international dispute settlement bodies. Already now, FTA labour provisions are increasingly referencing ILO instruments[104] and a growing number of FTAs is subjecting these provisions to DSMs.[105] The competent FTA dispute settlement bodies thus might come up with their own interpretations of ILO standards, potentially deviating from (or even conflicting with) interpretations adopted by ILO committees. This has raised concerns about an increasing fragmentation of international labour law.[106]

Systemically, the issue of fragmentation already exists with regard to present inter-state DSMs, albeit somewhat concealed by their general underperformance. It might become more pressing in the context of an individual complaint procedure that seeks to enhance efficacy and overcome the 'lowest common denominator approach' described above. Still, the 'danger' of fragmentation should not be understood as a particular problem of an individual complaint procedure, nor of FTA labour DSMs more generally: Even if FTA parties completely forgo any form of DSM, diverging interpretations might still occur in treaty practice simply because the FTA's substantive provisions are in many aspects open to diverging interpretations.

A number of FTAs explicitly envisage cooperation with ILO organs and committees that can be used to enhance consistent interpretation of ILO instruments.[107] Furthermore, even in the absence of such formal interlinkages, there are instances

[102] E.g. in international investment law, see Ripinsky and Williams (2008).

[103] E.g. pursuant to Art. 41 ECHR.

[104] Agustí-Panareda et al. (2014), p. 7.

[105] Agustí-Panareda et al. (2014), pp. 12–14.

[106] See Agustí-Panareda et al. (2014), p. 5 with further references.

[107] Agustí-Panareda et al. (2014), p. 12.

of inter-regime exchange between the ILO and other bodies. Other entities (e.g. human rights bodies) have relied on interpretations by ILO committees.[108] In return, ILO supervisory bodies have picked up and examined decisions of regional DSMs in their reports.[109] Some of these instances highlight potential frictions. Yet, at the same time, there are potential building blocks both for direct cooperation and for an inter-institutional indirect 'discourse *in absentia*' through decisions and reports. Both may not be able to entirely avoid conflicts, but nevertheless offer opportunities for contestation, correction and mutual 'review' and to collaboratively work towards coherence.

9 Final Remarks

Potentially the most difficult exercise will be to convince governments to agree on an individual complaint procedure, namely those with either significantly less economic weight than their negotiating partners, a poor record of labour protection or strong domestic sentiments of preserving sovereignty and shielding labour law and policy from external examination and review. It is to be understood that an individual complaint procedure is certainly no panacea for protecting and promoting labour standards and will not overcome all difficulties. On the other hand, some of its benefits might materialize even if workable and politically acceptable solutions cannot be found for all challenges. In this regard, much will depend on the particular design of any such procedure. From a political perspective, it is equally important that an individual complaint procedure is not understood narrowly as a mechanism for imposing sanctions and disguised protectionism, but rather as a tool to further the protection and promotion of labour standards, an exercise which necessarily entails dialogue and cooperation, but which also needs to give 'voice' to individuals and groups. As such, it offers an avenue to approach some of the key deficits of contemporary FTA labour DSMs.

References

Abel P (2017) Comparative conclusions on arbitral dispute settlement in trade-labour matters under US FTAs. In: Gött H (ed) Labour standards in international economic law. Springer International Publishing, Cham, this volume

Addo K (2015) Core labour standards and international trade – lessons from the regional context. Springer, Berlin/Heidelberg

[108] ECHR, *Case of Demir and Baykara v. Turkey*, Judgment of the Grand Chamber, Application no. 34503/97, 12 Nov 2008 and IACtHR, *Case of Ituango Massacres v. Colombia*, Judgment, 1 July 2006. Ebert and Oelz (2012) and Veldman (2013).

[109] E.g. ILO Report of the Committee of Experts on the Application of Conventions and Recommendations, International Labour Conference, 2010, p. 209.

Agustí-Panareda J, Ebert FC, LeClerq D (2014) Labour provisions in free trade agreements: fostering their consistency with the ILO standards system. Background paper social dimensions of free trade agreements. ILO, Geneva

Amerasinghe CF (2004) Local remedies in international law. Cambridge University Press, Cambridge

Banks K (2011) Trade, labor and international governance: an inquiry into the potential effectiveness of the new international labor law. Berkeley J Employ Labor Law 32:45–142

Bhagnani P (2015) Revisiting the countermeasures defense in investor-state disputes: approaches and analogies. In: Bjorklund AK (ed) Yearbook on international investment law and policy 2013–2014. Oxford University Press, Oxford, pp 437–472

Bieszczat FH (2008) Labor provisions in trade agreements - from the NAALC to now. Chicago-Kent Law Rev 83:1387–1408

Bolle MJ (2016) Overview of labor enforcement issues in free trade agreements. US Congressional Research Service. https://www.fas.org/sgp/crs/misc/RS22823.pdf. Accessed 29 May 2016

Churchill R, Khaliq U (2004) The collective complaints system of the European Social Charter - an effective mechanism for ensuring compliance with economic and social rights? Eur J Int Law 15(3):417–456

Compa LA (2001) NAFTA's labour side agreement and international labour solidarity. In: Waterman P, Wills J (eds) Place, space and the new labour internationalisms. Wiley-Blackwell, Oxford, pp 147–163

Dombois R (2006) Sozialklauseln in US-Freihandelsabkommen – ein wirksames Mittel internationaler Arbeitsregulierung? Indust Bezieh 13:238–252

Dombois R, Hornberger E, Winter J (2004) Internationale Arbeitsregulierung in der Souveränitätsfalle – Das Lehrstück des North American Agreement on Labor Cooperation zwischen den USA, Mexiko und Kanada. LIT, Münster

Ebert FC, Oelz M (2012) Bridging the gap between labour rights and human rights: the role of ILO Law in Regional Human Rights Courts. International Institute for Labour Studies Discussion Paper DP/212/2012. ILO, Geneva

Ebert FC, Posthuma A (2009) Rebalancing globalization: the role of labour provisions in existing international trade arrangements and development finance policies. World of Work Report. ILO, Geneva

Finbow RG (2006) The limits of regionalism – NAFTA's labour accord. Ashgate Publishing, Aldershot, Burlington

Gött H (2015) TTIP-Rechtsschutz zu Ende denken/Thinking out legal remedies under TTIP. http://verfassungsblog.de/ttip-rechtsschutz-zu-ende-denken/. Accessed 29 May 2016

Gött H (2016) "Legitimation durch den, den es angeht?" – Die Einbindung der Zivilgesellschaft in die geplante transatlantische Regulierungszusammenarbeit aus demokratischer Perspektive. In: Buszewski SE, Martini S, Rathke H (eds) Freihandel vs. Demokratie – Grundsätze transnationaler Legitimation, Partizipation, Reversibilität, Transparenz. Nomos, Baden-Baden, pp 199–218

Greven T (2012) Anforderungen an Legitimität und Effektivität von Sozialklauseln in Handelsverträgen. In: Scherrer C, Hänlein A (eds) Sozialklauseln in Handelsabkommen – Begründungen und Vorschläge aus juristischer, ökonomischer und politologischer Sicht. Nomos, Baden-Baden, pp 83–102

Hilf M, Salomon TR (2014) Margin of appreciation revisited: the balancing pole of multilevel governance. In: Cremona M, Hilpold P, Lavranos N, Schneider SS, Ziegler AR (eds) Reflections on the constitutionalisation of international economic law: Liber Amicorum for Ernst-Ulrich Petersmann. Martinus Nijhoffer Publishers, Leiden, pp 37–50

Human Rights Watch (2001) Trading away rights: the unfulfilled promise of NAFTA's labor side agreement. https://www.hrw.org/reports/2001/nafta/nafta0401.pdf. Accessed 29 May 2016

ILO (2006) Changing patterns in the world of work. ILO, Geneva

ILO (2013) Social dimensions of free trade agreements. ILO, Geneva

Kaufmann-Kohler G (2011) Interpretive powers of the free trade commission and the rule of law. In: Gaillard E, Bachand F (eds) Fifteen years of NAFTA chapter 11 arbitration. Juris Publishing, Huntington, pp 175–194

Kolben K (2004) Trade, monitoring, and the ILO: working to improve conditions in Cambodia's garment factories. Yale Hum Rights Dev Law J 7:79–107

La Hovary C (2017) The ILO's mandate and capacity: creating, proliferating and supervising labour standards for a globalized economy. In: Gött H (ed) Labour standards in international economic law. Springer International Publishing, Cham, this volume

Lazo Grandi P (2009) Trade agreements and their relation to labour standards: the current situation. International Centre for Trade and Sustainable Development, Geneva

Nolan Garcia KA (2009) Transnational advocacy and labor rights conditionality in the international trading order. University of New Mexico, Albuquerque

OECD (2012) Dispute settlement provisions in international investment agreements: a large sample survey. OECD Publishing, Paris

Polaski S (2003) Protecting labor rights through trade agreements: an analytical guide. Univ Calif Davis Law Rev 10:13–25

Polaski S, Vyborny K (2006) Labor clauses in trade agreements - policy and practice. Integr Trade 10:95–124

Ripinsky S, Williams K (2008) Damages in international investment law. British Institute of International and Comparative Law, London

Sands P, Mackenzie R (2008) International Courts and Tribunals, Amicus Curiae. In: Wolfrum (ed) Max Planck encyclopedia of public international law. Oxford University Press, Oxford. Available via DIALOG. http://opil.ouplaw.com/home/epil. Accessed 09 Aug 2017

Schreuer C (2009) The ICSID Convention: a commentary, 2nd edn. Oxford University Press, Oxford

Senghaas-Knobloch E (2004) Zwischen Überzeugen und Erzwingen – Nachhaltiger Druck für Geltung und Wirksamkeit internationaler Arbeits- und Sozialstandards. In: Zangl B, Zürn R (eds) Verrechtlichung - Baustein für Global Governance? Dietz Verlag, Bonn, pp 140–158

Stoll P-T, Holterhus TP, Gött H (2015) Die geplante Regulierungszusammenarbeit zwischen der Europäischen Union und Kanada sowie den USA nach den Entwürfen von CETA und TTIP. AK Wien, Vienna

Van den Putte L (2015) Involving civil society in social clauses and the decent work agenda. Glob Labour J 6:221–235

Van den Putte L, Orbie J, Bossuyt F, Martens D, de Ville F (2015) What social face of the new EU trade agreements? – Beyond the 'soft' approach. ETUI Policy Brief (European Economic, Employment and Social Policy) No. 13/2015. Available via DIALOG. https://www.etui.org/Publications2/Policy-Briefs/European-Economic-Employment-and-Social-Policy/What-social-face-of-the-new-EU-trade-agreements-Beyond-the-soft-approach. Accessed 29 May 2016

Van Roozendaal G, Voogsgeerd H (2011) International framework agreements versus labour rights included in trade agreements: models for empowerment of trade unions? Econ Environ Stud 11:339–371

Veldman A (2013) The protection of the fundamental right to strike within the context of the European Internal Market: implications of the forthcoming accession of the EU to the ECHR. Utrecht Law Rev 9:104–117

Vogt JS (2015) The evolution of labor rights and trade – a transatlantic comparison and lessons for the transatlantic trade and investment partnership. J Int Econ Law 18:827–860

Xu J (2017) The role of civil society in EU preferential trade agreements. European Society of International Law Conference Paper Series. Available via SSRN. https://ssrn.com/abstract=2912010. Accessed 2 Feb 2017

Zimmer R (2012) Sozialklauseln im Nachhaltigkeitskapitel des Freihandelsabkommens der Europäischen Union mit Kolumbien und Peru. In: Scherrer C, Hänlein A (eds) Sozialkapitel in Handelsabkommen – Begründungen und Vorschläge aus juristischer, ökonomischer und politologischer Sicht. Nomos, Baden-Baden, pp 141–156

Implications of CETA and TTIP on Social Standards

Reingard Zimmer

Contents

1 Introduction

The impact on European social standards of the trade agreements CETA (Comprehensive Economic and Trade Agreement) and TTIP (Trans-Atlantic Trade and Investment Partnership) has become the subject of a broad critical debate. States may reduce employee protection rights or deny (necessary) improvements of protection standards to obtain a competitive advantage against other countries.

R. Zimmer (✉)
Berlin School of Economics and Law, Berlin, Germany
e-mail: reingard.zimmer@hwr-berlin.de

H. Gött (ed.), *Labour Standards in International Economic Law*,
https://doi.org/10.1007/978-3-319-69447-4_11

This analysis looks at this very danger in relation to the free trade agreements CETA and TTIP.

The content of a new trade agreement is heavily influenced by those who determine the agenda for negotiations and their values and interests that become the principles on which negotiations are based. With the Lisbon Treaty, authority for negotiating international investment agreements moved away from individual member countries to the European Commission. The European Parliament takes an active part in political discussions, but is not formally involved in the negotiations. The Parliament has no influence on the content of an agreement, according to Art 218 VI (a) TFEU the European Parliament only has the right of veto whenever bi- or multinational agreements are concluded with third countries. As a result, an agreement can only be rejected in its entirety, but not modified.[1]

The ability to influence the negotiations of trade or investment agreements seems to be extremely unequal across society as in the case of TTIP for example, only companies and their interest groups have been involved in preliminary talks and negotiations, but not the civil society. In the first three rounds of consultation which the Commission has made public most of the input came from individual businesses and their associations or lobby groups which enjoy privileged access to the EU Commission.[2] This is also reflected in the composition of the preparatory group (High Level Working Group on Jobs and Growth, HLWG), where on the European side no experts on environmental or social issues were involved.[3] The lack of transparency of the whole negotiating procedure is also problematic and despite repeated questions from civil society,[4] the European Commission did not disclose the composition of the group and this information was finally published by the US side.[5] In addition, negotiations proceeded secretly and the relevant documents tended to be unavailable or only available to a limited audience.[6] Meanwhile, the Commission made available draft texts and 'fact sheets'.[7] Also the HLWG report from February 2013[8] and the EU negotiating mandate,[9] as adopted by the Council, have been made public in the meantime.

[1]For the conclusion of international agreements by the EU see Nawparwar (2009), pp. 25 et seqq.

[2]These are: ERT, TABD, Business Europe, European Services Forum (ESF), Association of German Banks, as well as the German Chamber of Commerce and Industry (Deutsche Industrie- und Handelskammer). Scherrer and Beck even quantify that 80% of the input came from the sphere of industry, compare Scherrer and Beck (2014), pp. 12, 50.

[3]Compare: Corporate Europe Observatory (2013).

[4]These questions were raised by the NGO *Corporate Europe Observatory*.

[5]The list of participants is available under: http://corporateeurope.org/sites/default/files/hlwg-members.pdf. Accessed 22nd November 2017.

[6]Not even MEPs have unfettered access to the documents, compare Bode (2015), pp. 29 et seqq.

[7]High Level Working Group on Jobs and Growth (2013).

[8]The HLWG was instituted at the EU/US summit in November 2011 and intended to propose measures to increase transatlantic trade and investment. See High Level Working Group on Jobs and Growth (2013).

[9]Council of the European Union (2013).

2 General Aspects

The general purpose of Free Trade Agreements is the elimination of trade barriers, in other words the elimination of government regulation seen as unnecessary or as mere obstacles to competition. Inherently, this is a normative commitment to free trade, i.e. trade liberalization. Competition for wages and welfare reduction are regarded as conducive to growth. As an overarching objective, this maxim was also the guiding principle of the TTIP and CETA negotiations. This means that those agreements aim primarily to extend market access for goods and services. Liberalization and investment protection provisions based on the highest level of liberalization and the highest protection levels (for investors) are dominant, as negotiated by the contracting parties in previous agreements, e.g. NAFTA and EU-Singapore. This approach runs counter to a basic assumption in labour law according to which the unequal power of the parties concerned makes employee protection laws imperative to provide protection for the weaker employees.

The bilateral High Level Working Group has recommended a broad concept for the EU-US agreement (TTIP), following the approach taken by the CETA agreement between the EU and Canada.[10] Apart from a further elimination of tariffs and restrictions in the trade of goods, it is also intended to liberalise the service sector in particular, to eliminate non-tariff (domestic) trade barriers or government regulations, to adapt, harmonise or accept the equivalence of regulatory (e.g. technical) standards, to provide the highest possible level of investment protection, to open up government procurement markets and to set competition policy measures such as the abolition of state preferences or provisions regarding the share of local added value (local content clauses).[11]

3 Historical Development

International free trade agreements have been concluded at both multilateral and bilateral level. The first one was the 1947 General Agreement on Tariffs and Trade (GATT) which led to the establishment of the World Trade Organization (WTO) in 1995.[12] Facing increasing difficulties to achieve multilateral trade agreements within the context of world trade rounds[13] on trade liberalization between countries of the Northern and Southern hemisphere and in addition, heavy protests against the WTO agenda by anti-globalization circles, there was a shift of further trade

[10] See High Level Working Group on Jobs and Growth (2013).

[11] Ibid., p. 6.

[12] On the development see https://www.wto.org/english/thewto_e/whatis_e/tif_e/fact4_e.htm. Accessed 26 Mar 2017.

[13] These were meetings of the representatives of WTO member countries, where further trade facilitation was negotiated. These ‘rounds’ are always named after the negotiating venue.

liberalization efforts from the WTO towards bilateral trade agreements. Moreover after the failure of the Multilateral Agreement on Investment (MAI) in the context of the OECD in 1998,[14] bilateral investment treaties (BITs) were increasingly concluded.[15] According to UNCTAD information, there are now 2950 of such agreements (BITs),[16] Germany having concluded 199 BITs.[17] With the exception of NAFTA, the combination of bilateral trade and bilateral investment agreements is a rather new phenomenon. So far, there is no bilateral trade (and investment) agreement with a trading region as large as that of TTIP, which after all would affect more than a third of world trade volume and would generate more than half the GDP of the world.[18]

4 Effect of 'Non-labour' Provisions on Labour Standards

4.1 Economic and Labour Market Political Impact

TTIP advocates argue that the new free trade agreements would offer a huge potential for growth. The EU Commission for example published in the CEPR-Report figures about enormous positive growth and employment stimuli provided by TTIP,[19] similar conclusions were reached by two IFO institute studies commissioned by the Bertelsmann Foundation and the German Federal Ministry of Economics and Technology, respectively.[20] But a closer look to the CEPR-Report shows that the expert opinion on behalf of the EU Commission assumes an average GDP growth of about 0.04 percentage points per year for the EU (0.03 percentage points for the USA).[21] Given the simulation period of 10 years, these stimuli would be marginal.[22] On closer inspection, no additional employment impulses can be expected as a result of TTIP because possible increasing demands for labour in expanding sectors contrast with a reduction of labour in others, so that in the long run employment levels are expected to remain constant.[23] The significant long-term

[14]Concerning MAI, see Burkard (2015), pp. 35 et seqq. and FES (1998).

[15]As a result of disputes between globalization opponents and the police, for example, the 1999 WTO meeting in Seattle could not be held as planned. Images of the protests went around the world at the time.

[16]According to the UNCTAD 2363 of these are still in force, compare http://investmentpolicyhub.unctad.org/IIA. Accessed 04 Nov 2017.

[17]Compare http://investmentpolicyhub.unctad.org/IIA/CountryBits/78. Accessed 27 Mar 2016.

[18]Krätke (2014), p. 5.

[19]Compare Francois et al. (2013).

[20]Compare Felbermayr et al. (2013a, b).

[21]Compare Francois et al. (2013).

[22]Schreyer (2014), p. 2 and Stephan (2014), p. 2.

[23]Stephan (2014), p. 2.

increase in per capita income forecast in the IFO studies about a comprehensive free trade agreement (measured in real GDP per head)[24] is considered unrealistic by other economists because of the underlying method of calculation.[25]

Critical economists arrive at different and emphatically more negative results because they take into account possible negative effects of the agreement which are not included in the other studies. Because of the social and macroeconomic costs of TTIP, some studies calculate the benefit to the national economy as 40% less than in the study undertaken on behalf of the EU Commission.[26] Some reports therefore expect adjustment and transition losses to occur, as job relocation is likely to exceed the scale mentioned in the IFO studies.[27] A Tufts university survey even forecasts net losses in exports and GDP after a decade, as well as a lowering of net take-home-pay and the loss of 600,000 jobs.[28] The forecast for Germany is for net export losses of −1.14%, a GDP reduction of −0.29%, a decrease in net earnings by −€3400 per employee and the loss of 134,000 jobs.[29]

4.2 *Liberalization Obligations and Investment Protection Rights*

4.2.1 Investment

Chapter 8 of CETA refers to investments, therefore the definition of Art. 8.1 of the CETA-draft is of vital importance. CETA uses a broad 'asset-based'-definition of investment which does not only protect the traditional foreign direct investment, but also portfolio investments.[30] Limitations exist merely in the way that only investments which had already been realized and are in accordance with national law will fall under the scope of the CETA investment chapter.[31] Other agreements like NAFTA apply a narrower definition of investment.[32] The EU-Commission narrows the definition of investment to that effect, that only investments of 'substantial business activities' in the country where the enterprise is registered are

[24]Compare Felbermayr et al. (2013a, b).

[25]See Capaldo (2014), pp. 9 et seqq. and Stephan (2014), pp. 3 et seqq.

[26]One such expert opinion was provided by the Austrian Research Foundation for International Development, see ÖFSE (2014).

[27]Capaldo (2014), pp. 4 et seqq.; Scherrer and Beck (2014), p. 58 and Stephan (2014), pp. 3 et seqq.

[28]The survey uses a calculation method employed by the United Nations which also evaluates trade impact, compare Capaldo (2014), pp. 4 et seqq.

[29]Ibid., p. 14.

[30]Krajewski (2014), p. 4 and Geiger (2014).

[31]These limitations are part of numerous agreements on investment; the principles were basically developed by ISDS decisions.

[32]Krajewski (2014), p. 4; concerning the definition of *investment*, see UNCTAD (2011), p. 22.

accepted. Local branches which are legally not independent and only function as offshore companies will not fall under the scope of application. Regrettably, there is no further definition of 'substantial business activities' by the EU (or the contracting parties), although these discussions are not new.[33]

4.2.2 Non-discrimination

Like other free trade and other investment agreements, Chapter 8 CETA includes the non-discrimination obligations of *national treatment* and *most favourable treatment* concerning investment. *National treatment* demands that foreign investors must not be treated any less favourably than national companies in a comparable situation:

> Each Party shall accord to investors of the other Party and to covered investments, treatment no less favourable than the treatment it accords, in like situations to its own investors and to their investments with respect to the establishment, acquisition, expansion, conduct, operation, management, maintenance, use, enjoyment and sale or disposal of their investments in its territory. (Chapter 8 Art. 8.6.1 CETA).

The above also applies to services.[34] Accordingly, all government measures giving preference to a national company over a foreign business are subject to this clause including, among others, preference given to a regional company, unless specific exemptions apply.[35] The same is true for most favoured treatment, see below. Given the horizontal direct effect of the fundamental freedoms in the EU,[36] this is nothing new. Nevertheless, one of the problems concerns factual discrimination as part of the national treatment obligation; unequal treatment does not necessarily have to be intentional. Even formally neutral state measures may be included if foreign investors are affected disproportionally.[37]

The *most favoured treatment* standardised in Chapter 8 Art. 8.7 CETA ('most-favoured nation, MFN') obliges the contractual parties as follows:

> Each Party shall accord to investors of the other Party and to covered investments, treatment no less favourable than the treatment it accords in like situations, to investors and to their investments of any third country (. . .).

This gives investors the opportunity to invoke other investment agreements concluded by the host country in question, should these offer more favourable treatment than the BIT concerned. While for TTIP 'the EU seeks to clarify that MFN does not allow procedural or substantive provisions to be imported from other

[33]Concerning the discussions on the definition of *investor* and *investment*, see OECD (2008).

[34]Krajewski and Kynast (2014), p. 34.

[35]Fritz (2015), p. 10; Krajewski (2014), p. 6 and Krajewski and Kynast (2014), pp. 27 et seq.

[36]Although this does not apply directly.

[37]Diebold (2010), p. 38. For further examples see Xiao (2006), pp. 141 et seqq.

agreements',[38] the corresponding wording of the limitations of the MFN standard in CETA refers only to rules of procedure, not to material protection standards.[39] Such a dynamic referral allows the import of future protection regulations for investors[40] even if this was not the original intention of the parties concerned.[41] Moreover, investors may rely upon investment protection rules from the past, although those rules might be bizarre and nearly forgotten from a current perspective, like e.g. those in the BIT between the Federal Republic of Germany and Ethiopia from 1951,[42] of which Art. VIII par. 5 codifies:

> Nationals and companies of either High Contracting Party which are permitted to establish or acquire enterprises within the territories of the other (. . .) Party shall enjoy the **right to continued control and management of such Enterprises**,

similar Art. 5 par 3 of the BIT with Oman from 1958[43] as well as Art. 5 par 3 of the BIT with Togo[44] from 1966. These clauses were initially created to protect German investors in countries like Ethiopia, Oman or Togo. From a current perspective such rules are highly problematic. Facing the MFN-standard in CETA and TTIP, the guarantee of '*continued control and management*' would allow investors to attack German statutory law concerning supervisory boards. Investors from Canada and the USA could therefore attack German codetermination, which enables an equal number of workers' representatives on supervisory boards, with arbitration proceedings.[45]

4.2.3 Fair and Equitable Treatment

A core part of investment protection rights is the standard of fair and equitable treatment (FET) in Chapter 8 Art. 8.10 CETA, on which most ISDS procedures are based.[46] So far, this standard was broadly interpreted in ISDS proceedings. Art. 8.10

---

[38]See Public consultation on modalities for investment protection and ISDS in TTIP. Consultation document, p. 4. http://trade.ec.europa.eu/doclib/docs/2014/march/tradoc_152280.pdf. Accessed 29 Mar 2016.

[39]Krajewski (2014), p. 6. See Art. X.2 (4) of the consultation document: 'For greater certainty, the 'treatment' referred to in Paragraph 1: a. does not include investor-to-state dispute settlement procedures provided for in other international investment treaties and other trade agreements, including compensation granted through such procedures (. . .)'.

[40]Compare on the MFN Mechanism UNCTAD (2010), pp. 107 et seqq.

[41]Fritz (2015), pp. 10 et seq. and Krajewski (2014), p. 6. Different view Schill (2014), p. 10.

[42]Trade Agreement between the Federal Republic of Germany and Ethiopia of 7 Sep 1951, TIAS 2864, 4 UST 2134.

[43]Trade Agreement with Muscat and Oman and Dependencies, 20 Dec 1958, TIAS 4530, 11 UST 1835.

[44]Trade Agreement with Togo, 8 Feb 1966, TIAS 6193, 18 UST 1.

[45]For the debate from the 1970th, see Wengler (1975).

[46]75% of ISDS proceedings won by US-Investors rely on FET standard violation, compare Wallach (2012).

par 2 CETA lists the facts which may provide grounds for claiming a breach of the treaty, among them: *'denial of justice', 'significant breaches of ordinary court proceedings', 'obvious arbitrariness', 'targeted discrimination' or 'improper use'*. Paragraph 4 makes in addition clear that *'legitimate expectations'* may be derived from *specific assurances* which may have been raised in the investors. Although, the list is in principle definite, nevertheless an extension pursuant to par 2 (at the end) in conjunction with Art. 8.10 par 3 CETA is possible under certain circumstances. The suitability for the purposes of limitation[47] of such phrasing therefore remains more than doubtful, particularly because the cases brought in the past actually relied on the facts and exactly the wording mentioned above and even NAFTA attempts at clarification did not effect a change in dispute settlement practice.[48]

Nevertheless, a more labour-friendly interpretation of the FET-standard in principle would be possible. In accordance with Art. 31.1 Vienna Convention on the Law of Treaties, the provisions and legal values of Chapter 23 (Trade and Labour) could be used for the systematical interpretation of the FET-standard, so that no obvious arbitrariness could be assumed, if the questionable governmental measure is in accordance with the ILO core labour standards or with the employment policy objectives as agreed upon in chapter 23. Given the outcome of arbitration proceedings in the past, such an interpretation is rather unlikely. In fact, the legally indeterminate nature of *legitimate expectations* based on *specific assurances* is seen as strengthening the interests of investors.[49]

4.2.4 Direct or Indirect Expropriation

An essential part of international investor protection is mandatory compensation in cases of direct or indirect expropriation which has to be *'prompt, adequate and effective'* (Chapter 8 Art. 8.12.1.d CETA).

> Indirect expropriation occurs where a measure or series of measures of a party has an effect equivalent to direct expropriation, in that it substantially deprives the investor of the fundamental attributes of property in its investment, including the right to use, enjoy and dispose of its investment, without formal transfer of title or outright seizure (Annex 8-A.1.b CETA).

A '*case-by-case fact-based inquiry*' is required which also looks at the economic impact of this measure, its duration, purpose, context and objective (Annex 8-A.2). Problematic is therefore, that even regulative measures reducing the value of an investment are affected, which might be relevant in terms of social standards.[50]

---

47 Fritz (2015), p. 11; Krajewski (2014), p. 7 and Sinclair et al. (2014), pp. 16 et seq.

48 ICSID, *Lone Pine vs. Canada*, Notice of Arbitration, ICSID Case No. UNCT/15/2, 6 Sep 2013. As well as ICSID, *Suez vs. Argentine*, Decision on Liability, ICSID Case No. ARB/03/17, 30 July 2010.

49 Porterfield (2013).

50 Fisahn and Ciftci (2015), p. 261 and Krajewski (2014), pp. 7 et seq.

'Non-discriminatory measures' aimed at *'legitimate public purposes'* such as *'health, safety and the environment'* are permissible, while social standards are not mentioned as grounds of justification. The annex has an additional reservation stating the measures taken should not be *'so severe (in light of its purpose) that they appear manifestly excessive'* (Annex 8-A.3. CETA). Only negative effects on the value of an investment are not enough for an indirect expropriation, but legitimate expectations of investors have to be acknowledged. From a legal analysis based upon constitutional law, the hurdle for a measure to have an effect which is comparable to the one of direct expropriation seems quite high. Examples from earlier jurisprudence of arbitral tribunals, however, show that in ISDS-cases, indirect expropriation is interpreted quite broadly (see under Sect. 4.3.2). Protective measures not subject to an exemption but associated with costs payable by employers therefore may be seen as indirect expropriation, e.g. significant increases in the minimum wage, considerable improvements in dismissal protection or full equal pay for temporary workers.[51] Also, the extension of co-determination rights of works councils in Germany might be seen, from the perspective of US or Canadian companies, as a measure which reduces the value of their investment.[52] As result of the broad margin of interpretation, ISDS procedures often rely on indirect expropriation.[53]

4.2.5 Exemption Clauses

State regulation can only be maintained or reintroduced under extremely limited conditions, if the investment protection provisions of CETA (or TTIP) are violated. The number of relevant exemption clauses is limited. Chapter 28 Art. 28.3.1 CETA incorporates those exemptions from the principle of non-discrimination which would be legitimate according to Art. XX.1 GATT (1994). Accordingly, permissible exemptions concern the protection of *public morals, human, animal or plant health, exhaustible natural resources, or products made by prison labour* (Art. XX a) b) e) GATT 1994). Measures of social and labour protection, by contrast, do not justify exemptions from the principle of non-discrimination. Only occupational safety measures might therefore be justifiable.[54]

Pursuant to Chapter 28 Art. 28.3.1 CETA, the justifications for relevant exemptions in Article XX GATT refer only to a part of the investment protection chapter in CETA; neither the protection against de facto expropriation nor the principle of fair and equitable treatment are included.

---

[51] New labour protection standards might for example be permissible, providing they do not appear 'manifestly excessive'.

[52] Broß (2015), p. 16.

[53] See e.g. Fritz (2015), pp. 12 et seq.

[54] Fritz (2015), p. 5.

Problematically seen might be as well the fixation of the respective level of liberalization. Exceptions of the obligation to liberalize as agreed upon in Chapter 8 (investments) and Chapter 9 (services) are to be found in comprehensive specific lists for both parties. Unlike the WTO General Agreement on Trade in Services (GATS), CETA (and TTIP) follow a so-called *negative list approach.* A positive list names the areas, which might be liberalized. In contrast to this, all areas which are not on the (negative) list of CETA (and TTIP), are basically open to liberalization. Limitations of liberalization are listed up in the Annexes of CETA. Although a provision has been included in the CETA investment chapter that reaffirms a government's right to regulate for legitimate policy objectives (Chapter 8 Art. 8.9.1 CETA),[55] it is doubtful, whether the interpretation of this new provision will actually lead to a limitation of liberalization, which is the maxim of the whole agreement. As legitimate policy objectives, the protection of public health and safety, public morals and social or consumer protection are listed in the norm. How far a legitimate social protection will be accepted in case of dispute, if company interests are affected, remains—facing previous outcomes of ICSID-cases—more than doubtful.

4.2.6 Impact on the Services Sector

The *negative list approach* chosen for the opening up of services in CETA and TTIP attracts major criticism. Unlike positive lists, where the areas and sectors to be liberalized are clearly defined, negative lists only exempt specifically named areas. This means that new services, such as crowd work[56] which are only emerging now or some which have simply been forgotten, can be fully liberalized.[57] The European Commission favours a narrow definition which only allows non-economic services of general interest for exemption of liberalization. The exemptions under CETA concern services rendered as a sovereign function (Chapter 9 Art. 9.2.2(a)). Areas which are partly privatized, such as water supply, education and health services are regarded as at least partly-commercialized and can therefore be provided by private operators as part of a general framework of economic competition. Specific exemptions for social standards are not included in this chapter.

The areas more strongly affected by CETA and TTIP comprise business-related services as well as communication and information services. In labour-intensive sectors, like health and social services in particular, increased activity can be

[55]Chapter 8 Art. 8.9.1 CETA: '[...] the Parties reaffirm their right to regulate within their territories to achieve legitimate policy objectives, such as the protection of public health, safety, the environment or public morals, social or consumer protection or the promotion and protection of cultural diversity'.

[56]Crowd workers are commissioned via internet platforms to check CD covers, describe products, draw up designs, develop cars etc. These are activities previously carried out by in-house staff and now outsourced. For more detail, see Benner (2015) and Däubler and Klebe (2015), p. 1032.

[57]Fritz (2015), p. 16 and Krajewski and Kynast (2014), pp. 32 et seqq.

expected by Canadian or US-based American service companies, and consequences for the quality of employment in Germany cannot be ruled out. Given rising demand and existing cost pressures in the health sector, increased competition and more labour intensification may entail the growth of precarious employment and sustained wage pressure accompanied by a decrease of union organising activities.[58]

4.2.7 Public Procurement

EU public procurement has an approximately 18% share of GDP[59] with a volume of roughly €350 billion. Public procurement allows the state to exert significant influence on social and ecological standards. These aspects were enhanced by EU directive 2014/24/EU[60] as Art. 18 Par. 2 stipulates:

> Member States shall take appropriate measures to ensure that in the performance of public contracts economic operators comply with applicable obligations in the fields of environmental, social and labour law established by Union law, national law, collective agreements or by the international environmental, social and labour law provisions listed in Annexe X.

This means that according to EU law social criteria in public procurement can no longer be termed 'procurement-unfriendly', but need to be considered when determining the most economically advantageous tender.[61]

CETA's Chapter 19 on public procurement does not pay similar attention to social criteria. Although according to Chapter 8, the rules governing non-discrimination, for example, do not apply in case of public procurement (Art. 8.1.5 CETA), the procurement chapter contains specific provisions which are quite similar. Art. 19.4.1 CETA e.g. demands, that suppliers located in the other economic area, are treated no less favourable than suppliers of the own territory. Furthermore, pursuant to Art. 19.4.6 CETA, so-called *offsets* are not allowed. Offsets are defined as 'any condition or undertaking that encourages local development or improves a Party's balance-of-payments accounts, such as the use of domestic content, the licensing of technology, investment, counter-trade and similar action or requirement' (Art. 19.1 CETA).

CETA hardly contains any provisions that allow to link public procurement tenders to social standards. Where permissible exemptions are concerned (*Security and General Exemptions*) Art. 19.3.2 CETA targets *public morals, order and safety* as well as *health, the disabled, charitable facilities, or goods and services provided by prison labour*. But there is no specific reference to labour or social standards. It is

---

[58]Scherrer and Beck (2014), p. 59 and Lethbridge (2011).

[59]European Parliament Public Procurement (2014).

[60]European Parliament and Council Directive 2014/24/EU *on public procurement and repealing Directive 2004/18/EC*, O.J. L 94/65 (2014). The directive has to be incorporated into national law by 18 April 2016.

[61]For more detail, see Glaser (2015), esp. pp. 32 et seqq., 77.

more than doubtful whether it is possible to group together compliance with 'collective bargaining regulations'[62] in procurement laws in Germany's regions (Länder) under the heading of '*public morals*',[63] although it might be justifiable to refer to provisions of occupational safety under '*health*'. However, it has to be examined whether procurement criteria are required and do not constitute unfair discrimination or unnecessary trade barriers[64] where the few permissible social regulations are concerned. As of now, once CETA and TTIP come into force, there is a danger that the new procurement directive 2014/94/EU, concluded after long debate, may be cancelled out.

4.3 Investor-State Dispute Settlement

4.3.1 General Aspects

Investor-State dispute settlement (ISDS) is a form of dispute resolution between foreign investors and the host state, which allows foreign investors to initiate dispute settlement proceedings against a host state if the investor sees a violation of investment law. Quite a number of free trade agreements contain investment chapters that provide for ISDS in case of investment-related disputes. There are currently more than 2700 international agreements[65] providing for ISDS. Rules of ISDS can also be found in domestic investment laws of some states and in specific contracts between a foreign investor and a state (or a state-affiliated agency),[66] some of these investment laws or contracts provide for dispute settlements at national courts. Figures of ISDS-cases have considerably risen in the last 15 years.[67]

Part of the central criticisms on TTIP (and CETA) concerns exactly the right of investors to turn to 'private arbitration'[68] and to claim damages from a state.[69] This criticism lead to a change of the CETA document, meanwhile the constitution of a specific tribunal for cases of disputes of Canadian or EU investors was stipulated,[70]

[62]Tariftreueregelungen.

[63]Similar Fritz (2015), p. 22.

[64]Compare in details ibid.

[65]Both free trade agreements and BITs.

[66]ICSID (2015), p. 1.

[67]As figures from the World Bank show, see ICSID (2015), pp. 4 et seq.

[68]'Private' in the sense, that the dispute settlement did not take place at national courts. The 'private' character of ISDS procedures is debated rather controversially. Due to the basis in international law, it is argued, that ISDS procedure would belong to public law or be a 'hybrid' form of law.

[69]For a comprehensive comparison Broß (2015) as well as v. Frankenberg (2014) or Krajewski (2015) and Hess (2015), pp. 163 et seqq.

[70]Chapter 8 Art. 8.27 et seqq. CETA.

similar proposals are discussed for TTIP. Initially, ISDS mechanisms were created to stimulate foreign direct investment in countries in which the judicial system was either very slow or not working at all (due to corruption).[71] When NAFTA was negotiated 20 years ago, US and Canadian negotiators insisted on ISDS rules to protect 'their' investors from expropriation in Mexico. In practice, US companies rather used the ISDS-rules to proceed against unwanted regulation in Canada, although Canada has a well-working judicial system. The same applies to Canadian companies. The Canadian group Lone Pine, e.g., sued his home country Canada with the help of a US letterbox company.[72] In general, private dispute settlement in developed countries significantly doubles legal protection for foreign companies, who have the possibility to sue against legislation before national courts as well as using ISDS mechanisms.[73] This does not change with the establishment of a new additional tribunal. Examples like Vattenfall[74] show that companies very well make use of these possibilities.[75] The general rule of international law that international courts can only be called after exhaustion of local remedies is not applicable to international investment disputes.[76] Meanwhile, agreements on investment do work as a protection against legal changes which reduce the value of an investment rather than as a protection against unlawful expropriation.[77]

In addition, international dispute settlement bodies tend to give a broad interpretation of the indeterminate legal concepts contained in BITs, as the examples below show. Decisions vary considerably and each case is an ad hoc ISDS-procedure which is based upon a specific BIT.[78] This is a strain on public authorities, partly because cases are lost, partly because the costs of the cases are enormous.[79] But the spectre of swinging damages means that a possibly high economic risk might influence future state regulation. Governments can therefore modify legal provisions because of the threat of proceedings against them, or they can be overeager and pass new regulations to be weaker from the outset in order to avoid later disputes proactively. ISDS procedures became a highly speculative and profitable market, where financial investors buy demands and lead cases

[71]v. Frankenberg (2014), p. 318.

[72]Eberhardt (2014), p. 6. See also ICSID, *Lone Pine vs. Canada*, ICSID Case No. UNCT/15/2.

[73]Krajewski (2015).

[74]Vattenfall sues on the one hand against the act on the termination of the use of nuclear power stations at the German Constitutional Court (BVerfG). At the same time, the company started an ISDS-case to obtain compensation. The amount in dispute is about €4.6 billion; ICSID, *Vattenfall (and others) vs. Federal Republik of Germany*, ICSID-Case No. ARB/09/6.

[75]This leads in practice to a disadvantage of national companies, who do only have the possibility to take legal action at national courts.

[76]Krajewski (2014), p. 10.

[77]Broß (2015), p. 11.

[78]Hess (2015), p. 166.

[79]The values of the claims ranged from several million to amounts exceeding US $1 billion; thus, in 2012, an arbitration panel obliged Ecuador to pay the so far unparalleled sum of US $2.4 billion in damages (including interest and legal costs), compare Eberhardt (2014), p. 6.

strategically and prepared to take risk.[80] Although the previous ISDS investment protection procedures will be replaced by an investment jurisdiction of the new tribunal, nevertheless, the problematic factors mentioned above, will not be solved, especially because it is not clear whether such a tribunal will not be orientated rather neoliberal and enterprise-friendly. The lack of democracy would be cured if such a new specialized court would be created. The question of the necessity of such an additional legal body still remains.

4.3.2 Examples for Lawsuits by Investors Against States

There have been a range of lawsuits in international arbitration bodies, brought by investors against protective rules referring to human rights or labour rights. Available decisions lack uniformity and coherence. The following cases are either pending or have recently been decided:

Proceedings due to indirect expropriation:

Goetz (u.a.) vs. Burundi In 1995, Belgian investors sued Burundi because Burundi changed its law and withdrew tax-privileges from companies which dealt with the extraction and commercialization of special metals, among others the Belgian company AFFIMET. The investors argued that they had legitimate expectations that their tax-privileges would not be changed. In 1999, the case was settled, after Burundi paid taxes and tariffs of about US $3 million back to AFFIMET.[81]

Noble Ventures vs. Romania In 2001, the US commodities group sued Romania; apart from indirect expropriation it claimed a violation of the full protection and security standard. The group had purchased a former state-owned company whose privatization had become more expensive as a result of worker protests. The American investors considered that the Romanian authorities had not given sufficient warning of strikes and 'site occupations', leading them to claim US $365 million in damages. Though breaches of the agreement were assumed to have occurred, Romania still managed to win the case in 2005 as no sufficient causality could be established between violations of contract and damage suffered. Even though it won the case, Romania still incurred high costs, as the legal costs were shared equally between the parties concerned.[82]

Paushok vs. Mongolia A Russian-owned Mongolian mining company, KOO Golden East-Mongolia, brought an action because of a windfall profit tax on gold sales introduced by Mongolia in 2006, and against a penalty tax amounting to ten times the national minimum wage per foreign worker after a 10% limit had been exceeded. Apart from indirect expropriation, the claim also asserted a FET standard

[80] Eberhardt and Olivet (2012), p. 57.

[81] ICSID, *Goetz (u.a) v. Republic of Burundi*, ICSID Case No. ARB/95/3.

[82] The average costs of an ISDS-case are about €8 million, see Hess (2015), p. 173. Concerning the case ICSID, *Noble vs. Rumänien*, Award, ICSID Case No ARB/01/11, 12 Oct 2005.

violation. This case is one example where a state emerged victorious from dispute settlement (in 2011), because the plaintiffs were unable to demonstrate satisfactorily that their expectation that the relevant tax in question would not be levied had been legitimate.[83]

Foresti (et al) vs. South Africa (non-discrimination) In 2007, Italian and Luxembourg investors sued South Africa for damages of US $350 million because a new mining act contained elements of anti-discrimination in favour of black workers based on the *Black Empowerment Act*. Businesses had been forced to sell company shares to 'historically disadvantaged South African'. The case was declared moot in 2010, after the investors received new licenses as a result of which they had to sell less shares.[84] The arbitration proceedings were put on hold on grounds of contractual assurances.

Achmea vs. Slovakia (public health insurance) In 2007, as part of a process of unification of the Slovak health insurance sector, Slovakia adopted a law which prohibited health insurance companies to take profit out of the public health insurance system. In 2008, the Dutch health company Achmea started an ISDS procedure based upon the BIT between Slovakia and the Netherlands. In 2012, Slovakia was held liable to pay €25 million on grounds of indirect expropriation.[85] Further claims because of intended changes of health insurances could be repelled in 2014.[86]

Centerra vs. Kyrgyzstan The Canadian mining company initiated arbitral proceedings in 2006, after the Kyrgyz government prescribed extra pay for miners having to work at altitude (Canterra's Kumto gold mine is 4000 m above sea level and is considered the second highest in the world). Further information is not publicly available.

Veolia vs. Egypt (minimum wage) The French utility company Veolia commenced arbitration against Egypt in 2012 on the basis of the BIT between France and Egypt, alleging breach of an agreement for waste disposal in the city of Alexandria. The city had refused contract changes Veolia wanted to introduce to counter higher costs—arising among others from the introduction of a national minimum wage. Media reports say Veolia is demanding €82 million in damages.[87] The case is still ongoing.

Examples with relation to labour standards are rare, but numerous examples concerning environmental standards may illustrate how companies made use of

[83]ICSID, *Paushok vs. Republik of Mongolia*, Award, ICSID Case No. ARB/04/10, 28 Apr 2011.

[84]ICSID, *Foresti vs. South Africa*, Award, ICSID Case No. ARB(AF)/07/01, 10 Aug 2010.

[85]PCA, *Achmea B.V. vs. the Slovak republic*, PCA-case no. 2008-13; for further information compare Reidl (2013).

[86]PCA, *Achmea B.V. vs. the Slovak republic*, Award on Jurisdiction and Admissibility, PCA-case no. 2013-12, 20 May 2014.

[87]Karadelis (2012).

investment protection law to attack new legislation with stronger environmental protection.[88]

5 Labour Law Standards in the Sustainability Chapter

CETA contains a chapter on trade and labour (Chapter 23) and it is also foreseen for TTIP. This is not new, as all recent US and EU investment protection or trade agreements include a sustainability or social chapter. In the past, labour standards have not been of greater importance in investment (protection) agreements. Only 5.5% of all BITs take labour standards into account (in percentage terms), with a trend towards a noticeable increase.[89] Free trade agreements more often contain a chapter on labour standards.[90] But do sustainability or social chapters of trade agreements help to ensure social standards? The chapters do not provide new norms on labour law, but rather rely upon conventions of labour standards which the parties have already ratified; mostly the parties 'reaffirm' their commitments under the ILO Declaration of 1998 on Core Labour Standards.[91]

The way sustainability chapters are accommodated can vary widely. Some agreements refer in general terms to sustainable development, corporate social responsibility (responsible business conduct) or human rights in the preamble. All EU free trade agreements exclude the sustainability or social chapter from the standard sanctions regime (e.g. recent agreements concluded with Colombia or South Korea). Besides an inter-state dialogue,[92] there is only a consultation or complaints mechanism, but complaints generally can only be made by the contracting parties (the other side of any agreement), not by representatives of civil society.[93] Recommendations on the subject matter of the dispute can be adopted (with follow-up monitoring), but no sanctions are available to address

[88]Due to a mining moratorium, the mining company Pacific Rim, e.g., initiated arbitral proceedings in 2009 against El Salvador, based upon investment protection rules in CAFTA. The moratorium was imposed because of massive protests of the local population against the destruction of the environment and water pollution because of mining. Since Pacific Rim therefore could not open the new mine 'El Dorado', the company demands U.S. $301 million in damages (which is more than 1% of the gross domestic product). Pacific Rim is situated in Canada and as Canada is not part of CAFTA, arbitration procedures were initiated via a subsidiary company in Nevada (USA), see Kirsch and Moore (2016).

[89]The study considers all BITs concluded before the end of 2013; compare Gordon et al. (2014), p. 15.

[90]In the middle of 2013, 58 of all 248 Free Trade Agreements registered at the WTO, contained a labour clause, see Ebert (2015), p. 19.

[91]Prislan and Zandvliet (2013), p. 23.

[92]The dialogue-mechanism in CETA is examined by Ebert (2017), pp. 305 et seqq. For such mechanisms in general see ILO (2013), pp. 67 et seqq.

[93]For a comprehensive analysis of the EU social chapter in the trade agreement with Columbia and Peru, see Zimmer (2011), pp. 625 et seqq. or Zimmer (2012), pp. 141 et seqq.

cases of persistent non-compliance, as the European Commission favours dialogue and incentive measures over enforcement action.[94]

Nevertheless, even if the regular dispute settlement mechanism is applicable to the sustainability chapter (as in nearly all US trade agreements[95]), the impact of the social chapter is questionable. In 2014, for the first time ever, the regular dispute settlement mechanism in a US trade agreement[96] reached the phase of arbitration because of continuous violations of labour rights in Guatemala. In the case, first complaints were already filed in 2009, the procedure therefore took more than 5 years.[97] Facing 13 US Free Trade Agreements with social chapters which contain labour law provisions, this is a rather disappointing outcome. All 37 complaints which were filed under NAALC (North American Agreement on Labor Cooperation)[98] stayed on the stage of consultations and public hearings, not a single sanction was imposed. The hurdle for sanctions is high, as in other trade or investment agreements, the violation of labour provisions or the derogation of labour law is only relevant in NAALC if it is trade-related. Art. 16.2.1 (a) NAALC thus requires 'a failure to effectively enforce its labor laws through a sustained or recurring course of action or inaction, in a manner effecting trade between the parties'.[99] The assassination of Guatemalan trade unionists however did not meet this condition[100] because trade was not affected. It would have been relevant e.g., if the trade unionists would have been murdered to attract investment—if they were murdered for other reason, this is not relevant.[101]

A 3-years study from the Washington Office on Latin America from 2009 that analyses the impact of CAFTA-DR on labour law could not find any improvements of labour conditions or a reduction of labour law violations. Not one dispute settlement procedure was started because of labour law violations, but 16 - investor-state dispute settlement-proceedings.[102]

The CETA chapter on trade and labour also includes only rules which are not subject to the arbitral procedures and presumably, the concept of the sustainability chapter in TTIP will be similar. Although an impact assessment of TTIP on labour is discussed, it is doubtful whether this will have any practical relevance in the

---

[94]Concerning labour rights in the EU-GSP-system, see critically Vogt (2015), pp. 285 et seq. who outlines, that even notorious labour law violators like Pakistan or Guatemala are granted GSP+.

[95]Concerning the US-approach, see ILO (2016), pp. 44 et seqq.

[96]Central American Free Trade Agreement, CAFTA-DR.

[97]Nevertheless, this process was interrupted because Guatemala in the meantime had signed an enforcement plan, whereupon the USA stopped the procedure. When Guatemala failed to implement the plan, the USA continued the proceedings.

[98]NAALC is the labour side agreement of NAFTA (North American Free Trade Agreement).

[99]The same requirement can be found in other agreements, e.g. in Art. 6 (4) (a) US-Jordan Trade Agreement or in Art. 15.2 (1) (a) US-Bahrain Trade Agreement.

[100]A complaint was filed, although Guatemala is not party of NAFTA.

[101]Similar (giving a different example) Prislan and Zandvliet (2013), p. 25.

[102]Washington Office on Latin America (2009).

future, as similar projects concerning other trade agreements, e.g. concerning the impact of CAFTA-DR, have shown.

6 Conclusion

The analysis of the free trade agreements CETA and TTIP illustrates the tense relationship between the state's interest in regulation for the protection of workers and investment protection rules aimed at protecting investors. The agreements promote privatisation tendencies and environmental and social standards considered 'obstacles' are sacrificed. In addition, the mechanism of mutual recognition of standards might trigger the dynamic of a competitive-based deregulation of standards.[103] This can be considered a tremendous threat for social standards in Europe.

References

Benner C (ed) (2015) Crowdwork – zurück in die Zukunft? Perspektiven digitaler Arbeit. Bund-Verlag, Frankfurt

Bode T (2015) TTIP – Die Freihandelslüge. Deutsche Verlags-Anstalt, München

Broß S (2015) Freihandelsabkommen, einige Anmerkungen zur Problematik der privaten Schiedsgerichtsbarkeit. HBS-Report Nr. 4, Düsseldorf

Burkard E-M (2015) Zum Spannungsverhältnis von Investitions- und Menschenrechtsschutz. Nomos, Baden-Baden

Capaldo J (2014) The Trans-Atlantic Trade and Investment Partnership: European disintegration, unemployment and instability. GDAE, Working Paper No. 14-03, Global Development and Environment Institute. http://ase.tufts.edu/gdae/policy_research/ttip_simulations.html. Accessed 05 Nov 2015

Corporate Europe Observatory (2013) Who's scripting the EU-US trade deal. https://corporateeurope.org/trade/2013/06/who-scripting-eu-us-trade-deal. Accessed 20 Mar 2016

Council of the European Union (2013) Directives for the negotiations on the Transatlantic Trade and Investment Partnership between the European Union and the United States of America, 11103/13. http://data.consilium.europa.eu/doc/document/ST-11103-2013-DCL-1/en/pdf. Accessed 15 Aug 2017

Däubler W, Klebe T (2015) Crowdwork: Die neue Form der Arbeit – Arbeitgeber auf der Flucht. Neue Zeitschrift für Arbeitsrecht 2015:1032–1041

Diebold N (2010) Non-discrimination in international trade in services. Cambridge University Press, Cambridge

Eberhardt P (2014) Investitionsschutz am Scheideweg, TTIP und die Zukunft des globalen Investitionsrechts. Friedrich-Ebert-Stiftung, Berlin

Eberhardt P, Olivet C (2012) Profiting from injustice. Corporate Europe Observatory and the Transnational Institute, Brussels/Amsterdam

Ebert F (2015) Social dimensions of free trade agreements, 2nd edn. Studies on growth with equity. ILO, Geneva

[103]Similar Scherrer and Beck (2014), p. 52.

Ebert FC (2017) The comprehensive economic and trade agreement (CETA): are existing arrangements sufficient to prevent adverse effects on labour standards? Int J Comp Labour Law Ind Relat 33(2):295–330

European Parliament Public Procurement (2014) Öffentliche Auftragsvergabe: Bessere Qualität und mehr Leistung für den Preis (press release). www.europarl.europa.eu/pdfs/news/expert/infopress/20140110IPR32386/20140110IPR32386_de.pdf. Accessed 09 Nov 2015

Felbermayr G, Heid B, Lehwald S (2013a) Die Transatlantische Handels- und Investitionspartnerschaft (THIP): Wem nutzt ein transatlantisches Freihandelsabkommen? Part 1: Makroökonomische Effekte. ifo-Institute study on behalf of Bertelsmann-Stiftung, Gütersloh

Felbermayr G, Larch M, Flach L, Yalcin E, Benz S (2013b) Dimensionen und Auswirkungen eines Freihandelsabkommens zwischen der EU und den USA. Study on behalf of the Federal Ministry of Economics and Technology, Munich

Fisahn A, Ciftci R (2015) CETA and TTIP: demokratische Bedenken zu einigen Aspekten. Kritische Justiz 2015(3):251–263

Francois J, Manchin M, Norberg H, Pindyuk O, Tomberger P (2013) Reducing transatlantic barriers to trade and investment. An economic assessment. CEPR Final Project Report commissioned by the EU Commission. Centre for Economic Policy Research, London

Friedrich Ebert Stiftung (ed) (1998) Das Multilaterale Investitionsabkommen MAI und die Umwelt. http://www.fes.de/pdf-files/iez/00192.pdf. Accessed 10 Mar 2015

Fritz T (2015) Analyse und Bewertung des EU-Kanada Freihandelsabkommens CETA. Expert opinion on behalf of Hans-Böckler-Stiftung, Berlin

Geiger R (2014) The Transatlantic Trade and Investment Partnership: a critical perspective. Columbia FDI Perspectives, No. 119. http://ccsi.columbia.edu/files/2013/10/No-119-Geiger-FINAL.pdf. Accessed 26 Mar 2016

Glaser A (2015) Zwingende soziale Mindeststandards bei der Vergabe öffentlicher Aufträge. Nomos, Baden-Baden

Gordon K, Pohl J, Bouchard M (2014) Investment treaty law, sustainable development and responsible business conduct: a fact finding survey. OECD Working Paper on International Investment 1/2014. OECD Publishing, Paris

Hess B (2015) Die Legitimitätskrise der Investitionsschiedsgerichtsbarkeit. In: Callies C (ed) Herausforderungen an Staat, Verfassung und Völkerrecht – Europarecht – Menschenrechte. Liber Amicorum für Torsten Stein zum 70. Geburtstag. Nomos, Baden-Baden, pp 163–175

High Level Working Group on Jobs and Growth (2013) Final Report. http://trade.ec.europa.eu/doclib/docs/2013/february/tradoc_150519.pdf. Accessed 24 Mar 2016

ICSID (2015) Background information on the International Centre for Settlement of Investment Disputes. https://icsid.worldbank.org/apps/ICSIDWEB/about/Documents/ICSID%20Fact%20Sheet%20-%20ENGLISH.pdf. Accessed 30 Mar 2016

ILO (2013) Social dimensions of free trade agreements. Studies on growth with equity. ILO, IILS, Geneva

ILO (2016) Assessment of labour provisions in trade and investment agreements. Studies on growth with equity. ILO, Geneva

Karadelis K (2012) Can Veolia trash Egypt at ICSID? Global Arbitration Review. http://globalarbitrationreview.com/news/article/30644/can-veolia-trash-egypt-icsid. Accessed 09 Nov 2015

Kirsch S, Moore J (2016) Mining, corporate social responsibility and conflict: OceanaGold and the El Dorado Foundation in El Salvador. http://miningwatch.ca/sites/default/files/el_dorado_foundation_report_2016_eng.pdf. Accessed 30 Mar 2016

Krajewski M (2014) Kurzgutachten: Zu Investitionsschutz und Investor-Staat-Streitbeilegung im Transatlantischen Handels- und Investitionspartnerschaftsabkommen (TTIP). https://www.gruene-bundestag.de/fileadmin/media/gruenebundestag_de/Veranstaltungen/140505-TTIP/Kurzgutachten_Investititionsschutz_TTIP_Endfassung_layout.pdf. Accessed 26 Mar 2016

Krajewski M (2015) Investor-Staat-Schiedsgerichtsbarkeit im TTIP. Europäische Zeitschrift für Wirtschaftsrecht 2015:105
Krajewski M, Kynast B (2014) Auswirkungen des Transatlantischen Handels- und Investitionsabkommens (TTIP) auf den Rechtsrahmen für öffentliche Dienstleistungen. Study on behalf of Hans-Böckler-Stiftung, Erlangen/Nürnberg
Krätke M (2014) TAFTA: Das Kapital gegen den Rest der Welt. Blätter für deutsche und internationale Politik I/2014:5-9
Lethbridge J (2011) Care services for older people in Europe – challenges for labour; Public Services International Research Unit (PSIRU), University of Greenwich
Nawparwar M (2009) Die Außenbeziehungen der Europäischen Union zu internationalen Organisationen nach dem Vertrag von Lissabon. Beiträge zum Europa- und Völkerrecht 4/2009
OECD (2008) International investment law: understanding concepts and tracking innovations. Chapter 1 – definition of investor and investment in international investment. OECD Publishing, Paris
ÖFSE (2014) ASSES_TTIP. Assessing the claimed benefits of the Transatlantic Trade and Investment Partnership, research report. ÖFSE – Austrian Foundation for Development Research, Vienna
Porterfield M (2013) A distinction without a difference? The interpretation of fair and equitable treatment under customary international law by investment tribunals, IISD. https://www.iisd.org/itn/2013/03/22/a-distinction-without-a-difference-the-interpretation-of-fair-and-equitable-treatment-under-customary-international-law-by-investment-tribunals/. Accessed 08 Nov 2015
Prislan V, Zandvliet R (2013) Labour provisions in international investment agreements: prospects for sustainable development. Grotius Centre Working Paper 2013/003-IEL. Available at SSRN. https://ssrn.com/abstract=2171716. Accessed 14 Aug 2017
Reidl P (2013) Die Slowakei wagt, was noch kein Land gewagt hat. Wirtschaftsblatt 11 Feb 2013
Scherrer C, Beck S (2014) Das transatlantische Handels- und Investitionsabkommen (TTIP) zwischen der EU und den USA. HBS-Arbeitspapier 30
Schill S (2014) Auswirkungen der Bestimmungen zum Investitionsschutz und zu den Investor-Staat-Schiedsverfahren im Entwurf des Freihandelsabkommens zwischen der EU und Kanada (CETA) auf den Handlungsspielraum des Gesetzgebers (Kurzgutachten). http://www.bmwi.de/BMWi/Redaktion/PDF/C-D/ceta-gutachten-investitionsschutz,property=pdf,bereich=bmwi2012,sprache=de,rwb=true.pdf. Accessed 09 Nov 2015
Schreyer M (2014) Die Transatlantische Handels- und Investitionspartnerschaft (TTIP): Kann das geplante Abkommen halten, was es verspricht? FES, WISO direkt, Bonn
Sinclair S, Trew S, Mertins-Kirkwood H (2014) Making sense of CETA. An analysis of the final text of the comprehensive economic and trade agreement. Canadian Centre for Policy Alternatives. https://www.policyalternatives.ca/publications/reports/making-sense-ceta. Accessed 08 Nov 2015
Stephan S (2014) TTIP – Das Märchen vom Wachstums- und Beschäftigungsmotor. FES, WISO direkt, Bonn
UNCTAD (2010) Most-favoured-nation treatment. UNCTAD Series on Issues in International Investment Agreements II, New York/Geneva
UNCTAD (2011) Scope and definition. UNCTAD Series on Issues in International Investment Agreements II, New York/Geneva
v. Frankenberg K (2014) Marktfähige Gerichtsbarkeit? Kritische Justiz 2014(3):316–329
Vogt J (2015) A little less conversation: the EU and (non) application of labour conditionality in the generalized system of preferency (GSP). Int J Comp Labour Law Ind Relat 31:285–304
Wallach L (2012) Fair and equitable treatment and investors' reasonable expectations: rulings in U.S. FTAs & BITs demonstrate FET definition must be narrowed. https://www.citizen.org/documents/MST-Memo.pdf. Accessed 08 Nov 2015

Washington Office on Latin America (2009) DR-CAFTA and workers' rights: moving from paper to practice. http://www.wola.org/sites/default/files/downloadable/Rights%20and%20Development/2010/WOLA_RPT_WorkersRights_FNL.pdf. Accessed 10 Dec 2015

Wengler W (1975) Die Mitbestimmung und das Völkerrecht. Nomos, Baden-Baden

Xiao Y (2006) Das Prinzip der Nichtdiskriminierung in einem künftigen multilateralen Investitionsabkommen. Nomos, Baden-Baden

Zimmer R (2011) Sozialklauseln im Freihandelsabkommen der EU mit Kolumbien und Peru. Recht der internationalen Wirtschaft 2011(9):625–631

Zimmer R (2012) Sozialklauseln im Nachhaltigkeitskapitel des Freihandelsabkommens der Europäischen Union mit Kolumbien und Peru. In: Scherrer C, Hänlein A (eds) Sozialkapitel in Handelsabkommen. Begründungen und Vorschläge aus juristischer, ökonomischer und politologischer Sicht. Nomos, Baden-Baden, pp 141–156

Mainstreaming Investment-Labour Linkage Through 'Mega-Regional' Trade Agreements

Henner Gött and Till Patrik Holterhus

Contents

H. Gött (✉) · T.P. Holterhus
Georg-August-University Göttingen, Institute of International and European Law, Göttingen, Germany
e-mail: hgoett@gwdg.de; tholter@gwdg.de

H. Gött (ed.), *Labour Standards in International Economic Law*,
https://doi.org/10.1007/978-3-319-69447-4_12

Abstract A growing number of large-scale free trade agreements, so-called 'mega-regionals', contain both investment and labour provisions. In this chapter, we argue that this bears the potential for mainstreaming investment-labour linkage into international investment law. Prompted by this prospect, we engage in an indepth analysis of the particular components of investment-labour linkages, their potentials and shortcomings. Our main observation is that the investment-labour linkage contained in the examined agreements has the potential to contribute to a more adequate balance between investors' and workers' interests. However, since the respective provisions largely leave this linkage to the stage of treaty interpretation and implementation, the tapping of this potential will eventually depend on the willingness and ability of investors and governments.

The inclusion of labour-related provisions in international economic treaties has been a recurring topic in political debates and legal analysis. However, the focus has largely been on international trade law, famously culminating in the struggle over including a 'social clause' in WTO law. By contrast, investment-labour linkage, i.e. the integration in an international treaty of provisions protecting and promoting foreign investments on the one hand and provisions aiming at protecting and promoting labour standards on the other, has not attained much attention. Presumably, one reason for this is that, until today, the bulk of international investment agreements (IIAs)[1], and especially the vast body of bilateral investment treaties (BITs), hardly ever contain references to labour issues.[2] Yet, despite investment-labour linkage generally remaining sidelined by its trade counterpart, there has been a steady and significant increase of investment-labour linkages in free trade agreements (FTAs). Economies like the US, Canada or Chile now regularly include both investment and labour provisions within their FTAs. The same linkage has appeared in recent EU agreements, although, at the time of writing, it is uncertain whether and to what extent the EU will continue to include investment provisons in its future FTAs.

[1]We use this term as a generic term for all treaties containing provisions of investment law, including bi- and plurilateral investment agreements, free trade agreements etc.

[2]Gordon et al. (2014), p. 12.

In this chapter, we argue that this proliferation bears the potential for mainstreaming investment-labour linkage into international investment law. Prompted by this prospect, we engage in an in-depth analysis of the particular components of investment-labour linkages, their potentials and shortcomings. Our main observation is that the investment-labour linkage contained in the examined agreements has the potential to contribute to a more adequate balance between investors' and workers' interests. However, since the respective provisions largely leave this linkage to the stage of treaty interpretation and implementation, the tapping of this potential will eventually depend on the willingness and ability of investors and governments.

Our analysis has a special focus on 'Mega-Regionals', i.e. FTAs with a particularly deep and comprehensive agenda for economic cooperation and integration. As will be discussed below, these agreements may have a significant impact on the future development of investment law and investment-labour linkages in particular. Though to some extent uncertain regarding their actual future conclusion, we will focus on three major contemporary endeavours: The EU-Canada Comprehensive Economic and Trade Agreement (CETA), the proposed EU-US Transatlantic Trade and Investment Partnership (TTIP) and the Trans-Pacific Partnership (TPP) between 12 Pacific rim states. The full text of TPP was published on 5 November 2015, the agreement itself was signed on 4 February 2016. The final CETA text was published alongside its signature on 30 October 2016. As to TTIP, while most parts are still undisclosed and negotiations apparently have been stalled at least temporarily, the European Commission has published some of its textual proposals, including the investment[3] and sustainable development[4] chapters, in late 2015. Although, at the time of writing, none of the treaties have entered into force, we will nevertheless refer to all three endeavours as 'treaties' for the sake of convenience.

As far as TPP is concerned, the recent withdrawal of the USA has rendered the future of this agreement highly uncertain. We will nonetheless include TPP in our analysis, as its extensively negotiated and signed text still resembles an important milestone in the development of FTAs, which arguably still allows at least a glimpse at potential future FTAs of the TPP signatories.

This chapter proceeds as follows: In the first section (Sect. 1), we will set the scene by arguing that investment-labour linkages currently undergo a process of 'generalization', i.e. they are about to become a more regular, rather than an exceptional, feature of international investment law. This trend is most visible in, and promoted by, current negotiations for mega-regionals. Building on this observation, we will examine core features of the investment-labour nexus in CETA, TPP and in the proposals for TTIP, as published by the European Commission, in the following sections. We will therefore examine the substantial provisions (Sect. 2), the institutional framework (Sect. 3) but also potentials for their circumvention (Sect. 4). We will finish with a conclusion (Sect. 5).

[3]Hereinafter 'TTIP Proposal (I)'.

[4]Hereinafter 'TTIP Proposal (SD)'.

1 Prologue: Towards a 'Generalization' of Investment-Labour Linkages

Our analysis builds on the assumption that contemporary large-scale FTA projects have the potential of predetermining and significantly influencing the development of the future international economic order by defining 'gold standards' (Sect. 1.1). It is our suggestion that this is also true with regard to the interrelation between international investment law and labour standards. We base this assertion on two observations: First, as has been shown elsewhere,[5] investment law in general is in a process of generalization, critically reinforced by current FTA endeavours and their respective investment chapters (Sect. 1.2). Second, provisions linking investment and labour standards are more frequent and often more elaborate in FTAs than in stand-alone BITs (Sect. 1.3). As a result, these FTAs do not only foster the generalization of investment law as such, but investment-labour linkages as well (Sect. 1.4).

1.1 FTAs as 'Game Changers'

With a persistent stalemate in WTO negotiations and with multilateral investment agreements currently being out of reach, major economies continue to strive for further economic liberalization and integration through comprehensive bilateral or plurilateral negotiations, covering not only genuine issues of trade, but an increasingly wide range of other issues as well. Among them are, to name only the two of relevance here, foreign investment and labour standards. Recent years have witnessed an intensifying struggle of leading economies to create ever larger free trade areas. Inter alia, these so-called 'mega-regional' FTAs are intended to create spill-over effects towards third states and to define 'gold standards' for future trade negotiations as well as, eventually, for the future world economic order as a whole. Accordingly, envisaged landmark agreements like CETA, TTIP and TPP are widely and rightly perceived as potential 'game changers'.[6] Obviously, whether any of them will actually live up to these expectations remains to be seen, even more so in light of the recent backlashes against TPP and TTIP[7] and the elusive truce between proponents and opponents that paved the way for CETA's signature in October 2016 (and its provisional application from September 2017). However, as a general observation, it seems fair to say that the way 'mega-regional' FTAs regulate and integrate trade, investment and other issues holds the potential to set the course for future developments in international economic law and policy.

[5] Stoll and Holterhus (2016).

[6] For example, TTIP would cover around 50% of global trade and 30% of global GDP, Vogt (2015).

[7] In the case of TPP, the withdrawal of the signature by the USA on 23 January 2017 and, in the case of TTIP, *inter alia*, the stagnating negotiations between the USA and the EU.

1.2 FTAs as Motors of a 'Generalization' of Investment Law

The integration of investment chapters into mega-regional FTAs makes investment law part of this 'game change' and accordingly provides a boost to what has been described as the 'generalization' of investment law.[8] For a long time, investment treaties were primarily perceived as tailor-made tools to protect investors from capital-exporting countries against arbitrary interference by capital-importing host states, predominantly in the global south. They hence had a defined and quite limited *raison d'être*. This 'traditional' perception of investment treaties is increasingly put into perspective by recent developments. First, investment chapters are increasingly included in agreements between developed economies.[9] Second, the ongoing struggle to set a 'gold standard' through the current negotiations adds momentum to the evolution and reform of investment law.[10] Both developments indicate a 'generalization' of investment law, which is about to become an established element of international economic law, moving it 'from splendid isolation to centre stage'.[11] As has already been observed elsewhere, current negotiations for mega-regionals serve as powerful catalysts for this generalization, forcefully combining both developments.[12] This particularly applies to large-scale free trade endeavours like CETA, TTIP and TPP, all of which include investment chapters, and are thus set to become decisive landmarks in the evolution of international investment law.

1.3 FTAs as Trailblazers of Investment-Labour Linkage

Mega-regional FTAs put investment law into a normative context with other areas of law, which are enshrined in other FTA chapters, provisions regarding labour standards being among them. The normative nexus between investment and labour provisions therefore needs to be considered as a 'generalized' element of a 'gold standard investment law'. Early FTAs, like the North American Agreement on Labor Cooperation (NAALC), approximated labour and investment by including labour provisions in a side accord to the main FTA comprising investment provisions.[13] From the early 2000s onwards, especially the USA and Canada have incorporated both investment and labour provisions as respective chapters in or as side agreements to comprehensive international economic treaties.[14]

---

[8]Stoll and Holterhus (2016). For an earlier account on multilateralization on the basis of most favoured nation-obligations see Schill (2009).

[9]Examples are, with respect to the USA and Canada, NAFTA, but also the three treaties examined here.

[10]Stoll and Holterhus (2016).

[11]Stoll and Holterhus (2016).

[12]Stoll and Holterhus (2016).

[13]For analyses, see e.g. Dombois et al. (2004) and Finbow (2006).

[14]See the survey by Van Duzer (2016a).

This stands in remarkable contrast to the role the investment-labour nexus played in traditional investment law, both in practice and scholarly research. According to a 2014 study, despite growing numbers,[15] only about 5.5% of all IIAs of the then 54 countries invited to participate in OECD-hosted investment dialogue included references to labour standards.[16] Accordingly, as compared to the overall number of investment treaty arbitrations, the number of cases in investment treaty and investment contract arbitration involving labour issues has remained rather low. As to scholarly research, while there is a considerable and growing body of scholarly writing on investment law and human rights, only few contributions focus on the particular related issue of investment and labour.[17]

It can further be observed that, compared to those few stand-alone BITs which actually include references to labour, FTAs often include more elaborate examples of labour provisions.[18] While many BITs refer to labour standards as a 'negative element', i.e. solely as a possible limitation of investment protection and investor rights,[19] FTAs, by contrast, do not only recognize labour standards as an investment/trade limitation, but in addition tend to set up a—albeit still limited—genuine labour agenda and include arrangements for the promotion of labour standards, as will be exemplified further below. While many of these arrangements have been underperforming, this nevertheless is an important conceptual difference.

1.4 Interim Conclusion: FTAs 'Mainstream' Investment-Labour Linkage

The aforementioned frequency and relative sophistication of labour provisions in FTAs have the potential of being more than just a statistical anecdote. Given that FTAs and their underlying rationale of pursuing a 'gold standard' are major drivers towards the generalization of investment law, they appear to foster generalizing a normative junction of investment and labour law as well. Additionally, the FTAs discussed above provide not only (interrelated) substantive provisions, but also a common conceptual and institutional framework. Design, benefits and shortcomings of these investment-labour linkage in mega regionals may therefore give a foretaste of treaty provisions governing the investment-labour nexus in the future.

[15]Of all IIAs concluded in 2012, around 40% contained labour provisions, see Gordon et al. (2014), p. 11.

[16]Gordon et al. (2014), p. 12.

[17]E.g. Prislan and Zandvliet (2013) and Zimmer (2017).

[18]Gordon et al. (2014), pp. 10 ff. and Van Duzer (2016a), p. 171.

[19]Van Duzer (2016a), p. 171.

2 The Substantive Dimension of the Investment-Labour Linkage in CETA, TTIP and TPP: Potentials in Need of Concretization

This section addresses the pivotal substantive provisions relevant to the investment-labour linkage in CETA, TTIP and TPP. These include significant overarching conceptual provisions applying to both chapters (Sect. 2.1), general provisions designed to preserve policy space (Sect. 2.2), provisions aiming at maintaining or enhancing the standards of labour protection and their possible repercussions on investment chapters (Sect. 2.3), the role of labour concerns in specific investment protection standards (Sect. 2.4), and finally, provisions on corporate social responsibility (Sect. 2.5).

2.1 Sustainable Development as a Common Conceptual Framework

A common observation regarding CETA, TTIP and TPP is that all three treaties, to varying extents, employ an overarching conceptual 'sustainability approach' to accommodate economic and other issues within an integrated conceptual framework.

The concept of sustainable development has rapidly proliferated during the last two decades and has encroached on an ever-growing number of international legal and political instruments as well as domestic laws.[20] In the words of the International Law Association's 2002 Declaration of Principles of International Law Relating to Sustainable Development:

> the objective of sustainable development involves a comprehensive and integrated approach to economic, social and political processes, which aims at the sustainable use of natural resources of the Earth and the protection of the environment on which nature and human life as well as social and economic development depend and which seeks to realize the right of all human beings to an adequate living standard on the basis of their active, free and meaningful participation in development and in the fair distribution of benefits resulting therefrom, with due regard to the needs and interests of future generations.[21]

There have been ongoing discussions concerning the role and the legal quality of the concept of sustainable development. While many regard it as a merely political

---

[20]See the references in Schrijver (2008) and Novitz (2017).

[21]ILA (2002), p. 212.

See also the 'classic' but more general definition in the World Commission on Environment and Development's Report 'Our Common Future' (the so-called Brundtland Report): 'We define [sustainable development] as paths of human progress that meet the needs and aspirations of the present generation without compromising the ability of future generations to meet their needs', WECD (1987).

concept, others have argued that sustainable development can at the same time be understood as a legal principle.[22]

With regard to investment law, suggestions have been made to include the concept in the actual text and the interpretation of investment treaties in order to overcome perceived biases in favour of investors and other shortcomings of the system of investment protection.[23] Likewise, sustainable development has expanded into a growing number of international labour governance instruments, including the ILO Decent Work Agenda, which are set to contribute to sustainable development.[24] The specific use of sustainable development as an overarching objective in FTAs is, however, a fairly recent phenomenon.

While essentially remaining instruments of international economic governance, CETA, TTIP and TPP all go way further than the limited references to sustainability in WTO- or investment law.[25] Most notably, CETA and TTIP prominently include the notion of sustainable development as a conceptual framework especially for environmental and labour issues, both in preambular language and in dedicated chapters.[26] The TPP uses the more ambiguous[27] term 'sustainable growth',[28] while mentioning sustainable development only with regard to environmental protection[29] and its development chapter.[30]

CETA and TTIP reflect the prevalent understanding of sustainable development and elevate it to the level of a treaty objective.[31] According to Art. 1 (1) TTIP Proposal (SD), headed 'Context', the parties would

> reaffirm their commitment to pursue sustainable development, the dimensions of which – economic development, social development and environmental protection – are interdependent and mutually reinforcing, and are committed to promote the development of international trade and investment in such a way so as to contribute to this overarching objective.

---

[22]See the thoughtful and in-depth analysis by Gehne (2011) and further Berner (2016), p. 182 f.

[23]See e.g. the contributions in Cordonier Segger et al. (2011) and Berner (2016).

[24]ILO Declaration on Social Justice for a Fair Globalization, adopted on 10 June 2008, preambular clause 5.

[25]On these see Schrijver (2008) and Van Duzer (2016a), p. 143.

[26]See e.g. Preamble Clause 9 CETA, which reads: 'The Parties [...] REAFFIRMING their commitment to promote sustainable development and the development of international trade in such a way as to contribute to sustainable development in its economic, social and environmental dimensions' (capitals in original). See also Chapters 22–24 CETA and TTIP (SD). For the EU, this marks a departure from including human rights clauses in its earlier agreements, see Bartels (2012) and Novitz (2017).

[27]See Schrijver (2008), p. 85.

[28]Preamble Clause 1 and Art. 19.10 (6) (b) TPP.

[29]Preamble Clause 12 TPP.

[30]Art. 23.1(5) and Art. 23.3(4) TPP.

[31]For example, Art. 22.1 CETA reads, in relevant parts: 'The Parties recognise that economic development, social development and environmental protection are interdependent and mutually reinforcing components of sustainable development [...].' See also Art. 1(1) and Art. 2 TTIP Proposal (SD).

The proposal contains a range of provisions on coordination, dialogue, impact assessments, consultation and participation of stakeholders and other cross-cutting activities to promote sustainable development.[32]

In remarkable contrast to the TTIP proposal, CETA does not explicitly name investment in its chapter on sustainable development, but only stipulates a

> commitment to promoting the development of international trade in such a way as to contribute to the objective of sustainable development, for the welfare of present and future generations.[33]

Apart from these differences in wording, it is noteworthy that all three agreements are silent on the particular role of the concept of sustainable development in the context of the respective investment chapters. Against this background, the implications of embedding the investment-labour nexus in this common conceptual framework are difficult to assess. As a general matter, provisions explicitly stating the parties' objectives may gain specific importance when establishing the treaty's object and purpose in treaty interpretation pursuant to Art. 31(1) VCLT.[34] For example, the NAFTA panels in *Canadian Agricultural Tariffs* and *Cross-Border Trucking Services* construed narrowly such treaty provisions that collided with NAFTA's 'principal objective' of trade liberalization laid down in its preamble and initial provisions, holding that '[a]ny interpretation adopted by the Panel must [...] promote rather than inhibit the NAFTA's objectives'.[35] In a similar vein, one could argue *mutatis mutandis* that the explicit objective to promote sustainable development requires to interpret the investment and labour chapters in the light of the common sustainability framework. Any such argument, however, would have to carefully examine the way sustainable development is framed as an objective in the particular wording of the FTA at hand. The aforesaid omission of the term 'investment' in CETA's sustainable development chapter could become relevant here. What is more, the objective of promoting sustainable development is usually just one of several FTA objectives, which would have to be duly accommodated. Finally, in any event, sustainable development is a contested and still rather broad concept. It is thus hardly foreseeable in what way, and to what extent, the common conceptual framework of sustainable development will have a traceable impact on the interpretation of FTAs and their specific chapters that would go beyond 'traditional' contextual interpretation as required anyway pursuant to Art. 31(1) and (2) VCLT. Yet, it is nevertheless conceivable that the objective of sustainable development will be given greater weight than under earlier international economic treaties. Eventually, this will depend on how the treaties will be applied and implemented.

---

[32]Further elaborated in the remaining articles of the TTIP Proposal (SD), see also Art. 22.1 CETA.

[33]Art. 22.1 CETA. CETA mentions 'investment' only on certain provisions of its labour and environmental chapters, e.g. in Art. 23.3(3), Art. 23.4, Art. 24.5 and Art. 24.8(1) CETA.

[34]Van Duzer (2016a), p. 148 et seq.

[35]NAFTA Arbitral Panel, *In the Matter of Tariffs Applied by Canada to Certain United States Origin Agricultural Products*, Final Panel Report, 2 Dec 1996, CDA 95-2008-01, para. 122 and NAFTA Arbitral Panel, *In the Matter of Cross Border Trucking Services*, Final Panel Report, 6 Feb 2001, USA-MEX-98-2008-01, paras. 219 and 237.

2.2 General Provisions Intended to Preserve Policy Space

FTAs frequently reserve policy space for trade and investment regulation. In the three particular agreements examined here, two techniques can be distinguished: Exception clauses (Sect. 2.2.1) and reaffirmations of the right to regulate (Sect. 2.2.2). As will be seen, these clauses can be construed to include labour issues, but it is uncertain if they add much to the current state of play when it comes to accommodate investment law and labour law.

2.2.1 'Negative Linkage': Exception Clauses

Inspired by (and building on) exception clauses in WTO law like Art. XX GATT, most FTAs include exception clauses that also apply to at least some of their investment provisions. These clauses provide for policy space by enumerating areas and excluding respective measures from the reach of FTA obligations, provided that they are non-discriminatory and not arbitrary. CETA, TTIP and TPP all include both general[36] and chapter- or provision-specific[37] exceptions to investment protection. For example, Art. 28.3 CETA incorporates Art. XX GATT in its section 1 and rephrases Art. XIV lit. (a)–(c) GATS in its section 2. Both sections apply to CETA's provisions on establishment of investment and non-discrimination of foreign investors, but not to the other parts of CETA's investment chapter, for example investment protection.

As per the current texts, none of the exception clauses in the three agreements will include an explicit exception for labour. In this regard, the situation under the three treaties will thus not be much different from the one under Art. XX GATT. Under that provision, measures affecting labour standards are only excluded to the extent they fall within one of the explicitly named areas, e.g. if they resemble measures necessary to protect public morals[38] or human, animal or plant life or health[39] or if they relate to the products of prison labour.[40]

2.2.2 Reaffirmations of the 'Right to Regulate'

As a reaction to critics and various reform proposals, all three treaties emphasize that the parties' capacity of regulating investment activities shall be maintained. Both CETA and TTIP seek to reserve policy spaces by explicitly reaffirming the

[36]Chapter 29 TPP; Art. 28.3 et seqq. CETA and Art. 9 TTIP Proposal (I) (drafters' note).

[37]E.g. Art. 8.15 CETA.

[38]Art. XX (a) GATT. See Blüthner (2004) and Cottier (2017).

[39]Art. XX (b) GATT.

[40]Art. XX (e) GATT.

parties' 'right to regulate'.[41] In this regard, CETA and TTIP contain a non-exhaustive enumeration of 'legitimate policy objectives', with CETA explicitly including 'social protection'.[42] While regulation in these areas is not excluded from the investment chapter, it is emphasized that regulation as such, even when it adversely affects investments, does not amount to a breach of obligations under the investment chapter.[43] TPP, for its part, stipulates that the parties may adopt, maintain or enforce measures they consider 'appropriate to ensure that investment activity [. . .] is undertaken in a manner sensitive to environmental, health or other regulatory objectives'.[44]

For the time being, it is difficult to assess the legal relevance, and thus potential impact, of these provisions. As a matter of general international law, parties retain their right to regulate as a corollary of state sovereignty to the extent they do not limit it by accepting treaty obligations. At least insofar as the aforesaid clauses in the three treaties reaffirm that right, they are binding restatements of the law. Whether they have legal relevance beyond such a binding restatement is a more complex question.[45] One the one hand, their genesis indicates that the respective clauses are intended to go beyond such a restatement and seek to strengthen the host state's regulatory autonomy. On the other hand, caution is warranted due to their somewhat minimalistic wording, which merely defines certain goals as legitimate objectives as such but does hardly include indicators as to the objectives' weight and importance in relation to investor rights. In this regard, it should be noted that, even in the absence of any comparable treaty language, earlier investment jurisprudence seems to have generally accepted that states may regulate investment activity and that labour protection in principle qualifies as a legitimate policy objective.[46] The pivotal issue in cases concerning the right to regulate was not so much the recognition of legitimate regulatory objectives as such, but rather to strike an adequate balance between these objectives and investor protection.[47] The clauses reaffirming the right to regulate will serve to overcome—often

[41]Art. 8.9 (1) CETA; Art. 3 (2) TTIP Proposal (SD) and Art. 2 (1) TTIP Proposal (I).

[42]Art. 8.9 (1) CETA and Art. 2 (1) TTIP Proposal (I). Surprisingly, the non-exhaustive list of 'legitimate public welfare objectives' in Annex 8-A(3) CETA (concerning indirect expropriation) does not name labour or social objectives (Cf. Annex I (3) TTIP Proposal (I)). The precise scope of the term 'social protection' contained in CETA remains open. There is a chance that the term covers at least certain labour objectives.

[43]Art. 8.9 (2) CETA and cf. the slightly different tone in Art. 2 (2) TTIP Proposal (I).

[44]Art. 9.15 TPP.

[45]As to TPP, the right to regulate is only reaffirmed with regard to 'measures otherwise consistent with this [i.e. the investment] Chapter' (Art. 9.15 TPP), arguably confining the clause's legal relevance to an explicit restatement.

[46]See the cases discussed below under Sect. 2.4. For a comparable example from outside the investment law context see ECJ, *International Transport Workers' Federation and Finnish Seamen's Union v. Viking Line ABP and OÜ Viking Line Eesti*, Judgment (Grand Chamber), 11 Dec2007, C-438/05, ECLI:EU:C:2007:772, para. 45.

[47]Dolzer and Schreuer (2012), p. 148 and Mills (2014), pp. 437 ff.

simplistic—arguments that regulation for certain reasons per se amounted to a violation of investor rights. However, they will hardly completely prevent overly investment-friendly interpretations of investment provisions by tribunals. To be sure, this is not to say that investment tribunals will not be induced by right to regulate clauses to strike a more nuanced balance between investment and labour interests, especially as there is existing case law on the balancing of investor rights and public policy objectives they can draw on.[48] The point is rather that the open wording of the clauses refers the questions if and how to balance and how to weigh the different aspects to the stage of treaty interpretation and implementation.[49]

2.3 Maintaining and Promoting Labour Protection in the Context of Investment

Besides the aforesaid 'negative' preservations of policy spaces, a number of FTAs include certain positive obligations to maintain or increase levels of labour protection. Some older agreements merely require the implementation and enforcement of domestic labour laws.[50] Some more recent treaties, among them the three texts examined here, also include provisions aiming at maintaining existing domestic labour standards or, although rather diffidently, to implement certain international minimum labour standards.

2.3.1 Non-Lowering of Standards Clauses

Among the most frequent treaty provisions linking investment and labour standards are so-called non-lowering of standards clauses (hereinafter 'NLS clauses'). NLS clauses seek to prevent a state from engaging in a 'race to the bottom', i.e. lowering its level of labour protection in order to offer a more attractive environment to foreign investors than other states. Therefore, they can be seen as a complement to the growing body of investment treaty provisions on establishment or market access of investments,[51] although most NLS clauses also apply in the post-entry phase.

[48] E.g. UNCITRAL, *Saluka Investments v. Czech Republic*, Partial Award, 17 March 2006, paras. 305–306.

[49] By exemplary comparison, the 2012 SADC Model BIT Template does not only stipulate the right to regulate, but also contains language on its reconciliation with investor rights through exceptions or balancing (Art. 20.1 and 20.2 SADC Model BIT Template).

[50] For an overview over FTA labour provisions see Lazo Grandi (2009) and ILO (2013).

[51] E.g. Art. 9.4, Art. 9.5 and Art. 9.9 TPP and Chapter 8 Section B CETA.

The recurring elements of NLS clauses include: first, a statement that lowering labour standards to encourage trade or investment is considered inappropriate,[52] second, the obligation not to lower or depart from domestic labour law and standards to encourage investment (or trade), and third, the obligation not to fail to effectively enforce these laws and standards as an encouragement for investment. NLS clauses are contained in TPP, CETA and TTIP.[53] TPP restricts the abovementioned obligations to certain enumerated labour standards.[54]

At first sight, the NLS clauses included in the three treaties offer a fairly broad scope of protection from derogation. Moreover, there are no limitations on the prohibited forms of the derogation. The clauses thus prohibit both adverse changes of legislation or administrative rules and other measures, e.g. contractual promises to relax standards or enforcement practice.[55]

On the other hand, however, there are important restrictions that might significantly limit the impact of the respective NLS clauses.

First, the NLS clauses tend to focus on systemic deteriorations of protection levels. Like a range of earlier FTAs,[56] all three treaties examined here only prohibit failures to enforce labour laws 'through a sustained or recurring course of action or inaction'.[57] Accordingly, occasional failures to enforce, arguably regardless of their gravity, do not violate the NLS obligation. This merely systemic protection is especially conspicuous when contrasted with the individual protection granted to foreign investors in FTA investment chapters.

Second, the NLS clauses contained in the three treaties seem to prohibit derogations primarily because of potential trade- or investment-distorting effects and not because of their negative impact on the situation of workers *per se*. For one part, the NLS clause contained in CETA only covers derogations from the current level of protection that were committed *to encourage trade or foreign investment*. The wording suggests that it is introducing a subjective element of regulatory intent, aiming at the motivation behind the derogation. This has two consequences: First, it is arguably not required that the derogation is actually making the host state economically more attractive to investors.[58] It seems to suffice that the state is *aiming* for such a result, regardless of whether it is actually achieved. Second, and perhaps more problematic from the viewpoint of labour protection, derogations that are pursued for different reasons but have a similarly investment-encouraging effect

[52]In some agreements, this is the sole content of NLS clauses, see e.g. Art. 5 (1) Austria-Kosovo-BIT; Art. 5 (1) Austria-Tadjikistan-BIT and Prislan and Zandvliet (2013), p. 24.

[53]Art. 23.4 CETA; Art. 17 TTIP Proposal (SD) and Art. 19.4 and Art. 19.5 TPP.

[54]Art. 19.4 TPP, thereby, however, expanding NLS obligations as compared to earlier US agreements, e.g. Art. 16.2 (2) CAFTA-DR, see Ebert (2017).

[55]All these points are also mentioned by Prislan and Zandvliet (2013), p. 25.

[56]E.g. Art. 16.2 (a) CAFTA-DR. See Abel (2017).

[57]Art. 23.4 CETA; Art. 17 TTIP Proposal (SD) and Art. 19.5(1) TPP.

[58]Prislan and Zandvliet (2013), p. 24.

remain permissible.[59] This turn to regulatory motives in CETA is somewhat surprising, as the core problem with the 'race to the bottom' is not so much the motivation of the derogating state, but rather the actual deterioration of the situation in that state as well as increased incentives for other states to follow suit. TPP's NLS clause, for its part, requires that a failure to enforce labour laws 'in a manner affecting trade or investment between the Parties',[60] indicating that an actual distortion needs to have occurred. Finally, the TTIP proposal combines both approaches.[61]

The intentional element embodied in CETA has the potential to significantly weaken the impact of NLS clauses. As a practical matter, an FTA party seeking to invoke the clause against another party has to establish the latter's motivation behind the derogation, which—in the absence of explicit statements—can prove burdensome. Moreover, many derogations from existing levels of protection could arguably be based on a broad range of interchangeable rationales. These may include the prohibited encouragement of trade and investment, but also other, still permissible objectives, e.g. considerations of labour market, social or fiscal policy, to name but a few.[62]

That being said, actual effects on economic relations, as required under TPP, are arguably no less burdensome to establish in a legal dispute. This applies both for the effect as such and for the derogation being its cause. While there are studies on possible interrelations between labour law derogations and trade-distorting effects,[63] such a connection is nonetheless difficult to prove, especially with regard to specific derogations, and might eventually impede the potential of NLS clauses.[64] Moreover, as the *US-Guatemala* labour arbitration under CAFTA-DR illustrates, the standard of 'affecting trade' is itself vague and open to differing interpretations.[65]

---

[59] Prislan and Zandvliet (2013), p. 24.

[60] Art. 19.4 and Art. 19.5 (1) TPP, see also e.g. Art. 16.2 (a) CAFTA-DR.

[61] Art. 17 TTIP Proposal (SD): '[The parties shall not derogate] in order to encourage, or in a manner affecting, trade or investment'.

[62] In this vein, the intentional element in CETA's NLS clause resembles a codification of the 'aims-and-effects test' discussed in WTO jurisprudence. In WTO, *Japan – Taxes on Alcoholic Beverages*, Report of the Panel, 11 July 1996, WT/DS8/R, para. 6.16–6.19, the panel rejected this test for the same reasons as given here, implicitly upheld by the Appellate Body in WTO, *Japan – Taxes on Alcoholic Beverages*, Report of the Appellate Body, 4 Oct 1996, WT/DS8/AB/R, para. 115.

[63] OECD (1996), Brown (2000) and Häberli et al. (2012).

[64] In this respect, a crucial—presently open—question will be whether the clause requires causation or merely coincidence, the latter arguably being easier to establish.

[65] Office of the Unites States Trade Representative, *In the Matter of Guatemala – Issues Relating to the Obligations Under Article 16.2.1(a) of the CAFTA-DR*, US Initial Written Submission, 3 Nov 2014, paras. 96–103; US Oral Statement, 2 June 2015, paras. 27–30; US Supplementary Written Submission, 17 June 2015, para. 8; Initial Written Submission of Guatemala, 2 Feb 2015, paras. 451–472 and Guatemala's Supplementary Submission and Replies to Panel Questions, 17 June 2015, paras. 16–20.

In sum, with their restricted focus on systemic and either intendedly or actually trade- and investment-distorting derogations, NLS clauses appear as instruments to maintain fair competition among capital-importing states in the first place, rather than to genuinely protect labour standards.

2.3.2 Minimum Standards and the 'High Standard of Protection'

A further kind of provisions in the three treaties require the parties to take positive action to maintain or even to strive to raise labour standards. One could speak of international 'duties to regulate'.[66] Some of these provisions require the parties to adopt bilateral minimum standards by explicitly referencing ILO instruments or defining related standards or regulatory obligations.[67] Others require the parties to pursue a 'high level of protection'.[68]

Unlike NLS clauses, these provisions are not explicitly linked to investment chapters. However, the minimum standard provisions may imply that investment chapters must to some extent be read in a 'labour protection-friendly' manner. As a general matter of treaty interpretation, treaty provisions ought to be interpreted in their context (Art. 31 (1) VCLT). Moreover, treaty provisions must not be interpreted in a way that would render them entirely meaningless.[69] Following these interpretative rules, an FTA obligation to reach a certain regulatory goal implies that other parts of the same FTA must not be interpreted in a way that would unreasonably impede—and thus render meaningless—the pursuit of this goal. In consequence, one could argue that, as a matter of principle, when FTA investment chapters are interpreted in context with the labour provisions on minimum standards or high levels of protection, the former must be interpreted to leave reasonable latitude to achieve the defined regulatory goals. A 'duty to regulate' imposed by FTA labour provisions thus necessarily entails the preservation of a certain policy space for the parties to fulfil it, and a corresponding interpretation of investor rights.

That being said, whether such an approach could actually determine the interpretation of investment chapters in practice crucially depends on the content and scope of the 'duties to regulate' in labour chapters. In this respect, indications are sobering: Whereas all three treaties exceed many previous FTAs in defining levels

---

[66] For a use of this expression in a domestic constitutional context, see Stoll et al. (2017).

[67] Art. 19.3 TPP; see also Art. 19.6 TPP on measures to discourage the importation of goods produced by forced or compulsory labour. The TTIP-Proposal contains issue-specific articles on core labour standards instead of referencing specific ILO Conventions, Arts. 4–8 TTIP Proposal (SD).

[68] Art. 23.2 CETA and Art. 3(2) TTIP Proposal (SD).

[69] See e.g. PCIJ, *Mavrommatis Palestine Concessions (Greece v. UK)*, 1924, PCIJ Series A No. 2, p. 34 and ICJ, *Dispute regarding Navigational and Related Rights (Costa Rica v. Nicaragua)*, Judgment, ICJ Reports 2009, p. 213, 238, para. 52; see also Tzanakopoulos and Ventouratou (2017).

and minimum standards,[70] most of the provisions nevertheless remain vague. The obligations to implement certain ILO instruments or other standards do not prescribe the means and procedures to achieve these regulatory goals. The 'high standard'-aim, for its part, is widely formulated in non-obligatory, hortatory language.[71] Moreover, in CETA, that aim is stunningly contrasted with the parties' right to regulate, arguably granting them wide discretion how to define and implement a high standard.[72] It is therefore unlikely that the 'duties to regulate' will have any significant practical impact regarding the interpretation and implementation of investment provisions. Quite to the contrary, particular measures of labour regulation taken by host states might become vulnerable to the challenge that the duty to adopt certain labour standards could be achieved in a more investment-friendly way.

2.4 *Labour Concerns in Specific Investment Protection Standards*

Typical substantive elements of investment treaties are provisions on expropriation (Sect. 2.4.1), fair and equitable treatment (Sect. 2.4.2) and full protection and security (Sect. 2.4.3). CETA, TTIP and TPP, to varying degrees, enhance and specify these standards, mostly in the light of current debates and in response to prior investment jurisprudence.[73] Yet, there is hardly any language explicitly linking these particular investor rights to labour standards.[74] Our focus will therefore lie on examples to explore potential inroads for labour standards by means of treaty interpretation and application.

2.4.1 Expropriation

Protection against unlawful expropriation is one of the pivotal elements of international investment law. At the outset, expropriations do not *per se* constitute violations of investment agreements. However, the legality of expropriations is made conditional on a range of requirements. Expropriating measures must be

[70] Cf. ILO (2013), Ebert (2017) and Vogt (2015).

[71] Art. 23.2 CETA reads: '[. . .] each Party shall seek to ensure those laws and policies provide for and encourage high levels of labour protection and shall strive to continue to improve such laws and policies with the goal of providing high levels of labour protection.' Cf. the somewhat stronger language ('[. . .] shall ensure [. . .]') in Art. 3 (2) TTIP Proposal (SD).

[72] Stoll et al. (2015), p. 17.

[73] See Alschner (2017), pp. 57 et seqq.

[74] For an exception which likely applies to at least some labour standards, see Annex I (3) TTIP Proposal (I) ('social protection').

taken 'for a public purpose, under due process of law, in a non-discriminatory manner; and on payment of prompt, adequate and effective compensation'.[75] Protection is provided against both direct and indirect[76] expropriation and against all kinds of state measures irrespective of their form or institutional provenience.[77]

Drawing a proper line between expropriation and the host state's regulatory margins is a long-standing issue in international investment law.[78] Often the point has been made that, under the cloak of indirect expropriation (or fair and equitable treatment, discussed below), investment protection would unduly interfere with legitimate host state regulations, including labour standards.[79] With regard to labour, this observation draws on several cases of investors challenging labour-related host state measures, such as *Veolia v. Egypt* (concerning legislation on minimum wages),[80] *Foresti v. South Africa* (concerning anti-discrimination legislation)[81] or *Goetz v. Burundi* (the reversion of previous derogations from national labour laws aimed at stimulating foreign investment).[82]

CETA, TTIP and TPP specify the concept of expropriation in dedicated annexes.[83] These annexes clarify, *inter alia*, that any finding of indirect expropriation requires a case-by-case, fact-based inquiry, taking into account factors such as the economic impact of the measure, its 'character' and the extent to which it interferes with distinct, reasonable investment-backed expectations.[84] Further, the annexes provide that:

> except in the rare circumstance when the impact of a measure or series of measures is so severe in light of its purpose that it appears manifestly excessive, non-discriminatory measures of a Party that are designed and applied to protect legitimate public welfare objectives [TTIP, unlike CETA and TPP, explicitly lists 'social protection' here] do not constitute indirect expropriations.[85]

However, whether these clarifications can provide an adequate protection for labour standards remains unclear. Given that at least some provisions explicitly name social concerns as legitimate public policy objectives, and given that the

[75]Art. 9.7 (1) TPP; Art. 8.12 (1) CETA and Art. 5 (1) TTIP Proposal (I). See also Art. 1110 NAFTA; Art. 13 Energy Charter Treaty and Reinisch (2008), p. 420 et seqq.

[76]On these terms see Reinisch (2008) and López Escarcena (2014).

[77]See the definition of 'measure' in Art. 1.1 CETA.

[78]See generally e.g. *Generation Ukraine v. Ukraine*, ICSID Case No. ARB/00/9, 16 Sep 2003, para. 20.29 and Reinisch (2008), p. 432.

[79]E.g. Sornarajah (2015), p. 210 and Zimmer (2017) with further references.

[80]*Veolia Propreté v. Egypt*, ICSID Case No. ARB/12/15, arbitration pending.

[81]*Piero Foresti, Laura de Carli & Others v. South Africa*, ICSID Case No. ARB(AF)/07/01, 4 Aug 2010.

[82]*Antoine Goetz et al. v. Burundi*, ICSID Case No. ARB/95/3, 10 Feb 1999.

[83]Annex 9-B TPP; Annex 8-A CETA and Annex I TTIP Proposal (I).

[84]Annex 9-B(3)(a) TPP.

[85]Quote from Annex 8-A (3) CETA, see also Annex I(3) TTIP Proposal (I) and Annex 9-B(3) (b) TPP.

labour chapters positively oblige the parties to maintain and improve labour standards, there can hardly be any doubt that labour standards generally qualify as 'measures designed and applied to protect legitimate public welfare objectives'.

Furthermore, earlier investment jurisprudence provides at least some general guidance on how annexes could be interpreted in the context of labour. For example, with regard to the criterion of reasonable expectations, the Iran-US Claims Tribunal held in *Starrett Housing* that:

> investors in Iran, like investors in all other countries, have to assume a risk that the country might experience strikes, lock-outs, disturbances, changes of the economic and political system and even revolution. That any of these risks materialized does not necessarily mean that property rights affected by such events can be deemed to have been taken.[86]

Yet, similar to the general provisions reaffirming the right to regulate described above, the language intended to safeguard regulatory latitudes remains again at a general level and widely leaves the application to labour-related issues to bilateral and national institutions, including the particularly delicate exercise of balancing and reconciling conflicting rights and interests.

2.4.2 Fair and Equitable Treatment (FET)

Besides expropriation, the fair and equitable treatment standard (FET) is the most widespread and practically relevant standard of international investment protection.

2.4.2.1 Defining (Contemporary) FET

There is no universally established definition of what constitutes FET (or an infringement thereof). Yet, certain elements are widely recognized as forming parts of the standard, such as legal consistency, stability and predictability, transparency, due process, freedom from coercion and harassment.[87] FET has also been invoked in labour-related arbitral practice. *Paushok v. Mongolia*, for example, concerned allegedly unpredictable legislative changes resulting in an increase of a foreign workers fee.[88] The claimants, which now had to pay an increased fee for employing non-Mongolian nationals beyond a certain quorum, complained against a 'lack of protection of their legitimate expectations, of transparency, of a stable and predictable regulatory framework, the discriminatory character of [the foreign workers fee] and its unreasonableness.'[89]

---

[86] IUSCT, *Starrett Housing Corp. v. The Government of the Islamic Republic of Iran*, Interlocutory Award, 4 Iran-US CTR 122 (158), 19 Dec 1983.

[87] See Dolzer and Schreuer (2012), p. 133 et seqq.

[88] UNCITRAL, *Sergei Paushok, CJSC Golden East Company and CJSC Vostokneftegaz Company v. Mongolia*, Award on Jurisdiction and Liability, 28 Apr 2011, paras. 350 et seqq.

[89] UNCITRAL, *Sergei Paushok, CJSC Golden East Company and CJSC Vostokneftegaz Company v. Mongolia*, Award on Jurisdiction and Liability, 28 April 2011, para. 362.

Besides indirect expropriation, FET is the standard most exposed to criticism in the current debate on investment law. This mainly derives from the fact that in many older agreements, FET was often included only in brief, vague and general language, leaving ample space for extensive (and sometimes excessive) interpretation by arbitral tribunals in favour of investors.[90]

CETA, TTIP and TPP all strive to further restrict the scope of FET protection. CETA and TTIP both define FET by including a catalogue of illegitimate measures: denial of justice, a fundamental breach of due process, manifest arbitrariness, a targeted discrimination on manifestly wrongful grounds or abusive treatment.[91] This enumeration is exhaustive, but amendable by decision of the respective treaty committees.[92] TPP does not contain an exhaustive list, but besides explicitly naming denial of justice, only grants FET protection as defined under customary international law,[93] which is a more volatile solution given the persisting uncertainty as to the scope of the customary FET standard.[94] None of the three treaties' explicitly links the (interpretation of the) FET clauses to labour standards.

2.4.2.2 Legitimate Expectations and Changes in Labour Legislation and Policy

Among those voicing criticism against FET, the protection of investors' expectations of a 'stable investment environment' attracted particular attention, as this protection may conflict with the host state's interest of changing its legal and regulatory framework to adapt to changing circumstances or policy priorities.[95] As the *Paushok* example shows, this can also concern labour legislation in the host state. That being said, arbitral practice under earlier BITs has predominantly accepted that host states retain their right to regulate according to legitimate public policy objectives. In this vein, it has e.g. been held in *Saluka v. Chech Republic* that a determination of a violation of FET 'requires a weighing of the Claimant's legitimate and reasonable expectations on the one hand and the Respondent's legitimate regulatory interests on the other.'[96]

As to the protection of legitimate expectations, all three treaties aim for adjusting the protection of investor expectations. TPP seeks to specify the host state's obligation by stipulating that 'the mere fact that a Party takes or fails to take an

---

[90] *Técnicas Medioambientales Tecmed v. Mexico*, ICSID Case No. ARB(AF)/00/2, 29 May 2003.

[91] Art. 8.10 (2) CETA and Sec. 2 Art. 3 (2) TTIP Proposal (I).

[92] Art. 8.10 (2) CETA and Sec. 2 Art. 3 (2) (f) TTIP Proposal (I).

[93] Art. 9.6 (1) and Annex 9-A TPP.

[94] On the debate on divergences and convergences between the customary FET standard and autonomous FET standards in IIAs and FTAs see Dralle (2011), p. 8 et seqq. and Dolzer and Schreuer (2012), p. 130 et seqq. with further references.

[95] See Dolzer and Schreuer (2012), p. 145 et seqq. with references to arbitral practice.

[96] UNCITRAL, *Saluka Investments v. Czech Republic*, 17 Mar 2006, paras. 305–306.

action that may be inconsistent with an investor's expectations does not constitute a breach of [FET]'.[97] CETA and TTIP, in an attempt to restrict the scope of protection of legitimate expectations, each provide that a tribunal 'may take into account whether a Party made a *specific representation* to an investor to induce a covered investment, that created a legitimate expectation, and upon which the investor relied in deciding to make or maintain the covered investment, but that the Party subsequently frustrated' (emphasis added).[98]

The absence of an explicit reference to labour standards in these provisions should not be understood as an indication for the fact that investors may legitimately expect no future impediments of their investments caused by a change of labour policy or an increasing level of labour protection whatsoever. Rather, existing arbitral practice in labour-relevant cases suggests that the investor has to bear to a certain extent the risk of changes in labour protection and remains responsible for making corresponding dispositions.[99] In this respect, the tribunal in *Paushok* rejected the FET claims brought before it, essentially reasoning that the change in labour legislation was predictable, that the claimants had failed to make prudent efforts to comply with the new laws and that investors could not reasonably expect that fees would not substantially change over time.[100] In particular, the tribunal considered it the claimants' fault not to have strived to conclude a stability agreement.[101] That investors' expectations can only be protected to a certain extent is even more the case with regard to FET clauses in FTAs that, like the three treaties examined here, explicitly call on the parties to maintain and strive to improve their labour standards. That being said, as noted above, the respective FTA labour provisions aiming for improving standards are mostly held in hortatory language. They neither oblige to take specific measures nor define a specific point in time at which the improvements have to be accomplished.

Given that both treaty language and hitherto jurisprudence only lay down in broad terms the criteria for determining the precise scope of legitimate investor expectations against changes in labour protection, considerable weight is—again—put on the stage of treaty implementation and interpretation, and thus on investor-state dispute settlement. CETA and TTIP even explicitly leave to the respective tribunal's discretion ('may take into account') whether to take into account host state conduct that could have generated investor expectations.

---

[97]Art. 9.6 (4) TPP.

[98]Art. 8.10 (4) CETA and Sec. 1 Art. 3 (4) TTIP (I).

[99]In this regard, the ICSID Tribunal in *El Paso* endorsed and applied in the context of FET the Iran-US Claims Tribunal's general findings in *Starrett Housing* concerning strikes, lock-outs and changes of the economic and social system, ICSID, *El Paso Energy International Company v. Argentina*, ICSID Case No. ARB/03/15, 31 October 2011, para. 363.

[100]UNCITRAL, *Sergei Paushok, CJSC Golden East Company and CJSC Vostokneftegaz Company v. Mongolia*, Award on Jurisdiction and Liability, 28 Apr 2011, paras. 363 et seqq.

[101]UNCITRAL, *Sergei Paushok, CJSC Golden East Company and CJSC Vostokneftegaz Company v. Mongolia*, Award on Jurisdiction and Liability, 28 Apr 2011, para. 370.

2.4.3 Protection and Security (FPS)

Alongside both customary international law and the vast majority of investment treaties, all three FTA treaties examined here require the host state to accord full protection and security (FPS) to the investor and its investments.

The FPS standard is different from the other two standards discussed above, as it not only requires the host state itself to refrain from interferences, but also obliges the host state to actively protect the investor against interferences from third persons.[102] It is this latter aspect that has become relevant in a number of investment cases involving labour issues, notably where fundamental worker rights were at stake, such as freedom of association or the right to take collective action. In these cases, investors claimed violations of the FPS standard, alleging insufficient protection against allegedly illegal worker or trade union action. Corresponding issues arose e.g. in *Noble Ventures v. Romania*[103] and *Plama v. Bulgaria,*[104] both concerning the question of inadequate protection by the host state's police against occupations of production sites and alleged worker riots.[105]

It is established in international jurisprudence that FPS is not an absolute standard and does not impose strict liability on the host state.[106] Rather, it has been held that the FPS standard is one of due diligence.[107] Accordingly, an infringement of FPS is given if it is established that the host state had to accord a higher level of protection than it actually did. In labour-related cases, this involves intricate distinctions between lawful conduct, e.g. between legitimate forms of worker and trade union protest that have to be respected by the host state, and excessive and unlawful conduct that has to be averted.[108]

Besides these legal uncertainties, the investor has to furnish evidence supporting his claim. He has to prove the circumstances warranting protection, the host state's alleged misconduct and, finally, that the alleged damages incurred could have been prevented. As the decisions in *Noble Ventures* and *Plama* illustrate, this is a considerable factual burden for the claiming investor. In both cases, the respective FPS claims were dismissed on factual grounds. In *Plama*, the claimants failed to prove that the alleged worker riots reached a level of intensity that would have

---

[102]Dolzer and Schreuer (2012), p. 161.

[103]ICSID, *Noble Ventures v Romania*, ICSID Case No. ARB/01/11, 12 Oct 2005, para 160 et seqq.

[104]ICSID, *Plama Consortium Limited v. Bulgaria*, ICSID Case No. ARB/03/24, 27 Aug 2008, para. 236.

[105]A similar situation was at stake in the *ELSI* case, ICJ, *Elettronica Sicula S.P.A. (ELSI) (United States v. Italy)*, Judgment, 20 July 1989, ICJ Reports 1989, p. 15 (63 et seqq.), paras. 103 et seqq.

[106]ICJ, *Elettronica Sicula S.P.A. (ELSI) (United States v. Italy)*, Judgment, 20 July 1989, ICJ Reports 1989, p. 15 (65), para. 108.

[107]ICSID, *Plama Consortium Limited v. Bulgaria*, ICSID Case No. ARB/03/24, 27 Aug 2008, para. 179 f. and ICSID, *Noble Ventures v Romania*, ICSID Case No. ARB/01/11, 12 Oct 2005, para 164 with further references. Dolzer and Schreuer (2012), p. 161.

[108]Prior international investment jurisprudence has not touched on these distinctions in greater detail, as the respective claims were dismissed on factual grounds.

amounted to illegal conduct.[109] In *Noble Ventures*, the claimants did not prove that their alleged losses could have been prevented.[110]

The three treaties seek to further restrict the scope of FPS obligations. TPP references the customary FPS standard.[111] CETA confines FPS to physical security.[112] Both will therefore counter extensive interpretations of FPS, e.g. to the effect that the standard provides protection against changes of legislation ('legal security').[113] These restrictions will likely preclude investors from successfully invoking FPS against changes in domestic labour legislation in the host state. By contrast, the limits of the exercise of workers' rights, notably collective action, remains a potential issue for FPS claims under the 'physical security' standard. In this regard, again, none of the three agreements offers normative guidance as to how to solve potential collisions. The exercise of balancing FPS protection and fundamental worker rights is thus left to the level of interpretation and implementation of the agreement.

2.5 Provisions Addressing Investor Conduct

Given the sometimes limited ability or willingness of host states to effectively ensure sufficient levels of domestic labour protection, the conduct of investors themselves with regard to labour standards has been the subject of political and scholarly debates. The key issue has been to enhance the accountability and responsibility of investors for violations of basic international labour standards, both with regard to their own conduct and to the conduct of subsidiaries, suppliers and subcontractors along global supply chains. In this regard, several schemes for responsible business conduct of investors have been created, designed to enhance compliance, *inter alia*, with labour standards.[114]

References to such schemes and the inclusion of investor obligations in investment treaties have remained the exception. A range of treaties use preambular language or references to CSR initiatives in the main text, usually in hortatory language.[115] Some agreements, like the 2008 EU-CARIFORUM Agreement, explicitly require its parties to ensure that investors act in accordance with core

[109]ICSID, *Plama Consortium Limited v. Bulgaria*, ICSID Case No. ARB/03/24, 27 Aug 2008, paras. 248–249.

[110]See ICSID, *Noble Ventures v Romania*, ICSID Case No. ARB/01/11, 12 Oct 2005, para. 166.

[111]Art. 9.6 (2) (b) TPP.

[112]Art. 8.10 (5) CETA.

[113]In the context of labour issues, this broader interpretation was e.g. pleaded by the claimants—but rejected by the tribunal—in UNCITRAL, *Paushok v. Mongolia* (*Sergei Paushok, CJSC Golden East Company and CJSC Vostokneftegaz Company v. Mongolia*, Award on Jurisdiction and Liability, 28 Apr 2011, para. 361. Unlike CETA, TTIP and TPP, some BITs explicitly include legal security, Dolzer and Schreuer (2012), p. 161.

[114]See the contributions by Gehne, Krause and Aghazadeh in this volume.

[115]Hepburn and Kuuya (2011), pp. 596–607.

labour standards and do not act in a manner circumventing the parties' international labour obligations.[116] As an example for more innovative approaches, the 2008 ECOWAS Supplementary Act for Investments imposes direct international obligations on investors, including with regard to labour standards, in a dedicated chapter.[117] Remarkably, the Act explicitly provides that failure to comply with these obligations can have an impact on the merits of investor claims, give rise to counterclaims or even entitle both the host and the home state to initiate proceedings against the investor before domestic courts or an international tribunal.[118] The 2012 SADC Model BIT Template contains similar provisions.[119] It should be noted, however, that these approaches are highly exceptional at present.

While none of the three treaties sets forth investor obligations regarding labour standards, they all refer to corporate social responsibility schemes. Yet, as to TPP and CETA, the treaty language remains vague. TPP only requires the parties to 'endeavour to encourage enterprises to voluntarily adopt corporate social responsibility initiatives on labour issues'.[120] CETA, while referencing the OECD Guidelines for Multinational Enterprises,[121] only stipulates that 'each Party shall strive to promote trade and economic flows and practices that contribute to enhancing decent work and environmental protection, including by: [...] encouraging the development and use of voluntary best practices of corporate social responsibility by enterprises [...] to strengthen coherence between economic, social and environmental objectives'.[122] Voluntary intergovernmental cooperation under both agreements may, but does not have to, include issues of Corporate Social Responsibility.[123] By comparison, the respective clauses in TTIP are more detailed.[124] It provides that the parties shall refer to and support a range of explicitly named schemes[125] and lays down specific activities the parties shall undertake with regard to the OECD Guidelines on Multinational Enterprises, the ILO Tripartite Declaration of Principles concerning Multinational Enterprises and Social Policy, the UN Guiding Principles on Business and Human Rights and the Global Reporting Initiative.[126]

---

[116]Art. 72 (b) and (c) EU-CARIFORUM.

[117]Chapter III, notably Art. 14 ECOWAS Supplementary Act.

[118]Art. 18 (3)–(5) ECOWAS Supplementary Act.

[119]Part 3 SADC Model BIT Template, especially Art. 15 and Art. 19.

[120]Art. 19.7 TPP. In a similar vein, in Art. 9.16 TPP, 'The Parties reaffirm the importance of each Party encouraging enterprises operating within its territory or subject to its jurisdiction to voluntarily incorporate into their internal policies those internationally recognised standards, guidelines and principles of corporate social responsibility that have been endorsed or are supported by that Party.'

[121]Preamble Clause 10 and Art. 22.3 (2) (b) CETA. With regard to labour, see especially Part 1 V of the Guidelines.

[122]Art. 22.3 (2) CETA.

[123]Art. 19.10 (6) (t) TPP.

[124]Art. 20 TTIP-Proposal (SD).

[125]Art. 20 (3) TTIP (SD).

[126]Art. 20 (4) and (5) TTIP (SD).

The wording in CETA and TPP remains at a very general level and employs hortatory language. What is more, all three treaties confine themselves to promote CSR *indirectly*, i.e. they require the state parties rather than the investors themselves to ensure socially responsible conduct.[127] Hence, while the three treaties acknowledge the significance of Corporate Social Responsibility, they lag behind more innovative approaches like the one taken by the ECOWAS Supplementary Act. That being said, it should not be inferred, at this stage, that this is necessarily deplorable. For one part, direct investor obligations under existing agreements are fairly new and have not been put to practice, leaving their potential advantages untested. For another part, indirect commitments to 'encourage' or to 'strive to promote' allow for creative interpretation and policy-making. States could e.g. require compliance with CSR schemes in investment contracts, or domestic administrative or tort law.[128]

In sum, the three treaties, notably the TTIP proposal, have a certain potential of promoting labour standards by means of corporate social responsibility schemes. Yet, whether this will actually become relevant for the investor-labour linkage crucially depends on how the respective clauses and their open language will be interpreted and applied.

2.6 *Interim Conclusion*

The substantive provisions of CETA, TTIP and TPP, while progressively bringing investment law and labour standards in a general normative context, leave crucial questions to the stage of application and implementation. Thus, what can be expected of the investment-labour linkages in the three treaties ultimately depends on how the respective provisions are dealt with by the parties and the respective bilateral institutions established. We will therefore address these institutional frameworks and their relevance for the investment-labour nexus in the next section.

3 Institutional Arrangements and Their Potential to Effectuate the Investment-Labour Linkage

Since, as shown above, the investment-labour linkage in the three treaties widely leaves it to the level of treaty implementation and interpretation to put investment and labour provisions into context, this section will focus on the institutional arrangements relevant for this implementation and interpretation and their potential

[127] The distinction between indirect obligations, addressed to the state parties, and direct obligations, addressing the investor, is borrowed from Hepburn and Kuuya (2011).

[128] Hepburn and Kuuya (2011), p. 609.

to give effect to the investment-labour linkage. 'Giving effect' is understood here as applying the FTA's investment and labour provisions in a way that strikes an adequate balance between the underlying interests of the affected groups, namely investors on the one hand and workers and trade unions on the other. We will look at the respective arrangements' organizational, jurisdictional and procedural setup in this regard.

Regarding the investment-labour nexus, the three treaties envisage institutional arrangements for two distinct purposes. The first purpose is the administration and implementation of the agreements, which is vested in bilateral intergovernmental committees and, as far as labour is concerned, in complementary institutionalized mechanisms for civil society participation (Sect. 3.1). The second purpose is dispute settlement, which, inasmuch as investment is concerned, falls within the jurisdiction of investor-state dispute settlement mechanisms, whereas the remaining topics, including labour, are either subject to inter-state arbitration or exempt from dispute settlement altogether (Sect. 3.2).

3.1 Administrative (and Political) Fora

The three treaties foresee both an intergovernmental committee structure (Sect. 3.1.1) and participatory mechanisms for stakeholders and civil society groups (Sect. 3.1.2). These mechanisms primarily aim at administering the implementation of the FTA, but have a certain potential of becoming political fora.

3.1.1 Intergovernmental Committees

As many other FTAs, TPP, CETA and TTIP will each establish an intergovernmental institutional framework for the administration of the agreements. They therefore create a two-level committee structure. The highest body is a main committee, meeting at ministerial level, serving as the supreme administrative body for the entire agreement and endowed with corresponding competences.[129] On a subordinate level, all three agreements foresee a range of subcommittees created under the auspices of the respective main committees and endowed with specific subject-matter competences. These subcommittees inter alia conduct preparatory work for the main committee.[130] The treaties predefine the committees' rules of procedure only in general terms and leave wide margins of procedural

[129]The 'Trans-Pacific Partnership Commission' (Art. 27.1 TPP), the 'CETA Joint Committee' (Art. 26.1 CETA) and the 'Joint Committee' (Art. X.1 TTIP (Inst)).

[130]Art. 26.2 CETA; Art. X.2 and Art. X.3 TTIP (Inst) and Art. 27.2 (2) (a) TPP.

flexibility to the committees.[131] The committees take consensual decisions, which in some cases can be legally binding.[132]

As to labour, all three treaties establish a subcommittee that is competent for issues of sustainable development (CETA and TTIP),[133] or, more specifically, for labour (TPP).[134] CETA and TTIP also foresee, quite unlike the majority of more traditional BITs, subcommittees for investment (also covering trade in services).[135] Under TPP, the Trans-Pacific Partnership Commission is competent to establish a similar subcommittee.[136] Accordingly, at least under CETA and TTIP, both labour and investment provisions will be on the agenda of institutionalized administrative fora. Moreover, these fora are institutionally interlinked via their subordination under the agreements' main committees. Whereas direct links between the subcommittees are scarce, this means that, at least on the main committee level, there is a permanent body competent to deal with labour and investment issues in context.

The implications of this specific institutional dimension of the investment-labour nexus remain yet to be seen, especially since there are many conceivable ways in which the committees might engage in activities regarding the investment-labour linkage. To pick one example which has gained some prominence in FTA committee practice under NAFTA, the main committees under all three agreements will be competent to adopt interpretations of investment chapter[137] and other FTA provisions.[138] These interpretations are legally binding in subsequent investment disputes and inter-state arbitration.[139] It is well conceivable that such interpretations will refer to investment and labour issues as well. This might include more concrete normative guidance on how investment chapter provisions are to be understood in the context of the FTAs' labour chapters, and might thus create a nucleus of a 'secondary investment and labour law' under the respective FTA. For example, it is conceivable that a committee will specify to what extent exception clauses cover labour-related measures, that it will elaborate on the scope of the

[131]The main committees in CETA and TTIP meet in regular intervals; the default rule foresees annual meetings, Art. 26.1 (2) CETA and Art. X.1 (2) TTIP (Inst). The meeting intervals of the TPP main committee is more flexible, Art. 27.4 (1) TPP. The same applies to some subcommittees under all three drafts (see e.g. Art. 22.4(2) CETA). The CETA and TTIP committees' standing orders are not predefined in the treaties but placed at their discretion (for the main committees see Art. 26.1 (4) (d) CETA and Art. X.1(5)(g) TTIP (Inst); for the subcommittees see Art. 26.2 (4) CETA and Art. X.3 (3) TTIP (Inst)), while Art. 27.4 TPP contains at least some general standing orders for the TPP committees.

[132]Art. 26.3 CETA; Art. X.4 TTIP (Inst) and Art. 27.3 TPP.

[133]Arts. 22.4 and Art. 26.2.1 (g) CETA and Art. X.3 (1) (c) TTIP (Inst).

[134]See the TPP Labour Council, Art. 19.12 TPP.

[135]Art. 8.44 CETA and Art. X.3 (b) TTIP (Inst).

[136]Art. 27.2 (2) (a) TPP.

[137]Art. 8.31 (3) CETA; Sec. 3, Art. 13 (5) TTIP (I) and Art. 9.24 (3) and Art. 27.2 (2) (f) TPP.

[138]Art. 26.1 (5) (e) CETA; Art. X.1 (6) (b) TTIP (Inst) and Art. 27.2 (2) (f) TPP.

[139]Art. 26.1 (5) (e) CETA; Art. X.1 (6) (b) TTIP (Inst) and Art. 9.24 (3) TPP.

parties' right to regulate or will provide further guidance on how to reconcile investor rights and labour concerns, for example regarding legitimate expectations or the scope of FPS protection against collective action. That being said, it should not be overlooked that the output of FTA committees concerned with labour issues has at best been modest under earlier agreements.[140]

3.1.2 Institutionalized Participatory Mechanisms for Civil Society

In addition to the intergovernmental committees, CETA and TPP (TTIP proposals on this issue have not yet been published) will, to varying degrees, install mechanisms for civil society participation in labour/sustainable development matters.[141] The 'European' model adopted by CETA provides for 'balanced representation of relevant interests' both on the domestic and bilateral level.[142] While, as *Orbie*, *van den Putte* and *Martens* point out in their contribution to this volume, the function of these mechanisms is far from being clear,[143] the overall purpose seems to be the provision of civil society input, improvement of decision-making, dialogue and legitimation. The TPP model is less pre-defined in the treaty and puts the institutional design largely at the discretion of the Labour Council[144] and the FTA parties,[145] respectively.

An in-depth assessment of the prospects and pitfalls of the aforementioned mechanisms goes beyond the scope of this chapter. Still, it is important to point out that under past treaty practice, trade unions and other civil society groups have been the main drivers behind putting to practice FTA labour provisions.[146] The proposed participatory mechanisms are the only institutionalized fora where these groups can proactively promote the protection and promotion of labour standards in the investment context. Yet, as has been pointed out elsewhere, it is uncertain if the mechanisms provided for in the treaties sufficiently remedy flaws of comparable mechanisms in earlier agreements.[147]

[140]For example, the intergovernmental Commission for Labor Cooperation established under NAALC has failed to ever ascertain a significant role in the implementation of the agreement.

[141]Further on these mechanisms van den Putte (2015), Gött (2016), Xu (2017) and Orbie et al. (2017).

[142]Art. 22.5 and Art. 23.8 (4) CETA.

[143]Orbie et al. (2017).

[144]For a mechanism at the bilateral level, Art. 19.14 (1) TPP.

[145]For domestic consultative mechanisms, Art. 19.14 (2) TPP.

[146]ILO (2013), p. 105.

[147]For an extensive case-study see Dombois et al. (2004), van den Putte (2015) and Gött (2016). See also the contributions by Abel and Gött (this volume).

3.1.3 Towards a Re-politicization of Investment Law?

It is worthwhile, at this stage, to briefly address a potential side-effect of the aforementioned inception of institutional frameworks. While it is unclear if and to what extent the FTA committees and the participatory mechanisms will use their potential to influence the concretization and implementation of the investment-labour linkage, the mere existence of this common institutionalized framework is noteworthy, as it might pave the way for a certain re-politicization of investment law in an international institutional setting.

All three texts characterize their respective institutional frameworks as 'administrative'. Yet, the respective provisions do not confine the committees' competences to purely 'technical' concerns. They rather employ open language that would also cover committee work on a more 'political' level. Depending on how the committees will work in practice, they could thus serve as gateways for introducing more (and, above all, more politically contentious) issues. This could, for example, be the case when an FTA main committee adopts a binding interpretation concerning a labour-relevant issue of investor rights. Whether made as a reaction to a preceding decision of an investor-state dispute settlement body or prospectively to guide future practice: A binding interpretation would in any event require that the parties reach political consensus over the respective subject-matter. The envisaged participation of civil society representatives might additionally contribute to opening up political space on the bilateral level.

Whether or not its full political potential will eventually be tapped, the mere inception of such an institutional framework is remarkable, bearing in mind that one of the reasons both for the establishment and the success of international investment law was its perceived de-politicizing nature.[148] Empowering investors to enforce substantive investor rights through investor-state dispute settlement led to the removal of investment disputes from the highly politicized area of intergovernmental diplomatic protection. By contrast, the common administrative framework envisaged in the three treaties opens an institutional setting for investment and investment-related issues to be again subject to intergovernmental political debate, this time in a more institutionalized setting. Both particular investment disputes and underlying more general questions could thus be re-politicized. This does not only apply to the contentious area of reconciling investment and labour law.

3.2 Dispute Settlement Mechanisms

Since other contributions in this volume look at FTA dispute settlement in greater detail, we will focus here on putting the developments and main characteristics in investor-state- and labour dispute settlement in the three treaties into perspective.

[148] Shihata (1986).

For a number of reasons, investor-state dispute settlement, as compared to dispute settlement procedures foreseen in FTA labour chapters, is clearly the more effective mechanism (Sect. 3.2.1). Hence, our enquiry will centre on the question whether, and to what extent, investor-state dispute settlement can be employed to effectuate investment-labour linkages (Sect. 3.2.2).

3.2.1 'Strong' Investment vs. 'Weak' Labour Dispute Settlement

When analysing dispute settlement with a particular focus on the investment-labour nexus in FTAs, a dichotomy between 'strong' adjudicatory investor-state dispute settlement and the comparably 'weak' FTA labour dispute settlement, with its many political rather than adjudicatory elements, becomes apparent.

On the investment side, it hardly needs to be restated that investor-state dispute settlement has added much to the overall efficacy of international investment law. Many major economies have used the occasion of recent free trade negotiations to readjust their foreign investment policy and to work on reformed investment provisions. Following numerous criticisms, notably the EU has made ambitious reform proposals. Arguably the most significant of these is the inclusion of a standing public investment court system in CETA and the EU-Vietnam-FTA as well as its proposed inclusion in TTIP.[149] While much of the reform agenda aims at correcting adverse impacts of ISDS, even a reformed system will be far from forfeiting its overall efficacy.

Quite to the contrary, international labour law has always had rather soft and 'political' mechanisms of implementation and enforcement. The ILO's supervisory system is essentially built on persuasion and moral pressure.[150] Those few FTAs that feature labour dispute settlement mechanisms clearly emphasize consensual intergovernmental settlement, rendering enforcement through inter-state arbitration and 'trade sanctions' an often highlighted but still rather remote possibility that has gained almost no practical relevance so far.[151] Contrary to individual investors in investor-state dispute settlement, individual workers, trade unions and other non-governmental stakeholders, while retaining the opportunity to file submissions concerning grievances, are by and large side-lined in inter-state labour dispute settlement procedures. As to labour dispute settlement in earlier FTAs, to the extent that the respective mechanisms have been activated at all, there is an overall record

[149] Chapter 8, Sec. F CETA and Sec. 3 TTIP (I). See also Chapter II, Sec. 3 EU-Vietnam-FTA (text on trade in services, investment and e-commerce).

[150] See Maupain (2013) and La Hovary (2017).

[151] The only FTA-labour case that has ever reached the stage of arbitration is the case before the Arbitral Panel established pursuant to Chapter Twenty of the CAFTA-DR, *In the Matter of Guatemala – Issues Relating to the Obligations Under Article 16.2.1(a) of the CAFTA-DR*, Final Report of the Panel, 14 June 2017. There is no reported case where FTA provisions on trade sanctions have ever been activated.

of under-performance.[152] Whereas namely the USA in some of its recent agreements subject trade and labour to the same dispute settlement mechanism[153] and have successfully pushed for an inclusion of a dispute settlement mechanism comprising arbitration and sanctions in TPP,[154] there is, at present, little evidence that this will substantially boost dispute settlement.[155] A number of recent EU trade agreements, including CETA, even completely exclude their labour provisions from the scope of their inter-state arbitral dispute settlement mechanisms and confine dispute settlement to consultations and the optional insertion of expert panels.[156]

3.2.2 Effectuating the Investment-Labour Linkage Through Investor-State Dispute Settlement?

Regarding this divergence, it is far more likely that, as far as dispute settlement is concerned, further concretization of the investment-labour linkage will appear in investor-state dispute settlement rather than in FTA labour dispute settlement procedures. We will therefore focus on potentials for effectuation by raising or opposing an investor claim in investor-state dispute settlement.

3.2.2.1 'Vicarious' Effectuation by Investors

To a limited extent, it is conceivable that investors 'vicariously' promote labour standards through investment claims. For example, in the NAFTA case of *UPS v. Canada*, Canada had derogated from certain collective bargaining rights, to the advantage of domestic competitors, but not extending that derogation to *UPS*. The latter challenged the derogation, invoking FET, national treatment and other standards. It argued that the derogation resulted in an unfair competitive advantage for its competitors.[157] The tribunal found that it lacked jurisdiction to entertain the FET claim, as the customary FET standard applicable under NAFTA did not protect against anticompetitive behaviour.[158] As to national treatment, the tribunal

---

[152] ILO (2013), p. 43 et seqq.

[153] Bolle (2016), p. 2 et seqq. and Abel (2017).

[154] USTR (2015). See Art. 19.15 (12) TPP.

[155] Abel (2017).

[156] Art. 23.11 CETA. The EU position prevailed over Canada's proposal to include monetary penalties as a last resort, Ebert (2017), p. 14.

[157] UNCITRAL, *United Parcel Service of America v. Canada*, Merits, 24 May 2007.

[158] It essentially reasoned that the customary FET standard protected under NAFTA did not require the host state from anticompetitive behaviour, UNCITRAL, *United Parcel Service of America v. Canada*, Jurisdiction, 22 Nov 2002, paras. 86–99.

dismissed some of *UPS's* claims, as it found UPS and domestic investors not to be 'in like circumstances'.[159] As to the remaining claims, the tribunal found that *UPS* had 'no sufficient interest' to pursue them,[160] following Canada's submission that *UPS* lacked standing to invoke labour standards that Canada owed to domestic workers and not foreign investors.[161]

While illustrating how investor-state dispute settlement could potentially be used with regard to the promotion of labour standards, the case is obviously exceptional. In general, the interest and incentive of investors to promote labour standards through investment arbitration will be rather limited. As another hurdle, a claimant would have to establish a connection between the alleged violation of labour standards and a violation of actionable investor rights, for example the national treatment standard. In this regard, it is not inconceivable that, in the *UPS* scenario, an investor would succeed in claiming to be in 'like circumstances'.[162] Yet, the *UPS* case also indicates that a host state's failure to fulfil its FTA labour obligations is not per se sufficient to constitute a 'sufficient interest' on which an investor claim can be based.[163] In sum, both the likeliness and the potential of effectuating the investment-labour linkage through investor claims seem limited.

3.2.2.2 Reactive Effectuation by the Respondent State or Other Actors

Leaving exceptional cases like *UPS* aside, the investment-labour linkage is much more likely to be invoked on the 'respondent side' of investment arbitration. Either, the respondent state itself will rely on the maintenance or promotion of labour standards as a justification for the alleged infringement of investor rights, invoking the substantive provisions discussed above, or third actors will attempt to make submissions in this respect. Third actor submissions offer an opportunity for trade unions and other non-governmental groups with a genuine labour agenda to introduce additional expertise or their respective points of view to the otherwise bipolar dispute.

Third actor participation has been steadily increasing in international investment disputes in recent years, mostly in the form of *amicus curiae* intervention.[164] In this regard, tribunals have on several occasions interpreted applicable procedural rules as permitting the admission of *amici curiae*, essentially requiring that the petitioners can contribute specific points of law or fact or that their participation can enhance the legitimacy of the dispute.[165] In the context of investment and labour,

[159]UNCITRAL, *United Parcel Service of America v. Canada*, Merits, 24 May 2007, para. 172.

[160]UNCITRAL, *United Parcel Service of America v. Canada*, Merits, 24 May 2007, para. 187.

[161]Prislan and Zandvliet (2013), p. 395 with further references.

[162]Prislan and Zandvliet (2013), p. 395.

[163]Prislan and Zandvliet (2013), p. 396.

[164]Viñuales (2013), p. 1726, para. 32.

[165]Viñuales (2013), p. 1728, para. 36.

admission was e.g. granted in *UPS* to the Canadian Union of Postal Workers and the Council of Canadians, an NGO with a social agenda,[166] and in *Foresti* to a number of (*inter alia* human rights) NGOs.[167] The 2013 UNCITRAL Transparency Rules, specifically designed to enhance transparency of arbitral proceedings, also contain provisions on the publication of documents[168] and tribunals' discretionary power to grant leave for third person submissions.[169]

In this respect, the reformed investor-state dispute settlement mechanisms in the three agreements, and CETA and TTIP in particular, seek to enhance the role of the public and persons or groups with particular interests. Increased transparency, enhanced avenues to introduce third views, the introduction of a permanent, public court with an appellate mechanism in the 'European' treaties all aim at addressing the potential impact of investor-state dispute settlement on third parties' or public interests. For example, CETA, building on earlier Canadian practice,[170] declares the UNCITRAL Transparency Rules applicable for all investment disputes.[171] It is likely that these arrangements will further enhance respondent's and third party's opportunities to invoke the investment-labour linkage in investment disputes.

That being said, the said effectuation of the investment-labour linkage by the respondent or third persons nevertheless remains 'reactive'. The decision if, and regarding which matters, investor-state dispute settlement mechanisms will be activated lies solely with the claiming investor. Actors seeking to invoke labour provisions must do so as a defensive argument within the confines of the investor's claim. While this is arguably an appropriate solution on the micro-level of the particular international investment dispute, it cannot overcome the limited opportunities to actively invoke investment-labour linkage, particularly by non-governmental actors, on the macro-level of the FTA.[172]

3.3 Interim Conclusion

As has been shown, the three treaties establish an institutional framework for administration and dispute settlement, through which the investment-labour linkage can be effectuated. The administrative fora offer a new institutional junction of

[166] UNCITRAL, *United Parcel Service of America v. Canada*, Decision on Petitions for Intervention and Participation as Amici Curiae, 17 Oct 2001, para. 73. By contrast, the tribunal refused to grant the petitioners standing as third parties, ibid. para. 43.

[167] ICSID, *Piero Foresti, Laura de Carli & Others v. South Africa*, ICSID Case No. ARB(AF)/07/01, Letter Regarding Non-Disputing Parties, 5 Oct 2009.

[168] Art. 3 UNCITRAL Transparency Rules, further modified and expanded by Art. 8.36 CETA.

[169] Art. 4 UNCITRAL Transparency Rules.

[170] Van Duzer (2016b), p. 9.

[171] Art. 8.36 (1) CETA.

[172] On this imbalance see Gött (2015) and Stoll et al. (2017).

investment and labour topics with a potential of concretizing and reconciling investment and labour law in bilateral dialogue and cooperation. As to dispute settlement, investment-labour linkages will most likely surface in investor-state dispute settlement, given the overall weakness (and, in the case of CETA: exclusion) of FTA labour issues from inter-state arbitral dispute settlement. In investor-state dispute settlement, labour issues will most likely be reactively invoked by the respondent state or third actors, whose participation is fostered by the three treaties.

However, looking at the institutional arrangements as a whole, there remains a discrepancy between the respective groups' standing and procedural capacity to invoke the investment-labour linkage in their interest, with investors being able to initiate investment proceedings, while workers, trade unions and other actors are essentially confined to non-adjudicatory participatory mechanisms for civil society. This imbalance can hamper the effectuation of the investment-labour linkages, as it resembles a systemic disadvantage for actors with a genuine labour agenda.

4 Potential Circumventions of Investment-Labour Linkage: Labour in Investment Contracts

Without marginalizing the shortcomings, investment-labour linkages in modern FTAs like CETA, TTIP and TPP, are holding a certain potential to foster a more adequate balance between investment protection and labour. Investors might therefore naturally be inclined to mitigate or avoid such 'adverse' labour effects on their investor rights. One option in this regard would be the conclusion of seperate investment contracts with the host state, aiming for 'protecting' the investor rights against the (balancing potentials of the) investment-labour linkage in the respective FTAs.

4.1 Common Features of Investment Contracts

An investment contract is—unlike an IIA, which is concluded among states—a contract between an individual investor and a host state, usually covering a specific investment project. Such an investment contract typically sets forth certain host state concessions on how a specific investment is to be treated and, in particular, how it is protected in case of adverse state interferences. The most common substantial provision in such investment contracts is the stabilization clause, essentially guaranteeing that the host state will not alter the investment's legal environment and conditions for a certain period of time. In its classic form (the so-called freezing clause), this means that the host state cannot issue *any* (labour) legislation or regulation which would adversely affect the investment after a certain date.

Although principally coverd by the domestic law of the contracting host state, investment contracts tend to refer to the general principles of international law (via a choice of law clause). They therefore have to be interpreted in the light of these principles in case of arbitration. Furthermore, investment contracts frequently comprise an arbitration clause, referring potential disputes regarding the host state's compliance with its specific contract concessions to international arbitration, rather than the host state's domestic courts.[173]

4.2 Potential Circumvention through Investment Contracts

If an investment contract including an arbitration clause is concluded, potential investment disputes are very likely to be directly (and solely) decided on the basis of the provisions in the particular investment contract. Accordingly, existing provisions in investment or labour chapters in FTAs would in principle not apply.

The already modest prospects of a more adequate balance between investment protection and labour through the respective FTAs would therefore be even less likely to materialize, since it is most unlikely that an investment contract would contain provisions on the protection of labour standards and legitimate labour regulation, but rather a stabilization clause guaranteeing that (labour) laws will *not* be changed.

The actual relevance of such investment contracts in arbitration can for example be observed in the ongoing investment dispute of *Veolia v. Egypt*.[174] In 2001, Veolia concluded a 15-year waste management contract with the city of Alexandria, Egypt, which was terminated in 2011. Besides other claims under the France-Egypt BIT, Veolia now argues that Egypt violated its investor rights by breaching a concession granted in the investment contract, namely the guarantee that Veolia will not be financially affected (which Veolia alleges has occurred) by adjustments to domestic labour laws, in particular the increase of minimum wages.

But even without such a stabilization clause, investment disputes based on investment contracts would most certainly forfeit the above described potentials of progressive cross-chapter investment-labour linkages in FTAs (like labour-relevant

[173]See extensively on the questions of the localization of investment contracts between national and international law as well as their common design von Walter (2015).

[174]ICSID, *Veolia Propreté v. Egypt*, ICSID Case No. ARB/12/15, arbitration pending.

clarifications on the right to regulate and the definitions of substantive investment protection standards, the enhanced institutional arrangements etc.[175]).

Additionally, even if we assume a potential investment contract not having an individual arbitration clause, the host state's concessions in the investment contract can still become the relevant standard of assessment in dispute settlement under FTAs' bi- or plurilateral investment chapters. For one part, this can be the case if these chapters include a so-called umbrella clause. An umbrella clause essentially requires the host state to adhere to its commitments under investment contracts. A breach of the contract therefore amounts, by virtue of the umbrella clause, also to a breach of investor rights under the treaty, and can therefore be claimed in investment treaty arbitration.[176] An umbrella clause is e.g. encompassed in the proposals for TTIP.[177] For another part, even in the absence of an umbrella clause, investment contracts can become relevant for the determination whether an investor's expectations as to the treatment of his investment were 'reasonable'. For example, TPP, in its definition of expropriation contained in Annex 9-B, explicitly clarifies:

> For greater certainty, whether an investor's investment-backed expectations are reasonable depends, to the extent relevant, on factors such as whether the government provided the investor with binding written assurances and the nature and extent of governmental regulation or the potential for government regulation in the relevant sector.[178]

In *Paushok v. Mongolia*, the tribunal held that the claimants' could not claim compensation for frustration of reasonable expectations *particularly because* they had failed to conclude a stabilizing investment contract to safeguard them against changes in Mongolian labour legislation.[179]

4.3 Limitations to Investment Contracts by NLS Clauses in CETA, TTIP and TPP?

Having shown the circumventing potentials of investment contracts regarding investment-labour linkages in FTAs, it suggests itself to come back to the NLS clauses in CETA, TTIP and TPP, stipulating that no domestic labour laws or standards shall be lowered or departed from to encourage investment (or trade), and that these laws and standards shall be effectively enforced.[180]

---

[175]See above (Sects. 2 and 3).

[176]On the controversy whether or not umbrella clauses actually make concessions in investment contracts part of the protection standards of applicable international investment treaties (and the sharply divided arbitral practice in this regard) see von Walter (2015).

[177]Art. 7 TTIP Proposal (I).

[178]Annex 9-B No. 3 (a) (ii) TPP (text taken from Fn. 36 in the relevant provision).

[179]UNCITRAL, *Sergei Paushok, CJSC Golden East Company and CJSC Vostokneftegaz Company v. Mongolia*, Jurisdiction and Liability, 28 Apr 2011, para. 370.

[180]See above, Sect. 2.3.1.

However, the odds are low that the perils of bypassing the balancing potentials of investment-labour linkages in CETA, TTIP and TPP through investment contracts can be prevented by these NLS clauses. This comes from two reasons: First, the NLS clauses provide for a non-*lowering* of labour standards, what makes it at least unclear whether or not stabilization clauses in investment contracts guaranteeing not to *increase* the standards of future domestic labour regulation would actually be in discrepancy. Second, even if assuming that investment contracts of the above described character would be covered by NLS clauses, it has been shown above that NLS clauses are far from being 'waterproof'.[181]

It will therefore depend to a significant extent on the political will of the respective host states not to negotiate separate investment contracts to allow for the potentials of investment-labour linkages of CETA, TTIP and TPP to fully unfold.

5 Conclusion: To the Future in Blind Flight

The investment-labour linkages in TPP, CETA and TTIP follow a trend from largely ignoring labour issues in earlier BITs towards their inclusion and integration in larger and more comprehensive FTA frameworks. Moreover, as has been shown, all three treaties open opportunities to strike a more adequate balance between the underlying interests of investors, workers and trade unions. Yet, the analysis has also shown that the three treaties' substantive provisions largely leave the balancing exercise to the stage of interpretation and implementation. On many accounts, the language included in the treaties themselves remains vague and reticent, opening potentials not only for action, but also for inaction or even 'misbalancing'. On the institutional side, the picture is similar concerning the treaties' administrative fora, which open space for technical and even political dialogue among the governments and non-governmental actors, but largely leave it to these actors whether and how to use these potentials. As to dispute settlement, the persisting weakness or, in the case of CETA, plain absence of FTA *labour* dispute settlement will cause the investment-labour linkage to surface most likely in investor-state dispute settlement. There, investors, through their decision when and on what matters to bring claims, will be able to predefine unilaterally to what extent investor-state dispute settlement's potential to effectuate investment-labour linkages will be tapped. The failure to endow actors with a genuine labour agenda with similarly effective institutional and procedural means may hinder the effectuation of the linkages in treaty practice. In addition, possible benefits of investment-labour linkages in the three treaties could be mitigated by the conclusion of investment contracts between investors and their respective host states, agreeing on more investment-friendly conditions. It will therefore depend on the host states to avoid such circumvention by not concluding seperate investment contracts.

[181]See above, Sect. 2.3.1.

In sum, investment-labour linkages in the three treaties offer opportunities to promote an adequate balance of investor and labour concerns, but, as they do not in themselves sufficiently steer towards this goal, also entail the risk of missing the mark. If the treaties are supposed to set a 'gold standard' for the future, this standard is in many regards built on the hope that treaty practice will actually arrive where presumably intended to. Given the institutional imbalance, the drafters seem to put their trust in the governments' and investors' will and ability to promote the linkage in good faith.

References

Abel P (2017) Comparative conclusions on arbitral dispute settlement in trade-labour matters under US FTAs. In: Gött H (ed) Labour standards in international economic law. Springer International Publishing, Cham. this volume

Alschner W (2017) The impact of investment arbitration on investment treaty design: myth versus reality. Yale J Int Law 42(1):1–66

Bartels L (2012) Human rights and sustainable development obligations in EU free trade agreements. University of Cambridge Faculty of Law Research Paper No.24/2012. Available via SSRN. https://papers.ssrn.com/sol3/papers2.cfm?abstract_id=2140033. Accessed 10 Aug 2017

Berner K (2016) Reconciling investment protection and sustainable development: a plea for an interpretative U-turn. In: Krajewski M, Hindelang S (eds) Shifting paradigms in international investment law. Oxford University Press, Oxford, pp 177–203

Blüthner A (2004) Welthandel und Menschenrechte in der Arbeit: the compatibility of human rights at work with the WTO-system. Peter Lang, Frankfurt am Main

Bolle MJ (2016) Overview of Labor Enforcement Issues in free trade agreements. US Congressional Research Service. https://fas.org/sgp/crs/misc/RS22823.pdf. Accessed 22 Jan 2017

Brown DK (2000) International Trade and Core Labour Standards: A Survey of the Recent Literature. OECD Labour Market and Social Policy Occasional Papers No. 43. https://doi.org/10.1787/677200103808

Cordonier Segger M-C, Gehring MW, Newcombe A (2011) Sustainable development in world investment law. Wolters Kluwer, Alphen aan den Rijn

Cottier T (2017) The implications of *EC – Seal Products* for the protection of core labour standards in WTO law. In: Gött H (ed) Labour standards in international economic law. Springer International Publishing, Cham. this volume

Dolzer R, Schreuer C (2012) Principles of international investment law, 2nd edn. Oxford University Press, Oxford

Dombois R, Hornberger E, Winter J (2004) Internationale Arbeitsregulierung in der Souveränitätsfalle – Das Lehrstück des North American Agreement on Labor Cooperation zwischen den USA, Mexiko und Kanada. LIT, Münster

Dralle TM (2011) Der Fair and Equitable Treatment-Standard im Investitionsschutzrecht am Beispiel des Schiedsspruchs Glamis Gold v. United States. Beiträge zum Transnationalen Wirtschaftsrecht Heft 115

Ebert FC (2017) The comprehensive economic and trade agreement (CETA) between the EU and Canada: are existing arrangements sufficient to prevent adverse effects on labour standards? Int J Comp Labour Law Ind Relat 33(2):295–329

Finbow RG (2006) The limits of regionalism – NAFTA's labour accord. Ashgate Publishing, Aldershot, Burlington

Gehne K (2011) Nachhaltige Entwicklung als Rechtsprinzip. Mohr Siebeck, Thüringen

Gordon K, Pohl J, Bouchard M (2014) Investment treaty law, sustainable development and responsible business conduct: a fact finding survey. OECD Working Papers on International Investment 2014/01. https://doi.org/10.1787/5jz0xvgx1zlt-en

Gött H (2015) TTIP-Rechtsschutz zu Ende denken. http://verfassungsblog.de/ttip-rechtsschutz-zu-ende-denken/. Accessed 22 Jan 2017

Gött H (2016) “Legitimation durch den, den es angeht?” - Die Einbindung der Zivilgesellschaft in die transatlantische Regulierungszusammenarbeit aus demokratischer Perspektive. In: Buszewksi S, Martini S, Rathke H (eds) Freihandel vs. Demokratie. Nomos, Baden-Baden, pp 199–218

Häberli C, Jansen M, Monteiro J-A (2012) Regional trade agreements and domestic labour market regulation. Employment Working Paper No. 120. ILO, Geneva

Hepburn J, Kuuya V (2011) Corporate social responsibility and investment treaties. In: Cordonier Segger M-C, Gehring MW, Newcombe A (eds) Sustainable development in world investment law. Kluwer Law International, Alphen aan den Rijn, pp 585–610

ILA (2002) Declaration of principles of international law relating to sustainable development. Paper presented at the 70th Conference of the International Law Association, New Delhi, 2–6 April 2002

ILO (2013) Social dimensions of free trade agreements. ILO, Geneva

La Hovary C (2017) The ILO’s mandate and capacity – creating, proliferating and supervising labour standards for a globalized economy. In: Gött H (ed) Labour standards in international economic law. Springer International Publishing, Cham. this volume

Lazo Grandi P (2009) Trade agreements and their relation to labour standards: the current situation. International Centre for Trade and Sustainable Development, Geneva

López Escarcena S (2014) Indirect Expropriation in International Law. Edward Elgar Publishing, Leuven

Maupain F (2013) The future of the International Labour Organization in the global economy. Hart, Oxford

Mills A (2014) The balancing (and unbalancing?) of interests in international investment law and arbitration. In: Douglas Z, Pauwelyn J, Viñuales JE (eds) The foundations of international investment law: bringing theory into practice. Oxford University Press, Oxford, pp 437–464

Novitz T (2017) Labour standards and trade: need we choose between ‘human rights’ and ‘sustainable development’? In: Gött H (ed) Labour standards in international economic law. Springer International Publishing, Cham. this volume

OECD (1996) Trade, employment and labour standards. A study of core workers’ rights and international trade. OECD Publishing, Paris

Orbie J, Van den Putte L, Martens D (2017) Civil society meetings in EU free trade agreements: the purposes unravelled. In: Gött H (ed) Labour standards in international economic law. Springer International Publishing, Cham. this volume

Prislan V, Zandvliet R (2013) Labour Provisions in International Investment Agreements: Prospects for Sustainable Development. Grotius Centre Working Paper 2013/003-IEL. Available via SSRN. https://papers.ssrn.com/sol3/papers2.cfm?abstract_id=2171716. Accessed 22 Jan 2017

Reinisch A (2008) Expropriation. In: Muchlinski P, Ortino F, Schreuer C (eds) The Oxford handbook of international investment law. Oxford University Press, Oxford, pp 407–458

Schill SW (2009) The multilateralization of international investment law. Cambridge University Press, Cambridge

Schrijver N (2008) The evolution of sustainable development in international law: inception, meaning and status. Brill/Nijhoff, Leiden/Boston

Shihata IFI (1986) Towards a greater depoliticization of investment disputes: the roles of ICSID and MIGA. Foreign Invest Law J ICSID Rev 1:1–25

Sornarajah M (2015) Resistance and change in the international law on foreign investment. Cambridge University Press, Cambridge

Stoll P-T, Holterhus T (2016) The ‘Generalization’ of international investment law in constitutional perspective. In: Krajewski M, Hindelang S (eds) Shifting paradigms in international investment law. Oxford University Press, Oxford, pp 339–356

Stoll P-T, Holterhus TP, Gött H (2015) Die geplante Regulierungszusammenarbeit zwischen der Europäischen Union und Kanada sowie den USA nach den Entwürfen von CETA und TTIP. AK Wien, Vienna

Stoll P-T, Holterhus TP, Gött H (2017) Investitionsschutz und Verfassung. Völkerrechtliche Investitionsschutzverträge aus der Perspektive des deutschen und europäischen Verfassungsrechts. Mohr Siebeck, Tübingen

Tzanakopoulos A, Ventouratou A (2017) Nicaragua in the international court of justice and the law of treaties. In: Sobenes E, Samson B (eds) Nicaragua before the International Court of Justice: Impacts on International Law (forthcoming). Available via SSRN. https://papers.ssrn.com/sol3/papers.cfm?abstract_id=2772648. Accessed 22 Jan 2017

United States Trade Representative (2015) The Trans-Pacific Partnership. Detailed Summary of US Objectives. https://ustr.gov/sites/default/files/TPP-Detailed-Summary-of-US-Objectives.pdf. Accessed 11 Aug 2017

Van den Putte L (2015) Involving civil society in social clauses and the decent work Agenda. Glob Labour J 6:221–235

Van Duzer JA (2016a) Sustainable development provisions in international trade treaties: what lessons for international investment agreements? In: Krajewski M, Hindelang S (eds) Shifting paradigms in international investment law. Oxford University Press, Oxford, pp 142–176

Van Duzer JA (2016b) Investor-State Dispute Settlement in CETA: Is It the Gold Standard? Ottawa Faculty of Law Working Paper No. 2016-44. Available via SSRN. https://ssrn.com/abstract=2860319. Accessed 22 Feb 2017

Viñuales JE (2013) Investment law and sustainable development: the environment breaks into investment disputes. In: Bungenberg M, Griebel J, Hobe S, Reinisch A (eds) International investment law. Nomos, Baden-Baden, pp 1763–1787

Vogt JS (2015) The evolution of labor rights and trade – a transatlantic comparison and lessons for the transatlantic trade and investment partnership. J Int Econ Law 18:827–860

Von Walter A (2015) Investor-state contracts in the context of international investment law. In: Bungenberg M, Griebel J, Hobe S, Reinisch A (eds) International investment law. Nomos, Baden-Baden, pp 129–141

WECD (1987) Our Common Future, The Brundtland Report. http://www.un-documents.net/our-common-future.pdf. Accessed 22 Jan 2017

Xu J (2017) The Role of Civil Society in EU Preferential Trade Agreements. European Society of International Law Conference Paper Series. Available via SSRN. https://ssrn.com/abstract=2912010. Accessed 2 Feb 2017

Zimmer R (2017) Implications of CETA and TTIP on social standards. In: Gött H (ed) Labour standards in international economic law. Springer International Publishing, Cham. this volume

Labour Standards and the World Bank. Analysing the Potential of Safeguard Policies for Protecting Workers

Franz Christian Ebert

Contents

Abstract Projects financed by the World Bank have, on a number of occasions, attracted criticism for involving violations of workers' rights. The revised World Bank safeguard policies, adopted in 2016, address some of these concerns by submitting projects financed by the Bank to specific labour standards requirements. The present chapter offers an in-depth analysis of the safeguard

---

This chapter draws on previous research by the author, in particular Ebert (2013, 2014). The author is grateful to Janelle Diller, Simon Hentrei, Violetta Ritz and the editor of this volume for useful comments and suggestions on earlier drafts of this paper. The usual disclaimer applies.

F.C. Ebert (✉)
Max Planck Institute for Comparative Public Law and International Law, Heidelberg, Germany
e-mail: ebert@mpil.de

H. Gött (ed.), *Labour Standards in International Economic Law*,
https://doi.org/10.1007/978-3-319-69447-4_13

policies' labour component. After providing some context, it examines the substantive labour standards requirements and looks at the procedural framework through which these requirements are to be implemented. The chapter also explores the safeguard policies' potential to positively affect labour standards in practice and points to some general features which may limit their effectiveness.

1 Introduction

The World Bank is a key actor in global economic governance. Over time, its activities have—similarly to those of the International Monetary Fund (IMF)—expanded significantly in terms of scope and 'now reach deep into policy-making within member governments'.[1] This also entails implications for labour standards, in particular in the 'Global South'.[2]

The World Bank has repeatedly been criticised for adopting policies that lead to a weakening of workers' protection in law and in practice.[3] Also, projects financed by the World Bank have been alleged to involve labour rights violations on the ground.[4] At the same time, the Bank has reacted to external criticism from civil society[5]—as well as internal pressure of 'labour-friendly' executive directors—by modifying its policy approach and instruments, including by adopting policies on labour standards.[6]

The term 'World Bank', as it is commonly understood, comprises two separate legal entities, the International Bank for Reconstruction and Development (IBRD)

[1]Woods (2001), p. 88.

[2]See e.g. O'Brien (2014), pp. 155-157. For an overview of the human rights implications of the World Bank activities see Darrow (2003), pp. 63–112.

[3]Various studies suggest that these structural adjustment programmes fostered by World Bank and IMF conditionality have come with a decline of labour rights protection in the countries concerned; see Abouharb and Cingranelli (2007), pp. 200–201 and Blanton et al. (2015), p. 9.

[4]See e.g. the report by Human Rights Watch (2014) on endemic forced labour in World Bank funded projects in the Uzbek cotton industry and the one by Bank Information Center (2015) on widespread child labour in a Bank-sponsored transport sector project in Uganda. In the latter case, the Bank eventually cancelled the project due to the numerous social issues it raised; see World Bank, World Bank Statement on Cancellation of the Uganda Transport Sector Development Project (TSDP), Press Release of 21 Dec 2015, available at http://www.worldbank.org/en/news/press-release/2015/12/21/wb-statement-cancellation-uganda-transport-sector-development-project. Accessed 9 Aug 2017.

[5]A key actor from civil society has been the International Trade Union Confederation (ITUC).

[6]See Murphy (2014), pp. 401, 409–410, 418–424.

and the International Development Association (IDA).[7] Sharing the same institutional framework and being served by the same staff,[8] these two institutions form part of the World Bank Group (WBG), which altogether comprises five different institutions.[9] For some time, the WBG's private sector arms, International Finance Corporation (IFC) and Multilateral Investment Guarantee Agency (MIGA), have integrated labour standards safeguards into some of their policies.[10] In August 2016, the World Bank followed suit by adopting new safeguard policies which, for the first time, expressly address labour standards concerns.[11]

The present chapter offers an analysis of the labour standards dimension of the revised World Bank safeguard policies.[12] For this purpose, Sect. 2 provides some context by outlining the World Bank's main policy instruments and sketches the Bank's approach to labour standards. It also provides an overview of the labour standards policies of IFC and MIGA, which to a large extent served as a blueprint for the World Bank's policies on this matter. Section 3 then reviews the Bank's policies in detail. It explores the substantive labour standards requirements and looks at the applicable procedural framework. Section 4 reflects on the safeguard policies' potential to positively affect labour standards in practice. For this purpose, it draws lessons from the application of IFC's and MIGA's labour standards policies as well as from the practice of the World Bank Inspection Panel, the Bank's quasi-judicial internal accountability mechanism. Also, some general features are highlighted which run the risk of limiting the safeguards' effectiveness. Section 5 concludes by pondering the potential and limitations of the World Bank's safeguard policies and points to the need for further improvement.

---

[7]See Ragazzi (2012), para. 2. The terms 'World Bank', 'Bank' and 'IBRD and IDA' are used in an interchangeable manner.

[8]See Guder (2011), para. 1.

[9]Apart from the IBRD and the IDA, these are the International Finance Corporation, the Multilateral Investment Guarantee Agency, and the International Centre for the Settlement of Investment Disputes. The latter institution is not directly relevant to the subject of the chapter and shall not be addressed in the following.

[10]For the purpose of this chapter, the term 'safeguard policies'shall be defined as comprising those instruments that set out obligations for WBG staff and borrowers with a view to avoiding adverse social and environmental impacts of activities supported by the WBG.

[11]World Bank (2016) Environmental and Social Framework.

[12]By contrast, the WBG's technical and political oversight mechanisms, such as the Independent Evaluation Group or the Executive Board, shall not be addressed here. Also, the question of whether the WBG's members are themselves subject to certain labour standards-related obligations under international law, including international human rights law, is beyond the paper's scope of analysis. See on this question in general McBeth (2010), pp. 178–184; Fujita (2013), pp. 7–12.

2 Contextualising the World Bank and Labour Standards

2.1 The World Bank's Key Instruments in a Nutshell

The World Bank influences the social and economic conditions in the countries concerned through a number of devices. These include instruments relating to financial assistance, development programming, policy advice, and technical cooperation.[13]

The IBRD provides a variety of loans and other financial services to its members,[14] in particular to middle-income countries.[15] Meanwhile, the IDA, which was established to provide assistance to the poorest countries, uses loans (so-called 'credits') at low or zero-rate interests or grants that do not have to be paid back.[16] In both cases, such financial assistance may aim at financing specific economic projects, including in the area of infrastructure ('project lending'), which is particularly relevant for the purpose of this chapter.[17] In addition, it may take the form of broader budget support, e.g. through 'development policy lending' (formerly known as 'structural adjustment lending') or the recent 'Program-For Results' instrument.[18] While the Articles of Agreement of IBRD and IDA envision project lending as the normal type of lending and non-project lending as the exception, the latter has taken an increasingly important role, sometimes amounting to about half of the Bank's financial activities.[19]

The World Bank's financial assistance typically takes place in the context of broader development programming instruments. The main device in this regard is

[13]The World Bank carries out a number of additional activities, e.g. the administration of specific trust funds. See Schlemmer-Schulte (2014), para. 87 et seq.

[14]Note that also the IBRD and the IDA can engage in activities with the private sector. Among others, the two institutions can issue guarantees for investments by private companies which are complementary to those issued by MIGA. See Schlemmer-Schulte (2014), paras. 56, 79–83 and Guder (2011), para. 17.

[15]See Schlemmer-Schulte (2014), para. 56. Its Articles of Agreement require the IBRD to act as a 'lender of last resort' and limit its financial services to countries that would otherwise have insufficient access to such loans. See ibid., referring to Art. III Sec. 4 (ii) IBRD Articles of Agreement.

[16]See Guder (2011), paras. 15–16. IBRD, too, provides some grants which are, however, small in number and volume, see Schlemmer-Schulte (2014), paras. 84–85.

[17]See World Bank (2013) Operational Policy 10.00—Investment Project Financing, revised July 2014.

[18]See World Bank (2012) Operational Policy 8.60—Development Policy Lending, revised July 2014, para. 9; World Bank (2015) Bank Policy. Program-for-Results Financing. For details on the latter see Malli (2014).

[19]See Schlemmer-Schulte (2014), para. 55.

the so-called 'Country Partnership Framework'.[20] Based on a 'Systematic Country Diagnostic',[21] it sets out the objectives to be accomplished and outlines the programme of the World Bank, IFC, and MIGA for the given timeframe.[22] In addition, the World Bank imparts policy advice in several ways. A prominent example in this regard is the World Bank's Doing Business Report which assesses domestic regulation for some 190 countries. Published by the World Bank on an annual basis,[23] Doing Business has quickly become an important source for policy-makers, especially regarding the Global South.[24] Finally, the Bank also provides technical assistance, especially in order to facilitate the implementation of other Bank activities.[25]

2.2 *The World Bank's Approach Towards Labour Standards*

The position of the World Bank regarding labour standards has changed significantly over time and has been described as an evolution from 'antagonism to [...] limited accommodation'.[26] Initially, the World Bank had declined to lend its support to the ILO's conception of the Core Labour Standards after their adoption in 1998,[27] raising concerns regarding the economic effects of trade unions rights.[28] In 2002, the Bank revised its stance and has since then fully endorsed, at least on paper, the ILO's Core Labour Standards.[29] Also, the Bank has come to accept that

[20]See the World Bank Group (2014) Directive on Country Engagement, OPCS 5.01-DIR.01. The CFP replaces the Bank's earlier Country Assistance Strategies. See on this Tan (2011), pp. 113–114. The Bank, jointly with the IMF, also used to employ Poverty Reduction Strategy Papers (PRSPs), in which low-income countries set out their development strategy, as the basis for the financial assistance provided to these countries by these two institutions. This device was also seen to serve as a tool to influence economic policy making at the domestic level at an early stage; see Tan (2011), pp. 3–5. The World Bank has discontinued this joint approach as of 2014 although the IMF carries on with a slightly adjusted Poverty Reduction Strategy. See IMF (2016), p. 1.

[21]See further IBRD/IDA/IFC/MIGA (2016) Guidance on the Systematic Country Diagnostic, OPS5.01-GUID.104).

[22]See Schlemmer-Schulte (2014), para. 98.

[23]Earlier reports feature the IFC and the World Bank as co-publishers; see e.g. IFC and World Bank (2013).

[24]See Berg and Cazes (2008), p. 350 and Michaels (2009), p. 772.

[25]See Schlemmer-Schulte (2014), para. 86.

[26]O'Brien (2014), p. 154.

[27]See the ILO Declaration on Fundamental Principles and Rights at Work and its Follow-up, International Labour Conference, adopted on 18 June 1998 and further La Hovary (2009), pp. 21 et seq.

[28]Murphy (2014), p. 405.

[29]See on this process Anner and Caraway (2010), pp. 156–159.

the scope of its mandate does not prevent it from taking labour standards matters into consideration when carrying out its activities[30]; although it remains reluctant to require labour standards compliance by countries as a precondition for obtaining finance.[31] In addition, the Bank has, together with the IMF, engaged in an institutional dialogue with global trade union organizations.[32]

Beyond minimum protection, the World Bank has tended to favour labour market flexibility as the main rationale for its engagement with labour law.[33] Along this line, a number of Country Assistance Strategies Papers have in practice pushed for reforms to reduce the protection of domestic labour laws.[34] Also, conditions which require rendering domestic labour laws more flexible have been attached to a number of the World Bank's development policy lending agreements.[35]

The tension between the Bank's policies and labour standards is particularly illustrated by the 'Employing Workers Index' (hereinafter 'EWI'), a component of the World Bank's Doing Business Report. Mainly three employment-related areas have been in its focus, including the recruitment of workers, conditions of employment,[36] and the laying-off of workers. By ranking countries based on the degree of 'flexibility' of relevant legislation, the EWI favoured a deregulatory agenda and wielded pressure on governments to deregulate domestic labour law in order not to put off potential investors, among other reasons.[37] Also, the EWI has been used by the World Bank and the IMF in their respective policy and lending instruments and has reportedly played an important role in obtaining IDA funding.[38] The EWI has been subject to severe criticism alleging, among others, methodological deficits, flawed assumptions and problems in terms of coherence with relevant ILO instruments.[39] After mounting resistance to the EWI by workers' organizations, other civil society actors and the ILO—as well as substantive lobbying efforts by pro-labour US politicians—the World Bank formally stopped utilizing it in its

[30] See on this issue Maupain (2013), pp. 72–79 and in general Darrow (2003), pp. 152–154. In this regard, the Bank's practice was to invoke the non-political interference clause of Art. IV (10) IBRD Articles of Agreement. For a historical account of the—often rather selective—application of this provision see Janse (2014).

[31] See on this question McBeth (2010), pp. 179–181.

[32] Murphy (2014), p. 407. This has also involved secondments of trade union officials to the World Bank. Ibid p. 409.

[33] Anner and Caraway (2010), p. 167.

[34] See Global Unions (2007), p. 7 for examples.

[35] See Bakvis (2009), p. 427. The following analysis on the Doing Business Report is based on Ebert (2014), pp. 239–241.

[36] This includes minimum wage issues, hours of work, and leave.

[37] See on this Santos (2009), pp. 63–64.

[38] See Global Unions (2007), pp. 8–11.

[39] See e.g. Santos (2009), pp. 68–73; Berg and Cazes (2008), p. 362 and Ebert (2013), pp. 81–82.

relevant activities in 2009.[40] Shortly thereafter, the Bank shifted the EWI into an appendix and eliminated the country ranking.[41] The 2016 version of Doing Business continues to provide comparative data on countries' labour laws and has added data on 'job quality', emphasizing the risks of both 'overregulation' and 'underregulation' of workers.[42]

In recent publications the World Bank has emphasized the 'challenge [...] to establish the right balance between workers' protection and flexibility'.[43] Such an approach is adopted, notably, in the Bank's 2013 World Development Report on 'Jobs'. While this report argues for the need to avoid the risk of overly intrusive labour market regulation that may curtail job creation, it recognizes that labour market regulation is not the main impediment in this regard and underlines the need to ensure social protection and basic labour rights.[44]

Of particular relevance for this chapter are labour standards-related problems that arise from the Bank's investment project financing. Many of these investments concern large-scale business projects in countries and sectors where labour standards are low and public labour institutions weak. This entails a significant risk that the Bank's investments contribute to labour standards violations by the borrower itself and its contractors as well as in the borrower's supply chain.[45] To assuage those risks—and related criticism from civil society—the World Bank has adopted safeguard policies, the most recent example of which is its Environmental and Social Framework of 2016.

2.3 *The Precursor of the World Bank's Safeguard Policies on Labour Standards: IFC's and MIGA's Sustainability Policies*

While IFC provides finance for specific business projects, among others,[46] MIGA provides guarantees to investors conducting business projects in developing countries.[47]

---

[40]See Independent Evaluation Group (2008), in particular pp. 6, 52 and World Bank (2009), pp. 1–2. For background see Murphy (2014), pp. 412–416.

[41]IFC and World Bank (2010), p. 94. According to the ITUC, the deregulatory impetus has nonetheless to some extent persisted. See Burrow (2014).

[42]See World Bank (2015), p. 118.

[43]Kuddo et al. (2015), p. 1.

[44]World Bank (2012), pp. 257–258, 292 and 297–298, respectively.

[45]For examples see ITUC (2011), pp. 19–26.

[46]IFC also engages in long-term investments through equity and provides financing through financial intermediaries. See Asrani and Dann (2014), para. 11 mentioning also some additional financial services provided by IFC.

[47]See Loewenfeld (2008), pp. 586–587.

With regard to labour standards policies for project finance, the IFC has been at the forefront within the WBG.[48] In 1998, the IFC issued internal guidelines, precluding any support of projects involving 'harmful child labour' and forced labour.[49] After consulting with a variety of stakeholders, the IFC expanded its approach by adopting the 'Performance Standards on Environmental & Social Sustainability' (hereinafter 'Performance Standards') in 2006, which were revised in 2012.[50] The Performance Standards contain, among others,[51] comprehensive labour standards requirements IFC's clients need to comply with. The relevant obligations of IFC's staff are set out in separate policies.[52] MIGA adopted largely identical policies in 2007,[53] which were revised in 2013.[54] The Performance Standards have also served as a model for similar policies adopted by regional and national development finance institutions as well as private banks.[55]

MIGA's and IFC's Performance Standard 2 comprises requirements relating to both local labour law and general minimum labour standards. Client companies are required to abide by any labour law norm of the host state, including international law rules that have been incorporated into the domestic legal system.[56] In addition, Performance Standard 2 spells out further requirements in a variety of sub-areas of labour law. This involves requirements relating to the ILO's Core Labour Standards,[57] occupational health and safety, employment and working conditions and

[48]The IFC has also partnered with the ILO for the so-called 'Better Work Programme'. This programme involves company-level monitoring, carried out by local ILO staff, of labour standards compliance in the textile sector of the participant countries, alongside training and advisory activities. See further on this Diller (2015), p. 335.

[49]IFC (1998) Policy Statement on Forced Labor and Harmful Child Labor.

[50]IFC (2012) Performance Standards on Social & Environmental Sustainability (hereinafter IFC, Performance Standards).

[51]The relevant areas consist of 'Resource Efficiency and Pollution Prevention, Community Health, Safety, and Security, Land Acquisition and Involuntary Resettlement, Biodiversity Conservation and Sustainable Management of Living Natural Resources, Indigenous Peoples, and Cultural Heritage', see IFC (2012) Performance Standards on Environmental and Social Sustainability.

[52]See IFC, Sustainability Policy, paras. 3–5; Also, IFC's ‚Access to Information Policies' establish what information the staff of the two institutions is to provide to the public.

[53]See on this Krajewski (2013), p. 207.

[54]MIGA (2013) Performance Standards on Environmental and Social Sustainability; MIGA (2013) Policy on Environmental and Social Sustainability (hereinafter MIGA, Sustainability Policy) and MIGA (2013) Access to Information Policy.

[55]See further Ebert (2014), pp. 233–234.

[56]IFC (2012) Performance Standard 1. Assessment and Management of Environmental and Social Risks and Impacts (hereinafter IFC, Performance Standard 1); MIGA (2013) Performance Standard 1. Assessment and Management of Environmental and Social Risks and Impacts (hereinafter MIGA, Performance Standard 1), para. 5, respectively.

[57]IFC (2012) Performance Standard 2. Labor and Working Conditions (hereinafter IFC, Performance Standard 2) and MIGA (2013) Performance Standard 2. Labor and Working Conditions (hereinafter MIGA, Performance Standard 2), paras. 13–17 and 21–22, respectively.

retrenchment procedures.[58] IFC's and MIGA's client companies must also set up a grievance mechanism through which concerns raised by workers can be tackled.[59]

The Performance Standards' implementation rests first and foremost on the due diligence obligations of both the client and IFC's and MIGA's staff.[60] In particular, the client company is required to undertake a social and environmental impact assessment of the project concerned and consult with relevant stakeholders.[61] If potential adverse impacts are identified, these must be addressed in an action plan devised by the client.[62] IFC and MIGA are required to conduct some additional due diligence[63] and, later on, carry out periodic monitoring of the client companies' compliance with the Performance Standards and any action plan after the project's approval.[64] In addition, various mechanisms exist for stakeholders to allege violations of IFC's and MIGA's environmental and social policies. Complaints can be filed informally with IFC's and MIGA's staff[65] or formally with the Compliance Advisor Ombudsman, the internal recourse mechanism of IFC and MIGA (see below).

3 The Labour Standards Dimension of the World Bank's Safeguard Policies

3.1 General Issues

The World Bank has been slower to integrate concerns relating to workers' protection into its policies than IFC and MIGA. Since 2007, bidders for works under World Bank projects, in principle, have to formally commit to certain labour standards.[66] In 2013, the World Bank adopted an adjusted version of the IFC Performance Standards for the (limited) private sector activities financed by

58 IFC/MIGA, Performance Standard 2, para. 10, 18–19, 23, respectively.

59 Ibid., para. 20.

60 IFC/MIGA, Sustainability Policy, para. 21, respectively.

61 IFC/MIGA, Performance Standard 1, para. 7, respectively.

62 Ibid., para. 16.

63 This may include an analysis of relevant documents, interviews, and on-site visits. IFC, Sustainability Policy, para. 28 and MIGA, Sustainability Policy, para. 26. Different—and somewhat reduced—requirements exist for operations relating to financial intermediaries and for advisory and certain technical activities. See IFC, Sustainability Policy, paras. 32–37 and 38–39 and MIGA, Sustainability Policy, paras. 30–37.

64 This involves, among others, 'annual monitoring reports' to be prepared by the client company, see IFC, Sustainability Policy, para. 45 and MIGA, Sustainability Policy, para. 43.

65 For example, IFC has created a Social and Environmental Development Department with which inquiries and complaints can be filed online. See ITUC (2011), p. 19.

66 World Bank (2007), pp. 149–154; 232–233.

it.[67] However, labour standards requirements were not protected by the World Bank's safeguard policies concerning the main bulk of its activities, dealing with the public sector. This contrasted with other areas[68] where specific World Bank safeguard policies had been adopted to protect people and the environment from adverse effects of the activities supported by the Bank.[69] Importantly, complaints alleging non-compliance by the World Bank with its safeguard policies in the context of a Bank-financed project are subject to the scrutiny of the World Bank Inspection Panel.[70]

The World Bank Environmental and Social Framework (ESF) adopted in August 2016 by the Bank's Board of Executive Directors thus contains the first safeguards requiring Bank borrowers to comply with specific labour standards when undertaking public sector projects. The ESF, which replaces several earlier Bank safeguards,[71] follows largely the model of the IFC's Sustainability Framework. Apart from a non-binding vision statement,[72] it contains an 'Environmental and Social Policy'[73] setting out the Bank's obligations, followed by ten 'Environmental and Social Standards' (ESS) which are directed to the borrower. The first ESS sets out the general framework for dealing with environmental and social issues while the following seven[74] address substantive matters, such as labour and environmental

[67]World Bank (2013) Operational Policy 4.03—Performance Standards for Private Sector Activities and World Bank (2013) Bank Procedures 4.03—Performance Standards for Private Sector Activities.

[68]Examples include indigenous peoples, involuntary resettlement, cultural resources, and environmental matters. See World Bank (2005), Operational Policy 4.10—Indigenous Peoples, revised April 2013; World Bank (2001), Operational Policy 4.12—Involuntary Resettlement, revised April 2013; World Bank (2001) Operational Policy 4.12—Involuntary Resettlement, revised April 2013; World Bank (2006) Operational Policy 4.11—Physical Cultural Resources, revised in April 2013 and World Bank (1999) Operational Policy 4.01—Environmental Assessment, revised in April 2013.

[69]See Bradlow and Naudé Fourie (2013), p. 18.

[70]See further below at 4.2.

[71]See World Bank (2016) Review and update of the World Bank's Safeguard Policies Environmental and Social Framework, proposed Third Draft, *Strengthening the effectiveness of our safeguard policies to enhance the development outcomes of Bank operations* (hereinafter 'Review and Update'), p. 8.

[72]World Bank (2016) A Vision for Sustainable Development.

[73]The full title is 'World Bank Environmental and Social Policy for Investment Project Financing' (hereinafter 'ES Policy').

[74]The first eight ESS are: Environmental and Social Standard 1. Assessment and Management of Environmental and Social Risks and Impacts (hereinafter 'ESS 1'); Environmental and Social Standard 2. Labor and Working Conditions (hereinafter 'ESS 2'); Environmental and Social Standard 3. Resource Efficiency and Pollution Prevention and Management; Environmental and Social Standard 4. Community Health and Safety; Environmental and Social Standard 5. Land Acquisition, Restrictions on Land Use and Involuntary Resettlement; Environmental and Social Standard 6. Biodiversity Conservation and Sustainable Management of Living Natural Resources; Environmental and Social Standard 7. Indigenous Peoples; Environmental and Social Standard 8. Cultural Heritage.

issues, local communities, and indigenous peoples-related concerns. ESS 9 contains specific requirements on financial intermediaries[75] whilst ESS 10 deals with engaging stakeholders as well as disclosure of information.[76]

Prior to adoption, the ESF had been subject to a revision process which the Bank described as involving 'the most extensive consultation ever conducted by the World Bank'.[77] Indeed, since 2012, the World Bank has conducted three consultation rounds with a wide range of stakeholders.[78] This included civil society representatives, donor countries, international organizations, and, in particular, borrowing countries, whose role the Bank's Executive Directors had emphasized.[79] Based on an 'approach paper',[80] a first consultation was held between October 2012 and March 2014. On this basis, World Bank staff subsequently prepared a draft of the safeguards which was subject to consultations between September 2014 and March 2015.[81] A revised draft of the safeguards was released for consultation purposes in August 2015, with consultations lasting until March 2016.[82] The final text of the safeguards was approved by the Bank's Board of Executive Directors on 4 August 2016.[83]

During the consultations, labour issues were addressed, among others, in country-level meetings and in meetings of dedicated 'expert focus groups' with international trade union organizations as well as the ILO.[84] Expectably, the views expressed by the actors consulted differed fundamentally on certain points. Among others, the ILO and certain donor countries advocated the insertion of references to the ILO's 1998 Declaration while borrowing countries emphasized the role of domestic law and the need to ensure the feasibility of the ESS' implementation.[85] This led to the necessity of reaching compromises on numerous fronts, which are reflected in ESS 2's provisions.

---

[75]Environmental and Social Standard 9. Financial Intermediaries (hereinafter 'ESS 9').

[76]Environmental and Social Standard 10. Stakeholder Engagement and Information Disclosure (hereinafter 'ESS 10').

[77]World Bank, Press Release, 'World Bank Board Approves New Environmental and Social Framework', 4 Aug 2016, available at http://www.worldbank.org/en/news/press-release/2016/08/04/world-bank-board-approves-new-environmental-and-social-framework. Accessed 9 Aug 2017.

[78]For comprehensive documentation see at https://consultations.worldbank.org/consultation/review-and-update-world-bank-safeguard-policies. Accessed 9 Aug 2017.

[79]See World Bank (2016) Review and Update, p. 11.

[80]See World Bank (2012) The World Bank's Safeguard Policies proposed review and update. Approach paper.

[81]World Bank (2014) Environmental and Social Framework. First Draft for Consultation.

[82]World Bank (2015) Environmental and Social Framework. Second Draft for Consultation.

[83]World Bank (2016) Environmental and Social Framework. Setting Environmental and Social Standards for Investment Project Financing.

[84]See World Bank, Review and Update, p. 22.

[85]Ibid.

3.2 *The Safeguard Policies' Labour Standards Component*

3.2.1 Substantive Labour Standards Requirements

The content of ESS 2, the part of the Bank's ESF dealing with labour standards, largely echoes the approach taken by IFC's and MIGA's Performance Standard 2. In terms of specific content, the ESS covers virtually all labour standards issues addressed by the IFC/MIGA Performance Standards.[86] This includes matters relating to the four ILO Core Labour Standards such as the prohibition of forced labour and child labour, workplace-related non-discrimination, as well as freedom of association and the right to collective bargaining. Conspicuously though, ESS 2 does, unlike the IFC/MIGA Performance Standards,[87] not refer to any ILO instrument.[88]

Other standards covered concern employment and working conditions, namely working time, leave, and wages issues.[89] In contrast to the IFC/MIGA Standards, these conditions only refer to 'national law' and 'labor management procedures' prepared by the borrower[90] without involving other points of reference, e.g. relevant collective agreements and the usual conditions of the industry.[91] By contrast, the requirements contained in ESS 2 relating to occupational safety and health[92] are more detailed than those in the corresponding IFC/MIGA Performance Standards.[93] Among others, the borrower needs to put in place measures to abate the risk of occupational injuries, diseases as well as other work-related hazards.[94] Further, a grievance mechanism for project workers and their organizations is provided for.[95]

In some respects, ESS 2 reproduces the limitations of the IFC/MIGA Performance Standard 2. This concerns notably the consistency with ILO standards.

[86]Under ESS 2, the requirements on retrenchment are now contained in the sub-section on "Terms and Conditions of Employment", rather than in a sub-section, and have been watered down in comparison to the IFC/MIGA Performance Standards; see ESS 2, para. 12. The latter require the client company to examine alternatives to the retrenchment and, where those are not viable, to set up a retrenchment plan complying with certain requirements. Also, the severance pay and outstanding salary payments have to be made within a reasonable timeframe. See IFC/ MIGA, Performance Standard 2, paras. 18–19, respectively.

[87]The Performance Standards note that they 'have been in part guided by a number of international conventions and instruments' and refer to the eight ILO Fundamental Conventions relating to the Core Labour Standards. See IFC Performance Standards, para. 2.

[88]See notably ESS 2, paras. 13–20.

[89]See ESS 2, paras. 10–12.

[90]Ibid., paras. 10–11.

[91]Cf. ibid., para. 11 and IFC/MIGA, Performance Standard 2, para. 10, respectively.

[92]See ESS 2, paras. 24–30.

[93]Cf. IFC Performance Standards, para. 23.

[94]See ESS 2, para. 25.

[95]Ibid., paras. 21–23.

Although the Board Paper states that ESS 2 'reflects the core principles of ILO's Fundamental Principles and Rights at Work',[96] the protection of these requirements is subject to significant constraints.[97] As under the IFC/MIGA PS 2,[98] this concerns in particular non-discrimination and workers' freedom of association issues whose observance is not fully required where the borrowing state's domestic law conflicts with these standards.[99] In particular, the requirements on non-discrimination are reduced in cases where the project takes place in countries whose domestic laws discriminate against certain groups of workers. In such cases, borrowers shall merely 'seek to carry out' their projects in accordance with the relevant requirements 'to the extent possible'.[100] Complete compliance with the relevant ILO standards is thus not required.[101] The situation is similar with regard to countries whose laws impose restrictions on or even prohibit trade unions. Rather than fully complying with the requirements as set out in the relevant ILO instruments,[102] borrowers must, in such scenarios, only refrain from impeding the workers concerned from creating 'alternative mechanisms' and must not engage in 'discriminat[ion] or retaliat[ion]' against workers that 'participate, or seek to participate' in such mechanisms.[103] The Bank's ESS 2 can therefore not be considered a full 'reflection' of the ILO's Core Labour Standards.

3.2.2 Coverage of Workers

The labour standards requirements as described above are not applicable to all workers involved in the project. Rather, they only apply to 'direct workers', i.e. those workers 'employed or engaged directly by the Borrower [...] to work specifically in relation to the project'.[104] While the term 'borrower' includes 'the

[96]See World Bank (2016) Review and Update, p. 31.

[97]The term 'Fundamental Principles and Rights at Work' was coined by the ILO Declaration on Fundamental Principles and Rights at Work 1998. In its para. 2, it refers to 'the principles concerning the fundamental rights [...], namely: (a) freedom of association and the effective recognition of the right to collective bargaining; (b) the elimination of all forms of forced or compulsory labour; (c) the effective abolition of child labour; and (d) the elimination of discrimination in respect of employment and occupation'. In this regard, the Declaration makes reference to eight 'Fundamental Conventions' which further specify these rights.

[98]See further Ebert (2014), pp. 235–237.

[99]See ESS 2, paras. 13 and 16.

[100]Ibid., para. 13.

[101]Cf., in particular, ILO Equal Remuneration Convention, 1951, No. 100 and ILO Discrimination (Employment and Occupation) Convention, 1958, No. 111.

[102]See, in particular, ILO Freedom of Association and Protection of the Right to Organise Convention, 1948, No. 87 and ILO Right to Organise and Collective Bargaining Convention, 1949, No. 98.

[103]See ESS 2, para 16.

[104]ESS 2, para. 3 (a) in conjunction with para. 4.

project proponent and the project implementing agencies',[105] many workers related to the project will not be covered by this definition, for example due to the outsourcing of project activities to third parties. For those workers, ESS 2 establishes three additional categories which are subject to different standards of protection. These are (1) certain types of workers employed by third parties ('contracted workers'), (2) workers employed by the borrowers' 'primary suppliers' ('primary supply workers'), and (3) workers 'providing community labor', including in the context of 'food for work programs and public works as safety nets programs' ('community workers').[106]

The requirements applying to these three types of workers are substantially lower than the ones that the borrower must meet in relation to 'direct workers'. As concerns contracted workers, borrowers are required to take certain precautionary measures rather than ensuring contractors' actual compliance with ESS 2.[107] More specifically, the borrower must take 'reasonable efforts' to ensure that contractors are 'legitimate and reliable entities' and have sufficient management systems in place to comply with ESS 2.[108] The borrower is also required to 'manag[e] and monito[r]' its contractors through appropriate procedures and ensure the availability of a grievance mechanism to the contractors' workers.[109] A lower standard is applicable to 'primary supply workers'. In this regard, the borrower's obligations are mainly limited to taking certain steps with regard to forced labour and child labour[110] as well as severe occupational safety issues.[111] A reduced set of requirements also applies to 'community workers'. In this regard, most ESS

---

[105]Ibid., para. 3 (a).

[106]Ibid., paras. 3 (b)–(d) and 34.

[107]See Ibid., para. 5 in conjunction with paras. 31–33.

[108]Ibid., para. 31.

[109]ESS 2, paras. 32 and 33. Some minor improvements regarding the level of protection are apparent in comparison to IFC/MIGA, Performance Standards 2. Notably, ESS 2 obligates borrowers to include the requirements contained in ESS 2 into their agreements with relevant contractors while the relevant IFC/MIGA standards only required the contractor to 'take commercially reasonable efforts' to do so. Cf. ESS 2, para. 32. with IFC, Performance Standard 2, para. 25. Another new feature of ESS 2 is an obligation incumbent on the borrower to ensure that contractors 'include equivalent requirements and non-compliance remedies in their contractual agreements with subcontractors', ESS 2, para. 32.

[110]See ESS 2, para. 40. The relevant requirements are weaker than those included into the IFC/MIGA Performance Standards as under ESS 2 the borrower does no longer have to identify the relevant risks himself but only has to 'require' its supplier to do so. Cf. ibid. with IFC/MIGA, Performance Standard 2, para. 27, respectively.

[111]See ESS 2, para. 41. Where it is not possible to bring the primary supplier into compliance, the borrower has to change to a supplier which demonstrably is in line with the relevant standards, see ESS 2, para. 42.

2 requirements are assessed on a case-by-case basis.[112] Only with regard to forced and child labour as well as basic occupational safety and health standards, the relevant requirements apply systematically to any case of community labour.[113]

Three broader problems seem apparent from the approach taken by ESS 2. First, the requirements incumbent on borrowers in relation to the three categories noted above are sometimes conspicuously vague. Among others, the borrowers' obligations regarding 'primary supply workers' only apply to 'significant risks', which, in the case of occupational safety must additionally concern a 'serious' problem.[114] Also, the application of the ESS 2 requirements to community workers is mainly based on this being 'proportionate' to 'a) the nature and scope of the project; (b) the specific project activities in which the community workers are engaged; and (c) the nature of the potential risks and impacts to the community workers.'[115] While this may increase 'implementability',[116] an objective emphasized by the Bank, this reduces foreseeability and may, depending on the pressures entailed by the project at hand, result in many ESS 2 requirements remaining unapplied.

Second, the less than clear-cut definitions of the terms 'contracted workers' and 'primary supply workers' grant borrowers and the Bank staff considerable discretion to determine which workers are covered by the relevant requirements in a given project. For example, the term 'contracted worker' is defined as any worker 'employed or engaged through third parties to perform work related to core functions of the project, regardless of location'.[117] The definition hinges thus heavily on the notion of the project's 'core functions'. These are in turn defined as 'those production and/or service processes essential for a specific project activity without which the project cannot continue'.[118] The question of which processes are 'essential' for the project's continuance is, however, a matter of judgment and difficult to decide in the abstract. It may in practice therefore be difficult to determine whether the activity the worker is involved in is so instrumental for the project at hand that it can be considered a part of a 'core function'. The definition thus provides little clarity and, without further specification, borrowers will easily be able to argue that many processes fall outside this definitional scope. Similar problems arise regarding the term 'primary supply workers'. 'Primary suppliers' are defined as any supplier 'who, on an ongoing basis, provide[s] directly to the project

[112]See ESS 2, para. 35. It is unclear whether the requirements concerning workers' organizations are applicable to community workers at all. While the ESS 2 requirements on conditions of employment and occupation safety and health are expressly mentioned in the relevant provision and subject to certain procedural requirements, this is not the case for workers' organizations.

[113]ESS 2, para. 37. With regard to occupational safety and health, only the general and industry-specific World Bank Group Environmental, Health and Safety Guidelines must be systematically applied; see ibid., para. 36.

[114]Ibid., paras. 40 and 41.

[115]ESS 2, para. 35.

[116]See World Bank, Review and Update, especially pp. 1, 10–11, 23.

[117]ESS 2, para. 3 (b).

[118]Ibid., footnote 4.

goods, and materials essential for the core functions of the project'.[119] In addition to the aforementioned problems concerning the term 'core functions', also the terms 'essential' and 'ongoing basis' may give rise to ambiguity and result in a situation where only few suppliers will be considered 'primary suppliers'. This entails the risk that a significant number of workers related to the project financed by the World Bank will not be covered by any aspect of ESS 2 at all.

Finally, ESS 2 does not set out any criterion concerning the project activities to be undertaken by 'direct workers' or any other restriction with regard to the outsourcing of project-related activities. As a result, the Bank's borrowers can, in principle, outsource any activity to third parties.[120] Borrowers can hence avoid the higher standards applicable to 'direct workers' merely by modifying their business structure. Indeed, the lower standards applicable to 'contracted workers' in comparison to 'direct workers' may, in the worst case, incentivize borrowers to outsource work to contractors or sub-contractors in order to avoid having to comply with the whole set of obligations under ESS 2.

By and large, the adoption of the Bank's ESS 2 constitutes an entry point for the protection of workers' rights which should, in light of the limitations and caveats mentioned above, however, be considered a rather modest step. Also, its potential will crucially depend on the actual implementation, which shall be addressed in the following section.

3.3 *Implementation Procedures*

Similar to MIGA's and IFC's policies, the implementation of ESS 2 relies primarily on the 'due diligence' the Bank is to perform prior to adopting the relevant project. This approach relies strongly on the concept of risk management which is common among financial institutions in the private sector.[121] This involves an assessment of the 'environmental and social risks and impacts' that the project at hand is likely to give rise to and possible avenues to address them.[122]

As under the IFC/MIGA Sustainability Policy, an emphasis is put on the borrowers' own risk assessment of the project,[123] which must in certain cases be carried out by 'independent specialists'.[124] The borrower is also obligated to

[119]ESS 2, para. 3 (c), footnote 5.

[120]Already IFC/MIGA Performance Standard 2 involved this problem, with the relevant Guidance Note merely noting that client companies ought not to take up 'disguised employment relationships'. See IFC, Guidance Note 2, para. 8.

[121]For some problems of this approach see Sarfaty (2012), pp. 137–139 and, specifically regarding labour standards, Trebilcock (2015), p. 107.

[122]ES Policy, paras. 30–32. Apart from the requirements under ESS2 also domestic law is to be 'take[n] into account'; see ESS 1, para. 26.

[123]Ibid., para. 32.

[124]See ESS 1, para. 25. This concerns notably 'High and Substantial Risk projects, as well as situations in which the Borrower has limited capacity'.

conduct consultations with relevant stakeholders.[125] The specific requirements for the due diligence depend in part on the risk classification the Bank undertakes for every specific project in light of factors such as the project's magnitude or its socio-political context.[126]

On this basis, an Environmental and Social Commitment Plan is agreed upon by the Bank and the borrower. The Plan sets out the measures which the borrower must take to bring the project into compliance with the ESS and also contains specific timelines.[127] The Plan is integrated into the legal agreement and is, hence, legally binding upon the borrower.[128] After the conclusion of the project agreement, the Bank's staff and the borrower are required to monitor the project's compliance with the Plan and any other aspect of the legal agreement.[129] The borrower also has to establish a grievance mechanism through which complaints related to the project can be addressed.[130]

While the ESF provides detailed rules regarding the due diligence to be conducted, certain limitations remain. The first one concerns the basis of the due diligence exercise. As under the IFC/MIGA Sustainability Policies, the primary basis in this regard is the borrower's own impact assessment of the project.[131] It has been argued that the Bank's dependence on the borrower's own assessment or assessments provided by consultants contracted by the borrower renders the independence of the due diligence exercise questionable.[132] Indeed, client companies may have an interest in detecting as little environmental and social risks as possible so as to trim down the costs arising from the implementation of the relevant requirements.[133] Furthermore, while in some cases external specialists are to carry out the assessment, the independence of their judgment may be relative if they are selected by the borrower himself, as the ES Policy stipulates.[134]

Second, throughout the due diligence process, Bank staff retains significant latitude.[135] For example, the degree of intensity and the modalities of the risk

[125]See ES Policy, para. 53. On the requirements the borrowers are to meet with regard to stakeholder consultations see also ESS 10, para. 6 et seq.

[126]See ES Policy, para. 20.

[127]Ibid., para. 46.

[128]See ibid. and ESS 1, para. 36 and for further analysis Dann and Riegner (2017), p. 12.

[129]See ES Policy, para. 56 and ESS 1, paras. 40, 45–50.

[130]See ES Policy, paras. 60–61.

[131]Ibid., para. 32 and IFC/ MIGA, Performance Standard 1, para. 7, respectively.

[132]See *mutatis mutandis* ITUC (2011), p. 13 on the relevant requirements of the IFC Performance Standards. See also Ebert (2014), p. 242.

[133]See on this argument relating to the IFC Performance Standards McBeth (2010), p. 215.

[134]ES Policy, para. 35.

[135]It is conspicuous that the relevant standards are framed as 'policies' rather than as legal requirements. Some authors attribute this to a general reluctance among WBG staff towards legal concepts and to a preference towards flexible arrangements, see Bradlow and Naudé Fourie (2013), p. 8.

assessment are largely left to the discretion of the relevant project staff.[136] Also, the time-limits under which the different requirements must be met are often kept in rather vague terms.[137] The due diligence procedure hence leaves considerable room for considerations that are unrelated to the environmental and social standards, such as the importance of the project to the Bank in economic or political terms.[138] This also highlights the potential importance of the Bank's quasi-judicial internal accountability mechanism, the Inspection Panel, to which persons affected by the Bank's projects have access and which is looked at below.

4 What to Expect from the Bank's Labour Standards-Related Safeguard Policies in Practice?

4.1 Insights from Labour-Related Cases Under the IFC's Performance Standards

This section draws some insights from the application of IFC's Sustainability Policies and Performance Standards with regard to labour standards issues.

The results of complaints filed with IFC's Social and Environmental Development Department seem highly case-specific. In some instances, IFC's investigations appear to have brought, if at all, few improvements for the workers' situations, also due to IFC's limited disclosure of related information and lack of clarity in the processes used.[139] In other cases, interventions by IFC appears to have helped to address labour-related compliance problems concerning the Performance Standards. A case in point deals with a Brazilian flight company which at the time benefited from financial support by the IFC. In this regard, trade unions had alleged incidents of company-sponsored anti-union activities. IFC staff reacted to these allegations by raising the matter with its client which, as union officials reported, led to a stop in the problematic activities.[140] In a similar case, trade unions brought a situation to the IFC's attention where a building firm in Uganda had failed to apply a collective agreement it had previously concluded. Reportedly, IFC's

[136]ESS 1 provides, for example that borrowers 'will assess, manage and monitor the environmental and social risks and impacts of the project [. . .] so as to meet the requirements of the ESSs *in a manner and within a timeframe acceptable to the Bank*' (emphasis added). See ESS 1, para. 14.

[137]For example, the ES Policy stipulates that any 'draft [Environmental and Social Commitment Plan] will be disclosed as early as possible, and before project appraisal', see ES Policy, para. 47. See for further examples Dann and Riegner (2017), p. 11.

[138]Regarding the labour-related IFC/MIGA Performance Standards, some authors have argued that the labour standards-related requirements of the Performance Standard will mostly be effective in cases where trade unions exist to scrutinize the client company's observance of these requirements. See Bakvis and McCoy (2008), p. 7.

[139]See, e.g. the cases reported in ITUC (2011), pp. 19–21 and 25–26. The information provided in this paragraph is based on Ebert (2014), pp. 245–246.

[140]See Bakvis and McCoy (2008), p. 6.

intervention with the company led to the application of the collective agreement.[141] Such results may, in part, have been fostered by internal measures adopted by the IFC in order to increase awareness among staff vis-à-vis labour standards issues in the course of its operations. Among others, the IFC has employed staff with labour expertise for the application of the Performance Standards and put in place a Labour Advisory Group to provide counsel on IFC's operations.[142]

Furthermore, the Compliance Advisor Ombudsman (CAO), the accountability mechanism for IFC and MIGA, has sometimes addressed labour standards matters.[143] Established in 1999 as a body of the WBG, the CAO reports to the WBG's president but is independent from the operational activities of the IFC and MIGA.[144] The CAO is vested with (1) a dispute resolution function for complaints filed by interested parties, (2) a compliance function involving the investigation of purported policy breaches by IFC and MIGA staff, and (3) an advisory function directed at the WBG President and IFC and MIGA senior management.[145] Any eligible complaint[146] will be assessed by the CAO who will facilitate an amicable dispute settlement based on information-sharing, joint fact-finding, and mediation, among others.[147] If no settlement is agreed upon, the CAO's compliance procedure is activated.[148] In the event of a positive 'compliance appraisal' by the CAO,[149] a 'compliance investigation' will be carried out.[150] The investigation involves a 'compliance panel' consisting of external experts[151] and culminates in an 'investigation report' determining whether the relevant policies have been observed by IFC or MIGA.[152] The CAO's findings do not entail any legal implications for the IFC's or the MIGA's management even though they may put political pressure on them to remedy possible violations.[153] The CAO monitors the case until the breach has, in its view, been remedied.[154]

[141]See Murie (2009), pp. 15–16.

[142]See Murphy (2014), p. 409.

[143]See further Ebert (2014), pp. 246–247.

[144]See Saper (2012), p. 1295. In 2015 the CAO disposed of a budget of about 4.5 million US dollars and 15 staff members. CAO (2015), pp. 64–68.

[145]See CAO (2013) Operational Guidelines (hereinafter CAO, Operational Guidelines 2013), pp. 4–5.

[146]See on the eligibility requirements CAO, Operational Guidelines 2013, p. 13.

[147]Ibid., pp. 13–15, 18. Relevant means in this regard can include document analysis, hearings, interviews, as well as on-site visits. See further Arp (2012), pp. 141–142.

[148]See CAO, Operational Guidelines 2013, pp. 14, 22. Furthermore, the CAO Vice President as well as the WBG President and MIGA's or IFC's senior management can set in motion the compliance procedure. See ibid., p. 22.

[149]Ibid., p. 23.

[150]See ibid., p. 24.

[151]The Compliance Panel will examine the case based on sources such as document review, interviews, and on-site observations. See ibid., pp. 23–24.

[152]Ibid., p. 25.

[153]Cf. ibid., p. 4. Also, while the reports of the CAO are, in principle, public, the WBG President may prohibit publication of the compliance reports, ibid., p. 25.

[154]Ibid., p. 25.

With regard to labour standards, the cases before the CAO have dealt with matters such as workers' freedom of association and collective bargaining, occupational safety and health as well as the payment of workers.[155] In some cases, the CAO's mediation efforts have yielded positive results.[156] A notable example pertains to Standard Profil, a Turkish automobile supplier, which raised issues regarding freedom of association, among others. On the basis of a comprehensive evaluation of the case, including site visits,[157] the CAO proposed several measures.[158] These measures, which found the acceptance of the parties involved, included labour-related capacity building and awareness raising activities regarding management and workers of IFC's client company. Also, an external assessment of the company's labour standards situation was undertaken.[159]

By contrast, other cases before the CAO have led to less tangible outcomes in terms of addressing labour standards-related cases, which underscores the complaint procedure's limitations. A recent case in point concerns the Colombian flight company Avianca. The company had received a loan from IFC about 50 million US dollars.[160] Submitted in 2011 to the CAO, the complaint involved issues pertaining to workers' freedom of association and collective bargaining rights.[161] After the company declined to engage in mediation by the CAO on the matter, the CAO initiated a compliance investigation in June 2012.[162] Published in April 2015, the CAO's 30-pages report provides a meticulous—and highly critical—review of the case. Among others, it states that 'IFC did not adequately understand the PS2 (ie. labour-related) risk attached to its investment prior to commitment' and noted severe deficiencies in IFC's due diligence exercise pertaining to Performance Standard 2.[163] The CAO also rebuked IFC for disbursing several tranches of the loan without observing the labour-related requirements of the loan agreement and IFC's sustainability policy and qualified IFC's labour audits as flawed.[164] In addition, the subsequent remedial measures taken by IFC were considered

[155]See the CAO's database on cases. http://www.cao-ombudsman.org/cases/. Accessed 9 Aug 2017. This paragraph is based on Ebert (2014), pp. 246–247.

[156]In general, the vast majority of cases filed with the CAO gets resolved at the dispute resolution stage. See Bradlow and Naudé Fourie (2013), p. 28.

[157]See CAO, *Turkey/Standard Profil-01/Duzce*, Regarding Labor Rights Concerns at Standart Profil, Stakeholder Assessment, 2 Feb 2009, p. 4.

[158]CAO, *Turkey/Standard Profil-01/Duzce*. Ombudsman Conclusion Report, June 2012, p. 2.

[159]See Berber Agtas (2009), pp. 38–89.

[160]See CAO, *Colombia/Avianca-01/Colombia*, Case Summary.

[161]Prior to this, the complainants had already raised these issues with IFC's staff which had not addressed the matters at hand to the satisfaction of the complainants. See further ITUC (2011), p. 23.

[162]See CAO, *Colombia/Avianca-01/Colombia*, Case Summary.

[163]CAO, *Complaint from Global Unions on behalf of unions representing employees of Avianca*, Investigation of IFC Investment in Avianca S.A., 27 Apr 2015, C-I-R9-Y12-F165, 27 April 2015 (hereinafter CAO, Avianca), pp. 16–17.

[164]CAO, Avianca, pp. 17–19.

insufficient and breaches of relevant disclosure requirements were established.[165] Interestingly, the CAO also analysed structural issues underlying the IFC's failure to observe the related labour requirements, such as a lack of skilled staff, relevant operational tools, and a tailored incentive system to induce company compliance as well as other limitations.[166] In terms of the legal analysis, it is interesting to note that the CAO engaged with and expressly challenged the IFC's interpretation of Performance Standards 1 and 2.[167] A major weakness of the case is the long duration of the procedure. The investigation report was rendered 4 years after the filing of the complaint with the CAO and almost 7 years after the initial complaint with IFC. This is not only problematic from a procedural efficiency perspective but also has concrete implications for the effectiveness of any remedial measures taken. Indeed, several of the workers concerned had to leave their trade union or were dismissed in the course of the industrial conflict. Moreover, Avianca already repaid the loan which significantly reduced IFC's leverage to induce any change in the company's trade union policy.[168] A CAO follow-up report from May 2017, which closed the case, concluded that no actions had been taken by IFC to address the issues at the project level while some—albeit insufficient—measures had been adopted to deal with the deficits regarding IFC's internal processes.[169]

On the whole, it would seem that although IFC's Sustainability Policies and Performance Standards show similar substantive and procedural limitations as the Bank's ESF,[170] these policies have sometimes helped to address labour standards issues, with specific outcomes varying from case to case.[171] Also, in some instances the CAO's interventions appear to have acted as a corrective to IFC's application of the relevant policies, thereby furthering their effective application.[172] Especially in contexts where effective remedies at the local level are scarce, IFC's and MIGA's policies can strengthen client companies' compliance with relevant labour standards. A general challenge, apart from the deficits mentioned above, is to ensure that those adversely affected by the respective projects have knowledge about IFC's involvement in the relevant project and the availability of the complaint procedure.[173]

---

165 Ibid., pp. 22–25.

166 Ibid., pp. 26–27.

167 Among others, the CAO stated that 'Similarly, CAO is unable to support IFC's argument that disclosure is discretionary in cases where a client has contentious relationships with its workers or their union representatives. Indeed, disclosure and consultation, while difficult, may be most important in such circumstances.' See ibid., p. 25. This has also occurred in some CAO cases not concerning labour standards; see e.g. Bradlow and Naudé Fourie (2013), p. 43.

168 See also ITUC (2015).

169 See CAO (2017), p. 9.

170 See further Ebert (2014), pp. 242–245.

171 This is also accepted by organizations that tend to have a critical attitude regarding the WBG. See for example ITUC (2011), p. 14.

172 See, for examples from other areas, Bradlow and Naudé Fourie (2013), pp. 48 and 59.

173 See Saper (2012), p. 1318 and Bradlow and Naudé Fourie (2013), p. 28.

4.2 Insights from the Experience with the World Bank's Inspection Panel

The Bank's ESF allows workers employed in the context of projects financed by the World Bank to file complaints with the World Bank's Inspection Panel. This is important, among others, because compliance by World Bank staff with its safeguard policies has been criticized as unsatisfactory by observers in the past.[174] Established after mounting criticism of the Bank's disregard of its own safeguard policies in the 1990s,[175] the Inspection Panel is the Bank's internal recourse body consisting of three members. Characterized by some as a 'quasi-judicial oversight mechanism',[176] the Inspection Panel examines allegations by individuals and groups. Any party has to show that 'its interests have been or are likely to be directly affected by an action or omission of the Bank as a result of a failure of the Bank to follow its operational policies and procedures with respect to the design, appraisal and/or implementation of a project financed by the Bank'.[177]

Reporting directly to the Bank's Executive Board, the Inspection Panel is autonomous from Bank management and staff.[178] The Panel enjoys hence a somewhat greater degree of autonomy than IFC's and MIGA's CAO, which it has aimed to preserve also in the face of occasional attempts of interference from Bank Management.[179] The Panel cannot issue injunctions to stop ongoing work or grant damages[180] and commentators have highlighted a number of flaws regarding the Panel's procedure.[181] That being said, its procedure is more formalized than that of the CAO and has been perceived as relatively independent and helpful for addressing project matters by a number of civil society actors.[182] An NGO lawyer has described it as 'an important tool in the matrix of protest and transnational organizing' '[d]espite the Panel's many infirmities'.[183]

The process can roughly be divided into an eligibility phase and an investigation phase.[184] Notwithstanding its quasi-judicial nature, the Inspection Panel's procedure contains—similarly to that of the CAO—several entry points for political considerations. Notably, the Panel has leeway to reject an investigation even in

[174]See, e.g. Tan (2008), p. 97.

[175]See Wong and Mayer (2015), p. 497.

[176]Naudé Fourie (2009), in particular pp. 323–328.

[177]See IBRD and IDA (1993), Resolution on the World Bank Inspection Panel (Res. No. IBRD 93-10, Res. No. IDA 93-6), para. 12.

[178]This does, of course, not amount to full independence from the Bank, also because the Panel has in part to rely on Bank Management and Staff to implement its findings. See on this Carrascott and Guernsey (2008), p. 600.

[179]See López-Jacoiste (2015), pp. 122–125.

[180]See further Carrascott and Guernsey (2008), pp. 595–597.

[181]See e.g. Wahi (2006), pp. 356–359.

[182]See Hunter (2003), pp. 209–210 and Lagerwall (2010), p. 419 with further references.

[183]See Kim (2008), p. 157.

[184]For further details, see Naudé Fourie (2009), in particular pp. 177–181.

cases where the request for investigation meets the 'technical eligibility criteria for an investigation',[185] taking into account, among others, the seriousness of the 'alleged harm and possible non-compliance by the Bank with its operational policies'.[186] Moreover, it is eventually the Board that must authorize the initiation of the Panel's investigation even though the Board usually does so without discussing the merits of the request.[187]

In practice, only a minor share of the cases received by the Panel is actually investigated.[188] This is in part due to technical eligibility issues but political considerations have also played a role in some instances.[189] In some cases, this was based on a prospect to have the matter of conflict resolved by the requesters of investigation and the Bank's management prior to the formal investigation.[190] Furthermore, observers have highlighted the limited possibilities of requesting parties to participate in the ongoing investigations.[191]

By contrast, in all cases where the investigations did occur by June 2014 some violations have been identified.[192] Typically, this has resulted in the elaboration of an Action Plan by the Bank's Management to be approved by the Board. In a number of cases, the Board has also requested implementation reports by the Bank's Management or, less frequently, has entrusted the Panel itself with the assessment of compliance of the implemented measures.[193] As experience with cases on non-labour matters decided by the Inspection Panel suggests, this can have a variety of effects: In a number of cases the Inspection Panel's reports appear to have put pressure on the Bank's operational staff to improve the monitoring of the relevant social requirements of the loan agreement at hand. In other cases, the Bank's staff has reacted to the Panel's report by adopting action plans or specific project policies addressing the issues raised by the complainants.[194] The Inspection Panel has also clarified the scope of the Bank's operational policies.[195] While short-term gains do not necessarily translate into long-term improvements especially regarding structural problems of the relevant projects,[196] the Inspection Panel's

[185]World Bank Inspection Panel (2014) Operating Procedures, para. 41.

[186]Ibid., para. 43 lit. a.

[187]World Bank Group (1999) Clarification of the Board's Second Review of the Inspection Panel, para. 9 and World Bank Inspection Panel (2014) Operating Procedures, para. 49.

[188]As of June 2014, out of the 77 cases completed by the Panel only 27 were reportedly investigated. See Wong and Mayer (2015), p. 504.

[189]Ibid., pp. 505–506.

[190]Ibid., p. 506. See on this approach Bugalski (2016), pp. 42–44, who also notes problems of this approach due to, among others, the absence of a fully-fledged framework for dispute settlement under the Panel's Operating Procedures.

[191]See Wahi (2006), p. 358 and Carrascott and Guernsey (2008), p. 601.

[192]See Wong and Mayer (2015), p. 506.

[193]Ibid., pp. 506–507.

[194]See Clark (1999), p. 17 and Bugalski (2016), pp. 36–38.

[195]See Barlas and Tassoni (2015), p. 493.

[196]See Hunter (2003), p. 210 and also Lagerwall (2010), p. 421.

interventions have arguably triggered a cultural change inside the Bank towards compliance in certain areas.[197] In other cases, the World Bank has withdrawn offers for financial support or revoked project contracts that were already being carried out, sometime resulting in a project stop altogether.[198]

In addition, in a number of cases the Panel's decisions have led to action by the Bank's Management to address alleged violations, such as the compensation of affected actors, the creation of protected areas, or the adoption of specific project-related policies.[199] Importantly, this has, in some cases, occurred even where no investigation has taken place.[200] One example is a complaint filed with the Inspection Panel which alleged child and forced labour to be occurring in projects funded by the World Bank in Uzbekistan. Despite the absence of a specific labour standards safeguard at the time, the Panel held that 'the Project is plausibly linked to the harms alleged in the Request, and that the Request raises important issues of harm and policy non-compliance'.[201] The decision on a fully-fledged investigation by the Panel was deferred though to give Bank staff time to take remedial measures, including monitoring by a third party and further dialogue between the Government and the World Bank.[202] In a follow-up report, the Inspection Panel noted that this led to an arrangement under which the ILO is to monitor forced and child labour regarding Bank projects.[203] Other measures reported by Bank management included putting in place a 'feedback mechanism' regarding the relevant violations, strengthening the Bank's own monitoring of the project sites, and creating an intensified dialogue with the Uzbek Government on these issues.[204] Bank Management has also committed to report on this issue to the Bank's Board of Directors. In this light, the Panel did not recommend starting an investigation.[205] Meanwhile, Uzbek civil society actors criticized that the measures were not sufficient to resolve forced labour in the agricultural sector.[206] They argued, in particular, that the Panel had ceded its scrutiny of the matter merely on the basis of commitments by the

[197]See Wong and Mayer (2015), p. 517.

[198]Ibid., p. 515 and Bugalski (2016), pp. 36–38 with specific examples.

[199]See Lukas (2015), p. 544.

[200]See further Wong and Mayer (2015), p. 516.

[201]See World Bank Inspection Panel (2013), Report and Recommendation, Republic Of Uzbekistan: Second Rural Enterprise Support Project (P109126) and Additional Financing for Second Rural Enterprise Support Project (P126962) (Report No. 83254-UZ), 9 Dec 2013, para. 101.

[202]See ibid., para. 104.

[203]World Bank Inspection Panel, Republic of Uzbekistan: Second Rural Enterprise Support Project (P 109126) and Additional Financing for the Second Rural Enterprise Support Project (P 126962), Final Eligibility Report and Recommendation, Report No. 93222·UZ, 19 Dec 2014, para. 19.

[204]Ibid., para. 18; see also paras. 20–24.

[205]Ibid., para. 37.

[206]Letter to the President of the World Bank by Cotton Campaign, 29 Jan 2015. http://www.cottoncampaign.org/uploads/3/9/4/7/39474145/letter_to_wb_president_january2015.pdf. Accessed 9 Aug 2017.

Bank that had not been implemented to that date.[207] A later statement by a large NGO coalition argued that the ILO's monitoring effort had been limited, also due to Government action discouraging individuals from reporting forced labour, and that forced labour remained widespread.[208] On the whole, this experience suggests that while the Inspection Panel can spark off useful dynamics to increase workers' protection, their overall impact will be modest at best unless the Panel decides to vigorously scrutinize the issues at hand and critically assess relevant remedial action taken by the Bank.

4.3 General Limitations of the Safeguard Policies

A number of general limitations need to be born in mind when considering the effectiveness of the ESF in terms of avoiding labour standards problems in the Bank's projects. An important one relates to the ESF's actual reach. The ESF allows for a significant shift of responsibility regarding environmental and social issues from the Bank to the borrower country.[209] The Bank's ESF may, under certain conditions (see below), be replaced by the borrower's own 'environmental and social framework', including its own domestic law.[210] In the same vein, the World Bank's due diligence and oversight mechanism can be substituted by the borrower's own institutions and procedural arrangements.[211] In such cases, the obligations regarding the Bank's due diligence and monitoring as well as the ESS do no longer apply to the project concerned. Also, the reach of the jurisdiction of the World Bank Inspection Panel in this regard has yet to be fully ascertained. In particular, it is unclear whether the Panel's jurisdiction will in those cases be limited to assessing the Bank's decision to rely on the borrower's framework or whether the Panel will examine the borrower's compliance with its own Environmental and Social

---

[207] See Press Release by Human Rights Watch, World Bank: No Probe of Link to Abuses in Uzbekistan. Decision on Forced Labor 'Shocking,' Rights Advocates Say, 2 Feb 2015, available at https://www.hrw.org/news/2015/02/02/world-bank-no-probe-link-abuses-uzbekistan. Accessed 9 Aug 2017 and Press Release by Bretton Woods Project, World Bank rejects investigation into Uzbek child and forced labour, 31 Mar 2015, available at http://www.brettonwoodsproject.org/2015/03/world-bank-rejects-investigation-into-uzbek-child-and-forced-labour/. Accessed 9 Aug 2017.

[208] See Joint Letter to the World Bank by The Cotton Campaign et al., 19 Nov 2015, available at https://www.hrw.org/news/2015/11/20/joint-letter-world-bank. Accessed 9 Aug 2017.

[209] See prominently ES Policy, paras. 23–29. For a critique of this proposed shift to a 'Country Systems Approach' under the earlier safeguards see already Tan (2008), pp. 97–98.

[210] See ES Policy, para. 24. Under the Bank's preceding safeguards this had only been exceptionally possible and been applied in a negligible fraction of Bank-supported projects. See World Bank (2015) Operational Policy 4.00, Piloting the Use of Borrower Systems to Address Environmental and Social Safeguard Issues in Bank-Supported Projects and World Bank Independent Evaluation Group (2010), Safeguards and Sustainability Policies in a Changing World. An Independent Evaluation of World Bank Group Experience, p. 85.

[211] See ES Policy, para. 24.

Framework to the extent that it replaces the Bank's ESF.[212] Importantly, such a replacement of the Bank's ESS is, in principle, possible for any project, including those labelled by the Bank as high risk activities.[213]

The condition for this is that the borrower's framework 'is likely to address the risks and impacts of the project, and enable the project to achieve objectives materially consistent with the ESSs'.[214] The specific meaning of this requirement has yet to be ascertained. Despite the fact that the use of the borrowers' framework is dealt with in several Bank documents[215] key aspects of the relevant criteria and procedure are not fully laid out. This includes, in particular, the question of when a borrower's legal and institutional framework is 'likely to address' relevant risks or to achieve 'objectives materially consistent' with the Bank's standards.[216] Further, while the Bank is required to assess the borrower's legal and institutional framework and consult with relevant stakeholders,[217] the assessment's content is largely left in the vague. For example, the Bank's Draft ES Procedure states that the assessment 'may include an evaluation of specific aspects of the Borrower's ES Framework', which is however to be 'carried out only where there is a reasonable likelihood that the specified aspects could be utilized'.[218] The leeway these provisions grant to the Bank's staff raises doubts as to whether the assessments will be sufficiently comprehensive to spot all existing deficiencies of the borrowers' frameworks. This applies particularly to areas where the Bank has accumulated limited expertise as in the area of labour standards and may not be able to anticipate relevant project risks or deficiencies in the borrower's framework. In order to prevent the Bank's ESF from being circumvented, it will therefore be crucial for the Bank to provide clear guidance on how the relevant requirements are to be applied.[219]

Also, the application of the ESS to 'subprojects' within the project financed by the Bank is largely left to the discretion of the Bank and its respective borrower. Only for 'high risk subprojects' a full assessment by the Bank's borrower is required.[220] For any other projects, including those involving 'substantial risks',

---

[212] See Dann and Riegner (2017), p. 16.

[213] Cf. ES Policy, para. 23.

[214] Ibid. This wording is reproduced in ESS 1, para. 19 and World Bank (2016) Bank Procedure. Environmental and Social Procedure. Deliberative Working Draft (hereinafter 'ES Procedure'), para. 45.

[215] See ES Policy, paras. 23–29; ESS 1, paras. 19–22; Draft ES Procedure, paras. 44–57 and World Bank (2016) Information Note, Assessing the Borrower's Environmental and Social Framework. Deliberative Working Draft, para. 4.

[216] ES Policy, para. 23.

[217] Ibid., paras. 25–26. Where 'gaps' between the borrower's 'environmental and social framework' and the ESS are apparent, the Bank can also assist the borrower to "address gaps[...] and strengthen the Borrower's ES Framework", ES Policy, para. 27.

[218] Draft ES Procedure, para. 46.

[219] For an argument in the same vein see Dann and Riegner (2017), p. 15.

[220] ES Policy, para. 37 (a).

merely the borrower's domestic law and 'any requirement of the ESSs that the Bank deems relevant to such subprojects' applies.[221] Depending on how the relevant requirements will be applied in practice, these features may render it rather easy for the Bank to discharge itself of the respective requirements. In addition, lower requirements also apply to the Bank's financial support to financial intermediaries.[222]

A broader limitation concerns the scope of the ESS in general. The World Bank Environmental and Social Policy defines as its scope of application the Bank's 'investment project financing'.[223] Other key activities of the Bank are expressly excluded from the scope. Examples are the Bank's aforesaid 'Development Policy Lending' and the 'Program-for-Results' lending.[224] While the Bank's relevant policies provide for a social impact assessment for these activities, the labour standards issues to be considered under such an assessment are not set out in detail[225] and no effective recourse mechanism is available to stakeholders.[226] Also, World Bank strategy documents, such as the 'Country Partnership Frameworks', are not covered by the ESF although these may include labour law reforms as part of the development agenda established for the country concerned.[227] Similarly, policy advice instruments, such as the aforesaid 'Doing Business Report', do not fall under the ESF. These World Bank instruments continue thus to not be subject to specific safeguard policies on labour standards.

5 Conclusion

This chapter has looked at the potential of the World Bank's labour standards safeguard policies for protecting workers employed in relation to projects financed by the Bank. The importance of such policies is highlighted by the problematic labour standards record of the Bank's activities, despite its discourse becoming gradually more labour-friendly.

---

[221] Ibid., para. 37 (b).

[222] See ESS 9, in particular paras. 7–9.

[223] ES Policy, para. 7. See for the scope of these operations World Bank (2013) Operational Policy 10.00—Investment Project Financing, revised July 2014, para. 1.

[224] ES Policy, para 7, Fn. 12.

[225] See, e.g., World Bank (2012) Operational Policy 8.60—Development Policy Lending, revised July 2014, para. 9 and World Bank (2015) Bank Policy. Program-for-Results Financing, section III, paras. 1 (c) and 8.

[226] On the Bank's Poverty and Social Impact Assessments and limitations see, e.g., Darrow (2003), pp. 265–267 noting significant implementation deficits in this regard.

[227] Such elements continue to be included into World Bank's development programming devices. See, e.g., the 2013 Country Assistance Strategy Paper on Benin, p. 44 which mentions the 'passage of a new labor code' as an envisaged 'milestone' under the results area on an 'Improved Investment Climate'.

The World Bank's overhauled safeguard policies, the Environmental and Social Framework, sets out, for the first time, detailed labour standards requirements for the Bank's staff and its borrowers regarding public sector projects. It comes with a comprehensive procedural framework, requiring Bank staff to systematically take into account labour standards matters in their project investments. Also, the new policy brings such labour standards issues under the scrutiny of the World Bank Inspection Panel which has in some cases triggered remedial action by the Bank, among other effects. The experience with the Inspection Panel—and its sister organization, the CAO—suggests that, at least in some cases, trade unions and NGOs may be able to use the safeguards to put pressure on the Bank with a view to remedying labour standards-related project deficiencies. In this sense, it represents a clear step forward for the protection of labour standards in the context of Bank-funded projects.

Nonetheless important limitations remain. For one, the adoption of labour standards safeguards by the WBG involves a process of appropriation in which the relevant standards are submitted to the institutions' operational logic and apparent market constraints.[228] Notably, the Bank deviates, contrary to what its policy statements suggest, from the ILO's Core Labour Standards in a number of respects, in particular where insisting on full compliance therewith might complicate the implementation of the project. Also, different standards are applied depending on the workers' link with the borrower, which enables borrowers to avoid the respective obligations by adjusting the structure of the project.

For another, a number of factors in-built in the World Bank's safeguard policies may impede their effective use to address labour standards violations. This includes, in particular, the outsourcing of responsibility for the implementation of the safeguard policies from the Bank to its borrowers by entrusting them with conducting the relevant due diligence on labour standards. A similar problem are the increased options for substituting the Bank's requirements and procedures by the borrowers' own legal and institutional framework. Also, the various discretionary elements in the complaint procedure before the Inspection Panel and in the safeguard policies themselves[229] limit their corrective potential vis-à-vis the Bank's operations. These features may also be read as an expression of the pressure that is incumbent on the Bank to ensure a rapid and uncomplicated disbursement of funds to remain a competitive lender and thereby ensure their 'organisational survival',[230]

[228] See for a general argument in this regard Wills (2012), pp. 13–14. For a similar point regarding human rights in general and the right to development in particular see Anghie (2000), pp. 253–254.

[229] For a similar point see also Bugalski (2016), p. 30, analysing an earlier draft of the ESF.

[230] Tan (2008), p. 93. In particular, the shift of responsibility for social and environmental assessments from the Bank to its borrowers can be seen as a reaction to concerns that the approach of the existing safeguards was too costly and put the Bank at a disadvantage vis-à-vis its competitors. See ibid., pp. 98–99.

also in the face of increasing competition from new development finance institutions.[231]

Finally, there is a risk that the debate revolving around the Bank's safeguard policies might result in a distraction from other policy fields pertaining to the Bank that are problematic from a labour standards perspective. Indeed, the World Bank's Draft Safeguard Policies expressly exclude the Bank's development policy lending and policy advice instruments. Moreover, the Bank's adoption of safeguard policies should not prevent reflections on how to create or strengthen external mechanisms to hold the Bank accountable for labour standards violations, be it in international or domestic fora.[232] More creative thinking about such outside mechanisms may also provide a political incentive for the Bank to further strengthen its internal mechanisms in this regard. It is clear though that pressure from trade unions and other civil society actors will be vital if any further progress is to occur regarding the alignment of World Bank operations with labour standards, both on paper and, more importantly, in practice.

References

Abouharb R, Cingranelli D (2007) Human rights and structural adjustment. Cambridge University Press, Cambridge

Anghie A (2000) Time present and time past: globalization, international financial institutions, and the third world. N Y Univ J Int Law Polit 32:243–290

Anner M, Caraway T (2010) International institutions and workers' rights: between labor standards and market flexibility. Stud Comp Int Dev 45:151–169

Arp B (2012) El Banco Mundial entre el apoyo a grandes inversiones y la protección de los derechos humanos. Estudios sobre el "Ombudsman" y Asesor en Materia de Observancia de la Corporación Financiera Internacional. Revista Instituto Interamericano de Derechos Humanos 55:123–146

Asrani S, Dann P (2014) International Finance Corporation (IFC). In: Wolfrum R (ed) Max Planck Encyclopedia of Public International Law. Oxford University Press, Oxford. Available via DIALOG. http://opil.ouplaw.com/home/epil. Accessed 9 Aug 2017

Bakvis P (2009) The World Bank's doing business report: a last fling for the Washington consensus? Tran Eur Rev Labour Res 15:419–438

Bakvis P, McCoy M (2008) Core labour standards and international organizations: what inroads has labour made? Friedrich Ebert Stiftung, Bonn

Barlas D, Tassoni T (2015) Improving service delivery through voice and accountability. The experience of the World Bank inspection panel. World Bank Leg Rev 6:477–493

Berber Agtas Ö (2009) Promoting core labour standards through the performance standards of the IFC: the case of Turkey, Global Union Research Network Discussion Paper No. 8. ILO, Geneva

Berg J, Cazes S (2008) Policymaking gone awry: the labor market regulations of the doing business indicators. Comp Labor Law Policy J 29:349–381

[231]This includes in particular the BRICS-led New Development Bank and the China-led Asia Infrastructure Investment Bank. See further Bugalski (2016), pp. 3–4.

[232]For a substantial analysis on human rights issues in general see Tan (2008), pp. 106–115.

Blanton RG, Blanton SL, Peksen D (2015) The impact of IMF and World Bank programs on labor rights. Polit Res Q 68(2):324–336
Bradlow D, Naudé Fourie A (2013) The operational policies of the World Bank and the international finance corporation. Int Organ Law Rev 10:3–80
Bugalski N (2016) The demise of accountability at the World Bank? Am Univ Int Law Rev 31 (1):1–56
Burrow S (2014) .World Bank's Investment Ratings Still at Odds with Human Rights and Poverty Reduction. http://www.rightingfinance.org/?p=848. Accessed 9 Aug 2017
CAO (2015) Annual Report 2015. Fifteen Years of Impact, Washington
CAO (2017) Compliance Monitoring Report. IFC Investment in Avianca S.A., Colombia. Project #25899, Washington
Carrascott ER, Guernsey AK (2008) The World Bank's inspection panel: promoting true accountability through arbitration. Cornell Int Law J 41:577–629
Clark DL (1999) A Citizen's guide to the World Bank inspection panel, 2nd edn. Center for International Environmental Law, Washington
Dann P, Riegner M (2017) Safeguard-Review der Weltbankgruppe. Ein neuer Goldstandard für das globale Umwelt- und Sozialrecht? Deutsche Gesellschaft für Internationale Zusammenarbeit (GIZ), Bonn/Eschborn
Darrow M (2003) Between light and shadow: the World Bank, the International Monetary Fund and international human rights law. Hart, Oxford
Diller JM (2015) Pluralism and privatisation in transnational labour regulation: experience of the International Labour Organization. In: Blackett A, Trebilcock A (eds) Research handbook on transnational labour law. Edward Elgar, Cheltenham, pp 329–342
Ebert FC (2013) Kohärenz der Weltbank mit den arbeitsrechtlichen Mindeststandards der Internationalen Arbeitsorganisation? In: Däubler W, Zimmer R (eds) Arbeitsvölkerrecht. Nomos, Baden-Baden, pp 72–83
Ebert FC (2014) The integration of labour standards concerns into the environmental and social policy of the international finance corporation. Verfassung und Recht in Übersee 47:229–249
Fujita S (2013) The World Bank, Asian Development Bank and human rights. Developing standards of transparency, participation and accountability. Edward Elgar, Cheltenham
Global Unions (2007) The role of the IFIs in supporting decent work and countering the risks of financial globalisation. In: Statement to the 2007 Annual Meetings of the IMF and World Bank. Washington DC
Guder L (2011) International development association (IDA). In: Wolfrum R (ed) Max Planck Encyclopedia of Public International Law. Oxford University Press, Oxford. Available via DIALOG. http://opil.ouplaw.com/home/epil. Accessed 9 Aug 2017
Human Rights Watch (2014) World Bank: Investigate Uzbekistan's Forced Labor. Inspection Panel Should Ensure Funds Not Used for Abuses. https://www.hrw.org/news/2014/12/17/world-bank-investigate-uzbekistans-forced-labor. Accessed 9 Aug 2017
Hunter D (2003) Using the World Bank inspection panel to defend the interests of project-affected people. Chic J Int Law 4:201–211
IBRD, IDA (1993) The World Bank Inspection Panel Resolution (Res. No. IBRD 93-10, Res. No. IDA 93-6). http://siteresources.worldbank.org/EXTINSPECTIONPANEL/Resources/ResolutionMarch2005.pdf. Accessed 9 Aug 2017
IFC, World Bank (2010) Doing business 2011. Making a difference for entrepreneurs. World Bank, Washington
IFC, World Bank (2013) Doing business 2014. Understanding regulations for small and medium-size enterprises. World Bank, Washington
IMF (2016) Poverty Reduction Strategies in IMF-supported Programs. Available via DIALOG. https://www.imf.org/en/About/Factsheets/Sheets/2016/08/01/16/32/Poverty-Reduction-Strategy-in-IMF-supported-Programs. Accessed 9 Aug 2017
Independent Evaluation Group (2008) Doing business: an independent evaluation. Taking the measure of the World Bank- IFC doing business indicators. World Bank, Washington

ITUC (2011) Labour standards in World Bank Group lending. Lessons learned and next steps. ITUC, Brussels
ITUC (2015) Avianca-Colombia: IFC Should Follow Ombudsman's Recommendations for Labour Standards Compliance, Say Unions. Press Release of 19 May 2015. http://www.ituc-csi.org/avianca-colombia-ifc-should-follow?lang=de. Accessed 9 Aug 2017
Janse R (2014) (Why) was the World Bank supposed to be a nonpolitical organization? An interpretation of the original meaning and rationale of article 4(10) of the articles of agreement of the International Bank for reconstruction and development, 1941–1948. J Hist Int Law 16:113–155
Kim ET (2008) Unlikely formation: contesting and advancing Asian/African "Indigenousness" at the World Bank inspection panel. N Y Univ J Int Law Polit 41:131–158
Krajewski M (2013) Investment guarantees and international obligations to reduce poverty: a human rights perspective. In: Nadakavukaren Schefer K (ed) Poverty and the International Economic Legal System. Duties to the world's poor, pp 189–210
Kuddo A, Robalino D, Weber M (2015) Balancing regulations to promote jobs. From employment contracts and unemployment benefits. World Bank, Washington
Lagerwall A (2010) Le Panel d'Inspection. Jouit-il de l'independance necessaire pour controler les agissements de la Banque Mondiale? Revue Belge de Droit International 2010(2):389–422
La Hovary C (2009) Les droits fondamentaux au travail. Origines, statut et impact en droit international. Presses Universitaire de France, Paris
Loewenfeld A (2008) International economic law. Oxford University Press, Oxford
López-Jacoiste E (2015) El control *cuasi jurisdiccional* del Panel de Inspección del Banco Mundial. Anuario Español de Derecho Internacional 29:111–164
Lukas K (2015) The inspection panel of the World Bank. An effective extrajudicial complaint mechanism? World Bank Leg Rev 6:531–544
Malli M (2014) Assessing capacity development in World Bank 'program-for-results' financing. Verfassung und Recht in Übersee 47:250–269
Maupain F (2013) The future of the International Labour Organization in the global economy. Hart, Oxford/Portland
McBeth A (2010) International economic actors and human rights. Routledge, London/New York
Michaels R (2009) Comparative law by numbers? Legal origins thesis, doing business reports, and the silence of traditional comparative law. Am J Comp Law 57:765–795
Murie F (2009) BWI strategies to promote decent work through procurement: the example of the Bujagali dam project in Uganda. GURN Discussion Paper No. 9. ILO, Geneva
Murphy H (2014) The World Bank and Core labour standards: between flexibility and regulation. Rev Int Polit Econ 21:399–431
Naudé Fourie A (2009) The World Bank Inspection Panel and Quasi-Judicial Oversight. In Search of the 'Judicial Spirit' in Public International Law. Eleven International Publishing, Utrecht
O'Brien R (2014) Antagonism and accommodation: the labor-IMF/World Bank relationship. In: Kaasch A, Stubbs P (eds) Transformations in global and regional social policies. Springer, Heidelberg, pp 153–174
Ragazzi M (2012) World Bank Group. In: Wolfrum R (ed) Max Planck Encyclopedia of Public International Law (Vol. X). Oxford University Press, Oxford, pp 909–912
Santos A (2009) Labor flexibility – legal reform and economic development. Va J Int Law 50:43–106
Saper B (2012) The international financial corporation's Compliance Advisor/Ombudsman (CAO): an examination of accountability and effectiveness from a global administrative law perspective. Int Law Polit 44:1279–1329
Sarfaty GA (2012) Values in transition. Human rights and the culture of the World Bank. Stanford University Press, Stanford
Schlemmer-Schulte S (2014) International Bank for Reconstruction and Development (IBRD). In: Wolfrum R (ed) Max Planck Encyclopedia of Public International Law. Oxford University Press, Oxford. Available via DIALOG. http://opil.ouplaw.com/home/epil. Accessed 9 Aug 2017

Tan C (2008) Mandating rights and limiting mission creep: holding the World Bank and the International Monetary Fund Accountable for human rights violations. Hum Rights Int Legal Discourse 2:79:116
Tan C (2011) Governance through development. Poverty reduction strategies, international law and the disciplining of third world states. Routledge, Abingdon
Trebilcock A (2015) Due diligence on labour issues – opportunities and limits of the UN guiding principles on business and human rights. In: Blackett A, Trebilcock A (eds) Research handbook on transnational labour law. Edward Elgar, Cheltenham, pp 93–107
Wahi N (2006) Human rights accountability of the IMF and the World Bank: a critique of existing mechanisms and articulation of a theory of horizontal accountability. U C Davis J Int Law Policy 12(2):331–407
Wong Y, Mayer B (2015) The World Bank's inspection panel. A tool for accountability? World Bank Legal Rev 6:495–530
Wills J (2012) The world turned upside down? Neo-liberalism, socioeconomic rights, and hegemony. Leiden J Int Law 27:11–35
Woods N (2001) Making the IMF and the World Bank more accountable. Int Aff 77:83–100
World Bank (2007) Standard bidding Documents – Procurement of Works and User's Guide. http://siteresources.worldbank.org/INTPROCUREMENT/Resources/Works-4-07-ev1.pdf. Accessed 9 Aug 2017
World Bank (2009) Guidance note for World Bank Group staff on the use of the doing business employing workers indicator for policy advice. World Bank, Washington
World Bank (2012) World development report 2013. Jobs. World Bank, Washington
World Bank (2015) Doing business 2016: measuring regulatory quality and efficiency. World Bank, Washington
World Bank Inspection Panel (2013) Report and Recommendation, Republic Of Uzbekistan: Second Rural Enterprise Support Project (P109126) and Additional Financing for Second Rural Enterprise Support Project (P126962) (Report No. 83254-UZ). http://siteresources.worldbank.org/EXTINSPECTIONPANEL/Resources/PanelReport_Uzbekistan_SRESP_Dec9_2013.pdf. Accessed 9 Aug 2017

Part III
Business Conduct and Labour Standards

Soft Standards and Hard Consequences: Why Transnational Companies Commit to Respect International Labour and Social Standards, and How This Relates to Business and Regulation

Katja Gehne

Contents

Abstract Companies increasingly promise to respect widely recognized labour and social standards, mostly referring to well-established international standards in this field. This commitment can create a hard law effect of an originally soft law commitment. While there are key drivers behind this development such as customer and investor requirements or risks of brand-damage, companies have begun to broaden their business perspective: they seek 'shared value' for the company and the society when respecting international labour standards, thereby building valuable social and human capital that represents an important element of business success and resilience. This short contribution aims to shed some light on this phenomenon of private regulation as part of transnational regulation, its drivers, and the sustainability management approach.

This article is issued at the responsibility of the author alone, and does not reflect views of her professional work context. I am grateful to Nazli Aghazadeh for her kind and knowledgeable support.

K. Gehne (✉)
BASF, Ludwigshafen, Germany
e-mail: katja.gehne@gmx.net

H. Gött (ed.), *Labour Standards in International Economic Law*,
https://doi.org/10.1007/978-3-319-69447-4_14

1 Introduction

Responsible business conduct has a long standing tradition, going back to antiquity.[1] Business discovered what is nowadays called social or human capital in the early twentieth century when developing social benefits schemes for employees or investing in local communities to build trust, commitment and motivation with respect to the company.[2] Around the same time, newly established international organizations, such as the International Labour Organization (ILO) and later the United Nations (UN), inspired by the epoch's rising humanism, started forging international legal standards in the field of workers' protection and labour law. While both the business approach and the normative approach of international organizations engaging in global standard setting spring from the same humanist *zeitgeist*, their motivations have been different in character and effect. Business sees and seeks related benefits (e.g. employee commitment to the company, effectiveness, and stability of workforce) or tries to mitigate business harm (e.g. through strikes or reputational damage) responding to what relates as business opportunity or risk. Public international regulation, on the other hand, coins standards of conduct out of the *zeitgeist* through a complex process of decision-making and debate with protection of human dignity and liberty being strong ethical drivers. The latter normative approach creates a binding, non-relative frame, not necessarily responsive to business needs, but constituting an important standard of protection. The business approach is non-binding and has been ethically questioned by some stakeholders, as business interest remains a key driver behind responsible business conduct in practice. Nevertheless, as we will see below, this approach has a potential to create positive 'shared value'[3] for the society and has a capacity to be at the same time well-tailored to companies' flexibility needs and rightsholders' demands.

A relatively new phenomenon in this context is companies' public commitment or claim to respect widely recognized international labour and social standards, sometimes referring to related international soft law instruments such as the UN Guiding Principles on Business and Human Rights,[4] the Organization for Economic

---

[1]Schwalbach and Klink (2015), pp. 178 et seq.

[2]The widespread term 'Corporate Social Responsibility (CSR)' that can be related to this business approach has been interpreted in numerous ways and put into a broad variety of business concepts, including, for example, the CSR definition of the European Union, see European Commission (2011) A renewed EU strategy 2011–2014 for Corporate Social Responsibility, COM(2011) 681, p. 6. The term CSR can thus hardly be converged to one common definition or approach (see on the variety of approaches Schwartz and Carroll (2003), p. 503 and on CSR as a continuously developing concept Schneider (2015), p. 23). The strength of the term is, however, that it groups and explains on the basis of all its interpretations most business activities related to socially responsible behavior and activities, and can thus be seen as some kind of general superscription to those activities. See on CSR and social/human capital building Habisch and Schwarz (2015), pp. 113 et seq.

[3]Porter and Kramer (2011), p. 6.

[4]Report of the Special Representative of the Secretary, Guiding Principles on Business and Human Rights: Implementing the United Nations 'Protect, Respect and Remedy' Framework, UN Human Rights Council, A/HRC/17/31, 21 March 2011.

Cooperation and Development (OECD) Guidelines for Multinational Enterprises[5] or the ILO Tripartite Declaration of Principles Concerning Multinational Enterprises and Social Policy (ILO MNE Declaration).[6,7] These kinds of commitments are often related to so-called 'non-financial reporting' as a complement to the usual annual 'financial reporting'.[8] Thereby, a company reports on its activities in the domain of socially responsible business conduct, most often according to a benchmark of sustainability indicators and business evaluation as provided by, for example, the Global Reporting Initiative (GRI). Recent regulatory initiatives in this domain establish companies' obligations to non-financial reporting.[9] This kind of reporting and positioning creates external expectations (e.g. by customers, investors, civil society) that put pressure on the company to effectively respect these norms. Mainly customers that seek procurement from responsibly acting firms increasingly ask for evidenced commitment related to international labour and social standards, and make adherence to the standards part of or condition to the business relationship. This may result in a rather 'hard' binding effect of an originally voluntary or 'soft' commitment to international labour and social standards.[10] This 'private regulation' phenomenon seems an interesting twist in companies' history of responsible business conduct in the field of labour and social standards. Global trade unions have responded to that trend by urging for so called transnational company agreements (TCA) by which employers and unions agree upon an international industrial relations instrument regarding the respect for international labour and social standards.[11] Other NGO-related initiatives offer support for companies in managing related challenges, such as Social Accountability International (SAI)[12] or the Fair Labor Association (FLA)[13] which include auditing and certification. The following sections aim to give background information from a practitioner's perspective and a possible explanation to the 'private regulation' trend in the field of international labour and social standards that has a potential to play a useful complementary role in transnational regulation.

---

[5]OECD (2011).

[6]ILO (2017).

[7]See Blackett (2001), pp. 406 et seq.

[8]See as an example on this issue the 'Accountability for Sustainability' Initiative by the Prince of Wales, https://www.accountingforsustainability.org/. Accessed 12 Oct 2016 and the Global Reporting Initiative (GRI), https://www.globalreporting.org/. Accessed 9 Aug 2017. In terms of company practice see KPMG (2012).

[9]See for example EU Parliament and Council Directive 2014/95/EU *amending Directive 2013/34/EU as regards disclosure of non-financial and diversity information by certain large undertakings and groups*, O.J. L 330/1 (2014).

[10]See on possible legal consequences of 'soft commitments' Johnsen and Ramadori (2016).

[11]Fick (2014), pp. 11 et seq. and Hadwiger (2014), pp. 9 et seq.

[12]SAI that established the wide spread standard Social Accountability (SA) 8000 that serves as a basis for certification, see http://www.sa-intl.org/index.cfm?fuseaction=Page.ViewPage&pageId=1689. Accessed 12 Oct 2016.

[13]See http://www.fairlabor.org/. Accessed 12 Oct 2016.

2 The Drivers

In a nutshell, there are three main drivers of companies' commitment to and reporting of international labour and social standards. First of all, from a customer's perspective: more and more customers make proven respect for international labour and social standards a condition for business. This reflects a trend in end-users' demand: more and more people are concerned about working conditions related to what they buy. Global media coverage gives instant and colourful insights in exploitive working conditions in so-called 'sweatshops' that constitute forms of modern slavery under conditions of severe poverty.[14] Companies selling to end-users are increasingly driven by risks of brand-damage due to complicity in human rights violations. They put pressure on their suppliers to guarantee responsible business conduct, including on-site controls via audits.[15]

Secondly, the financial market gets more and more influenced by non-financial (environmental, social and governance) factors of responsible business conduct.[16] This includes respect for widely recognized international labour and social standards. There is an increasing number of firms' rankings with respect to their social performance and responsibility that are used as benchmarks for responsible investment, such as the Dow Jones Sustainability Index (DJSI)[17] or the Principles of Responsible Investment (PRI).[18] Besides, principles of responsible business conduct, such as the Equator Principles[19] related to the financial sector, closely linked to the International Financial Corporation's (IFC) performance standards,[20] have become part of investment decisions as a tool to manage environmental and social risks in investment projects. Decisions on credits or investment guarantees, e.g. Hermes' guarantees granted by the German government for foreign investments, include criteria on responsible business conduct.[21]

Finally, civil society plays an important role, expressed in the ethical claim to respect international labour and social standards, voiced by civil society organizations, parliaments and people, and fuelled by modern media: social networks spread news quickly, show pictures brusquely, cameras film and photos are taken quickly

[14]Under conditions of severe poverty people are dependent on anything they can get to survive. This allows for conditions of exploitation and human rights abuse such as child labour, excessive working hours and overtime, no living wage, sexual abuse, harassment and violence, or careless exposition to hazards and toxic substances. For an exemplary analysis of labour conditions related to the electronic industry in China, see China Labor Watch (2012).

[15]Examples of quickly growing platforms that support companies in monitoring these requirements: SEDEX, http://www.sedexglobal.com/; Together for Sustainability (TfS), http://tfs-initiative.com/; Business Social Compliance Initiative (BSCI), http://www.bsci-intl.org/ and ECOVADIS, http://www.ecovadis.com/. All accessed 12 Oct 2016.

[16]White (2015).

[17]See for more information http://www.sustainability-indices.com/. Accessed 12 Oct 2016.

[18]See for more information https://www.unpri.org/. Accessed 12 Oct 2016.

[19]See for more information http://equator-principles.com/. Accessed 12 Oct 2016.

[20]See IFC (2012).

[21]See for more information http://www.agaportal.de/. Accessed 12 Oct 2016.

everywhere. As for politics, legitimacy and success of business actions depend on peoples' acceptance and demand: if society does not approve of business conduct, it is difficult for a business to survive (license to operate).[22] If a business does not seize and seek opportunities to innovate, compete and differentiate in line with societal demand, it will fail on the markets.

3 Sustainability Management: Minimizing Risks and Creating Value

While for some companies the pressure through customers' requirements is the key driver, others have taken an explicit sustainability management approach that starts out with a sustainability business strategy with related responsible business values and business goals.[23] The key idea is to broaden the business perspective: not only numbers, marketing and sales determine business, but also an aim to contribute to societal needs that are related to environmental and social challenges and concerns. This does not mean that businesses' purpose becomes a contribution to the society. Businesses' role remains to earn money, sell and grow. The sustainability business concept is a broadened approach to business opportunities and value creation, taking into account societal challenges. As business in this context works with social or environmental concerns and needs, there is a high potential of business cases that create value for business *and* the society,[24] be it with respect to products (increasing demand and need for socially responsible goods or solutions to upcoming environmental (e.g. soil degradation, emissions) or social (e.g. accessibility to clean water) problems, be it in relation to employees (create and maintain continuous workforce capacity, motivation and commitment through social benefits, openness and care)[25] or the public (report on business responsibility and dilemmas to create social capital of brand trust). In sum, the scope of business to find solutions or react to challenges and problems related to all aspects along the value chain is widened and with that the potential of value creation.

There are roughly two key starting points of sustainability driven business. First, the so-called materiality analysis, a stakeholder-based methodology to identify and prioritize material aspects that reflect a company's economic, social and environmental impacts that have significant influence on relevant stakeholders' decisions.[26]

---

[22]Business needs the ongoing approval of its stakeholders, including broad social acceptance as a condition for survival and success, see for a definition Lin-Hi (2017) and Sustainable Business Council/BusinessNZ Major Companies Group (2013/14).

[23]See for example BASF (2015).

[24]Porter and Kramer (2011), p. 6.

[25]Doyé (2016).

[26]See the G4 Sustainability Reporting Guidelines, https://www.globalreporting.org/information/g4/Pages/default.aspx. Accessed 12 Oct 2016.

Internal and external stakeholders of a company are systematically interviewed with respect to pre-selected possible relevant topics to choose the most relevant sustainability topics for the company. Given the increasing concern of customers and investors regarding human rights and the related business impact, international labour and social standards will for most businesses be a likely part of the so-determined key sustainability topics of a company that undertakes the materiality analysis.[27] Second, sustainability management means systematic scanning of the business context (stakeholders, markets, customers' needs) to identify business opportunities, potential values or risks with respect to a valuable contribution to the environment or the society.

International labour and social standards as a sustainability topic touch upon human resources management and, if a company has committed to adhere to standards, it forms part of compliance.[28] In terms of risks, there is the business risk of not responding to customers' needs of products or services issued on a proven basis of responsible business conduct, and thus losing a stake in the relevant markets. Another prominent risk relates to a company's reputation: if cases of child labour or other severe violations of international labour and social standards are attributed to a company, this harms a company's brand, all the more so if the company has positioned itself as a responsibly acting firm. Respect for widely recognized international labour and social standards has become something like a credibility baseline for responsibly acting employers or firms. At the same time, there is the opportunity to differentiate on markets through responsibly produced products. International labour and social standards may also inspire performance in human resources management through value adding approaches such as, for example, related to social benefits (e.g. pension schemes, medical care, accident insurance, health programs), employee development, knowledge management, or principles of a diverse and inclusive workplace that fosters innovation and exchange.[29]

4 Management Processes to Respect International Labour and Social Standards

4.1 Which Standards?

There are numerous standards, platforms and processes in place that support companies' approaches to responsible business management, all of them including international labour and social standards. Some have been established by customers to create platforms that help managing suppliers by setting a common standard and procedure for mutual recognition and to share results of supplier controls to achieve

[27] See for example BASF (2013).
[28] Doyé (2016).
[29] Ibid.

synergies. Examples are SEDEX, a not-for-profit membership organization that aims at improving responsible business conduct in supply chains. Member companies are enabled to share supply chain information on the basis of a common standard called Sedex Members Ethical Trade Audit (SMETA). Another example is Together for Sustainability (TfS), an initiative of the chemical industry that elaborated a standard and audit procedure to improve responsible supply chain management, with the results shared among members. As mentioned above, there are not-for-profit organizations that have started standards initiatives to offer guidance for socially responsible business conduct and certification (e.g. Social Accountability International (SAI)) or issued guidelines for non-financial sustainability reporting (e.g. the Global Reporting Initiative, GRI). There are bodies and organizations that offer sustainability performance evaluation for investors (e.g. DJSI) or developed guidelines for responsible investment (e.g. Equator Principles, International Finance Corporation (IFC) Performance Standard). International organizations have issued guidelines for responsible business conduct, e.g. the International Standards Organization's (ISO) ISO 26000 standard,[30] the OECD Guidelines for Multinational Enterprises, the Global Compact under the auspices of the UN.[31] Companies are confronted with a variety of standards required by stakeholders (mainly investors and customers), including a wide range of additional individual customer codes of responsible business conduct. This complexity implies a relatively high administrative effort to deal with diverse and sometimes very detailed indicators, questions and related audits.

Generally, in the field of international social and labour standards one will meet a certain core set of standards, mostly related to the International Bill of Human Rights and the Covenants and/or the ILO Declarations regarding responsible business conduct and the Declaration on Fundamental Rights and Principles at Work[32] setting out core labour standards or principles concerning multinational enterprises and social policy.[33] On this basis, it seems natural that one should seek to reduce this complexity of standards through mutual recognition and synergies among the standards and stakeholder requirements. There are increasing trends that indicate respective developments, such as common platforms, open choice of standards content with core requirements or the possibility to negotiate mutual recognition.

[30]See http://www.iso.org/iso/home/standards/iso26000.htm. Accessed 12 Oct 2016.

[31]See https://www.unglobalcompact.org/. Accessed 12 Oct 2016.

[32]See ILO Declaration on Fundamental Principles and Rights at Work and its Follow-up, International Labour Conference, adopted on 18 June 1998 and Annex revised 15 June 2010.

[33]See ILO (2017).

4.2 Which Management Process?

In 2008, the Human Rights Council of the UN appointed a Special Representative on Business and Human Rights (Prof. John Ruggie) in an aim to clarify roles and responsibilities of governments and business organizations with regard to human rights. Informed by a thorough research basis, extensive consultations with all implied stakeholders (business, academia, civil society, states and international organizations) his work resulted in the so called 'Protect, Respect and Remedy' Framework on human rights and business that culminated into the adoption of the resulting UN Guiding Principles on Business and Human Rights by the Human Rights Council in 2011, thereby issuing a global standard to deal with risks of human rights violations related to irresponsible business conduct that has been supported by all relevant stakeholders. This marked a milestone in responsible business conduct management. Not only did many existing standards almost instantly align with the UN Guiding Principles that thereby became an important harmonizing factor in the international standards landscape.[34] The UN Guiding Principles also contained an apt-to-practice tool for business: they defined business' responsibility to be distinguished from states' duties regarding human rights and provided a management approach to deal with human rights risks that corresponded to familiar general company risk management such as the Committee of Sponsoring Organizations of the Treadway Commission (COSO) Enterprise Risk Management (ERM).[35]

In a nutshell, according to the UN Guiding Principles, states have the duty to protect human rights, and businesses have the corporate responsibility to respect human rights which is generally translated with 'do no harm' to human rights. To ensure this, companies are supposed to have a three-pronged management process in place that starts out with a policy commitment to respect human rights. Secondly, on this basis, through human rights due diligence, business should identify, prevent, mitigate and remedy actual and potential adverse human rights impacts through effective management processes; at a minimum regarding those rights that are laid down in the International Bill of Human Rights and the ILO's Declaration on Fundamental Principles and Rights at Work. Business is to account for human rights due diligence management processes, including how challenges are addressed.[36] Thereby, management processes and solutions can be flexible and imply solutions over time, mainly regarding specific challenges and dilemma situations; for example, when national law or local conditions hinder respect for human rights. Finally, as a third element, impartial grievance mechanisms and social dialogue are promoted as effective means to identify, address and remedy adverse human rights impacts.

---

[34]See for example the OECD Guidelines for Multinational Enterprises. On the occasion of their 2011 review, a Human Rights Chapter was included in the Guidelines that correspond to the UN Guiding Principles and explicitly refers to these, see OECD (2011), p. 31.

[35]See COSO (2004) and Martens and Perraglia (2016).

[36]Backer (2015), pp. 491 et seq. and Blitt (2012), pp. 43 at seq.

International labour and social standards form part of human rights requirements. The UN Guiding Principles thus equally apply to management processes with respect to international labour and social standards.

5 Conclusion

Although international social and labour standards are not binding for companies, external stakeholder pressure makes that they have become an inherent factor of companies' non-financial risk management. In this context, soft standards at the international level have emerged as a standard of responsible business management. 'Hard regulation' often bears the risk of setting norms that are as the result of a multiple political and private interest debate less responsive to business needs and effective apt-to-practice solutions when it comes to addressing specific challenges of international labour standards. This is why 'private regulation' tendencies in this field merit a closer look as a phenomenon of a legal pluralist system of transnational law.[37] Some go as far as calling this a 'new paradigm' of legal pluralism,[38] a complement to local and national governance structures with tripartism—meaning collaboration among workers/unions, employers and the government—having a potential of complementary cosmopolitan democratic approach to governance.[39]

In this sense, the described companies' initiatives and management approaches related to international labour and social standards could be seen as an element of effective private regulation that smartly embeds natural driving forces of business, a self-regulatory phenomenon that complements public (international or transnational) regulation. As such, this soft law phenomenon merits a closer look when it comes to regulatory challenges in this field, not least with respect to the ongoing national action plan elaboration on the basis of the UN Guiding Principles. What should be sought are principles[40] that allow for targeted flexibility against the backdrop of smartly intertwined private and public remedy systems; what should be avoided are inefficiencies and ineffectiveness of rules through inflexible, detailed and interest-driven 'one-size-that-do-not-fit-all' rules that hinder good shared value solutions for human rights and business. The aim should be not to regulate this private regulation phenomenon but to find ways to smartly embed its natural driving forces in regulation. This could be part of a (para-)legal answer to deficiencies of national states' human rights protection systems that reach their limits when facing globalization.[41]

[37] See for a detailed and historical overview on legal pluralism Tamanaha (2008) and Giudice (2014).

[38] Blackett (2001), p. 421.

[39] Blackett (2001), p. 434.

[40] See with respect to roles of rules and principles in law Gehne (2011), pp. 200 et seq. and 297 et seq.

[41] See with respect to the limits of transnational governance institutions, theoretical underpinnings of mixed approaches to law, and the role of private law in transnational governance Calliess and Zumbansen (2010), pp. 17 and 25.

References

Backer L (2015) Moving forward the UN guiding principles for business and human rights: between enterprise social norm, state domestic legal orders, and the treaty law that might bind them all. Fordham Int Law J 38:456–542

BASF (2013) Report: Economic, Environmental and Social Performance. Available via DIALOG. http://report.basf.com/2013/en/servicepages/filelibrary/files/collection.php. Accessed 12 Oct 2016

BASF (2015) Report: Economic, Environmental and Social Performance. http://www.reports.basf.de/2015/en/servicepages/downloads/files/BASF_Report_2015.pdf. Accessed 12 Oct 2016

Blackett A (2001) Global governance, legal pluralism, and the decentered state: a labor law critique of codes of corporate conduct. Indiana J Glob Legal Stud 8(2):401–447

Blitt R (2012) Beyond Ruggie's guiding principles on business and human rights: charting an embracive approach to corporate human rights compliance. Texas Int Law J 48:33–62

Calliess G-P, Zumbansen P (2010) Rough consensus and running code. A theory of transnational private law. Hart, Oxford

China Labor Watch (2012) Tragedies of Globalization: The Truth Behind Electronics Sweatshops. http://www.chinalaborwatch.org/report/52. Accessed 12 Oct 2016

COSO (2004) Unternehmensweites Risikomanagement: Übergreifendes Rahmenwerk (Zusammenfassung). Available via DIALOG. http://www.coso.org/documents/COSO_ERM_ExecutiveSummary_German.pdf. Accessed 12 Oct 2016

Doyé T (2016) Mit gesellschaftlichem Engagement zum Erfolg, Human Resources Manager. http://www.humanresourcesmanager.de/ressorts/artikel/mit-gesellschaftlichem-engagement-zum-erfolg-835254145?utm_source=www.humanresourcesmanager.de&utm_medium=personalszene&utm_campaign=20160926-szene-hrm-25716&utm_content=641741. Accessed 12 Oct 2016

Fick B (2014) Corporate social responsibility for enforcement of labor rights: are there more effective alternatives. J Articles 9(30):1–25

Gehne K (2011) Nachhaltige Entwicklung als Rechtsprinzip: Normativer Aussagegehalt, Rechtstheoretische Einordnung, Funktionen im Recht. Mohr Siebeck, Tübingen

Giudice M (2014) Global legal pluralism: what's law got to do with it? Oxf J Leg Stud 34 (3):589–608

Habisch A, Schwarz C (2015) CSR als Investition in Human- und Sozialkapital. In: Schneider A, Schmidpeter R (eds) Corporate social responsibility, 2nd edn. Springer, Berlin/Heidelberg, pp 113–134

Hadwiger F (2014) Why Do Multinational Companies Sign Transnational Company Agreements? DFG Graduiertenkolleg (GRK 1597/2): The Economics of the Internationalization of the Law. http://www.siecon.org/online/wp-content/uploads/2014/10/Hadwiger-198.pdf. Accessed 9 Aug 2017

IFC (2012) Performance Standards on Environmental and Social Sustainability. http://www.ifc.org/wps/wcm/connect/c8f524004a73daeca09afdf998895a12/IFC_Performance_Standards.pdf?MOD=AJPERES. Accessed 12 Oct 2016

ILO (2017) Tripartite declaration of principles concerning multinational enterprises and social policy, 5th edn. ILO, Geneva

Johnsen M, Ramadori H (2016) CSR und Recht sind noch immer zwei verschiedene Dinge. Im Blickpunkt: die Diskussion um die Verbindlichkeit und das Zusammenspiel von CSR und Compliance. Deutscher AnwaltSpiegel 2016(5):15–17

KPMG (2012) Sustainability Reporting Systems. A Market Review. https://assets.kpmg.com/content/dam/kpmg/pdf/2012/08/S_CG_5e.pdf. Accessed 12 Oct 2016

Lin-Hi N (2017) Licence to operate. In: Gablers Wirtschaftslexikon. http://wirtschaftslexikon.gabler.de/Definition/licence-to-operate.html. Accessed 9 Aug 2017

Martens F, Perraglia SJ (2016) Risk Through the Eyes of Strategy: How the COSO ERM Framework looks at the relationship between risk and strategy from three perspectives.

https://www.pwc.com/gx/en/services/advisory/consulting/risk/resilience/publications/connecting-risk-and-strategy-in-the-coso-erm-framework.html. Accessed 12 Oct 2016

OECD (2011) OECD guidelines for multinational enterprises. OECD Publishing, Paris

Porter M, Kramer M (2011) Creating shared value. Harv Bus Rev (January-February)4–17

Schneider A (2015) Reifegradmodell CSR – eine Begriffserklärung und -abgrenzung. In: Schneider A, Schmidpeter R (eds) Corporate social responsibility, 2nd edn. Springer, Berlin/Heidelberg, pp 21–42

Schwalbach J, Klink D (2015) Der ehrbare Kaufmann als individuelle Verantwortungskategorie in der CSR-Forschung. In: Schneider A, Schmidpeter R (eds) Corporate social responsibility, 2nd edn. Springer, Berlin/Heidelberg, pp 177–197

Schwartz M, Carroll A (2003) Corporate social responsibility: a three-domain approach. Bus Ethics Q 13(4):503–530

Sustainable Business Council/BusinessNZ Major Companies Group (2013/14) Social Licence to Operate Paper. https://www.sbc.org.nz/__data/assets/pdf_file/0005/99437/Social-Licence-to-Operate-Paper.pdf. Accessed 12 Oct 2016

Tamanaha B (2008) Understanding legal pluralism: past to present, local to global. Sydn Law Rev 30:375–411

White A (2015) Why Sustainability Ratings Matter. MITSloan Management Review. http://sloanreview.mit.edu/article/why-sustainability-ratings-matter/. Accessed 12 Oct 2016

The Promotion of Labour Standards Through International Framework Agreements

Rüdiger Krause

Contents

1 Introduction

Globalization of the economy is not an entirely new phenomenon but can be traced back centuries ago to the conquest of the New World.[1] Nevertheless, its extent and intensity has dramatically increased since the 1990s.[2] Fuelled by the economic interests of firms, enabled by technological developments like the internet, and facilitated by the liberalization of world trade, the number of multinational enterprises (MNEs) as central actors of global economy and the relevance of global supply chains as a consequence of the increasing fragmentation of production has steadily grown.[3] In 2004, the World Commission on the Social Dimension of Globalization identified some 65,000 MNEs with around 850,000 foreign

[1]Cf. Supiot (2003), p. 118.

[2]Even the term 'globalization' did not become popular until the 1990s.

[3]Cf. Baldwin (2013), pp. 13–59; ILO (2016), p. 5, no. 14; Perraton et al. (1998), pp. 134–168; UNCTAD (2013), pp. 121–139 and World Commission on the Social Dimension of Globalization (2004), pp. 24–35, nos. 131–169. For the rise of global value chains, see also WTO (2014), pp. 78–127 and further Gereffi (2005), pp. 1–16, who dates the beginning of offshore outsourcing back to the 1970s.

R. Krause (✉)
Georg-August-University Göttingen, Institute of Labour Law, Göttingen, Germany
e-mail: Lehrstuhl.Krause@jura.uni-goettingen.de

H. Gött (ed.), *Labour Standards in International Economic Law*,
https://doi.org/10.1007/978-3-319-69447-4_15

affiliates.[4] Global supply chains in the broad sense of any cross-border organization of investment, production, and services or the delivery of goods are estimated to count for 60–80% of international trade[5] and over 20% of jobs globally.[6]

The general question whether globalization of economy is an inevitable outcome of the existence of markets and undermines the traditional instruments to limit and regulate market forces at national level is an extensively and controversially debated topic.[7] The same is true with regard to the more specific issue of the impact of globalization on working conditions and labour rights. While not denying that there is a regulatory competition between states which want to attract and retain investors, some scholars challenge that this competition necessarily leads to a 'race to the bottom'.[8] Other scholars are less optimistic and claim to observe a transnational regulatory competition for lowering labour standards.[9] The International Labour Office has given an ambiguous account[10]: On the one side, globalization of the economy has in many cases created jobs that have higher job specifications and remuneration levels[11] and has contributed to compliance with existing labour standards or even to their amelioration. On the other side, there is sufficient evidence that in many cases the pressure on producer prices and delivery times as well as a fierce competition between suppliers account for a deterioration of working conditions and a disregard of labour rights.[12]

In any case, there can be no doubt that globalization has shifted the balance of power between capital and labour,[13] because the traditional actors who limit the managerial power, namely legislator, labour administration, and trade unions, are embedded within national borders. In contrast, MNEs now have an easily accessible exit-option to evade national regulations or national trade unions as bargaining counterparts by relocating their investments.[14] Moreover, the public bodies in developing countries, where MNEs frequently move their production, often lack the resources to monitor compliance with labour standards at workplaces or even

[4]World Commission on the Social Dimension of Globalization (2004), p. 33, no. 159. See also UNCTAD (2009), p. 2: 79,000 MNEs with around 790,000 foreign affiliates with 81.6 million employees in the year 2007.

[5]UNCTAD (2013), p. 135.

[6]ILO (2015), p. 132.

[7]Cox (1997), p. 23 and Held and McGrew (eds) (2003), pp. 19–28.

[8]Deakin (2005), pp. 38–51 and Hepple (2005), pp. 251–276.

[9]Banks (2006), pp. 77–107 and Trubek (2006), pp. 725–733.

[10]ILO (2015), pp. 140–146 and ILO (2016), pp. 2, 17–26.

[11]Empirically affirmed by Powell and Skarbek (2006), pp. 263–274. Positive account from a moral standpoint by Zwolinski (2007), pp. 689–727, who argues on the grounds of autonomy and preferences of sweatshop workers.

[12]Negative account (in the case of trade openness) by Mosley and Uno (2007), pp. 923–948. For a more distinguished understanding of the varieties of exploitation, see Snyder (2010), pp. 187–213.

[13]Trubek (2006), p. 725; see also World Commission on the Social Dimension of Globalization (2004), p. 46, no. 210.

[14]Nice description of capital strategies by Beck (2002), pp. 185–252.

lack the will to do so in order to support domestic enterprises.[15] Terrible examples of grave failures in maintaining sufficient levels of workplace safety are factory fires in *Ali Enterprises*[16] and *Tazreen Fashions*[17] in Pakistan and Bangladesh in 2012 and the collapse of *Rana Plaza* in Bangladesh in 2013[18] which took the lives of more than 1500 people.

To sum up, globalization of economy has led to a 'governance deficit' that can analytically be divided into three categories: (1) a governance deficit in terms of a mismatch between a globalized economy and national institutions in developed countries, (2) a governance deficit due to the weak institutions in developing countries, and (3) a governance deficit as result of the limited scope and regulatory capacity of international and intergovernmental institutions.[19]

Since the end of the 1980s, trade unions have developed a new strategy as a response to the challenges of globalization of the economy and the end of conventional 'embedded liberalism'.[20] Following the ground-breaking agreement between the International Food and Allied Workers' Association (IUF) and the French transnational food company Danone (back then BSN) in 1988, Global Union Federations (GUFs)[21] have increasingly concluded so-called International Framework Agreements (IFAs) (also known as Global Framework Agreements = GFAs). A study of June 2015 identified 112 of such IFAs or GFAs.[22] Compared to the 65,000 MNEs in total this appears to be only a drop in the ocean. However, many large companies have signed those kind of agreements and numbers are increasing.

This chapter addresses the question whether IFAs are an appropriate and effective instrument to promote labour standards in the global economy. The first parts are descriptive. They give a short overview of the development, the content, and the scope of IFAs (Sect. 2), look at the motivation of the actors, i.e. unions and management (Sect. 3), and present the implementation and monitoring mechanisms (Sect. 4). The following part is more theoretical and argues that IFAs are an important element of an emerging global labour governance regime (Sect. 5). The final part is empirical and points out the real impact of IFAs (Sect. 6).

[15]For the complex reasons for this phenomenon, see Kolben (2015), p. 435. See also in this context ITUC (2016).

[16]Cf. CCC (2013a).

[17]Cf. CCC (2013b).

[18]Cf. CCC (2013c).

[19]Gereffi and Mayer (2005), pp. 47–49.

[20]Ruggie (1982), pp. 379–415.

[21]For a comprehensive description, see Platzer and Müller (2009), pp. 111–403.

[22]Hadwiger (2015), p. 77. The European Commission has actually listed in its database on transnational company agreements 267 agreements. http://ec.europa.eu/social/main.jsp?catId=978. Accessed 14 Aug 2017. However, this list contains not only IFAs but also other agreements (e.g. at the European level).

2 Development of International Framework Agreements

The first IFA, as mentioned, dates from 1988 and was concluded between BSN (renamed Danone in 1994) and the IUF.[23] This so-called Common Viewpoint IUF/BSN was an important step in an ongoing discussion process between BSN and the IUF since 1984. In this document, the parties agree to promote coordinated initiatives in four issues, namely (1) training for skills of employees as regards the introduction of new technologies or industrial restructuring, (2) achieve the same level and quality of information both in the economic and social fields, (3) real equality between men and women at work, and (4) the implementation of trade union rights as defined in ILO Conventions Nos. 87, 98 and 135. Furthermore, it was agreed that the operations of the whole BSN group should be covered worldwide. In the next decade, only few IFAs were concluded, in particular because GUFs pursued mainly the political strategy to incorporate ILO standards into the WTO system ('social clause'-debate).[24] After the failure of these attempts, trade unions have turned again to the strategy to influence directly the labour policies in MNEs.[25] To be more precise, GUFs have followed a company-centered approach, which utilizes as a first step the influence of trade unions on the central management of specific companies and as a second step the central management's influence on the periphery of the group. Thus, nearly all existing IFAs have been concluded since the year 2000.

Regarding the signatories to these agreements, on the trade unions side only a handful of GUFs have signed more than 90% of all IFAs.[26] In other words, there is a concentration on specific sectors (metal industry, chemical and energy industry, building and timber industry, and service industry). On the company side, the vast majority of these agreements has been signed by MNEs headquartered in Europe. Among them are 25 companies from Germany, 15 companies from France, 12 companies from Spain, and 10 companies from Sweden. This account demonstrates that the conclusion of IFAs is favoured by the long tradition of social dialogue between management and labour which characterizes the European Social Model[27] and may be described as 'conflict partnership'.[28] In contrast, IFAs are much less frequent in systems with more adversarial industrial relations as they have developed in the

[23]Cf. Gallin (2008), pp. 26–27.

[24]Cf. Anner (2001), pp. 43–63 and Hepple (2005), pp. 56–67. This demand was raised as early as 1970 by Ford, the then General Secretary of the International Textile, Garment and Leather Workers' Federation. For the vast literature on the linkage between global trade and labour standards, see only Barry and Reddy (2006), pp. 545–639; Kolben (2007), pp. 203–256 and Roozendaal (2002).

[25]Fichter et al. (2011), p. 73. Various other union strategies are depicted by Moldof (2005), pp. 119–154.

[26]BWI, IndustriALL (formerly ICEM and IMB), IUF and UNI.

[27]Hadwiger (2016), p. 21.

[28]Fichter et al. (2011), p. 78.

U.S. corporate culture. Correspondingly, the conclusion of IFAs reflects the power resources of trade unions vis-à-vis the central management of MNEs.[29]

The substantive content of IFAs can, generally speaking, be divided into two parts: On the one side, unlike 'normal' national collective agreements or the transnational agreements of the International Transport Workers' Federation in the maritime sector on hours and wages,[30] IFAs have referred, from the very beginning of their emergence and in line with the ICFTU/ITS model code of 1997,[31] to pre-existing international instruments and principles. Moreover, this reference seems to play an increasing role in the wording of IFAs. This means that IFAs do not create own labour standards but try to enhance the efficacy of internationally acknowledged standards by establishing an additional channel for their application at the workplace. Most of these agreements refer, though in differing wording and sometimes only vaguely, to the ILO Core Labour Standards (CLS) set out in the—though hardly expressly mentioned—ILO Declaration on Fundamental Principles and Rights at Work of 1998 (Annex revised in 2010).[32] This approach mirrors the fundamental position of the GUFs not to conclude any IFA that does not contain the CLS.[33] However, there is a significant trend to include other international instruments and principles that have not attained the same level of importance as the CLS.[34] Thus, an increasing number of IFAs refer also to the ILO Tripartite Declaration of Principles concerning Multinational Enterprises and Social Policy (MNE Declaration) of 1977 (amended in 2000 and 2006 and revised in 2017), which is the only ILO tool that provides direct guidance to enterprises on social policy and workplace practices. Beyond ILO standards, many IFAs incorporate UN instruments like the Universal Declaration of Human Rights of 1948 or the Global Compact of 1999. Last but not least, numerous IFAs refer to the OECD Guidelines for Multinational Enterprises of 1976 (updated in 2000 and 2011).[35] On the other side, various IFAs focus on more company-specific issues and contain, by way of example, guidelines for the qualification of employees in order to enhance their skills.

---

[29]For a listing of mainly company-specific conditions which favor the conclusion of IFAs, see Platzer and Müller (2009), p. 738.

[30]For these agreements, see Ojeda-Avilés (2015), pp. 238–240.

[31]Available at http://training.itcilo.it/actrav_cdrom1/english/global/guide/icftuco.htm. Accessed 14 Aug 2017.

[32]Hadwiger (2016), p. 20; see also the list of substantive provisions in Papadakis (ed) (2008), pp. 271–275. These 'Fundamental Principles and Rights at Work' are recognized in the ILO-Conventions Nos. 29, 87, 98, 100, 105, 111, 138 and 182. In detail, the CLS encompass (i) freedom of association and the effective recognition of the right to collective bargaining, (ii) the elimination of all forms of forced or compulsory labour, (iii) the effective abolition of child labour, and (iv) the elimination of discrimination in respect of employment and occupation.

[33]Cf. IndustriALL (2012): 'must explicitly include'.

[34]Cf. IndustriALL (2012): 'it is important [. . .] to seek formal recognition'.

[35]Hadwiger (2016), p. 19.

Another important trend is the growing awareness of poor labour practices in global supply chains.[36] Whereas some IFAs do not mention suppliers and subcontractors and thus are limited to the operations of the MNEs itself, there is a considerable number of agreements (some 40%) that include an obligation for the MNE to inform its suppliers and subcontractors of the IFA and encourage them to adhere to the standards set out in the agreement. One third of the agreements provides for sanctions in the case of a (serious) violation of the standards stipulated in the IFA by a supplier or a subcontractor and declares that non-compliance will lead to a termination of the contractual relationship. However, this instrument is a double-edged sword. On the one hand, the threat with a termination of business relations may be a strong incentive for suppliers or subcontractors to comply with the IFA and may be much more effective than any threat of being fined by the domestic labour administration, especially in those countries in which state authorities are weak or, even worse, are not interested to protect workers' rights. On the other hand, the termination of the contractual relationship may be detrimental for the employees who work in the affected companies because termination increases the risk that they will be dismissed. Moreover, the MNE loses any opportunity to influence the conduct of the supplier or subcontractor in the future.[37] Last but not least, most of the IFAs mention only direct suppliers and subcontractors, whereas only few agreements address the entire global supply chain and expect from the business partners of MNEs to care for the compliance with the labour standards set out in the agreement also in the relationships with their own contractors.

3 Motivation of Unions and Management

Although IFAs are voluntary collective arrangements between MNEs and GUFs, they are clearly union-driven. As regards the motivation of the GUFs,[38] IFAs are, generally speaking, the response of labour to the growing influence of MNEs on industrial relations. In that respect, they originate in the—unsuccessful—attempts of three international trade union secretariats to get into negotiations with some MNEs as early as in the 1960s and 1970s.[39] During the first few years of the emergence of IFAs, unions pursued two main objectives: Firstly, the recognition of and the compliance with ILO labour standards by managements and, secondly, the recognition of GUFs as social partners at MNE level with the purpose to establish a continuous social dialogue. The first goal derives from the dissatisfaction of trade unions with the slow progress of the implementation of international labour standards in many countries and MNEs on the one side and the corporate codes of

[36]Comprehensive overview by Hadwiger (2016), pp. 23–28.

[37]Hadwiger (2016), p. 25.

[38]For the motives and interests of the signatory parties, see also Eurofound (ed) (2008), pp. 38–47.

[39]Gallin (2008), pp. 16–26.

conduct movement on the other side. Concerning corporate codes of conducts, which became popular in the early 1990s and which were mainly NGO-driven,[40] trade unions realized that only few of these codes expressly dealt with clear-cut labour standards, let alone enabling rights such as freedom of association and collective bargaining as centrepieces of employee rights.[41] Moreover, corporate codes of conduct are unilaterally adopted by the management of MNEs and do not require the consent of the labour side. Thus, trade unions suspected that this paternalistic top-down approach was often only a marketing instrument to influence public opinion, whereas in serious conflicts profit would always trump moral issues and the legitimate interests of workers.[42] In this dimension, IFAs were intended to make labour standards more effective. The second goal reflected the experience of trade unions that corporate power has shifted from the national to the international level and therefore unions also had to enter the international level in order to stay at equal footing with the employer side,[43] although IFAs were not intended to substitute but to complement collective bargaining at national level. An additional purpose of GUFs became evident in the aftermath of the conclusion of the first generation of IFAs when it was observed that the latter had only had little impact in the day-to-day activities of management, in particular at the periphery of MNEs. Facing this situation, GUFs began to use IFAs as a lever to increase the organizational power of trade unions by gaining new union members at the various sites of the MNE[44] and by promoting transnational cooperation between unions.[45] Moreover, a trade union representative stated that from the very beginning the principal objective was not the conclusion of IFAs as an end in itself but to increase unions' strength at MNE level.[46] This statement expresses plainly the realistic assessment that the pursuing of their members' interests as a main goal of trade unions is most promising if the union can act from a position of power and not of weakness. This is particularly true when it comes to collective bargaining.

Management has of course had other motives. The conclusion of the first IFA, the already mentioned Common Viewpoint IUF/BSN, was apparently for a large extent influenced by the personal convictions of the back-then-CEO of the company who has been described as a 'progressive Catholic with links to the French Socialist Party' and as having a preference for strong unions.[47] However, this situation is understandably very unique and not representative for IFAs taken as a whole. In general, IFAs may be qualified as tools in the Corporate Social Responsibility

[40]For a comprehensive description of this movement, see Jenkins (2001).

[41]Blackett (2001), p. 411 and Egels-Zandén and Merk (2014), pp. 464–470.

[42]Cf. Frundt (2004), pp. 36–69.

[43]Gallin (2008), p. 25.

[44]For the diverging strategic goals of GUFs and the different interests of European and U.S. trade unions, see Platzer and Müller (2009), pp. 731–732.

[45]Cf. Coleman (2010), pp. 604–607 and Drouin (2015), p. 219.

[46]Gallin (2008), p. 25.

[47]Gallin (2008), p. 29.

(CSR) policy of MNEs to protect and improve the legitimacy of the company's conduct. Some authors state that these agreements signal to investors, employees, customers, government agencies, and NGOs that the company is committed to observe the abovementioned labour standards.[48] But, at least with regard to external actors and in particular to the market, the relevance of 'signaling virtue'[49] in terms of 'doing good to do well'[50] is apparently low because it is often hard to find a hint on the IFA on the websites of companies.[51] Unlike codes of conduct, these agreements are often not openly communicated to the public. Thus, it is more plausible that management finds it reasonable not to refuse the request of a GUF for the conclusion of an IFA but to shift the social dialogue which is familiar to European-based MNEs to the global level in order to gain the benefits of resilient relations to the workforce not only in Europe but globally.[52] Another purpose may be the harmonization of human resource policies throughout the worldwide operations of the group. In that respect, IFAs may serve as an instrument for a more centralized human resource management. Moreover, an IFA may be a tool in the risk management because there is a growing awareness in the public regarding labour abuses and violations of workers' rights caused by the activities of MNEs and their suppliers and subcontractors which could damage the reputation of the company and, in the long run, to a decrease of credit and profit by investors and consumers. More specifically, on the one hand, the instruments provided by these agreements may help to detect bad labour practices before they became public and thus function as an 'early warning system'.[53] On the other hand, the IFA may serve as a tool to channel labour conflicts and curtail their destructive effects on production. Last but not least, the existence of an IFA in combination with robust relations to the employee side at MNE level may shield the group as such when it comes to media investigations and public accusations. However, this aspect should not be overestimated, as a cynical comment of a previous *Apple* manager demonstrates.[54]

[48]Fichter et al. (2011), p. 76.

[49]Cf. Mundlak and Zvi (2011), pp. 603–663.

[50]Cf.—however skeptical—Vogel (2005), p. 21.

[51]See e.g. the Website of *Siemens*. The more positive assessment of this issue by Hauch (2015), pp. 121–123 cannot be confirmed. In future, a change is conceivable, as IFAs may be used in the context of disclosure of non-financial information according to European Parliament and Council Directive 2014/95/EU *amending Directive 2013/34/EU as regards disclosure of non-financial and diversity information by certain large undertakings and groups*, O.J. L 330/1 (2014).

[52]Egels-Zandén (2009), pp. 540–543.

[53]Brandl (2006), p. 272.

[54]'We've known about labor abuses in some factories for four years, and they're still going on [...]. Why? Because the system works for us. Suppliers would change everything tomorrow if Apple told them they didn't have another choice [...]. If half of iPhones were malfunctioning, do you think Apple would let it go on for four years?' Former Apple executive quoted in *The New York Times*, cf. Duhigg and Barboza (2012). By the way, in the first quarter of 2016 *Apple* achieved a record net profit of more than US $18 billion.

4 Implementation and Monitoring Mechanism

The most crucial issue concerns the implementation and enforcement of IFAs. As this kind of agreements is concluded at the top level of an MNE, there is a great risk that it remains only a piece of paper without any effect on labour practices, in particular at the worldwide periphery of the group and at its suppliers and subcontractors.

From a strictly legal point of view, especially from the perspective of German labour law that qualifies collective agreements regularly both as contracts and as norms, the decisive question is only whether IFAs could be directly or indirectly enforced at a (labour) court. This topic has been addressed in depth in another article[55] and shall not be reiterated in detail here. In short, depending on the concrete wording of the agreement at stake, the enforcement of an IFA by a GUF against an MNE by means of litigation appears not unpromising, at least at a German labour court. However, this strategy has remained in the realm of theory, because until now no case has become public in which a GUF has brought an IFA to a court. Moreover, the enforcement of an IFA via litigation could have negative repercussions, because it may undermine the willingness of the MNE's top management to cooperate in good faith with the GUF any longer and, upon becoming public, may be a strong disincentive for other MNEs to enter into an IFA.[56] Therefore, it is conceivable that, depending on the social embedding of economic interests in an overall consideration, soft law can generate more concrete effects than hard law.[57]

In any case, from the perspective of GUFs, the question whether IFAs can be qualified as hard law or 'only' as soft law is too narrow. Trade unions are—of course—not interested in artificial legal constructions but in practical results which are beneficial for employees. Thus, from their point of view, it is much more important that the IFA itself contains efficient mechanism through which the agreement becomes an integrated part of the labour policy within the MNE and the global supply chain. Indeed, since the year 2000, GUFs have put increasing emphasis on the implementation and follow-up procedures,[58] because they were not fully satisfied with the real impact of the first generation of IFAs.[59] According to the voluntaristic policy approach, the outcomes of these efforts vary strongly from

[55]Krause (2012), pp. 749–773. See also Dzida and Reinhard (2012), pp. 2241–2246 and Thüsing (2010), pp. 78–93.

[56]Thus, the situation differs from the increasing number of litigation by victims of human rights violations against MNEs which are mostly supported by NGOs, cf. Meeran (2011), pp. 1–41 and see also Weschka (2006), pp. 625–661.

[57]The relevance of social embeddedness of economic actions is stressed by Granovetter (1985), pp. 481–510.

[58]Cf. IndustriALL (2012): 'Effective mechanism for implementation, enforcement and a procedure for binding dispute resolution.'

[59]Hadwiger (2015), p. 89, names a 'second generation' of IFAs. A slightly different assessment regarding two 'generations' of IFAs is given by Fornasier (2015), p. 295.

agreement to agreement.[60] Three recently concluded IFAs may serve as examples for the different aspects,[61] namely (1) dissemination/implementation, (2) review/monitoring, and (3) dispute settlement/sanctions.

With regard to all of these categories, the IFA of *Ford* of 2012 uses very general terms. It provides basically only the establishment of an ongoing discussion process between the parties and also between the company and the regional unions on the principles set out in the agreement. This is—from a GUF perspective—better than nothing but far away from a robust implementation and enforcement mechanism. Such a wording may reflect a strong and trustful relationship between the top management and the union side. However, it is more likely that it indicates the weakness of labour.[62] In contrast, the IFA of *Siemens* of 2012 provides the dissemination of the agreement by informing all employees of the group verbally or in writing. The responsibility for complying with the principles laid down in the agreement shall rest with the regional business units. Moreover, the compliance shall be monitored through an internal company controlling mechanism. A Central Works Council negotiating team ('Verhandlungsdelegation') shall have the task of supporting the worldwide implementation of the agreement and advising on suitable measures. Furthermore, the IFA stipulates that in the event of grievances, employees and employee representative bodies should first exhaust the internal and local/national complaint and arbitration facilities. However, if complaints cannot be resolved at local or national level the *Verhandlungsdelegation* shall have the task to pursue them at central level. The IFA of *ThyssenKrupp* of 2015 goes into the same direction, but it is more advanced. For instance, the agreement provides that it must be translated in eight most spoken languages. Moreover, the IFA expressly states that employee representatives shall be involved in the implementation process. The Human Resources executive board member shall report on the basis of suitable documents to the so-called International Committee which has the task to monitor the implementation of the agreement and to propose appropriate measures to be taken in the event of violations if local or national level mediation remains unsuccessful. Interestingly, the representatives of the International Committee shall be free to visit production sites of their choosing each year in consultation with the Human Resources executive board member. Furthermore, the IFA stipulates an internal whistleblowing system through which employees can report violations of the agreement and must not be subject of any disadvantage as reaction of such a report.

These few examples show that one of the central purposes of IFAs lies in the creation of a permanent social dialogue between the social partners, though the

[60] Detailed analysis by Felkl (2010), pp. 132–152 and Hauch (2015), pp. 62–74. See also the list of procedural provisions in Papadakis (ed) (2008), pp. 279–288. For a comparison between IFAs and European Framework Agreements at Company Level, see Marassi (2015), pp. 69–187.

[61] Available at the EU database on transnational company agreements. http://ec.europa.eu/social/main.jsp?catId=978. Accessed 14 Aug 2017.

[62] Cf. Fichter et al. (2011), p. 78.

concrete role of trade unions or other employee representatives within the process of implementation of the agreement differs considerably. Moreover, it is a significant pattern that IFAs provide a multi-level mechanism for the resolution of labour disputes, if they deal with this issue at all: Conflicts shall regularly be resolved firstly with the local management, in the case of failure with the national management, and as a last option with the central management.

5 International Framework Agreements as Part of an Emerging Global Labour Governance Regime

Governance is the key word of modern regulatory theory.[63] Though there are numerous governance theories, it is a common feature that the state should no longer be recognized as the only law-maker. In contrast, governance theorists put much emphasis on the decoupling of law and state and the existence of private regulatory regimes, mixtures of public and private ordering, de-centred self-regulation, non-state actors, soft law, and the like, in other words on 'governance *without* government' (instead of 'governance *by* government' or 'governance *with* government') or 'private law beyond the state'.[64] For labour law, this conception is everything but new, because for decades, collective bargaining had been qualified as a form of governance of the workplace without substantive state-made law. From this perspective, it appears that IFAs are basically not novel because they only transfer the concept of self-regulation by social partners from the national into the international arena.

However, there are important differences. Firstly, the partners of conventional collective bargaining in developed countries are acting against the backdrop of a functioning national legal framework with existing and enforceable workers' rights. Thus, a collective agreement which provides that the company has to comply with existing labour law would not make sense. The company simply must obey the law. The employees can claim the violation of a right before domestic courts and the labour administration enforces public labour law like health and safety regulations. Therefore, national collective agreements are not needed to promote pre-existing protective rights of employees but to establish new rights for workers above the minimum legal standards in order to pursue distributive goals. Hence, if existing international labour standards like the CLS, enshrined in the ILO Declaration of 1998 and binding even upon those ILO member states which have not ratified the corresponding ILO Conventions, would be backed by strong public bodies in every country and at every plant where MNEs operate, IFAs would be more or less superfluous, nice to have but not necessary for the effectiveness of these standards.

---

[63] See in general Levi-Faur (ed) (2012); further Black (2001), pp. 103–146; Lobel (2004), pp. 342–470; Stoker (1998), pp. 17–28.

[64] See Jansen and Michaels (eds) (2008).

Indeed, the very concept of international standards with effective enforcement as an appropriate response to the internationalization of the economy is by no means new but known for decades.[65] The G8 Labour and Employment Ministers were fully right when they declared in 2007 on global social standards: 'It is primarily the task of governments to implement and improve human rights and labour standards'.[66] From this perspective, IFAs are only a second best solution in comparison to social rights which are guaranteed by state bodies or robust international public bodies.[67] Secondly, in contrast to collective agreements at national level, IFAs operate within a legal vacuum. While national labour law regulates who is the capable actor of collective agreements, what is their valid content and their legal effect, all of these questions remain unclear when it comes to IFAs. Therefore, due to the lack of a functioning legal framework for IFAs at global level, it is uncertain according to which law or which general principles disputes on the interpretation or the effect of such an agreement shall be decided.[68] In other words, there is a 'governance gap'[69] at the transnational level and IFAs have the function to fill this gap regardless to the fact that they are not framed by domestic or international law like, for instance, the ILO Maritime Labour Convention (MLC) of 2006.[70]

IFAs are, as a matter of course, not the only response to the 'governance gap' with regard to the regulation of global labour. In the past few decades a plethora of other policy tools have been developed, such as ILO instruments, Codes of Conduct, global supply chain-related national legislation like the California Transparency in Supply Chains Act of 2012 or the UK Modern Slavery Act of 2015, and so on,[71] which establish a global labour governance regime[72] in the meaning of a 'set of implicit or explicit principles, norms, rules, and decision-making procedures around which actors' expectations converge in a given area of international relations'.[73] However, IFAs as an expression of global legal pluralism[74] and as particular instruments of 'social governance'[75] have some characteristic features. First, these agreements are intended to promote pre-existing international labour

[65]Cf. Feis (1927), pp. 491–518.

[66]G8 Labour and Employment Ministers Conference (2007), Chair's Conclusions, para. 22.

[67]Mund and Priegnitz (2007), pp. 671–677.

[68]On these questions, from the perspective of German and European law, see in depth Krause (2012), pp. 749–773.

[69]Cf. ILO (2016), pp. 39, 62.

[70]For the MLC, see Asante and Chigara (2015), pp. 343–356.

[71]Overview at ILO (2016), pp. 40–61; see also Bakvis and McCoy (2008); Blecher (2017); Hendrickx et al. (2016), pp. 339–355.

[72]Cf. Hassel (2008), pp. 236–243; see also O'Rourke (2003), pp. 1–29.

[73]See the 'classical' definition by Krasner (1982), p. 186.

[74]Cf. Berman (2012); Michaels (2009), pp. 243–262 and Zumbansen (2010), pp. 141–189. The insufficiency of 'pluralism' as a guideline without taking into account other principles like freedom, equality, and so forth, which hinder the collapse into relativism, is stressed by Isiksel (2013), p. 195 and Peters (2016), p. 1023.

[75]See Gereffi and Lee (2016), p. 30.

standards by means of internal governance. With regard to the content of these standards this approach has therefore a 'derivative' character, as the parties do not create own labour standards but adopt such standards which have been developed by international institutions. Thus, the GUFs act as 'transmission agencies'[76] and use the authority of public international law to confer more legitimacy on their own agreements. Moreover, this regulatory model combines public and private law elements and can be qualified as a 'contractualization'[77] of fundamental labour standards or as development of a 'hybrid' global labour law.[78] Concerning the transfer of the referred labour standards from a paper text into the real worklife, this approach intends that the management of MNEs at the central and, as much as possible, at the local level should acknowledge these standards and integrate them into the human resources policy of the group. With regard to this aim, the trade unions try to use the central managerial power to influence labour practices within the MNE. Due to the evident weakness of external structures charged with the enforcement of international labour standards, internal governance structures have been created, such as frequent meetings, special committees, reporting systems, and whistleblowing hotlines. Moreover, IFAs intend to employ the economic power of MNEs to influence the labour practices in the global supply chain as well. In this regard, the extension of the scope of at least some IFAs indicate that the MNE assumes to a certain extent responsibility for the workers of suppliers or subcontractors who are not legally but socially connected with the lead firm.[79]

Secondly, IFAs function as tools for capacity-building. Thus, they express the development from the traditional compliance to the more advanced capability model.[80] As these agreements put much emphasis on the guarantee of freedom of association and collective bargaining, they serve as instruments to strengthen the union power in two dimensions: On the one hand, at the sites of the MNEs vis-à-vis the local management and, on the other hand, within the whole group via collaboration between the national trade unions which represent the global workforce vis-à-vis the central management in order to counter the organization of internal competition for investments between different plants.[81] In this respect, IFAs have the character of 'reflexive law' in the sense that they do not only employ a simple 'command and control'-approach but establish a framework that facilitates the shaping of industrial relations by the social partners at local or global level.[82] In that respect, IFAs can be conceptualized as mechanism to regulate the self-regulation of industrial relations in other social spheres. The workers should not

[76]Cf. Platzer and Rüb (2014), p. 3.

[77]Drouin (2015), pp. 221–222.

[78]Mückenberger (2014), pp. 471–477.

[79]Cf. Dahan et al. (2011), pp. 452–464.

[80]For the background, see Locke (2013), pp. 80–85.

[81]Herrnstadt (2007), p. 190.

[82]Rogowski (2015), pp. 72–90 and see also Rogowski (2013). Critical to the concept of reflexive labour law Arthurs (2007), pp. 27–35.

only be beneficiaries of protective rights but also be the subjects of a law-making process.[83] Hereby, IFAs express the concept of workplace democracy. From another theoretical point of view, these agreements bring the fundamental capability approach[84] of *Amartya Sen*[85] and *Martha Nussbaum*[86] to the ground by providing social rights which enable the employee side to exercise real and not only formal personal freedom.[87]

Nevertheless, this approach has some ambiguities or even disadvantages which should not be neglected. To begin with, trade unions are regularly focused on members' interests and less keen to pursue the interests of non-members. Thus, for GUFs and their affiliates, freedom of association and collective bargaining are standing in the foreground while (other) human rights[88] enjoy less attention. Hence, with the conclusion of IFAs trade unions fill a loophole which is left by other actors, such as NGOs, whose focus on human rights violations of MNEs tends to neglect traditional labour rights and is often pursued in short campaigns instead of a sustainable strategy.[89] But, due to the limited number and scope of IFAs, only a small minority of employees benefits from this strategy. An overwhelming majority of workers is neither directly nor indirectly covered by IFAs though at least the CLS are impartible and not a privilege for those employees who are working at MNEs or at their suppliers and subcontractors.[90] Thus, a company-centred approach must be aware that this strategy cannot substitute the effective enforcement of labour law by strong public institutions. Furthermore, the question can be raised whether GUFs are representative as a voice of the whole workforce of MNEs and within the global supply chain. In this respect, some scholars claim a democratic deficit of IFAs.[91] Moreover, as IFAs are a mainly European-based phenomenon, there is the risk that they are regarded as paternalistic instruments which the 'North' exports to the 'South'.[92] Last not least, the problem of tensions between the content of an IFA and domestic law is not perfectly resolved. However, this aspect should not be overexaggerated.

---

[83]Drouin (2010), p. 611.

[84]Cf. Robeyns (2011).

[85]Sen (1999, 2009).

[86]Nussbaum (2011).

[87]Generally discussed recently by Del Punta (2016), pp. 383–405. For a critical assessment of the capabilities approach, see Bogg (2015), pp. 86–95.

[88]For the contested question of qualifying labour rights as human rights, see the debate between Youngdahl (denying) (2009) and Compa (affirming) (2009). Further Compa (2008), pp. 99–123. Comprehensive discussion by Kolben (2010), pp. 449–484 and see also Mantouvalou (2013), pp. 151–172 distinguishing between a positivistic, an instrumental, and a normative approach.

[89]For the differences between NGO-pressure and union-pressure on companies see Braun and Gearhart (2004), pp. 183–196 and Egels-Zandén (2009), pp. 541–542.

[90]A comprehensive account on the 'pros' and 'cons' of CLS is delivered by Sengenberger (2005).

[91]Niforou (2014), pp. 381–383.

[92]Cf. Platzer and Rüb (2014), p. 16.

6 Real Impact of International Framework Agreements

The general effectiveness of the mentioned implementation mechanisms is hard to assess. Industrial relations research gives the account that the implementation depends very much on the will of central management to develop a robust global HR-policy and to incorporate the IFA into this policy. Conversely, a non-interventionist approach regarding local industrial relations is detrimental for the impact of an IFA.[93] However, a successful implementation requires more than a simple top-down order but will be influenced by the general standing of central management with regard to its power, capacity, and resources.[94] As IFAs are agreements at the top level of MNEs, the likelihood of an effective implementation is larger if the group has generally a centralized and hierarchical structure whereas a fragmented structure and relatively independent affiliates in the various countries where the MNE operates is disadvantageous for the implementation process. In short, the efficacy of the implementation of the IFA is directly linked to the corporate governance of the MNE. Moreover, the involvement of local actors in the process of negotiation and implementation is an important factor for the future effectiveness of the IFA when it comes to concrete labour disputes.

Much harder to assess is the question whether and to which extent IFAs lead to a real change in labour practices throughout the MNEs and the global supply chain. In this respect, some case studies shed light on this issue.[95] First of all, these studies show that most conflicts have concerned the right to freedom of association and collective bargaining. Furthermore, they demonstrate on the one side that there are MNEs in which neither the employees nor the management at local level have knowledge of the IFA. In such situations, the agreement can of course not influence the conduct in particular of local management and has to be qualified as a simple piece of paper without any practical relevance. On the other side, in the past few years, there have been several labour conflicts in which the GUFs have invoked the IFA as an instrument in order to protect and pursue workers' rights and interests. These conflicts occurred in countries like the US, Brazil, and India and concerned different branches like the cement industry, a supplier of a car manufacturer, and a provider of international security services. Though the GUFs were not successful in every case, in most of the reported conflicts they achieved some improvement for the employees. Admittedly, it is difficult to evaluate to which degree this success rests on the existence of the IFA. In contrast to the decision of a court which rests, at least theoretically, on exactly those arguments which the court delivers as reasons, the outcome in a concrete labour conflict is the result of various empirical factors. However, there can be no doubt that the IFA has regularly played a considerable

---

[93]Niforou (2012), p. 370.

[94]Fichter et al. (2011), p. 79.

[95]E.g. Eurofound (ed) (2008), pp. 73–83 and Papadakis (ed) (2011), pp. 85–198. Overview by Hadwiger (2015), pp. 88–89.

role.[96] Nevertheless, it is important to realize that the invoking of an IFA has to be embedded in a pre-existing strong position of labour if such a strategy is meant to be successful. It is not very likely that the mere text of an IFA will change bad labour practices in a union-hostile climate with economic, political, and not least legal obstacles. This is in particular true in regard to the situation in the US[97] However, depending on the power resources and other factors like the general trust between the conflicting parties, an IFA can help to resolve a labour dispute in a way which recognizes the rights and interests of workers in an appropriate manner.[98]

7 Conclusion

International Framework Agreements can be regarded as an important policy instrument in the emerging global labour governance regime. They step in the 'governance gap' which exists in regard to MNEs and global supply chains. The virtue of IFAs is not their often doubtful legal effect but their potential as a tool to influence labour practices, and thus to 'civilize globalization'[99] by not only selecting the black sheep but by taming the wolves. However, not every IFA has the same impact. Its efficacy depends to some extent on the wording of the agreements that, with regard to the referred labour standards and in particular to the implementation and monitoring mechanism, can either be vague or robust. The content of the IFA reflects on the one side the negotiating power of the employee side vis-à-vis the employer side. On the other side, and due of the lack of a transnational legal framework which supports enforcement, it is just the power of the union which determines whether the agreement can be employed successfully when it comes to a labour dispute at the periphery of the MNE or in the global supply chain. Thus, an IFA as soft law unsurprisingly works best if it is embedded in strong and resilient industrial relations in precisely that arena in which the dispute occurs. In such an environment the agreements function as a living instrument, which stimulate the actors who are involved in the conflict to find new common solutions. Conversely, without such a convenient environment an IFA

[96] See also Williams et al. (2015), pp. 181–203: successful use of an IFA in a case concerning the South African construction industry.

[97] Cf. Stevis and Fichter (2012), pp. 682–687 and more details by Fichter and Stevis (2013). See also Liebman (2016), pp. 143–157 and Sherrard and Wisskirchen (2014), pp. 256–262. For a more optimistic view, see Rosado Marzán (2014a), pp. 725–780. A non-binding arbitration based on ILO norms as instrument to resolve disagreements, as proposed by Rosado Marzán (2014b), pp. 1749–1804, would theoretically ameliorate the situation. However, it is unlikely that just US-based MNEs will follow their European counterparts (cf. the IFA of the Swedish company Skanska of 2001 which provides even a binding arbitration) and will stipulate such a clause as part of an IFA.

[98] Drouin (2010), pp. 599–621.

[99] Cf. Kinley (2009).

risks to remain a mere piece of paper. Besides that, IFAs are not the only negotiated arrangements with which the situation of workers can be improved. The terrible disasters in Bangladesh mentioned at the outset have led in the year 2013 to the 'Accord on Fire and Building Safety in Bangladesh' which has been signed by over 200 apparel brands, retailers, and importers from over 20 countries in Europe, North America, Asia, and Australia, two global trade unions, eight Bangladeshi trade unions, and four NGO witnesses.[100] This example shows that many different policy tools must be developed in order to cope with the challenges of global labour. Nevertheless, IFAs are *one* possible instrument which can, dependent on the individual case, be quite effective and therefore GUFs should continue to follow this path and conclude more robust agreements in the future.

References

Anner M (2001) The international trade union campaign for core labor standards in the WTO. WorkingUSA: J Labor Soc 5(1):43–63

Arthurs H (2007) Corporate self-regulation: political economy, state regulation and reflexive labour law. In: Bercusson B, Estlund C (eds) Regulating labour in the wake of globalisation. Hart, Oxford, pp 19–35

Asante A, Chigara B (2015) Emergent maritime labour law: possible implications for other transnational labour fields. In: Blacket A, Trebilcock A (eds) Research handbook on transnational labour law. Edward Elgar, Cheltenham, pp 343–356

Bakvis P, McCoy M (2008) Core labour standards and international organizations: what inroads has labour made? Friedrich-Ebert-Stiftung, Briefing Papers No. 6. http://library.fes.de/pdf-files/iez/05431.pdf. Accessed 11 Jan 2017

Baldwin R (2013) Global supply chains: why they emerged, why they matter, and where they are going. In: Elms DK, Low P (eds) Global value chains in a changing world. WTO, Geneva, pp 13–59

Banks K (2006) The impact of globalization on labour standards. A second look at the evidence. In: Craig JD, Lynk SM (eds) Globalization and the future of labour law. Cambridge University Press, Cambridge, pp 77–107

Barry C, Reddy SG (2006) International trade and labour standards: a proposal for linkage. Cornell Int Law J 39:545–639

Beck U (2002) Macht und Gegenmacht im globalen Zeitalter. Neue weltpolitische Ökonomie. Suhrkamp, Frankfurt am Main, pp 185–252

Berman PS (2012) Global legal pluralism. A jurisprudence of law beyond borders. Cambridge University Press, Cambridge

Black J (2001) Decentering regulation: understanding the role of regulation and self-regulation in a 'post-regulatory' world. Curr Leg Probl 54:103–146

Blackett A (2001) Global governance, legal pluralism and the decentered state: a labor law critique of codes of corporate conduct. Indiana J Glob Leg Stud 8:401–447

Blecher L (2017) Codes of conduct: the trojan horse of international human rights law? Comp Labor Law Policy J 38:437–476

[100] Cf. CCC (2013d). For more information on this issue, see Diller (2015), pp. 336–337; Zimmer (2016).

Bogg A (2015) Labour law and the trade unions: autonomy and betrayal. In: Blogg A, Costello C, Davies ACL, Prassl J (eds) The autonomy of labour law. Bloomsbury Publishing, London, pp 73–106
Brandl S (2006) Nachholende Internationalisierung? Zur Dynamik Internationaler Rahmenvereinbarungen. Indust Bezieh 13:270–281
Braun R, Gearhart J (2004) Who should code your conduct? Trade union and NGO differences in the fight for workers' rights. Dev Pract 14:183–196
Clean Clothes Campaign (2013a) Fire kills 286 – despite social responsibility certificate. https://cleanclothes.org/ua/2012/cases/ali-enterprise. Accessed 11 Jan 2017
Clean Clothes Campaign (2013b) Tazreen Fire. https://cleanclothes.org/ua/2012/cases/tazreen. Accessed 11 Jan 2017
Clean Clothes Campaign (2013c) Rana Plaza. https://cleanclothes.org/safety/ranaplaza. Accessed 11 Jan 2017
Clean Clothes Campaign (2013d) Frequently Asked Questions (FAQ) about the Bangladesh Safety Accord. https://cleanclothes.org/issues/faq-safety-accord. Accessed 11 Jan 2017
Coleman S (2010) Enforcing international framework agreements in U.S. courts: a contract analysis. Columbia Hum Rights Law Rev 41:601–634
Compa L (2008) Labor's new opening to international human rights standards. WorkingUSA: J Labor Soc 11:99–123
Compa L (2009) Solidarity and human rights: a response to Youngdahl. New Labor Forum 18 (1):31–47
Cox RW (1997) A perspective on globalization. In: Mittelman JE (ed) Globalization: critical reflections. Lynne Rienner, Boulder, pp 21–30
Dahan Y, Lerner H, Milman Sivan F (2011) Global justice, labor standards and responsibility. Theor Inq Law 12:439–464
Deakin S (2005) Social rights in a globalized economy. In: Alston P (ed) Labour rights as human rights. Oxford University Press, Oxford, pp 25–60
Del Punta R (2016) Labour law and the capability approach. Int J Comp Labour Law Ind Relat 32:383–405
Diller JM (2015) Pluralism and privatization in transnational labour regulation: experience of the International Labour Organization. In: Blacket A, Trebilcock A (eds) Research handbook on transnational labour law. Edward Elgar, Cheltenham, pp 329–342
Drouin RC (2010) Promoting fundamental labor rights through international framework agreements: practical outcomes and present challenges. Comp Labor Law Policy J 31:591–636
Drouin RC (2015) Freedom of association in international framework agreements. In: Blacket A, Trebilcock A (eds) Research handbook on transnational labour law. Edward Elgar, Cheltenham, pp 217–229
Duhigg C, Barboza D (2012) In China, human costs are built into an iPad. In: The New York Times, 25 Jan 2012. http://www.nytimes.com/2012/01/26/business/ieconomy-apples-ipad-and-the-human-costs-for-workers-in-china.html. Accessed 11 Jan 2017
Dzida B, Reinhard C (2012) Globale Rahmenabkommen: zwischen Corporate Social Responsibility und gewerkschaftlichen Kampagnen. Betriebs-Berater 36:2241–2246
Egels-Zandén N (2009) TNC motives for signing international framework agreements: a continuous bargaining model of stakeholder pressure. J Bus Ethics 84:529–547
Egels-Zandén N, Merk J (2014) Private regulation and trade union rights: why codes of conduct have limited impact on trade union rights. J Bus Ethics 123:461–473
Eurofound (ed) (2008) Codes of conduct and international framework agreements: new forms of governance at company level. Public Office, Luxembourg
Feis H (1927) International labour legislation in the light of economic theory. Int Labour Rev 15:491–518
Felkl J (2010) Rechtliche Bedeutung der Internationalen Rahmenvereinbarungen. Dissertation, University of Freiburg

Fichter M, Helfen M, Sydow J (2011) Regulating labor relations in global production networks: insights on international framework agreements. Internationale Politik und Gesellschaft 2:69–86
Fichter M, Stevis D (2013) Global framework agreements in a union-hostile environment: the case of the USA. Friedrich-Ebert-Stiftung. http://library.fes.de/pdf-files/id/10377.pdf. Accessed 11 Jan 2017
Fornasier M (2015) Transnational collective bargaining: the case of international framework agreements – a legal analysis. Europäische Zeitschrift für Arbeitsrecht 8:281–296
Frundt HJ (2004) Unions wrestle with corporate codes of conduct. WorkingUSA: J Labor Soc 7:36–69
G8 Labour and Employment Ministers Conference (2007) Shaping the social dimensions of globalisation, Chair's conclusions. Dresden
Gallin D (2008) International framework agreements: a reassessment. In: Papadakis K (ed) Cross-border social dialogue and agreements: an emerging global industrial relations framework? International Institute for Labour Studies, ILO, Geneva, pp 15–41
Gereffi G (2005) An overview of the contemporary global labour market. In: Gereffi G (ed) The new offshoring of jobs and global development. ILO Social Policy Lectures, Geneva, pp 1–16
Gereffi G, Lee J (2016) Economic and social upgrading in global value chains and industrial clusters: why governance matters. J Bus Ethics 133:25–38
Gereffi G, Mayer F (2005) Globalization and the demand for governance. In: Gereffi G (ed) The new offshoring of jobs and global development. ILO Social Policy Lectures, Geneva, pp 39–58
Granovetter M (1985) Economic action and social structure: the problem of embeddedness. Am J Sociol 91:481–510
Hadwiger F (2015) Global framework agreements: achieving decent work in global supply chains? Int J Labour Res 7:75–94
Hadwiger F (2016) Global framework agreements: achieving decent work in global supply chains. Background paper. ILO, Geneva
Hassel A (2008) The evolution of a global labor governance regime. Governance 21:231–251
Hauch ET (2015) International Framework Agreements: Hintergrund, Rechtsnatur und Justiziabilität. Dissertation, University of Bonn
Held D, McGrew AG (eds) (2003) The global transformations reader: an introduction to the globalization debate, 2nd edn. Cambridge, Blackwell Publishing
Hendrickx F, Marx A, Rayp G, Wouters J (2016) The architecture of global labour governance. Int Labour Rev 155(3):339–355
Hepple B (2005) Labour laws and global trade. Hart, Oxford
Herrnstadt OE (2007) Are international framework agreements a path to corporate social responsibility? Univ Pa J Bus Employ 10:187–224
ILO (2015) World employment and social outlook. ILO, Geneva
ILO (2016) Decent work in global supply chains. ILO, Geneva
IndustriALL (2012) Global union's guidelines for global framework agreements (GFAs) of 2012. http://www.industriall-union.org/sites/default/files/uploads/documents/GFAs/industriall_gfa_guidelines_final_version_exco_12-2014_english.pdf. Accessed 15 Aug 2017
Isiksel T (2013) Global legal pluralism as fact and norm. Glob Constitutionalism 2:160–195
ITUC (2016) Global rights index. The world's worst countries for workers. https://www.ituc-csi.org/IMG/pdf/survey_ra_2016_eng.pdf. Accessed 11 Jan 2017
Jansen N, Michaels R (eds) (2008) Beyond the state: rethinking private law. Mohr Siebeck, Tübingen
Jenkins R (2001) Corporate codes of conduct: self-regulation in a global economy. United Nations Research Institute for Social Development, Geneva
Kinley D (2009) Civilising globalisation: human rights and the global economy. Cambridge University Press, Cambridge
Kolben K (2007) Integrative linkage: combining public and private regulatory approaches in the design of trade and labor regimes. Harv Int Law J 48:203–256

Kolben K (2010) Labor rights as human rights? Va J Int Law 50:449–484
Kolben K (2015) Dialogic labor regulation in the global supply chain. Michigan J Int Law 36:425–464
Krasner SD (1982) Structural causes and regime consequences: regimes as intervening variables. Int Organ 36:185–205
Krause R (2012) International framework agreements as instruments for the legal enforcement of freedom of association and collective bargaining? Comp Labor Law Policy J 33:749–773
Levi-Faur D (ed) (2012) The Oxford handbook on governance. Oxford University Press, Oxford
Liebman WB (2016) U.S. trade unions and German subsidiaries. Soziales Recht 4:143–157
Lobel O (2004) The renew deal: the fall of regulation and the rise of governance in contemporary legal thought. Minn Law Rev 89:342–470
Locke RM (2013) The promise and limits of private power: promoting labor standards in a global economy. Cambridge University Press, Cambridge
Mantouvalou V (2013) Are labour rights human rights? Eur Labour Law J 3:151–172
Marassi S (2015) Globalization and transnational collective labour relations. Kluwer Law International, Alphen aan den Rijn
Meeran R (2011) Tort litigation against multinational corporations for violation of human rights: an overview of the position outside the United States. City Univ Hong Kong Law Rev 3:1–41
Michaels R (2009) Global legal pluralism. Annu Rev Law Soc Sci 5:243–262
Moldof SB (2005) Unions responses to the challenges of an increasingly globalized economy. Richmond J Glob Law Bus 5:119–154
Mosley L, Uno S (2007) Racing to the bottom or climbing to the top? Economic globalization and collective labor rights. Comp Pol Stud 40:923–948
Mückenberger U (2014) Ein globales Hybridarbeitsrecht. In: Calliess G-P (ed) Transnationales Recht. Mohr Siebeck, Tübingen, pp 457–477
Mund H, Priegnitz K (2007) Soft law – second best solution or privatisation of social rights? Some pointers for a future discussion. Transfer 13:671–677
Mundlak G, Zvi IR (2011) Signaling virtue? A comparison of corporate codes in the fields of labor and environment. Theor Inq Law 12:603–663
Niforou C (2012) International framework agreements and industrial relations governance: global rhetoric versus local realities. Br J Ind Relat 50:352–373
Niforou C (2014) International framework agreements and the democratic deficit of global labour governance. Econ Ind Democr 35:367–386
Nussbaum M (2011) Creating capabilities: the human development approach. Harvard University Press, Cambridge
Ojeda-Avilés A (2015) Transnational labour law. Kluwer Law International, Alphen aan den Rijn
O'Rourke D (2003) Outsourcing regulation: analyzing nongovernmental systems of labor standards and monitoring. Policy Stud J 31(1):1–29
Papadakis K (ed) (2008) Cross-border social dialogue and agreements: an emerging global industrial relations framework? International Institute for Labour Studies, ILO, Geneva, pp 271–275
Papadakis K (ed) (2011) Shaping global industrial relations: the impact of international framework agreements. ILO, Geneva
Perraton J et al (1998) Die Globalisierung der Wirtschaft. In: Beck U (ed) Politik der Globalisierung. Suhrkamp, Frankfurt am Main, pp 134–168
Peters A (2016) Fragmentation and constitutionalization. In: Orford A, Hoffmann F, Clark M (eds) The Oxford handbook of the theory of international law. Oxford University Press, Oxford, pp 1011–1031
Platzer H-W, Müller T (2009) Die globalen und europäischen Gewerkschaftsverbände: Handbuch und Analysen zur transnationalen Gewerkschaftspolitik. Sigma, Berlin
Platzer H-W, Rüb S (2014) International framework agreements: an instrument for enforcing social human rights? Friedrich-Ebert-Stiftung. http://library.fes.de/pdf-files/iez/10474.pdf. Accessed 11 Jan 2017

Powell B, Skarbek D (2006) Sweatshops and third world living standards: are the jobs worth the sweat? J Lab Res 27:263–274

Robeyns I (2011) The capability approach. The Stanford encyclopedia of philosophy. https://plato.stanford.edu/entries/capability-approach/. Accessed 11 Jan 2017

Rogowski R (2013) Reflexive labour law in the world society. Edward Elgar, Cheltenham

Rogowski R (2015) The emergence of reflexive global labour law. Indust Bezieh 22:72–90

Rosado Marzán CF (2014a) Organizing with international framework agreements: an exploratory study. UC Irvine Law Rev 4:725–780

Rosado Marzán CF (2014b) Labor's soft means and hard challenges: fundamental discrepancies and the promise of non-binding arbitration for international framework agreements. Minn Law Rev 98:1749–1804

Ruggie JG (1982) International regimes, transactions, and change: embedded liberalism in the postwar economic order. Int Organ 36:379–415

Sen A (1999) Development as freedom. Oxford University Press, Oxford

Sen A (2009) The idea of justice. Harvard University Press, Boston

Sengenberger W (2005) Globalization and social progress: the role and impact of international labour standards. Friedrich-Ebert-Stiftung, Bonn

Sherrard MG, Wisskirchen G (2014) Next up for North American employers and unions? International and corporate social responsibility. J Labor Employ Law 29:245–282

Snyder J (2010) Exploitation and sweatshops labor: perspectives and issues. Bus Ethics Q 20:187–213

Stevis D, Fichter M (2012) International framework agreements in the United States: escaping, projecting, or globalizing social dialogues? Comp Labor Law Policy J 33:667–690

Stoker G (1998) Governance as theory: five propositions. Int Soc Sci J 50:17–28

Supiot A (2003) The labyrinth of human right: credo or common resource? New Left Rev 21:118–136

Thüsing G (2010) International Framework Agreements: rechtliche Grenzen und praktischer Nutzen. Recht der Arbeit 2:78–93

Trubek DM (2006) Review essay: the emergence of transnational labor law. Am J Int Law 100:725–733

UNCTAD (2009) Training manual on statistics for FDI and the operations of TNCs, vol II. United Nations, New York/Geneva

UNCTAD (2013) World investment report. United Nations, New York/Geneva

Van Roozendaal G (2002) Trade unions and global governance: the debate on a social clause. Continuum, London

Vogel DJ (2005) Is there a marker for virtue? The business case for corporate social responsibility. Calif Manag Rev 47(4):19–45

Weschka M (2006) Human rights and multinational enterprises: how can multinational enterprises be held responsible for human rights violations committed abroad? Zeitschrift für ausländisches öffentliches Recht und Völkerrecht 66:625–661

Williams G, Davies S, Chinguno C (2015) Subcontracting and labour standards: reassessing the potential of international framework agreements. Br J Ind Relat 53:181–203

World Commission on the Social Dimension of Globalization (2004) A fair globalization: creating opportunities for all. ILO, Geneva

WTO (2014) World trade report, trade and development: recent trends and the role of the WTO. WTO, Geneva

Youngdahl J (2009) Solidarity first: labor rights are not the same as human rights. New Labor Forum 18(1):31–47

Zimmer R (2016) Corporate responsibility in the "Bangladesh-Accord". Friedrich-Ebert-Stiftung. http://library.fes.de/pdf-files/id-moe/13072.pdf. Accessed 11 Jan 2017

Zumbansen P (2010) Transnational legal pluralism. Transl Leg Theory 1:141–189

Zwolinski M (2007) Sweatshops, choice, and exploitation. Bus Ethics Q 17:689–727

Transnational Labour Litigation: The Ups and Downs Under the Alien Tort Statute

Anja Seibert-Fohr

Contents

Abstract When we consider the protection of labour rights, international standard-setting is only one aspect that deserves attention. What is equally important is the enforcement of these rights. Unfortunately, however, enforcement mechanisms are insufficient or unavailable in many developing countries. Therefore, victims of labour rights violations have turned to those jurisdictions where transnational corporations are incorporated in order to seek damages.

The contribution by Anja Seibert-Fohr addresses the question of how labour standards can be enforced by individuals in such domestic courts. Taking the example of the US Alien Torts Act (ATS) she describes the experience gained under this over 200 years-old statute which gives district courts jurisdiction of civil action by aliens for torts committed in violation of international law. While ATS litigation initially focused on grave human rights violations, such as torture and genocide, a number of civil suits have been brought by foreigners seeking damages

This article is written in the author's personal capacity. It does not express opinions on behalf of the UN Human Rights Committee. The author is grateful to Torsten Stirner for his very thorough editing assistance.

A. Seibert-Fohr (✉)
Ruprecht-Karls-University, Heidelberg, Germany
e-mail: sekretariat.seibert-fohr@jurs.uni-heidelberg.de

H. Gött (ed.), *Labour Standards in International Economic Law*,
https://doi.org/10.1007/978-3-319-69447-4_16

for the violation of international labour standards over the past decade. The contribution describes what obstacles are faced by the plaintiffs and asks to what extent private litigation can contribute to the protection of labour standards abroad.

1 Introduction

The preceding chapters have considered international labour standards and the relevant institutional framework at the international level. However international standard-setting is only one aspect that deserves attention when the protection of labour rights is considered. What is equally important is the enforcement of these rights. Unfortunately enforcement mechanisms are insufficient or unavailable in many developing countries. In the absence of strong international dispute settlement mechanisms victims of labour rights violations have turned increasingly to those jurisdictions where transnational corporations are incorporated in order to seek civil damages in domestic courts.[1] Most prominently, victims of human rights abuses have sued for damages in United States courts on the basis of the Alien Tort Statute (ATS).[2] For example, in *Doe I v. Unocal Corp*., Burmese peasants sought redress for forced labour and other serious human rights violations which had been committed by the Burmese army while securing a pipeline project with the alleged knowledge of Unocal and Total.[3]

In *Estate of Rodriguez v. Drummond Co.*, a trade union and the family of three union leaders who had been killed in the midst of bargaining negotiations sued because the paramilitary forces had allegedly been hired by employees of the defendant company in an effort to put pressure on the bargaining process.[4] Another example is *Licea v. Curacao Drydock Co,* Inc where a group of Cuban plaintiffs sued a company for conspiracy in a Cuban forced labour scheme. The Court entered a default judgement and awarded $80 million in compensatory and punitive damages.[5]

In the following contribution, I will give an overview over ATS litigation and describe the experience gained with transnational labour litigation in the United States over the past two decades. I will first describe the legal scope of the Alien Tort Statue and the obstacles faced by plaintiffs in order to explore to what extent such litigation is feasible. In a second step, I will evaluate whether private litigation can contribute to the protection of labour standards abroad and what lessons can be learned for future transnational labour litigation.

[1]Schaffer et al. (2014), chapter 19; Stephens (2014), pp. 179–198; Parrish (2013), pp. 25–43; Clapham (2014), pp. 535–538; Collingsworth (2002), p. 203 and Bradley (2001), p. 458.

[2]Wuerth (2013), p. 601; Young (2015), pp. 1023–1127. In a number of cases suits have also been based on common law or the Torture Victim Protection Act.

[3]Seibert-Fohr (2003), pp. 195–204. The case was eventually settled out of court.

[4]U.S. District Court N.D. Alabama, *Estate of Lacarno Rodriquez v. Drummond*, 256 F.Supp.2d 1250 (N.D. Ala. 2003).

[5]U.S. District Court S.D. Florida, *Licea v. Curaçao Drydock Co., Inc.,* 584 F. Supp. 2d 1355 (S.D. FLA. 2008).

2 Alien Tort Statute

The Alien Tort Statute was enacted by US Congress more than 200 years ago, in 1789.[6] It provides the basis for civil suits by foreigners seeking damages for violations of public international law in US federal courts and reads: 'The district courts shall have original jurisdiction of any civil action by an alien for a tort only, committed in violation of the law of nations or a treaty of the United States'. The rationale for this law is unclear as there is no record of congressional discussion.[7] Presumably it was designed to cover violations of safe conducts, infringements of the rights of ambassadors, and piracy.[8] For almost 200 years the Act was hardly ever resorted to in litigation.[9] It only gained importance in 1980 when a Paraguayan family filed a suit for damages against a Paraguayan police officer for the kidnapping, torture and death of a Paraguayan national. At this point of time the plaintiffs and the defendant were in the United States. In *Filártiga v. Peña-Irala* the U.S. Court of Appeals for the Second Circuit Court held that the ATS had to be read in light of current international law.[10] Since the prohibition of torture was part of customary international law the Court of Appeals concluded that the ATS provides federal jurisdiction whenever an alleged torturer is found and served with process by an alien within the borders of the United States.

The combination of this jurisdictional provision with contemporary international law offered victims of international law violations an avenue to seek damages in domestic courts. Suddenly the door to US courts seemed open and numerous cases were brought challenging serious violations of human rights[11] including labour rights,[12] and even environmental harm.[13] While early cases were brought against individual perpetrators, the ATS has also been relied on since the 1990s to sue transnational corporations for their involvement in various abuses committed

---

[6]28 U.S.C. § 1350. The following account is based on a comprehensive update of my contribution in the Max Planck Encyclopedia of Public International Law. Seibert-Fohr (2015) and see also Seibert-Fohr and Wolfrum (2005), pp. 153–186.

[7]For the history of the ATS, see Dodge (1996), pp. 221–258 and Paust (2004), pp. 249–66.

[8]U.S. Supreme Court, *Sosa v. Alvarez-Machain,* 542 US 692, 723, 724 (2004) and Steinhardt (2004), pp. 587 et seq.

[9]For a detailed account see Steinhardt and D'Amato (1999).

[10]U.S. Court of Appeals, *Filartiga v. Pena-Irala*, 630 F.2d 876 (2d Cir. 1980).

[11]U.S. Court of Appeals, *Kadic v. Karadzic,* 70 F.3d 232 (2d Cir. 1995); U.S. Court of Appeals, *In re Estate of Ferdinand E. Marcos Human Rights Litigation*, 25 F.3d 1467, 1475 (9th Cir. 1994) and U.S. Court of Appeals, *Doe I v. Unocal Corporation*, 395 F.3d 932 (9th Cir. 2002).

[12]See e.g. California Superior Court, *Union of Needletrades Industrial and Textiles Employees v. The Gap,* Case No. 300474 (Cal. Sup. Ct. 1999) and U.S. District Court N.D. Alabama, *Rodriguez v. Drummond Co.*, 256 F. Supp. 2d 1250 (N.D. Ala. 2003).

[13]U.S. Court of Appeals, *Flores v. Southern Peru Copper Corp.*, 414 F.3d 233 (2d Cir. 2003); U.S. District Court C.D. California, *Sarei et al. v. Rio Tinto Plc et al.*, 221 F.Supp.2nd 1116, 1140 (C.D. Cal. 2002) and U.S. Court of Appeals, *Beanal v. Freeport-McMoran Inc.*, 197 F.3d 161, 167 (5th Cir. 1999). See also Anderson (2002), pp. 399–425.

abroad.[14] For example several enterprises were sued for their involvement in the *apartheid* regime in South Africa.[15] Other cases were filed against American private military contractors for alleged abuses committed in Iraq including in detention facilities, such as the Abu Ghraib prison.[16] There were further cases of alleged complicity in terrorism[17] and against an internet company for disclosing information to Chinese authorities.[18] Some ATS suits led to out of court settlements and compensation packages.[19] In total more than 150 ATS cases have been filed in federal courts against corporations in different industry sectors for alleged abuses in various regions of the world.[20]

3 Causes of Action

In order to successfully trigger federal jurisdiction under the ATS, claims need to meet three basic requirements: the plaintiff must be an alien (1), the defendant must be responsible for a tort (2), and the tort must be in violation of the law of nations or a treaty to which the United States are a party (3). With respect to the third requirement the question arose what is meant by the 'law of nations' and which rules of international law could be referred to under the ATS: only those which had been recognized in 1789 or also those of modern international law. In an effort to specify the causes of action, the US Supreme Court in *Sosa v Alvarez-Machain* held in 2004 that the Statute is based on the understanding that common law provides a cause of action for all violations of international law that carry personal liability.[21] Though it allowed civil suits for modern customary international law violations, it

[14]ExxonMobil, Coca Cola, DelMonte, Nike, Royal Dutch/Shell, Texaco/Chevron, DaimlerChrysler, DynCorp, Drummond Company, Unocal, Occidental Petroleum und Total have been amongst the defendants.

[15]The dismissal of the case was recently confirmed by the 2nd U.S. Circuit Court of Appeals because Ford and IBM had not been sufficiently engaged in wrongdoings in the United States to hold them responsible for killings, torture and other serious human rights violations in South Africa under the ATS. U.S. Court of Appeals, *Balintulo v. Ford Motor Co.*, No. 14-4104 (2d Cir. 2015).

[16]U.S. Court of Appeals, *Saleh v. Titan Corp.*, 580 F.3d 1 (D.C. Cir. 2009) and U.S. Court of Appeals, *Al Shimari v. CACI Premier Technology, Inc*, 758 F.3d 516 (4th Cir. 2014).

[17]U.S. District Court E.D. New York, *Almog v. Arab Bank*, 471 F. Supp. 2d 257 (E.D.N.Y. 2007).

[18]U.S. District Court N.D. California, *Wang Xiaoning v. Yahoo!, Inc.*, Case No. 4:2007cv02151, 36 Media Law Reporter 1589 (Cal. Northern District Court 2007) (The Case was settled out of court).

[19]E.g. suits brought by German forced labour victims. U.S. Court of Appeals, *Princz v. Federal Republic of Germany*, 26 F.3d 1166 (D.C. Cir. 1994). See for the 1995 compensation agreement http://www.justice.gov/archive/opa/pr/1997/January97/029fcs.htm. Accessed 15 Nov 2015.

[20]Childress (2012), p. 713.

[21]U.S. Supreme Court, *Sosa v. Alvarez-Machain,* 542 US 692 (2004), part IV, B.

narrowed the scope of the ATS by further requiring that the international norm has a definite content and is broadly accepted internationally.[22]

In practice, federal courts have admitted genocide,[23] war crimes,[24] crimes against humanity,[25] slavery,[26] torture,[27] extrajudicial killings,[28] enforced disappearances, rape,[29] forced labour[30] and prolonged cruel, inhuman treatment[31] as causes of action which can be the subject of ATS suits. However, they have been more reserved with respect to socio-economic rights.[32] For example, the right to health was not deemed to be precise enough for a cause of action by the U.S. Court of Appeals for the Second Circuit.[33]

The high threshold pronounced in *Sosa v Alvarez-Machain* also has implications for the enforcement of labour standards in U.S. federal courts.[34] Many of these standards are unlikely to qualify as customary international law in the first place. Even if they do, they have to be universal, specific and of mutual concern in order to satisfy the *Sosa* test for ATS suits. Therefore, even the core labour rights pronounced in the 1998 ILO Declaration on Fundamental Principles and Rights at

---

[22]Similarly, accepted as the offences which the drafters of the law had in mind, namely offences against ambassadors and piracy: prohibition of arbitrary arrest does not fall under this modest number of international law violations carrying personal liability.

[23]U.S. Court of Appeals, *Kadic v. Karadzic,* 70 F.3d 232, 242–243 (2d Cir. 1995).

[24]Ibid. See also U.S. District Court N.D. Alabama, *Estate of Lacarno Rodriquez v. Drummond*, 256 F.Supp.2d 1250 (N.D. Ala. 2003), para 3. b I and U.S. District Court C.D. California, *Sarei et al. v. Rio Tinto Plc et al.*, 221 F.Supp.2nd 1116, 1139–1142 (C.D. Cal. 2002).

[25]U.S. Court of Appeals, *Quinn v. Robinson*, 783 F.2d 776, 799 (9th Cir. 1986) and U.S. District Court C.D. California, *Sarei et al. v. Rio Tinto Plc et al.*, 221 F.Supp.2nd 1116, 1149–1151 (C.D. Cal. 2002).

[26]U.S. District Court of New Jersey, *Iwanova v. Ford Motor Co.*, 67 F. Supp. 2d 424 (D.N.J. 1999) and U.S. District Court C.D. California, *National Coalition Gov't of the Union of Burma v. Unocal, Inc.*, 176 F.R.D. 329, 349 (C.D. Cal. 1997).

[27]U.S. Court of Appeals, *Kadic v. Karadzic,* 70 F.3d 232 (2d Cir. 1995) and U.S. District Court C.D. California, *Sarei et al. v. Rio Tinto Plc et al.*, 221 F.Supp.2nd 1116, 1140 (C.D. Cal. 2002).

[28]U.S. District Court S.D. New York, *Wiwa et al. v. Royal Dutch Petroleum Co. et al.*, 2002 WL 319887 (S.D.N.Y. 2002), para 6 and U.S. Court of Appeals, *United States v. Matta-Ballesteros*, 71 F.3d 754, 764 n.5 (9th Cir. 1995).

[29]U.S. Court of Appeals, *Kadic v. Karadzic*, 70 F.3d 232, 243–244 (2d Cir. 1995) and U.S. Court of Appeals, *Doe I v. Unocal Corporation*, 395 F.3d 932 (9th Cir. 2002).

[30]U.S. Court of Appeals, *Doe I v. Unocal Corporation*, 395 F.3d 932, 946 (9th Cir. 2002).

[31]U.S. District Court S.D. New York, *Wiwa et al. v. Royal Dutch Petroleum Co. et al.*, 2002 WL 319887 (S.D.N.Y. 2002), para 6.

[32]U.S. Court of Appeals, *Flores et al. v. Southern Peru Copper Corporation*, 414 F 3d 233 (2d Cir. 2003); U.S. Court of Appeals, *Beanal v. Freeport-McMoran Inc.*, 197 F.3d 161 (5th Cir. 1999) and U.S. District Court C.D. California, *Sarei et al. v. Rio Tinto Plc et al.*, 221 F.Supp.2nd 1116, 1160 (C.D. Cal. 2002).

[33]U.S. Court of Appeals, *Flores et al. v. Southern Peru Copper Corporation*, 414 F 3d 233 (2d Cir. 2003).

[34]For labour standards under the ATS, see Köbele (2009), pp. 123–149.

Work[35] are only partly able to pass this test. For example, the prohibition on discrimination is unlikely to be recognized as actionable under the ATS.[36] The same applies to the freedom of association. A comparison of this right to the prohibition of arbitrary arrest which was rejected as a cause of action in *Sosa v Alvarez-Machain*[37] suggests that the freedom of association will neither be recognized as actionable in federal court. Though the 1948 ILO Convention on the Freedom of Association and Protection of the Right to Organise[38] and the 1949 Convention on the Right to Organise and Collective Bargaining[39] guarantee the right of workers to establish and join trade unions, they arguably lack the specificity and universal acceptance required by the U.S. Supreme Court in *Sosa.*[40]

There is at least a minimum core of labour protection that overlaps with basic human rights and arguably is able to satisfy the *Sosa* test.[41] For example, if corporations are involved in serious human rights violations, such as forced labour,[42] torture or prolonged cruel, inhuman treatment, victims are more likely to be able to make an ATS case.[43]

Whether the prohibition of child labour forms part of this actionable minimum core is not yet fully settled.[44] This question is at issue in *Doe v. Nestle.*[45] The lawsuit was brought by plaintiffs alleging that they had been forced to work on a large cocoa plantation in Côte d'Ivoire after having been trafficked from Mali as

[35]ILO Declaration on Fundamental Principles and Rights at Work and its Follow-up, International Labour Conference, adopted on 18 June 1998 and Annex revised 15 June 2010.

[36]Köbele (2009), p. 134. But see Pagnattaro (2004), pp. 250–254.

[37]U.S. Supreme Court, *Sosa v. Alvarez-Machain,* 542 US 692 (2004), part IV, C.

[38]ILO Convention No. 87 on the Freedom of Association and Protection of the Right to Organise, adopted 9 July 1948 and entry into force 4 July 1950, 68 UNTS 17.

[39]ILO Convention No. 98 on the Right to Organise and Collective Bargaining, adopted 1 July 1949 and entry into force 18 July 1951, 96 UNTS 257.

[40]Köbele (2009), p. 142. See also U.S. District Court S.D. Florida, *Villeda Aldana v. Fresh Del Monte Produce, Inc.*, 305 F. Supp. 2d 1285 (S.D. Fla. 2003). But see U.S. District Court N.D. Alabama, *Estate of Lacarno Rodriquez v. Drummond*, 256 F.Supp.2d 1250 (N.D. Ala. 2003) and U.S. District Court S.D. Florida, *Estate of Winston Cabello v. Fernandez-Larios*, 157 F. Supp. 2d 1359 (S.D. Fla. 2001).

[41]Pagnattaro (2004), pp. 230–254.

[42]With respect to child forced labour see U.S. District Court S.D. Indiana, *Roe v. Bridgestone*, 492 F.2d 988, 1010–1015 (S.D. Ind. 2007). The case was later dismissed on other grounds. For an early recognition of forced labour as a possible cause of action see U.S. District Court of New Jersey, *Iwanova v. Ford Motor Co.*, 67 F. Supp. 2d 424 (D.N.J. 1999) and U.S. District Court C.D. California, *National Coalition Gov't of the Union of Burma v. Unocal, Inc.*, 176 F.R.D. 329 (C.D. Cal. 1997). See also U.S. Court of Appeals, *Doe I v. Unocal Corporation*, 395 F.3d 932, 946 (9th Cir. 2002).

[43]Köbele (2009), pp. 146, 148.

[44]Wendle (2014), pp. 447–483. According to the Court of Appeals for the Seventh Circuit in *Flomo v. Firestone Natural Rubber Co.*, 643 F.3d 1013, 1022 (7th Cir. 2011), the prohibition of child labour was too vague for customary international law.

[45]U.S. Court of Appeals, *Doe v. Nestlé USA*, 766 F.3d 1013, 1028 (9th Cir. 2014). For another child labour case see Bergman (2011), pp. 455–479.

child slaves. They were allegedly forced to work long hours without pay and kept in locked rooms after work suffering from severe physical abuse from their guards. According to the ILO Convention concerning the Prohibition and Immediate Action for the Elimination of the Worst Forms of Child Labour such forms of child exploitation are clearly prohibited.[46] The Convention's precise scope and its unanimous adoption as well as its broad ratification suggest that the prohibition of the worst forms of child labour as spelled out in Art. 3 of the Convention is able to satisfy the *Sosa* test.[47] At any rate, child forced labour is more likely to be recognized as actionable than non-violent abuses of other labour rights.[48] At the time of writing in 2015 the *Nestle Chocolate Case* is still pending and it remains to be seen whether the claim of child forced labour will be recognized by the court.

4 Corporate Liability

An issue which also is still unsettled is the question whether liability under the ATS extends to individuals only (e.g. corporate executives) or also to corporations as such. The issue has been on the docket of various federal courts for some time now. The US Court of Appeals for the Eleventh Circuit in *Sinaltrainal v. Coca-Cola* recognized that corporate defendants are subject to liability under the ATS and may be liable for violations of customary international law.[49] However the Second Circuit held in *Kiobel v. Royal Dutch Petroleum* that no corporation had ever been subject to liability under customary international law so that there was no room for corporate liability under the ATS.[50]

The controversy is due to the mix of domestic and international law under the Alien Tort Statute. Since it recognizes a civil remedy on the basis of international law the relationship between the two sources of law and the question which liability

[46]ILO Convention No. 182 Concerning the Prohibition and Immediate Action for the Elimination of the Worst Forms of Child Labor, adopted 17 June 1999, entry into force 19 November 2000, 2133 UNTS 161.

[47]Köbele (2009), p. 139. But see U.S. Court of Appeals, *Flomo v. Firestone Natural Rubber Co.*, 643 F.3d 1013, 1022 (7th Cir. 2011).

[48]Wendle (2014), p. 482. See also U.S. District Court C.D. California, *Doe v. Nestle SA*, 748 F. Supp. 2d 1057, 1075 (C.D. Cal. 2010) and U.S. Court of Appeals, *Flomo v. Firestone Natural Rubber Co.*, 643 F.3d 1013, 1022, 1023 (7th Cir. 2011). For the difficulty to distinguish between child labour that violates customary international law from those rules which do not constitute such violations see U.S. District Court S.D. Indiana, *Roe v. Bridgestone*, 492 F.2d 988, 1020 (S.D. Ind. 2007).

[49]U.S. Court of Appeals, *Sinaltrainal v Coca-Cola Co.*, 578 F 3d 1252 (11th Cir. 2009). See also U.S. Court of Appeals, *Flomo v. Firestone Natural Rubber Co.*, 643 F.3d 1013, 1021–1022 (7th Cir. 2011); U.S. Court of Appeals, *Sarei v. Rio Tinto PLC*, 671 F.3d 736, 748 (9th Cir. 2011); U.S. Court of Appeals, *Romero v. Drummond Co.*, 552 F.3d 1303, 1315 (11th Cir. 2008); U.S. Court of Appeals, *Doe v. Exxon Mobil Corp.*, 654 F.3d 11, 57 (D.C. Cir. 2011) and U.S. Court of Appeals, *Doe v. Nestlé USA*, 766 F.3d 1013, 1021–1023 (9th Cir. 2014).

[50]U.S. Court of Appeals, *Kiobel v. Royal Dutch Petroleum*, 621 F.3d 111, 145, 176 (2d Cir. 2010).

standard should govern is contentious. Most international law commentators consider corporations not to be bound by international law.[51] Therefore, without a customary international law rule, which binds transnational corporations, arguably there cannot be a customary international law violation to trigger ATS jurisdiction in the first place. On the other hand, corporate liability is firmly recognized in U.S. common law. Since common law provides for the cause of action in ATS suits a combination of international and common law suggests itself.

As both lines of argument are feasible it does not surprise that different Circuits of the Court of Appeal have taken different positions on corporate liability under the ATS. The Supreme Court has not taken a position on this issue so far. It decided the *Kiobel Case* on a different ground and thus avoided the issue of corporate liability.[52] Future Supreme Court jurisprudence is likely to address this issue. At the time of this chapter's publication the case *Jesner v. Arab Bank, PLC*, which presents the question whether the ATS forecloses corporate liability, is still pending before the Supreme Court.

5 Extraterritoriality

Another issue, which has steered debate, is the question of extraterritoriality. Most cases against transnational corporations concern abuses committed abroad. Therefore, granting damages for such extraterritorial abuses has been criticized as an interference with foreign internal matters.[53] In reaction to this criticism, the Supreme Court cautioned federal courts already in *Sosa v. Alvarez-Machain* of the potentially adverse foreign relations implications and asked them to give serious weight to the Executive Branch's view.[54] In its 2013 judgment in *Kiobel v. Royal Dutch Petroleum* the Supreme Court even went beyond, finding a presumption against extraterritoriality under the ATS.[55] The Court required that a claim must 'touch and concern' the territory of the United States 'with sufficient force' in order to overcome this presumption.[56]

Though the precise parameters of the 'touch and concern' test were not spelled out, the Court mentioned that the mere corporate presence in the US would be insufficient to trigger jurisdiction under the ATS because corporations are often present in many countries.[57] In *Kiobel* the defendant had not been a domestic but

[51] Paust (2002), pp. 801–826; Ratner (2001), pp. 443–545; Schmalenbach (2001), pp. 57–81; Frey (1997), pp. 153–188; Cassel (1996), pp. 1963–1984; Mock (2000), pp. 15–26 and Wood and Scharffs (2002), pp. 531–566.

[52] U.S. Supreme Court, *Kiobel v. Royal Dutch Petroleum*, 133 S.Ct. 1659, 1663 *et seq.* (2013).

[53] For further details see Seibert-Fohr (2015).

[54] U.S. Supreme Court, *Sosa v. Alvarez-Machain,* 542 US 692, 695 (2004).

[55] U.S. Supreme Court, *Kiobel v. Royal Dutch Petroleum*, 133 S.Ct. 1659, 1669 (2013).

[56] Ibid. See also Giegerich (2014), pp. 335–367.

[57] U.S. Supreme Court, *Kiobel v. Royal Dutch Petroleum*, 133 S.Ct. 1659, 1669 (2013).

foreign corporation. The plaintiffs, Nigerian citizens, had sued Royal Dutch Shell for aiding and abetting in the commission of serious human rights violations committed by the Nigerian Government in Nigeria. As the case had been brought by an alien against a foreign corporation for acts committed on foreign soil, the Court denied jurisdiction.[58]

While *Kiobel v. Royal Dutch Petroleum* was a rather clear-cut case, the outcome is less obvious in other cases which show some sort of connection to the United States.[59] Arguably the nationality of the defendant company could play a role. But the Second Circuit in *Balintulo et al. v. Daimler AG* found that it is insufficient to overcome the presumption of extraterritoriality if a claim is brought against a US company.[60] Other Circuits have considered nationality at least as one aspect to be considered.[61] In other words, US nationality of a corporation may be a relevant factor supporting ATS jurisdiction, but not sufficient *per se* according to this line of jurisprudence.

The question how much more territorial nexus is needed for ATS suits is still controversial. Justice Kennedy recognized in his concurrence in *Kiobel* that the judgment left open significant questions regarding the reach of the ATS.[62] It is essential to specify additional parameters (beyond nationality) for a claim to touch and concern the territory of the United States. But so far it is unclear what exactly constitutes 'relevant conduct' for the determination of extraterritoriality. Is it sufficient if a claim generally exhibits significant contacts with the United States or is it necessary for the violation itself to take place within U.S. territory? The most rigid analysis of the touch and concern test was proposed by the concurrent opinion of Justices Alito and Thomas in *Kiobel*. They required that the domestic conduct itself be in violation of international law.[63]

The case most likely to overcome the presumption of extraterritoriality thus is a tort which involves corporate conduct in the United States.[64] If abuses are planned

---

[58]Ibid.

[59]For cases in which the presumption of extraterritoriality could be overcome see Cleveland (2014), pp. 567 et seq.

[60]U.S. Court of Appeals, *Balintulo et al. v. Daimler AG*, 727 F.3d 174 (2d Cir. 2013). See also U.S. Court of Appeals, *Mastafa v. Chevron Corp., 770 F.3D 170 (2D CIR. 2014).*

[61]U.S. District Court D. Massachusetts, *Sexual Minorities Uganda v. Lively*, 960 F.Supp.2d 304, 321 (D. Mass. 2013); U.S. District Court D. Maryland, *Daobin v. Cisco Sys., Inc.*, 2 F. Supp. 3d 717, 728 (D. MD. 2014) and U.S. Court of Appeals, *Al Shimari v. CACI Premier Technology, Inc*, 758 F.3d 516 (4th Cir. 2014).

[62]U.S. Supreme Court, *Kiobel v. Royal Dutch Petroleum*, 133 S.Ct. 1659, 1669 (2013).

[63]Ibid. See also U.S. Court of Appeals, *Mastafa v. Chevron Corp., 770 F.3D 170 (2D CIR. 2014)*, which is based on the 'focus test'. But see U.S. Court of Appeals, *Al Shimari v. CACI Premier Technology, Inc*, 758 F.3d 516 (4th Cir. 2014) and U.S. Court of Appeals, *Doe v. Nestlé USA*, 766 F.3d 1013, 1028 (9th Cir. 2014). For the focus test see U.S. Supreme Court, *Morrison v. - Australian National Bank*, 561 U.S. 247 (2010).

[64]One example is the fundraising and hosting of meetings in support of a foreign terror organization. See U.S. District Court District of New Jersey, *Krishanti v. Rajaratnam*, No. 2:09-cv-05395, 2014 U.S. Dist. Lexis 58314 (D.N.J. 2014), p. 10. For further examples see Coleman and Holland (2013) with reference to U.S. District Court District of Columbia, *Mwani v. Bin Laden*, 947 F. Supp.2d 1, 5 (D.D.C. 2013).

and managed to a substantial degree on its territory, a claim for damages arguably touches and concerns the United States with sufficient force. One example is *Sexual Minorities Uganda v. Lively* in which an Ugandan Non-Profit Organisation sued a US citizen for allegedly assisting, encouraging and consulting from the United States the persecution of LGBTI persons in Uganda. The US District Court in 2013 rejected a motion to dismiss this case as extraterritorial because defendant's *domestic* conduct had violated international law.[65] A later motion to dismiss was denied by the US Court of Appeals for the First Circuit in 2014.[66] A further appeal to the First Circuit Court of Appeals against the District court's renewed dismissal of the case is still pending at the time of this chapter's publication. Another case which was not dismissed for the presumption of extraterritoriality was *Al Shimari v. CACI Premier Technology*. The Fourth Circuit allowed this ATS suit against an American military contractor for abuses and torture in the Abu Ghraib prison to proceed.[67]

However, in *Cardona v. Chiquita Brands* the US Court of Appeals for the Eleventh Circuit dismissed an ATS suit for illegal payments to Colombian paramilitaries who were allegedly responsible for killings and enforced disappearances despite the fact that some steps had been taken in the United States.[68] On a similar basis the Second Circuit in *Balintulo v. Daimler* held that supplying computer systems and cars to the apartheid regime in South Africa was insufficient to overcome the presumption of extraterritoriality as the human rights violation had occurred in South Africa.[69]

Though since 2013 a number of ATS suits have been dismissed, it appears that the strict interpretation of *Kiobel* by the U.S. Court of Appeals for the Second Circuit is not shared by all circuits. The above cited cases reveal that jurisprudence diverges on the issue what is required to fulfill the touch and concern test.[70] Ultimately this matter is likely to be determined by the Supreme Court some time in the future in order to clarify for which conduct a transnational company can be sued under the ATS.

---

[65]U.S. District Court D. Massachusetts, *Sexual Minorities Uganda v. Lively*, 960 F.Supp.2d 304, 321 (D. Mass. 2013).

[66]See http://www.masslive.com/news/index.ssf/2014/12/scott_lively.html. Accessed 13 Nov 2015.

[67]U.S. Court of Appeals, *Al Shimari, v. CACI Premier Tech.*, 758 F.3d 516, 528, 530–531 (4th Cir. 2014). In this case the contract had substantial ties to the United States and managers in the United States had allegedly implicitly encouraged the abuses.

[68]U.S. Court of Appeals, *Cardona v. Chiquita Brands Int' l, Inc.*, 760 F.3d 1185 (11th Cir. 2014). See also U.S. Court of Appeals, *Baloco v. Drummond Co.*, 767 F.3d 1229 (11th Cir. 2014).

[69]U.S. Court of Appeals, *Balintulo et al. v. Daimler AG*, 727 F.3d 174 (2d Cir. 2013).

[70]Coleman and Holland (2013).

6 Conclusion

In the absence of an effective international enforcement mechanism for labour rights domestic courts can arguably provide for an alternative for the enforcement of international standards. But, though the U.S. Alien Tort Statute which combines international standards with domestic judicial remedies seemed to open up this avenue, the latest experience under this statute is sobering.[71] Since *Sosa* and *Kiobel* the Supreme Court has narrowed this avenue substantially. The canon of international norms which can serve as a basis for a tort claim under the ATS is reduced to a core of well-established customary human rights rules. Apart from this substantive restriction, the territorial scope has been limited by requiring that a claim has sufficient contacts with the United States which effectively precludes universal civil litigation under the Statute. As a result, the avenue for enforcing international labour rights has been narrowed to a small set of core protections and plaintiffs need to demonstrate a territorial nexus to the United States territory for which the nationality of the defendant corporation alone is insufficient. Only a few federal courts have found sufficient contacts with the United States to deny dismissal of pending cases so far.

Nevertheless, the door is not closed and federal courts are still in the process of delimiting the exact scope of ATS litigation. I would argue that if a rule of international law is sufficiently established, such as forced labour, and if an abuse has been aided and abetted in on U.S. territory, federal courts should recognize their jurisdiction under the Statute. There are good reasons to interpret the ATS in a way that prevents transnational corporations from abusing U.S territory as a safe harbour for abusive conduct abroad.[72]

While the ATS was criticized for being overly broad in past decades, I would argue that its interpretation is now overly rigid. International human rights institutions show an increasing awareness of transnational corporations' human rights records.[73] Since the notion of direct corporate accountability has been met with resistance by national States, it is consequent to call on them to exercise their jurisdiction to prevent serious human rights violations abroad and to provide remedies effectively. For this reason the UN Human Rights Committee encouraged Germany in 2012 'to set out clearly the expectation that all business enterprises domiciled in its territory and/or its jurisdiction respect human rights standards in accordance with the Covenant throughout their operations'.[74] It also encouraged Germany 'to take appropriate measures to strengthen

[71]Even if jurisdiction under the ATS can be established, suits for civil damages incurred abroad face additional procedural obstacles regarding justiciability, such as the political question doctrine, *forum non-conveniens*, the doctrine of international comity and the rules on sovereign immunity. See Seibert-Fohr (2015).

[72]For this rationale see also Justice Breyer in U.S. Supreme Court, *Kiobel v. Royal Dutch Petroleum*, 133 S.Ct. 1659, 1674 (2013).

[73]Human Rights Council (2011); UN Committee on Economic, Social and Cultural Rights (2005), para. 52 et seq. and UN Commission on Human Rights, Sub-Commission on the Promotion and Protection of Human Rights (2003), p. 52.

[74]Human Rights Committee (2012), para 16.

the remedies provided to protect people who have been victims of activities of such business enterprises operating abroad'.[75] If this recommendation is taken seriously and followed up on by States, there is hope that new potentials for transnational labour litigation will ensue in the future.[76]

References

Anderson M (2002) Transnational corporations and environmental damage: is tort law the answer? Washburn Law J 41:399–425

Bergman J (2011) The Alien Tort Statute and Flomo v. Firestone Natural Rubber Company: the key to change in global child labor practices? Indiana J Glob Leg Stud 18:455–479

Bradley CA (2001) The costs of international human rights litigation. Chicago J Int Law 2:457–474

Cassel D (1996) Corporate initiatives: a second human rights revolution? Fordham Int Law J 19:1963–1984

Childress DE (2012) The Alien Tort Statute, federalism, and the next wave of transnational litigation. Transnat Litig 100:709–757

Clapham A (2014) Non-state actors. In: Moeckli D, Shah S, Sivakumaran S (eds) International human rights law. Oxford University Press, Oxford, pp 531–549

Cleveland S (2014) After Kiobel. J Int Crim Just 12:551–574

Coleman TJ, Holland EB (2013) Touching and concerning 'Kiobel': continuing implications. N Y Law J 253

Collingsworth T (2002) Boundaries in the field of human rights, the key human rights challenge: developing enforcement mechanisms. Harv Hum Rights J 15:183–204

Dodge WS (1996) The historical origins of the Alien Tort Statute: a response to the 'Originalists'. Hast Int Comp Law Rev 19:221–258

Frey BA (1997) The legal and ethical responsibilities of transnational corporations in the protection of international human rights. Minn J Glob Trade 6:153–188

[75]Ibid. See also Human Rights Committee (2015) para. 6, where the Committee based its recommendation on the fact that Canadian enterprises had received support from the government. The recommendation reads: 'While appreciating information provided, the Committee is concerned about allegations of human rights abuses by Canadian companies operating abroad, in particular mining corporations and about the inaccessibility to remedies by victims of such violations. The Committee regrets the absence of an effective independent mechanism with powers to investigate complaints alleging abuses by such corporations that adversely affect the enjoyment of the human rights of victims, and of a legal framework that would facilitate such complaints (art. 2). The State party should: a) enhance the effectiveness of existing mechanisms to ensure that all Canadian corporations, in particular mining corporations, under its jurisdiction respect human rights standards when operating abroad; b) consider establishing an independent mechanism with powers to investigate human rights abuses by such corporations abroad; c) and develop a legal framework that affords legal remedies to people who have been victims of activities of such corporations operating abroad.'

[76]As demonstrated by a 2013 comparative study, the existing remedies are still flawed in many respects. Skinner et al. (2013), pp. 66–67.

Giegerich T (2014) Demise of a 'Legal Lohengrin'? An international lawyer's question mark over Kiobel v. Royal Dutch Petroleum. In: Delbrück J (ed) Aus Kiel in die Welt: Kiel's contribution to international law. Dunckler & Humblot, Berlin, pp 335–367
Human Rights Committee (2012) Concluding observations on the Sixth Periodic Report of Germany, adopted 15 Oct-2 Nov 2012, CCPR/C/DEU/CO/6
Human Rights Committee (2015) Concluding observations on the Sixth Periodic Report of Canada, adopted 20 July 2015, CCPR/C/CAN/CO/6
Human Rights Council (2011) Human rights and transnational corporations and other business enterprises, Res. A/HRC/RES/17/4
Köbele M (2009) Corporate responsibility under the Alien Tort Statute: enforcement of international law through US torts law. Martinus Nijhoff, Leiden, pp 123–149
Mock W (2000) Corporate transparency and human rights. Tulsa J Comp Int Law 8:15–26
Pagnattaro MA (2004) Enforcing international labor standards: the potential of the Alien Tort Claims Act. Vanderbilt J Transnat Law 37:203–264
Parrish AL (2013) State court international human rights litigation: a concerning trend? UC Levine Law Rev 3:25–43
Paust JJ (2002) Human rights responsibilities of private corporations. Vanderbilt J Transnat Law 35:801–826
Paust JJ (2004) The history, nature, and reach of the Alien Tort Claims Act. Fla J Int Law 16:249–266
Ratner SR (2001) Corporations and human rights: a theory of legal responsibility. Yale Law J 111:443–545
Schaffer R, Agusti F, Dhooge L, Earle B (2014) International business law and its environment, 9th edn. Cengage Learning, Stamford
Schmalenbach K (2001) Multinationale Unternehmen und Menschenrechte. Archiv des Völkerrechts 39:57–81
Seibert-Fohr A (2003) Die Deliktshaftung von Unternehmen für die Beteiligung an im Ausland begangenen Völkerrechtsverletzungen- Anmerkungen zum Urteil Doe I v. Unocal Corp. des U.S. Court of Appeals (9th Circuit). Zeitschrift für ausländisches öffentliches Recht und Völkerrecht 63:195–204
Seibert-Fohr A (2015) United States Alien Tort Statute. In: Wolfrum R (ed) Max Planck encyclopedia of public international law. Oxford University Press, Oxford. Available via DIALOG. http://opil.ouplaw.com/home/epil. Accessed 09 Aug 2017
Seibert-Fohr A, Wolfrum R (2005) Die einzelstaatliche Durchsetzung völkerrechtlicher Mindeststandards gegenüber transnationalen Unternehmen. Archiv des Völkerrechts 43 (2):153–186
Skinner G, McCorquodale R, De Schutter O (2013) The third pillar: access to judicial remedies for human rights violations by transnational business. http://icar.ngo/wp-content/uploads/2013/02/The-Third-Pillar-Access-to-Judicial-Remedies-for-Human-Rights-Violation-by-Transnational-Business.pdf. Accessed 13 Nov 2015
Steinhardt RG (2004) The Alien Tort Claims Act: theoretical and historical foundations of the Alien Tort Claims Act and its discontents. St. Thomas Law Rev 16:585–605
Steinhardt RG, D'Amato A (eds) (1999) The Alien Tort Claims Act: an analytical anthology. Transnational Publisher, New York
Stephens B (2014) Human rights litigation in U.S. courts against individuals and cooperations. In: Blecher L, Stafford NK, Bellamy GC (eds) Corporate responsibility for human rights impacts: new expectations and paradigms. ABA Publishing, Chicago, pp 179–198
UN Commission on Human Rights, Sub-Commission on the Promotion and Protection of Human Rights (2003) Responsibility of transnational corporations and other business enterprises with regard to human rights, Res. 2003/16, UN Doc. E/CN.4/Sub.2/2003/L.11

UN Committee on Economic, Social and Cultural Rights (2005) General Comment No. 18 - Right to Work, UN Doc. E/C.12/GC/18
Wendle K (2014) Establishing liability for the enslavement and forced labour of children under the Alien Tort Statute. Syracuse J Int Comp Law 41:447–483
Wood SG, Scharffs BG (2002) Applicability of human rights standards to private corporations: an American perspective. Am J Comp Law Suppl 50:531–566
Wuerth I (2013) Kiobel v. Royal Dutch Petroleum Co.: The Supreme Court and the Alien Tort Statute. Am J Int Law 107:601–621
Young EA (2015) Universal jurisdiction, the Alien Tort Statute, and transnational public law litigation after Kiobel. Duke Law J 64:1023–1127

Promoting Labour Standards in Global Supply Chains Through Consumers' Choice: Is Social Labelling Effective?

Nazli Aghazadeh

Contents

Abstract This chapter will focus on social labelling schemes implemented by non-governmental organizations (NGOs), which are one form of private regulatory initiatives for the promotion of labour standards in global supply chains. From a theoretical perspective, these schemes are based on information asymmetries in terms of social conditions in production, which exist between consumers and producers.

N. Aghazadeh (✉)
Georg-August-University Göttingen, Institute of International and European Law, Göttingen, Germany
e-mail: nazli.aghazadeh@stud.uni-goettingen.de

H. Gött (ed.), *Labour Standards in International Economic Law*,
https://doi.org/10.1007/978-3-319-69447-4_17

They aim to minimize this information asymmetry, as equal levels of information enable consumers to decide in favour of products made under good conditions over those made under bad conditions. However, in practice there remains an information asymmetry, primarily between the producers and the labelling NGOs, but inevitably being passed on to the consumers. This results mainly from a deficient oversight capacity of the implementing NGOs to ensure that their standards are met. Therefore, the effectiveness of the labelling schemes is limited. This will be shown by means of three existing schemes, namely GoodWeave, Fairtrade, and the Forest Stewardship Council (FSC). Hence, it will be argued that transparency with regard to the NGOs' actual oversight capacity is necessary to make labelling schemes more effective. This might be achieved through a regulatory approach addressing the information provided by the labels. Furthermore, the International Labour Organization (ILO) could play a significant role by supporting labelling NGOs with necessary resources to strengthen their oversight capacity.

1 Introduction

Globalization and the expansion of internationally dispersed production has been a growing challenge for the regulation of labour conditions in production. Traditionally, regulation has been accomplished by public entities such as states and international organizations. However, those entities are bound to their jurisdiction, while multinational corporations are able to take advantage of so-called regulatory arbitrage. Since the 1990s, regulation therefore seems to be getting a second wing in form of private regulatory initiatives. Those have been emerging in response to perceived failures of public entities due to political obstructions.[1] Started by non-state actors, either by industry itself ('self-regulation') or third parties, they verify corporations' compliance with labour standards in production.[2] One form of such private regulatory initiatives are social labelling schemes implemented by non-governmental organizations (NGOs).

Social labelling 'connote[s] a mean of communicating information, through a physical label, about the social conditions surrounding the production of a product or rendering of a service'.[3] This information is meant to enable consumers to distinguish between products in ethical terms and not only with regard to the price. Consumers can thereby decide in favour of products which were produced under equitable social conditions. Consumers' preference of those products could in turn incentivize producers to introduce or maintain such conditions.[4] Richard Freeman shows that up to a certain point consumers would be willing to pay an

[1]See O'Rourke (2003), pp. 4–5.

[2]See Bartley (2007), pp. 297–298.

[3]Urminsky (2001), p. 38.

[4]Cf. Zadek et al. (1998), p. 16.

additional amount for products made under good social conditions.[5] The label verifies these conditions and thereby serves as a valuable intermediary between consumers and producers by reducing transaction costs on both sides. Transaction costs would arise on the one hand for consumers if they had to search for the information they are interested in by themselves and on the other hand for producers if they had to convince consumers of their good social performance.[6] The higher efforts on the producers' side and respectively the higher price on the consumers' side would therefore be worth it.

Social labelling schemes have been spreading rapidly,[7] as the public demand for Corporate Social Responsibility (CSR) has grown and reputation has become an increasingly important aspect for business. By participating in social labelling schemes, companies can prevent public accusations, consumer boycotts, and even legal charges for indecent or unlawful social practices.[8] Therefore, it has become an attractive instrument for firms, which in turn has led to a huge amount of labelled products on the market.

The attraction of social labelling, and thus the quantity of labelled products on the market, has made scholars call into question its actual efficacy. Yet, the evaluation whether or not social labelling schemes are 'effective' depends on the assumptions this assessment is based on. In other words: Whether their performance is regarded as effective may vary with the purpose that is subscribed to them.

Many authors assume that social labelling schemes are supposed to enforce labour standards in global supply chains.[9] Enforcement is, in this context, understood as induction of compliance or at least an increase in the level of compliance.[10] Accordingly, social labelling schemes are viewed as 'effective', if they induce compliance or increase the level of compliance with labour standards.

Given the limited resources of NGOs in relation to the complexity of the political and socio-economic context of today's issues,[11] this view appears to overestimate the capacity of social labelling schemes. In contrast, this chapter will argue that their capacity is restricted to market-based incentives and should therefore be merely considered as such. This becomes especially important for the evaluation of their potential and the discussion on how to strengthen it. For this aim, the chapter takes another perspective:

George Akerlof developed a theory on asymmetric information in the market, which provides a useful framework to understand the purpose and mechanism of social labelling. This framework will be used to determine under what condition social labelling schemes are 'effective' (2). By applying this framework, the

[5]See Freeman (1994), pp. 80–84.

[6]Cf. Chestnut (2013), p. 347.

[7]See Hicks (2012), pp. 165–166.

[8]Cf. Diller (1999), pp. 100–101.

[9]See e.g. Marx and Wouters (2016), p. 3.

[10]Marx and Wouters (2016), p. 6.

[11]See Nooruddin and Sokhey (2012), pp. 83–84.

effectiveness of three existing labels will be assessed. It will become apparent that their effectiveness is limited because of certain aspects (3). The attention is focused on labelling schemes initiated by NGOs and covering (inter alia or solely) labour issues. Nevertheless, both Fair Trade labels and Ethical Trade labels,[12] as well as different sectors are represented. In a further step, a proposal will be given on how to overcome the current limitations of social labelling schemes (4). The chapter will end with a conclusion (5).

2 The Idea of Minimizing Asymmetric Information in the Market

In this section, the objective is to facilitate an understanding of the idea behind social labelling, that is to say what social labelling is actually supposed to do. As, in general, social labelling tries to influence market developments in support of social objectives and is, in this respect, a market-based regulatory initiative (see Sect. 1), it seems appropriate to look at it from an economic perspective. In this context, George Akerlof's theory[13] on asymmetric information in the market provides valuable findings.

For his research on asymmetric information on the market George Akerlof received the 2001 Nobel Prize in Economics.[14] His paper 'The Market for 'Lemons'' (1970) has become a fundamental point of reference in the economics of information in particular, but also in social sciences in general.

Akerlof's theory has been applied to various markets, such as the financial market, the insurance market, and the labour market.[15] This is understandable seeing that these examples were given by Akerlof himself.[16] However, Akerlof also mentioned the consumer goods market.[17] Still, the application of his theory on social labelling has not been considered adequately in light of the fact that—as may become apparent below—social labelling precisely targets the problem Akerlof analyses with regard to the consumer goods market.

There are, indeed, explanations of eco- and food labelling, which are based on the notion of information asymmetry, and—either explicitly or implicitly—refer to

[12]For this distinction see Zadek et al. (1998), pp. 24–27.

[13]The term 'theory' is used for the sake of delineation from 'practice', which is dealt with in the next section. To be precise, Akerlof has actually built a 'model' which is the basis for the more far-reaching neo-institutional theory of economics and the school of thought of New Institutional Economics.

[14]Jointly with Michael Spence and Joseph Stiglitz.

[15]For an (early) overview of the contributions see e.g. Löfgren et al. (2002), pp. 206–209.

[16]Cf. Akerlof (1970), pp. 492–499.

[17]Ibid., pp. 495–496.

Akerlof's theory.[18] These contributions have served as inspirations for this chapter. Yet, unfortunately, their implications with respect to the question of the effectiveness of labelling are rather scarce and Akerlof's theory has not been used at its full potential.

Therefore, in the following Akerlof's relevant core findings are first presented more in-depth and subsequently applied to social labelling. From that perspective, it is possible to derive the condition that has to be met in order to regard social labelling schemes as 'effective'.

Akerlof uses 'lemons', a common American term for used cars with poor quality,[19] as an example to illustrate the economic implications of asymmetric information in the market. The seller of a used car has in general more knowledge about the quality of the car than any potential buyer, as she or he has better knowledge of the history of the car. Accordingly, there is an information asymmetry between owners and potential buyers in the used car market.[20]

The effects caused by this information asymmetry are problematic. Akerlof notes that potential buyers usually assume that any used car is of lower quality than a new one. This is because 'it is impossible for a buyer to tell the difference between a good car and a bad car; only the seller knows'.[21] Therefore, owners of used cars reduce their prices, in order to encourage people to buy their used cars. At the same time, Akerlof observes that there are some sellers who *have to* offer a high quality car for sale, for example because they are moving abroad. Since potential buyers are unable to distinguish between high and low quality cars, their decision is based solely on the price. Assuming that sellers price their used cars according to the quality, high quality cars are more expensive than low quality cars. Therefore, sellers with high quality cars on offer do either not receive an appropriate price or they are unwilling to offer their cars on the market. This finding of Akerlof—'lemons' driving out high quality used cars from the market—is associated with the term 'adverse selection'. In view of this process, Akerlof comes to the conclusion that the information asymmetry in the market results in a market inefficiency.[22]

'Numerous institutions arise to counteract the effects of quality uncertainty'.[23] Social labelling can be understood as one of those institutions. It is meant to address the problem of asymmetric information which exists between consumers and producers. Due to globalization and dispersed production, consumers are presumably not familiar with the social conditions in production. Social labels aim to provide this information for consumers, as they are not in a position to observe the social conditions by themselves. The idea then is that a certain level of information

[18]See e.g. Chestnut (2013), pp. 345–347; Golan et al. (2001), pp. 136–137 and Hartman (2014), p. 53.

[19]See Akerlof (1970), p. 489.

[20]Cf. Löfgren et al. (2002), p. 197.

[21]Akerlof (1970), p. 490.

[22]Cf. Barkley Rosser (2003), p. 10.

[23]Akerlof (1970), p. 490.

regarding the products enables consumers to decide in favour of those products which have been produced under good social conditions. Meanwhile, a lack of this information might rather render a decision in favour of products that are cheaper, but produced under bad social conditions. Through the lens of Akerlof's theory, an adverse selection of 'high quality products'—meaning produced under good social conditions—might be caused. Clearly this is not how an efficient market is supposed to work. Thus, in order to avoid this market inefficiency, social labelling schemes aim to minimize the information asymmetry between consumers and producers and thereby turn the selection in favour of 'high quality products'.

In this sense, labelling schemes are 'effective' if they minimize the information asymmetry between consumers and producers. In contrast to the assumption that social labelling schemes are supposed to enforce labour standards in global supply chains, this view seems to grasp the capacity of labelling schemes in a more confined way. It points out their influence on market developments and thereby shows their actual potential, which is to provide market-based incentives. Even though the ultimate aim of providing market-based incentives might be to induce compliance with labour standards, this view is probably still more realistic with regard to their expected impact. It recognizes the fact that between the provision of market-based incentives and the influence on market developments on the one hand, and ultimately the induction of compliance with labour standards on the other hand, there is a step—or some steps—in between. One does not necessarily cause the other. Therefore, it appears more accurate to explore on a limited ground whether the labelling schemes in question are able to minimize the information asymmetry between consumers and producers. If this is the case, they can be regarded as 'effective'. This notion of effectiveness is taken as the basis for the following analysis. It determines the labelling schemes' 'target', which shall now be compared to their actual 'performance'.

3 The Limitations of Social Labelling Schemes

With the aforementioned framework in mind, it is the aim of this section to assess three existing labelling schemes in terms of their effectiveness. The focus will be on one specific characteristic of each scheme to argue that its effectiveness is limited. Although in each case there might be other characteristics that could give reason for concern, the characteristics referred to here may be considered as the most problematic ones with regard to the purpose of labelling schemes as it is determined here (see Sect. 2).

The selection of the labelling schemes that shall be examined is based on three criteria: First, they are all initiated by NGOs. Second, they apply to different sectors. Third, they focus on different labour issues. The use of these criteria resulted in the selection of the labelling schemes GoodWeave (formerly known as RugMark), Fairtrade and the Forest Stewardship Council (FSC).

Each case will be analysed by following the same structure to facilitate a comparison. First of all, the labelling scheme in question will be briefly introduced by describing its aims and approach. Afterwards, its problematic characteristic and the subsequent constraints to achieve its purpose are pointed out. Finally, some concluding remarks about its effectiveness can be formulated with reference to the applied framework. At the end of the section, interim conclusions from the whole assessment will be recapitulated.[24]

3.1 *GoodWeave*

GoodWeave is a social labelling scheme that is administered by GoodWeave International (GWI). GWI is a non-profit organization[25] which is incorporated in the United States.[26] The organization was founded in 1994 as the RugMark Foundation. Accordingly, the labelling scheme was named RugMark at the time. In 2009 the RugMark Foundation changed to GWI and the labelling scheme became GoodWeave.[27]

GoodWeave operates in the carpet industry. Its main issue of concern is the use of child labour in carpet production. GoodWeave addresses manufacturers in the carpet exporting countries India, Nepal, and Afghanistan. On the other hand, it draws on consumers' awareness for child labour in the carpet importing countries Germany, the United Kingdom and the United States.[28]

3.1.1 Aims and Approach

'GoodWeave's mission is to end child labour in the carpet industry'.[29] In pursuit of this, it attempts to give carpet manufacturers an incentive not to employ children for production. That incentive is consumers' preference for child-labour-free carpets.[30]

GoodWeave labels carpets which apparently have been produced without child work. 'The certification claim is that no child labour [...] was used in the production of the certified carpet'.[31]

---

[24]Since the argument of this chapter is of a conceptual nature, the following assessment is not an empirical study. It rather builds on other sources for relevant empirical information. The conceptual implications are the focus of interest though.

[25]See http://www.goodweave.net/index.php?cid=156. Accessed 5 Mar 2016.

[26]See GWI (2016b), p. 3.

[27]See GWI (2009).

[28]See http://www.goodweave.net/index.php?cid=156. Accessed 5 Mar 2016.

[29]GWI (2016b), p. 2.

[30]See GWI (2013), pp. 4–5 and GWI (2016b), p. 2.

[31]GWI (2016b), p. 5.

In order to get a label, manufacturers have to register their sites on which their carpets are made. The registration gives the GWI-Certification Division (GWI-CD), GoodWeave's certification body, the permission to inspect those sites on a regular, unannounced, and random basis. In case the inspectors do not find any children working on carpets, the GWI-CD allows them to label their carpets. Each label has a number that allows consumers to trace its origin.[32]

3.1.2 Constraints Within the Monitoring System

GoodWeave's monitoring system strikes as a point of concern, which is mainly for two reasons: One is the structure of the carpet industry compared to GoodWeave's personnel resources, and the other is the dependence of GoodWeave's competence to check production sites from the willingness of manufacturers to register those sites. In the following it shall be looked at these aspects in more detail.

First, the carpet industry is geographically[33] as well as structurally[34] dispersed. Furthermore, production is not exclusively confined to factories, but there are also activities taking place outside of factories.[35] In comparison to that, GoodWeave currently employs 13 inspectors for all three countries in which it operates.[36] For this reason, doubts have been expressed that this small number of inspectors is able to monitor all activities related to the production of the labelled carpets.[37]

Secondly, GoodWeave's inspectors are able to visit only those production sites that are registered with GoodWeave. Even though GoodWeave requires from participating manufacturers that they register all their production sites and use only registered sites for production,[38] due to GoodWeave's lack of monitoring resources it seems difficult to control the compliance with this requirement. In practice, the factories are therefore often registered on a selective basis. It is also possible that children are displaced to unregistered factories. Registration of factories is hence de facto voluntary.[39]

It must therefore be recognized that there might be potential sources of infractions, which are not covered by the scope of GoodWeave's monitoring system.[40] Thus, GoodWeave is not able to ensure that the labelled carpets have been produced without any child work.

[32]GWI (2016b), pp. 3–7 and also http://www.goodweave.net/about/child_labor_free_rugs. Accessed 5 Mar 2016.

[33]See Seidman (2012), p. 1035.

[34]See Ballet et al. (2014), p. 93.

[35]Cf. Seidman (2009).

[36]See http://www.goodweave.org/about/certification-division. Accessed 5 Mar 2016.

[37]See e.g. Seidman (2012), p. 1035.

[38]See GWI (2016a), p. 10.

[39]See Dumas (2013), p. 87.

[40]Ibid.

3.1.3 Implications for Its Effectiveness

GoodWeave's ability to minimize the information asymmetry between consumers and producers is, hence, limited which results from its rather poorly equipped monitoring system for the operation in the carpet industry. As a consequence, there remains an information asymmetry between carpet manufacturers and GWI. At the same time, communicating to consumers that there were certainly no children involved in the making of the labelled carpets maintains an information asymmetry between GWI itself and the consumers. This information asymmetry can turn into mistrust towards the label in case consumers realize that there was actually a chance for child labour being involved.

3.2 *Fairtrade*

Fairtrade is a social labelling scheme that was originally run by several national Fair Trade[41] organizations. In 1997 they established the umbrella organization called Fairtrade International (FI). In 2002 a common Fairtrade label was launched.[42] FI is a not-for-profit association and is based in Germany.[43]

Fairtrade operates mainly in the field of agricultural commodity production, but the label can also be found on other products such as drinks, textiles, and jewellery.[44] It is concerned with the economic and social situation of 'disadvantaged' farmers and workers in developing countries and seeks to avoid a production that is harmful to the environment.[45]

3.2.1 Aims and Approach

Fairtrade's main objective is to enable farmers and workers in developing countries to produce in an environmentally sustainable way, and likewise to improve their own social and economic situation. This objective is pursued by the principle 'Aid through Trade' which suggests to facilitate 'the access to markets for the goods and services

[41]There is a difference between the terms 'Fair Trade' and 'Fairtrade'. While Fair Trade represents the broad movement 'that seeks greater equity in international trade', Fairtrade refers specifically to 'the product certification system operated by Fairtrade International'. See Fair Trade Glossary (2011), p. 1.

[42]See http://www.fairtrade.net/about-fairtrade/history-of-fairtrade.html. Accessed 5 Mar 2016.

[43]See FI (2007), p. 3.

[44]See http://www.fairtrade.net/about-fairtrade/the-fairtrade-marks/fairtrade-mark.html. Accessed 5 March 2016.

[45]See FI (2007), p. 4.

coming from these target groups' and to obtain 'trade under fair conditions'.[46] These aspects as well as the fact that consumers can identify through the label that the products have been made under desirable conditions,[47] and hence choose those products, shall serve producers as incentives to participate in the scheme.

FI sets standards adherence to which is meant to develop the communities' social and economic situation and to maintain environmentally sustainable production.[48] Producers have to meet a minimum scope of standards in order to be accepted into the scheme. This is checked by the certification body FLO-CERT. In case of conformity with the Fairtrade standards, FLO-CERT grants a Fairtrade label,[49] though the labels are licensed by FI or a National Fairtrade Organization.[50] Fairtrade labels are usually attached on the packaging of products.[51] In order to ensure further compliance and improvement of the producers' performance, FLO-CERT conducts regular unannounced audits.[52]

In return, producers benefit from a guaranteed minimum price that aims to enable them to cover the costs of sustainable production, even when world market prices drop. Moreover, they benefit from a premium that is paid by consumers on top of the minimum price. The premium flows into a communal fund. Producers within the farmers' organization or a workers' committee on a plantation can decide democratically how to use the amount. It is supposed to be invested in projects to enhance education, healthcare, and the infrastructure in the local community.[53]

3.2.2 Constraints Within the System of Distribution of Benefits

The marketing of Fairtrade is focused on the imagery of the disadvantaged farmer. When Fairtrade points to 'the producer', the farmer in particular is implied.[54] This may trace back to the fact that Fairtrade predominantly works with small farmers. According to the latest available data from FI, 80% of the producer organizations holding a Fairtrade label are small farmer organizations.[55]

However, not to underestimate is the fact that the production of agricultural commodities is very labour-intensive. Therefore, there are often much more, and

[46]Ibid.

[47]Ibid.

[48]See FI (2007), p. 4.

[49]See FLO-CERT (2015), p. 8.

[50]Ibid., p. 4.

[51]See http://www.fairtrade.net/about-fairtrade/the-fairtrade-marks/using-the-fairtrade-mark.html. Accessed 5 Mar 2016.

[52]See FLO-CERT (2016), p. 7.

[53]See http://www.fairtrade.net/about-fairtrade/what-is-fairtrade.html. Accessed 5 Mar 2016.

[54]Cf. Raynolds (2014), p. 503.

[55]See FI (2015a), p. 8.

also different actors involved in the production processes than solely the farmer.[56] Even though coffee and cacao might be produced on small farms, fruits and tea, for example, are most commonly produced on plantations with many hired workers.[57] In 2014 the number of people working in hired labour organizations holding a Fairtrade label was 204,000. Most of these workers were on the aforementioned plantations, 5400 of them in factories in which Fairtrade soccer balls are made.[58] Those hired workers are named in FI documents, but they 'tend to disappear in the core small farmer narrative'.[59]

With Fairtrade's expansion to plantations and other large producer organizations with hired labour, FI introduced specific standards for hired labour.[60] These, indeed, pay special attention to workers, being defined as

> waged employees, whether they are permanent or seasonal/temporary, migrant or local, subcontracted or directly employed. Workers include all hired personnel whether they work in the field, in processing sites, or in administration. The term is restricted to personnel that can be unionised and therefore middle and senior and other professionals are generally not considered workers.[61]

Yet, it has to be taken into account that the relationship between these workers and the employing farmers is hierarchical.[62] The workers are in general reliant on wages. In the case of temporary, migrant or seasonal workers there is, moreover, the fact that they frequently do not have a connection to the local area. Therefore, they cannot benefit from any social development projects which are supposed to be facilitated by the Fairtrade premium. It is only possible for them to benefit from the Fairtrade system if the farmers' benefits are translated into higher wages or into their inclusion in long-term projects.[63]

Given these circumstances, it is questionable if the benefits from the Fairtrade system, which in the first instance accrue to the farmers, are adequately distributed with the workers. Section 2.1. of the standards for hired labour (titled 'Management of Fairtrade Premium') sets this ambition:

> The intent of this section is to ensure that the direct beneficiaries of Fairtrade, through the Fairtrade Premium in particular, are workers and their families and the communities they live in. This includes permanent, migrant, seasonal and temporary workers.[64]

For this purpose, the standards provide that

[56]Cf. Cramer et al. (2014), pp. 10–11.

[57]Cf. Dragusanu et al. (2014), p. 231.

[58]See FI (2015a), p. 17.

[59]Raynolds (2014), p. 503.

[60]See Dragusanu et al. (2014), p. 231 and Raynolds (2014), p. 502.

[61]FI (2015b), p. 6.

[62]See Davenport and Low (2012), pp. 344–345.

[63]Cf. ibid., p. 332.

[64]FI (2015b), p. 10.

> [a] Fairtrade Premium Committee (FPC), with elected FPC worker members and appointed advisors from the management is created, with the purpose of managing the Fairtrade Premium (FP) for the benefits of all workers.[65]

The Fairtrade Premium, which consumers pay, has to be used for

> projects that address [workers', their families' and their communities'] needs and preferences as decided and adequately justified by workers.[66]

In practice, the standard of proper distribution of the Fairtrade benefits with workers, their families and their communities is not necessarily met. Recently, a research team based at the School of Oriental and African Studies in London conducted a study in which they examined whether 'a poor rural person dependent on access to wage employment for their (and their family's) survival is better served by employment opportunities in areas where there is a Fairtrade certified producer organization or in areas where there is none'.[67] For this purpose, they comparatively analysed the social conditions of workers living in areas including Fairtrade certified production and of workers living in areas without such certification. Although their research is confined to the rural areas of Ethiopia and Uganda in which agricultural commodities are produced,[68] their findings are comprehensible irrespective of the place in which the study was undertaken and might similarly apply to other places in which Fairtrade operates. The findings of the research are alarming:

> This research was unable to find any evidence that Fairtrade has made a positive difference to the wages and working conditions of those employed in the production of the commodities produced for Fairtrade certified export [. . .] In some cases, indeed, the data suggest that those employed in areas where there are Fairtrade producer organizations are significantly worse paid, and treated, than those employed for wages in the production of the same commodities in areas without any Fairtrade certified institutions [. . .].[69]

Even though Fairtrade continuously improves its standards, for instance most lately through developing living wage benchmarks and requiring employers to pay the living wage or at least to make progress to achieve this objective,[70] the evidence seems to indicate that certain constraints remain. Fairtrade is not able to control that its standards are actually respected. Especially in terms of distribution of benefits it is likely that the benefits are not translated into benefits for workers given the hierarchic employment relations. Therefore, Fairtrade cannot ensure that '[w]hen you buy products with any of the FAIRTRADE Marks, you support farmers and workers as they improve their lives and their communities'.[71]

---

[65] FI (2015b), p. 10.

[66] Ibid., p. 16.

[67] Cramer et al. (2014), p. 5.

[68] See ibid., p. 6.

[69] Cramer et al. (2014), pp. 15–16.

[70] See FI (2015a), p. 24.

[71] See http://www.fairtrade.net/about-fairtrade/the-fairtrade-marks.html. Accessed 5 Mar 2016.

3.2.3 Implications for Its Effectiveness

Fairtrade faces a limitation in minimizing the information asymmetry in the market, resulting from its lack of capacity to ensure an adequate distribution of benefits. Just as the case of GoodWeave, this information asymmetry inevitably passes on to the consumers. These expect that by buying products with the Fairtrade label they help to improve the lives of workers and their communities besides the farmers. In light of the evidence, which shows that there is a chance that this is not the case, such claims do not appear conducive to the organizations' 'work [which] is driven by informed consumer choices'.[72] It is unlikely that consumers choose Fairtrade products, if they have the impression that they are not accurately informed about the actual impact of their purchase. Instead, they might even generate mistrust towards the label.

3.3 *Forest Stewardship Council (FSC)*

The Forest Stewardship Council (FSC) is a not-for-profit, non-governmental organization.[73] It was created in 1993[74] and is domiciled in Mexico.[75]

The FSC is based on concerns about environmental degradation, misuse of natural resources, and the rights of indigenous peoples.[76] It therefore operates in the forest industry and runs a labelling scheme for wood and non-timber forest products.[77]

3.3.1 Aims and Approach

'The mission of the Organization is to promote environmentally appropriate, socially beneficial and economically viable management of the world's forests.'[78] To this end, the FSC sets respective standards for forest management.[79] Products are allowed to be sold with the FSC label if they were made in accordance with these standards.[80] Consumers' preference for such products shall give forest managers an incentive to follow these standards in their practice.

---

[72]See http://www.fairtrade.net/about-fairtrade/our-vision.html. Accessed 5 Mar 2016.

[73]See FSC (2015b), p. 2.

[74]Ibid., p. 6.

[75]See FSC (2015a), p. 1.

[76]Ibid.

[77]See FSC (2015b), p. 8.

[78]FSC (2015a), p. 2.

[79]See FSC (2015b), p. 7.

[80]Ibid., p. 6.

While the FSC sets standards for the certification process, it does neither conduct the audit process nor does it issue the labels itself. It rather accredits third 'independent' bodies that carry out the audits and take the certification decisions.[81] A forest manager, who wants to receive FSC labels, contracts a FSC accredited certification body himself. The certification body assesses his operation and awards FSC labels in case his operation meets the FSC's standards. Further compliance with the standards is audited on an annual basis.[82]

3.3.2 Constraints Within the Certification System

In recent years, the FSC has been facing a lot of critique, resignation of important stakeholders, and even a creation of a watchdog group, FSC-Watch,[83] aimed to critically observe its operation. They all call into question the credibility of the FSC.[84]

These developments mainly trace back to the FSC's certification system. The FSC's accredited certification bodies are for-profit firms, like SGS in Switzerland and SCS Global Services in the United States. They are not only chosen by the companies that apply for FSC certification themselves, but also paid by them. Moreover, it is possible for both parties to maintain their business relations for a long-term period.[85] Certification bodies have, therefore, an incentive to acquire more clients. For the same reason, they might be influenced by their clients, bringing forward their potential future cooperation.[86] In view of this close business relation between the forest companies and the certification bodies, doubts about the impartiality of the latter in their audits have been expressed.[87]

Furthermore, certification has become a business itself. There are many firms operating as certification bodies for the FSC. In order to remain competitive, certification bodies might tend to reduce their prices. To be able to offer lower prices, they have to keep their certification costs as low as possible. Lower certification costs, in turn, can only result from lower audit efforts. Less audit efforts implicate lower audit quality. In this way, it is possible that the competition among certification bodies results in a 'race to the bottom' in assessment quality.[88]

No matter how high or low the audit quality is, the same FSC label is affixed on the products. The label is only attributed to the FSC and not to a specific certification body. Thus, consumers cannot tell the standard the producers had chosen for

[81]See FSC (2015c), p. 2.

[82]See https://ic.fsc.org/en/certification. Accessed 5 Mar 2016.

[83]See http://fsc-watch.com. Accessed 5 Mar 2016.

[84]See Moog et al. (2015), pp. 474–475.

[85]Cf. Moog et al. (2015), p. 480.

[86]Cf. Chestnut (2013), p. 356.

[87]See Boström (2012), p. 11.

[88]See Moog et al. (2015), pp. 480–481.

the assessment of their performance.[89] Consequently, there is no incentive—neither for applying companies nor for certification bodies—to choose high quality audits. The information on this choice remains between the two parties—the applying company and the certification body—and does not reach the consumers.

Moreover, even the FSC might not dispose of that information. Although the certification bodies have to meet certain requirements during the certification process,[90] the FSC does not have the capacity to control their performance in a concrete context.[91] On this basis, it may be inferred that the FSC cannot guarantee that the conditions in production had been audited with high performance.

3.3.3 Implication for Its Effectiveness

There persists an information asymmetry, due to the certification through third, for-profit bodies. For the reason of constraints within this certification system, the information asymmetry exists firstly between the applying producers and the certification bodies, then passes on to the FSC, and ultimately reaches the consumers. Similar to the cases of GoodWeave and Fairtrade, claims as, for example, its accredited certification bodies being 'independent' and conducting high quality audits are undifferentiated, as the aforementioned circumstances give reason to question if the FSC can actually ensure this. They may generate mistrust towards the labels as it has already happened with the creation of a watchdog-group.

3.4 *Interim Conclusions*

The cases of GoodWeave, Fairtrade and the FSC have shown that the effectiveness of social labelling schemes in minimizing the information asymmetry between consumers and producers is limited. In each case this limitation is related to constraints within a particular system of the labelling scheme: GoodWeave's monitoring system, Fairtrade's system of distribution of benefits, and the FSC's certification system.

Despite the difference in the roots of their limitation, the consequence of their limitation is similar in each case. There seems to remain an information asymmetry, which the labelling NGOs are unable to eliminate because of their deficient oversight capacity.

The insight about the deficient oversight capacity of NGOs is nothing new. Nor is it the aim of this chapter to blame NGOs for their lack of control resources.

[89]Cf. Chestnut (2013), p. 357.
[90]See FSC (2015d), pp. 10–44.
[91]Cf. Boström (2012), p. 11.

However, the crucial question is how to deal with the fact that it is hardly possible for them to ensure good social performance by the producers.

Usually, the NGOs do not reveal precise information on their actual capacity to control whether their standards are met (no child involved in production, direct benefits for all actors involved in production, high quality audit by certification bodies). As seen in the cases of GoodWeave, Fairtrade and the FSC, they rather tend to give 'big promises' to consumers, while the evidence indicates that there is a good chance that these promises cannot be kept. Suspicions of overstated or even deceptive claims may induce mistrust in social labels. Consequently, consumers might not prefer those products over unlabelled products anymore, which—seen from the lens of Akerlof's theory—indicates an adverse selection of the former. This effect can frustrate the social purpose of labelling schemes and render them ineffective.

Hence, the question that follows is: How should the labelling NGOs deal with the issue of their deficient oversight capacity? What is needed to make social labelling schemes live up to their actual purpose as can be derived from Akerlof's theory, and thus make them more effective?

4 A Possible Solution

In this section, it will be argued that labelling NGOs should deal with the problem of deficient oversight capacities by enhancing transparency vis-à-vis consumers. They should transparently disclose what they can truly ensure. This would give consumers more certainty about the correctness of their statements and strengthen their trust towards the labels. This transparency might be pursued through a regulatory approach. A regulation could require to provide clear information on what the labelling NGOs can actually guarantee. It might also give producers an incentive to compete for more transparency of their supply chains as this would then be revealed through the labels. The International Labour Organization (ILO) could play a significant role by supporting NGOs with the necessary resources to better or more widely oversee the single stages of supply chains.

4.1 Transparency with Respect to the NGOs' Capacity to Minimize the Information Asymmetry

First and foremost, labelling NGOs need to confine their claims to what they are truly able to ensure. This has also been recommended by the research team which conducted a study to see if Fairtrade has made any difference in the social conditions of workers:

> Fairtrade labelling and branding information needs to be changed substantially to reflect the limitations of the claims made and an inability to monitor the wages and working conditions of people employed on the farms of members of small producers' organisations.[92]

Beyond that, the specific suggestion here is that labelling NGOs should reveal transparently vis-à-vis consumers up to which stage of the supply chain they were able to strictly control all critical aspects like the production as such, the certification process, and the distribution of benefits.

There are two (actual or at least potential) developments which can be imagined due to the current limitations of social labelling schemes, but could be addressed by enhancing transparency as proposed here.

First, the proliferation of social labels might generate confusion for consumers. As Ballet et al. clarify, it is likely that consumers do not even understand the meaning of each label and its difference to other labels.[93] In contrast, transparency as outlined here would enable consumers to grasp the actual meaning of each label, since it would then be clear for them what they actually guarantee. Each social labelling scheme might assert to have overseen the distinct processes up to a different stage of supply chain. Thereby, it would also be possible for consumers to distinguish the labels among each other.

Second, the practice of giving 'big promises' by the labelling NGOs might reduce consumers' confidence in social labels. Opposed to this practice, transparent and differentiated information about their actual oversight capacity would strengthen the reliability of social labels. Consumers would probably feel more certain about the accuracy of their statements, and hence, trust the labels to a higher degree.

4.2 *Regulation of the Information Provided by Social Labels*

In pursuit of transparency, standards for social labels might be useful. The labels would need to meet these standards in order to be allowed to be placed on products. Such standards could require, for instance, that labels need to reveal the stage of the supply chain up to which they can guarantee to have overseen all crucial aspects like the production as such, the certification process, and the distribution of benefits.

This proposal has to be distinguished from what has been brought forward by some others as 'harmonization' of labelling policies. Ballet et al. have concluded harmonization to be the right way to address the (actual or potential) developments mentioned above.[94] Also the European Commission has recommended a harmonization of the approaches being followed by environmental labelling

---

[92]Cramer et al. (2014), p. 124.

[93]See Ballet et al. (2014), p. 96.

[94]See Ballet et al. (2014), p. 97.

schemes.[95] The idea of harmonization implies basically to introduce 'standards for standards', meaning that the standards which the corporations are required to comply with in order to receive a label and/or the standards which are followed by the implementing organizations during the certification process shall be standardized among different labelling schemes. This suggestion is not approved here, for the reason that the determination of these standards and their implementation depend on the organizations' objectives and resources.[96] Those standards must therefore remain at their discretion.

Instead, the standards proposed here are meant to regulate the transparency of the labels itself, in other words the 'outcomes' of the labelling schemes. Such regulation may first appear as a harsh treatment of labelling NGOs since they would need to meet the respective requirements in terms of transparency when issuing the labels. Yet, there are several reasons for arguing in favour of a regulatory approach to achieve the transparency as outlined above rather than, for instance, simply expressing recommendations towards labelling NGOs:

The suggestion to regulate the information provided by social labels indicates that labelling NGOs would all have to meet the requirements to be allowed to issue the labels. This can give them power towards the participating corporations. First, NGOs can only issue the labels if the according transparency of the corporations' supply chains is provided since only then the requirements of the regulation could be met. Second, there would be no alternative for the corporations to seek a collaboration with another NGO in case they are not willing to provide the transparency, as the regulation would apply to all labelling NGOs without exception. Supposed the corporations strive for getting a label, whether because of the reputation of being 'good producers' or the extra premium on top of the prices they receive by the label (incentives), there would be higher requirements to fulfil in order to get a label.

In addition, revealing detailed information, e.g. on the percentage of supply chain stages that have been overseen with certainty, would perhaps even incentivize producers to give auditors for social labels a deeper look into their supply chains, since producers would then compete for transparency. For example, producer A made 80% of its supply chain transparent, whereas producer B already revealed 95%. The difference in the transparency of their supply chains and therefore apparently higher level of compliance with labour standards—it can be assumed that otherwise they would not disclose the critical stages—may justify different amounts of the premium consumers pay. Higher implementation efforts are unsurprisingly costlier. Therefore, the better the producers' performance, the higher the product's end price could be in order to compensate their efforts.

[95] See European Commission Recommendation 2013/179/EU *on the use of common methods to measure and communicate the life cycle environmental performance of products and organizations*, O.J. L 124/1-4 (2013).

[96] Again, the issue of available resources to labelling NGOs seems not to be sufficiently taken into account.

At the same time, consumers would be precisely informed about the producers' performance and would probably therefore develop more confidence in social labels because of the NGOs' more differentiated claims about their capacity. Ideally, the 'selection' according to Akerlof could then be turned in favour of products which were made under the best social conditions.

4.3 *Support from the ILO with Necessary Resources*

Regulation may be a possibility to achieve transparency, but obviously it is simple to call for such a measure without taking into consideration its practicability for the labelling NGOs. One big problem remains, which is the issue of the NGOs' limited recourses to get access to the information required by the proposed standards. It is, indeed, difficult for the labelling NGOs to consistently control all critical aspects, even in only one supply chain stage.

In this context, the ILO could play a crucial role. The ILO could support—possibly selected, most credible—labelling NGOs with the resources they need to be able to better control the corporations' compliance with their standards in one supply chain stage and likewise to more widely control their performance along the whole supply chain. The resources may be of personnel, financial, or technical nature. However, they would strengthen the NGOs' oversight capacity. The series of programmes launched after the Rana Plaza collapse in 2013 set a good example for a fruitful collaboration between the ILO and NGOs to enforce commonly pursued social standards.[97]

The proposal of such involvement of the ILO in social labelling schemes is not to be understood as a call for the ILO to be an initiator or an administrator of a social labelling scheme.[98] If the ILO ran an own social labelling scheme, it would not be able to address corporations directly, as that is not covered by its mandate, but only states as 'hosts' of private actors.[99] Thus, the ILO would 'label' countries as a whole for complying with labour standards in their legislation and practice, rather than specific firms in their 'narrow radius' of business performance.[100] As a consequence, the ILO would implicitly approve the demand for products from those ('labelled') countries as being produced under desirable labour standards, while disapproving the demand for products from other ('unlabelled') countries. Labour standards would thereby be connected to international trade, raising the issue of non-tariff barriers to trade and triggering the rules of the World Trade Organization (WTO).[101]

[97]See ILO (2016).

[98]Baccaro and Mele (2012), pp. 206–207 describe how the proposal of an ILO social label was considered, but failed within the ILO at the end of the 2000s.

[99]Cf. Baccaro and Mele (2012), p. 206.

[100]Cf. Bartley (2003), p. 450.

[101]Cf. Baccaro and Mele (2012), p. 206.

By contrast, what is proposed here is the sole provision of resources by the ILO for social labelling schemes, which are initiated as well as administered by NGOs themselves. While (inter-)governmental—i.e. public and mandatory—regulation of the requirements for products to be imported into a market or the commercialization of products within a market falls under the purview of WTO rules, non-governmental—i.e. private and voluntary—regulatory efforts are not covered by the scope of WTO rules.[102] Given that condition, it is—at least currently—favourable that social labelling schemes remain in NGOs' hands.

The WTO case law shows the tensions that can arise when social labelling schemes are adopted by public entities. The most recent example is *US-Tuna II (Mexico)*. In this case, the WTO's Appellate Body decided on a dispute between Mexico and the United States. Subject matter of the dispute was a public regulation which was introduced by the US and meant to establish a labelling regime. The regulation at issue specifies conditions that need to be met for tuna products to be sold in the US market with a label indicating that 'dolphin-safe' fishing methods were applied. The WTO's Appellate Body found that the regulation effected the competitive conditions in the US market to the detriment of Mexican tuna products. It declared the regulation to be inconsistent with WTO rules[103] and, thus, ruled in favour of Mexico.[104]

In light of the conflict with international trade law, which arises when states get directly involved in social labelling schemes,[105] it appears more promising to maintain social labelling schemes as a form of private regulatory initiatives. Also, to preserve their own agenda, it seems advisable for the labelling NGOs to keep the dividing line between their own approach and governments' policies.

5 Conclusion

This chapter dealt with the issue of social labelling as an increasingly expanding type of private regulatory initiatives. Observing this expansion, the central question in academia is about the effectiveness of social labelling schemes. In this context, it is sometimes assumed that social labelling schemes are supposed to enforce labour

---

[102]See Lopez-Hurtado (2002), p. 720 and Vogel (2008), p. 265. On the other hand, Mizulin and Zhu (2015), p. 138 argue that WTO rules oblige the member states to 'control' private labelling schemes in order 'to ensure that they are not misused as a disguised discrimination in international trade'.

[103]Specifically, inconsistent with Art. 2.1. TBT Agreement and Art. I:2 and II:4 GATT 1994 and not applied consistently with the chapeau of Art. XX GATT 1994.

[104]See WTO, *United States—Measures Concerning the Importation, Marketing and Sale of Tuna and Tuna Products*, Report of the Appellate Body, 20 Nov 2015, WT/DS381/AB/R.

[105]For a basic and comprehensive disquisition of the legal aspects under the WTO system in terms of state-sponsored social labelling schemes see Lopez-Hurtado (2002). Additional case law since then has to be considered though.

standards in globalized supply chains. This view seems to neglect two aspects: On the one hand, NGOs regularly face a lack of resources. On the other hand, the problems to be targeted are embedded in a complex political and socio-economic context.

As social labelling is an initiative arising from the idea of making use of market mechanisms and is, thus, a market-based initiative, it is appropriate to look at it from an economic perspective in order to better understand its function. George Akerlof's theory on asymmetric information in the market provides a useful framework for this purpose. From that viewpoint, this chapter formulated the optimal condition under which social labelling can be regarded as effective. Starting from that optimal condition, three exemplary labelling schemes were assessed, drawing on pre-existing empirical works.

With this approach, the chapter explored that the target of social labelling schemes is to minimize the information asymmetry that exists in the market between consumers and producers in terms of the social conditions in production. By providing this information to consumers, social labels aim to enable consumers to support the promotion of labour standards with their purchase. Their preference for products made under decent social conditions shall give producers an incentive to introduce or maintain such conditions.

However, comparing this target to the actual performance of social labelling schemes, it becomes apparent that those are barely able to reduce the information asymmetry between consumers and producers. In fact, there remains an information asymmetry. Their effectiveness is therefore limited which in each case can be mainly traced back to constraints within a specific system of the labelling scheme in question (GoodWeave: monitoring system; Fairtrade: system of distribution of benefits; FSC: certification system). The limitations result from a lack of control resources of the implementing NGOs as a recurring issue under all three labelling schemes.

Obviously, this issue cannot be ignored. The question that comes up is, therefore, how to deal with it. Subsequently, a possibility was considered on how to deal with the issue of lack of resources. More broadly, it was asked how to close the gap between the target and the actual performance of social labelling schemes and thereby make them more effective in the sense as understood here. The proposal given here indicated to transparently reveal vis-à-vis consumers to what extent the information asymmetry between them and producers can be minimized, in order to enable them to qualify the information given by the labels. In pursuit of transparency, a regulation of the information which is to be provided by the labels was considered to be helpful. For the NGOs' capability to minimize the information asymmetry to a higher level, a collaboration with the ILO appeared to be beneficial, since the ILO more likely possesses the necessary resources for a deeper supervision of the producers' performance.

Primarily, the chapter tried to confine the understanding of the capacity of social labelling to market-based incentives. It showed that even by applying such narrow understanding, social labelling schemes are limited in their effectiveness—let alone if we assumed that they are supposed to enforce labour standards in global supply chains. Although social labelling can be a powerful market tool, it cannot replace public authority. Private regulatory initiatives can only complement, but not substitute public regulation. They can promote a culture of compliance, but they cannot enforce labour standards in global supply chains. Enforcement in the sense of ensuring compliance, for instance through imposing sanctions in case of non-compliance which can hurt the corporations, is the task of public entities and should not be ascribed to private regulatory initiatives. This distracts responsibility from public entities and is, moreover, misleading in assessing the potential of social labelling schemes and discussing how to strengthen it.

However, the solution brought forward in this chapter needs to be scrutinized more profoundly as to whether it could be realized and how it could be realized. Especially in terms of the suggested regulation of the information provided by social labels, it has to be considered from a legal point of view at which level, i.e. by whom, such regulation could be introduced. It also needs to be dealt with the question whether the regulation should be binding or not. Finally, the ultimate goal should be to increase market transparency in terms of social conditions in production, the quality of the product, and the environmental impacts of the production process. Social labelling schemes are meant to be institutions to achieve this goal. However, as shown above, in order to achieve this, it is necessary that they provide themselves the sufficient transparency. For this purpose, the suggested regulation could be the basis for further research.

References

Akerlof G (1970) The market for "Lemons": quality uncertainty and the market mechanism. Q J Econ 84(3):488–500

Baccaro L, Mele V (2012) Pathology of path dependency? The ILO and the challenge of new governance. Ind Labor Relat Rev 65(2):195–224

Ballet J, Bhukuth A, Carimentrand A (2014) Child labor and responsible consumers: from boycotts to social labels, illustrated by the Indian Hand-Knotted Carpet Industry. Bus Soc 53 (1):71–104

Barkley Rosser J (2003) A Nobel prize for asymmetric information: the economic contributions of George Akerlof, Michael Spence and Josph Stiglitz. Rev Polit Econ 15(1):3–21

Bartley T (2003) Certifying forests and factories: states, social movements and the rise of private regulation in the apparel and forest product fields. Polit Soc 31:433–464

Bartley T (2007) Institutional emergence in an era of globalization: the rise of transnational private regulation of labor and environmental conditions. Am J Sociol 113(2):297–351

Boström M (2012) The problematic social dimension of sustainable development: the case of the Forest Stewardship Council. Int J Sustain Dev World Ecol 19(1):3–15

Chestnut B (2013) 'Cherry' trees or 'Lemon' trees: conflicts of interest in forest certification. Georgetown Int Environ Law Rev 25:341–366

Cramer C, Johnston D, Oya C, Sender J (2014) Fairtrade, employment and poverty reduction in Ethiopia and Uganda. SOAS, London

Davenport E, Low W (2012) The labour behind the (Fair Trade) label. Crit Perspect Int Bus 8 (4):329–348

Diller J (1999) A social conscience in the global marketplace? Labour dimensions of codes of conduct, social labelling and investor initiatives. Int Labour Rev 138(2):99–129

Dragusanu R, Giovannucci D, Nunn N (2014) The economics of fair trade. J Econ Perspect 28 (3):217–236
Dumas M (2013) Three misunderstandings about consumocratic labor law. Comp Labor Law Policy J 35(1):67–92
Fairtrade International (FI) (2007) Constitution of the association. https://www.fairtrade.net/fileadmin/user_upload/content/2009/about_us/documents/151014-Constitution-Fairtrade-International-EN.pdf. Accessed 15 Aug 2017
Fairtrade International (FI) (2015a) Monitoring the scope and benefits of Fairtrade, 7th edn. https://www.fairtrade.net/fileadmin/user_upload/content/2009/resources/2015-Monitoring_and_Impact_Report_web.pdf. Accessed 15 Aug 2017
Fairtrade International (FI) (2015b) Fairtrade standard for hired labour. https://www.fairtrade.net/fileadmin/user_upload/content/2011-12-29-HL_EN.pdf. Accessed 15 Ag 2017
FLO-CERT (2015) Application for Fairtrade certification - standard operating procedure. http://www.flocert.net/wp-content/uploads/2014/02/CERT-Application-SOP-15-en.pdf. Accessed 5 Mar 2016
FLO-CERT (2016) Certification - standard operating procedure. http://www.flocert.net/wp-content/uploads/2016/01/CERT-Certification-SOP-30-en.pdf. Accessed 5 Mar 2016
Forest Stewardship Council (FSC) (2015a) Statues. Available via DIALOG. https://ic.fsc.org/preview.fsc-statues.a-646.pdf. Accessed 5 Mar 2016
Forest Stewardship Council (FSC) (2015b) FSC principles and criteria for forest stewardship. https://ic.fsc.org/preview.fsc-principles-and-criteria-for-forest-stewardship-fsc-std-01-001-v5-2-enwebversion.a-4846.pdf. Accessed 5 Mar 2016
Forest Stewardship Council (FSC) (2015c) Report on the structure of the FSC certification system – version 2-1. https://ic.fsc.org/preview.report-on-the-structure-of-the-fsc-certification-system.a-5358.pdf. Accessed 5 Mar 2016
Forest Stewardship Council (FSC) (2015d) General requirements for FSC accredited certification bodies – version 4-0. https://ic.fsc.org/preview.fsc-std-20-001-v4-0-en-general-requirements-for-fsc-accredited-certification-bodies.a-5352.pdf. Accessed 5 Mar 2016
Freeman R (1994) A hard-headed look at labour standards. In: Sengenberger W, Campbell D (eds) International labour standards and economic interdependence. International Institute for Labour Studies, Geneva, pp 79–92
Golan E, Kuchler F, Mitchell L (2001) Economics of food labeling. J Consum Policy 24:117–184
GoodWeave International (GWI) (2009) RugMark introduces GoodWeave. http://www.goodweave.de/fileadmin/user_upload/pdfs/GoodWeave_Press_Release.pdf. Accessed 15 Aug 2017
GoodWeave International (GWI) (2013) GoodWeave Annual Report 2013: picturing an end to child labor. Available via DIALOG. https://goodweave.org/about/annual-reports/. Accessed 15 Aug 2017
GoodWeave International (GWI) (2016a) Generic international standard for rug producers v.3.0. Available via DIALOG. https://goodweave.org/proven-approach/standard/. Accessed 15 Aug 2017
GoodWeave International (GWI) (2016b) Licensing and Certification Policy v.1.2. http://comments.goodweave.org/wp-content/uploads/GWI-Licensing-and-Certification-Policy-v.1.2.pdf. Accessed 5 Mar 2016
Hartman K (2014) GMO labeling: a case of asymmetric information and the 'Nudge'. Policy Perspect 21:48–59
Hicks R (2012) Product labeling, consumer willingness to pay, and the supply chain. In: Boone T, Jayaraman V, Ganeshan R (eds) Sustainable supply chains - models, methods, and public policy implications. Springer, New York, pp 165–174
ILO (International Labour Organization) (2016, January) Bangladesh - Improving working conditions in the ready made garment industry: progress and achievements. http://www.ilo.org/dhaka/Whatwedo/Projects/WCMS_240343/lang–en/index.htm. Accessed 5 Mar 2016

Löfgren KG, Persson T, Weibull J (2002) Markets with asymmetric information: the contributions of George Akerlof, Michael Spence and Joseph Stiglitz. Scand J Econ 104(2):195–211

Lopez-Hurtado C (2002) Social labelling and WTO law. J Int Econ Law 5(3):719–746

Marx A, Wouters J (2016) Redesigning enforcement in private labor regulation. Will it work? Int Labour Rev 155:435–459

Mizulin N, Zhu H (2015) Non-tariff barriers and private conduct: the case of labelling. In: Herman C (ed) European yearbook of international economic law. Springer, Berlin, pp 137–159

Moog S, Spicer A, Böhm S (2015) The politics of multi-stakeholder initiatives: the crisis of the Forest Stewardship Council. J Bus Ethics 128(3):469–493

Nooruddin I, Sokhey S (2012) Credible certification of child labor free production. In: Gourevitch P, Lake D, Gross Stein J (eds) The credibility of transnational NGOs - when virtue is not enough. Cambridge University Press, Cambridge, pp 62–85

O'Rourke D (2003) Outsourcing regulation: analyzing nongovernmental system of labor standards and monitoring. Policy Stud J 31(1):1–29

Raynolds L (2014) Fairtrade, certification, and labor: global and local tensions in improving conditions for agricultural workers. Agric Hum Values 31(3):499–511

Seidman G (2009) Social labeling in export supply chains: can voluntary certification programs end child labor? http://casi.sas.upenn.edu/iit/seidman. Accessed 7 Dec 2015

Seidman G (2012) Regulation at work: globalization, labor rights, and development. Soc Res 79 (4):1023–1044

Urminsky M (2001) Self-regulation in the workplace: codes of conduct, social labeling and socially responsible investment. ILO, Geneva

Vogel D (2008) Private global business regulation. Annu Rev Pol Sci 11:261–282

World Fair Trade Organization, Fairtrade International, FLO-Cert (2011) Fair trade glossary. https://www.fairtrade.net/fileadmin/user_upload/content/2009/about_fairtrade/2011-06-28_fair-trade-glossary_WFTO-FLO-FLOCERT.pdf. Accessed 15 Aug 2017

Zadek S, Lingayah S, Forstater M (1998) Social labels: tools for ethical trade. Report for the European Commission, New Economics Foundation. Cinnamon House, London

Part IV
Labour Standards in International Economic Law: A Proposal for Practice

A Model Labour Chapter for Future EU Trade Agreements

Peter-Tobias Stoll, Henner Gött, and Patrick Abel

Contents

1 Introduction

This chapter contains a textual proposal for a model labour chapter to be included into future EU trade agreements. The chapter was commissioned by Friedrich-Ebert-Stiftung, in collaboration with the Chairman of the European Parliament's International Trade Committee (INTA), Mr. Bernd Lange, MEP. It was first presented publicly in Brussels on 28 June 2017.

The model chapter is the result of extensive research conducted at the Institute of International and European Law's Department of International Economic and Environmental Law at the University of Göttingen. It aims at translating insights gained in in-depth academic research into workable practical solutions for future trade negotiations. It thereby seeks to assist practitioners who are concerned with shaping

---

This chapter is, apart from minor changes, a reproduction of Stoll/Gött/Abel, Model Labour Chapter for EU Trade Agreements, first published online on http://www.fes-asia.org/news/model-labour-chapter-for-eu-trade-agreements/ as a draft by Friedrich-Ebert-Stiftung on 28 June 2017. We are grateful to Friedrich-Ebert-Stiftung and MEP Bernd Lange for their consent to include it in this volume.

P.-T. Stoll (✉) · H. Gött · P. Abel
Georg-August-University Göttingen, Institute of International and European Law, Göttingen, Germany
e-mail: pstoll@gwdg.de; hgoett@gwdg.de; mail@patrickabel.de

H. Gött (ed.), *Labour Standards in International Economic Law*,
https://doi.org/10.1007/978-3-319-69447-4_18

globalization in a way that is mindful of—and, in the best case, is conducive to—the protection and promotion of labour standards in identifying well-reasoned policy solutions within considerably short windows of time and political opportunity.

The model labour chapter presents a progressive and ambitious approach to secure and enhance the protection of workers in future EU trade agreements. It provides a comprehensive model containing both substantive labour standards and rights and an institutional and procedural framework to enforce them. The social partners and civil society organizations are empowered to participate and monitor all labour related activities of the Parties under the respective free trade agreement.

Importantly, while presenting one comprehensive and consistent policy option, the chapter is intended to be a template to be used in all trade negotiations to come. It is not a chapter tailored to the relations between the EU and one particular trading partner. It hardly needs any further explanation that, depending on the particular negotiating partner at hand, the inclusion of some of the model chapter's provisions can make more or less sense. In a similar vein, Part VI on pre-ratification conditionality is designed as a flexible tool: Whether any of the model chapter's provisions (or any other obligations outside the chapter) should be made a condition for the entry into force of the trade agreement strongly depends on the respective trading partner and cannot be settled in abstract terms in a model chapter.

The model chapter is based on five core ideas:

1) **Integration and Implementation of International Rules and Guidelines on Labour Protection**

   The chapter comprehensively integrates international rules and standards on labour issues. The Parties undertake not only to ratify and implement the fundamental ILO Conventions, but agree to go beyond. The model chapter notably includes important, yet often under-represented, standards on occupational safety and health, decent living wages and working hours. Special regard is given to horizontal challenges for labour protection, such as the status and rights of social partners and their organizations, global supply chains and specific modes of labour.

2) **Institutional Framework for an Effective Participation of Social Partners and Civil Society**

   Essential for the success of a labour chapter in practice is the comprehensive and effective involvement of social partners and civil society. The model chapter assures their continuous participation in all labour-related activities of the Parties under the trade agreement. Representation and participation are realised in particular through the establishment of reformed Domestic Advisory Groups and a bilateral Civil Society Forum. Detailed rules on competences and procedures are provided to ensure an effective and prominent role for organizations and give employees and employers a balanced and equal say.

3) **Detailed Cooperative and Promotional Activities**

   The model chapter takes up and improves the traditional focus of EU trade agreements on cooperative and promotional activities in labour matters. It provides a framework for a continuous and guided cooperation aimed at successively furthering labour protection. This includes periodic bilateral cooperation meetings between the Parties in consultation with the social partners and organized civil society, flanked by capacity building and technical assistance essential for developing partners. A public submissions procedure allows for an uncomplicated exchange of views between the Parties and any person or organization, which allows for unbureaucratic solutions. A periodic mandatory review of the chapter is coupled with an innovative impact assessment carried out by an independent Rapporteur, inspired by EU practice and model procedures developed at UN level.[1]

4) **Effective Dispute Settlement Between the Parties and a Collective Complaint Procedure**

Separately and in addition to cooperative and promotional activities, the model chapter provides for dispute settlement procedures, designed to address concrete cases of violations of the substantive obligations included in the chapter. The chapter thus complements the traditional EU cooperative and promotional approach with adjudicatory dispute settlement procedures known from labour chapters of US trade agreements. The model chapter provides for two different dispute settlement procedures: Firstly, labour dispute settlement between the Parties, and, secondly, an innovative collective complaint procedure, allowing workers', employers' or other civil society organizations to directly enforce the agreed labour standards against a Party.

Dispute settlement between the Parties involves a legal review of adherence to labour obligations under this chapter with a legally binding report by an independent Panel of Experts. The available remedies include consensual compensation, monetary assessment and the suspension of obligations. Priority is given to monetary assessment.

The new collective complaint procedure is a progressive and ambitious approach to empower social partners to enforce labour obligations under this chapter on their own and with full control over the proceedings. They can, after the exhaustion of all adequate and affordable local remedies, initiate legal review as to a violation of an obligation by a Party, which results in a legally binding report by an independent Panel of Experts. The report may include the award of a monetary just satisfaction which is enforceable before domestic courts of both Parties without any further examination by any domestic institution. This procedure aims for giving the social partners the means to actively defend their rights on an international level.

5) **Treaty Language Integrating and Improving Existing and Established Texts**

The model labour chapter aims at providing balanced language for inclusion into future EU trade agreements. For that purpose, it draws primarily on existing EU agreements and EU textual proposals published by the European

[1]Notably the UN Special Rapporteur on the Right to Food (2011) Guiding Principles on Human Rights Impact Assessments of Trade and Investment Agreements, UN Doc. A/HRC/19/59/Add.5.

Commission. The central point of reference is the final text of the EU-Canadian Comprehensive Economic and Trade Agreement (CETA), as signed on 30 October 2016, and the Commission's textual proposals for the currently stalled Transatlantic Trade and Investment Partnership (TTIP) between the EU and the USA. Where appropriate, other EU trade agreements and instruments have been taken into account. The model chapter aims at addressing the shortcomings of labour chapters in earlier agreements while preserving accomplished progress. Occasionally, recourse has been had to trade agreements of the EU's most important trading partners, notably the signed text for the Trans-Pacific Partnership (TPP). To the extent that language had not existed before, the model chapter closely follows existing established texts, notably ILO and Council of Europe conventions.

2 Textual Proposal with Comments

Part I – General Provisions

Overview on Part I: Part I contains overarching provisions which set out the context (Art. X.1) and rules on cross-cutting issues (Arts. X.2 – X.6). The provisions reproduce, with minor amendments, the language of CETA and the EU's TTIP Proposal.

Article X.1 – Context and Objectives

1. The Parties recognise the value of international cooperation and agreements on labour affairs as a response of the international community to economic, employment and social challenges and opportunities resulting from globalisation and as fundamental instruments to promote and achieve decent work for all. The Parties stress the need to enhance the mutual supportiveness between trade, investment and labour policies and rules. They recognise the contribution that international trade and investment could make to full and productive employment and decent work for all. Accordingly, they agree to promote the development of their trade and investment relations in a manner conducive to the realisation of the Decent Work Agenda, as expressed through the International Labour Organization (ILO) 2008 Declaration on Social Justice for a Fair Globalisation, in its four strategic objectives:

   a) employment promotion,
   b) social protection,
   c) social dialogue,
   d) fundamental principles and rights at work, and the cross-cutting issues of gender equality and non-discrimination.

   The Parties commit to consulting and cooperating as appropriate on trade- and investment-related labour and employment issues of mutual interest.

2. Affirming the value of greater policy coherence in decent work, encompassing labour standards, and high levels of labour protection, coupled with their effective enforcement, the Parties recognise the beneficial role that those areas can have on economic efficiency, innovation and productivity, including export performance. In this context, they also recognise the importance of social dialogue on labour matters among workers and employers, and their respective organizations, and governments, and commit to the promotion of such dialogue.
3. The Parties reaffirm their commitment to pursue sustainable development, the dimensions of which – economic development, social development and environmental protection – are inter-dependent and mutually reinforcing, and are committed to promote the development of international trade and investment in such a way so as to contribute to this overarching objective. The Parties recall the Rio Declaration and the Agenda 21 on Environment and Development of 1992, the ILO Declaration on Fundamental Principles and Rights at Work of 1998 and its Follow-up, the Johannesburg Plan of Implementation on Sustainable Development of 2002, the Ministerial Declaration of the UN Economic and Social Council on Full Employment and Decent Work of 2006, the ILO Declaration on Social Justice for a Fair Globalisation of 2008, the Outcome Document of the UN Conference on Sustainable Development of 2012 entitled 'The Future We Want', and the outcome of the UN Summit on Sustainable Development of 2015 entitled 'Transforming Our World: the 2030 Agenda for Sustainable Development'. The Parties underline the benefit of considering labour issues, including those which are trade and investment-related, as part of a global approach to trade and sustainable development.
4. The Parties recognise that the violation of fundamental principles and rights at work cannot be invoked or otherwise used as a legitimate comparative advantage and that labour standards should not be used for arbitrary or unjustifiable discrimination or protectionist trade purposes.
5. The Parties are mindful of their common history, including colonialism. Against this backdrop, the Parties affirm that this chapter is in no way seeking to exert pretended superiority through standards. They recognize that the provisions of this chapter build upon and serve to further principles and rights that are universal and accepted globally.
6. The Parties recognise the benefits of commerce in fair and ethical trade products and the importance of facilitating such commerce between them.
7. The Parties recall the UN Guiding Principles on Business and Human Rights, the OECD Guidelines for Multinational Enterprises, the ILO Tripartite Declaration of Principles concerning Multinational Enterprises and Social Policy and the 2016 ILO Resolution on Decent Work in Global Supply Chains and reaffirm the responsibilities of businesses to safeguard human rights as laid down in these instruments. The Parties reaffirm their commitment to promote decent work and ensure compliance with applicable labour standards with a particular view to the specific labour-related challenges arising in connection with global supply chains.

Comments: Art. X.1 provides context and sets out the specific objectives of the chapter. It does not contain specific obligations, but provides context that can be taken into account when interpreting the chapter according to the Vienna Convention on the Law of Treaties rules. Para. 1, a combination of language from Art. 23.1 CETA and Art. 4 TTIP, contains a commitment to the ILO Decent Work agenda and highlights the beneficial contributions of trade and investment to the protection and promotion of labour standards. Para. 2, based on Art. 23.1 CETA, emphasizes the beneficial economic effects of labour protection. Para. 3 reproduces language from Art. 1 TTIP and links the model chapter to the Parties' commitments to pursue sustainable development. Para. 4 is taken from Art. 4 TTIP and interlinks the two statements that labour standards violations must not be relied upon as a comparative advantage and that labour standards must not be abused for protectionism. Para. 5, which contains new language, aims at countering sentiments of continued colonialist dominance by the EU and its member states in FTAs with former colonies or developing countries. Para. 6 is based on Art. 191 para. 5 of the EU-CARIFORUM Agreement. Para. 7 contains new language and addresses issues of corporate social responsibility and responsible business conduct, especially in global value chains.

Article X.2 – Right to Regulate; High Levels of Protection

1. The Parties recognise the right of each Party to determine its labour policies and priorities, to set and regulate its levels of domestic labour protection, and to adopt or modify relevant policies and laws accordingly. The right to regulate shall be exerted in a manner which fully conforms with the obligations under this chapter, including the international instruments referred to therein.
2. Each Party shall ensure that its domestic labour policies and laws provide for and encourage high levels of workers' protection and shall strive to continue to improve those policies and laws and their underlying levels of protection.

Comments: Art. X.2 reproduces Art. 3 TTIP Proposal with minor modifications to enhance clarity.

Article X.3 – Social Partners and Civil Society

1. The Parties highlight and reinforce the central importance of social partners and civil society for achieving the objectives of this Chapter. The Parties agree on promoting and ensuring a high level of effective participation and integration of social partners and civil society in all phases and modes of application of this Chapter. The Parties commit to giving due regard to the views of social partners and civil society in their policy decisions on issues under this Chapter.

2. Social partners and civil society organizations shall participate both in cooperative and promotional activities and in dispute settlement proceedings as provided for under this Chapter. Participation of social partners and civil society in cooperative and promotional activities shall be realised in particular through the Domestic Advisory Groups and the Civil Society Forum as laid down in Article X.24 (Domestic Advisory Groups and Civil Society Forum). Their participation in dispute settlement proceedings shall be realized in particular through their role and the role of the Domestic Advisory Groups and the Civil Society Forum in dispute settlement between the Parties pursuant to Part V Section 1 of this Chapter and the collective complaint procedure pursuant to Part V Section 2 of this Chapter.
3. The Parties agree to respect, protect and ensure the independence and the freedom of association of social partners and civil society in conformity with the ILO Convention on Freedom of Association and Protection of the Right to Organise of 1948 (No. 87), the ILO Convention concerning the Application of the Principles of the Right to Organise and to Bargain Collectively of 1949 (No. 98), the International Covenant on Civil and Political Rights of 1966 and the International Covenant on Economic, Social and Cultural Rights of 1966. In particular, the Parties commit to respect, protect and ensure independence and the freedom of association of social partners and civil society in the selection and nomination as well as the treatment of participants of the Domestic Advisory Groups and Civil Society Forum under Article X.24 (Domestic Advisory Groups and Civil Society Forum).
4. The Parties agree to ensure a balanced representation and consideration of organizations of social partners and civil society, giving equal weight to organizations representing or relating to employers' as well as employees' interests, and allowing for adequate representation of organizations with a general scope of activities, in particular employers' organizations and trade union federations, and of those with sectoral scope of activities.
5. For greater certainty, nothing in this Article shall be read to permitting infringements on the status or rights of the social partners and civil society organizations enshrined in other provisions of domestic or international law.

Comments: Art. X.4 is a cross-cutting provision on the role of the social partners and civil society organizations in the context of the model chapter. It serves as a reference point for further provisions touching on these organizations, notably Art. X.24 (Domestic Advisory Groups and Civil Society Forum). Para. 2 highlights their role both in the cooperative and promotional and the sanctions-backed dispute settlement dimensions of the chapter. Para. 3 guarantees basic freedoms and independence of the respective organizations, in particular with a view to avoiding undue state influence. Para. 5 is a safeguard to ensure that Art. X.4 does not have any negative impact on any more favourable provisions on social partners and civil society organizations in other areas of international or domestic law

Article X.4 – Non-Lowering of Standards

1. The Parties shall not encourage trade or investment by weakening or reducing the levels of protection afforded in their labour law and standards.
2. A Party shall not waive or otherwise derogate from, or offer to waive or otherwise derogate from, its labour law and standards, to encourage trade or the establishment, acquisition, expansion or retention of an investment. A Party shall not waive or otherwise derogate from, or offer to waive or otherwise derogate from, its labour law and standards which implement its obligations under this Chapter.
3. A Party shall not fail to effectively enforce its labour law and standards, including those which implement obligations under this Chapter.
4. For greater certainty, this Article applies to the entirety of each Party's territorial or other jurisdiction, including in particular any regional divisions and zones with special status such as export processing zones.

Comments: Art. X.4 builds on Art. 23.4 CETA. That provision aims at preventing a 'race to the bottom' in labour protection via deregulation by a Party in order to attain comparative advantages. Art. 23.4 CETA has been criticized for only prohibiting derogations made with the specific intent of encouraging trade and investment. This focus on a specific regulatory intent implies e contrario that derogating measures taken with other intents remain permissible. This opens the door to abusive invocations of other regulatory intentions which in many instances will be hard to contest. Accordingly, the last sentences in paras. 2 and 3, respectively, were inserted to clarify that the Parties may in no case derogate from or fail to enforce provisions that implement their obligations under the model chapter, regardless of their regulatory intent. Insofar as a Party creates 'autonomous' labour standards which are not required by this chapter, the Party remains free to lower these standards at a later stage in accordance with Art. X.2 (Right to Regulate; High Levels of Protection), safe that it may not do so in order to encourage trade or investment, i.e. in order to attain a comparative advantage.

Article X.5 – Global Supply Chains and Similar Economic Arrangements

1. The Parties recognize that cross-border organization of supply, production and distribution of goods and provision of services, in particular in global supply chains, poses distinct and significant challenges to the protection and promotion of decent work for all. In particular, they recognize challenges resulting from economic dependency between contracting enterprises, excessive competition among subcontractors and suppliers and difficulties in implementing and enforcing domestic and pertinent international labour standards and rights.
2. The Parties shall maintain and enhance their domestic and bilateral efforts to address the challenges referred to in paragraph 1. The Parties affirm and agree to promote and effectively implement international efforts, decisions and

instruments to address the challenges mentioned in paragraph 1, such as the UN Guiding Principles on Business and Human Rights, the OECD Guidelines for Multinational Enterprises, and the ILO Tripartite Declaration of Principles concerning Multinational Enterprises and Social Policy and the 2016 ILO Resolution on Decent Work in Global Supply Chains and its follow-up, in accordance with Section 3 of Part II.

3. The Parties shall

   (a) effectively assume and exercise jurisdiction under their internal laws over all participants involved in cross-border organization of supply, production and distribution of goods and provision of services, including global supply chains, which have their nationality or operate from or on their territory, and
   (b) effectively implement and enforce their domestic labour law and regulations and international obligations, including arising under this Chapter, with particular regard to cross-border organization of supply, production and distribution of goods and provision of services, in particular in global supply chains, and the accompanying challenges to the protection and promotion of decent work for all.

Comments: Art. X.5 contains a cross-cutting obligation of the Parties to effectuate the chapter with special regard to the specific challenges of global supply chains and other forms of cross-border production.

Article X.6 – Specific Modes of Labour

1. The Parties recognize that specific modes of labour may encompass a specific vulnerability of workers and lead to challenges for the attainment of decent work for all, and they are mindful that economic globalization may have the inadvertent side-effect of aggravating such vulnerability. The specific modes of labour include

   (a) economic activities by workers and economic units that are – in law or in practice – not covered or insufficiently covered by formal arrangements, excluding illicit activities,
   (b) domestic work,
   (c) work carried out by migrant workers,
   (d) maritime labour, or
   (e) hired labour.

2. The Parties agree to implement and enforce this Chapter with a view to secure and promote decent work for all in specific modes of labour. They agree to promote, in accordance with their obligations under international law, efforts that have been made to secure and promote decent work for all in specific modes of labour. The Parties recognize the importance of international instruments on this matter, such as the ILO Domestic Workers Convention, 2011 (No. 189), the ILO Transition from the Informal to the Formal Economy Recommendation, 2015 (No. 204) and the Maritime Labour Convention, 2006.

Comments: Art. X.6 contains a cross-cutting obligation to implement the model chapter taking into account the increased vulnerability of workers employed in certain specific modes of labour.

Part II – Substantive Provisions

Overview on Part II: Part II contains substantive obligations of the Parties. It builds upon Arts. 4-9 and 18 TTIP and Arts. 23.3 and 23.5 CETA, with certain modifications and amendments as explained further below. The Part follows an integrated two-tier approach: On the one hand, the Parties commit to adhere to certain central ILO instruments (Art. X.7). On the other hand, the chapter creates genuine obligations with regard to certain subject matters, especially core labour standards and working conditions (Arts. X.8 – X.15). This follows the EU TTIP proposal's approach. It reconciles the need for coherence with key ILO instruments to avoid fragmentation and the need to genuine FTA safeguards concerning certain minimum standards in the designated subject areas even insofar as the Parties have not ratified or do not implement ILO instruments. To the extent that this two-tiered approach contains overlapping obligations, the obligation to interpret them coherently and in the light of pertinent ILO standards, explicitly enshrined in Art. X.30 para. 12, ensures a sound and uniform application.
Section 3 of Part II sets forth provisions on the domestic implementation of the obligations in Sections 1 and 2. Issues covered are transparency in regulation, labour inspection, review and domestic enforcement proceedings. It largely builds on pre-existing language in CETA and the TTIP Proposal.

Section 4 sets forth the parties' obligations in regard to corporate social responsibility and responsible business conduct.

Section 1: Instruments of the International Labour Organization

Article X.7 – Adherence to ILO Instruments; Further Ratification of ILO Conventions

1. The Parties reaffirm and commit to fulfil their respective obligations as ILO members, including under the ILO Constitution, the Declaration of Philadelphia of 1944, the ILO Declaration on Fundamental Principles and Rights at Work of 1998 and its Follow-up, and the ILO Decent Work Agenda, as expressed in the ILO Declaration on Social Justice for a Fair Globalisation of 2008. Each Party shall at all times ensure that its laws and practices respect, promote, and realise within an integrated strategy, in its whole territory and for all, the internationally recognised core labour standards which are the subject of the fundamental ILO Conventions.
2. Each Party, to the extent it has not yet done so, shall ratify, without undue delay, all fundamental ILO Conventions and their Protocols. The Parties shall regularly exchange information on their respective situation and advancements as regards the ratification of these as well as of priority and other ILO Conventions that are classified as up to date by the ILO and their Protocols.

3. Each Party shall effectively implement in its laws and practices and in its whole territory all ILO Conventions it has ratified. For all areas covered by up-to-date Conventions each Party shall implement its policies in the relevant areas bearing in mind the Recommendations adopted by the ILO, where they exist.
4. The obligations set forth in this Article shall not be read as to prejudice or limit in any way the Parties' obligations and their timely and comprehensive implementation under other provisions of this Chapter, especially under Sections 2 and 3 of this Part, nor shall they be read as to prejudice or limit in any way the Parties' commitment to high levels of protection and the Partiers' right to enhance their domestic labour policies, laws and protection levels pursuant to Article X.2 [Right to regulate; High Levels of Protection].

Comments: Art. X.7 embodies the 'instrument-focused' obligations of the Parties, i.e. the Parties' obligations to adhere to certain key ILO instruments.

Para. 1 contains a commitment to observe the Parties' obligations as ILO members as framed by the ILO Constitution and the ILO's three declarations of principles cited there.

Para. 2 and 3 contain obligations regarding ILO conventions. Para. 2 refers to their ratification. Continued ratification of ILO conventions is highly recommendable for four reasons: first, it serves the economic goal of countering a 'race to the bottom' and the broader goal of improving labour standards at the same time, second, the ILO's regular supervisory mechanisms apply, improving monitoring, third, it improves the legitimacy of the ILO and, fourth, it enhances the 'gold standard' the EU is aiming to set with its trade agreements. In this vein, para. 2 calls for the ratification without undue delay of the eight fundamental ILO conventions, which refer to universally recognized core labour standards and include:

- Freedom of Association and Protection of the Right to Organise Convention, 1948 (No. 87)
- Right to Organise and Collective Bargaining Convention, 1949 (No. 98)
- Forced Labour Convention, 1930 (No. 29)
- Abolition of Forced Labour Convention, 1957 (No. 105)
- Minimum Age Convention, 1973 (No. 138)
- Worst Forms of Child Labour Convention, 1999 (No. 182)
- Equal Remuneration Convention, 1951 (No. 100), and
- Discrimination (Employment and Occupation) Convention, 1958 (No. 111).

All of these conventions have already been ratified by all EU Member States. The phrase 'without undue delay' emphasizes the urgency of ratification while preserving latitude for conducting an adequate ratification procedure within reasonable time.

Art. X.7 does not oblige the Parties to ratify any other ILO convention, including those classified as 'priority' by the ILO. Following CETA and TTIP, the model chapter calls for an exchange of information concerning the Parties' progress and the state of ratifications of such other conventions.

Para. 3 concerns the effective implementation of all – i.e. not only the fundamental – ILO conventions a Party has ratified.

Para. 4 defines the relation between Art. X.7 and the subsequent, subject-specific articles of Part II. In particular, adherence to ILO instruments as required by Art. X.7 does not relief the Parties from fulfilling their obligations under the subsequent articles. This is of relevance since these subsequent articles, which were taken from the EU's TTIP proposal, contain some obligations which reflect well-established ILO practice albeit not explicitly mentioned in the conventions.

Section 2: Core Labour Standards and Working Conditions
Comments on Arts. X.8 – X.11: Arts. X.8 – X.11 resemble Arts. 5-8 TTIP, with minor clarifications. As mentioned above, these articles set forth subject-specific obligations.

Article X.8 – Freedom of Association and Right to Collective Bargaining

1. The Parties underline their commitment to protecting the freedom of association and the right to collective bargaining, and recognise the importance of international rules and agreements in this area, such as ILO Conventions 87 and 98, the UN Universal Declaration of Human Rights of 1948, the UN International Covenants on Civil and Political Rights and on Economic, Social and Cultural Rights of 1966.
2. Accordingly, the Parties shall uphold and implement in their laws and practices:
   a) the right to form and join trade unions and the inherent corollary of the right to strike,
   b) the right to establish and join employers' organizations,
   c) the effective recognition of the right to collective bargaining and the right to collective action,
   d) effective social dialogue and tripartite consultations, as referred to in the instruments under paragraph 1.
3. To this end, the Parties shall:
   a) implement effective domestic policies and measures for social dialogue by involving employers and workers representatives in the formulation of or consultation on domestic labour policies and laws;
   b) implement effective domestic policies and measures for information and consultation of workers through dialogue with workers including through permanent worker representation bodies in companies, such as works councils and encourage their active functioning in accordance with domestic laws;

c) provide effective protection against acts of anti-union discrimination in respect of workers' employment;
d) maintain the right to negotiate, conclude and enforce collective agreements as well as to take collective action in accordance to domestic laws and practices;
e) enable and promote the organization of employers' and workers' representation;
f) facilitate dialogue and exchanges between employers' and workers' organizations established in their territories;
g) promote and facilitate information and consultation of workers in companies at a transnational level;
h) promote worldwide implementation of the principles under paragraph 2, in particular through promoting adherence to relevant international instruments, including with regard to ratification where appropriate, as well as participation in relevant international processes and initiatives.

Article X.9 – Forced and Compulsory Labour

1. The Parties underline their commitment to eliminate forced or compulsory labour, and recognise the importance of international rules and agreements in this area, such as ILO Convention 29 and its Protocol, ILO Convention 105, the UN Universal Declaration of Human Rights of 1948, the UN International Covenants on Civil and Political Rights and on Economic, Social and Cultural Rights of 1966.
2. Accordingly, the Parties shall uphold and implement in their laws and practices:

   a) the effective suppression of forced or compulsory labour, in all its forms, including with regard to trafficking in persons,
   b) the prevention of the use of forced or compulsory labour,
   c) the provision to victims of protection and access to appropriate and effective remedies, as referred to in the instruments under paragraph 1.

3. To this end, the Parties shall:

   a) implement effective domestic policies and measures, including the establishment and application of adequate deterrent measures for offences, to prevent and eliminate forced or compulsory labour, and provide protection to the victims;
   b) exchange information and cooperate, as appropriate, on the prevention and elimination of forced or compulsory labour worldwide, including through the promotion of comprehensive approaches and international cooperation in this regard;
   c) promote worldwide implementation of the principles under paragraph 2 in particular through promoting adherence to relevant international instruments, including with regard to ratification where appropriate, as well as participation in relevant international processes and initiatives.

Article X.10 – Effective Abolition of Child Labour

1. The Parties underline their commitment to protect the rights of the child and to the abolition of child labour, and recognise the importance of international rules and agreements in this area, such as ILO Conventions 138 and 182, the UN Universal Declaration of Human Rights of 1948, the UN Declaration on the Rights of the Child of 1959, the UN International Covenant on Economic Social and Cultural Rights of 1966, the UN Convention on the Rights of the Child of 1989, and the Brasilia Declaration on Child Labour of 2013.
2. Accordingly, the Parties shall uphold and implement in their laws and practices:
   a) the immediate and effective prohibition and elimination of the worst forms of child labour,
   b) the effective abolition of all child labour,
   c) the protection of children of compulsory schooling age from performing labour, as referred to in the instruments under paragraph 1
3. To this end, the Parties shall:
   a) implement effective domestic policies and measures to protect children from performing hazardous work;
   b) promote access to quality basic education to all children;
   c) promote decent working conditions for young people in employment;
   d) exchange information and cooperate, as appropriate, on the elimination of the worst forms of child labour worldwide, including through the promotion of comprehensive approaches in this regard;
   e) promote worldwide implementation of the principles under paragraph 2, in particular through promoting adherence to relevant international instruments, including with regard to ratification where appropriate, as well as participation in relevant international processes and initiatives.

Article X.11 – Equality and Non-Discrimination in Respect of Employment and Occupation

1. The Parties underline their commitment to equality and non-discrimination at the workplace, and recognise the importance of international rules and agreements in this area, such as ILO Conventions 100 and 111, the UN Universal Declaration of Human Rights of 1948, the UN International Covenants on Civil and Political Rights and on Economic Social and Cultural Rights of 1966, the UN Convention on the Elimination of All Forms of Discrimination against Women of 1979, the UN Convention on the Rights of Persons with Disabilities of 2006.
2. Accordingly, the Parties shall in their laws and practices:
   a) ensure equal opportunity and treatment in employment and occupation for all,

b) ensure protection against all forms of direct and indirect discrimination as regards employment and occupation,
c) promote gender equality,
d) ensure equal remuneration for men and women for work of equal value, as referred to in the instruments under paragraph 1.

3. To this end, the Parties shall:

a) implement effective domestic policies and measures to ensure equal opportunity and equal treatment in employment and occupation for all, with a view to preventing and eliminating any discrimination, direct and indirect, in respect thereof;
b) ensure the application of equal remuneration for women and men for work of equal value;
c) exchange information and cooperate, as appropriate, including through the promotion of integrated approaches in this regard, on:

i) the worldwide elimination of discrimination in employment and occupation,
ii) gender equality at the workplace worldwide;

d) share experiences and information on measures to eliminate direct and indirect discrimination in the workplace and to ensure equal remuneration for women and men for work of equal value;
e) take adequate measures to ensure that persons with disabilities can enjoy their right to work on equal basis with others;
f) promote worldwide implementation of the principles under paragraph 2, in particular through promoting adherence to relevant international instruments, including with regard to ratification where appropriate, as well as participation in relevant international processes and initiatives.

Article X.12 – General Obligation to Ensure and Promote Decent Working Conditions
In accordance with the ILO Decent Work Agenda, as expressed in the ILO Declaration on Social Justice for a Fair Globalisation of 2008, and in accordance with its other international commitments, each Party shall ensure and promote decent working conditions.

Comments: Art. X.12 serves as a 'catch-all' general obligation to maintain and promote decent working conditions, including those not covered by the specific issues covered by the next three articles.

Article X.13 – Occupational Safety and Health

1. The Parties underline their commitment to ensure and promote occupational safety and health, and recognise the importance of international rules and agreements in this area, such as ILO Conventions 155 and 187 and other

instruments of the International Labour Organization relevant to the promotional framework for occupational safety and health, the UN Universal Declaration of Human Rights of 1948 and the UN International Covenants on Civil and Political Rights and on Economic, Social and Cultural Rights of 1966.

2. Accordingly, in line with the ILO Decent Work Agenda, as expressed in the ILO Declaration on Social Justice for a Fair Globalisation of 2008, and in conformity with its other international commitments, each Party shall protect health and safety at work, including through relevant policies, systems and programmes, the fostering and promotion of a preventive safety and health culture and the adoption of risk-based and precautionary approaches.
3. In particular, each Party shall ensure that its labour law and practices embody and provide protection for working conditions that respect the health and safety of workers, including by formulating and implementing policies that promote principles aimed at preventing accidents and injuries that arise out of or in the course of work, and that are aimed at developing a preventive safety and health culture where the principle of prevention is accorded the highest priority.
4. The Parties shall exchange information and cooperate, as appropriate, on occupational safety and health worldwide, including through the promotion of comprehensive approaches in this regard. They shall promote worldwide implementation of the principles underlying paragraphs 1, 2 and 3, in particular through promoting adherence to relevant international instruments, including with regard to ratification where appropriate, as well as participation in relevant international processes and initiatives.

Comments: Art. X.13 is based on language in Art. 23.3 CETA and the TTIP Proposal. It requires the Parties to provide for decent occupational safety and health in accordance with pertinent international standards, aiming at a preventive culture.

Article X.14 – Decent Living Wages and Minimum Wages

1. The Parties underline their commitment to ensure and promote decent living wages and equal remuneration for work of equal value. They recognise the importance of international rules and agreements in this area, such as the UN International Covenant on Civil and Political Rights of 1966, the International Covenant on Economic, Social and Cultural Rights of 1966, the ILO Equal Remuneration Convention, 1951 (No. 100), the ILO Protection of Wages Convention, 1949 (No. 95), the ILO Minimum Wage Fixing Convention, 1970 (No. 131), the ILO Protection of Workers' Claims (Employer's Insolvency) Convention, 1992 (No. 173) and further instruments of the International Labour Organization, as well as other instruments pertaining to decent living wages or equal remuneration for work of equal value. The

Parties affirm that decent living wages are an important factor in reducing poverty.

2. Accordingly, in line with the ILO Decent Work Agenda, as expressed in the ILO Declaration on Social Justice for a Fair Globalisation of 2008, and in conformity with its other international commitments, each Party shall promote and strive to ensure decent living wages, regardless of their form of employment and including those not covered by collective agreements with a view to enable wage earners and their families to afford a basic, but decent, living that is considered acceptable by society at its current level of economic development.
3. The Parties affirm the central importance of setting decent living wages by collective means, including collective bargaining. In addition to their obligations under Art. X.8 (Freedom of Association and Right to Collective Bargaining), the Parties shall ensure a robust and fair environment for collective bargaining and shall promote, without limiting the autonomy rights of the social partners, the determination of decent living wages by collective bargaining.
4. Notwithstanding their further obligations under the preceding paragraphs of this Article, the Parties shall, in accordance with their respective international commitments and the principles enshrined in the instruments referred to in paragraph 1, establish and maintain an effective and fair system for minimum wages covering all wage earners, regardless of their form of employment and including those not covered by collective agreements. Insofar as a Party chooses to provide for statutory minimum wages, it shall ensure the full consultation and, insofar as possible, direct participation, on a basis of equality, of the social partners in the establishment and operation of minimum wage systems.
5. Further to their obligations under Art. X.17 (Domestic Enforcement Procedures, Administrative Proceedings and Review of Administrative Action), paragraph 1(b), each Party shall ensure that the administrative and judicial proceedings mentioned in that provision provide for easily accessible, prompt and effective remedies to enforce justified claims to back pay, in order to secure a timely receipt of at least the pertinent minimum wage as defined in paragraph 4 of this Article to all wage earners.

Article X.15 – Working Hours

1. The Parties underline their commitment to ensure and promote decent hours of work and adequate rest periods to ensure high productivity while safeguarding workers' physical and mental health. They recognise the importance of international rules and agreements in this area, such as the ILO Conventions and Recommendations on the subjects of working hours, weekly rest and paid holidays.

2. Accordingly, in line with the ILO Decent Work Agenda, as expressed in the ILO Declaration on Social Justice for a Fair Globalisation of 2008, and in conformity with its other international commitments, each Party shall:

   a) uphold and implement in their laws and practices decent working hours, oriented towards the principle of the 40-hour workweek and at least ensure a general standard of a maximum of 48 regular hours of work per week, with a general maximum of ten hours per day and lower maximum hours per day for sectors with particularly strenuous work demands;
   b) uphold and implement in their laws and practices that workers enjoy a rest period of at least 24 consecutive hours every seven days;
   c) in their laws and practices take appropriate measures required by the nature of night work for the protection of night workers;
   d) ensure that part-time workers receive the same protection, basic wage and social security, as well as employment conditions equivalent to those accorded to comparable full-time workers.
   e) uphold and implement in their laws and practices the entitlement of all workers to an annual paid holiday of a minimum length specified by law which should aim for at least three working weeks of annual paid holiday for one year of service.

Section 3: Domestic Implementation and Enforcement

Article X.16 – Transparency and Public Participation in Domestic Labour Regulation

1. Each Party, in accordance with Chapter *[##] [The Agreement's Transparency Chapter, e.g. Chapter 27 of CETA]*, shall ensure that any measures pursuing labour objectives, particularly measures to protect labour conditions, that may affect trade or investment – or trade or investment measures that may affect the protection of labour conditions -, are developed, introduced, implemented and reviewed in a transparent manner.
2. To this end, each Party shall:

   a) encourage public dialogue with and among stakeholders, particularly non-state actors, including social partners, as regards the development and definition of priorities that may lead to the adoption by public authorities of such measures;
   b) take account of relevant scientific and technical information and international standards, guidelines or recommendations if they exist, including on risk management and precautionary approaches;
   c) ensure timely communication to, and consultation of, stakeholders, particularly non-state actors, including social partners, on such measures and their administration and review;
   d) promote, once they are adopted, awareness of these measures, including related enforcement and compliance procedures, by ensuring the availability of information to the public;

e) recognise the role of stakeholders, particularly non-state actors, including social partners concerning the respect and enforcement of relevant domestic measures.

Comments: Art. X.16 is based on Art. 18 TTIP Proposal.

Article X.17 – Domestic Enforcement Procedures, Administrative Proceedings and Review of Administrative Action

1. The Parties recognise the importance of international rules and agreements, such as the ILO governance conventions, which comprise the Labour Inspection Convention (No. 81) the Employment Policy Convention (No. 122), the Labour Inspection (Agriculture) Convention (No. 129) and the Tripartite Consultation (International Labour Standards) Convention (No. 144). Bearing these instruments in mind, each Party shall promote compliance with and shall effectively enforce its labour law, including by:

   (a) maintaining a system of labour inspection in accordance with its international commitments aimed at securing the enforcement of legal provisions relating to working conditions and the protection of workers which are enforceable by labour inspectors; and
   (b) ensuring that administrative and judicial proceedings are available in a particular matter to persons with a legally recognised interest and their legal representatives who maintain that a right is infringed, in order to permit effective action against infringements of its labour law, including appropriate remedies for violations of such law.

2. Each Party shall fulfil its obligations under subparagraph 1(a) through appropriate government action, such as:

   (a) establishing and maintaining effective and adequately staffed, funded and resourced labour inspection services, including by appointing and training inspectors;
   (b) monitoring compliance and investigating suspected violations, including through onsite inspections;
   (c) requiring record keeping and reporting;
   (d) encouraging the establishment of worker-management committees to address labour regulation of the workplace;
   (e) providing or encouraging mediation, conciliation and arbitration services; and,
   (f) initiating, in a timely manner, proceedings to seek appropriate sanctions or remedies for violations of its labour law.

3. Each Party shall, in accordance with its law, ensure that the proceedings referred to in subparagraph 1(b) are not unnecessarily complicated or prohibitively costly, do not entail unreasonable time limits or unwarranted

delays, provide injunctive relief, if appropriate, and are fair and equitable, including by:

(a) providing defendants with reasonable notice when a procedure is initiated, including a description of the nature of the proceeding and the basis of the claim;
(b) providing the parties to the proceedings with a reasonable opportunity to support or defend their respective positions, including by presenting information or evidence, prior to a final decision;
(c) providing that final decisions are made in writing and give reasons as appropriate to the case and based on information or evidence in respect of which the parties to the proceeding were offered the opportunity to be heard; and
(d) allowing the parties to administrative proceedings an opportunity for review and, if warranted, correction of final administrative decisions within a reasonable period of time by a tribunal established by law, with appropriate guarantees of tribunal independence and impartiality.

Comments: Paras. 1 and 3 were taken from Art. 23.5 CETA. Para. 1 includes, in line with the structure of the previous articles, a definition of the overall objective and recalls pertinent international instruments. The express mentioning of the ILO governance conventions seeks to define international reference points without obliging the Parties to ratify these conventions. Para. 2 aims at specifying para. 1 a) and is based on a proposal tabled by Canada in the CETA negotiations.

Section 4: The Parties' Obligations Regarding the Conduct of Enterprises

Overview on Section 4: The text of the articles of Section 4 is based on Art. 20 and 21 of the EU proposal on TTIP with minor modifications, partly inspired by other international documents. Section 4 addresses the Parties' obligations with regard to the conduct of MNEs, employers and investors with reference to relevant international standards and guidelines and to the consultative participation of stakeholders. The main reason why this section has been included is to maintain the standard of previous agreements and proposals, with some suggestions for modest improvement. This is, however, not to be understood as providing a comprehensive and exhaustive proposal on corporate conduct and social responsibility. Such a proposal would exceed the limits of a labour chapter and would perhaps be best located in a separate, dedicated chapter, which could also deal with the issue of obligations of enterprises.

Article X.18 – Corporate Social Responsibility and Responsible Business Conduct

1. The Parties recognise that Corporate Social Responsibility (CSR) and responsible business conduct, which refer to companies taking responsibility for their impact on society and their employees and to their actions over and

above their legal obligations towards society and their employees, strengthen the contribution of trade and investment to a sustainable growth and contribute to the objectives of this Agreement to support high levels of labour protection. The Parties further recognise that CSR and responsible business conduct, by their voluntary nature build on and supplement the respect of domestic laws in these areas.

2. The Parties agree to promote CSR and responsible business conduct, including with regard to accountability and to adherence to, implementation, follow-up and dissemination of internationally agreed guidelines and principles. They agree to encourage the incorporation of these guidelines and principles into public initiatives by governments and into corporate policies and practices by companies and investors, including with regard to global supply chains, including through exchange of information and best practices. They agree to improve the legal, institutional and regulatory framework for CSR and responsible business conduct. They agree to consider transforming norms of CSR and responsible business conduct into binding domestic law.
3. In this regard, the Parties shall refer to and support internationally recognised guidelines and principles on CSR and responsible business conduct, including by endorsing, adhering to, or participating in, according to the nature of the instrument, the OECD Guidelines for Multinational Enterprises, the UN Global Compact, the UN Guiding Principles on Business and Human Rights, ISO 26000, and the ILO Tripartite Declaration of Principles concerning Multinational Enterprises and Social Policy, as revised in 2017, as well as specific or sectoral standards of responsible practice where these exist. The Parties equally agree to facilitate progress in responsible business conduct by supporting actions which can allow for a greater uptake of these internationally recognised instruments among companies established in their respective territories.
4. Accordingly, the Parties shall cooperate to foster among both governments and private sector actors adherence, implementation, follow-up, and dissemination of internationally recognised instruments on CSR and responsible business conduct, including by promoting:

   a) communication and exchanges of best practices between the National Contact Points established under the OECD Guidelines for Multinational Enterprises,
   b) awareness and encouragement of use of the tools and dialogue practices established under the 2017 ILO Tripartite Declaration of Principles concerning Multinational Enterprises and Social Policy
   c) sharing of experiences and best practices on the development and implementation of National Action Plans on the implementation of the UN Guiding Principles on Business and Human Rights or their integration in national CSR strategies.

5. The Parties agree to encourage disclosure by companies of social information, including by relying on the international frameworks referred to in paragraph 3, the Global Reporting Initiative, and other relevant frameworks.
6. The Parties agree to consult and exchange information on CSR and Responsible Business Conduct on a regular basis with the Civil Society Forum and the ILO in the Committee on Labour Matters.

Comments: The Article on CSR and Responsible Business Conduct stresses the importance of these non-binding instruments and oblige the Parties to promote and encourage their use, as well as to improve the regulatory framework for their application. As one possible and voluntary policy option, the Parties agree to consider transforming non-binding CSR and Responsible Business Conduct standards into binding domestic law. The Article emphasizes the relevance of a series of key international CSR and Responsible Business Conduct instruments of the UN, OECD and ILO in their latest versions and any future international standards equally or more progressively according social responsibility to companies. It provides for regular consultation with stakeholders in the Civil Society Forum and the ILO in the Committee on Labour Matters.

Article X.19 – Voluntary Labour Standards Protection Schemes

The Parties recognise that impartial, open and transparent voluntary initiatives to protect the labour rights through codes of conduct, standard schemes, labelling, certification, verification fair trade schemes and other related corporate policies or public initiatives can contribute to the achievement and maintenance of high levels of labour protection and complement domestic regulatory measures, and agree to encourage, with involvement of stakeholders, the development of and participation in such initiatives, including voluntary sustainable assurance schemes such as fair and ethical trade schemes and eco-labels.

Part III – Institutional Provisions

Overview on Part III: Part III contains provisions on the institutional framework of the model chapter. It includes the Committee on Labour Matters, the Domestic Contact Points, the Domestic Advisory Groups and the Civil Society Forum. Part III provides rules on their roles, structure and ways of working.

Article X.20 – Committee on Labour Matters

1. A Committee on Labour Matters shall be established, as provided for under Article *[##] [Article in FTA's general institutional provisions on specialised intergovernmental committees, e.g. Art. 26.2 CETA]*, and shall be comprised of high level representatives of the Parties competent for labour matters. The Committee on Labour Matters shall oversee the implementation of this Chapter and address issues relevant to this chapter which arise in the implementation of other parts of this Agreement, including cooperative activities and the review of the impact of this Agreement on labour, and address in an

integrated manner any matter of common interest to the Parties in relation to the interface between economic development and labour matters.

2. The Committee on Labour Matters shall meet within the first year of the entry into force of this Agreement, and shall be convened at least once a year. The contact points referred to in Article X.21 (Domestic Contact Points) are responsible for the communication between the Parties regarding the scheduling and the organization of those meetings.
3. Each regular meeting of the Committee on Labour Matters includes a public session to discuss matters relating to the implementation of the relevant Chapters.
4. The Committee on Labour Matters shall promote transparency and public participation. To this end:

   (a) any decision or report of the Committee on Labour Matters shall be made public, unless it decides otherwise;
   (b) the Committee on Labour Matters shall present updates on any matter related to this Chapter, including its implementation, to the Civil Society Forum referred to in Article X.24 (Domestic Advisory Groups and Civil Society Forum). Any view or opinion of the Civil Society Forum shall be presented to the Parties directly, or through the Domestic Advisory Groups referred to in Article X.24 (Domestic Advisory Groups and Civil Society Forum). The Committee on Labour Matters shall report annually on the follow-up to those communications;
   (c) the Committee on Labour Matters shall report annually on any matter that it addresses.

5. The Committee on Labour Matters may establish standing or other subsidiary bodies and appoint rapporteurs in order to assist it in the performance of its tasks. It may change or undertake the tasks assigned to such bodies and rapporteurs. It may dissolve such bodies and dismiss such rapporteurs.

Comments: Art. X.20 is based on Article 22.4 CETA with modifications. The Committee on Labour Matters is one of the specialized committees which operate under the auspices of a joint main committee under all EU trade agreements. The Committee on Labour Matters is the intergovernmental administrative body of the model chapter and entrusted with important competences in various provisions of the Chapter. Art. X.20 lays down the general objectives of the Committee on Labour Matters and ensures that it is convened on a regular basis. It also safeguards the transparency of the Committee's work and the participation of the public and stakeholders. Para. 5 is based on Art. 26.1 CETA. It ensures that the Committee on Labour Matters can fulfil its tasks.

Apart from Art. X.20, the Committee on Labour Matters is also governed by the FTA's general administrative institutional provisions (see as a reference point Chapter 26 CETA, notably Art. 26.2 CETA), which are not reproduced here.

Article X.21 – Domestic Contact Points

1. Each Party shall designate an office to serve as the contact point with the other Party for the implementation of this Chapter, including with regard to:
   (a) cooperative programmes and activities in accordance with Part IV (Bilateral Labour Cooperation),
   (b) the receipt of public submissions in accordance with Article X.23 (Public Submissions), consultation requests in accordance with Article X.29 (Consultation Between the Parties) and the request for an establishment of a Panel of Experts in accordance with Article X.30 (Complaint Procedure Between the Parties Before a Panel of Experts); and
   (c) information to be provided to the other Party, the Panels of Experts and the public.
2. Each Party shall inform the other Party, in writing, and shall inform the public by appropriate means, of the contact point referred to in paragraph 1.

Comments: Art: X.21 is based on Art. 23.8 CETA.

Article X.22 – Cooperation and Coherence with the International Labour Organization and Other Intergovernmental Entities

1. In all matters under this chapter, the Parties, including through the Committee for Labour Matters, shall communicate and cooperate with the ILO wherever appropriate. They shall take into account the activities of the ILO so as to promote greater cooperation and coherence between the work of the Parties under this Chapter and the ILO. For that purpose, the Committee for Labour Matters shall invite the Director-General of the International Labour Office or its representative to participate in its meetings on a consultative basis to maintain coherence between the work of the Parties under this Chapter and the ILO. The Parties should seek to make arrangements with the ILO to promote cooperation and coherence between the work of the Parties and the ILO. In reports submitted to the International Labour Organization pursuant to an obligation under the ILO Constitution or other ILO instrument, the Parties shall include information on the implementation of this Chapter.
2. The Parties, including through the Committee for Labour Matters, may decide to communicate or cooperate with other international organizations and other intergovernmental bodies as they deem appropriate in all matters under this Chapter so as to promote greater cooperation and coherence between the work of the Parties and such organizations and bodies.

Comments: Art. X.22 is based on language contained in Art. 23.7 CETA. Given that there are potential overlaps between the work of the ILO and the Parties under the Chapter on Trade and Labour, Art. X.22 aims for providing principles and procedures for international cooperation with the ILO and coherence of the work of the Parties under the Chapter on Trade and Labour and the ILO. Para. 2 concerns communications with other international organizations which may work in fields touched upon by this chapter.

Article X.23 – Public submissions

1. Each Party, through its Domestic Contact Point designated under Article X.21 (Domestic Contact Points), shall provide for the receipt and consideration of written submissions from persons on matters related to this Chapter in accordance with its domestic procedures.
2. Each Party shall make readily accessible and publicly available its procedures, including timelines, for the receipt and consideration of written submissions. A Party may provide in its procedures that, to be eligible for consideration, a submission should, at a minimum:

   (a) raise an issue directly relevant to this Chapter, and
   (b) clearly identify the person or organization making the submission.

3. Each Party shall:

   (a) consider matters raised by the submission and provide a timely response to the submitter, including in writing as appropriate, and thereby shall strive to resolve the matter raised; and
   (b) make the submission and the results of its consideration available to the other Party, its Domestic Advisory Group, the Civil Society Forum and the public in a timely manner.

4. A Party may request from the person or organization that made the submission additional information that is necessary to consider the substance of the submission.
5. The making or abstention from making of a submission under this Article shall not prejudice in any way rights of the social partners or civil society organizations to raise the same or other matters in accordance with Article X.24 (Domestic Advisory Groups and Civil Society Forum) or Part V, Section 2 of this Chapter.

Comments: Art. X.22 is based on language in CETA and on Art. 19.9 TPP. Public submissions with Domestic Contact Points provide an easily accessible and flexible recourse for persons to articulate concerns and matters related to the Chapter on Trade and Labour to a Party. It is a communication channel which may raise Parties' awareness and facilitate quick solutions on matters of trade and labour. Public submissions do not require the Parties to act in a certain manner, but call for a communicative response only, and are without prejudice to any other dispute settlement procedures and institutional participatory procedures of this Chapter.

Article X.24 – Domestic Advisory Groups and Civil Society Forum

1. Each Party shall convene a new or consult its existing standing Domestic Advisory Group and the Parties shall facilitate and convene a joint Civil Society Forum, to seek views and advice on labour issues relating to this Agreement, to monitor and evaluate the functioning and implementation this Agreement with a focus on labour issues, to provide a space for participation and deliberation and to conduct a domestic and bilateral dialogue between civil society and the Parties and among the members of civil society on the labour aspects of this Agreement.
2. The Domestic Advisory Groups shall comprise independent representative organizations of civil society in a balanced representation of employers, unions, their respective federations, and other non-governmental organizations working on matters covered by this Chapter, as well as other relevant stakeholders as appropriate. Balanced representation of the representative organizations of civil society shall be mirrored in equal and balanced rights to participate in meetings of the Domestic Advisory Groups. Each Party's Domestic Advisory Group shall comprise such organizations and stakeholders which are that Party's nationals or established in that Party's territory. All participants in the Domestic Advisory Group shall be organizations in the sense of Article X.3 (Social Partners and Civil Society) and shall in particular enjoy at least the status and rights as mentioned in paragraph 3 of that Article. Out of the total number of members of a Domestic Advisory Group, at least one third shall be employers' organizations and at least one third shall be trade unions or their respective federations. Employers' organizations and trade unions shall be represented in equal numbers. The Parties shall ensure, including by ensuring adequate funding, that all members of their Domestic Advisory Groups can participate on equal conditions in its meetings. With a view to enhancing efficiency and accessibility of the Domestic Advisory Groups, each Party, in consultation with any affected existing Domestic Advisory Groups, may provide that its Domestic Advisory Group may also fulfil functions under other international agreements which are equivalent to the functions of the Domestic Advisory Group under this Agreement.
3. The Civil Society Forum shall be convened at least once a year. The Civil Society Forum shall comprise independent representative organizations of participants in the Advisory Groups of both Parties in a balanced representation of employers, unions their respective federations, and other non-governmental organizations working on matters covered by this Chapter, including, as well as other relevant stakeholders as appropriate. All members of the Civil Society Forum shall be organizations in the sense of Article X.3 (Social Partners and Civil Society) and shall in particular enjoy at least the status and rights as mentioned in paragraph 3 of that Article. The Civil Society Forum shall comprise an equal number of members from each Party. The Parties shall ensure, including by ensuring adequate funding, that all members of the Civil Society Forum can participate on equal

conditions in its meetings. With a view to enhancing efficiency and accessibility of the Civil Society Forum, the Parties may facilitate participation by electronic means. For the same purposes, they shall strive to include equivalent standards for civil society fora or equivalent mechanisms in other international agreements that provide for such a forum or equivalent mechanisms, taking into account experiences made under previous mechanisms and any views of the Civil Society Forum on this matter.

4. With a view to facilitate the immediate and proper functioning of the Civil Society Forum, the Parties, in consultation with their domestic advisory groups, shall adopt Rules of Procedure for the Civil Society Forum no later than the first meeting of the Civil Society Forum. The Civil Society Forum, at its first meeting or anytime thereafter, may choose to approve or amend its Rules of Procedure. The Rules of Procedure shall at all times comply with this Agreement.
5. The members of the Civil Society Forum shall make every effort to take decisions and adopt statements by consensus. In case consensus cannot be reached on the taking of a decision, the decision may be taken by a majority of the members of the Civil Society Forum, comprising at least a majority of employers' and a majority of workers' representatives. In any case of disagreement on the adoption of a statement, the Conclusions and the minutes of the meeting should reflect that disagreement and display the views of every member of the Civil Society Forum that wishes to include them.
6. Each Domestic Advisory Group and the Civil Society Forum may submit opinions and make recommendations to the Parties, the Committee on Labour Matters, the *[FTA Main Committee]* or any other *[FTA specialized committee]* on any labour issues relating to this Agreement on their own initiative. If opinions or recommendations are submitted to the Committee on Labour Matters, they shall be placed on the agenda of its next meeting. The Party addressed or the Committee on Labour Matters or the addressed Committee, respectively, shall consider matters raised by any Domestic Advisory Group and the Civil Society Forum and shall provide a timely response in writing, no later than 90 days from the date of the receipt. The submission or recommendation and the response shall be made available to the Parties and to the public in a timely manner.

Comments: Art. X.24 is based on Art. 22.5 and 23.8 CETA. Para. 5 is taken from the Rules of Procedure of the EU-Korea Civil Society Forum. The aforesaid provisions were modified to account for experience made with mechanisms under earlier FTAs. Art. X.24 institutes bodies for the balanced and representative participation of civil society in the application and implementation of the model chapter. These organs are referenced in other provisions of this chapter. The Domestic Advisory Groups provide for representation of the domestic civil society of each Party separately, whereas the Civil Society Forum provides for joint representation of both Parties' civil societies. The Article stipulates rules on the composition and procedure of these organs in order to ensure transparency, balanced representation and effective participation.

Part IV – Bilateral Labour Cooperation

Overview on Part IV: Part IV contains provision on diplomatic cooperation between the Parties in labour matters. It follows the EU's traditional dialogue-seeking promotional approach in FTAs which aims for continuous progress by successive mutual agreements and coordination between the Parties on labour issues.

Section 1: Cooperation in Labour Matters

Article X.25 – Bilateral Cooperation in Labour Matters

The Parties recognise the importance of working together on trade-related aspects of labour policies in order to achieve the objectives of this Agreement. In this context, they shall consult and cooperate as appropriate at bilateral, regional, and global levels, paying specific attention to developing countries and in particular Least Developed Countries (LDCs), with respect to trade-related labour matters of mutual interest. In addition to areas and activities of cooperation identified elsewhere in this chapter, priority areas and activities in this regard may include, inter alia, the following:

a) cooperation with and within international fora dealing with issues relevant for both trade and labour and employment policies, including in particular the WTO, the ILO, and *[depending on the trade partner, further international fora can be highlighted here, e.g. the G20]*;
b) cooperation on aspects of the ILO Decent Work Agenda relevant for the interlinkages between trade, decent work and full and productive employment freely chosen by the employee;
c) exchange of information on each Party's experience in implementing ILO standards and Conventions;
d) exchange of information on data and statistics concerning labour inspections;
e) exchange of views and experiences on the information and consultation of workers at the workplace;
f) exchange of information concerning health and safety at work measures and occupational diseases;
g) cooperation with and in third countries, with a view to promoting respect and giving effect to the ILO core labour standards and to promoting ratification and effective implementation of fundamental and ratified other ILO Conventions;
h) exchange of information on each Party's experience in implementing labour provisions in Free Trade Agreements concluded with third countries, including with regard to technical assistance, and, where appropriate, cooperation in this regard in countries and regions of common interest;
i) exchange of views on the impacts of this Agreement on labour and employment, on tools to jointly or individually assess such impacts, and on ways to enhance, prevent or mitigate them, taking into account impact assessments carried out by the Parties;

j) cooperation on the analysis of the trade impact of labour laws and standards, as well as the labour impacts of trade and investment rules including on the development of domestic labour laws and policy;
k) cooperation on the promotion of decent work in global supply chains.

Section 2: Technical Assistance and Capacity Building
Overview on Section 2: This Section gives special regard to the need for technical assistance and capacity building for developing countries. It is based on language of Chapter 21 TPP on Cooperation and Capacity Building with modifications and language of Art. 196 EU-Cariforum EPA.

Article X.26 – General Provisions

1. The Parties recognize that technical assistance and capacity building are central elements and essential factors in the realization of the objectives of this Chapter. The Parties shall undertake and strengthen these activities, also recognizing that the involvement of the private sector is important in these activities.
2. Technical assistance and capacity building shall seek to complement and build on existing agreements or arrangements between the Parties.
3. Technical assistance and capacity building shall include financial and non-financial forms and may inter alia be conducted in modes such as: dialogue, workshops, seminars, conferences, collaborative programmes and projects; technical assistance to promote and facilitate capacity building and training; the sharing of best practices on policies and procedures; and the exchange of experts, information and technology.
4. Technical assistance and capacity building shall be coordinated by the national contact points of the Parties in consultation with the Domestic Advisory Groups and the Civil Society Forum.

Article X.27 – Areas of Technical Assistance and Capacity Building

1. The Parties agree to undertake and strengthen technical assistance and capacity building to assist in:

    (a) implementing the provisions of this Chapter; and
    (b) enhancing each Party's ability to safeguard and improve labour standards as envisaged in this Chapter.

2. Technical assistance and capacity building shall be undertaken inter alia in the following areas:

    (a) exchange of information on the respective social and labour legislation and related policies, regulations and other measures;
    (b) the formulation of national social and labour legislation and the strengthening of existing legislation, as well as mechanisms for social dialogue, including measures aimed at promoting the Decent Work Agenda as defined by the ILO;

(c) educational and awareness-raising programmes, including skills training and policies for labour market adjustment, and raising awareness of health and safety responsibilities, workers' rights and employers' responsibilities; and
(d) enforcement of adherence to national legislation and work regulation, including training and capacity building initiatives of labour inspectors, and promoting corporate social responsibility through public information and reporting.

Article X.28 – Resources
Recognizing the different levels of development of the Parties, the Parties shall work to provide the appropriate financial or in-kind resources for technical assistance and capacity building activities conducted under this Chapter, subject to the availability of resources and the comparative capabilities that the Parties possess to achieve the goals of this Chapter.

Part V – Dispute Settlement Procedures
Overview on Part V: Part V covers two different dispute settlement procedures in two different Sections. Section 1 covers Dispute Settlement between the Parties, which consists of three steps: Consultations, a complaint procedure before a Panel of Experts, and a compliance procedure. The adjudicatory complaint procedure leads to a final report with legally binding force. Enforcement is possible through three alternative types of temporary measures: Consensual compensation, monetary assessment and suspension of obligations. Monitoring is provided by the Committee on Labour Matters.

Section 2 covers a collective complaint procedure which follows the example of the European Convention of Human Rights and ILO dispute settlement with modifications. It consists of two steps: An adjudicatory complaint procedure between a workers', employers' or other civil society organization and a Party before a Panel of Experts, and a compliance phase. The adjudicatory complaint procedure leads to a final report with legally binding force and may grant just satisfaction to the Complainant, this is to say monetary payment for damages suffered. Enforcement is possible through direct enforcement of the final report in the Parties' domestic legal system. Monitoring is provided by the Committee on Labour Matters.

The text of Section 1 is largely based on the dispute settlement provisions of the CETA Chapter on Trade and Labour with modifications and refers to the Agreement's general dispute settlement chapter. The text of Section 2 is based on Art. X.30 (Complaint procedure between the Parties before a Panel of Experts) and contains a series of modifications which are in part sui generis, in part draw on inter alia the European Convention on Human Rights, ILO supervisory mechanisms, the European Social Charter's monitoring system and on minor aspects of CETA's Investment Chapter.

Section 1: Dispute Settlement between the Parties

Overview on Section 1: Section 1 is divided into three Sub-Sections which reflect the three phases of dispute settlement between the Parties.

Sub-Section A: Consultations

Article X.29 – Consultations between the Parties

1. A Party may request consultations with the other Party regarding any matter arising under this Chapter by delivering a written request to the Domestic Contact Point of the other Party. A Party shall request consultations with the other Party if its Domestic Advisory Group adopts a corresponding decision with a majority of three quarters of its participants, comprising at least a majority of employers' and a majority of workers' representatives, regarding the matter arising under this Chapter specified in the decision of the Domestic Advisory Group. The Party shall present the matter clearly in its request, identify the questions at issue and provide a brief summary of any claims under this Chapter. Consultations must commence promptly after a Party delivers a request for consultations.
2. During consultations, each Party shall provide the other Party with sufficient information in its possession to allow a full examination of the matters raised, subject to its law regarding confidential personal and commercial information.
3. If relevant, and if both Parties consent, the Parties shall seek the information or views of any person, organization or body, including the ILO, that may contribute to the examination of the matter that arises.
4. If a Party considers that further discussion of the matter is required, that Party may request that the Committee on Labour Matters be convened to consider the matter by delivering a written request to the contact point of the other Party. The Committee on Labour Matters shall convene promptly and endeavour to resolve the matter. If appropriate, it shall seek the advice of the Parties' Domestic Advisory Groups or the Civil Society Forum through the consultative mechanisms referred to in Article X.24 (Domestic Advisory Groups and Civil Society Forum).
5. Each Party shall make publicly available any solution or decision on a matter discussed under this Article.

Comments: Art. X.29 is based on Art. 23.9 CETA. Consultations allow for case-related discussions between the Parties on alleged violations of labour obligations under this Chapter with the possibility to involve stakeholders. They form a necessary first phase for a request for the establishment of a Panel of Experts under the subsequent Art. X.30 (Complaint Procedure Between the Parties Before a Panel of Experts).

Sub-Section B: Panel of Experts

Article X.30 – Complaint Procedure between the Parties before a Panel of Experts

1. For any matter on the alleged violation of obligations under this Chapter that is not satisfactorily addressed through consultations under Article X.29 (Consultations Between the Parties), a Party may, 90 days after the receipt of a request for consultations under Article X.29 (Consultations Between the Parties), request that a Panel of Experts be convened to examine that matter, by delivering a written request to the contact point of the other Party. The requesting Party shall notify the Director-General of the International Labour Office and the Domestic Advisory Groups of both Parties of its request.
2. The rules on general dispute settlement in Chapter *[Chapter of the FTA on general dispute settlement, e.g. CETA Chapter 29]* apply, including the Rules of Procedure and Code of Conduct set out in Annexes *[Annexes of the FTA on Rules of Procedure and Panellists' Code of Conduct, e.g. Annexes 29-A and 29-B of CETA]*, subject to the following modifications.
3. If the request concerns an alleged breach of the Agreement by the European Union or a Member State of the European Union, the procedure for determination of the responding Party for disputes with the European Union or its Member States laid out in Article *[Article of the FTA's dispute settlement or investment protection chapter addressing the selection of the responding Party in case of the EU and its member states, e.g. Art. 8.21 CETA]* applies mutatis mutandis.
4. The Panel of Experts is composed of three panellists.
5. The Parties shall consult with a view to reaching an agreement on the composition of the Panel of Experts, nominated from the list established as provided in paragraph 7, within 10 working days of the receipt by the responding Party of the request for the establishment of a Panel of Experts.
6. If the Parties are unable to decide on the composition of the Panel of Experts within the period of time specified in paragraph 5, the selection procedure set out in Article *[Provisions of the FTA's general dispute settlement chapter on the composition of an arbitral panel, e.g. Art. 29.7 CETA]* applies in respect of the list established in accordance with paragraph 7.
7. The Committee on Labour Matters shall, at its first meeting after the entry into force of this Agreement, establish a list of at least nine individuals chosen for their objectivity, reliability and sound judgment, who are willing and able to serve as panellists. For that purpose, the Committee on Labour Matters shall consult with the Director-General of the International Labour Office or its delegate and the Civil Society Forum. Each Party shall name at least three individuals to the list to serve as panellists. The Parties shall also name at least three individuals who are not nationals of either Party and who

are willing and able to serve as chairperson of a Panel of Experts. The Committee on Labour Matters shall ensure that the list is always maintained at this level. The Committee on Labour Matters may decide to increase or to decrease the number of the Experts by multiples of three. Additional appointments shall be made on the same basis as provided in this paragraph.

8. The experts proposed as panellists must have specialised knowledge or expertise in labour law, other issues addressed in this Chapter, or in the resolution of disputes arising under international agreements. Furthermore, they must be independent, serve in their individual capacities and not take instructions from any organization or government with regard to the matter in issue or be affiliated with the government of either Party, and must comply with the Code of Conduct set out in Annex *[FTA's Annex on Code of Conduct, e.g. Annex 29-B of CETA]*.
9. Unless the Parties decide otherwise, within five working days of the date of the selection of the panellists, the terms of reference of the Panel of Experts are as follows:

'to examine, in the light of the relevant provisions of Chapter *[##]* (Trade and Labour), the matter referred to in the request for the establishment of the Panel of Experts, and to deliver a report, in accordance with Article X.30 (Complaint Procedure Between the Parties before a Panel of Experts) of Chapter *[##]* (Trade and Labour).'

10. The Tribunal shall not have jurisdiction to determine the legality of a measure, alleged to constitute a breach of this Agreement, under the domestic law of the disputing Party. For greater certainty, in determining the consistency of a measure with this Agreement, the Tribunal may consider, as appropriate, the domestic law of the disputing Party as a matter of fact. In doing so, the Tribunal shall follow the prevailing interpretation given to the domestic law by the courts or authorities of that Party and any meaning given to domestic law by the Tribunal shall not be binding upon the courts or the authorities of that Party.
11. In considering the complaint, the Panel of Experts shall have due regard to ongoing and finalised procedures of other international bodies, in particular of the ILO, and strive for international coordination and coherence.
12. In respect of matters related to other international treaties, the Panel of Experts shall take into account relevant available international practice in conformity with the Vienna Convention on the Law of Treaties. In respect of matters related to or covered by ILO instruments, the Panel of Experts shall seek information from the ILO, including any pertinent available interpretative guidance, findings or decisions adopted by the ILO. The International Labour Office shall be invited by the Panel of Experts to appoint representatives to participate, in a consultative capacity, in the meetings of the Panel of Experts. The Panel of Experts can invite representatives of other international bodies to participate, in a consultative capacity, in the meetings of the Panel of Experts.

13. The Panel of Experts shall consult with Domestic Advisory Groups and give due regard to their submissions. The Panel of Experts shall receive written submissions or any other information from persons with relevant information or specialised knowledge, in particular by relevant stakeholders such as employers' organizations and trade unions, and may request such submissions or information.
14. For determining a relevant violation of obligations of this Chapter, the Panel of Experts shall take into consideration any report issued against the responding Party by a Panel of Experts through collective complaints under Article X.37 (Collective Complaint Procedure before a Panel of Experts).
15. The Panel of Experts shall issue to the Parties an interim report and a final report in accordance with the general dispute settlement procedure in Article *[Article in FTA's general provisions on reports of dispute settlement panels, e.g. Art. 29.9 f. CETA]*. They shall set out the findings of fact, the applicability of the relevant provisions of this Agreement and the rationale behind any findings and determinations. The final report shall determine any violation of obligations under this Chapter and order the cessation of the violation. The Panel of Experts shall deliver to the Parties the interim report within 120 days after the last panellist is selected. The Parties may provide comments to the Panel of Experts on the interim report within 45 days of its delivery. After considering these comments, the Panel of Experts may reconsider its report or carry out any further examination that it considers appropriate. The Panel of Experts shall deliver the final report to the Parties via their Domestic Contact Points within 60 days of the submission of the interim report. The final report has binding legal force between the Parties.
16. The Panel of Experts shall also deliver the final report to the Domestic Advisory Groups and to the Civil Society Forum. If the final report of the Panel of Experts determines that a Party has not conformed with its obligations under this Chapter, the Committee on Labour Matters shall discuss the final report on its first meeting after delivery of the final report, consult with the Civil Society Forum and consider appropriate consensual measures, including a mutually agreed action plan.

Comments: Art. X.30 is based on CETA's Chapter on Trade and Labour which provides in its Article 23.10 for the establishment of a Panel of Experts. The procedure was modified and developed to a full international adjudicatory procedure which applies the general dispute settlement provisions of the Agreement with modifications. Special regard is given to participation by stakeholders and the involvement of the ILO throughout all steps of the procedure.

By reference to the Agreement's general dispute settlement chapter which has been modelled along CETA's chapter 29, a series of important procedural aspects and safeguards are understood to be regulated by that Chapter, including inter alia general rules of procedure, transparency of proceedings and reports, time periods, the selection procedure of Experts by lot (Art. 29.7 CETA), etc. Some procedural questions are covered by reference to other CETA provisions, i.e. the procedure for determination of the responding Party in case it is supposed to be either the EU or one (or more) of its Member States (Art. 8.21 CETA).

Sub-Section C: Compliance

Overview: Sub-Section C comprehensively regulates compliance in the dispute settlement procedure between the Parties. It is based on Sub-Section B (Compliance) of CETA's General Dispute Settlement Chapter 29 with modifications. It provides for the subsidiary compliance measures of mutually agreed compensation and suspension of obligations covered by CETA's General Dispute Settlement Chapter 29, and adds monetary assessment as an additional temporary remedy for non-compliance following the model of Art. 28.20 TPP. Monetary assessment is given priority over the suspension of benefits, as it is considered to result in more constructive effects.

The three different types of temporary enforcement measures are available to compel the responding Party to comply. Firstly, the payment of mutually agreed compensation to the complaining Party, as envisaged in CETA's Chapter on general dispute settlement 29 with modifications. Secondly, as a labour-specific addition and modification, monetary assessment following the example of Art. 28.20 TPP. Thirdly, suspension of obligations (also called trade sanctions) by the complaining Party against the responding Party, as stipulated in CETA's Chapter on general dispute settlement with modifications. The relation between monetary assessment and the suspension of obligations is as follows: If a complaining Party notifies its intent to suspend obligations, the responding Party can request the payment of a monetary assessment as a replacement for the suspension of obligations. The monetary assessment then is to be paid into a fund which shall use the money for supporting initiatives to improve labour standards of the Parties. The use of the money is determined by the Civil Society Forum. Therefore, in practice, monetary assessment is given priority over the suspension of benefits. Only if recourse to monetary assessment fails, suspension of obligations is available. None of these temporary enforcement measures alter the obligation to comply with the Panel of Expert's final report.

Article X.31 – Compliance with the Final Panel Report

The responding Party shall take any measure necessary to comply with the final report. No later than 20 days after the receipt of the final report by the Parties, the responding Party shall inform the other Party and the Committee on Labour Matters of its intentions in respect of compliance.

Article X.32 – Reasonable Period of Time for Compliance

1. If immediate compliance is not possible, no later than 20 days after the receipt of the final report by the Parties, the responding Party shall notify the complaining Party and the Committee on Labour Matters of the period of time it will require for compliance.

2. In the event of disagreement between the Parties on the reasonable period of time in which to comply with the final panel report, the requesting Party shall, within 20 days of the receipt of the notification made under paragraph 1 by the responding Party, request in writing the Panel of Experts to determine the length of the reasonable period of time. Such request shall be notified simultaneously to the other Party, to the Committee on Labour Matters, to the Domestic Advisory Groups and the Civil Society Forum. The Panel of Experts shall issue its ruling to the Parties, to the Committee on Labour Matters, to the Domestic Advisory Groups and to the Civil Society Forum within 30 days from the date of the request.
3. The reasonable period of time may be extended by mutual agreement of the Parties.
4. At any time after the midpoint in the reasonable period of time and at the request of the complaining Party, the responding Party shall make itself available to discuss the steps it is taking to comply with the final report.
5. The responding Party shall notify the other Party, the Committee on Labour Matters, the Domestic Advisory Groups and the Civil Society Forum before the end of the reasonable period of time of measures that it has taken to comply with the final panel report.

Article X.33 – Temporary Remedies in Case of Non-Compliance
If:

(a) the responding Party fails to notify its intention to comply with the final report under Article X.31 or the time it will require for compliance under Article X.32;
(b) at the expiry of the reasonable period of time, the responding Party fails to notify any measure taken to comply with the final report; or
(c) the Panel of Experts referred to in Article X.36 paragraph 5 establishes that a measure taken to comply is inconsistent with that Party's obligations under the provisions of this Chapter,

the temporary remedies of

- mutually agreed compensation as laid down in Article X.34 (Mutually Agreed Compensation),
- monetary assessment as laid down in Article X.35 (Monetary Assessment), or
- suspension of obligations as laid down in Article X.36 (Suspension of Obligations)

shall be available to bring about compliance of the responding Party. None of these measures shall relieve the responding Party from its obligations under this Chapter, in particular the full implementation of the Panel of Experts' final report. These measures shall be temporary and shall be applied only until the measure found to be inconsistent with the provisions under this Chapter has been withdrawn or amended so as to bring it into conformity with those provisions.

Article X.34 – Mutually Agreed Compensation

At any time, subject to Article X.33 (Temporary Remedies in Case of Non-Compliance), the complaining Party may request the responding Party to provide an offer for temporary compensation and the responding Party shall present such offer. Any agreement shall be delivered by the Parties to the Committee on Labour Matters, the Domestic Advisory Groups and the Civil Society Forum.

Article X.35 – Monetary Assessment

1. Subject to Article X.33 (Temporary Remedies in Case of Non-Compliance) and the requirements of this Article, monetary assessment is available as a temporary compliance measure. The Parties agree that monetary assessment should have priority over the suspension of obligations which is understood to be a measure of last resort only, as spelled out in this Article and Article X.36 (Suspension of Obligations). The complaining Party shall not suspend obligations pursuant to Article X.36 (Suspension of Obligations) if and as long as the responding Party resorts to the payment of a monetary assessment in accordance with this Article.
2. The responding Party may pay a monetary assessment if it provides written notice to the complaining Party, the Committee on Labour Matters, the Domestic Advisory Groups and the Civil Society Forum within 30 days after the complaining Party provided written notice of intent to suspend obligations under Article X.36 paragraph 1, or after the Panel of Experts provided its determination under Article X.36 paragraph 5.
3. The disputing Parties shall begin consultations no later than 10 days after the date on which the responding Party has given notice that it intends to pay a monetary assessment with a view to reaching agreement on the amount of the assessment. If the disputing Parties are unable to reach an agreement within 30 days after consultations begin, the amount of the assessment shall be set at a level equal to 50 per cent of the level of the obligations the Panel of Experts has determined under Article X.36 paragraph 5 to be of equivalent effect or, if the Panel of Experts has not determined the level, 50 per cent of the level that the complaining Party has proposed to suspend under Article X.36 paragraph 1.
4. A monetary assessment shall be paid in equal, quarterly instalments beginning 60 days after the date on which the responding Party gives notice that it intends to pay an assessment. At the same time the responding Party shall provide to the complaining Party a plan of the steps it intends to take to cease the violation of this Chapter as found by the Panel of Experts in its final report.
5. The assessment is to be paid into a fund designated by the disputing Parties for appropriate initiatives to improve labour conditions of the Parties in accordance with and in the spirit of this Chapter. The selection of initiatives and use of the monetary assessment by the fund shall be determined by the Civil Society Forum which shall convene for that purpose in an extraordinary session.

6. A responding Party may pay a monetary assessment in lieu of suspension of obligations by the complaining Party for a maximum of 12 months from the date on which the responding Party has provided written notice under paragraph 2.
7. The complaining Party may suspend the application of obligations in accordance with Article X.36 (Suspension of Obligations) if:

   (a) the responding Party fails to make a payment under para. 4; or
   (b) the responding Party fails to provide the plan as required under para. 4; or
   (c) the Civil Society Forum cannot bring about a decision on the selection of labour standard initiatives and the use of the monetary assessment under para. 5 within 90 days after the responding Party has made its first instalment under para. 4; or
   (d) the monetary assessment period has lapsed and the responding Party has not yet ceased the violation under this Chapter.

Article X.36 – Suspension of Obligations

1. Subject to Article X.33 (Temporary Remedies in Case of Non-Compliance), Art. X.35 (Monetary Assessment) and the requirements of this Article, the complaining Party may suspend obligations owed to the other Party. The suspension of obligations shall be a measure of last resort, priority understood to be given to monetary assessment as spelled out in this Article and Art. X.35 (Monetary Assessment). Before suspending obligations, the complaining Party shall notify the responding Party, the Committee on Labour Matters, the Domestic Advisory Groups and the Civil Society Forum of its intention to do so, including the level of obligations it intends to suspend.
2. The suspension of obligations may concern any provision in Chapters *[specify trade-related Chapters to the exclusion of obligations for the protection of public interest, in particular this Chapter on Trade and Labour]* of this Agreement and shall be equivalent to the violation of the obligation under this Chapter by the responding Party, taking into account the gravity of the violation of the obligation under this Chapter and of the labour rights in question.
3. The requesting Party may implement the suspension 10 working days after the date of receipt of the notification referred to in paragraph 1 by the responding Party unless a Party has requested a Panel of Experts under paragraphs 5 and 6.
4. A disagreement between the Parties concerning the existence of any measure taken to comply or its consistency with the provisions of this Chapter ('disagreement on compliance'), or on the equivalence between the level of suspension and the violation of the obligation under this Chapter ('disagreement on equivalence'), shall be referred to the Panel of Experts.

5. A Party may reconvene the Panel of Experts by providing a written request to the Panel of Experts, the other Party, the Committee on Labour Matters, the Domestic Advisory Groups and the Civil Society Forum. In case of a disagreement on compliance, the Panel of Experts shall be reconvened by the complaining Party. In case of a disagreement on equivalence, the Panel of Experts shall be reconvened by the responding Party. In case of disagreements on both compliance and on equivalence, the Panel of Experts shall rule on the disagreement on compliance before ruling on the disagreement on equivalence.
6. The arbitration panel shall notify its ruling to the Parties, the Committee on Labour Matters, the Domestic Advisory Groups and the Civil Society Forum accordingly:

   (a) within 90 days of the request to reconvene the Panel of Experts, in case of a disagreement on compliance;
   (b) within 30 days of the request to reconvene the Panel of Experts, in case of a disagreement on equivalence;
   (c) within 120 days of the first request to reconvene the Panel of Experts, in case of a disagreement on both compliance and equivalence.

7. The complaining Party shall not suspend obligations until the Panel of Experts reconvened under paragraphs 5 and 6 has delivered its ruling. Any suspension shall be consistent with the Panel of Expert's ruling.

Section 2: Collective Complaint Procedure

Article X.37 – Collective Complaint Procedure before a Panel of Experts

1. Any workers', employers' and other civil society organizations in the sense of Article X.3 (Social Partners and Civil Society), including the members of the Domestic Advisory Groups and the Civil Society Forum, can file a collective complaint against a Party claiming the violation of an obligation of this Chapter by the Party

   (a) if the organization is affected by the alleged violation, on its own behalf; or
   (b) if one of its members is affected by the alleged violation, on the member's behalf and request a Panel of Experts to be convened.

2. The provisions on Dispute Settlement in Labour Matters between the Parties of Article X.30 paragraphs 2-3, 7-8, 10-13, 16 (Complaint Procedure between the Parties Before a Panel of Experts) apply mutatis mutandis subject to the provisions of this Article. Article X.30 paragraphs 4-6 (Complaint Procedure between the Parties Before a Panel of Experts) apply mutatis mutandis with the premise that at least one expert nominated from the sub-list of experts of each Party is represented in the Panel.

3. The complaint is to be filed with the Chair of the Committee on Labour Matters or its delegate which delivers it to the Party against which the complaint is raised and notifies the Director-General of the International Labour Office and the Domestic Advisory Groups of the Parties of the complaint. The complaint should, at a minimum,

   (a) clearly identify the person or organization making the complaint;
   (b) elaborate on the facts constituting a violation of this Chapter by a Party, and specify the action or omission of the Party to which the complaint refers; and
   (c) state the provisions of this chapter which are alleged to be violated.

4. The terms of reference of the Panel of Experts are as follows:

'to examine, in the light of the relevant provisions of Chapter *[##]* (Trade and Labour), the matter referred to in the request for the establishment of the Panel of Experts, and to deliver a report, in accordance with Article X.37 (Collective Complaint Procedure before a Panel of Experts) of Chapter *[##]* (Trade and Labour).'

5. The Panel of Experts shall declare inadmissible any collective complaint submitted if:

   (a) it considers the complaint to be manifestly ill-founded or an abuse of the right of a collective complaint;
   (b) the Complainant has not or not yet exhausted all reasonably available domestic remedies in accordance with generally recognised rules of international law. If and to the extent the responding Party has not fulfilled its obligations under Article X.17 (Domestic Enforcement procedures, administrative proceedings and review of administrative action), especially if no reasonably affordable and expeditious access to domestic remedies is available to the Complainant, it shall be assumed that domestic remedies were not reasonably available; or
   (c) the claimant files the complaint more than six months after the date on which the final decision under the available domestic remedies was taken.

6. In any proceedings of a Panel of Experts under this Article, any Party which is not a party to the proceedings has the right to submit written comments and to take part in hearings. The Panel of Experts may invite any Party which is not a party to the proceedings to submit written comments or take part in hearings.
7. The Panel of Experts shall issue to the parties an interim report and a final report in accordance with the general dispute settlement procedure in Article *[Article in FTA's general provisions on reports of dispute settlement panels, e.g. Art. 29.9 et seq. CETA]*. It shall set out the findings of fact, the applicability of the relevant provisions of this Agreement and the rationale behind any findings and determinations. The final report shall determine any violation of obligations under this Chapter and order the cessation of the violation. The Panel of Experts shall, if necessary, afford just satisfaction to the injured

party which may include pecuniary damage, non-pecuniary damage as well as costs and expenses if the internal law of the responding Party concerned allows only partial reparation to be made. In the case that the complainant filed the complaint on behalf of one of its members, just satisfaction shall be determined with a view to that member's situation, and the claimant shall ensure that any payment obtained from the responding Party is transferred to the member in question. The final report has binding legal force between the parties.

8. Each Party shall recognize a final report rendered pursuant to this Article as binding and enforce the pecuniary obligations imposed by that final report within its territories as if it were a final judgment of a court in its domestic legal system. A Complainant seeking recognition or enforcement in the territories of a Party shall furnish to a competent court or other authority which such State shall have designated for this purpose a copy of the final report. Each Party shall notify the Committee of Labour Matters, the Civil Society Forum and the Domestic Advisory Groups of the designation of the competent court or other authority for this purpose and of any subsequent change in such designation and make such information publicly available. The responding Party shall also separately provide such information to the claimant after a final report was issued finding for a violation under this Chapter. Execution of the final report shall be governed by the laws concerning the execution of judgments in force in the Party in whose territories such execution is sought.

Article X.38 – Compliance

In the event of disagreement between the disputing parties on compliance with the report of the Panel of Experts, the Complainant can bring the matter to the attention of the Committee on Labour Matters which shall investigate the matter on its next meeting. The other Party may take any instance of alleged non-compliance as a basis for consultations in accordance with Article X.29 (Consultations Between the Parties) and for Dispute Settlement in Labour Matters between the Parties, including the compliance procedure, in accordance with Article X.30 (Complaint Procedure Between the Parties Before a Panel of Experts).

Comments: The collective complaint procedure provides for international adjudication open to workers', employers' and other civil society organizations. The collective complaint procedure builds on Article X.30 (Complaint Procedure Between the Parties Before a Panel of Experts) with modifications and assures a similar level of participation by stakeholders and involvement of the ILO.

- The Article strikes a balance between providing international labour protection to natural and legal persons in the context of the Agreement through an international adjudicatory procedure and giving due regard to the Parties' representation in the procedure and to their sovereignty and sovereign equality.

- Collective complaints lead to legally binding reports which order the cessation of the violation. Complainants can profit from the political pressure arising from the publicly available report. The reports may also provide for just satisfaction following the example set by the European Convention of Human Rights. The Complainant can claim pecuniary as well as non-pecuniary damage, costs and expenses. Complainants can directly enforce these reports in the domestic legal systems of all Parties. As Parties accept final reports to have the status of binding final domestic judgments, domestic courts must generally enforce final reports without further examination, which provides for an effective enforcement tool at the disposal and initiative of the Complainant. Moreover, the Complainant can bring non-compliance to the attention of the Committee on Labour Matters which carries out a monitoring function.
- Separate and in addition to the Complainant's own option to directly enforce just satisfaction awarded in a final report in the Parties' domestic legal system, a Party can also decide to file a separate complaint in accordance with Article X.30 (Complaint procedure between the Parties before a Panel of Experts). It can base this complaint on the non-compliance of the other Party with a report initiated by a workers', employers' or other civil society organization which may then result in enforcement through temporary enforcement measures as stipulated in Article X.33-X.36. This allows for an additional and optional linkage between the two different procedures in Section 1 and Section 2 of Part V.

Part VI – Conditions for Entry into Force and for Maintenance of Benefits

Overview on Part VI: This Part sets out general rules applicable to labour protection related action plans agreed upon by the Parties during the negotiation of this Agreement. It contains rules on their binding character, their conditional character for the entry into force of the Agreement, and their relationship with other parts of the Agreement. The actual conditions will be negotiated between the Parties and may be laid down in a separate Annex. This Part also addresses Action Plans which do not contain pre-ratification conditions and also provides for an accelerated procedure for the amendment of such action plans which allows for flexible modifications and amendments provided their conformity with the Agreement and the conformity with any internal requirements, e.g. constitutional prerequisites, of the Parties.

Article X.39 – Pre-ratification Conditionality and Action Plans

1. The Parties emphasise the role of legal and institutional reforms agreed upon by the Parties during the negotiation of this Agreement in labour protection related Action Plans which refer to this Agreement, and reaffirm their legally binding character. The entry into force of this Agreement is contingent upon the full realisation of the commitments under these Action Plans by the Parties, except where provisions of these Action Plans explicitly provide for otherwise.

2. To the extent that any labour protection related Action Plan which refers to this Agreement provides that obligations set forth by that Action Plan do not need to be enacted and realised before entry into force of this Agreement, these obligations shall be fulfilled at the latest until the date set forth in the respective Action Plan and shall be open to dispute settlement procedures under Part V (Dispute Settlement Procedures).
3. The Committee on Labour Matters, in consultation with the Civil Society Forum, may, on agreement of the Parties and after completion of their respective internal requirements and procedures, adopt and amend labour protection related Action Plans provided the conformity of any adoption and amendment with this Agreement. Any obligation set forth by an Action Plan, including any future amendments and any new obligation, shall define a precise date until which the respective obligation must be implemented. Such date shall be ambitious and adequate, taking into account the subject matter concerned and the current political, legal and economic situation in the region concerned. Paragraph 2 applies mutatis mutandis.

Part VII – Evaluation of the Chapter, Impact Assessments, Amendments

Overview on Part VII: The text of Article X.40 (Review of the Chapter on Trade and Labour) is based partly on Art. 8.44.1 CETA and on Art. 246.1 of the EU-Cariforum EPA with modifications and additions. The text of Article X.41 (Ex Post Impact Assessment of the Chapter on Trade and Labour) is based on language from the EU Commission's Handbook for Trade Sustainability Impact Assessment, 2nd edition, 2016 with modifications which build on the 2011 UN Guiding Principles on Human Rights Impact Assessments of Trade and Investment Agreements, A/HRC/19/59/Add.5.

Part VII entails rules on the evaluation and consensual amendments of the Chapter on Trade and Labour on the basis of an obligatory ex-post impact assessment.

Article X.40 – Review of the Chapter on Trade and Labour

1. The Committee on Labour Matters shall provide a forum for the Parties to consult on difficulties which may arise in the implementation of this Chapter and possible improvements of this Chapter, in particular in the light of experience and developments in other international *fora*, in particular the International Labour Organization and international human rights bodies, and under the Parties' other agreements. The Parties agree to consider extending this Agreement with the aim of broadening and supplementing its scope in accordance with their respective legislation. The Committee on Labour Matters shall conduct such consultations in the spirit of progression of labour standards and labour protection and international coordination of such efforts. The Committee on Labour Matters shall consult and take into account the views of the Civil Society Forum and the Director-General of the International Labour Office, and may consult and take into account the views of other international bodies. At least every five years, the Committee on

Labour Matters shall conduct a general evaluation of this Chapter. This evaluation shall be based on the impact assessment report under Article X.41 (Ex-Post Impact Assessment of the Chapter on Trade and Labour). The Parties shall provide reasoned statements on the report's findings and recommendations in the course of the evaluation.

2. The Committee on Labour Matters may, on agreement of the Parties and after completion of their respective internal requirements and procedures, adopt and amend this Chapter (Part II), provided that any adoption or amendment brings about a progression of labour standards and labour protection in the spirit of international cooperation and coherence of efforts, and provided that any adoption or amendment does not lower the balanced procedural role and influence of relevant stakeholders, in particular employers, unions, labour and business organizations.

Comments: The Article on review of the Chapter on Trade and Labour enables the Parties to amend the Chapter on Trade and Labour in a simplified procedure on the basis of scientific expertise subject to compliance with internal domestic requirements and procedures of the Parties. For that purpose, the Article provides for an obligatory evaluation of the Chapter and according consultations at least every five years on the basis of the results of an impact assessment analysis which must be conducted by an independent Rapporteur nominated one year in advance.

Article X.41 – Ex-Post Impact Assessment of the Chapter on Trade and Labour

1. The Parties recognise the importance of basing the periodical review of the Chapter on Trade and Labour under Article X.40 (Review of the Chapter on Trade and Labour) on an economic and social impact assessment, including the impact on labour-related human rights, which is integrated, independent, evidence-based, transparent, participatory and proportionate. The Parties recognise the importance of the 2011 UN Guiding Principles on Human Rights Impact Assessments of Trade and Investment Agreements which shall inform the understanding of this Article. The impact assessment report drafted in accordance with this Article shall be taken into consideration by the Committee on Labour Matters in line with Article X.40 (Review of the Chapter on Trade and Labour) and complement Parties' national impact assessments as required under their domestic legislation.
2. At least one year before the review under Article X.40 (Review of the Chapter on Trade and Labour) is to be carried out, the Parties in the Committee on Labour Matters shall consensually nominate a Rapporteur on the Impact Assessment of the Chapter on Trade and Labour who shall carry out the impact assessment within one year. The Rapporteur shall be an individual or an institution who or which meets the requirements for experts proposed as panellists for the Panel of Experts under Article X.30 paragraph 8 (Complaint Procedure Between the Parties Before a Panel of Experts).

3. The impact assessment process shall be
   (a) transparent, making all communication available to the public, with due regard for exceptional and appropriate protection of confidentially;
   (b) evidence-based, resting on sound methodology and the investigation of the relevant facts and applicable law and standards, carried out by experts in order to conduct a high-quality assessment;
   (c) proportionate, calibrating the scope and depth to the importance and the type of measures analysed and the magnitude of the expected impacts, mindful of the high importance of a timely finalisation of the process within one year after nomination of the Rapporteur;
   (d) independent, the Rapporteur being accorded the same independent status as panellists of the Panel of Experts under Article X.30 paragraph 8 (Complaint Procedure Between the Parties Before a Panel of Experts). The Parties assure full support to the Rapporteur, including adequate funding; and
   (e) participatory, working as a platform for systematic dialogue between stakeholders and the Parties, through in-depth consultation in line with paragraph 7 in which all stakeholders are given an opportunity to participate, paying due and adequate regard to the manifold and diverse involved and affected interests and rights.
4. The impact assessment shall first conduct a preliminary screening and scoping analysis aiming at identifying significant labour impacts. Screening shall involve identifying key labour issues, measures and sectors to be assessed in further detail, mindful of the high relevance of a finalisation of the impact assessment in time. Scoping shall involve the identifying and analysing of components of measures under the Agreement and of the Parties which are likely to be the main drivers of the impact. Furthermore, the methodological approach of the impact assessment procedure shall be carved out and a draft consultation plan outlined which includes a preliminary list of key stakeholders. The preliminary phase shall result in a short and concise draft inception report which is made public for comments, submitted to the Committee on Labour Matters, the Civil Society Forum, the Domestic Advisory Groups, the Parties' National Contact Points and the Director-General of the ILO. The draft inception report is made subject to consultations in line with paragraph 7. After consultation, the inception report is finalised, latest three months after nomination of the Rapporteur, and made public as well as submitted to the Committee on Labour Matters, the Civil Society Forum, the Domestic Advisory Groups and the Parties' National Contact Points.
5. On the basis of the inception report, the methodological approach proposed therein is implemented in an interim phase. The economic and social impact assessment is carried out which involves evidence gathering and analysis. Evidence gathering shall include the use of both quantitative and qualitative research in order to determine the impacts as precisely as possible. Analysis determines the impacts of this Chapter on trade and labour, including labour-related economic, social and human rights impacts. Explicit reference shall be made to normative content of international binding and non-binding legal

instruments, in particular those covered in this Chapter. The interim phase results in an interim report, finalised latest nine months after nomination of the Rapporteur, which encompasses the interim economic and social impact assessment. The interim report is made public, submitted to the Committee on Labour Matters, the Civil Society Forum, the Domestic Advisory Groups, the Parties' National Contact Points and the Director-General of the ILO. The interim report is made subject to consultations in line with paragraph 7.

6. Building on the previous phases, the Rapporteur in a final phase refines the overall analyses performed so far on the basis of the ongoing consultations, and after further consultations in line with paragraph 7 produces a final report which must be clear and understandable, taking into account the need to address both experts and non-expert readers. The final report recapitulates the outcomes and findings of the impact assessment, together with a summary of the methodological approach adopted to arrive at those outcomes. It must summarise and exploit stakeholders' comments in a transparent manner. In the final report, the Rapporteur shall make recommendations and proposals for measures to maximise the benefits of the Labour Chapter and the Agreement and prevent or minimise negative impacts. Such recommendations shall include an analysis of feasibility, costs and possible impact. The final report is made public and submitted to the Committee on Labour Matters, which shall send it to the Civil Society Forum, the Domestic Advisory Groups, the Parties' National Contact Points and the Director-General of the ILO.
7. Through consultation of stakeholders, the Rapporteur aims for actively engaging with all interested parties in order to reflect their experience, priorities and concerns, contributing to the transparency of the impact assessment analysis and helping to identify priority areas and key issues of trade and labour. For that purpose, the Rapporteur provides regular information to Civil Society Forum, the Domestic Advisory Groups and the Parties' National Contact Points, and regularly seeks their input. In addition, it provides regular information to the Director-General of the ILO or its delegate, and regularly seeks its input in order to enhance international cooperation and coherence of efforts. The Rapporteur may in addition consult other international bodies. Consultation shall include a wide range of complementary activities, including inter alia interviews, meetings, written comments, digital communication and local inspections. Consultation shall be

   (a) continuous, conducting consultations throughout all phases of the impact assessment procedure, on a regular basis providing for and seeking information, with an emphasis on the consultation of the different reports described in the paragraphs;
   (b) comprehensive, by giving all relevant stakeholders, the ILO and representatives of other consulted international bodies the opportunity to express their views;
   (c) balanced, ensuring an adequate and balanced and representative coverage of all relevant interested parties during the consultation, mindful of the tripartite representation in labour matters;

(d) timely, in order to maximise the usefulness of stakeholders', ILO's and other consulted international bodies' contributions, starting at an early stage of the impact assessment process and ensuring the completion of the process within one year;
(e) tailored, adapting activities and documents to the needs of all target audiences and ensuring that they are easily understandable, concise and clear; and
(f) incorporated, appropriately taking stakeholders', ILO's and other consulted international bodies' contributions into account, responding to and exploiting them in the impact assessment process.

Comments: Article X.41 (Ex-Post Impact Assessment of the Chapter on Trade and Labour) imposes an obligation to conduct an ex-post economic and social impact assessment on the Chapter on Trade and Labour which also involves labour-related human rights aspects. The final report shall be completed within one year in order to provide a basis for the mandatory periodic evaluation laid down in Article X.40 (Review of the Chapter on Trade and Labour). It draws upon the established practice and principles of the EU on internal impact assessment analyses of trade agreements and establishes an international independent and structured expert impact assessment procedure based on the 2011 UN Guiding Principles on Human Rights Impact Assessments of Trade and Investment Agreements. The Article ensures transparency and continuous participation of stakeholders and the ILO.

3 Labour-Relevant Model Provisions for Other FTA Chapters

Comments: The following provisions relate to the protection and promotion of labour standards outside the actual labour chapter and within the wider FTA framework. In order to enhance the interconnection between provisions on labour and the rest of the FTA, these provisions should be inserted into other parts of the FTA, as indicated below.

3.1 Exceptions Chapter

Article *[##]* – General Exceptions

1. For the purposes of Article 30.8.5 (Termination, suspension or incorporation of other existing agreements), Chapters Two (National Treatment and Market Access for Goods), Five (Sanitary and Phytosanitary Measures), and Six (Customs and Trade Facilitation), the Protocol on rules of origin and origin procedures and Sections B (Establishment of investment) and C (Non-discriminatory treatment) of Chapter Eight (Investment), Article XX

of the GATT 1994 is incorporated into and made part of this Agreement. Acknowledging that the maintenance of minimum labour conditions in the way they have been defined by the ILO core labour standards represent a public concern anchored in the morality of society, the Parties understand that the measures referred to in Article XX (a) of the GATT 1994 include measures necessary to protect public morals in this regard. The Parties understand that the measures referred to in Article XX (b) of the GATT 1994 include environmental measures necessary to protect human, animal or plant life or health. The Parties understand that Article XX (g) of the GATT 1994 applies to measures for the conservation of living and non-living exhaustible natural resources.

2. For the purposes of Chapters Nine (Cross-Border Trade in Services), Ten (Temporary Entry and Stay of Natural Persons for Business Purposes), Twelve (Domestic Regulation), Thirteen (Financial Services), Fourteen (International Maritime Transport Services), Fifteen (Telecommunications), Sixteen (Electronic Commerce), and Sections B (Establishment of investments) and C (Non-discriminatory treatment) of Chapter Eight (Investment), subject to the requirement that such measures are not applied in a manner which would constitute a means of arbitrary or unjustifiable discrimination between the Parties where like conditions prevail, or a disguised restriction on trade in services, nothing in this Agreement shall be construed to prevent the adoption or enforcement by a Party of measures necessary:

   (a) to protect public security or public morals or to maintain public order;[2]
   (b) to protect human, animal or plant life or health; or
   (c) to secure compliance with laws or regulations which are not inconsistent with the provisions of this Agreement including those relating to:

      (i) the prevention of deceptive and fraudulent practices or to deal with the effects of a default on contracts;
      (ii) the protection of the privacy of individuals in relation to the processing and dissemination of personal data and the protection of confidentiality of individual records and accounts; or
      (iii) safety.

Comments: This Article is based on Art. 28.3 CETA. Closely following the line of reasoning in recent WTO jurisprudence, it includes an acknowledgement that the maintenance of minimum labour conditions is not only a matter of international law, but also of public morals. Para. 1 adopts this modification for trade in goods, whereas para. 2 applies to trade in services, including the investment chapter provisions on establishment and non-discrimination. All references contained in this Article refer to the respective rules in CETA.

---

[2]The public security and public order exceptions may be invoked only where a genuine and sufficiently serious threat is posed to one of the fundamental interests of society, including to see minimum labor conditions maintained, as they are defined by the ILO Core Labour Standards.

The scope of application of this clause, as laid down in para. 1, is adopted without changes from CETA. The model clause does not seek to improve these references, although it is submitted that the various general and special exceptions clauses in CETA might be in need of improvement, especially regarding their consistency and coherence.

3.2 Public Procurement Chapter

Article [##] – Security and General Exceptions [to be inserted into the Agreement's Chapter of Investment, here following the example of Art. 19.3 CETA]

"(. . .)

3. For greater certainty, public morals as under section 2 lit. a encompass the fundamental interest in society to see minimum labour conditions maintained, as they have been defined by the ILO core labour standards."

3.3 Investment Chapter

Preambular language

Insertion into the Agreement's preamble [here: modification of CETA's preamble]:

"(. . .)

RECOGNISING that the provisions of this Agreement protect investments and investors with respect to their investments, and are intended to stimulate mutually-beneficial business activity, without undermining the right of the Parties to regulate in the public interest within their territories, recognising and underlining at the same time the high relevance of corporate social responsibility of protected investments and investors;

(. . .)"

Article *[##]* – Corporate Social Responsibility of Investors

The Parties underline that investors bear a corporate social responsibility in line with, in particular, the UN Guiding Principles on Business and Human Rights, the OECD Guidelines on Multinational Enterprises and the ILO Tripartite Declaration concerning Multinational Enterprises and Social Policy and any applicable sector-specific corporate social responsibility norms. Accordingly, investors should incorporate into their internal policies internationally recognised voluntary standards, guidelines and principles of corporate social responsibility that have been endorsed or are supported by that Party, including the corporate social responsibility norms laid down in Article X.18 and X.19 of Chapter *[##]* on Trade and Labour.

Article [##] – Investment and Regulatory Measures [to be inserted into the Agreement's Chapter of Investment, here following the example of Art. 8.9 CETA]

"(. . .)

5. For greater certainty, nothing in this Section shall be construed as preventing a Party from conforming with and applying provisions of the Chapter on Trade and Labour."

Comments: This language is to be inserted as a new paragraph into the general provision on the right to regulate in investment chapters, such as Art. 8.9 CETA.

Article [##] – Final Award [to be inserted into the Agreement's Chapter of Investment, here following the example of Art. 8.39 CETA]

"(. . .)

3. Monetary damages shall not be greater than the loss suffered by the investor or, as applicable, the locally established enterprise, reduced by any prior damages or compensation already provided. For the calculation of monetary damages, the Tribunal may also reduce the damages to take into account any restitution of property or repeal or modification of the measure. The Investment Tribunal shall consider in the determination of the amount of monetary damages due to the investor any non-compliance of the investor with standards of CSR and responsible business conduct as laid down in Article X.18 (Corporate Social Responsibility and Responsible Business Conduct).

4. (. . .)"

Comments: This language is based on Art. 8.39 para. 3 CETA and on Policy Option 7.1.3 of the 2015 UNCTAD Investment Policy Framework for Sustainable Development (p. 110). The provision indirectly binds investors to CSR standards. If the investor does not comply with CSR norms, the Investment Tribunal can reduce the damages awarded down to 0 %. This applies to all investment obligations and thus has a comprehensive effect on the Investment Chapter. Thereby, a strong incentive is provided to investors to conform with CSR norms if they do not want to lose investment protection. At the same time, it allows for a more nuanced and balanced consideration and proportionate weighing of CSR-norms, as the tribunal can e.g. award 25 % or 50 % of the damages depending on the scale and intensity of wrongdoing by the investor in contrast to an all-or-nothing solution. This will lower any potential reluctance of the Tribunal to give effect to CSR-norms when applying the investment chapter.

Kolibri 360 GmbH
Ferdinand-Jühlke-Straße 7
99095 Erfurt, Deutschland
produktsicherheit@kolibri360.de